THE INTERNATIONAL LIBRARY OF PSYCHOLOGY,
PHILOSOPHY AND SCIENTIFIC METHOD

Edited by C.

The Mind and Its Place in Nature

By C. D. BROAD, M.A., Litt.D.

About the Series

THE PURPOSE of *The International Library* is to give expression, in a convenient form and at a moderate price, to the remarkable developments which have recently occurred in Psychology and its allied sciences. The older philosophers were preoccupied by metaphysical interests which, for the most part, have ceased to attract the younger investigators, and their forbidding terminology too often acted as a deterrent for the general reader. The attempt to deal in clear language with current tendencies, has met with a very encouraging reception, and not only have accepted authorities been invited to explain the newer theories, but it has been found possible to include a number of original contributions of high merit.

LITTLEFIELD, ADAMS & CO.
Paterson, New Jersey

INTERNATIONAL LIBRARY OF PSYCHOLOGY, PHILOSOPHY AND SCIENTIFIC METHOD

Edited by C. K. Ogden

The Mind
and its Place in Nature

By

C. D. BROAD, M.A., Litt.D.

Fellow and Lecturer in the Moral Sciences, Trinity College, Cambridge
Author of *Perception, Physics, and Reality*, and *Scientific Thought*

1960

LITTLEFIELD, ADAMS & CO.
Paterson, New Jersey

THE INTERNATIONAL LIBRARY OF PSYCHOLOGY,
PHILOSOPHY AND SCIENTIFIC METHOD

Edited by C. K. OGDEN

1 9 6 0

PUBLISHED BY LITTLEFIELD, ADAMS & CO.
Reprinted by arrangement with Humanities Press, Inc.
For sale only in the U.S.A., its possessions, and territories.

●

●

First published in the English language by Routledge and Kegan Paul,
Ltd., London, in 1925 and reprinted in 1929, 1937, 1947, 1949, and 1951.
Cloth edition available from Humanities Press, Inc., New York, in the
United States of America.

To
J. A. CHADWICK

PREFACE

My duties as Tarner Lecturer and as Lecturer in the
Moral Sciences at Trinity College, Cambridge, began
together and overlapped during the Michaelmas term
of 1923. It was therefore impossible for me to devote
as much time to the preparation of the Tarner Lectures
as I could have wished; and I was profoundly dis-
satisfied with them. So I determined to spend the
whole of the Long Vacation of 1924, and all my spare
time in the Michaelmas term of that year, in rewriting
what I had written, and in adding to it. However
bad the book may seem to the reader, I can assure
him that the lectures were far worse; and however
long the lectures may have seemed to the audience,
I can assure them that the book is far longer.

I had no intention of inflicting another book on
the public so soon after my *Scientific Thought;* and
I should certainly not have done so had I not been
asked to give the Tarner Lectures. I think I can
promise that it will be long before I offend again.
In the meanwhile I retire to my well-earned bath-
chair, from which I shall watch with a fatherly eye
the philosophic gambols of my younger friends as
they dance to the highly syncopated pipings of Herr
Wittgenstein's flute.

I am, as always, deeply indebted to the works of
Mr Johnson, Dr M'Taggart, Dr Moore, Mr Bertrand
Russell, and Prof. Stout. I have to thank my friend,
Mr J. A. Chadwick of Trinity, for kindly reading the
proofs. I have also learned much from him in the
many conversations which we have had together, and
I am indebted to him especially for certain suggestions

which I have tried to work out in Chapter XIII. Part of Chapter II. and part of Chapter VIII. are based on papers which have been published in the *Proceedings* of the Aristotelian Society. Part of Chapter III. is based on an article which appeared in *The Monist;* and part of Chapter XII. is based on an article which appeared in *The Hibbert Journal.* I have to thank the editors of these publications for kind permission to make use of the articles in question.

I shall no doubt be blamed by certain scientists, and, I am afraid, by some philosophers, for having taken serious account of the alleged facts which are investigated by Psychical Researchers. I am wholly impenitent about this. The scientists in question seem to me to confuse the Author of Nature with the Editor of *Nature;* or at any rate to suppose that there can be no productions of the former which would not be accepted for publication by the latter. And I see no reason to believe this.

I am only too well aware how inadequate the book is to its rather ambitious title. Many subjects which ought to have been discussed are not touched upon; and those subjects which are discussed are not exhausted, even if the reader be so. But it is the best that I can do at present; and I hope that some parts of it, at any rate, may form starting-points for fruitful controversies among philosophers, psychologists, biologists and psychical researchers.

C. D. BROAD.

Trinity College, Cambridge,

CONTENTS

CONTENTS

SECTION D

*The Alleged Evidence for Human Survival
of Bodily Death*

SECTION E

The Unity of the Mind and the Unity of Nature

CHAPTER I

"She's a rum 'un is Natur'," said Mr Squeers. . . .
"Natur' is more easier conceived than described."
(DICKENS, *Nicholas Nickleby*)

CHAPTER I

Introduction. General Remarks on Method. Pluralism and Monism

Introduction. The aim of the Tarner Benefaction is to found a course of lectures on "the relation or lack of relation between the various sciences." Dr Whitehead, who gave the first course, dealt with applied geometry and chronometry, dynamics, and the Theory of Relativity. He left to his immediate successor a delicate and invidious task. Dr Whitehead's *Concept of Nature* is an epoch-making book by a man who is a complete master of the technical part of his subject and an original philosophic thinker of the highest order. Taken in conjunction with its predecessor, *The Principles of Natural Knowledge*, and its sequel, *The Principle of Relativity*, it forms the most important contribution which has been made for many years to the philosophy of mathematical physics. For me to attempt to cover the same ground again in these lectures would be to expose myself to the most unflattering comparisons. Moreover, I have lately dealt with these matters to the best of my ability in my *Scientific Thought*; and, whilst I am well aware how much room there is for improvement in that book, my readers must be as tired of seeing my views on this subject as I am at present of writing them down. I therefore determined to choose a problem which should be supplementary to Dr Whitehead's work and should overlap it as little as possible.

Now the limitations which the first Tarner Lecturer deliberately imposed on himself at once suggest a subject for discussion by his immediate successor. He quite explicitly confined himself to the study of Nature as an *object* of Mind. He refused to complicate his problem by dealing with the stuff and structure of mind as such, or with its place within the physical world which it contemplates and acts upon. And, beside this, Dr Whitehead confined himself to the most general characteristics of the physical world, to those which are shared by stones, trees, and animal or human bodies. He did not consider in detail the very great apparent differences which there are between such objects as these. In these self-imposed limitations he was, I think, wholly justified. The problem of the external world as such is a terribly hard one, and it has certainly been made harder in the past by being mixed up to a needless extent with psychological and physiological questions. I found it necessary to follow much the same course, so far as I could, in my *Scientific Thought*. Nevertheless, it seems clear to me (and I do not suppose that Dr Whitehead would seriously dissent) that all sharp divisions of Reality into water-tight compartments, and all confinement of our attention to the *common* characteristics of things which *also* differ profoundly, are practically necessary rather than theoretically satisfactory. Minds do arise, to all appearance, within the physical world; and they do remain, to all appearance, tightly bound to certain special physical objects, viz., living animal organisms. And, having arisen and being connected with such organisms, they do then proceed to perceive, think about, act upon, feel emotions toward, and approve or disapprove of things and events in the physical world. Nor do they confine their attention to such objects. A mind may perform all these acts towards itself and towards other minds as well as towards physical things and events; and the minds which we know most about are concerned almost as much with themselves and with other minds as with matter. Nor does even this exhaust the objects with which minds are apparently concerned from time to time. Some minds, and especially Dr Whitehead's, seem to spend a good deal of their time in contemplating, reasoning about, and feeling approval or disapproval towards objects which are, on the face of them, neither material nor mental, *e.g.*, numbers, propositions, and the formal relations of such objects among themselves. And it is certainly arguable that a mind could go little if any distance in cognising objects which *are* physical or mental if it did not have the power of cognising objects which are neither.

Now these are vitally important facts which must presumably shed some further light on the stuff and structure of the world as a whole, and even on that part of it which consists of physical things and processes and is called " Nature." When we treat any one part of Reality in isolation from the rest, or when we concentrate on the common features of things which also differ profoundly, it is certain that our results will not be the whole truth and probable that they will not be wholly true. The speculative philosopher and the scientific specialist are liable to two opposite mistakes. The former tends to deliver frontal attacks on Reality as a whole, armed only with a few wide general principles, and to neglect to isolate and master in detail particular problems. The latter tends to forget that he has violently abstracted one part or one aspect of Reality from the rest, and to imagine that the success which this abstraction has given him within a limited field justifies him in taking the principles which hold therein as the whole truth about the whole world. The one cannot see the trees for the wood, and the other cannot see the wood for the trees. The result of both kinds of mistake is the same, viz., to produce philosophical theories which may be self-consistent but which must be described as " silly ". By a " silly " theory I mean one which may be held at the time when one is talking or writing professionally, but which only an inmate of a lunatic asylum would think of carrying into daily life.

I should count Behaviourism, taken quite strictly, and certain forms of Idealism as "silly" in this sense. No one in his senses can in practice regard himself or his friends or enemies simply as ingenious machines produced by other machines, or can regard his arm-chair or his poker as being literally societies of spirits or thoughts in the mind of God. It must not be supposed that the men who maintain these theories and believe that they believe them are "silly" people. Only very acute and learned men could have thought of anything so odd or defended anything so preposterous against the continual protests of common-sense.

General Remarks on Method. In view of these dangers it seems to me that the best plan for the philosopher is somewhat as follows. He must start by considering separately those departments of Reality which seem *prima facie* to be susceptible of fairly elaborate treatment by themselves without detailed knowledge of their relations to each other. He must then analyse and reflect upon each of these in turn as carefully and exhaustively as he can until he finds himself nearing a point at which no further progress can be made in understanding one without a detailed study of its relations to the others. In the meanwhile he will always bear in mind that the departments which he is treating separately are in fact connected with each other, and that any results which he has reached about one of them will probably need some correction and modification when he takes into account those relations with the rest which he has hitherto been ignoring. Again, within each department he will begin by considering those most abstract and pervasive features which are common to all things that fall within it and so exhibit its general structure and ground-plan. When he has done this he will pass on to consider the most striking and apparently fundamental differences between different objects which fall into the same department.

Here again he will do well to remember that the study of the detailed differences may force him to modify his original conclusions about the common structure of the department in question. Thus the general procedure is (1) gradually to work forward from the parts to the whole and from the common features of each part to the characteristic differences within it; and (2) at every stage to look back on one's earlier results and see how far and in what direction they need to be modified in the light of the later ones.

Now it might be objected at this stage that the suggested method prejudges the question of Pluralism or Monism. I do not think that it does. The plain fact is that if the world be too much or too little of a unity there is not the least chance of our ever being able to understand it. If it were as pluralistic as Leibniz thought or as monistic as Mr Bradley seems to have believed, I do not see how knowledge would be possible. What we find is that Reality as a whole does seem to show a mixture of unity and relative isolation; and it is reasonable to begin with the departments which seem relatively independent and work at them in detail before considering the connexions which they undoubtedly also have with each other. So long as we know what we are doing, and clearly recognise that what seems at first sight closely connected may prove to be separable and that what seems at first sight independent may prove to be intimately connected, we shall not go far wrong.

I have said that at each stage of our work we must look back to see whether the results of the earlier stages need correction or modification. I want now to explain this possibility a little further. In the first place, the results of our earlier and more abstract investigations may be seen to be positively wrong in some respects when we take into account the more special and concrete aspects of Reality which we had formerly been ignoring. But there is a second alternative which may arise if we have been lucky in our original division of Reality into separate departments and cautious in the statement of our conclusions about these departments. We may find, in this case, that we have not positively to *correct* anything that we have already asserted, but have only to *choose between alternatives* which we have already recognised as possible. So long as we confine ourselves to each department in isolation from the rest, and so long as we investigate only the general ground-plan of each department, we may well find that a number of alternative theories are open to us and that we have no means of deciding between them. As we go on to consider the relations of one department to the others and the detailed differences within each department, we may find that this new knowledge favours certain of these alternatives and excludes others. In that event we shall not be correcting past errors, but merely replacing true but less determinate theories by true and more determinate theories. This is of course the ideal path of philosophic progress ; but we cannot assume that we shall strike it. Our chance of doing so depends partly on initial luck and insight in our division of the subject-matter, and partly on the power of recognising a number of alternatives and not thinking at any stage that our knowledge is more determinate than it really is.

I will now illustrate my meaning with an example. In Dr Whitehead's Lectures and in my *Scientific Thought* we are concerned with matter only as known to the physicist, and with mind only as something which perceives and thinks about matter. The main problem at that level is to state clearly what is meant by " sensible appearance ", and to reconcile what we know about the sensible appearances and their qualities and mutual relations with what physics asserts about the matter which appears to us in this way. Now it seems to me that, so long as we confine ourselves to these data, many alternative theories about the nature of matter and of mind are possible. But, in the first place, we have to remember that matter seems to have differences of kind within it beside the common features which are studied by the mathematical physicist. *E.g.*, there seem to be a number of different chemical elements ; there seems to be a fundamental difference between living organisms and inorganic matter ; and so on. Again, within the region of mind there are apparently very profound differences. Oysters, perhaps, can only feel ; cats, perhaps, can only feel and perceive ; men can feel, perceive and reason ; and so on. Secondly, we have to notice that there is in fact a most intimate relation between minds and living bodies. The minds that we know about are not disembodied spirits ; they seem to be tied to organisms, to grow and decay with these, and to cease when these die. Moreover, in our part of the world at any rate, there seems to have been a gradual historic development of mind going hand in hand with a growth in the complexity of living matter. Any theory of Reality which can claim to be even approximately adequate must take such apparent facts into account, and must contain a doctrine of matter and mind which shall be consistent with them. Now it may well be that, of the various theories which were possible when we considered merely the common properties of mind and of matter and when we looked on mind merely as a contemplator of matter, some will be ruled out when we take account of the different sorts of mind and of matter and the apparent relation of dependence between these two departments of Reality. And it may be that some of the remaining alternatives will be better adapted than others to this new and more concrete situation.

I propose therefore to consider in these lectures the Mind and its Place in Nature. As minds are specially closely connected with those peculiar bodies called "animal organisms" I shall also have to consider the apparent differences between living and non-living matter. This line of inquiry seems to fall quite naturally into the scheme of the Tarner Benefaction ; for it amounts to considering the "relation or want of relation" between physics, physiology, and psychology. I shall in certain places assume that the reader is acquainted with my *Scientific Thought;* but I shall take no special pains to make the outcome of this inquiry square with the outcome of that. If they should turn out to be mutually consistent, so much the better. But I shall follow my argument whithersoever it may lead ; and, if fragments of my works should survive the downfall which Western civilisation is so busily preparing for itself, it will perhaps be the pleasing task of the Negro commentators of the future universities of central Africa to excogitate a consistent system of thought from my scattered remains.

I propose to attack the problem in the following order. (*A*) I shall begin by taking quite traditional and commonplace views about matter and mind, and shall discuss at that level the old questions of Mechanism and Vitalism and of the Relation of Mind and Body. (*B*) Next I shall consider critically the sources of our alleged knowledge of Matter, of our own Minds, and of other Minds. In this section I shall also discuss Memory, which is involved in all our knowledge. This should enable us to decide how much we are probably justified in asserting about the nature of Matter and of Mind, taken in isolation from each other. (*C*) It will then be profitable to say something about what seem to be common features of living organisms and minds, or to be on the borderline between merely vital and obviously mental phenomena. I allude here to Mnemic Phenomena and the "Unconscious". At the end of this section we shall see that there are certain alternative possibilities between which we cannot decide unless we know whether minds ever survive the destruction of the organisms which they have animated. Therefore (*D*) I then proceed to discuss the arguments for and against human survival of bodily death. Finally (*E*) I shall consider the internal unity of the mind, and its position and probable prospects in Nature.

Dangers of the Genetic Method. In dealing with living organisms and with minds there is a complication which does not arise to the same extent in considering non-living matter. This is the fact of evolution. Each mind and each organism that we know of has developed gradually from very simple beginnings. And, again, there is some reason to think that the most complex minds and organisms which have appeared up to a given date are less and less complex as that date is pushed further back in the earth's history, and that the more complex organisms of later date are the descendants of less complex organisms of earlier date. However this may be, it is certain that at the present time there are minds and organisms of very various degrees of complexity, ranging from amœbas through cats and dogs to men. Now, in trying to analyse and understand any complex state of affairs which has gradually grown up from simpler beginnings, there are two alternative orders of treatment. One is to start by considering the most perfect and highly developed instances of the phenomenon in question. Another is to treat the problem genetically, devoting great attention to its earliest, simplest, and crudest forms. The latter is of course the more popular order at the present time. My own view is that neither line of approach can be dispensed with, but that the former is the more fundamental of the two. In the first place, if we want to study the nature and structure of some important item in Reality it is surely more sensible to begin by studying it in its most characteristic and developed forms than in those elementary beginnings in which it is barely distinguishable from other factors in Reality. Even if one's main interest be in the development of something it is at least as important to know what it has developed into as what it has developed out of. Secondly, if we start from the other end, we are liable to fall into two errors. (*a*) We are extremely likely to underestimate the complexity and ignore the peculiarities of the final stage, because we cannot see how they could have developed out of the earlier and simpler stages. It certainly seems to me that evolutionary accounts of Mind very often fail altogether to take due account of the most characteristic features of the most highly developed minds. Now it is much more disastrous to slur over differences which are really irreducible than to recognise differences and wrongly think them to be irreducible. If we make the latter error we still have in hand all the data for the solution of our problem, and we or others will solve it when we have pushed our analysis a little further. But, if we make the former mistake, our data are incomplete and the problem cannot possibly be solved until we have recognised this fact. My first objection then to starting from the lower end and working to the higher is that this way of approach tends to prevent one from viewing the latter with an unprejudiced eye, and to make one commit the greatest of all mistakes in philosophy, that of over-simplifying the facts to be explained.

(*b*) A second danger is the following. When I study the evolution of anything, be it an animal or an institution or a mental process, I am simply learning about the *history* of it and its "ancestors" in a wide sense of that word. I learn that A developed into B, B into C, and C into the thing in question. Now we are all extremely liable to confuse a history of the becoming of a thing with an analysis of the thing as it has become. Because C *arose out of* B, and B out of A, people are inclined to think that C is *nothing but A in a disguised form*. Thus, suppose we could show that action from a sense of duty developed out of action from fear of public opinion, that this developed out of action from fear of the ghosts of dead ancestors, and that this developed out of action from fear of living chiefs. All that we

should really have done would be to give a *history* of
the process of becoming which ended in action from a
sense of duty. But we should be very liable to think
that we had *analysed* the sense of duty as it now exists,
and proved that it is just a disguised form of fear of
punishment by tribal chiefs. This would be simply a
gross mistake. To analyse anything you must examine
and reflect upon *it;* and the most elaborate account of
what preceded it in the course of history is no substitute
for this. At the best a study of the history of a thing
may make you look for factors in the thing which you
might otherwise have missed. But, on the other hand,
as I have already pointed out, it is just as likely to
make you turn a blind eye to factors in it which were
not present in the earlier stages. And, in any case,
you have no right whatever to say that the end is just
the beginning in disguise if, on inspecting the end as
carefully and fairly as you can, you do *not* detect the
characteristics of the beginning in it and *do* detect
characteristics which were not present in the beginning.

There is a certain kind of pretentious futility which is
closely connected with this error and is highly typical
of some of the sillier psycho-analysts. Suppose we are
told that a taste for music is due to suppressed sexual
desire or to Dr Ernest Jones's family pet, "infantile anal-
erotic sensations". What is the precise cash-value of
such a statement? It cannot mean that this is a *sufficient*
condition of a taste for music, since the psycho-analyst
would be the first to assure us that suppressed sexual
desire can exist in people who show no taste for music
but an excessive fondness for pet animals. Thus other
factors must be needed to account for the taste for music
in one person and the mania for keeping cats in the
other. And these other factors will plainly be the more
characteristic cause-factors, since the suppressed sexual
desire is supposed to be the *common* condition of *both*,
whilst the other factors determine *which of the two* shall
result. So the most that can be said is that the sup-

pressed sexual desire is a *necessary* condition of a taste for music. Now it is obvious that the more different states the psycho-analyst ascribes to suppressed sexual desire the more trivial his statement becomes about any one of them. If this desire be a necessary condition of fifty different tastes, accomplishments, diseases, and crotchets, it is of extremely little interest to say of any one of them that it is " due to " suppressed sexual desire. It is about as useful as to say that committing a murder is " due to " being born. This is true, since you could not commit a murder without having been born. But it is not very interesting or important, since it is equally true that being born is a necessary condition of saving another man's life at the risk of your own.

Thus, one characteristic mistake of the incautious user of the genetic method is to give a rather trivial necessary condition of some highly developed state as if it were the sufficient condition. He then proceeds to ignore the other conditions, which are equally necessary and much more characteristic. The next move is to confuse a list of the historical conditions out of which a thing arose with an analysis of the thing itself. And so, from the perfectly trivial, even if true, proposition that suppressed sexual desire is a necessary condition of a taste for music, he jumps by these two steps to the interesting but extremely doubtful assertion that a taste for music is just a disguised form of sexual desire. For these reasons I think I am justified in the order which I propose to adopt, *i.e.*, in discussing the apparent features of highly developed minds at an early stage, and not considering the borderline of Instinct and the Unconscious until later. And perhaps it is relevant to add that I fancy I can imagine what it feels like to be a highly developed mind much better than I can imagine what it feels like to be a flea or an amœba. But, of course, that may just be my conceit.

Value of the Abnormal. Before leaving this subject I must make one further remark about method, which

eem to be inconsistent with what I have just been
g but is not, I think, really so. I hold that it is
the utmost value for the philosopher to study the
abnormal in all subjects. *E.g.*, it is such facts as
dreams, hallucination, mirror-images, etc., which
prevent (or should prevent) us from taking too simple-
minded a view of the external world and our perception
of it. If we start with a theory made to fit the normal
cases alone, we shall probably never be able to square
the abnormal cases with it. If, on the other hand, we
take the abnormal cases into account from the very first,
we may be able to devise a general theory which covers
both them and the normal cases. The normal cases
may then be seen to arise from the fulfilment of certain
special conditions which do *in fact* generally hold, but
which do not hold *of necessity* and are not in fact fulfilled
in the abnormal cases. A simple example from mathematics will make this clear. If we had started by con-
fining our attention to circles, and had then insisted on
regarding all other conic-sections as circles which had
more or less "gone to the bad", it seems unlikely that
we should ever have had a very satisfactory theory of
conic-sections. The alternative and much better plan
is to start with the general equation of a conic-section,
and to see that circles, ellipses, hyperbolas, etc., are
special cases which arise through special values of, or
special relations between, the co-efficients in this general
equation.

Now this general principle is just as important in
considering minds as it is in considering the external
world and our perception of it. This fact may be
illustrated in three ways. (1) If we study sane human
beings in their waking moments we find a very high
degree of unity in their minds. And, if we confine
ourselves to them, we shall be tempted to think that
psychical events *can* exist only as states of selves, and
that each human body *can* have only one self connected
with it. Now these conclusions may be true; but they

begin to look much less plausible when we co
abnormal phenomena, such as automatic wr.
multiple personality, etc. Moreover, a study of su
phenomena may lead us to scrutinise more carefully the
normal human mind, and we may then find that even
the mind of a healthy young Scotsman "on the make"
is a good deal less unified than it seemed to be. In
the end we may decide that the facts as a whole are best
explained by supposing that psychical events *need not*
be states of selves and that one human body *need not* be
connected with only one self. The considerable degree
of mental unity which we find as a rule, and the normal
assignment of one self to one body, may then be regarded as due to the fulfilment of certain special
conditions which *generally* hold but need not and sometimes do not. It will still be a most important fact
that these conditions tend to be approximately fulfilled
in the vast majority of cases, so that there will be no
excuse for neglecting the study of normal minds. But
the study of the abnormal will have had two excellent
effects. It will have presented alternative hypotheses
to us which we should otherwise not have contemplated
as possible, and it will have made us notice certain facts
about the normal mind which we should otherwise not
have looked for. (2) Under normal circumstances one
mind seems to be incapable of knowing what is going
on in another except by listening to the speech or
watching the gestures of the body with which this other
mind is connected. Most theories of mind assume that
this very roundabout method is the *only possible* way in
which one mind can communicate with another. Now
it seems to me that the existence of telepathy between
specially sensitive subjects and between ordinary minds
under special conditions has been firmly established by
the work of the S.P.R., and I consider that I have met
with undoubted instances of it in sittings which I have
had with the medium Mrs Osborne Leonard. The
establishment of such facts opens up many possibilities

which would otherwise have had to be rejected, and it suggests that even in normal human intercourse a telepathic factor may play some part. (3) Lastly, there are the more debatable cases in which it looks as if a human mind were communicating after the death of its body. At present it would be very unwise to philosophise about the mind with such cases mainly in view. But it seems to me to be almost equally rash to put forward a theory of mind and its relation to body which totally ignores these phenomena and assumes that they can all be explained away.

Now I do not think that there is any inconsistency between my present contention that philosophy must attend most carefully to the abnormal and my former assertion that it must start by considering the most highly developed, and therefore the most characteristic, minds and mental processes. In the first place, many of the phenomena dealt with by Psychical Research may be fairly regarded as *super*normal, *i.e.*, as instances in which a mind shows powers which no mind was suspected of having. And, even in the merely pathological abnormalities which the psycho-analyst and the student of multiple personality treat, we are concerned with derangements which can happen only to a mind of a fairly high order. We should not expect to find multiple personality in a guinea-pig or suppressed complexes in an amœba; a mind must be fairly highly developed before it can go wrong in an interesting and instructive way.

Pluralism and Monism. I have now said all that I want to say about method. In doing so, however, I have introduced the notion of Reality falling into relatively isolated, though connected, "departments". I have also talked of apparently fundamental differences of kind among things which belong to the same department. To explain these notions further it will be necessary to say something about the traditional antithesis of "Pluralism" and "Monism". These words are terribly ambiguous, and I think it will be both useful and relevant to clear up their ambiguities at this stage. In doing so I shall be throwing some light on the principles which I have been asserting, shall sketch out the possible alternatives which have to be considered in detail in later chapters, and shall show something of the conditions on which the "connexion or lack of connexion of the various sciences" depends.

Existents and Abstracta. The first great division within Reality as a whole which strikes one is the distinction between the part which *exists* and the part which is *real but not existent*. The contents of the latter I call "Abstracta". The names "Pluralism" and "Monism" are usually confined to different views about the nature of the Existent; but a prior question arises, for some philosophers have held that the difference between Abstracta and Existents is not ultimate, since in their view there are no Abstracta. A Nominalist, who holds that there are no universals but only words used in a certain way, would be a Monist, in a sense in which a Realist, who holds that there are real universals whether *ante rem* or only *in re*, would not. However, we have the words "Realist", in the mediæval sense, and "Anti-Realist" (covering Nominalists and Conceptualists) to mark this distinction; and we can therefore keep the words "Monist" and "Pluralist" for differences of opinion about the Existent. Nevertheless, I will briefly explain what I understand by the distinction, which seems to me to be a real and irreducible one.

I do not think that "Existence" can be defined, but I think that it can be unambiguously described. (*a*) Whatever exists can occur in a proposition *only* as a logical subject. Of course the *name* of an existent may appear in a *sentence* as a grammatical *object* and in other positions too. *E.g.*, in the sentence "Smith dislikes Jones" the only grammatical subject is the word

"Smith", and the word "Jones" counts as a grammatical object. Nevertheless, the men Smith and Jones are both logical subjects of the proposition for which this sentence stands. This property, however, cannot safely be taken by itself to mark out existents. If there be such entities as propositions they are certainly Abstracta and not Existents; yet it would seem that the only part which one proposition can play in another proposition is that of logical subject. *E.g.*, if the sentence "Edwin will marry Angelina" stands for a single complex entity, a proposition, then it can only appear in such other propositions as: It is probable that Edwin will marry Angelina, or: Smith believes that Edwin will marry Angelina. And in these secondary propositions it is plain that the original proposition about Edwin and Angelina is present as a logical subject. (*b*) A second characteristic which belongs to all Existents and to no Abstracta is that they are *either* literally and directly in time; *or*, if time be unreal, have those characteristics, whatever they may be, which make them appear to human minds to be directly and literally in time. I put the matter in this way because, although I see no reason to doubt the reality of time, there are philosophers who deny it and yet believe that there are existents. If then I had said that all existents are literally and directly in time I should have prejudged this question. But I think that even those philosophers who deny the reality of time would accept the second part of the above alternative.

I do not think that Abstracta can even be unambiguously described except by saying that they are real but non-existent. But they can be indicated enumeratively. This class of realities includes qualities, relations, numbers, and also propositions and classes if there be such entities. Abstracta of course do not exist, and neither are nor appear to be literally and directly in time. But some at least of them are very closely connected with existents, and thereby become indirectly connected with time. This happens in two different ways. (*a*) Certain qualities characterise certain things or events from time to time Again, certain relations relate now one set of existents and now another. And many propositions are about things and events which exist in time. (*b*) Any Abstractum may from time to time become the object of someone's thought. The proposition that Charles I was beheaded is not in time directly and literally, as Charles I and the axe are ; but it is connected indirectly with time, both because it is about temporal things and events and because I began to think of it a moment ago and shall cease to think of it a few minutes hence. All that can happen to a quality is that it sometimes characterises one, sometimes another, and sometimes perhaps no existent ; and that it is sometimes thought of by me, sometimes by you, and sometimes perhaps by no one. The realm of Abstracta, as such, forms the inexhaustible subject-matter of the *a priori* sciences of Pure Logic and Pure Mathematics.

On this matter, which it would be irrelevant to pursue further here, I am *certainly* a Realist to the extent of accepting *universalia in re* as absolutely irreducible factors in Reality. And I am inclined to be a Realist in the stronger sense of believing that we cannot do without *universalia ante rem*, *i.e.*, simple and unanalysable universals which will never have instances. But I think it possible that we may be able to devise a means of dispensing with such universals, though I do not at present see how to do the trick.

Pluralism and Monism about the Existent.—I will first illustrate the ambiguities of these terms by taking examples. (1) Leibniz is commonly counted as a typical pluralist. And in one sense he certainly was. Descartes is commonly regarded as a typical dualist. But, in the sense in which Descartes is a dualist, Leibniz is a monist. Leibniz held that all that appears as matter is really mind, whilst Descartes held that mind and matter are equally real and quite irreducible to each other. We therefore say that Leibniz was a monist in the sense in which Descartes was a dualist. But Leibniz was equally certain that there is a very large number of minds, each of which is an independent substance ; and in this Descartes agreed with him. In this sense they were both pluralists. Let us next consider the case of Spinoza, who is commonly regarded as a typical monist. In the sense in which Leibniz was a monist, and Descartes was a dualist, Spinoza was an extreme pluralist. For he not only held that thought and extension were both real and mutually irreducible ; he held that these were just two out of an infinite number of equally real and mutually irreducible "Attributes". On the other hand, Spinoza was a monist in the sense in which Leibniz was a pluralist. He held that minds are not independent substances but are simply "modes" of the "attribute" of thought ; and he meant roughly by this that there is a single psychic continuant of which all minds are merely occurrent states. Of course he held a similar view about bodies. In this sense Descartes was a pluralist about mind and a monist about matter, for he agreed with Leibniz that minds are continuants and with Spinoza that bodies are occurrents.

These examples illustrate some, but not all, of the ambiguities. Let us imagine two materialists who both believed that there are many independent material particles. So far they would both be monists, in the sense in which Leibniz is and Spinoza is not a monist. And they would both be pluralists, in the sense in which Leibniz is and Spinoza is not a pluralist. Now let us suppose that one of these materialists holds that there is a plurality of irreducibly different *kinds* of material particle, *e.g.*, Oxygen atoms, Hydrogen atoms, and so on. And let us suppose that the other thinks that there is ultimately only one kind of material particle, and that the differences between Oxygen,

Hydrogen, etc., are simply differences in the structure and movements of different *groups* of these particles. Then the second materialist would be a monist in a certain sense. And, in this sense, the first materialist would be a pluralist. Leibniz was a pluralist in this sense ; for he held that there were ultimately different *orders* of mind, *e.g.*, "bare monads", the souls of animals, and human minds.

Let us now try to draw the necessary distinctions and to define our terms. (*a*) There are certain attributes which anything must have if it is to be a substance at all. I should say that anything that is a substance must have some duration and must be capable of standing in causal relations. Or, since some people deny the reality of time and of causation, let us say that anything that is a substance must have those characteristics, whatever they may be, which appear to human minds as duration and causation. I will call these "Substantial Attributes". There are other attributes which a thing need not have in order to be a substance. It need not be extended and it need not even appear to be so. Again, it need not have the power of feeling or cognising, and it need not even seem to have this.

(*b*) Now it must be admitted that every actual substance must have *some* special attribute or other beside the substantial attributes which are essential to all substances. This special attribute will make it a substance of such and such a kind, *e.g.*, a material or a mental substance. Let us call such attributes "Differentiating Attributes". It will be necessary to describe the nature of a differentiating attribute a little more fully. (1) It must not be essential to substance as such, even if in fact it be possessed by all substances. *E.g.*, if materialism be true, extension is an attribute which is in fact possessed by all substances. But it is a differentiating attribute for all that, since it is not essential for a substance as such to be extended. (2)

It is a determinable which is not itself a determinate under any higher determinable. This condition is needed for the following reason. Suppose that the properties of being gold, being silver, and so on, are ultimate and irreducible. We do not want to count these as differentiating attributes; but, if we did not add the present condition, it is difficult to see why we should not have to do so. But these properties would be determinates under the higher determinable "matter", and so they will not have to be counted as differentiating attributes if we add the condition that such attributes must be determinables of the highest order. (3) If it belongs to any complex substance as a whole it must belong also to all its parts. This has to be added in view of the doctrine of "emergent qualities", about which more will be said in what follows. An emergent quality is roughly a quality which belongs to a complex as a whole and not to its parts. Some people hold that life and consciousness are emergent qualities of material aggregates of a certain kind and degree of complexity. If there be such qualities we do not want to have to count them as differentiating attributes. (4) It must be a simple attribute, *i.e.*, it must not be analysable into a conjunction or disjunction of other attributes.

We can now define the first kind of Pluralism and Monism. This I will call "Pluralism and Monism about Differentiating Attributes". A "Differentiating-Attribute Monist" holds that there is in fact only one differentiating attribute. Materialists, like Hobbes, and Mentalists, like Leibniz, are monists of this kind. A "Differentiating-Attribute Pluralist" holds that there are two or more differentiating attributes. Pluralists of this kind can be further subdivided according to two different principles. (1) We may take the trivial principle of dividing them according to the number of differentiating attributes which they accept. *E.g.*, Descartes was a dualist and accepted two only; Spinoza accepted an infinite number; and there seems no obvious reason why there should not be Trialists or Hendekal-ists in this sense, though I cannot call any to mind at the moment. (2) A much more important principle of division is the following. Some people who accept a plurality of differentiating attributes hold that one and the same substance can have several or all of these attributes. Thus Spinoza held that God has all the infinite number of differentiating attributes. Others consider the various differentiating attributes to be in-compatible with each other. This view was held by Descartes of the two differentiating attributes which he accepted. The first kind of differentiating-attribute pluralist can (though he *need* not) believe that there is only one substance, as Spinoza did. The second kind of differentiating-attribute pluralist *must* admit at least as many different substances as there are differentiating attributes, and he *may* of course admit more. Descartes could not consistently have accepted less than two sub-stances; and in fact he accepted a great many more, since he thought that each individual mind is a distinct substance. On the other hand, a man can be a differ-entiating-attribute monist, like Leibniz, and yet accept an infinite plurality of substances.

We have now to consider a second meaning of the antithesis between Pluralism and Monism. Just as every actual substance has some differentiating attribute as well as the substantial attributes, so too every actual substance has its differentiating attribute in some specific form. No material substance is *just* a bit of matter; it has the Oxygen properties, or the Hydrogen properties, or the Silver Chloride properties, and so on. Similarly, no mind is *just* a thinking substance; it has the charac-teristic properties of an oyster's mind, or of a dog's, or of a man's, or of an angel's, and so on. I will call these more specific features, which distinguish different " natural kinds " of substances having the same differ-entiating attribute, " Specific Properties ". And I will call the aggregate of substances which have a common differentiating attribute, taken together, a "Realm of Being". *E.g.*, we can talk of the "Mental Realm" and the "Material Realm". The question can then be raised : "Are there several ultimately different kinds of substance within a single realm of being, or are all the apparently different specific properties within a realm of being really reducible to a single one? *E.g.*, must the Oxygen-property and the Hydrogen-property simply be accepted as ultimate ; or can they both be derived from certain common properties of all matter, such as extension, spatial arrangement, motion of particles, etc.?" We might call a man who accepted the first alternative a "Pluralist about the Specific Properties of Matter", and one who accepted the second alternative a "Monist about the Specific Properties of Matter". It would of course be quite consistent to be a differentiating-attribute pluralist and a specific-property monist about some or all of the realms of being. And the opposite combination of views would also be quite consistent. *E.g.*, Leibniz was a differentiating-attribute monist ; but he was a specific-property pluralist, since he believed in ultimately different kinds of mind. Descartes, on the other hand, was a differentiating-attribute dualist. But he was a specific-property monist about the realm of matter, for he thought that the apparently different kinds of matter differ only in the arrangement and motion of the parts of a single homogeneous material substance. He was a specific-property pluralist about the realm of mind, for he certainly held that God's mind differs in kind from human minds. It is evident that, if a man believes in a plurality of *kinds* of substance within a single realm of being, he must accept at least as great a plurality of *substances ;* and he may of course accept a much greater plurality of substances than of kinds.

This brings us to a third sense of "Monism" and "Pluralism". On the face of it there can be a plurality of substances having the same specific properties. *E.g.*, it is plainly true, in some sense, that there is a large number of human minds and a large number of hydrogen atoms in the universe. Now some men hold that the minds of Smith, Brown, Jones, and Robinson actually are distinct and independent substances; others hold that they are not strictly substances at all, but only states of a single substance. Similarly, some men hold that atoms or electrons are not strictly substances; but are merely different states of vortex-motion in a single substance, the ether. We might call the former class of people "Substantival Pluralists" and the latter class "Substantival Monists". Spinoza and Mr Bradley are examples of substantival monists; for both of them regard chairs and tables and minds, not as substances, but as "modifications", "differentiations", or "states" of a single Substance. But, whereas Spinoza is an extreme pluralist about differentiating attributes, Mr Bradley is a differentiating-attribute monist; for he thinks that the Absolute consists wholly of mental stuff or "experience", as he calls it.

Let us now sum up the results of this attempt at clarification. We have distinguished and exemplified three different kinds of opposition under the vague disjunction of Pluralism and Monism. (i) *Differentiating-attribute Pluralism and Monism*. This kind of pluralism may take two forms (apart altogether from the question of how many differentiating attributes are accepted). (*a*) It may allow that the differentiating attributes are all compatible with each other; in which case it is consistent with, though it does not entail, Substantival Monism. (*b*) It may deny the compatibility of some or of all combinations of differentiating attributes, in which case it entails some degree at any rate of Substantival Pluralism. (ii) *Specific-Property Pluralism and Monism*. This is the question whether there are or are not irreducibly different kinds of substance within the same realm of being, *i.e.*, with the same differentiating attributes. Monism about differentiating attributes is compatible with pluralism about specific properties (cf. Leibniz); and pluralism about differentiating attributes is compatible with monism about specific properties in some or in all realms of being (cf. Descartes' view of matter). Specific-property Monism is consistent with, but does not entail, Substantival Monism. Specific-property Pluralism does entail some degree at any rate of Substantival Pluralism. (iii) *Substantival Pluralism and Monism.* This is the question whether the apparent plurality of substances of the same kind is really a plurality of *substances* or only of the states or occurrents of a single Substance. As we have seen, Substantival Monism is not entailed by either of the other kinds of monism, but some degree of Substantival Pluralism is entailed by each of the other forms of pluralism. And, just as it is possible to be a Specific-property Monist for one realm of being and a Specific-property Pluralist for another realm, so it is possible to be a Substantival Monist for one realm and a Substantival Pluralist for another (cf. Descartes' views on Matter and Mind respectively).

Pluralism and Monism about Differentiating Attributes will be discussed in Section E of this book. Pluralism and Monism about Specific Properties in the realm of matter will be discussed in the next chapter. But I may not have another opportunity of saying anything about Substantival Monism and Pluralism, so I will end this chapter with some remarks about this antithesis.

The controversy between Substantival Monists and Pluralists seems to me to be partly verbal, and to depend on taking the word "substance" in a wider or a narrower sense. Suppose we define a *substance* simply as a particular existence, which is practically what Dr M'Taggart does. Then twinges of toothache, flashes of lightning, and so on, must be counted as substances. For they certainly exist or appear to exist literally in time, and they cannot occupy any position in a proposition except that of logical subject. But most people would refuse to call them "substances". They would call such objects "events in" or "states of" substances. Evidently these people mean by a "substance" something more specific than a particular existent. They would say that all substances are particular existents, but that the converse is not true. It is not very easy to say exactly what more is needed. One feature that seems to be assumed is that a substance must last for a considerable time. In fact, whatever else it may be, it would seem that it is supposed to be at least a series of events having a certain kind of internal unity and continuity both causal and spatio-temporal, and lasting at least long enough for this unity to be fully manifested. I think that it is also assumed by most people that all events which do not themselves last long enough to count as substances are parts of some series of interconnected events which is a substance.

It will be seen that, under these circumstances, the distinction between a substance and a mere event is likely to be hard to draw in practice, and that a certain particular existent will be asserted to be a substance by some and denied to be a substance by others. Moreover, we must notice that, when two things are very closely interconnected, some people would call them "two substances" whilst others would call the whole which they together form "one substance". *E.g.*, we generally think of a man's body as a single substance, though, from another point of view, his head is one substance and his trunk is another. Bearing these facts in mind, let us compare the ordinary view of the world as consisting of a plurality of substances with the view of a typical Substantival Monist, such as Spinoza. The ordinary man would count the various chairs in his room as so many distinct substances ; and he would take the same view about his own and his neighbours' minds. But he probably would not count the falling of a chair or a passing twinge of toothache as substances; he would say that they are only states or modifications of substances. And he would say this partly because they are so transitory, and partly because he thinks that they could not have existed by themselves; *e.g.*, that a fall can exist only as part of the history of some body, and that a feeling of toothache can exist only as part of the history of some mind. The plain man thus takes long duration, and the possibility of independent existence, as marks of a substance; and he takes transitoriness and incapacity for independent existence as marks of a mere state or modification of a substance.

Now it is very easy for a Substantival Monist to attack this position. How long must a particular last in order to count as a substance? The plain man says that a flash of lightning or a twinge of toothache is too transitory to be a substance, but holds that a human body lasts long enough to be a substance. But this is obviously rather arbitrary. The duration of a human body is very small as compared with that of the pyramids and almost negligible as compared with that of a mountain. Thus, if the distinction is to turn on mere duration, it seems difficult to find any safe resting-place between the two extreme views of Dr M'Taggart and of Spinoza, viz., that every particular existent, however transitory, is a substance, and that no existent can count as a substance unless it be eternal.

The common-sense view does not fare very much better if we take the capacity for independent existence as the characteristic mark of a substance. No doubt it is extremely difficult to conceive of a perfectly isolated twinge of toothache, forming no part of a longer and wider whole, called a "mind". But is it much easier to conceive the existence of a perfectly isolated human body, when you clearly understand what you are trying to do? Eating, breathing, sleeping, walking, etc., are all characteristic features of a living human body; and it is hard to see how anything with these properties could be conceived to exist without air to breathe, ground to walk on, and so on. Thus the radical distinction which common-sense draws between the twinge of toothache, as a mere state incapable of independent existence, and the human body as a genuine substance capable of existing independently, seems rather arbitrary on reflection. A Substantival Monist, like Spinoza, would meet the difficulty by saying that *no* finite particulars are capable of independent existence and that therefore none of them deserves the name of "substance". According to this view, nothing less than the whole material world throughout Space and Time would deserve the name of "substance". All finite bodies are merely states or modifications of this, which last for longer or shorter times and then break up, giving place to other modifications.

Probably many people would be ready to accept this mode of statement as on the whole the best way of expressing the known facts about the material realm. Perhaps we might, however, put the case somewhat differently. We might hold that, whilst the difference between a substantive and an adjective is a difference of kind, that between substances and states is a matter of degree. Anyone who held Substantival Monism to mean that chairs or minds are literally *adjectives*, *i.e.*, universals and not particulars, would plainly be talking nonsense. It is plain that the proposition : John Smith exists, does not mean : The Universe has a John-Smithy character, for this is either meaningless or false. It must be admitted that some Monists have talked as if they meant to assert some such nonsense as this; but it is charitable to suppose that they were merely expressing themselves badly. The difference between an adjective and a substantive is that between a universal and a particular, and it is irreducible. On the other hand, what would commonly be called a "substance" and what would commonly be called a "mere state" are both particulars. Now I would suggest that it is quite reasonable to talk of "degrees of substantiality". *Cæteris paribus*, an existent is more of a substance the longer it lasts and the less dependent it is on anything else. I should then agree with Spinoza to the following extent. I should say that the solar system is much more substantial than my body; and that my body is much more substantial than a sneeze; and that the whole material world, if it forms a single self-contained physical system, is still more of a substance than the solar system. So far I should agree with the more reasonable Substantival Monists, though I should state the facts in rather different language.

But, although the question at issue is thus *largely* verbal, it is not *wholly* so. There are three closely connected points to be noticed which are not merely verbal. (1) Spinoza took a similar view about mind to that which I have just been stating in my own way about matter. He held that finite minds are not genuine substances any more than finite bodies; they are just states or modifications of a single mind-substance. (He would of course have said "mind-*attribute*", but for the present purpose there is no important distinction between what Spinoza calls an "attribute" and what I am calling a "substance".) Now I can accept the negative part of this statement tentatively, but I see very little reason to accept the positive part. I think it is perfectly true that finite minds have a comparatively low degree of substantiality, unless they are very different from what they appear in this life to be. No doubt my mind is more substantial than a twinge of toothache. But, in the first place, it apparently begins and ends in time. Again, it is apparently not existing during large parts of the time between my birth and my death. Lastly, it seems to be extremely dependent on my body. These appearances may of course be decep-tive; we shall have to consider the question in greater detail in a future chapter. But I think we may fairly say that a human mind, taken at its face-value, is a poor sort of substance.

So far I should agree with Spinoza. But I cannot see much reason to think that there is anything mental which is *more* substantial than finite minds, poor things as they are ; or that finite minds are states of some one mental substance which is more substantial than themselves. The material realm does seem to form one single system in a fairly definite sense. All finite bodies have spatial relations to each other, and all physical events are causally interconnected by gravitation and other forces which bridge the spatio-temporal gaps between them. Moreover, the whole seems to be of much the same nature as the parts. The spatial and causal relations *within* a finite body and between its parts are of much the same nature as the spatial and causal relations *between* two finite bodies and within the material realm as a whole. Now, so far as one can see, there is very little analogy to this within the mental realm. No doubt some groups of minds form societies which last longer than any of their individual members ; and probably all human minds do belong to such societies. I think it would be perfectly correct to call Trinity College or the Judicial Committee of the Privy Council a "mental substance". But we must remember (*a*) that a society is in many ways less substantial than the minds which compose it ; (*b*) that it is not a mental substance, in the sense that it *is* a mind, but only in the sense that its *constituents* are minds. A society of minds is not a big mind ; but a system of bodies (such as the solar system) is just a big body ; (*c*) there is no one society which includes all minds ; and (*d*) the minds which are included in any one society are also as a rule included in others which are not parts of the first. The essential point is that the relations *within* a mind and between its states seem to be different in kind from the relations *between* several minds and within a society, and that no society is at once all-inclusive and very highly unified. I therefore can see no good ground for believing in a single mental substance of which all finite minds could be regarded as states or modifications. I think that this notion would become plausible only if we had reason to believe that all minds are in some kind of intimate telepathic union, analogous to gravitation in the material realm, and that the system thus formed was itself of the nature of a mind.

(2) The second qualification that must be made to my tentative acceptance of a form of Substantival Monism is this. I have granted that the typical material substances of ordinary life, viz., human bodies, chairs, trees, etc., are only imperfectly substantial, since they are transitory and incapable of existing in isolation. And I have granted that the solar system, and still more the whole material realm, can claim a higher degree of substantiality. But might we not say that some things which are much smaller than the material substances of daily life, viz., molecules, atoms, electrons, etc., can claim a very high degree of substantiality? If this be so, we could not agree with Spinoza in holding that *only* the material realm as a whole deserves to be called a material substance ; we should have to hold that there are also certain parts of the material realm which have just as good claims to this name. And I think that this must be admitted. We took endurance and capacity for independent existence as two tests for substantiality. Now a thing may be enduring and self-subsistent for two different reasons. (*a*) It may be so because it is so very inclusive. The solar system is more enduring and self-subsistent than my body because there is so very little outside it to upset it. (*b*) A thing may not include very much, but it may be extremely stable. This may happen in two different ways. (i) It may be that, although there are many things outside it, it is indifferent to nearly all of them, so that they have

no hold on it.   (ii) It may be that, although it is influenced by other things, it has an intense degree of internal unity and can be destroyed by these things only under very special circumstances which very seldom arise.   Now it seems to be a fact that, as you divide up the material realm in Space and Time, there are certain definite stages of division below which disintegrating forces which were formerly effective cease to be so, *e.g.*, a chair can be broken up by many means, including an axe.   A molecule cannot be split up by mechanical means, but it can be by heat or chemical reagents.   The ordinary atoms are so stable that only heroic methods will break them up.   I should say that, at the stages of molecules, atoms, and electrons, we come across genuine natural units each of which may fairly claim a high degree of substantiality.

(3) There is one other remark to be made.   We have said that the notion of a substance involves the persistence of something through a lapse of time, and that the longer this something persists the more substantial it is said to be.   But common-sense distinguishes between the mere persistence of *form* and the persistence of *stuff*.   We can identify a certain ripple on a sheet of water and follow it as it moves along just as well as we can identify a certain speck of dust and follow it as it rests or moves through the air.   But the persistence of the ripple is known to be just the fact that a certain kind of movement successively affects a continuous series of *different* particles of water; whilst the persistence of the speck of dust is the fact that *the same bit of stuff* occupies successively the same or a continuous series of successive places.   Now it is commonly held that the two kinds of persistence are essentially different; and that things which have the latter kind are substances, whilst those which have only the former are not.   On this view, if an electron could be shown to be merely a persistent vortex in the ether it would be denied to be a substance, even though it could be

shown that such a vortex must go on for ever. For, it would be said, an electron on this theory fails to fulfil the second condition of substantiality. From the nature of the case a vortex in the ether could not exist without the ether existing to move in whirlpools, but the ether could quite well have existed without moving in this or any other way. Hence the ether is the only genuine substance concerned, and the electrons would be counted merely as states, though endless and indestructible states, of the ether.

I doubt whether this sharp distinction between substances and mere states, based on the difference between the two kinds of persistence, can be upheld. (i) We must notice that there are border-line cases in which there is persistence of form with gradual change of stuff. Here common-sense does not hesitate to hold that we have a persistent substance. A human body is a fairly obvious instance. No doubt at two moments near together the bulk of the stuff of which it is composed is the same; but there is always some difference, and we all know that after a few years scarcely any of the same stuff remains. Yet, if the outward form and the characteristic ways of behaving are kept, no one hesitates to call it the same body or attempts to deny that it is a substance. (ii) Common-sense presumably regards a mind as a persistent substance; yet it may fairly be doubted whether in this case there is anything corresponding to the notion of persistent stuff. (iii) These, however, are merely examples of the fact that common-sense is not perfectly consistent in practice, which we all knew before. The important question is whether there is really any fundamental difference between persistence of stuff and persistence of form. If this distinction can be got rid of, it must be by reducing persistence of stuff to persistence of form, I think. Let us consider the case of what would be called "the same bit of stuff" resting for a time in one place and then moving to another. We must first distinguish between its purely spatial, properties, *i.e.*, its shape and size at any moment, and what I will call its "material qualities," *i.e.*, its colour, weight, chemical and physical constants, and so on. Now, if the persistence of this bit of stuff is to be reduced to persistence of form, in a wide sense, this reduction must be made somewhat as follows. We should have to say that all that is meant by the persistence of a certain bit of stuff is that certain determinable characteristics are manifested throughout a period of time in one or in a continuous series of determinate forms throughout one or a continuous series of places.

This attempted reduction of persistence of stuff to persistence of form seems most plausible when we confine our attention to solid bodies with sharp outlines which rest or move about *in vacuo* or in a fluid medium markedly different from themselves. It is much less plausible when we try to apply it to a homogeneous fluid. Imagine a homogeneous incompressible fluid with no solid bodies in it. Let us consider a small volume at any place within this fluid. Then, whether the fluid were wholly at rest or there were currents steadily circulating within it, precisely the same properties would continue to be manifested throughout the small volume that we have chosen for investigation. On the principles suggested above we should have to say in *both cases* that this volume contains a single persistent bit of stuff. But actually we always distinguish in theory the two cases (*a*) where the constancy of the properties manifested in any small volume is due to the fluid being at rest, so that nothing is flowing into or out of this volume; and (*b*) where this constancy is due to the fact that the fluid is in a steady state of internal motion, and the matter which flows into the volume is always exactly like the matter which it displaces therefrom. Since we plainly do distinguish these two cases in thought, even if we cannot always distinguish them in practice, it would seem that the attempted reduction of persistence of stuff to persistence of form has failed. (Of course it would be quite easy to distinguish the two cases in practice as well as in theory if we put a drop of highly coloured liquid into our fluid and saw whether the colour merely diffused slowly and equally in all directions or streamed out in one direction.)

I am inclined to think that there is a more ultimate objection than this, which applies as much to the attempted reduction for solids as to its application to homogeneous fluids. It seems to me that the theory in question presupposes the existence of Absolute Space, in a quite crude and literal sense. When it is said that certain properties continue to pervade "the same place", or that they successively pervade "a continuous series of different places", we presuppose the existence and persistence of these places. We are in fact thinking of Space as a kind of persistent homogeneous medium, which differs from the homogeneous-fluid ether only in the fact that it has nothing but spatial properties and that all its parts are eternally at rest. And we are thinking of the material properties as being manifested now in one part and now in another of this medium. But this just amounts to saying that the stuff of all material substances is Space. We shall still have to distinguish between a plurality of different bits of stuff, for each different volume in Space will now be a different bit of stuff. We have thus not got rid of the notion of stuff, nor dissolved persistence of stuff into persistence of form, nor avoided the necessity of accepting a plurality of different bits of stuff. The difference between this view and the more usual one is not that the former avoids the notion of stuff altogether whilst the latter uses it. The real differences are these. (a) On the present view no bit of stuff can move about; and the motion of a body becomes the successive inherence of the same or a continuous series of determinate qualities in a continuous series of different bits of stuff;

whilst, on the more usual view, bits of stuff themselves move about. And (*b*) on the present view the various bits of stuff are just different volumes within a single continuum ; whilst, on the more usual view, the various bits of stuff are not all in contact with each other at any time. The former type of theory, as I have said, requires Absolute Space, in the literal substantival sense ; whilst the latter fits in with a Relational Theory of Space. But neither can do without the notion of stuff or without accepting a plurality of different bits of stuff ; since Absolute Space becomes the stuff of the former theory, and the different parts of Absolute Space become the plurality of different bits of stuff.

My conclusion then is that in the long run we cannot be *Substantival* Monists about the material realm. For, if it be true that Absolute Space would be one substance and that space is the only *kind* of stuff in the material world, it is equally true that every part of Absolute Space is a distinct substance, so that there will be as many *bits* of stuff as there are different spaces within Absolute Space. The differences between a hydro-dynamic and an atomic view of the material world are no doubt important ; but it is a mistake to think that they are differences about *Substantival* Monism or Pluralism. For, as I have tried to show, both types of view presuppose Substantival Pluralism, though at different places. Really the question at issue between them is whether there is one *kind* of material stuff or many ; and this is the question of Specific-Property Monism or Pluralism.

SECTION A

Introductory Remarks

" Est quædam . . . . etiam nesciendi ars et scientia ; nam, si
turpe est nescire quæ possunt sciri, non minus turpe est scire se
putare quæ sciri nequeunt." (Lobeck, *Aglaophamus*, Bk. III :
Proœm.)

SECTION A

ALTERNATIVE THEORIES OF LIFE AND MIND AT THE LEVEL OF ENLIGHTENED COMMON-SENSE

Introductory Remarks

IN this section I propose to consider the problem of the mind's place in Nature, as it presents itself to educated persons who are acquainted in outline with the concepts and results of modern science. The restriction that I here impose on myself is that I take matter and mind to be very much as they appear to be to educated common-sense, and do not for the present consider in detail the modifications which philosophic criticism may introduce into those concepts. It will of course be necessary to remove this restriction at a later stage of the book; and this may entail considerable modifications in any tentative conclusions that we may reach here. A discussion at the present level, though necessarily imperfect, would be by no means useless, even though it were not to be corrected by later and more accurate investigations. For there really is a good deal to be said, and a good many confusions to be cleared up, in the ordinary discussions about Mechanism and Vitalism or Interaction and Parallelism.

The section is divided into two chapters; the first on *Mechanism and its Alternatives*, and the second on *The Traditional Problem of Body and Mind*. I should like to point out that the first of these chapters is essentially a discussion of Specific-Property Monism and Pluralism within the material realm; and that it has a most important bearing on "the connexion or lack of connexion between the various sciences ". If we give one kind of answer to the questions which are raised in that chapter we can hold that strictly there is one and only one science of matter, and that all the apparently different sciences which deal with various aspects of the material realm are merely departments of it. If we give the other kind of answer we shall have to hold that, even within the realm of matter, there is a plurality of sciences which are irreducible to each other, though they can be arranged in a hier-archical order.

CHAPTER II

Mechanism and its Alternatives

In this chapter I want to consider some of the characteristic differences which there seem to be among material objects, and to inquire how far these differences are ultimate and irreducible. On the face of it the world of material objects is divided pretty sharply into those which are alive and those which are not. And the latter seem to be of many different kinds, such as Oxygen, Silver, etc. The question which is of the greatest importance for our purpose is the nature of living organisms, since the only minds that we know of are bound up with them. But the famous controversy between Mechanists and Vitalists about living organisms is merely a particular case of the general question : Are the apparently different kinds of material objects irreducibly different?

It is this general question which I want to discuss at present. I do not expect to be able to give a definite answer to it ; and I am not certain that the question can ever be settled conclusively. But we can at least try to analyse the various alternatives, to state them clearly, and to see the implications of each. Once this has been done it is at least possible that people with an adequate knowledge of the relevant facts may be able to answer the question with a definite Yes or No ; and, until it has been done, all controversy on the subject is very much in the air. I think one feels that the disputes between Mechanists and Vitalists are unsatisfactory for two reasons. (i) One is never quite sure what is meant by " Mechanism " and by " Vitalism"; and one suspects that both names cover a multitude of theories which the protagonists have never distinguished and put clearly before themselves. And (ii) one wonders whether the question ought not to have been raised long before the level of life. Certainly living beings behave in a very different way from non-living ones; but it is also true that substances which interact chemically behave in a very different way from those which merely hit each other, like two billiard-balls. The question: Is chemical behaviour ultimately different from dynamical behaviour? seems just as reasonable as the question: Is vital behaviour ultimately different from non-vital behaviour? And we are much more likely to answer the latter question rightly if we see it in relation to similar questions which might be raised about other apparent differences of kind in the material realm.

The Ideal of Pure Mechanism. Let us first ask ourselves what would be the ideal of a mechanical view of the material realm. I think, in the first place, that it would suppose that there is only one fundamental kind of stuff out of which every material object is made. Next, it would suppose that this stuff has only one intrinsic quality, over and above its purely spatio-temporal and causal characteristics. The property ascribed to it might, *e.g.*, be inertial mass or electric charge. Thirdly, it would suppose that there is only one fundamental kind of change, viz., change in the relative positions of the particles of this stuff. Lastly, it would suppose that there is one fundamental law according to which one particle of this stuff affects the changes of another particle. It would suppose that this law connects particles by pairs, and that the action of any two aggregates of particles as wholes on each other is compounded in a simple and uniform way from the actions which the constituent particles taken by pairs would have on each other. Thus the essence of Pure Mechanism is (*a*) a single kind of stuff, all of whose parts are exactly alike except for differences of position and motion ; (*b*) a single fundamental kind of change, viz., change of position. Imposed on this there may of course be changes of a higher order, *e.g.*, changes of velocity, of acceleration, and so on ; (*c*) a single elementary causal law, according to which particles influence each other by pairs ; and (*d*) a single and simple principle of composition, according to which the behaviour of any aggregate of particles, or the influence of any one aggregate on any other, follows in a uniform way from the mutual influences of the constituent particles taken by pairs.

A set of gravitating particles, on the classical theory of gravitation, is an almost perfect example of the ideal of Pure Mechanism. The single elementary law is the inverse-square law for any pair of particles. The single and simple principle of composition is the rule that the influence of any set of particles on a single particle is the vector-sum of the influences that each would exert taken by itself. An electronic theory of matter departs to some extent from this ideal. In the first place, it has to assume at present that there are two ultimately different kinds of particle, viz., protons and electrons. Secondly, the laws of electro-magnetics cannot, so far as we know, be reduced to central forces. Thirdly, gravitational phenomena do not at present fall within the scheme ; and so it is necessary to ascribe masses as well as charges to the ultimate particles, and to introduce other elementary forces beside those of electro-magnetics.

On a purely mechanical theory all the apparently different kinds of matter would be made of the same stuff. They would differ only in the number, arrangement and movements of their constituent particles. And their apparently different kinds of behaviour would not be ultimately different. For they would all be deducible by a single simple principle of composition from the mutual influences of the particles taken by pairs; and these mutual influences would all obey a single law which is quite independent of the configurations and surroundings in which the particles happen to find themselves. The ideal which we have been describing and illustrating may be called "Pure Mechanism".

When a biologist calls himself a "Mechanist" it may fairly be doubted whether he means to assert anything so rigid as this. Probably all that he wishes to assert is that a living body is composed only of constituents which do or might occur in non-living bodies, and that its characteristic behaviour is wholly deducible from its structure and components and from the chemical, physical and dynamical laws which these materials would obey if they were isolated or were in non-living combinations. Whether the apparently different kinds of chemical substance are really just so many different configurations of a single kind of particles, and whether the chemical and physical laws are just the compounded results of the action of a number of similar particles obeying a single elementary law and a single principle of composition, he is not compelled as a biologist to decide. I shall later on discuss this milder form of "Mechanism," which is all that is presupposed in the controversies between mechanistic and vitalistic biologists. In the meanwhile I want to consider how far the ideal of Pure Mechanism could possibly be an adequate account of the world as we know it.

Limitations of Pure Mechanism. No one of course pretends that a satisfactory account even of purely physical processes in terms of Pure Mechanism *has* ever been given; but the question for us is: How far, and in what sense, *could* such a theory be adequate to all the known facts? On the face of it external objects have plenty of other characteristics beside mass or electric charge, *e.g.*, colour, temperature, etc. And, on the face of it, many changes take place in the external world beside changes of position, velocity, etc. Now of course many different views have been held about the nature and status of such characteristics as colour; but the one thing which no adequate theory of the external world can do is to ignore them altogether. I will state here very roughly the alternative types of theory, and show that none of them is compatible with Pure Mechanism as a complete account of the facts. (1) There is the naïve view that we are in immediate cognitive contact with parts of the surfaces of external objects, and that the colours and temperatures which we perceive quite literally inhere in those surfaces independently of our minds and of our bodies. On this view Pure Mechanism breaks down at the first move, for certain parts of the external world would have various properties different from and irreducible to the one fundamental property which Pure Mechanism assumes. This would not mean that what scientists have discovered about the connexion between heat and molecular motion, or light and periodic motion of electrons would be wrong. It might be perfectly true, so far as it went; but it would certainly not be the whole truth about the external world. We should have to begin by distinguishing between "macroscopic" and "microscopic" properties, to use two very convenient terms adopted by Lorentz. Colours, temperatures, etc., would be macroscopic properties, *i.e.*, they would need a certain minimum area or volume (and perhaps, as Dr Whitehead has suggested, a certain minimum duration) to inhere in. Other properties, such as mass or electric charge, might be able to inhere in volumes smaller than these minima and even in volumes and durations of any degree of smallness. Molecular and electronic theories of heat and light would then assert that a certain volume is pervaded by such and such a temperature or such and such a colour if and only if it contains certain arrangements of particles moving in certain ways. What we should have would be laws connecting the macroscopic qualities which inhere in a volume with the number, arrangement, and motion of the microscopic particles which are contained in this volume.

On such a view how much would be left of Pure Mechanism? (i) It would of course not be true of macroscopic properties. (ii) It might still be true of the microscopic particles in their interactions with each other. It might be that there is ultimately only one kind of particle, that it has only one non-spatio-temporal quality, that these particles affect each other by pairs according to a single law, and that their effects are compounded according to a single law. (iii) But, even if this were true of the microscopic particles in their relations *with each other*, it plainly could not be the *whole truth* about them. For there will also be laws connecting the presence of such and such a configuration of particles, moving in such and such ways, in a certain region, with the pervasion of this region by such and such a determinate value of a certain macroscopic quality, *e.g.*, a certain shade of red or a temperature of $57°$ C. These will be just as much laws of the external world as are the laws which connect the motions of one particle with those of another. And it is perfectly clear that the one kind of law cannot possibly be reduced to the other; since colour and temperature are irreducibly different characteristics from figure and motion, however close may be the causal connexion between the occurrence of the one kind of characteristic and that of the other. Moreover, there will have to be a number of different and irreducible laws connecting microscopic with macroscopic characteristics; for there are many different and irreducible determinable macroscopic characteristics, *e.g.*, colour, temperature, sound, etc. And each will need its own peculiar law.

(2) A second conceivable view would be that in

perception we are in direct cognitive contact with parts of the surfaces of external objects, and that, so long as we are looking at them or feeling them, they do have the colours or temperatures which they then seem to us to have.   But that the inherence of colours and temperatures in external bodies is dependent upon the presence of a suitable bodily organism, or a suitable mind, or of both, in a suitable relation to the external object.

On such a view it is plain that Pure Mechanism cannot be an adequate theory of the external world of matter.   For colours and temperatures would belong to external objects on this view, though they would characterise an external object only when very special conditions are fulfilled.   And evidently the laws according. to which, *e.g.*, a certain shade of colour inheres in a certain external region when a suitable organism or mind is in suitable relations to that region cannot be of the mechanical type.

(3) A third conceivable view is that physical objects can seem to have qualities which do not really belong to any physical object, *e.g.*, that a pillar-box can seem to have a certain shade of red although really no physical object has any colour at all.   This type of theory divides into two forms.   (*a*) It might be held that, when a physical object seems to have a certain shade of red, there really is *something* in the world which has this shade of red, although this something cannot be a physical object or literally a part of one.   Some would say that there is a red mental state—a "sensation"—; others that the red colour belongs to something which is neither mental nor physical.*   On either of these alternatives it would be conceivable that Pure Mechanism was the whole truth about matter considered in its relations with matter.   But it would be certain that it is not the whole truth about matter when this limitation is removed.   Granted that bits of matter only *seem* to be red or to be hot, we still claim to know a good deal about the conditions under which one bit of matter will

* (*b*) It might be held that *nothing* in the world really has colour, though certain things *seem* to have certain colours.   The relation of "seeming to have" is taken as ultimate.

seem to be red and another to be blue and about the
conditions under which one bit of matter will seem to
be hot and another to be cold.   This knowledge belongs
partly to physics and partly to the physiology and
anatomy of the brain and nervous system.   We know
little or nothing about the mental conditions which have
to be fulfilled if an external object is to seem red or
hot to a percipient ; but we can say that this depends
on an unknown mental factor x and on certain physical
conditions a, b, c, etc., partly within and partly outside
the percipient's body, about which we know a good
deal.   It is plain then that, on the present theory,
physical events and objects do not merely interact
mechanically with each other ; they also play their
part, along with a mental factor, in causing such and
such an external object to seem to such and such an
observer to have a certain quality which really no
physical object has.   In fact, for the present purpose,
the difference between theories (2) and (3) is simply
the following.   On theory (2) certain events in the
external object, in the observer's body, and possibly
in his mind, cause a certain quality to inhere in the
external object so long as they are going on.   On
theory (3) they cause the same quality to *seem* to inhere
in the same object, so long as they are going on,
though *actually* it does not inhere in any physical
object.   Theory (1), for the present purpose, differs
from theory (2) only in taking the naïve view that
the body and mind of the observer are irrelevant to
the *occurrence* of the sensible quality in the external
object, though of course it would admit that these
factors are relevant to the *perception* of this quality
by the observer.   This last point is presumably
common to all three theories.

I will now sum up the argument.   The plain
fact is that the external world, as perceived by us,
seems not to have the homogeneity demanded by
Pure Mechanism.   If it *really* has the various irreduc-

ibly different sensible qualities which it *seems* to have, Pure Mechanism cannot be true of the whole of the external world and cannot be the whole truth about any part of it. The best that we can do for Pure Mechanism on this theory is to divide up the external world first on a macroscopic and then on a microscopic scale; to suppose that the macroscopic qualities which pervade any region are causally determined by the microscopic events and objects which exist within it; and to hope that the latter, in their interactions with *each other* at any rate, fulfil the conditions of Pure Mechanism. This result may remind the reader of the carefully qualified compliment which Mr Gibbon pays to the morality of the Negroes in a foot-note which I forbear from quoting. We must remember, moreover, that there is no *a priori* reason why microscopic events and objects should answer the demands of Pure Mechanism even in their interactions with each other; that, so far as science can tell us at present, they do not; and that, in any case, the laws connecting them with the occurrence of macroscopic qualities *cannot* be mechanical in the sense defined.

If, on the other hand, we deny that physical objects have the various sensible qualities which they seem to us to have, we are still left with the fact that some things *seem* to be red, others to be blue, others to be hot, and so on. And a complete account of the world must include some explanation of such events as "seeming red to me", "seeming blue to you", etc. We can admit that the ultimate physical objects may all be exactly alike, may all have only one non-spatio-temporal and non-causal property, and may interact with each other in the way which Pure Mechanism requires. But we must admit that they are also cause-factors in determining the *appearance*, if not the *occurrence*, of the various sensible qualities at such and such places and times. And, in these transactions, the laws which they obey *cannot* be mechanical.

We may put the whole matter in a nutshell by saying that the appearance of a plurality of irreducible sensible qualities forces us, no matter what theory we adopt about their status, to distinguish two different kinds of law. One may be called "intra-physical" and the other "trans-physical". The intra-physical laws may be, though there seems no positive reason to suppose that they are, of the kind required by Pure Mechanism. If so, there is just one ultimate elementary intra-physical law and one ultimate principle of composition for intra-physical transactions. But the trans-physical laws cannot satisfy the demands of Pure Mechanism; and, so far as I can see, there must be at least as many irreducible trans-physical laws as there are irreducible determinable sense-qualities. The nature of the trans-physical laws will of course depend on the view that we take about the status of sensible qualities. It will be somewhat different for each of the three alternative types of theory which I have mentioned, and it will differ according to which form of the third theory we adopt. But it is not necessary for our present purpose to go into further detail on this point.

The Three Possible Ways of accounting for characteristic Differences of Behaviour. So far we have confined our attention to pure qualities, such as red, hot, etc. By calling these "pure qualities" I mean that, when we say "This is red", "This is hot", and so on, it is no part of the meaning of our predicate that "this" stands in such and such a relation to something else. It is *logically* possible that this should be red even though "this" were the only thing in the world; though it is probably not *physically* possible. I have argued so far that the fact that external objects seem to have a number of irreducibly different pure qualities makes it certain that Pure Mechanism cannot be an adequate account of the external world. I want now to consider differences of *behaviour* among external

objects.   These are not differences of pure quality.
When I say "This combines with that", "This eats
and digests", and so on, I am making statements which
would have no meaning if "this" were the only thing
in the world.   Now there are apparently extremely
different kinds of behaviour to be found among external
objects.   A bit of gold and a bit of silver behave quite
differently when put into nitric acid.   A cat and an
oyster behave quite differently when put near a mouse.
Again, all bodies which would be said to be "alive",
behave differently in many ways from all bodies which
would be said not to be "alive".   And, among non-
living bodies, what we call their "chemical behaviour"
is very different from what we call their "merely physical
behaviour".   The question that we have now to discuss
is this : "Are the differences between merely physical,
chemical, and vital behaviour ultimate and irreducible
or not?   And are the differences in chemical behaviour
between Oxygen and Hydrogen, or the differences in
vital behaviour between trees and oysters and cats,
ultimate and irreducible or not?"   I do not expect to
be able to give a conclusive answer to this question, as
I do claim to have done to the question about differences
of pure quality.   But I hope at least to state the possible
alternatives clearly, so that people with an adequate
knowledge of the relevant empirical facts may know
exactly what we want them to discuss, and may not
beat the air in the regrettable way in which they too
often have done.

We must first notice a difference between vital behaviour, on the one hand, and chemical behaviour, on
the other.   On the macroscopic scale, *i.e.*, within the
limits of what we can perceive with our unaided senses
or by the help of optical instruments, *all* matter seems
to behave chemically from time to time, though there
may be long stretches throughout which a given bit
of matter has no chance to exhibit any marked chemical
behaviour.   But only a comparatively few bits of matter

ever exhibit vital behaviour. These are always very complex chemically; they are always composed of the same comparatively small selection of chemical elements; and they generally have a characteristic external form and internal structure. All of them after a longer or shorter time cease to show vital behaviour, and soon after this they visibly lose their characteristic external form and internal structure. We do not know how to make a living body out of non-living materials; and we do not know how to make a once living body, which has ceased to behave vitally, live again. But we know that plants, so long as they are alive, do take up inorganic materials from their surroundings and build them up into their own substance; that all living bodies maintain themselves for a time through constant change of material; and that they all have the power of restoring themselves when not too severely injured, and of producing new living bodies like themselves.

Let us now consider what general types of view are possible about the fact that certain things behave in characteristically different ways. (1) Certain characteristically different ways of behaving may be regarded as absolutely unanalysable facts which do not depend *in any way* on differences of structure or components. This would be an absurd view to take about vital behaviour, for we know that all living bodies have a complex structure even on the macroscopic scale, and that their characteristic behaviour depends *in part* at least on their structure and components. It would also be a foolish view to take about the chemical behaviour of non-living substances which are known to be compounds and can be split up and re-synthesised by us from their elements. But it was for many years the orthodox view about the chemical elements. It was held that the characteristic differences between the behaviour of Oxygen and Hydrogen are due in no way to differences of structure or components, but must simply be accepted as ultimate facts. This first alternative can hardly be counted as one way of *explaining* differences of behaviour, since it consists in holding that there are certain differences which cannot be explained, even in part, but must simply be swallowed whole with that philosophic jam which Professor Alexander calls "natural piety". It is worth while to remark that we could never be logically compelled to hold this view, since it is always open to us to suppose that what is macroscopically homogeneous has a complex microscopic structure which wholly or partly determines its characteristic macroscopic behaviour. Nevertheless, it is perfectly possible that this hypothesis is not true in certain cases, and that there are certain ultimate differences in the material world which must just be accepted as brute facts.

(2) We come now to types of theory which profess to explain, wholly or partly, differences of behaviour in terms of structure or components or both. These of course all presuppose that the objects that we are dealing with are at any rate microscopically complex: an hypothesis, as I have said, which can never be conclusively refuted. We may divide up these theories as follows. (*a*) Those which hold that the characteristic behaviour of a certain object or class of objects is in part dependent on the presence of a peculiar *component* which does not occur in anything that does not behave in this way. This is of course the usual view to take about the characteristic chemical behaviour of compounds. We say that Silver Chloride behaves differently from Common Salt because one contains Silver and the other Sodium. It is always held that differences of microscopic *structure* are also relevant to explaining differences of macroscopic chemical behaviour. *E.g.*, the very marked differences between the chemical behaviour of acetone and propion aldehyde, which both consist of Carbon, Hydrogen, and Oxygen in exactly

the same proportions, are ascribed to the fact that the
former has the structure symbolised by

$$CH_3—C—CH_3$$
$$\|$$
$$O$$

and that the latter has the structure symbolised by

$$CH_3 \cdot CH_2 \cdot C \overset{O}{\underset{H}{\diagdown}} .$$

The doctrine which I will call "Substantial Vitalism"
is logically a theory of this type about vital behaviour.
It assumes that a necessary factor in explaining the
characteristic behaviour of living bodies is the presence
in them of a peculiar component, often called an
"Entelechy", which does not occur in inorganic
matter or in bodies which were formerly alive but
have now died. I will try to bring out the analogies
and differences between this type of theory as applied
to vital behaviour and as applied to the behaviour of
chemical compounds. (i) It is not supposed that the
presence of an entelechy is *sufficient* to explain vital
behaviour; as in chemistry, the structure of the complex is admitted to be also an essential factor. (ii) It
is admitted that entelechies cannot be isolated, and
that perhaps they cannot exist apart from the complex
which is a living organism. But there is plenty of
analogy to this in chemistry. In the first place,
elements have been recognised, and the characteristic
behaviour of certain compounds has been ascribed to
their presence, long before they were isolated. Secondly,
there are certain groups, like CH_3 and C_6H_5 in organic
chemistry, which cannot exist in isolation, but which
nevertheless play an essential part in determining the
characteristic behaviour of certain compounds. (iii) The
entelechy is supposed to exert some kind of directive
influence over matter which enters the organism from
outside. There is a faint analogy to this in certain
parts of organic chemistry. The presence of certain

groups in certain positions in a Benzene nucleus makes it very easy to put certain other groups and very hard to put others into certain positions in the nucleus. There are well-known empirical rules on this point.

Why then do most of us feel pretty confident of the truth of the chemical explanation and very doubtful of the formally analogous explanation of vital behaviour in terms of entelechies? I think that our main reasons are the following, and that they are fairly sound ones. (i) It is true that some elements were recognised and used for chemical explanations long before they were isolated. But a great many other elements had been isolated, and it was known that the process presented various degrees of difficulty. No entelechy, or anything like one, has ever been isolated; hence an entelechy is a *purely* hypothetical entity in a sense in which an as yet unisolated but suspected chemical element is not. If it be said that an isolated entelechy is from the nature of the case something which could not be perceived, and that this objection is therefore unreasonable, I can only answer (as I should to the similar assertion that the physical phenomena of mediumship can happen only in darkness and in the presence of sympathetic spectators) that it may well be true but is certainly very unfortunate. (ii) It is true that some groups which cannot exist in isolation play a most important part in chemical explanations. But they are *groups* of known composition, not mysterious simple entities; and their inability to exist by themselves is not an isolated fact but is part of the more general, though imperfectly understood, fact of valency. Moreover, we can at least pass these groups from one compound to another, and can note how the chemical properties change as one compound loses such a group and another gains it. There is no known analogy to this with entelechies. You cannot pass an entelechy from a living man into a corpse and note that the former ceases and the latter begins to behave vitally. (iii) Entelechies are supposed to differ in kind from material particles; and it is doubtful whether they are literally in Space at all. It is thus hard to understand what exactly is meant by saying that a living body is a compound of an entelechy and a material structure; and impossible to say anything in detail about the structure of the total complex thus formed.

These objections seem to me to make the doctrine of Substantial Vitalism unsatisfactory, though not impossible. I think that those who have accepted it have done so largely under a misapprehension. They have thought that there was no alternative between Biological Mechanism (which I shall define a little later) and Substantial Vitalism. They found the former unsatisfactory, and so they felt obliged to accept the latter. We shall see in a moment, however, that there is another alternative type of theory, which I will call "Emergent Vitalism", borrowing the adjective from Professors Alexander and Lloyd Morgan. Of course positive arguments have been put forward in favour of entelechies, notably by Driesch. I do not propose to consider them in detail. I will merely say that Driesch's arguments do not seem to me to be in the least conclusive, even against Biological Mechanism, because they seem to forget that the smallest fragment which we can make of an organised body by cutting it up may contain an enormous number of similar microscopic structures, each of enormous complexity. And, even if it be held that Driesch has conclusively *dis*proved Biological Mechanism, I cannot see that his arguments have the least tendency to *prove* Substantial Vitalism rather than the Emergent form of Vitalism which does not assume entelechies.

(*b*) I come now to the second type of theory which professes to explain, wholly or partly, the differences of behaviour between different things. This kind of theory denies that there need be any peculiar *component* which is present in all things that behave in a certain way and is absent from all things which do not behave in this way. It says that the components may be exactly alike in both cases, and it tries to explain the difference of behaviour wholly in terms of difference of structure. Now it is most important to notice that this type of theory can take two radically different forms. They differ according to the view that we take about the laws which connect the properties of the components with the characteristic behaviour of the complex wholes which they make up. (i) On the first form of the theory the characteristic behaviour of the whole *could* not, even in theory, be deduced from the most complete know-ledge of the behaviour of its components, taken separately or in other combinations, and of their proportions and arrangements in this whole. This alternative, which I have roughly outlined and shall soon discuss in detail, is what I understand by the "Theory of Emergence". I cannot give a conclusive example of it, since it is a matter of controversy whether it actually applies to anything. But there is no doubt, as I hope to show, that it is a logically possible view with a good deal in its favour. I will merely remark that, so far as we know at present, the characteristic behaviour of Common Salt cannot be deduced from the most complete know-ledge of the properties of Sodium in isolation ; or of Chlorine in isolation ; or of other compounds of Sodium, such as Sodium Sulphate, and of other compounds of Chlorine, such as Silver Chloride. (ii) On the second form of the theory the characteristic behaviour of the whole is not only completely *determined by* the nature and arrangement of its components ; in addition to this it is held that the behaviour of the whole could, in theory at least, be *deduced* from a sufficient knowledge of how the components behave in isolation or in other wholes of a simpler kind. I will call this kind of theory "Mechanistic". A theory may be "mechanistic" in this sense without being an instance of Pure Mechanism, in the sense defined earlier in this chapter. *E.g.*, if a biologist held that all the characteristic behaviour of living beings could be deduced from an adequate knowledge of the physical and chemical laws which its components would obey in isolation or in non-living complexes, he would be called a "Biological Mechanist" even though he believed that the different chemical elements are ultimately different kinds of stuff and that the laws of chemical composition are not of the type demanded by Pure Mechanism.

The most obvious examples of wholes to which a mechanistic theory applies are artificial machines. A clock behaves in a characteristic way. But no one supposes that the peculiar behaviour of clocks depends on their containing as a component a peculiar entity which is not present in anything but clocks. Nor does anyone suppose that the peculiar behaviour of clocks is simply an emergent quality of that kind of structure and cannot be learnt by studying anything but clocks. We know perfectly well that the behaviour of a clock can be deduced from the particular arrangement of springs, wheels, pendulum, etc., in it, and from general laws of mechanics and physics which apply just as much to material systems which are not clocks.

To sum up. We have distinguished three possible types of theory to account wholly or partly for the characteristic differences of behaviour between different kinds of material object, viz., the Theory of a Special Component, the Theory of Emergence, and the Mechanistic Theory. We have illustrated these, so far as possible, with examples which everyone will accept. In the special problem of the peculiar behaviour of living bodies these three types of theory are represented by Substantial Vitalism, Emergent Vitalism, and Biological Mechanism. I have argued that Substantial Vitalism, though logically possible, is a very unsatisfactory kind of theory, and that probably many people who have accepted it have done so because they did not recognise the alternative of Emergent Vitalism. I propose now to consider in greater detail the emergent and the mechanistic types of theory.

Emergent Theories. Put in abstract terms the emergent theory asserts that there are certain wholes, composed (say) of constituents A, B, and C in a relation R to each other ; that all wholes composed of constituents of the same kind as A, B, and C in relations of the same kind as R have certain characteristic properties ; that A, B, and C are capable of occurring in other kinds of complex where the relation is not of the same kind as R ; and that the characteristic properties of the whole R(A, B, C) cannot, even in theory, be deduced from the most complete knowledge of the properties of A, B, and C in isolation or in other wholes which are not of the form R(A, B, C). The mechanistic theory rejects the last clause of this assertion.

Let us now consider the question in detail. If we want to explain the behaviour of any whole in terms of its structure and components we *always* need two independent kinds of information. (*a*) We need to know how the parts would behave separately. And (*b*) we need to know the law or laws according to which the behaviour of the separate parts is compounded when they are acting together in any proportion and arrangement. Now it is extremely important to notice that these two bits of information are quite independent of each other in every case. Let us consider, *e.g.*, the simplest possible case. We know that a certain tap, when running by itself, will put so many cubic centimetres of water into a tank in a minute. We know that a certain other tap, when running by itself, will put so many cubic centimetres of water into this tank in the same time. It does not follow logically from these two bits of information that, when the two taps are turned on together, the sum of these two numbers of cubic centimetres will be added to the contents of the tank every minute. This might not happen for two reasons. In the first place, it is quite likely that, if the two taps came from the same pipe, less would flow from each when both were turned on together than when each was turned on separately ; *i.e.*, the separate factors do not behave together as they would have behaved in isolation. Again, if one tap delivered hot water and the other cold water, the simple assumption about composition would break down although the separate factors continued to obey the same laws as they had followed when acting in isolation. For there would be a change of volume on mixture of the hot and cold water.

Next let us consider the case of two forces acting on a particle at an angle to each other. We find by experiment that the actual motion of the body is the vector-sum of the motions which it would have had if each had been acting separately. There is not the least possibility of deducing this law of composition from the laws of each force taken separately. There is one other fact worth mentioning here. As Mr Russell pointed out long ago, a vector-sum is not a sum in the ordinary sense of the word. We cannot strictly say that each force is doing what it would have done if it had been alone, and that the result of their joint action is the sum of the results of their separate actions. A velocity of 5 miles an hour in a certain direction does not literally contain as parts a velocity of 3 miles an hour in a certain other direction and a velocity of 4 miles an hour in a direction at right angles to this. All that we can say is that the effect of several forces acting together is a fairly simple mathematical function of the purely hypothetical effects which each would have had if it had acted by itself, and that this function reduces to an algebraical sum in the particular case where all the forces are in the same line.

We will now pass to the case of chemical composition. Oxygen has certain properties and Hydrogen has certain other properties. They combine to form water, and the proportions in which they do this are fixed. Nothing that we know about Oxygen by itself or in its combinations with anything but Hydrogen would give us the least reason to suppose that it would combine with Hydrogen at all. Nothing that we know about Hydrogen by itself or in its combinations with anything but Oxygen would give us the least reason to expect that it would combine with Oxygen at all. And most of the chemical and physical properties of water have no known connexion, either quantitative or qualitative, with those of Oxygen and Hydrogen. Here we have a clear instance of a case where, so far as we can tell, the properties of a whole composed of two constituents could not have been predicted from a knowledge of the properties of these constituents taken separately, or from this combined with a knowledge of the properties of other wholes which contain these constituents.

Let us sum up the conclusions which may be reached from these examples before going further. It is clear that in *no* case could the behaviour of a whole composed of certain constituents be predicted *merely* from a knowledge of the properties of these constituents, taken separately, and of their proportions and arrangements in the particular complex under consideration. Whenever this *seems* to be possible it is because we are using a suppressed premise which is so familiar that it has escaped our notice. The suppressed premise is the fact that we have examined other complexes in the past and have noted their behaviour; that we have found a general law connecting the behaviour of these wholes with that which their constituents would show in isolation; and that we are assuming that this law of composition will hold also of the particular complex whole at present under consideration. For purely dynamical transactions this assumption is pretty well justified, because we have found a simple law of composition and have verified it very fully for wholes of very different composition, complexity, and internal structure. It is therefore not particularly rash to expect to predict the dynamical behaviour of any material complex under the action of any set of forces, however much it may differ in the details of its structure and parts from those complexes for which the assumed law of composition has actually been verified.

The example of chemical compounds shows us that we have no right to expect that the same simple law of composition will hold for chemical as for dynamical transactions. And it shows us something further. It shows us that, if we want to know the chemical (and many of the physical) properties of a chemical compound, such as silver-chloride, it is absolutely necessary to study samples of *that particular compound*. It would of course (on any view) be useless merely to study silver in isolation and chlorine in isolation ; for that would tell us nothing about the law of their conjoint action. This would be equally true even if a mechanistic explanation of the chemical behaviour of compounds were possible. The essential point is that it would also be useless to study chemical compounds in general and to compare their properties with those of their elements in the hope of discovering a *general* law of composition by which the properties of *any* chemical compound could be foretold when the properties of its separate elements were known. So far as we know, there is no general law of this kind. It is useless even to study the properties of other compounds of silver and of other compounds of chlorine in the hope of discovering one general law by which the properties of silver-compounds could be predicted from those of elementary silver and another general law by which the properties of chlorine-compounds could be predicted from those of elementary chlorine. No doubt the properties of silver-chloride are completely *determined* by those of silver and of chlorine ; in the sense that whenever you have a whole composed of these two elements in certain proportions and relations you have something with the characteristic properties of silver-chloride, and that nothing has these properties except a whole composed in this way. But the law connecting the properties of silver-chloride with those of silver and of chlorine and with the structure of the compound is, so far as we know, an *unique* and *ultimate* law. By this I mean (*a*) that it is not a special case which arises through substituting certain determinate values for determinable variables in a general law which connects the properties of *any* chemical compound with those of its separate elements and with its structure. And (*b*) that it is not a special case which arises by combining two more general laws, one of which connects the properties of *any* silver-compound with those of elementary silver, whilst the other connects the properties of *any* chlorine-compound with those of elementary chlorine. So far as we know there are no such laws. It is (*c*) a law which could have been discovered *only* by studying samples of silver-chloride itself, and which can be extended inductively *only* to other samples of the same substance.

We may contrast this state of affairs with that which exists where a mechanistic explanation is possible. In order to predict the behaviour of a clock a man need never have seen a clock in his life. Provided he is told how it is constructed, and that he has learnt from the study of *other* material systems the general rules about motion and about the mechanical properties of springs and of rigid bodies, he can foretell exactly how a system constructed like a clock must behave.

The situation with which we are faced in chemistry, which seems to offer the most plausible example of emergent behaviour, may be described in two alternative ways. These may be theoretically different, but in practice they are equivalent. (i) The first way of putting the case is the following. What we call the "properties" of the chemical elements are very largely propositions about the compounds which they form with other elements under suitable conditions. *E.g.*, one of the "properties" of silver is that it combines under certain conditions with chlorine to give a compound with the properties of silver-chloride. Likewise one of the "properties" of chlorine is that under certain conditions it combines with silver to give a compound with the properties of silver-chloride. These "properties" cannot be deduced from any selection of the other properties of silver or of chlorine. Thus we may say that we do not know all the properties of chlorine and of silver until they have been put in presence of each other; and that no amount of knowledge about the properties which they manifest in other circumstances will tell us what property, if any, they will manifest in these circumstances. Put in this way the position is that we do not know all the properties of any element, and that there is always the possibility of their manifesting unpredictable properties when put into new situations. This happens whenever a chemical compound is prepared or discovered for the first time. (ii) The other way to put the matter is to confine the name "property" to those characteristics which the elements manifest when they do not act chemically on each other, *i.e.*, the physical characteristics of the isolated elements. In this case we may indeed say, if we like, that we know all the properties of each element; but we shall have to admit that we do not know the laws according to which elements, which have these properties in isolation, together produce compounds having such and such other characteristic properties. The essential point is that the behaviour of an as yet unexamined compound cannot be predicted from a knowledge of the properties of its elements in isolation or from a knowledge of the properties of their other compounds; and it matters little whether we ascribe this to the existence of innumerable "latent" properties in each element, each of which is manifested only in the presence of a certain other element; or to the lack of any general principle of composition, such as the parallelogram law in dynamics, by which the behaviour of any chemical compound could be deduced from its structure and from the behaviour of each of its elements in isolation from the rest.

Let us now apply the conceptions, which I have been explaining and illustrating from chemistry, to the case of vital behaviour. We know that the bits of matter which behave vitally are composed of various chemical compounds arranged in certain characteristic ways. We have prepared and experimented with many of these compounds apart from living bodies, and we see no obvious reason why some day they might not all be synthesised and studied in the chemical laboratory. A living body might be regarded as a compound of the second order, *i.e.*, a compound composed of compounds ; just as silver-chloride is a compound of the first order, *i.e.*, one composed of chemical elements. Now it is obviously possible that, just as the characteristic behaviour of a first-order compound could not be predicted from any amount of knowledge of the properties of its elements in isolation or of the properties of other first-order compounds, so the properties of a second-order compound could not be predicted from any amount of knowledge about the properties of its first-order constituents taken separately or in other surroundings. Just as the only way to find out the properties of silver-chloride is to study samples of silver-chloride, and no amount of study of silver and of chlorine taken separately or in other combinations will help us ; so the only way to find out the characteristic behaviour of living bodies may be to study living bodies as such. And no amount of knowledge about how the constituents of a living body behave in isolation or in other and non-living wholes might suffice to enable us to predict the characteristic behaviour of a living organism. This possibility is perfectly compatible with the view that the characteristic behaviour of a living body is completely determined by the nature and arrangement of the chemical compounds which compose it, in the sense that any whole which is composed of such compounds in such an arrangement will show vital behaviour and that nothing else will do so. We should merely have to recognise, as we had to do in considering a first-order compound like silver-chloride, that we are dealing with an *unique* and *irreducible* law ; and not with a special case which arises by the substitution of particular values for variables in a more general law, nor with a combination of several more general laws.

We could state this possibility about living organisms in two alternative but practically equivalent ways, just as we stated the similar possibility about chemical compounds. (i) The first way would be this. Most of the properties which we ascribe to chemical compounds are statements about what they do in presence of various chemical reagents under certain conditions of temperature, pressure, etc. These various properties are not deducible from each other ; and, until we have tried a compound with every other compound and under every possible condition of temperature, pressure, etc., we cannot possibly know that we have exhausted all its properties. It is therefore perfectly possible that, in the very special situation in which a chemical compound is placed in a living body, it may exhibit properties which remain "latent" under all other conditions. (ii) The other, and practically equivalent, way of putting the case is the following. If we confine the name "property" to the behaviour which a chemical compound shows in isolation, we may perhaps say that we know all the "properties" of the chemical constituents of a living body. But we shall not be able to predict the behaviour of the body unless we also know the laws according to which the behaviour which each of these constituents *would have* shown in isolation is compounded when they are acting together in certain proportions and arrangements. We can discover such laws only by studying complexes containing these constituents in various proportions and arrangements. And we have no right to suppose that the laws which we have discovered by studying non-living complexes can be carried over without modification to the very different case of living complexes. It may be that the only way to discover the laws according to which the behaviour of the separate constituents combines to produce the behaviour of the whole in a living body is to study living bodies as such. For practical purposes it makes little difference whether we say that the chemical compounds which compose a living body have "latent properties" which are manifested only when they are parts of a whole of this peculiar structure; or whether we say that the properties of the constituents of a living body are the same whether they are in it or out of it, but that the law according to which these separate effects are compounded with each other is different in a living whole from what it is in any non-living whole.

This view about living bodies and vital behaviour is what I call "Emergent Vitalism"; and it is important to notice that it is quite different from what I call "Substantial Vitalism". So far as I can understand them I should say that Driesch is a Substantial Vitalist, and that Dr J. S. Haldane is an Emergent Vitalist. But I may quite well be wrong in classifying these two distinguished men in this way.

Mechanistic Theories. The mechanistic type of theory is much more familiar than the emergent type, and it will therefore be needless to consider it in great detail. I will just consider the mechanistic alternative about chemical and vital behaviour, so as to make the emergent theory still clearer by contrast. Suppose it were certain, as it is very probable, that all the different chemical atoms are composed of positive and negative electrified particles in different numbers and arrangements; and that these differences of number and arrangement are the only ultimate difference between them. Suppose that all these particles obey the same elementary laws, and that their separate actions are compounded with each other according to a single law which is the same no matter how complicated may be the whole of which they are constituents. Then it would be *theoretically* possible to deduce the characteristic behaviour of any element from an adequate knowledge of the number and arrangement of the particles in its atom, without needing to observe a sample of the substance. We could, *in theory*, deduce what other elements it would combine with and in what proportions; which of these compounds would be stable to heat, etc.; and how the various compounds would react in presence of each other under given conditions of temperature, pressure, etc. And all this should be *theoretically* possible without needing to observe samples of these compounds.

I want now to explain exactly what I mean by the qualification "theoretically". (1) In the first place the mathematical difficulties might be overwhelming in practice, even if we knew the structure and the laws. This is a trivial qualification for our present purpose, which is to bring out the *logical* distinction between mechanism and emergence. Let us replace Sir Ernest Rutherford by a mathematical archangel, and pass on. (2) Secondly, we cannot directly perceive the microscopic structure of atoms, but can only infer it from the macroscopic behaviour of matter in bulk. Thus, in practice, even if the mechanistic hypothesis were true and the mathematical difficulties were overcome, we should have to start by observing enough of the macroscopic behaviour of samples of each element to infer the probable structure of its atom. But, once this was done, it should be possible to deduce its behaviour in macroscopic conditions under which it has never yet been observed. That is, if we could infer its microscopic structure from a *selection* of its observed macroscopic properties, we could henceforth *deduce* all its other macroscopic properties from its microscopic structure without further appeal to observation. The difference from the emergent theory is thus profound, even when we allow for our mathematical and perceptual limitations. If the emergent theory of chemical compounds be true, a mathematical archangel, gifted with the further power of perceiving the microscopic structure of atoms as easily as we can perceive hay-stacks, could no more predict the behaviour of silver or of chlorine or the properties of silver-chloride without having observed samples of those substances than we can at present. And he could no more deduce the rest of the properties of a chemical element or compound from a selection of its properties than we can.

Would there be any theoretical limit to the deduction of the properties of chemical elements and compounds if a mechanistic theory of chemistry were true? Yes. Take any ordinary statement, such as we find in chemistry books; *e.g.*, "Nitrogen and Hydrogen combine when an electric discharge is passed through a mixture of the two. The resulting compound contains three atoms of Hydrogen to one of Nitrogen; it is a gas readily soluble in water, and possessed of a pungent and characteristic smell." If the mechanistic theory be true the archangel could deduce from his knowledge of the microscopic structure of atoms all these facts but the last. He would know exactly what the microscopic structure of ammonia must be; but he would be totally unable to predict that a substance with this structure must smell as ammonia does when it gets into the human nose. The utmost that he could predict on this subject would be that certain changes would take place in the mucous membrane, the olfactory nerves and so on. But he could not possibly know that these changes would be accompanied by the appearance of a smell in general or of the peculiar smell of ammonia in particular, unless someone told him so or he had smelled it for himself. If the existence of the so-called "secondary qualities," or the fact of their appearance, depends on the microscopic movements and arrangements of material particles which do not have these qualities themselves, then the laws of this dependence are certainly of the emergent type.

The mechanistic theory about vital behaviour should now need little explanation. A man can hold it without being a mechanist about chemistry. The minimum that a Biological Mechanist need believe is that, *in theory*, everything that is characteristic of the behaviour of a living body could be deduced from an adequate knowledge of its structure, the chemical compounds which make it up, and the properties which these show in isolation or in non-living wholes.

Logical Status of Emergence and Mechanism. I have now .stated the two alternatives which alone seem worthy of serious consideration. It is not my business as a philosopher to consider detailed empirical arguments for or against mechanism or emergence in chemistry or in biology. But it is my business to consider the logical status of the two types of theory, and it is relevant to our present purpose to discuss how far the possibility of science is bound up with the acceptance of the mechanistic alternative.

(1) I do not see any *a priori* impossibility in a mechanistic biology or chemistry, so long as it confines itself to that kind of behaviour which can be completely described in terms of changes of position, size, shape, arrangement of parts, etc. I have already argued that this type of theory cannot be the whole truth about all aspects of the material world. For one aspect of it is that bits of matter have or seem to have various colours, temperatures, smells, tastes, etc. If the occurrence or the appearance of these "secondary qualities" depends on microscopic particles and events, the laws connecting the latter with the former are certainly of the emergent type. And no complete account of the external world can ignore these laws.

(2) On the other hand, I cannot see the least trace of self-evidence in theories of the mechanistic type, or

in the theory of Pure Mechanism which is the ideal towards which they strive. I know no reason whatever why new and theoretically unpredictable modes of behaviour should not appear at certain levels of complexity, or why they *must* be explicable in terms of elementary properties and laws of composition which have manifested themselves in less complex wholes.

(3) At the back of the Mechanist's mind there is undoubtedly a notion that there is something radically unscientific and superstitious about non-mechanistic theories. It will be well worth while to consider this vague belief carefully, and to see if there be anything in it. (*a*) In the first place, I think that the ordinary Biological Mechanist does not clearly distinguish between the Substantial and the Emergent forms of Vitalism; in fact he generally identifies Vitalism with Substantial Vitalism. Now there are grave objections to the first type of theory, which I have already pointed out. But it does not follow that they apply to the second type of Vitalism.

(*b*) How far does the Biological Mechanist's vaguely felt objection to Vitalism remain when we confine ourselves to the emergent form of the theory? I think that the parallel case of chemistry may help us to answer this question. It is perfectly certain that chemistry is a subject about which there is a great deal of scientific knowledge, and that this is constantly increasing. Now of course it *may* be true as a matter of fact that the atoms of the various elements are wholes composed of various numbers of similar particles with various arrangements and movements. And it may be true as a matter of fact that the laws of chemical combination, the properties of compounds and so on, are mere consequences of the laws of electro-magnetics and of the particular number, arrangement and movements of the particles which compose each kind of atom. It may even be true that all chemists now hold this opinion as a matter of scientific faith. But it is perfectly obvious that the progress of chemistry in the past has not depended either on the *truth* of this proposition, or on the *general acceptance* of it by chemists. For chemistry had become a science of great extent and certainty long before the electron theory was thought of; and great advances were made in it by workers who utterly scouted the notion that the various elements were all made of a single kind of stuff, and that their differences were due simply to different arrangements of the particles of this stuff. And to this day chemists who accept the electronic theory can make scarcely any use of it in their chemical investigations. If then chemistry can be a scientific subject and can make steady progress without using the assumption that a mechanistic explanation of chemical phenomena is possible, it would presumably have made precisely the same progress if in fact no such explanation had been possible. And, if neither the possibility of mechanistic explanation nor the belief in it is essential to the progress of chemistry, it is hard to see how a parallel belief about vital phenomena can be essential to the progress of physiology.

(*c*) Reflexion on chemistry will teach us another important fact, which applies equally to physiology. I have said that to learn the properties of silver-chloride we *must* at present study samples of *that substance;* and that we cannot deduce them from a knowledge of the properties of silver and of chlorine by themselves or in other combinations, by help of some general law connecting the properties of any compound with those of its elements and with its structure. It does not follow that there are no general laws connecting *some* of the properties of compounds with those of their constituents and with their structure. There are plenty of such laws, and organic chemists in particular study them. For instance the presence of Carbon, Oxygen, and Hydrogen

in the grouping $C\!\!\diagup\!\!\diagdown\!\!\begin{smallmatrix}O\\OH\end{smallmatrix}$ is known to give a compound with acidic properties. Obviously the way to find such laws is to keep the structure and all but one constituent fixed, and then to vary this constituent; or to keep all the constituents fixed, and to vary the structure; and so on. There might, *e.g.*, be certain general properties which are common to all compounds of a certain structure which contain Chlorine, and these might vary in a perfectly characteristic way when the structure is kept fixed and Bromine or Iodine is substituted for the Chlorine. What we have to admit is that such laws have to be discovered independently by an actual study and comparison of the compounds; they cannot be deduced from a mere knowledge of the properties which the constituents would have in isolation or in other wholes; and they cannot be reduced to so many special cases of a single general law.

Now laws like this could exist and could be discovered in Physiology on the emergent form of Vitalism, just as they can exist and be discovered in Chemistry. But they will have to be discovered by studying living beings, as such, and varying their constituents so far as possible one at a time while keeping the structure as constant as may be. If emergence be true they *could* not have been deduced from any amount of reflexion on the properties of these constituents taken separately or in non-living wholes; nor, when they have been discovered, can they be reduced to so many special cases of a single general law which applies equally to the living and the non-living. I do not see that such a view conflicts with the actual procedure of any physiologist. No physiologist in practice professes to deduce the laws of living matter simply from what he knows of the properties which the constituents of living bodies, or substances more or less like them, exhibit in non-living wholes; any more than a chemist in practice professes to deduce the properties of a compound wholly from the properties of its elements when free or in other combinations and from the supposed structure of its molecules.   Thus, whatever the ultimate truth of the matter may be, both the chemist and the physiologist are forced in practice to behave as if the complexes with which they deal had emergent properties.

(d) Let us now sum up the theoretical differences which the alternatives of Mechanism and Emergence would make to our view of the external world and of the relations between the various sciences.   The advantage of Mechanism would be that it introduces a unity and tidiness into the world which appeals very strongly to our æsthetic interests.   On that view, when pushed to its extreme limits, there is one and only one kind of material.   Each particle of this obeys one elementary law of behaviour, and continues to do so no matter how complex may be the collection of particles of which it is a constituent.   There is one uniform law of composition, connecting the behaviour of groups of these particles as wholes with the behaviour which each would show in isolation and with the structure of the group.   All the apparently different kinds of stuff are just differently arranged groups of different numbers of the one kind of elementary particle ; and all the apparently peculiar laws of behaviour are simply special cases which could be deduced in theory from the structure of the whole under consideration, the one elementary law of behaviour for isolated particles, and the one universal law of composition.   On such a view the external world has the greatest amount of unity which is conceivable.   There is really only one science, and the various "special sciences" are just particular cases of it.   This is a magnificent ideal ; it is certainly much more nearly true than anyone could possibly have suspected at first sight ; and investigations pursued under its guidance have certainly enabled us to discover many connexions within the external world which would otherwise have escaped our notice.   But it has no trace of self-evidence ; it cannot be the *whole* truth about the external world, since it cannot deal with the existence or the appearance of "secondary qualities" until it is supplemented by laws of the emergent type which assert that under such and such conditions such and such groups of elementary particles moving in certain ways have, or seem to human beings to have, such and such secondary qualities; and it is certain that considerable scientific progress can be made without assuming it to be true. As a practical postulate it has its good and its bad side. On the one hand, it makes us try our hardest to explain the characteristic behaviour of the more complex in terms of the laws which we have already recognised in the less complex. If our efforts succeed, this is sheer gain. And, even if they fail, we shall probably have learned a great deal about the minute details of the facts under investigation which we might not have troubled to look for otherwise. On the other hand, it tends to over-simplification. If in fact there are new types of law at certain levels, it is very desirable that we should honestly recognise the fact. And, if we take the mechanistic ideal too seriously, we shall be in danger of ignoring or perverting awkward facts of this kind. This sort of over-simplification has certainly happened in the past in biology and physiology under the guidance of the mechanistic ideal; and it of course reaches its wildest absurdities in the attempts which have been made from time to time to treat mental phenomena mechanistically.

On the emergent theory we have to reconcile ourselves to much less unity in the external world and a much less intimate connexion between the various sciences. At best the external world and the various sciences that deal with it will form a kind of hierarchy. We might, if we liked, keep the view that there is only one fundamental kind of stuff. But we should have to recognise aggregates of various orders. And there would be two fundamentally different types of law, which might be called "intra-ordinal" and "trans-ordinal" respectively. A trans-ordinal law would be one which connects the properties of aggregates of adjacent orders. A and B would be adjacent, and in ascending order, if every aggregate of order B is composed of aggregates of order A, and if it has certain properties which no aggregate of order A possesses and which cannot be deduced from the A-properties and the structure of the B-complex by any law of composition which has manifested itself at lower levels. An intra-ordinal law would be one which connects the properties of aggregates of the same order. A trans-ordinal law would be a statement of the irreducible fact that an aggregate composed of aggregates of the next lower order in such and such proportions and arrangements has such and such characteristic and non-deducible properties. If we consider the properties of a given aggregate of high order we could then divide them into three classes. (i) Those which are characteristic of this order, in the sense that all aggregates of the order possess them, that no aggregate of lower order does so, and that they cannot be deduced from the structure of the aggregate and the properties of its constituents by any law of composition which has manifested itself in lower orders. These might be called the "ultimate characteristics" of the order. (ii) Those which are characteristic of this order; but which could in theory be deduced from the structure of the aggregate, the properties of its constituents, and certain laws of composition which have manifested themselves in lower orders. These might be called "reducible characteristics" of the order. (iii) Properties which aggregates of this order share with those of lower orders. These might be called "ordinally neutral properties". I will now illustrate these conceptions.

Suppose, *e.g.*, that living bodies form an order of aggregates in the sense defined. Then the power of reproduction might be an example of an Ultimate Characteristic of this order. The law which asserts that all aggregates composed of such and such chemical substances in such and such proportions and relations have the power of reproduction would be an instance of a Trans-ordinal Law. The laws connecting the reproduction of living bodies with other ultimate characteristics of living bodies would be instances of Intra-ordinal Laws. A great many, though not perhaps all, of the facts about the beating of the heart might be Reducible Characteristics of this order. *I.e.*, although they are characteristic of living beings, they might in theory be deduced from what we know of the chemical, physical, and mechanical properties of non-living aggregates, and from the special structure of the living body. Lastly, the conservation of energy, the property of inertial and gravitational mass, etc., would be examples of Ordinally Neutral Properties, since they appear unchanged in living bodies, chemical compounds, elements, etc.

There is nothing, so far as I can see, mysterious or unscientific about a trans-ordinal law or about the notion of ultimate characteristics of a given order. A trans-ordinal law is as good a law as any other ; and, once it has been discovered, it can be used like any other to suggest experiments, to make predictions, and to give us practical control over external objects. The only peculiarity of it is that we must wait till we meet with an actual instance of an object of the higher order before we can discover such a law ; and that we cannot possibly deduce it beforehand from any combination of laws which we have discovered by observing aggregates of a lower order. There is an obvious analogy between the trans-ordinal laws which I am now discussing and the trans-physical laws which I mentioned in considering Pure Mechanism and said must be recognised in any complete account of the external world. The difference is this. Trans-physical laws, in the sense in which we are using the term, are *necessarily* of the emergent type. For they connect the configurations and internal motions of groups of microscopic particles, on the one hand, with the fact that the volume which contains the group is, or appears to be, pervaded by such and such a secondary quality. Since there are many irreducibly different *kinds* of secondary quality, *e.g.* colour, smell, temperature, etc., there *must* be many irreducible laws of this sort. Again, suppose we confine our attention to one *kind* of secondary quality, say colour. The concepts of the various colours—red, blue, green, etc.—are not contained in the general concept of Colour in the sense in which we might quite fairly say that the concepts of all possible motions are contained in the general concepts of Space and of Motion. We have no difficulty in conceiving and adequately describing determinate possible motions which we have never witnessed and which we never shall witness. We have merely to assign a determinate direction and a determinate velocity. But we could not possibly have formed the concept of such a colour as blue or such a shade as sky-blue unless we had per-ceived instances of it, no matter how much we had reflected on the concept of Colour in general or on the instances of other colours and shades which we *had* seen. It follows that, even when we know that a certain *kind* of secondary quality (*e.g.*, colour) pervades or seems to pervade a region when and only when such and such a *kind* of microscopic event (*e.g.*, vibrations) is going on within the region, we still could not possibly predict that such and such a determinate event of the kind (*e.g.*, a circular movement of a certain period) would be connected with such and such a determinate shade of colour (*e.g.*, sky-blue). The trans-physical laws are then *necessarily* of the emergent type.

On the other hand, emergent laws are not necessarily trans-physical, and it cannot be positively proved that any intra-physical law is emergent. (i) The process of breathing is a particular kind of movement which goes on in living bodies. And it can be described without any essential reference to secondary qualities.   Yet in its details it may be such that it could not be deduced from any amount of knowledge about non-living wholes and the movements that take place in them.   If so it is an "ultimate characteristic" of the vital order, and it is determined by a trans-ordinal law.   But this law is not trans-physical, in the sense defined.   (ii) On the other hand, since it is a movement and since the characteristic movements of some complex wholes (*e.g.*, clocks) *can* be predicted from a knowledge of their structure and of other complex wholes which are not clocks, it cannot be positively *proved* that breathing is an "ultimate characteristic" or that its causation is emergent and not mechanistic.   Within the physical realm it always remains logically possible that the appearance of emergent laws is due to our imperfect knowledge of microscopic structure or to our mathematical incompetence.   But this method of avoiding emergent laws is not logically possible for trans-physical processes, as I have tried to show.

Teleology, Mechanism, and Design.   I have so far discussed Mechanism and its alternatives in a perfectly general way ; and have said nothing in detail concerning those peculiar facts about living organisms which make it plausible to distinguish a "Vital Order" with "ultimate characteristics" of its own.   Now the peculiarities of living organisms are often summed up in the phrase that organisms are "Teleological Systems".   And there is thought to be some special connexion between Teleology and Design, and some special opposition between Teleology and Mechanism. I shall end this chapter by trying to clear up these points.

Teleology is an observable characteristic which certainly belongs to some things in the world.   Design is a particular cause which certainly produces teleology in some cases.   I want to begin by defining "teleology" in such a way that there shall be no doubt of its existence and that the admission of this fact shall not presuppose the acceptance of any special theory.   Suppose that a system is composed of such parts arranged in such ways as might have been expected *if* it had been constructed by an intelligent being to fulfil a certain purpose which he had in mind.   And suppose that, when we investigate the system more carefully under the guidance of this hypothesis, we discover hitherto unnoticed parts or hitherto unnoticed relations between the parts, and that these are still found to accord with the hypothesis.   Then I should call this system "teleological".   It will be noticed that there are two clauses in the definition.   The first is that our more or less superficial knowledge of the system suggests that it was designed for a special purpose which a rational mind might be likely to entertain.   The second is that, if we use this hypothesis as a clue to more minute investigation, we continue to find that the system is constructed as if the hypothesis were true.   I think that probably both factors are necessary.   Of any system whatever we might suppose that it was designed to do what we actually find it doing.   But in general we should not find that this gave us any clue to investigating its more minute structure or predicting its unobserved behaviour.

Now it seems to me perfectly certain that the world contains systems which are teleological, in this sense. The most obvious examples of such systems are machines, like watches, motor-cars, etc.   In this case of course we start by knowing that they have in fact been designed by intelligent beings for a certain purpose, such as telling the time or conveying people quickly along roads.   Knowing this we can explain, as we say, "what each part is for."   Suppose now we were to meet with a certain machine for the first time and to know nothing about the purpose of its constructor.   As we have met with plenty of other machines (though none exactly like this); as we know that all of these have been made by some human being for some purpose; and as we know of no machines which have arisen in any other way; we may legitimately infer that this one also was constructed by a human being for some purpose. By studying the action of the machine we may then be able to guess what the purpose probably was. We can then predict how it will probably be constructed in detail, and how it will probably work under various circumstances. And, if our predictions are found to be true, it is likely that we have hit on the true purpose of the machine. I will call the kind of teleology which is shown by watches, motor-cars, and other artificial machines, "external teleology". By this I mean that the purpose for which such systems were constructed, and by which their minute structure can be anticipated, is not wholly or mainly to keep themselves going or to produce other machines like themselves. Their main function is to do something, such as telling the time, which is of interest not to themselves but to their makers or other men.

Now it seems to me equally clear that living organisms are teleological systems in the sense defined. The most superficial knowledge of organisms does make it look as if they were very complex systems designed to preserve themselves in face of varying and threatening external conditions and to reproduce their kind. And, on the whole, the more fully we investigate a living organism in detail the more fully does what we discover fit in with this hypothesis. One might mention, *e.g.*, the various small and apparently unimportant glands in the human body whose secretions are found to exercise a profound influence over its growth and well-being. Or again we might mention the production in the blood of antitoxins when the body is attacked by organisms likely to injure it. I will call this kind of teleology "internal teleology". Whatever be the right explanation of it, it is plainly a fact.

We have now to consider the relation between Teleology and Design.   (i) The definition of "teleology" involves a hypothetical reference to design. The system is teleological provided it acts *as if* it were designed for a purpose. But it does not involve anything more than this. It remains a question of fact whether the system was actually the result of a design in someone's mind. (ii) So far as we know, the teleology of non-living machines is always due to design.   They behave in the characteristic way in which they do behave simply because their parts are constructed and fitted together in certain special ways, and we have no reason to suppose that this special arrangement could arise spontaneously without the intervention of a mind which deliberately chose it.   (iii) The real paradox about organisms is that they are teleological systems which seem nevertheless to arise without design.   It is this last fact which we must now discuss.

Many organisms have minds connected with them. But we know that, if they were designed at all, the mind which designed them was certainly not the mind which animates them, unless this be extraordinarily different from what it appears to be both to itself and to others. The highest type of mind which we are acquainted with is that which animates a human body. If we designed our own organisms we are quite unaware of the fact. And the enterprise seems altogether beyond our powers. The most skilled physiologist does not know how to make a living body ; but, if we say that his mind designed his own organism, we must suppose that it performed as an embryo a feat which it is totally incapable of performing in its developed state. We must say then that, if organisms are designed by minds, either (*a*) the designing mind is altogether different from and enormously wiser and more skilful than the animating mind ; or (*b*) that the animating mind, as known to itself by introspection and to others by communication, is the merest fragment of the total animating mind, and that the part of it which does not appear to itself or to others is of superhuman wisdom and in-genuity. Of course it might be held that the designing mind, or the designing part of the animating mind, though extraordinarily clever at its own particular job, takes no interest in anything else ; or that it works in a wholly different way from the minds which are known to us. But this will not help us. If the con-ception of design is to provide any explanation of the peculiarities of organisms we must mean by "design" something of the same nature as the only designs that we know anything about, viz., our own. Otherwise we are merely playing with words. Now we have designs only when we imagine a possible state of affairs, apply our knowledge of the properties and laws of matter to discover how it might be brought about, and then use our technical skill to shape the material and to arrange it in those ways which we have seen to be necessary for our purpose. If the minds which design organisms act in this way they must have a superhuman knowledge of the laws and properties of matter, superhuman mathe-matical ability to work out the consequences of various possible combinations, and superhuman technical skill ; and all analogy makes it most unlikely that a mind which took no interest in anything but the one job of manufacturing organisms would have these powers. If, on the other hand, the minds which design organisms act in some quite different and to us unknown way, then we have no right to call them "minds" or to call their mode of operation "design". We are merely assuming a wholly mysterious cause for the teleology of organisms, and tricking ourselves into the belief that it is an explanation by using the familiar words "mind" and "design". I conclude then that, if organisms be the result of design in any intelligible sense, their designers may fairly be called "gods"; and either we are gods in disguise or there are superhuman beings who make organisms.

These considerations remove one positive argument in favour of the theory of entelechies. I am sure that many people who look with a friendly eye on entelechies do so because of the teleological nature of organisms. They think of entelechies as little minds which design organisms and direct and control their growth and reactions. But they modestly regard entelechies as very inferior minds or as the inferior parts of the minds which animate organisms. Now, if I am right, this modesty is wholly out of place. If the hypothesis of an entelechy is to explain anything, we must suppose that an entelechy is a very superior mind or the very superior part of the mind which animates an organism. The theory insinuates itself into our confidence by pretending that the entelechy is so lowly a mind as scarcely to deserve the name; but it can explain the facts only if it supposes the entelechy to be so exalted a mind as to deserve the name of a "god".

I pass now to the relations between Teleology and Design, on the one hand, and Biological Mechanism, on the other. It is evident that, up to a point, there is no opposition between teleology and mechanism. Nothing can be more thoroughly teleological than a watch or a motor-car; yet these are machines, and their characteristic behaviour is wholly deducible from the special arrangement of their parts and from the general laws which these parts would equally obey in isolation or in other and non-teleological complexes. We may say then that, so long as we take a material system as a going concern and do not raise questions about its origin, there is no reason whatever why its characteristic behaviour should not be at once teleological and capable of complete mechanistic explanation. Now the mechanistic biologist regards organisms as very complex machines; and indeed if we were not very familiar with artificial self-acting and self-regulating machinery it would never have entered our heads to suggest a mechanistic theory of vital behaviour. So long as he confines his attention to a developed organism there is nothing preposterous in this theory.   It is only when we consider the *origin* of teleological systems that a legitimate doubt arises whether teleology and mechanistic explanation are *ultimately* consistent with each other.

(i) Every system which is *certainly known* to be at once teleological and mechanistic is an artificial machine; and, if we follow its history far enough backwards, we always come to one or more *organisms*, which are teleological but not *certainly* mechanistic systems.   It is true that many machines are themselves made by machines; but sooner or later in this chain we come to human bodies which made these machines and were not themselves made by machinery.   Thus, apart altogether from any question of minds and their designs, there is something dangerously like a vicious circle in professing to explain the teleology of organisms by analogy with artificial machines.   For, the moment we begin to consider the *origin* of organisms in general or of any particular organism, we have to admit that *all* artificial machines were ultimately made by organisms whilst *no* organism is ever made by an artificial machine.

To this objection I think that the following answer might be made.   It might be said: " Admittedly we must distinguish two kinds of machines, viz., natural and artificial.   We can quite well admit the general principle that *all* machines are made by other machines. Natural machines (*i.e.*, organisms) are always made by other natural machines; artificial machines may be made proximately by other artificial machines, but in the long run in the history of any artificial machine we come to a natural machine.   We admit then that natural machines are *causally* prior to artificial machines; but this involves no logical circle.   We first derive the general notion of machinery and of a mechanistic explanation of teleological behaviour from the specially simple and obvious case of artificial machines, at a time when we do not suspect that our bodies are themselves natural machines. Eventually we *apply* the notion thus derived to our bodies, and find that it fits them perfectly. There is no inconsistency between the facts (*a*) that the recognition of artificial machines is psychologically prior to the recognition of natural machines, and (*b*) that the existence of natural machines is causally prior to the existence of artificial machines". I think that this is a valid answer to the particular logical objection raised above. But it does not exhaust the difficulties of Biological Mechanism ; and this brings us to our next point.

(ii) It is true, but it is not the whole truth, to say that in the history of every system which is positively known to be both teleological and mechanistic (*i.e.*, of every artificial machine) we come at length to an organism. We also come to the mind which animates this organism ; to a design in this mind ; and to the deliberate arrangement of matter in view of an end. And this seems to be essential for the production of a teleological system out of non-teleological materials. On a mechanistic theory the teleological behaviour of a system must be due wholly to the initial configuration of its parts ; and, if matter has only the properties which physicists and chemists ascribe to it, it has no tendency by itself to fall into those extraordinarily special arrangements which alone can give rise to teleological behaviour. Now, if the analogy of organisms to artificial machines is to be used at all, it must be used fairly ; we must not ignore one essential part of the facts about the origin of artificial machines. Let us then apply the whole analogy to organisms. It is certain that, when one organism produces another by ordinary processes of generation, the mind of the first does not design and construct the second, as it would if it were producing an artificial machine like a watch or a type-writer. This in itself need cause no trouble to the Mechanist. When one artificial machine produces another the mind of the first does not design the second, for artificial machines have no minds. The Biological Mechanist will therefore simply say that the generation of one organism by another is analogous to the production of one artificial machine by another. But, as we have seen, the latter series eventually brings us back to a mind with designs. Hence, if the Biological Mechanist is to apply his analogy fairly, there are only two courses open to him. The first is to say that there always have been organisms, and that organisms have never arisen from inorganic matter. On this alternative he has a series of natural machines going back to infinity. In that case of course every artificial machine will also have an infinite ancestry of other machines, since the production of an artificial machine eventually brings one back to a natural machine. Such a theory would be self-consistent; though it would still leave the awkward difference that design enters into the history of *every* artificial machine and of *no* natural machine. It is of course an alternative that most mechanists would be very loath to take; for one of the advantages claimed for Biological Mechanism over Substantial Vitalism is that the former does and the latter does not render the development of living from non-living matter conceivable.

The other possible alternative is to admit that organisms arose in the remote past out of non-living matter. This means, on the mechanistic view, that natural machines arose from matter which was not arranged in the form of a machine. And this can be consistently held *only* if the Biological Mechanist will postulate at that point the intervention of a mind which deliberately designed and arranged non-living matter in the form of a natural machine. For, as we have seen, the only systems which we positively *know* to be machines have all arisen in this way; and, if matter has no properties except those which chemists and physicists assign to it, there is not the least reason to suppose that it can

spontaneously fall into the extremely special configuration which is needed if the resulting system is to behave
teleologically. Thus the proper complement to a completely mechanistic theory about organisms is some
form of the doctrine of Deism; a result which accords
very well with that simple piety which is so characteristic of Biological Mechanists.

But, even if we are willing to go thus far with the
Biological Mechanist, we cannot allow him to leave
the matter there. Every system which is positively
known to be a machine has been ultimately made, not
by a pure spirit, but by a mind which animates an
organism which it did not design or construct. This mind
formed a design; in consequence of this the organism
which it animates has moved in various ways; and it is
thus and thus only that the design has been realised in
foreign matter. Once more, if we are to use the analogy
of machines at all, we must use it fairly and not ignore
these parts of it which, so far as we can see, are
essential but which are not convenient. The Biological
Mechanist, having been brought willingly or unwillingly
to Deism, must now take a further step and ascribe to
God an organism which God's mind animates. And by
all analogy we must suppose that God did not design
or construct his own organism; since, so far as our
experience goes *no* mind designs or constructs the
organism which it animates. Thus, in the end, we
shall be brought to one organism at least, viz., God's,
which presumably has not arisen out of non-living
matter either spontaneously or by design. This seems
to be the final result of seriously and fairly applying
the analogy between organisms and machines, when
we cease to confine our attention to the organism as a
going concern and try to account also for the origin of
organisms, as Biological Mechanism would wish to do.

**Tentative Decision between the Three Theories
of Organisms.** When we consider the teleological

characteristics of organisms the three possible theories of Substantial Vitalism, Emergent Vitalism, and Biological Mechanism cease to be on a level. In the first place, there seems to be nothing to be said for Substantial Vitalism, and a great deal to be said against it. We may therefore provisionally reject it, and confine our attention to Emergent Vitalism and Biological Mechanism. It seems to me that, so long as we merely consider the behaviour of the organism as a going concern, there is no strong argument for deciding between the two types of theory. For it is quite certain that a material system, once it is in being, can be teleological and at the same time mechanistic in its behaviour. Hence, even if we did not see our way to explain certain teleological characteristics of developed organisms mechanistically, the Biological Mechanist could always answer that this is merely because we do not yet know enough about the minute structure of the machine or about the more obscure physico-chemical properties of non-living matter. And this is what he *is* continually occupied in saying. But, when we come to consider the *origin* of organisms as well as their behaviour, the case is altered. We find that Biological Mechanism about the developed organism cannot consistently be held without an elaborate Deistic theory about the origin of organisms. This is because Biological Mechanism is admittedly a theory of the organism based on its analogy to self-acting and self-regulating machines. These, so far as we can see, neither do arise nor could have arisen without design and deliberate interference by someone with matter. And, in applying our analogy, we have no right whatever to ignore this side of it. I do not of course assert that this is a conclusive objection to Biological Mechanism. Deism has always seemed to me a much more sensible theory than most of its more pretentious successors. But I do wish to make it quite clear that Biological Mechanism is committed logically to a great deal more than is commonly supposed. If Emergent Vitalism could dispense with the need for all this Deistic supplementation it would *pro tanto* score over Biological Mechanism. But can it?

It might well be thought that in this matter Emergent Vitalism is no better off than Biological Mechanism. On both theories the peculiar behaviour of an organism is completely determined by its structure and its components and by nothing else. The only difference is that on the Emergent View the peculiar behaviour of such systems must be "seen to be believed", whilst on the Mechanistic View it could in theory have been foretold from the structure and the behaviour of the components in isolation or in non-living wholes. If you make it an objection to the Mechanistic Theory that the characteristic behaviour of the organism depends on the arrangement of its parts, and that this arrangement could only have happened by design, does not the objection apply equally strongly to the Emergent Theory? This argument is plausible, but I do not think that it is sound. The Biological Mechanist points to the analogy between organisms and artificial machines, and asks us to believe on this ground that organisms are machines. To this we answered that matter has no natural tendency to arrange itself in the form of *machines* (*i.e.*, of teleological systems whose characteristic behaviour is *mechanistically* explicable) ; and that therefore, *if* organisms be of the nature of machines, there is no reason to suppose that they could have arisen spontaneously and without design. But it is perfectly consistent for a man to hold that matter has *no* tendency to fall spontaneously into the form of *machines* and that it *has* a natural tendency to fall into the form of *organisms;* provided he holds, as the Emergent Vitalist does, that organisms are not machines but are systems whose characteristic behaviour is emergent and not mechanistically explicable. Thus the real difference is that a possibility is open to the Emergent

Vitalist, who recognises two fundamentally different kinds of teleological system, and that this possibility is closed to the Biological Mechanist, who recognises only one kind.

Of course this possibility, which is open to the Emergent Vitalist and not to the Biological Mechanist, is very vague and needs to be worked out in much greater detail. This would be the task of the empirical scientist rather than the critical philosopher. I will content myself with saying that the Emergent Vitalist should not rest with nothing better than the vague statement that matter has a natural tendency to fall into that kind of structure which has vital behaviour as its emergent characteristic. If Emergence be true at all there are probably many Orders below the Vital Order. What must be assumed is not a special tendency of matter to fall into the kind of arrangement which has vital characteristics, but a general tendency for complexes of one order to combine with each other under suitable conditions to form complexes of the next order. At each stage in this process we shall get things with new and irreducibly characteristic properties and new intra-ordinal laws, whilst there will probably remain certain complexes of all the lower orders. The universe would thus grow continually more varied, so long as the special conditions necessary for this combination of complexes of lower order to give complexes of higher order continued; and at every new stage new possibilities of further development would begin. It would be the business of the believer in Emergence to determine the precise condition under which the passage from one order to the next can take place; to state definitely what are the irreducibly characteristic features of each order; and to deduce those characteristic features which can be deduced.

It seems to me then that on the whole Emergent Vitalism is distinctly to be preferred to Biological Mechanism. It does not *necessitate* a complicated

Deistic supplement, as Biological Mechanism does; and this seems to me to be an advantage. At the same time it is perfectly *consistent with* the view that there is a God who created and controls the material world; so that, if there should be any good reason to believe in such a Being, the Emergent Vitalist could meet the situation with a quiet mind.

CHAPTER III

The Traditional Problem of Body and Mind

IN the last Chapter we considered organisms simply as complicated material systems which behave in certain characteristic ways. We did not consider the fact that some organisms are animated by minds, and that all the minds of whose existence we are certain animate organisms. And we did not deal with those features in the behaviour of certain organisms which are commonly supposed to be due to the mind which animates the organism. It is such facts as these, and certain problems to which they have given rise, which I mean to discuss in the present Chapter. There is a question which has been argued about for some centuries now under the name of "Interaction"; this is the question whether minds really do act on the organisms which they animate, and whether organisms really do act on the minds which animate them. (I must point out at once that I imply no particular theory of mind or body by the word "to animate". I use it as a perfectly neutral name to express the fact that a certain mind is connected in some peculiarly intimate way with a certain body, and, under normal conditions with no other body. This is a fact even on a purely behaviouristic theory of mind; on such a view to say that the mind M animates the body B would mean that the body B, in so far as it behaves in certain ways, *is* the mind M. A body which did not act in these ways would be said not to be animated by a mind. And a different Body B', which acted in the same general way as B, would be said to be animated by a different mind M'.)

The problem of Interaction is generally discussed at the level of enlightened common-sense; where it is assumed that we know pretty well what we mean by "mind", by "matter" and by "causation". Obviously no solution which is reached at that level can claim to be ultimate. If what we call "matter" should turn out to be a collection of spirits of low intelligence, as Leibniz thought, the argument that mind and body are so unlike that their interaction is impossible would become irrelevant. Again, if causation be nothing but regular sequence and concomitance, as some philosophers have held, it is ridiculous to regard psycho-neural parallelism and interaction as mutually exclusive alternatives. For interaction will mean no more than parallelism, and parallelism will mean no less than interaction. Nevertheless I am going to discuss the arguments here at the common-sense level, because they are so incredibly bad and yet have imposed upon so many learned men.

We start then by assuming a developed mind and a developed organism as two distinct things, and by admitting that the two are now intimately connected in some way or other which I express by saying that "this mind *animates* this organism". We assume that bodies are very much as enlightened common-sense believes them to be; and that, even if we cannot define "causation", we have some means of recognising when it is present and when it is absent. The question then is: "Does a mind ever act on the body which it animates, and does a body ever act on the mind which animates it?" The answer which common-sense would give to both questions is: "Yes, certainly." On the face of it my body acts on my mind whenever a pin is stuck into the former and a painful sensation thereupon arises in the latter. And, on the face of it, my mind acts on my body whenever a desire to move my arm arises in the former and is followed by this movement in the latter. Let us call this common-sense view "Two-sided Interaction". Although it seems so obvious it has been denied by probably a majority of philosophers and a majority of physiologists. So the question is: "Why should so many distinguished men, who have studied the subject, have denied the apparently obvious fact of Two-sided Interaction?"

The arguments against Two-sided Interaction fall into two sets:—Philosophical and Scientific. We will take the philosophical arguments first; for we shall find that the professedly scientific arguments come back in the end to the principles or prejudices which are made explicit in the philosophical arguments.

Philosophical Arguments against Two-sided Inter-action. No one can deny that there is a close correlation between certain bodily events and certain mental events, and conversely. Therefore anyone who denies that there is action of mind on body and of body on mind must presumably hold (*a*) that concomitant variation is not an adequate criterion of causal connexion, and (*b*) that the other feature which is essential for causal connexion is absent in the case of body and mind. Now the common philosophical argument is that minds and mental states are so extremely unlike bodies and bodily states that it is inconceivable that the two should be causally connected. It is certainly true that, if minds and mental events are just what they seem to be to introspection and nothing more, and if bodies and bodily events are just what enlightened common-sense thinks them to be and nothing more, the two *are* extremely unlike. And this fact is supposed to show that, however closely correlated certain pairs of events in mind and body respectively may be, they cannot be causally connected.

Evidently the assumption at the back of this argument is that concomitant variation, together with a high enough degree of likeness, is an adequate test for causation ; but that no amount of concomitant variation can establish causation in the absence of a high enough degree of likeness. Now I am inclined to admit part of this assumption. I think it is practically certain that causation does not simply *mean* concomitant variation. (And, if it did, *cadit quæstio*.) Hence the existence of the latter is not *ipso facto* a proof of the presence of the former. Again, I think it is almost certain that concomitant variation between A and B is not in fact a sufficient sign of the presence of a *direct* causal relation between the two. (I think it may perhaps be a sufficient sign of *either* a direct causal relation between A and B *or* of several causal relations which indirectly unite A and B through the medium of other terms C, D, etc.) So far I agree with the assumptions of the argument. But I cannot see the least reason to think that the other characteristic, which must be added to concomitant variation before we can be sure that A and B are causally connected, is a high degree of likeness between the two. One would like to know just how unlike two events may be before it becomes impossible to admit the existence of a causal relation between them. No one hestitates to hold that draughts and colds in the head are causally connected, although the two are extremely unlike each other. If the unlikeness of draughts and colds in the head does not prevent one from admitting a causal connexion between the two, why should the unlikeness of volitions and voluntary movements prevent one from holding that they are causally connected? To sum up. I am willing to admit that an adequate criterion of causal connexion needs some other relation between a pair of events beside concomitant variation ; but I do not believe for a moment that this other relation is that of qualitative likeness.

This brings us to a rather more refined form of the argument against Interaction. It is said that, whenever we admit the existence of a causal relation between two events, these two events (to put it crudely) must also form parts of a single substantial whole. *E.g.*, all physical events are spatially related and form one great extended whole. And the mental events which would commonly be admitted to be causally connected are always events in a single mind. A mind is a substantial whole of a peculiar kind too. Now it is said that between bodily events and mental events there are no relations such as those which unite physical events in different parts of the same Space or mental events in the history of the same mind. In the absence of such relations, binding mind and body into a single substantial whole, we cannot admit that bodily and mental events can be causally connected with each other, no matter how closely correlated their variations may be.

This is a much better argument than the argument about qualitative likeness and unlikeness. If we accept the premise that causal relations can subsist only between terms which form parts of a single substantial whole must we deny that mental and bodily events can be causally connected? I do not think that we need. (i) It is of course perfectly true that an organism and the mind which animates it do not form a physical whole, and that they do not form a mental whole; and these, no doubt, are the two kinds of substantial whole with which we are most familiar. But it does not follow that a mind and its organism do not form a substantial whole of *some* kind. There, plainly, is the extraordinary intimate union between the two which I have called "animation" of the one by the other. Even if the mind be just what it seems to introspection, and the body be just what it seems to perception aided by the more precise methods of science, this seems to me to be enough to make a mind and its body a substantial whole. Even so extreme a dualist about Mind and Matter as Descartes occasionally suggests that a mind and its body together form a quasi-substance; and, although we may quarrel with the language of the very numerous philosophers who have said that the mind is "the form" of its body, we must admit that such language would never have seemed plausible unless a mind and its body together had formed something very much like a single substantial whole.

(ii) We must, moreover, admit the possibility that minds and mental events have properties and relations which do not reveal themselves to introspection, and that bodies and bodily events may have properties and relations which do not reveal themselves to perception or to physical and chemical experiment. In virtue of these properties and relations the two together may well form a single substantial whole of the kind which is alleged to be needed for causal interaction. Thus, if we accept the premise of the argument, we have no right to assert that mind and body *cannot* interact; but only the much more modest proposition that introspection and perception do not suffice to assure us that mind and body are so interrelated that they *can* interact.

(iii) We must further remember that the Two-sided Interactionist is under no obligation to hold that the *complete* conditions of any mental event are bodily or that the complete conditions of any bodily event are mental. He needs only to assert that some mental events include certain bodily events among their necessary conditions, and that some bodily events include certain mental events among their necessary conditions. If I am paralysed my volition may not move my arm; and, if I am hypnotised or intensely interested or frightened, a wound may not produce a painful sensation. Now, if the complete cause and the complete effect in all interaction include both a bodily and a mental factor, the two wholes will be related by the fact that the mental constituents belong to a single mind, that the bodily constituents belong to a single body, and that this mind animates this body. This amount of connexion should surely be enough to allow of causal interaction.

This will be the most appropriate place to deal with the contention that, in voluntary action, and there only, we are immediately acquainted with an instance of causal connexion. If this be true the controversy is of course settled at once in favour of the Interactionist. It is generally supposed that this view was refuted once and for all by Mr Hume in his *Enquiry concerning Human Understanding* (Sect. VII, Part I). I should not care to assert that the doctrine in question is true; but I do think that it is plausible, and I am quite sure that Mr Hume's arguments do not refute it. Mr Hume uses three closely connected arguments. (1) The connexion between a successful volition and the resulting bodily movement is as mysterious and as little self-evident as the connexion between any other event and its effect. (2) We have to learn from experience which of our volitions will be effective and which will not. *E.g.*, we do not know, until we have tried, that we can voluntarily move our arms and cannot voluntarily move our livers. And again, if a man were suddenly paralysed, he would still expect to be able to move his arm voluntarily, and would be surprised when he found that it kept still in spite of his volition. (3) We have discovered that the immediate consequence of a volition is a change in our nerves and muscles, which most people know nothing about; and is not the movement of a limb, which most people believe to be its immediate and necessary consequence.

The second and third arguments are valid only against the contention that we know immediately that a volition to make a certain movement is the *sufficient* condition for the happening of that movement. They are quite irrelevant to the contention that we know immediately that the volition is a *necessary* condition for the happening of just that movement at just that time. No doubt many other conditions are also necessary, *e.g.*, that our nerves and muscles shall be in the right state; and these other necessary conditions can be discovered only by special investigation. Since our volitions to move our limbs are in fact followed in the vast majority of cases by the willed movement, and since the other necessary conditions are not very obvious, it is natural enough that we should think that we know immediately that our volition is the *sufficient* condition of the movement of our limbs. If we think so, we are certainly wrong; and Mr Hume's arguments prove that we are. But they prove nothing else. It does not follow that we are wrong in thinking that we know, without having to wait for the result, that the volition is a *necessary* condition of the movement.

It remains to consider the first argument. Is the connexion between cause and effect as mysterious and as little self-evident in the case of the voluntary production of bodily movement as in all other cases? If so, we must hold that the first time a baby wills to move its hand it is just as much surprised to find its hand moving as it would be to find its leg moving or its nurse bursting into flames. I do not profess to know anything about the infant mind; but it seems to me that this is a wildly paradoxical consequence, for which there is no evidence or likelihood. But there is no need to leave the matter there. It is perfectly plain that, in the case of volition and voluntary movement, there *is* a connexion between the cause and the effect which is not present in other cases of causation, and which does make it plausible to hold that in this one case the nature of the effect can be foreseen by merely reflecting on the nature of the cause. The peculiarity of a volition as a cause-factor is that it involves as an essential part of it the idea of the effect. To say that a person has a volition to move his arm involves saying that he has an idea of his arm (and not of his leg or his liver) and an idea of the position in which he wants his arm to be. It is simply silly in view of this fact to say that there is no closer connexion between the desire to move my arm and the movement of my arm than there is between this desire and the movement of my leg or my liver. We cannot detect any analogous connexion between cause and effect in causal transactions which we view wholly from outside, such as the movement of a billiard-ball by a cue. It is therefore by no means unreasonable to suggest that, in the one case of our own voluntary movements, we can see without waiting for the result that such and such a volition is a necessary condition of such and such a bodily movement.

It seems to me then that Mr Hume's arguments on this point are absolutely irrelevant, and that it may very well be true that in volition we positively know that our desire for such and such a bodily movement is a necessary (though not a sufficient) condition of the happening of just that movement at just that time. On the whole then I conclude that the philosophical arguments certainly do not disprove Two-sided Inter-action, and that they do not even raise any strong presumption against it. And, while I am not prepared definitely to commit myself to the view that, in voluntary movement, we positively *know* that the mind acts on the body, I do think that this opinion is quite plausible when properly stated and that the arguments which have been brought against it are worthless. I pass therefore to the scientific arguments.

Scientific Arguments against Two-sided Interaction. There are, so far as I know, two of these. One is supposed to be based on the physical principle of the Conservation of Energy, and on certain experiments which have been made on human bodies. The other is based on the close analogy which is said to exist between the structures of the physiological mechanism of reflex action and that of voluntary action. I will take them in turn.

(1) *The Argument from Energy.* It will first be need-ful to state clearly what is asserted by the principle of the Conservation of Energy. It is found that, if we take certain material systems, *e.g.*, a gun, a cartridge,

and a bullet, there is a certain magnitude which keeps approximately constant throughout all their changes. This is called "Energy". When the gun has not been fired it and the bullet have no motion, but the explosive in the cartridge has great chemical energy. When it has been fired the bullet is moving very fast and has great energy of movement. The gun, though not moving fast in its recoil, has also great energy of movement because it is very massive. The gases produced by the explosion have some energy of movement and some heat-energy, but much less chemical energy than the unexploded charge had. These various kinds of energy can be measured in common units according to certain conventions. To an innocent mind there seems to be a good deal of "cooking" at this stage, *i.e.*, the conventions seem to be chosen and various kinds and amounts of concealed energy seem to be postulated in order to make the principle come out right at the end. I do not propose to go into this in detail, for two reasons. In the first place, I think that the conventions adopted and the postulates made, though somewhat suggestive of the fraudulent company-promoter, can be justified by their coherence with certain experimental facts, and that they are not simply made *ad hoc*. Secondly, I shall show that the Conservation of Energy is absolutely irrelevant to the question at issue, so that it would be waste of time to treat it too seriously in the present connexion. Now it is found that the total energy of all kinds in this system, when measured according to these conventions, is approximately the same in amount though very differently distributed after the explosion and before it. If we had confined our attention to a part of this system and *its* energy this would not have been true. The bullet, *e.g.*, had no energy at all before the explosion and a great deal afterwards. A system like the bullet, the gun, and the charge, is called a "Conservative System"; the bullet alone, or the gun and the charge, would be called

" Non-conservative Systems ". A conservative system might therefore be defined as one whose total energy is redistributed, but not altered in amount, by changes that happen within it. Of course a given system might be conservative for some kinds of change and not for others.

So far we have merely defined a " Conservative System", and admitted that there are systems which, for some kinds of change at any rate, answer approximately to our definition. We can now state the Principle of the Conservation of Energy in terms of the conceptions just defined. The principle asserts that every material system is either itself conservative, or, if not, is part of a larger material system which is conservative. We may take it that there is good inductive evidence for this proposition.

The next thing to consider is the experiments on the human body. These tend to prove that a living body, with the air that it breathes and the food that it eats, forms a conservative system to a high degree of approximation. We can measure the chemical energy of the food given to a man, and that which enters his body in the form of Oxygen breathed in. We can also, with suitable apparatus, collect, measure and analyse the air breathed out, and thus find its chemical energy. Similarly, we can find the energy given out in bodily movement, in heat, and in excretion. It is alleged that, on the average, whatever the man may do, the energy of his bodily movements is exactly accounted for by the energy given to him in the form of food and of Oxygen. If you take the energy put in in food and Oxygen, and subtract the energy given out in waste-products, the balance is almost exactly equal to the energy put out in bodily movements. Such slight differences as are found are as often on one side as on the other, and are therefore probably due to unavoidable experimental errors. I do not propose to criticise the interpretation of these experiments in detail, because, as I shall show soon, they are completely irrelevant to the problem of whether mind and body interact. But there is just one point that I will make before passing on. It is perfectly clear that such experiments can tell us only what happens on the average over a long time. To know whether the balance was accurately kept at every moment we should have to kill the patient at each moment and analyse his body so as to find out the energy present then in the form of stored-up products. Obviously we cannot keep on killing the patient in order to analyse him, and then reviving him in order to go on with the experiment. Thus it would seem that the results of the experiment are perfectly compatible with the presence of quite large excesses or defects in the total bodily energy at certain moments, provided that these average out over longer periods. However, I do not want to press this criticism ; I am quite ready to accept for our present purpose the traditional interpretation which has been put on the experiments.

We now understand the physical principle and the experimental facts. The two together are generally supposed to prove that mind and body cannot interact. What precisely is the argument, and is it valid? I imagine that the argument, when fully stated, would run somewhat as follows: "I will to move my arm, and it moves. If the volition has anything to do with causing the movement we might expect energy to flow from my mind to my body. Thus the energy of my body ought to receive a measurable increase, not accounted for by the food that I eat and the Oxygen that I breathe. But no such physically unaccountable increases of bodily energy are found. Again, I tread on a tin-tack, and a painful sensation arises in my mind. If treading on the tack has anything to do with causing the sensation we might expect energy to flow from my body to my mind. Such energy would cease to be measurable. Thus there ought to be a noticeable decrease in my bodily energy, not balanced by increases anywhere in the physical system. But such unbalanced decreases of bodily energy are not found." So it is concluded that the volition has nothing to do with causing my arm to move, and that treading on the tack has nothing to do with causing the painful sensation.

Is this argument valid? In the first place it is important to notice that the conclusion does not follow from the Conservation of Energy and the experimental facts alone. The real premise is a tacitly assumed proposition about causation ; viz., that, if a change in A has anything to do with causing a change in B, energy must leave A and flow into B. This is neither asserted nor entailed by the Conservation of Energy. What *it* says is that, *if* energy leaves A, it must appear in something else, say B ; so that A and B together form a conservative system. Since the Conservation of Energy is not itself the premise for the argument against Interaction, and since it does not entail that premise, the evidence for the Conservation of Energy is not evidence against Interaction. Is there any independent evidence for the premise? We may admit that it *is* true of many, though not of all, transactions within the physical realm. But there are cases where it is not true even of purely physical transactions ; and, even if it were always true in the physical realm, it would not follow that it must also be true of transphysical causation. Take the case of a weight swinging at the end of a string hung from a fixed point. The total energy of the weight is the same at all positions in its course. It is thus a conservative system. But at every moment the direction and velocity of the weight's motion are different, and the proportion between its kinetic and its potential energy is constantly changing. These changes are caused by the pull of the string, which acts in a different direction at each different moment. The string makes no difference to the total energy of the weight; but it makes all the difference in the world to the particular way in which the weight moves and the particular way in which the energy is distributed between the potential and the kinetic forms. This is evident when we remember that the weight would begin to move in an utterly different course if at any moment the string were cut.

Here, then, we have a clear case even in the physical realm where a system is conservative but is continually acted on by something which affects its movement and the distribution of its total energy. Why should not the mind act on the body in this way? If you say that you can see how a string can affect the movement of a weight, but cannot see how a volition could affect the movement of a material particle, you have deserted the scientific argument and have gone back to one of the philosophical arguments. Your real difficulty is either that volitions are so very unlike movements, or that the volition is in your mind whilst the movement belongs to the physical realm. And we have seen how little weight can be attached to these objections.

The fact is that, even in purely physical systems, the Conservation of Energy does not explain what changes will happen or when they will happen. It merely imposes a very general limiting condition on the changes that are possible. The fact that the system composed of bullet, charge, and gun, in our earlier example, is conservative does not tell us that the gun ever will be fired, or when it will be fired if at all, or what will cause it to go off, or what forms of energy will appear if and when it does go off. The change in this case is determined by pulling the trigger. Likewise the mere fact that the human body and its neighbourhood form a conservative system does not explain any particular bodily movement; it does not explain why I ever move at all, or why I sometimes write, sometimes walk, and sometimes swim. To explain the happening of these particular movements at certain times it seems to be problem. Suppose that B is some artificial object, like a book or a bridge. If we admit that this could not have come into existence unless a certain design and volition had existed in a certain mind, we could interpret the facts in two ways. (*a*) We could hold that the design and volition are themselves an indispensable link in the chain of causation which ends in the production of a bridge or a book. This is the common view, and it requires us to admit the action of mind on body. (*b*) We might hold that the design and the volition are not themselves a link in the chain of causation which ends in the production of the artificial object; but that they are a necessary accompaniment or sequent of something which *is* an indispensable link in this chain of causation. On this view the chain consists wholly of physical events; but one of these physical events (viz., some event in the brain) has a complex consequent. One part of this consequent is purely physical, and leads by purely physical causation to the ultimate production of a bridge or a book. The other is purely mental, and consists of a certain design and volition in the mind which animates the human body concerned. If this has any consequences they are purely mental. Each part of this complex consequent follows with equal necessity; this particular brain-state could no more have existed without such and such a mental state accompanying or following it than it could have existed without such and such a bodily movement following it. If we are willing to take some such view as this, we can admit that certain objects could not have existed unless there had been designs of them and desires for them; and yet we could consistently deny that these desires and designs have any effect on the movements of our bodies.

It seems to me then that the doctrine which I will call "One-sided Action of Body on Mind" is logically possible; *i.e.*, a theory which accepts the action of body on mind but denies the action of mind on body. But I do not see the least reason to accept it, since I see no reason to deny that mind acts on body in volition. One-sided Action has, I think, generally been held in the special form called "Epiphenomenalism." I take this doctrine to consist of the following four propositions : (1) Certain bodily events cause certain mental events. (2) No mental event plays any part in the causation of any bodily event. (3) No mental event plays any part in the causation of any other mental event. Consequently (4) all mental events are caused by bodily events and by them only. Thus Epiphenomenalism is just One-sided Action of Body on Mind, together with a special theory about the nature and structure of mind. This special theory does not call for discussion here, where I am dealing only with the relations between minds and bodies, and am not concerned with a detailed analysis of mind. In a later chapter we shall have to consider the special features of Epiphenomenalism.

Arguments in Favour of Interaction. The only arguments *for* One-sided Action of Body on Mind or for Parallelism are the arguments *against* Two-sided Interaction ; and these, as we have seen, are worthless. Are there any arguments in favour of Two-sided Interaction ? I have incidentally given two which seem to me to have considerable weight. In favour of the action of mind on body is the fact that we seem to be immediately aware of a causal relation when we voluntarily try to produce a bodily movement, and that the arguments to show that this cannot be true are invalid. In favour of the action of body on mind are the insuperable difficulties which I have pointed out in accounting for the happening of new sensations on any other hypothesis. There are, however, two other arguments which have often been thought to prove the action of mind on body. These are (1) an evolutionary argument, first used, I believe, by William James ; and (2) the famous "telegram

argument." They both seem to me to be quite obviously
invalid.

(1) The evolutionary argument runs as follows: It is
a fact, which is admitted by persons who deny Two-
sided Interaction, that minds increase in complexity
and power with the growth in complexity of the brain
and nervous system. Now, if the mind makes no
difference to the actions of the body, this development
on the mental side is quite unintelligible from the point
of view of natural selection. Let us imagine two
animals whose brains and nervous systems were of the
same degree of complexity; and suppose, if possible,
that one had a mind and the other had none. If the
mind makes no difference to the behaviour of the body
the chance of survival and of leaving descendants will
clearly be the same for the two animals. Therefore
natural selection will have no tendency to favour the
evolution of mind which has actually taken place. I
do not think that there is anything in this argument.
Natural selection is a purely negative process; it simply
tends to eliminate individuals and species which have
variations unfavourable to survival. Now, by hypothesis,
the possession of a mind is not *unfavourable* to survival;
it simply makes no difference. Now it may be that the
existence of a mind of such and such a kind is an
inevitable consequence of the existence of a brain and
nervous system of such and such a degree of complexity. Indeed we have seen that some such view is
essential if the opponent of Two-sided Interaction is to
answer the common-sense objection that artificial objects
could not have existed unless there had been a mind
which designed and desired them. On this hypothesis
there is no need to invoke natural selection twice over,
once to explain the evolution of the brain and nervous
system, and once to explain the evolution of the mind.
If natural selection will account for the evolution of the
brain and nervous system, the evolution of the mind
will follow inevitably, even though it adds nothing to

the survival-value of the organism. The plain fact is that natural selection does not account for the origin or for the growth in complexity of anything whatever; and therefore it is no objection to any particular theory of the relations of mind and body that, if it were true, natural selection would not explain the origin and development of mind.

(2) The "telegram argument" is as follows: Suppose there were two telegrams, one saying "Our son has been killed", and the other saying: "Your son has been killed". And suppose that one or other of them was delivered to a parent whose son was away from home. As physical stimuli they are obviously extremely alike, since they differ only in the fact that the letter "Y" is present in one and absent in the other. Yet we know that the reaction of the person who received the telegram might be very different according to which one he received. This is supposed to show that the reactions of the body cannot be wholly accounted for by bodily causes, and that the mind must intervene causally in some cases. Now I have very little doubt that the mind does play a part in determining the action of the recipient of the telegram; but I do not see why this argument should prove it to a person who doubted or denied it. If two very similar stimuli are followed by two very different results, we are no doubt justified in concluding that these stimuli are not the complete causes of the reactions which follow them. But of course it would be admitted by every one that the receipt of the telegram is not the complete cause of the recipient's reaction. We all know that his brain and nervous system play an essential part in any reaction that he may make to the stimulus. The question then is whether the minute structure of his brain and nervous system, including in this the supposed traces left by past stimuli and past reactions, is not enough to account for the great difference in his behaviour on receiving two very similar stimuli. Two keys may be very much alike,

essential to take into account the volitions which happen from time to time in my mind; just as it is essential to take the string into account to explain the particular behaviour of the weight, and to take the trigger into account to explain the going off of the gun at a certain moment. The difference between the gun-system and the body-system is that a little energy does flow into the former when the trigger is pulled, whilst it is alleged that none does so when a volition starts a bodily movement. But there is not even this amount of difference between the body-system and the swinging weight.

Thus the argument from energy has no tendency to disprove Two-sided Interaction. It has gained a spurious authority from the august name of the Conservation of Energy. But this impressive principle proves to have nothing to do with the case. And the real premise of the argument is not self-evident, and is not universally true even in purely intra-physical transactions. In the end this scientific argument has to lean on the old philosophic arguments; and we have seen that these are but bruised reeds. Nevertheless, the facts brought forward by the argument from energy do throw some light on the *nature* of the interaction between mind and body, assuming this to happen. They do suggest that all the energy of our bodily actions comes out of and goes back into the physical world, and that minds neither add energy to nor abstract it from the latter. What they do, if they do anything, is to determine that at a given moment so much energy shall change from the chemical form to the form of bodily movement; and they determine this, so far as we can see, without altering the total amount of energy in the physical world.

(2) *The Argument from the Structure of the Nervous System*. There are purely reflex actions, like sneezing and blinking, in which there is no reason to suppose that the mind plays any essential part. Now we know

the nervous structure which is used in such acts as these. A stimulus is given to the outer end of an efferent nerve; some change or other runs up this nerve, crosses a synapsis between this and an afferent nerve, travels down the latter to a muscle, causes the muscle to contract, and so produces a bodily movement. There seems no reason to believe that the mind plays any essential part in this process. The process may be irreducibly vital, and not merely physico-chemical; but there seems no need to assume anything more than this. Now it is said that the whole nervous system is simply an immense complication of interconnected nervous arcs. The result is that a change which travels inwards has an immense number of alternative paths by which it may travel outwards. Thus the reaction to a given stimulus is no longer one definite movement, as in the simple reflex. Almost any movement may follow any stimulus according to the path which the afferent disturbance happens to take. This path will depend on the relative resistance of the various synapses at the time. Now a variable response to the same stimulus is characteristic of deliberate as opposed to reflex action.

These are the facts. The argument based on them runs as follows. It is admitted that the mind has nothing to do with the causation of purely reflex actions. But the nervous structure and the nervous processes involved in deliberate action do not differ in kind from those involved in reflex action; they differ only in degree of complexity. The variability which characterises deliberate action is fully explained by the variety of alternative paths and the variable resistances of the synapses. So it is unreasonable to suppose that the mind has any more to do with causing deliberate actions than it has to do with causing reflex actions.

I think that this argument is invalid. In the first place I am pretty sure that the persons who use it have before their imagination a kind of picture of how mind and particular form which interaction probably takes if it happens at all. They suggest that what the mind does to the body in voluntary action, if it does anything, is to lower the resistance of certain synapses and to raise that of others. The result is that the nervous current follows such a course as to produce the particular movement which the mind judges to be appropriate at the time. On such a view the difference between reflex, habitual, and deliberate actions for the present purpose becomes fairly plain. In pure reflexes the mind cannot voluntarily affect the resistance of the synapses concerned, and so the action takes place in spite of it. In habitual action it deliberately refrains from interfering with the resistance of the synapses, and so the action goes on like a complicated reflex. But it *can* affect these resistances if it wishes, though often only with difficulty ; and it is ready to do so if it judges this to be expedient. Finally, it may lose the power altogether. This would be what happens when a person becomes a slave to some habit, such as drug-taking.

I conclude that, at the level of enlightened common-sense at which the ordinary discussion of Interaction moves, no good reason has been produced for doubting that the mind acts on the body in volition, and that the body acts on the mind in sensation. The philosophic arguments are quite inconclusive ; and the scientific arguments, when properly understood, are quite compatible with Two-sided Interaction. At most they suggest certain conclusions as to the form which interaction probably takes if it happens at all.

Difficulties in the Denial of Interaction. I propose now to consider some of the difficulties which would attend the denial of Interaction, still keeping the discussion at the same common-sense level. If a man denies the action of body on mind he is at once in trouble over the causation of new sensations. Suppose that I suddenly tread on an unsuspected tin-tack. A new sensation suddenly comes into my mind. This is an event, and it presumably has some cause. Now, however carefully I introspect and retrospect, I can find no other mental event which is adequate to account for the fact that just that sensation has arisen at just that moment. If I reject the common-sense view that treading on the tack is an essential part of the cause of the sensation, I must suppose either that it is uncaused, or that it is caused by other events in my mind which I cannot discover by introspection or retrospection, or that it is caused telepathically by other finite minds or by God. Now enquiry of my neighbours would show that it is not caused telepathically by any event in their minds which they can introspect or remember. Thus anyone who denies the action of body on mind, and admits that sensations have causes, must postulate either (a) immense numbers of unobservable states in his own mind; or (b) as many unobservable states in his neighbours' minds, together with telepathic action; or (c) some non-human spirit together with telepathic action. I must confess that the difficulties which have been alleged against the action of body on mind seem to be mild compared with those of the alternative hypotheses which are involved in the denial of such action.

The difficulties which are involved in the denial of the action of mind on body are at first sight equally great; but I do not think that they turn out to be so serious as those which are involved in denying the action of body on mind. The *prima facie* difficulty is this. The world contains many obviously artificial objects, such as books, bridges, clothes, etc. We know that, if we go far enough back in the history of their production, we always do in fact come on the actions of some human body. And the minds connected with these bodies did design the objects in question, did will to produce them, and did believe that they were initiating and guiding the physical process by means of these designs and volitions. If it be true that the mind does not act on the body, it follows that the designs and volitions in the agents' minds did not in fact play any part in the production of books, bridges, clothes, etc. This appears highly paradoxical. And it is an easy step from it to say that anyone who denies the action of mind on body must admit that books, bridges, and other such objects *could* have been produced even though there had been no minds, no thought of these objects and no desire for them. This consequence seems manifestly absurd to common-sense, and it might be argued that it reflects its absurdity back on the theory which entails it.

The man who denies that mind can act on body might deal with this difficulty in two ways: (1) He might deny that the conclusion *is* intrinsically absurd. He might say that human bodies are extraordinarily complex physical objects, which probably obey irreducible laws of their own, and that we really do not know enough about them to set limits to what their unaided powers could accomplish. This is the line which Spinoza took. The conclusion, it would be argued, *seems* absurd only because the state of affairs which it contemplates is so very unfamiliar. We find it difficult to imagine a body like ours without a mind like ours; but, if we could get over this defect in our powers of imagination, we might have no difficulty in admitting that such a body could do all the things which our bodies do. I think it must be admitted that the difficulty is not so great as that which is involved in denying the action of body on mind. There we had to postulate *ad hoc* utterly unfamiliar entities and modes of action; here it is not certain that we should have to do this.

(2) The other line of argument would be to say that the alleged consequence does not necessarily follow from denying the action of mind on body. I assume

that both parties admit that causation is something more than mere *de facto* regularity of sequence and concomitance. If they do not, of course the whole controversy between them becomes futile ; for there will certainly be causation between mind and body and between body and mind, in the only sense in which there is causation anywhere. This being presupposed, the following kind of answer is logically possible. When I say that B could not have happened unless A had happened, there are two alternative possibilities. (*a*) A may itself be an indispensable link in any chain of causes which ends up with B. (*b*) A may not itself be a link in any chain of causation which ends up with B. But there may be an indispensable link a in any such chain of causation, and A may be a necessary accompaniment or sequent of a. These two possibilities may be illustrated by diagrams. (*a*) is represented by the figure below :—

$$A_0 \qquad A \qquad A_1 \qquad A_2 \qquad B$$
$$\cdot \longrightarrow \cdot \longrightarrow \cdot \longrightarrow \cdot \longrightarrow \cdot$$

The two forms of (*b*) are represented by the two figures below :—

Evidently, if B cannot happen unless a precedes, and if a cannot happen without A accompanying or immediately following it, B will not be able to happen unless A precedes it. And yet A will have had no part in causing B. It will be noticed that, on this view, a has a complex effect AA_1, of which a certain part, viz., A_1 is sufficient by itself to produce A_2 and ultimately B. Let us apply this abstract possibility to our present problem.   Suppose that B is some artificial object, like a book or a bridge.   If we admit that this could not have come into existence unless a certain design and volition had existed in a certain mind, we could interpret the facts in two ways.   (*a*) We could hold that the design and volition are themselves an indispensable link in the chain of causation which ends in the production of a bridge or a book.   This is the common view, and it requires us to admit the action of mind on body.   (*b*) We might hold that the design and the volition are not themselves a link in the chain of causation which ends in the production of the artificial object ; but that they are a necessary accompaniment or sequent of something which *is* an indispensable link in this chain of causation.   On this view the chain consists wholly of physical events ; but one of these physical events (viz., some event in the brain) has a complex consequent.   One part of this consequent is purely physical, and leads by purely physical causation to the ultimate production of a bridge or a book.   The other is purely mental, and consists of a certain design and volition in the mind which animates the human body concerned.   If this has any consequences they are purely mental.   Each part of this complex consequent follows with equal necessity ; this particular brain-state could no more have existed without such and such a mental state accompanying or following it than it could have existed without such and such a bodily movement following it.   If we are willing to take some such view as this, we can admit that certain objects could not have existed unless there had been designs of them and desires for them ; and yet we could consistently deny that these desires and designs have any effect on the movements of our bodies.

It seems to me then that the doctrine which I will call "One-sided Action of Body on Mind" is logically possible ; *i.e.*, a theory which accepts the action of body on mind but denies the action of mind on body.   But I do not see the least reason to accept it, since I see no reason to deny that mind acts on body in volition. One-sided Action has, I think, generally been held in the special form called "Epiphenomenalism." I take this doctrine to consist of the following four propositions : (1) Certain bodily events cause certain mental events. (2) No mental event plays any part in the causation of any bodily event. (3) No mental event plays any part in the causation of any other mental event. Consequently (4) all mental events are caused by bodily events and by them only. Thus Epiphenomenalism is just One-sided Action of Body on Mind, together with a special theory about the nature and structure of mind. This special theory does not call for discussion here, where I am dealing only with the relations between minds and bodies, and am not concerned with a detailed analysis of mind. In a later chapter we shall have to consider the special features of Epiphenomenalism.

Arguments in Favour of Interaction. The only arguments *for* One-sided Action of Body on Mind or for Parallelism are the arguments *against* Two-sided Interaction ; and these, as we have seen, are worthless. Are there any arguments in favour of Two-sided Interaction ? I have incidentally given two which seem to me to have considerable weight. In favour of the action of mind on body is the fact that we seem to be immediately aware of a causal relation when we voluntarily try to produce a bodily movement, and that the arguments to show that this cannot be true are invalid. In favour of the action of body on mind are the insuperable difficulties which I have pointed out in accounting for the happening of new sensations on any other hypothesis. There are, however, two other arguments which have often been thought to prove the action of mind on body. These are (1) an evolutionary argument, first used, I believe, by William James; and (2) the famous "telegram argument." They both seem to me to be quite obviously invalid.

(1) The evolutionary argument runs as follows: It is a fact, which is admitted by persons who deny Two-sided Interaction, that minds increase in complexity and power with the growth in complexity of the brain and nervous system. Now, if the mind makes no difference to the actions of the body, this development on the mental side is quite unintelligible from the point of view of natural selection. Let us imagine two animals whose brains and nervous systems were of the same degree of complexity; and suppose, if possible, that one had a mind and the other had none. If the mind makes no difference to the behaviour of the body the chance of survival and of leaving descendants will clearly be the same for the two animals. Therefore natural selection will have no tendency to favour the evolution of mind which has actually taken place. I do not think that there is anything in this argument. Natural selection is a purely negative process; it simply tends to eliminate individuals and species which have variations unfavourable to survival. Now, by hypothesis, the possession of a mind is not *unfavourable* to survival; it simply makes no difference. Now it may be that the existence of a mind of such and such a kind is an inevitable consequence of the existence of a brain and nervous system of such and such a degree of complexity. Indeed we have seen that some such view is essential if the opponent of Two-sided Interaction is to answer the common-sense objection that artificial objects could not have existed unless there had been a mind which designed and desired them. On this hypothesis there is no need to invoke natural selection twice over, once to explain the evolution of the brain and nervous system, and once to explain the evolution of the mind. If natural selection will account for the evolution of the brain and nervous system, the evolution of the mind will follow inevitably, even though it adds nothing to

the survival-value of the organism. The plain fact is that natural selection does not account for the origin or for the growth in complexity of anything whatever; and therefore it is no objection to any particular theory of the relations of mind and body that, if it were true, natural selection would not explain the origin and development of mind.

(2) The "telegram argument" is as follows: Suppose there were two telegrams, one saying "Our son has been killed", and the other saying: "Your son has been killed". And suppose that one or other of them was delivered to a parent whose son was away from home. As physical stimuli they are obviously extremely alike, since they differ only in the fact that the letter "Y" is present in one and absent in the other. Yet we know that the reaction of the person who received the telegram might be very different according to which one he received. This is supposed to show that the reactions of the body cannot be wholly accounted for by bodily causes, and that the mind must intervene causally in some cases. Now I have very little doubt that the mind does play a part in determining the action of the recipient of the telegram; but I do not see why this argument should prove it to a person who doubted or denied it. If two very similar stimuli are followed by two very different results, we are no doubt justified in concluding that these stimuli are not the complete causes of the reactions which follow them. But of course it would be admitted by every one that the receipt of the telegram is not the complete cause of the recipient's reaction. We all know that his brain and nervous system play an essential part in any reaction that he may make to the stimulus. The question then is whether the minute structure of his brain and nervous system, including in this the supposed traces left by past stimuli and past reactions, is not enough to account for the great difference in his behaviour on receiving two very similar stimuli. Two keys may be very much alike,

but one may fit a certain lock and the other may not. And, if the lock be connected with the trigger of a loaded gun, the results of "stimulating" the system with one or other of the two keys will be extremely different. We know that the brain and nervous system are very complex, and we commonly suppose that they contain more or less permanent traces and linkages due to past stimuli and reactions. If this be granted, it is obvious that two very similar stimuli may produce very different results, simply because one fits in with the internal structure of the brain and nervous system whilst the other does not. And I do not see how we can be sure that anything more is needed to account for the mere difference of reaction adduced by the "telegram argument."

The Positive Theory of Parallelism. The doctrine of Psycho-physical Parallelism, or, as I prefer to call it, "Psycho-neural Parallelism", has two sides to it. One is negative; it is the denial that mind acts on body and the denial that body acts on mind. With this side of it I have now dealt to the best of my ability, and have argued that there is no reason to believe it and tolerably good reason to disbelieve it. But Psycho-neural Parallelism has also a positive side, which might be accepted by one who rejected its negative side. The positive assertion of Parallelism is that there is a one-one correlation between events in a mind and events in the brain and nervous system of the body which it animates. Is there any reason to believe this on empirical grounds?

I think we must say that it *may* be true, but that it is a perfectly enormous assumption unless there be some general metaphysical ground for it; and that the empirical evidence for it is, and will always remain, quite inadequate. The assertion is that to every particular change in the mind there corresponds a certain change in the brain which this mind animates, and that to every change in the brain there corresponds a certain change in the mind which animates this brain. What kind of empirical evidence *could* there be for such an assertion? At best the evidence would be of the following kind: "I have observed a number of brains and the minds which animate them; and I have never found a change in either which was not correlated with a specific change in the other. And all other people who have made similar observations have found the same thing." *If* we had evidence of this sort the positive side of Parallelism would be a straightforward inductive generalisation of it; *i.e.*, an argument from "A has never been observed to happen without B" to "A never does happen without B". But actually we have *no* evidence whatever of this kind. No one person in the world ever has observed, or probably ever will observe, a brain and *its* mind. The only mind that he can observe is his own and the only brains that he can observe are those of others. Nor is this the worst. We can very rarely observe other men's brains at all, and never when they are alive and in a state of normal consciousness. Thus the actual empirical data for the positive side of Parallelism consist of observations on brains which are no longer animated by minds at all or whose animating minds are in abeyance. And these minds could not be directly observed by us even if they were present and functioning normally.

It will therefore be worth while to consider carefully what amount of parallelism we really are justified on empirical grounds in assuming. (1) We have fairly good reasons for thinking that the existence and general integrity of a brain and nervous system is a necessary condition for the manifestation of a mind to itself and to other minds. We do not positively know that it is a sufficient condition; and the question whether it be so or not will have to be discussed later in this book. Our evidence is all of the following kind: (i) In the absence of a brain and nervous system we see none of those external actions which we know in our own case to be accompanied by consciousness. (ii) The brain and nervous system are known to increase in complexity up to a certain age, and we have observed in ourselves and can infer from the behaviour of others a corresponding growth in mental complexity. (iii) Soon after men have ceased to show signs of consciousness by their external behaviour their brains and nervous systems break up. It must be admitted that it might be maintained with almost equal plausibility that these last facts show that the integrity of the brain and nervous system is dependent on the presence of the mind. We might just as well argue that the brain begins to break up because the mind has ceased to animate it, as that the mind has ceased to manifest itself because the brain has begun to break up. In fact, seeing the order in which we actually get our knowledge of the two facts, the former is *prima facie* the more plausible interpretation. (iv) In many cases where men's behaviour has been so odd as to suggest that their minds are abnormal, it is known that their brains have been injured or it has been found after their death that their brains were in an abnormal state. On the other hand, it must be admitted that the brains of some lunatics on dissection show no systematic differences from those of normal people. It would obviously be absurd to talk of "Parallelism" in reference to this very general relation between the integrity and complexity of the brain and nervous system, on the one hand, and the manifestation of a human mind, on the other.

(2) There is, however, empirical evidence which goes rather further than this. It is found that wounds in certain parts of the brain make specific differences to the mind. *E.g.*, a wound in one part may be followed by a loss of memory for spoken words, and so on. Unfortunately, similar results can often be produced by causes like hypnotism or like those which

psycho-analysts discuss.   And here there is no positive empirical evidence that these specific areas of the brain are affected.   Again, there seems to be some evidence that, after a time and within certain limits, another part of the brain can take over the functions of a part that has been injured.   Thus the most that we can say is that the general integrity of certain parts of the brain seems to be at least a temporarily necessary condition for the manifestation of certain specific kinds of mental activity.   It remains doubtful how far any given area is indispensable for a given kind of mental activity, and whether there may not be some kinds of activity which, though dependent like all others on the general integrity of the brain, are not specially correlated with any particular area.   We might sum up these facts by saying that there is good evidence for a considerable amount of " Departmental Parallelism " between mind and brain.

(3) The orthodox Parallelist, however, goes much further than this, and much beyond the most rigid departmental parallelism.   He would hold, not merely that there is a strict correlation between each distinguishable *department* of mental life and some specific *area* of the brain, but also that there is a strict parallelism of *events*.   *E.g.*, he holds, not merely that I could not remember at all unless a certain area of my brain were intact, but also that if I now remember eating my breakfast there is a certain event in this area uniquely correlated with this particular mental event.   And by "unique correlation" he means that if some other mental state had happened now instead of this particular memory there would necessarily have been a different brain-event, and conversely.   So far as I know there is not, and could not possibly be, any empirical evidence for this " Parallelism of Events ", as I will call it.   For (i), while a man is conscious and can observe events in his own mind, his brain is not open to inspection by himself or by anyone else.   And, when his brain is

open to inspection, he is not likely to be in a position to introspect or to tell others what is going on in his mind, even if something is happening there at the time. (ii) In any case the events in the brain which are supposed to correspond to particular events in the mind would be admitted to be too minute to be observable even under the most favourable circumstances. They are as purely hypothetical as the motions of electrons, without the advantage that the assumption of them enables us to predict better than we could otherwise do what states of mind a man will probably have under given circumstances.

It seems to me then that there is no empirical evidence at all for a Parallelism of Events between mind and brain. If this doctrine is to be held, the grounds for it must be general. *E.g.* psycho-*neural* parallelism might be plausible if, on other grounds, we saw reason to accept psycho-*physical* parallelism ; *i.e.*, the doctrine that *every* physical event is correlated with a specific mental event, and conversely. And the wider doctrine might be defended as helping to explain the apparent origin of life and mind from apparently non-living and non-conscious matter. This is a question which we shall have to discuss later ; all that I am concerned to argue at present is that, at the level of enlightened common-sense and apart from some general metaphysical theory of the nature of matter and mind, there is no adequate evidence for a psycho-neural parallelism of events. And, as parallelism has commonly been defended on the ground that it is established by empirical scientific investigation of the brain and nervous system, this fact is worth pointing out.

If there is no reason *for* psycho-neural parallelism of events, is there any positive reason *against* it ? Some philosophers have held tnat there is. They have held that, while it is possible and even probable that *some* mental events are correlated with specific neural events, it is impossible that this should be true of *all* mental events. Those who take this view generally hold that there probably is psycho-neural parallelism of events for sensations, but that there certainly cannot be such parallelism for comparison, introspection, attentive inspection, and so on. This view is taken by Mr Johnson in his *Logic* (Part III); and it will be worth while to consider his arguments. They are contained in Chapter VII, § 6 of that work. Mr Johnson's argument, if I rightly understand it, comes to this: We must distinguish, *e.g.*, between the *fact* that I am having two sensations, one of which is light red and the other dark red, and my *recognition* that both are red and that one is darker than the other. We must likewise distinguish, *e.g.*, between the *fact* that the dark one started before the light one, and my recognition of this fact; and between the *fact* that the dark one is to the left of the light one in my visual field and my recognition of this fact. Finally, we must notice that we have to distinguish different degrees of clearness and determinateness with which a perfectly determinate fact may be recognised. We may merely judge that one sensum is separate from another, or we may judge that one is to the left of the other, or we may judge that the first is as much to the left of the second as the second is to the right of a third, and so on. Now Mr Johnson contends that the sensations themselves have neural correlates, and that the determinate qualities and relations which the sensations actually have are determined by the qualities and relations of these neural correlates. But he holds that there is then nothing left on the neural side for the *recognition* of these qualities and relations to be correlated with. Still less is there anything left on the neural side to be correlated with the infinitely numerous different degrees of determinateness with which the qualities and relations of the sensations may be apprehended. Hence he concludes that mental events above the level of sensations *cannot* be correlated one to one with specific neural events. He does not explicitly draw the distinction which I have done between Departmental Parallelism and Parallelism of Events; but I think it is plain that his argument is meant only to deny the latter. He would probably admit that, if certain specific areas of our brains were injured, we should lose altogether the power of making judgments of comparison and of recognising spatio-temporal relations; but he would hold that, given the general integrity of those areas, there is not some one specific event within them corresponding to each particular judgment of comparison or of spatio-temporal relation.

Before criticising this argument we must notice that Mr Johnson does not explicitly distinguish sensations and sensa. By a "sensation" I think he means what I should call a "sensed sensum". And he thinks that, from the nature of the case, there can be no unsensed sensa. Thus a sensation for him is a sensum, regarded as existentially mind-dependent; and, in virtue of its supposed existential mind-dependence, it counts as a mental event belonging to the mind on which its existence depends. If we like to distinguish between mental *states* and mental *acts* we can say that a sensation, for Mr Johnson, is apparently a mental *state* having certain sensible qualities, such as colour, position in the visual field, and so on. To recognise that one is having a sensation, that it is of such and such a kind, and that it stands in such and such spatio-temporal relations to other sensations, would be to perform a cognitive mental *act*. And his contention is that, whilst there is a parallelism of events for mental states, there cannot for this very reason be also a parallelism of events for mental acts. This at least is how I understand him.

Now I must confess that Mr Johnson's argument seems to me to be so extremely weak that (knowing Mr Johnson) I hesitate to believe that I can have properly understood it. Let us suppose that the actual relative position of two sensa s_1 and s_2 in a visual sense-field is determined by the relative position of two excited areas in the brain, b_1 and b_2. Let us suppose that the actual relative date of the two sensa in the sense-history of the experient is determined by the relative date of the excitement of these areas. And let us suppose that the determinate sensible qualities of the two sensa (*e.g.*, the particular shade of the particular colour possessed by each) is determined by the particular kind of movement which is going on in the microscopic particles within these two areas. Mr Johnson's contention seems to be that, when we have mentioned the positions of the excited areas, the dates at which they begin to be excited, and the particular kind of movement which is going on within them, we have said all that can be said about the neural events. There is nothing left on the neural side to be correlated with our acts of recognition, of qualitative comparison, and of spatio-temporal judgment ; and therefore these events can have no special neural correlate. To this there are two answers which seem so obvious that I am almost ashamed to make them.

(1) At the very utmost the argument would show only that there is nothing left *within the two areas* b_1 *and* b_2 to be correlated with any judgments which we happen to make about the sensations s_1 and s_2. But these two areas do not exhaust the whole of the brain and nervous system. Why our acts of judgment about these two sensations should not have neural correlates in some other part of the brain I cannot imagine. The situation on the mental side is that we may, but need not, make these judgments if we do have the sensations ; and that we cannot make them unless we have the sensations. This is exactly what we might expect if the neural correlates of the acts of judgment were in a different part of the brain from the neural correlates of the sensations themselves : and if a certain kind of disturbance in the latter were a necessary but insufficient condition of a certain kind of disturbance in the former.

(2) But we could answer the argument without needing even to assume that the neural correlates of judgments about sensations are in a different area of the brain from the neural correlates of the sensations themselves. We have to remember that the same area may contain at the same time microscopic events of different scales of magnitude. Let us take a purely physical analogy. The same piece of metal may be at once hot and glowing. We have extremely good reasons to believe that *both* these apparent characteristics are correlated with microscopic motions which are going on throughout the whole volume occupied by the bit of metal. The heat is supposed to be correlated with the random movements of molecules and the light with the jumps of electrons from one stable orbit to another. The large-scale events can go on without the small-scale events (a body may be hot without glowing); but the more violent the large-scale events the more frequent will be the small-scale events (a body begins to glow if it be heated enough). Now I cannot imagine why the same thing might not be true of the neural correlates of sensations and the neural correlates of our judgments about our sensations. Suppose that the neural correlates of sensations were large-scale events in a certain area of the brain ; and suppose that the neural correlates of our judgments about these sensations were small-scale events in the same area. Then I should expect to find that sensations could happen without our making judgments about them ; that we could not make the judgments unless we had the sensations ; and that it would be more difficult not to make the judgments as the sensations became more intense, other things being equal. And this is exactly what I do find. It seems to me then, either that I have altogether misunderstood Mr Johnson's argument, or that there is nothing whatever in it.

There remains one other point to be discussed before leaving the subject. It is true, as Mr Johnson points out, that we make judgments of various degrees of determinateness about the same perfectly determinate fact. Does this raise any particular difficulty against the view that every act of judgment has a specific neural correlate? I do not think that it does, if we avoid certain confusions into which it is very easy to fall. I suppose that the difficulty that is felt is this: " Every neural event is perfectly determinate; how can an indeterminate judgment have a determinate neural correlate; and how can there be different determinate neural correlates for all the different degrees of determinateness in judgments?" To this I should answer (i) that of course the differences on the neural side which would correspond to different degrees of determinateness in the judgment are not themselves differences of determinateness. But why should they be? The differences on the neural side which correspond to differences of shade in sensations of colour are not themselves differences of shade. If, *e.g.*, the area which is correlated with judgments about our sensations be different from the area which is correlated with the sensations themselves, we might suppose that differences in the determinateness of the judgment were correlated with differences in the extent or the intensity of the disturbance within this area. If, on the other hand, we supposed that our sensations were correlated with large-scale events, and our judgments about these sensations with small-scale events in the same region of the brain, we might suppose that differences in the determinateness of the judgment are correlated with differences in the frequency of these small-scale events. There is thus no difficulty, so far as I can see, in providing neural correlates to every different degree of determinateness in our judgments. (ii) It is perhaps necessary to point out that what is called an "indeterminate judgment" is not an indeterminate event; every event, whether mental or physical, is no doubt perfectly determinate of its kind. *E.g.*, whether I merely judge that *some one* has been in the room or make the more determinate judgment that *John Smith* has been in the room, either judgment as a psychical event has perfectly determinate forms of all the psychical determinables under which it falls. The indefiniteness is in what is asserted, not in the act of asserting as such. Hence the problem is not, as it might seem to a careless observer, to find a determinate neural correlate to an indeterminate psychical event; the problem is merely to find a determinate neural correlate to a determinate psychical event which consists in the asserting of a relatively indeterminate characteristic.

I conclude then that no adequate reason has been produced by Mr Johnson to prove that there *cannot* be specific neural correlates to mental *acts* as well as to mental *states*. I have also tried to show that there neither is nor is likely to be any empirical evidence *for* the doctrine that all mental events have specific neural events as their correlates. Hence the positive doctrine of Psycho-neural Parallelism of Events seems to me to be a perfectly open question. This is not perhaps a wildly exciting result. But it is not altogether to be despised, since it leaves us with a perfectly free hand when we try to construct a speculative theory of the relations of matter and mind which shall do justice to all the known facts. For the known facts neither require nor preclude complete Psycho-neural Parallelism of Events.

Summary and Conclusions. I wish to make quite clear what I do and what I do not claim to have done in this chapter. I have definitely assumed that the body and the mind are two distinct entities, which are now in a very intimate union, which I express by saying that the former is "animated by" the latter. I have raised no question about the exact nature or origin of this relation of "animation"; and I have not considered the apparent growth of mind in the individual or the apparent development of consciousness from the non-conscious in the course of the earth's history. Again, I have taken the body to be very much as common-sense, enlightened by physical science, but not by philosophical criticism, takes it to be; I have supposed that we know pretty well what a mind is; and I have assumed that causation *is* not simply regular sequence and concomitant variation, though these are more or less trustworthy *signs* of the presence of a causal relation. These are the assumptions on which the question of Interaction has commonly been discussed by philosophers and by scientists; and it would be idle for me to conceal my opinion that it has been discussed extraordinarily badly. The problem seems to have exercised a most unfortunate effect on those who have treated it; for I have rarely met with a collection of worse arguments on all sides. I can only hope that I have not provided yet another instance in support of this generalisation.

My conclusion is that, subject to the assumptions just mentioned, no argument has been produced which should make any reasonable person doubt that mind acts on body in volition and that body acts on mind in sensation. I have tried to show the extreme diffi-culties which are involved in attempting to deny that body acts on mind. And I have tried to show that the apparently equal difficulties which seem to be in-volved in attempting to deny that mind acts on body could be evaded with a little ingenuity. Thus One-sided Action of Body on Mind is a possible theory. But there seems to me to be no positive reason for accepting it, and at least one reason for doubting it, viz., the conviction which many men have (and which Mr Hume's arguments fail altogether to refute) that we *know* directly that our volitions are necessary con-ditions for the occurrence of our voluntary movements.

If these conclusions be sound, Parallelism, con-sidered as an *alternative* which excludes Interaction, has no leg left to stand upon.   But Parallelism has a positive side to it which is perfectly compatible with Interaction, and is therefore worth discussing for its own sake.   I distinguished between the metaphysical doctrine of Psycho-*physical* Parallelism and the more restricted doctrine of Psycho-*neural* Parallelism.   And I divided the latter into Departmental Parallelism and Parallelism of Events.   It seemed to me that there was good empirical evidence for a considerable amount of Departmental Parallelism, but that there was not and is not likely to be adequate empirical evidence for Parallelism of Events.   On the other hand, I came to the conclusion that Mr Johnson's arguments to prove that complete parallelism between mental and neural events is *impossible* were quite unsound.

This, I think, is as far as the discussion can be carried at this level.   One thing seems to me to emerge clearly even at this point.   If interaction has to be denied at a later stage it can only be because the relation between mind and body turns out to be so intimate that "interaction" is an unsuitable expression for the connection between a particular mental event and its correlated bodily event.   This would be so if, *e.g.*, Materialism were true, so that the mind was just some part of the body.   It might be so on a Double-aspect Theory, or on a theory of Neutral Monism. But we cannot decide between such general theories until we know more about the true nature of Mind and of Matter, and have taken into consideration questions about origin and development of minds which we have hitherto explicitly left out of account. Thus the final discussion of the question can come only near the end of the book.

SECTION B

Introductory Remarks

" If there's a screw loose in a heavenly body, that's philosophy;
and if there's a screw loose in a earthly body, that's philosophy
too; or it may be that there's sometimes a little metaphysics in
it, but that's not often. Philosophy's the chap for me. If a
parent asks a question in the classical, commercial, or mathematical line, says I gravely, 'Why, sir, in the first place, are
you a philosopher?' 'No, Mr Squeers,' he says, 'I ain't.'
'Then, sir,' says I, 'I am sorry for you, for I shan't be able to
explain it.' Naturally the parent goes away and wishes he was
a philosopher, and, equally naturally, thinks I'm one."

(DICKENS, Nicholas Nickleby)

SECTION B

THE MIND'S KNOWLEDGE OF EXISTENTS

Introductory Remarks

IN this Section I am going to consider the knowledge which a human mind has of matter, of itself, and of other minds. Knowledge is a transaction with two sides to it, the mind which knows and the objects known. A critical discussion of the mind's alleged knowledge of anything should therefore help to clear our ideas both of the nature of the mind and its activities and of the nature of the objects which it knows. Thus, in discussing the mind's knowledge of matter through perception, we ought to learn something both of the nature of the mind as a percipient and of the nature and reality of matter. And, when we consider the mind's knowledge of itself and of other minds, we ought to learn something of the nature of the mind from two sides. Common-sense believes itself to know pretty well what mind is and what matter is, though it might have great difficulties in putting its beliefs into clear and consistent language. So far we have accepted these claims without question, and have discussed certain problems subject to this condition. We have now to pass from the level of enlightened common-sense to that of Critical Philosophy. By this I mean that we have to consider carefully the sources of our alleged knowledge of matter and of mind, and to see how far we can still accept the common-sense view of these two entities in the light of this additional information. Even if the common-sense view should not need *correction*, it will certainly need careful and explicit *statement*; and, when stated, it may seem unfamiliar and even shocking to common-sense.

It would, I think, be admitted by every one that such knowledge as we have of matter is based on sense-perception and memory. Each man's sense-perception and memory are supplemented by communication with other minds which claim to tell him what they have perceived and remembered. Thus the problem of our knowledge of matter inevitably involves the problem of our knowledge of other minds. There is less agreement about the sources of our knowledge of other minds. But I suppose that every one would admit that a necessary, if not a sufficient, condition of such knowledge is that we should listen to the sounds and note the gestures of other human bodies. So the problem of our knowledge of other minds is in turn bound up with the problem of our knowledge of matter. The exact connexion between these two problems will have to be considered in some detail. There is, again, a lack of agreement about the sources of a mind's knowledge of itself. I suppose that every one would admit that memory is involved here as much as in our knowledge of matter. But, on the one hand, some people deny the existence of a mental activity, called "introspection," by which a mind observes itself or the events belonging to it. And those who admit the existence of this activity differ a good deal about its limitations; for some think that we can introspect both acts and states, whilst others seem to hold that we can introspect states but not acts. On the other hand, some people who admit the existence of introspection and give it extensive powers would hold that it is not the only or the main source of our knowledge of our own minds.

In any case we can see at once that the three problems are most intimately linked, and that no treatment of one can be satisfactory without a treatment of the rest.

I have already tried to show this linkage between the problem of our knowledge of matter and the problem of our knowledge of other minds. There seems to be an equally close connexion between the problem of our knowledge of our own minds and that of our knowledge of other minds. For, even if it be not the whole truth, it certainly seems an important part of the truth to say that our beliefs about other minds are based on analogies with what we know of our own. The other point which is already clear is that memory is involved in all three kinds of knowledge. Hence the divisions of this Section will be the following : First I shall treat *Sense-perception*, then *Memory*, then *Our Knowledge of our own Minds*, and then *Our Knowledge of other Minds*. The reader will remember that this division is necessary, because we cannot say everything at once, but that none of these four chapters is likely to be satisfactory when taken by itself.

CHAPTER IV

Sense-perception and Matter

In this chapter I propose to give a sketch of the problem of the mind's knowledge of matter through the senses. I shall necessarily be covering again ground which I have already been over in my *Scientific Thought*, and I must refer the reader to the Second Part of that book for a detailed statement and defence of my views on the subject. Here I shall be as brief as possible, and in consequence somewhat dogmatic. I shall, however, be approaching the problem from a slightly different angle, so that I hope that this chapter will not be mere vain repetition.

Perceptual Situations. Let us begin with something that every one, whatever his philosophical views may be, would admit to be a fact. Some people would raise doubts about the existence of physical objects, such as chairs, tables, bells, etc. Some people would raise doubts about the existence of selves or minds which perceive such objects. But no one doubts that such phrases as " I see a bell ", " I feel a bell ", " I hear a bell ", indicate states of affairs which actually exist from time to time. People do not begin to quarrel till they try to *analyse* such situations, and to ask what must be meant by " I ", by the " bell ", and by " hearing ", if it is to be true that " I hear a bell ". When they do this they are liable to find that the only senses of " I ", " bell ", and " hear ", which will make the statement true are very different from those which we are wont to attach to those words. If this should happen, it still remains true, of course, that the phrases "I hear a bell" and "I see a chair" stand for real states of affairs which differ in certain specific ways from each other; but these states of affairs may be extremely different in their structure and their components from what the form of words which is used to indicate them would naturally suggest to us.

I will call such situations as are naturally indicated by phrases like "I am seeing a chair" or "I am hearing a bell" by the name of "Perceptual Situations". I take it then that every one agrees that there are such things as Perceptual Situations. Can we all agree to go any further together before parting company? I think we obviously can. (i) There are certain situations, which undoubtedly arise from time to time, which are indicated by such phrases as "I feel tired" or "I feel cross". I think that every one would admit that perceptual situations differ radically from these. Suppose we compare the situations indicated by the two phrases "I feel cross" and "I hear a bell". When we feel cross we are not feeling some*thing* but are feeling some*how*. When we hear a bell we no doubt are feeling some*how*, but the important point about the perceptual situation is that we claim to be in cognitive contact with some*thing* other than ourselves and our states. This claim is just as obvious in those perceptual situations which are commonly believed to be delusive as in those which are commonly believed to be veridical. The two situations "I am hearing a bell" and "I am seeing pink rats" agree completely in this respect, and both differ in this respect from the situation "I feel cross". I will express the difference between the two kinds of situation by saying that the one does and the other does not have an "epistemological object". The bell-situation and the pink-rat-situation both have epistemological objects; the situation indicated by "I feel cross" has no epistemological object. My motive in adding the qualifying word "epistemological" is that other-

wise some bright spirit will at once complain that the
pink-rat situation has no object. What he really means
is of course that there is no *ontological* object, corresponding to the *epistemological* object which the situation
certainly has ; *i.e.*, that the situation involves a certain
claim which the physical world refuses to meet. I had
better take this opportunity to anticipate another purely
verbal objection which someone is sure to make. Someone is certain to say : "We don't really *see* pink rats,
for there are none ; we only *think* that we see them."
To this I answer by admitting that words like "seeing",
"hearing", etc., do, most unfortunately, introduce the
"fallacy of many questions" like the barrister's query :
"When did you leave off beating your wife?" The
phrase "I see so-and-so" *is* taken in ordinary life to
mean : "There is a perceptual situation of the visual
kind of which I am subject. This has such and such
an epistemological object. And there is a physical
object corresponding to this epistemological object".
If a second person has reason to believe that the third
of these propositions is false, he will be inclined to say :
"You are not really seeing so-and-so ; you only think
that you are seeing it". Now words like "seeing" and
"hearing" are hopeless for our present purpose if they
are to be interpreted in this way. I therefore wish it to
be clearly understood that I shall depart so far from
common usage as to say that a man *sees* a pink rat,
provided he is subject of a perceptual situation which
has a pink rat as an epistemological object and is of
the visual kind, regardless of whether there is a
physical pink rat corresponding to this epistemological
object. With these verbal explanations I think that
every one would admit that there are perceptual situations and that all perceptual situations necessarily have
epistemological objects. Common language, though
far from consistent, expresses the difference between
the two kinds of situation in the following way : It
tends to express a situation which has no epistemo-

logical object by the verb "to feel" followed by an adjective or adverb, such as "cross" or "crossly". It tends to express a situation which has an epistemological object by some special transitive verb, such as "see" or "hear", and by a substantive-name which, in an inflected language, would be put in the accusative case. In order to know what is the epistemological object of any situation it is only necessary to know the meaning of this substantive-word in the phrase which expresses the situation. In order to know whether the situation has an *ontological* as well as an *epistemological* object it is plainly not enough to consider the meanings of *words*; the question can be settled only, if at all, by a careful enquiry into the nature and connexions of *things*.

(ii) It would further be admitted by every one that not all situations which have an epistemological object are perceptual. (*a*) In the first place there are situations whose epistemological objects are such that no *physical* object could correspond to them, though ontological objects of a different kind might correspond to them. *E.g.*, the situation expressed by the phrase "I notice that I am acting spitefully" has an epistemological object. But, if there be an ontological object which corresponds to this epistemological object, it certainly cannot be any purely physical thing or event. It must be some process which is going on in my mind. I will say that the epistemological object of a situation which has such an object may be "of the physical kind", or "of the psychical kind", or possibly of many other kinds. It would be agreed, I think, that the epistemological object of any perceptual situation must be of the physical kind ; and this simply means that, if there be an ontological object corresponding to it, it must be a physical object or event.

(*b*) It would further be admitted that a situation may have an epistemological object of the physical kind and yet not be a perceptual situation. Compare the two phrases "I am hearing a bell" and "I am thinking of a bell". The epistemological objects of the two situations which are expressed by these two phrases are both of the physical kind ; they might, so far as one can see, even be identical. But every one recognises that there is a deep difference between the situations. We should vaguely express one part of this difference by saying that in the perceptual situation we are "in more immediate touch with" the bell than in the thought - situation. This difference is indicated in speech by the fact that the phrase which expresses the thought-situation contains a preposition like "of" or "about" before the substantive-word which expresses the epistemological object of the situation, whilst there is in general no such word in the phrase which stands for the perceptual situation. I will express this difference by saying that a perceptual situation is "intuitive", whilst a thought-situation with the same kind of epistemological object is "discursive". Here again I suppose that every one would admit the distinction which I am drawing, though different philosophers would differ violently about the proper analysis of it. I do not wish to deny that there may be something intuitive in every thought - situation and something discursive in every perceptual situation. But I think that it is plainly true that what strikes us about the situation called "hearing a bell" is its intuitive character, and that what strikes us about the situation called "thinking about a bell" is its discursive character.

(c) We must next notice that there are situations which have an epistemological object of the physical kind, and are intuitive and not discursive, and yet would not be called perceptual. The most obvious examples are memory-situations. I may have a genuine memory of the tie which my friend was wearing yesterday. This situation has an epistemological object of the physical kind. And it is intuitive, in the sense in which seeing his tie would be intuitive and merely thinking of his tie would not be. But it is quite different from a perceptual situation. And one important difference, at any rate, is this. It is of the essence of a perceptual situation that it claims to reveal an object as it *is* at the time when the situation is going on ; and it is of the essence of a memory-situation that it claims to reveal an object as it *was* some time before the memory-situation began. It is perfectly true that, when I see a distant star, this is an instance of a perceptual situation ; and it is true that there is strong reason to believe that, if the situation reveals a physical object at all, it reveals it as it *was* long before the situation began. But this does not affect the truth of my statement. For it is certainly true that, so long as we remain at the level of perception and do not introduce inferences, the situation *does claim* to reveal the star as it now is ; and, if it did not, it would not be a perceptual situation.

(iii) There is one other point which I suppose that every one would admit to be common and peculiar to perceptual situations. This is the fact that sensation plays an unique and indispensable part in them. I do not think it is possible to define "sensation". But it is possible to give illustrations which every one will recognise. Such statements as " I am aware of a red flash ", " I am aware of a squeaky noise ", and so on, are certainly sometimes true ; and they express a kind of situation which is perfectly familiar to every one. Whenever such a statement is true, there exists a sensation. And it would be admitted that there cannot be perceptual situations without sensations. I think that it would also be admitted that sensations play a part in perceptual situations which they do not play in any other kind of situation. I will express this fact by saying that perceptual situations are " sensuous ".

We may now sum up the points on which every one is really agreed, however much they may differ in their language, as follows : There certainly are perceptual situations ; they are intuitive and sensuous and they have epistemological objects of the physical kind, which are given as simultaneous with the situation itself. This is of course neither a definition of the perceptual situation nor an analysis of it; it is simply a set of propositions which are admittedly all true of perceptual situations and not all true of anything else. Does the agreement stretch any further than this? I think that it can be carried one step further. I think that every one is really agreed about the irreducible minimum of characteristics that a thing would have to possess in order to count as a physical object. Now it is agreed that all perceptual situations claim to reveal objects of this kind, for that is what we mean when we say that they all have epistemological objects of the physical kind. Let us then raise the question:

What do we understand by a "Physical Object"? The following marks seem to characterise anything that we should be willing to call a "physical object". (i) It is conceived to be a strand of history of reasonably long duration, as compared with that of our specious present, and possessed of a certain characteristic unity and continuity throughout the period during which it is said to last. A mere flash would hardly be counted as a physical *object;* a penny, if it has the characteristics which it is commonly believed to have, would count as one. (ii) It is conceived to be quite literally extended in space. It has some size and some shape, an inside as well as an outside, and it stands in spatial relations to other physical objects. Strictly speaking, we ought rather to say that each momentary cross-section of the history of the object has these characteristics, and that the nearer together two such cross-sections are in time the more nearly alike they will be in their spatial properties. It may happen, as a particular case, that all the momentary cross-sections of a certain physical object within a certain stretch of time are exactly alike in all their spatial characteristics. In this case we should say that, for this stretch of time, the object had kept its shape and position unchanged. (iii) It is conceived to persist and interact with other physical objects when no one perceives it. "Being perceived" is regarded as something which happens from time to time to physical objects, but which is not essential to their existence, and makes no further difference to their qualities either at the time or afterwards. (iv) It is conceived to be perceptible by a number of different observers at the same time, as well as by one observer at various times. (v) It is supposed to combine a number of other qualities beside the spatio-temporal characteristics already mentioned. Some of these qualities reveal themselves in one way, others in another way; thus colour reveals itself to sight, hardness and temperature to touch, and so on. In order that a certain kind of quality may reveal itself to a certain mind it seems necessary that the body which this mind animates shall be gifted with appropriate sense-organs. Thus it is held to be quite possible that physical objects may have many qualities which are never revealed to us, simply because we lack the necessary sense-organs. If there be no things which have all these characteristics, there are, strictly speaking, no physical objects; and all perceptual situations are delusive. But of course there might still be things which literally possessed some of these characteristics and to which the rest could be ascribed in various more or less Pickwickian senses. In that case it would be a matter of taste whether we still said that we believed in physical objects; but it would be a matter of fact that all perceptual situations are delusive in certain respects. *E.g.*, if the ordinary scientific view, as commonly interpreted, were right, all perceptual situations would be delusive in so far as they claim to reveal objects which literally have colour, taste, smell, etc. But they would be veridical in so far as they claim to reveal objects which literally have shape, size, position, and motion. If Berkeley be right, all perceptual situations are delusive in every respect except in their claim to reveal *something* independent of and common to percipients. This "something" will be the permanent habits of volition according to which God sends us such and such sensations on such and such occasions.

Analysis of Perceptual Situations. The typical linguistic expression for a perceptual situation is a sentence like "I see the chair" or "I hear the bell". This mode of expression inevitably suggests a certain mode of analysis for the perceptual situation. It suggests that it consists of me and the physical object whose name appears in the phrase, related directly by an asymmetrical two-term relation which is indicated by the verb. And this suggests that the admitted existence of the situation guarantees the existence of me and of the physical object. How far can this simple-minded view be maintained?

In philosophy it is equally silly to be a slave to common speech or to neglect it. When we remember that it represents the analyses made unconsciously for practical ends by our prehistoric ancestors we shall not be inclined to treat it as an oracle. When we remember that they were probably no greater fools than we are, we shall recognise that it is likely to accord at any rate with the more obvious facts, and that it will be wise to take it as our starting-point and to work from it. It is plausible to suppose that the perceptual situation which language describes by the phrase "I see a chair" does contain two outstanding constituents related by an asymmetrical two-term relation. But it is quite another question whether these two constituents can possibly be what is commonly understood by "me" and by "chair". Let us now consider this question, first as regards the object and then as regards the subject.

The Objective Constituent. Even if we had never had any reason to believe that some perceptual situations are delusive, this extremely simple-minded analysis would need to be modified considerably. / (*a*) It would be admitted that in any one perceptual situation I am never aware of the *whole* of the surface of a physical object, in the sense in which I do seem to be aware of a part of it.   Nobody who was looking at a bell would seriously maintain that, at a given moment, he is aware of the far side and the inside of the bell, in the same sense in which he would claim to be aware of a certain part of the outside which is facing him at the time. And by a "bell" we certainly mean something which has a closed surface with an inside as well as an out-side, and not merely a patch with indefinite boundaries. Thus the most we could say is : "The perceptual situation contains as a constituent something which is in fact part of the surface of a bell ".   (*b*) A similar limitation with regard to time must be put on the naïve analysis of the perceptual situation.   By a "bell" we mean something of considerable duration ; something which certainly may, and almost certainly does, stretch out in time beyond the limits of the perceptual situation in which I am aware of it.   Now no one would maintain that the parts of the history of the bell which come before the beginning and after the end of a certain perceptual situation are "given" to him in that per-ceptual situation in the same sense in which the con-temporary slice of the bell's history is "given".   Thus we have no right to say that the situation, described by the phrase "I am seeing the bell" contains the *bell* as a constituent ; at most we can say that it contains as a constituent a short event which is in fact a slice of a longer strand of history, and that this longer strand is the history of a certain bell.   (*c*) It would be admitted by every one that a bell is something more than a coloured surface, more than a cold hard surface, and so on.   Now, so long as I merely look at a bell, its colour only is revealed to me ; its temperature or hardness are certainly not revealed in the same sense at that time. Similarly, when I merely touch the bell, only its temperature and hardness are revealed to me; its colour is certainly not revealed to me in the same sense at that time. Once again then I have no right to say that the *bell* is a constituent of either of these perceptual situations. At most I may say there is a constituent which displays certain qualities, and that this same constituent has in fact other qualities which would be displayed under other conditions.

Thus we are forced to modify the first naïve analysis of "I see a bell" at least in the following respects: We cannot hold that this situation literally contains the bell itself as a constituent. The most we can say is that the situation contains me and *something* related by an asymmetrical two-term relation; that this something is in fact a part of a larger surface, and is also a short slice of a longer strand of history; that it has in fact other qualities beside those which are sensuously revealed to me in this situation; and that this spatially larger and temporally longer whole, with the qualities which are not revealed sensuously in this situation, is a certain bell. This whole is the epistemological object of the situation expressed by the phrase " I am seeing the bell ". And, even if it be granted that there is an ontological object which corresponds accurately to the epistemological object, we cannot admit that *it* is bodily a constituent of the situation. The most that we can grant is that a small spatio-temporal fragment of the ontological object is literally a constituent of the situation, and that a small selection of the qualities of this fragment is sensuously revealed in the situation.

Now of course the existence of any complex whole entails the existence of anything that really is a constituent of it. There is no doubt that such situations as are described by the phrase "I see a bell" exist. And there is no doubt that the epistemological object of such a situation is something having all the characteristics which are connoted by the word "bell". If then the perceptual situation did contain as a constituent

something which accurately corresponds to its epistemological object, the existence of the former would
guarantee that of the latter. But it is now clear that
the situation does not and could not contain as a constituent anything that could properly be denoted by
the word "bell". Hence the existence of the situation
denoted by the phrase "I see the bell" does not suffice
to guarantee the existence of a certain thing denoted
by the phrase "the bell". It is plain then that there
is involved in every perceptual situation another factor
beside me and a certain spatio-temporally extended
particular. This is the conviction that this particular
something is not isolated and self-subsistent, and is not
completely revealed in all its qualities ; but that it is
spatio-temporally a part of a larger whole of a certain
characteristic kind, viz., a certain physical object, and
that this whole has other qualities beside those which
are sensuously manifested in the perceptual situation.

Let us call the constituent about which we believe
these propositions "the objective constituent of the perceptual situation". And let us call this conviction
which we have about the objective constituent "the
external reference of the situation". I give it this
name because it clearly points spatially, temporally,
and qualitatively, beyond the situation and what is
contained in and sensuously manifested in it. I will
now say something more about the external reference
of a perceptual situation.

The External Reference. (*a*) It would be false psychologically to say that we *infer* from the nature of the
objective constituent and from any other knowledge that
we may have that it is part of a larger spatio-temporal
whole of a certain specific kind. It is perfectly evident
that we do nothing of the sort. Of course we can talk
of "unconscious inferences", if we like ; but at most
this means that we in fact reach without inference the
kind of conclusion which could be defended by inference
if it were challenged. (*b*) It would be false logically

to say that the beliefs which are an essential factor in a perceptual situation, though not reached by inference, could be justified by inference. I can see no way of validly inferring from the mere presence of an objective constituent, which sensuously manifests such and such qualities, that this constituent is part of a larger spatio-temporal whole which is not a constituent of the situation and has other qualities. It might perhaps be argued that, although this cannot be inferred with certainty from any one or from any number of perceptual situations taken separately, it might be inferred with probability from a number of such situations taken together and considered in their mutual relations. I shall go further into this question a little later in the chapter. But it is evident that, even if the general validity of such inferences be admitted, their conclusion would be something much less definite than the belief that the objective constituent of a perceptual situation is a spatio-temporal part of a larger whole which corresponds accurately to the epistemological object of the situation. Strictly speaking, the most that could be directly inferred from a study of perceptual situations and their mutual relations is that probably such and such a perceptual situation will be accompanied by such and such others, belonging to different observers; or that it will probably be succeeded by such and such other perceptual situations, provided I make such and such movements. The notion of persistent physical objects is logically merely a hypothesis to explain such correlations between perceptual situations; and the common-sense belief that the objective constituents of perceptual situations are literally spatio-temporal parts of persistent physical objects is logically one very special form of this hypothesis. It is tolerably obvious that the actual strength of our conviction that in perception we are in direct cognitive contact with literal spatio-temporal parts of a physical object, which corresponds to the epistemological object of the situation, could not be justified by inference. (c) Lastly, we

express the position far too intellectually, when we say
that in a perceptual situation we are acquainted with an
objective constituent which sensuously manifests certain
qualities, and that this acquaintance gives rise to and
is accompanied by a belief that the constituent is part
of a larger spatio-temporal whole of a specific kind.
We must remember that ignorant men, and presumably
animals, perceive as well as philosophers ; and we must
beware of mixing up our *analysis* of the perceptual
situation with the situation as it actually exists.   It
would be nearer the truth to say that, at the purely
perceptual level, people do not have the special experience called "belief" or "judgment".   To believe so
and so at this level really means to act as it would be
reasonable to act *if* one believed so and so, and to be
surprised if the action turns out to be a failure.   We
automatically adjust our sense-organs in a certain way ;
we make incipient movements ; and so on.   These are
of course accompanied by characteristic bodily feelings.
Again, traces left by former experiences will be excited,
and this may give rise to images.   More often it gives
rise only to vague feelings of familiarity and to vague
expectations.   An example of what I mean is provided
if we see what looks like a heavy weight, but is really
a hollow object made of skilfully painted cardboard.
We generally do not have any distinct images of what
it would feel like to lift such a weight ; still less do
we make explicit judgments about its heaviness.   But,
if we start to lift it, we shall find that we have automatically adjusted our bodies as it would be reasonable
to do if we had judged it to be heavy.   And the feelings
connected with this adjustment will be part of the total
experience of external reference.   When we start to
lift it we almost overbalance, and we feel our expectations frustrated, though these expectations were not
really present at the time as distinct beliefs about the
future.

I shall have to carry this analysis a little further

when I come to consider the subjective side of the perceptual situation, to which it more properly belongs. But it was necessary to ward off certain probable misunderstandings at once. To sum up: In all perceptual situations there is an external reference beyond the objective constituent; and, if you asked the ordinary man to make this reference explicit, he would say that the objective constituent is literally part of a certain physical object of larger size and longer duration, which possesses many qualities beside those which are sensuously manifested to him in the perceptual situation. It is in virtue of this external reference that the perceptual situation has the epistemological object which it does have; for the epistemological object just is this whole of which the objective constituent is believed to be a part. But it would be false psychologically to say that this belief is reached by a process of inference. For in fact we cannot detect any such process, and we ascribe perception to beings who would be quite incapable of making inferences of the kind required. It would also be false psychologically to say that this belief exists at the purely perceptual level in the form of an explicit judgment; we must rather say that the percipient adjusts himself automatically in ways that would be reasonable *if* he held this belief, and that the belief is represented at this stage by the bodily feelings which accompany these adjustments and by the feelings of satisfaction or frustration which arise according to the results of acting as if one held the belief. Lastly, it would be false as a matter of logic to maintain that this belief, in the precise form and in the actual strength in which it is held, could be justified by any known process of reasoning from any available premises.

So far we have used no argument which would not be equally valid if no perceptual situations were in the least delusive. But of course it is held that there are delusive perceptual situations, and that in some cases the epistemological object is wildly different from the ontological object.   The drunkard says that he sees pink rats, just as the sober man says that he sees a penny.   And the former means by "pink rats" something which lasts beyond the duration of the perceptual situation, which could be felt as well as seen, which could be seen and felt by other men, which would eat corn and excite fox-terriers, and so on.   We call this perceptual situation "delusive," because none of these expectations, which form an essential factor in the situation, are verified by the contemporary perceptions of other observers or by the subsequent perceptions of the drunkard himself.   We must remember that, although no amount of perceptual verification can prove that the objective constituent of a perceptual situation *is* a part of a physical object of a certain specified kind, complete failure of such verification may make the contradictory of this almost certain.   It may be doubtful whether there are such things as pennies, in the sense in which the unphilosophical teetotaller asserts that there are ; and it may be doubtful whether the objective constituent of the situation which we call "the teetotaller's perception of a penny" is literally part of a penny, as he believes it to be.   But it is practically certain that there are no such things as pink rats, in the sense in which the unphilosophical drunkard asserts that there are, when he is in the situation called "seeing pink rats."

Now the existence of wildly delusive perceptual situations, such as we have been describing, is important for our present analysis in several ways : (*a*) It supports the conclusion, which we have already reached independently, that language is a partly misleading guide to the analysis of perceptual situations. The perceptual situation, described as "I am seeing a penny," does seem likely to contain the penny as a constituent if we follow the guidance of the phrase. We have already seen that this cannot be literally true, without needing to take into account the existence of delusive perceptual situations. But this is more glaringly obvious in the case of delusive perceptual situations. The drunkard says "I see a pink rat", just as the sober man says "I see a brown penny"; and, *mutatis mutandis*, they mean exactly the same kind of thing by their two statements. So long as we follow the suggestions of language, there is just as much reason for holding that a pink rat is a constituent of the drunkard's perceptual situation as for holding that a brown penny is a constituent of the sober man's perceptual situation. But this analysis *must* be wrong in the former case, since there is almost certainly no pink rat to be a constituent of anything. And, since there is no relevant internal difference between the veridical and the delusive perceptual situation, it is reasonable to suppose that in no case does a perceptual situation contain as a constituent the physical object which corresponds to its epistemological object, even when there is such a physical object.

(*b*) No doubt each perceptual situation does contain an objective constituent of a characteristic kind. And in each case this is bound up with the practical belief that this constituent is part of a larger and more enduring whole which possesses certain other qualities beside those which are sensuously manifested in the situation. The difference is that this practical belief, which goes beyond the present situation and its contents, is *certainly* wrong in the one case, whilst (so far as we have yet seen) it might possibly be right in the other. And there is absolutely nothing in the two situations as such to distinguish the case where the belief is certainly false from the case where it is possibly true. Now this cuts out an alternative which we have not yet refuted. We have indeed seen that the external reference of a perceptual situation cannot be regarded as a valid logical inference from the existence of the situation and the nature of its objective constituent. But, if there had been no delusive perceptual situations, the following alternative might have been maintained. It might have been held that every perceptual situation is as such accompanied by an infallible revelation that its objective constituent is part of a larger and more enduring whole of a certain specific kind. All such situations certainly involve this claim ; and, if there had been no reason to think that any of them are delusive, it might have been held that this is not a mere *claim* but an infallible *revelation*. So far as I can see, such a position cannot be maintained in face of perceptions of pink rats. The claim made here is of precisely the same kind as is made when teetotallers perceive pennies. And it is made just as strongly. Here the claim proves to be false. And, if it be false in *some* cases, it cannot be accepted as true merely at its face-value in *any* case. Of course, if we water down the claim enough, it may at last be put in such an attenuated form as to be invulnerable to all refutation. If we claim merely that the objective constituents in all perceptual situations are correlated in *some* way with *something* larger and more enduring than themselves, and that every variation in the former is a sign of a change of *some* kind *somewhere or other* in the latter, we can hardly be refuted. There is, no doubt, some such correlation between the objective constituent of the drunkard's perceptual situation and the alcohol in his stomach or something that is happening in his brain. But I think it is perfectly clear that perceptual situations do involve a more specific claim than this ; and that, since this specific claim is certainly wrong in some cases and since there is no internal distinction between these cases and others, it may be wrong in all.

The Alternative Theories. So far I have granted that, in some cases at least, the objective constituent of a perceptual situation *may* in fact be literally a part of a larger external object of a certain specific kind, having other qualities beside those which are sensuously manifested in the situation. I have shown only (a) that this object, as such, is never a constituent of the situation ; (b) that this claim can never be accepted at its face-value, because it is certainly sometimes false in situations which differ in no relevant internal respect from those in which it might be true ; and (c) that the claim cannot be proved to be true, as it stands, by logical inference from any premises which are available to us. It now remains to see whether we can hold that it is *ever* true. Let us confine ourselves for the present to visual situations. I think we can prove that in this case we are tied down to two alternatives, neither of which accords very well with common-sense. Either (a) the objective constituent of a visual situation does not have some of the properties which it seems on careful inspection to have, and does have properties inconsistent with these ; or (b) the larger external whole of which it is a part is so different from what it is commonly supposed to be that it hardly deserves the name of " physical object ". Of course it is possible that both alternatives might have to be combined. Let us now try to prove this.

A penny is believed by common-sense to be a round flat object whose size and shape are independent of the observer, his position, and his movements. A certain observer may move about, and may hold that in all the perceptual situations in which he is placed he sees the whole of the top of a certain penny. If he carefully inspects the objective constituents of these perceptual situations he will certainly find that they seem to be of different shapes and sizes. Most of them will seem elliptical and not round, and the direction of their major-axes and their eccentricity will seem to vary as he moves. Now, if these objective constituents are to be identified with different short slices of the history of the top of the penny, one of two views must be taken. (a) One alternative is to suppose that these objective constituents *really are* all round and all of one size, although they *seem*, on careful inspection, to be elliptical and of various sizes and eccentricities. (*b*) The other alternative is to suppose that the penny is not of constant size and shape, as is commonly believed, but that it varies in these respects as the observer walks about.

Now the latter alternative might be the reasonable one to take if only one observer had to be considered, and only his successive visual situations. But in fact there may be a number of observers who can compare notes. They may agree that they are all seeing the whole of the top of the same penny. And, as we have said, it is certainly part of the notion of a physical object that it is capable of being perceived by several observers at once. Now suppose that one of these observers stands still, whilst another moves about. The objective constituent of the stationary observer's perceptual situation will seem constant in size and shape; the objective constituents of the moving observer's successive perceptual situations will seem to differ in size and shape. Evidently, if we suppose that these objective constituents really do have the characteristics which they seem to have; that the observers really are seeing the whole of the top of the same penny; and that the objective constituents of their respective perceptual situations really are identical with slices of the history of the top of the penny, we shall have to suppose that the penny *both* changes and keeps constant in shape and size during the same stretch of time. And this seems at first sight impossible. If you give up the view that two different observers can both literally see the same part of the same physical object at the same time, you have given up the neutrality and publicity which are part of the notion of a physical object. If you accept this publicity and neutrality, and identify the objective constituents of the various visual situations with the neutral and public top of the penny, you *must* hold either (*a*) that the objective constituents have certain qualities which differ from and are inconsistent with those which they seem on careful inspection to have; or (*b*) that the top of the penny both varies and keeps constant in shape and size within the same stretch of time. The second alternative may seem impossible; but let us not rashly reject it, since the first is not very much more attractive.

A like result is reached if we consider a single observer in two different kinds of perceptual situation. A man may feel a penny, and at the same time move his head about whilst he continues to look at it. The objective constituent of the tactual situation seems on inspection to be constant in shape and size. Those of the successive visual situation seem on inspection to differ in shape and size. Now common-sense holds that it is the same surface which we see and which we touch; though certain non-spatial qualities, such as colour, are sensuously manifested only in one kind of situation, whilst other non-spatial qualities, such as temperature, are sensuously manifested only in another kind of situation. If we wish to keep the common-sense notion of physical objects, we *must* hold either (*a*) that the objective constituents of some perceptual situations have certain qualities which differ from and are inconsistent with those which they seem on careful inspection to have; or (*b*) that one and the same surface can vary and keep constant in shape and size within the same stretch of time.

I think that I have now proved that we are tied down to three alternatives, each almost as distasteful to common-sense as the others. (*a*) We may try to keep the common-sense view that the objective constituents of some visual situations are literally spatio-temporal parts of a certain physical object, which we are said to be "seeing". But, if we do this, we must hold either (*a*) that this physical object can be both constant and variable in its spatial characteristics within the same stretch of time; or (*β*) that the objective constituents of the visual situations can have qualities which are different from and inconsistent with those which they seem on careful inspection to have. Or (*b*) we may drop the common-sense view that the objective constituent of a visual situation may be, and in some cases actually is, literally a spatio-temporal part of a certain physical object which we are said to be "seeing". I will now take these alternatives in turn.

(*a*, α) *Theory of Multiple Inherence.* It might be held that this alternative is so absurd that it is not worth discussing. Is it not a plain contradiction that the same part of the same thing should be at once variable and constant in size, round and elliptical, and so on? It seems to me that this is possible, if and only if what we commonly regard as pure qualities are really relational properties. We all know that the same man can be at the same time generous (to his family) and stingy (to his workmen). The only question is whether we could possibly deal with such propositions as "This is round", "This is elliptical", etc., where "This" is an objective constituent in a visual situation, in a similar way. Let us first state what characteristics the objective constituent of a visual situation seems on careful inspection to have. I think we may fairly say that it seems to be a spatially extended patch, having a certain determinate size and shape, situated in a certain determinate position out from the body, and now occupied and marked out by a certain determinate shade of a certain colour. Of course, the colour need not be uniform throughout the region ; but this raises no question of principle, so I will assume for simplicity that it is uniform. We have then four things to consider : the apparent colour, the apparent shape and size, the apparent position, and the apparent date at which the colour inheres in the place.

Now it has been suggested that the objective constituent of a visual situation can be regarded as a certain region of physical space which is pervaded by a certain determinate shade of colour at a certain time, *provided that* we recognise that the relation of "pervasion" is of a peculiar kind. It must not be a two-term relation, involving only the pervading colour and the pervaded region, as we commonly suppose. It must be at least a three-term relation, involving the pervading colour, the pervaded region, and another region which we might call the "region of projection". Theories of this kind have been suggested lately by Dr Whitehead and by Professor Kemp Smith ; and it seems to me that such a theory in a very crude form may be detected by a very charitable interpreter in the writings of Malebranche. I propose now to discuss it in my own way without further reference to the eminent men who have suggested it. I will call this type of theory "The Theory of Multiple Inherence".

The impression which it makes on me at the outset is that it can be made to work very well for secondary qualities, like colour, provided we raise no questions about shape, size, position, and date ; but that it is more difficult to deal with these apparent characteristics of the objective constituents of perceptual situations in terms of the theory. Let us begin with colour. According to the theory the proposition "This is sensibly of such and such a shade of red" (where "this" is an objective constituent of a visual situation) *could not* be true if "this" were the only thing in the world, any more than "This is a shareholder" could be true if "this" were the only thing in the world. And by "could not" here I mean, not merely that it is *causally* impossible, but also that it is *logically* impossible. Red, on the present view, is a characteristic of such a kind that it cannot inhere in a place simply ; it can only "inhere-in-a-place-from-a-place", and this relation, which needs such a complex phrase to express it, is simple and unanalysable. Now, supposing that this were true, it would be perfectly possible that one and the same region of physical Space should be pervaded at one and the same time by different determinate shades of red. For the minimum complete statement about pervasion by a colour would be of the form: "The determinate shade r_1 inheres in the place s from the place s_1 at the time t". And this is perfectly compatible with: "The determinate shade r_2 inheres in the place s from the place s_2 at the time t". What *would* be inconsistent with the first proposition is the proposition: "The determinate shade r_2 inheres in the place s from the place s_1 at the time t". But there is no reason to suppose that this complication ever arises, so it need not trouble us.

It would now be perfectly easy to define a meaning for the phrase "s *is* red" without reference to any other particular place. We might, *e.g.*, define "s *is* red" to mean "From *every* place *some* shade of red inheres in s". This is no doubt only a first approximation to a satisfactory definition. For "every place" we should certainly have to substitute "every place that fulfils such and such conditions". But the general principle of the definition is obvious enough, and I do not think that there would be much difficulty in mentioning the conditions. The full statement would not, I think, differ very much from the following:—"s is physically red" means "From every place which is physically occupied by a normal human brain and nervous system in a normal condition and is near enough to s some shade of red sensibly inheres in s." The first condition is put in to deal with colour-blind men and men drugged with santonin ; the second is put in to cut out complications about coloured spectacles, and so on.

The essence of the theory, so far as we have gone, is this: We must distinguish between the "sensible" and the "physical" inherence of a colour in a place. The former is the fundamental and indefinable relation ; and it is irreducibly triadic, involving an essential reference to the pervading shade of colour, the pervaded region, and the region of projection. The latter is a two-term relation ; but it is not ultimate, for it is definable in terms of the former. And the definition is of the following kind : " R inheres physically in *s* " means " From every place s_n, which fulfils certain conditions C, some determinate form r_n of the determinable R sensibly inheres in *s* ". With these definitions we could perfectly well maintain the common-sense view that a physical object cannot have two different colours at once, and yet admit that it does have different colours at once. We should simply need to clear up the ambiguities of our statements. The truth will be (1) that two different colours cannot *sensibly* inhere in the same place *from the same place* at once ; (2) that two different colours cannot *physically* inhere in the same place at once ; but (3) that different colours or different shades of the same colour can *sensibly* inhere in the same place from *different* places at once. Perhaps I ought to say a word or two in further explanation of the second of these propositions. To say that the same place was at once physically red and physically green would be to say that from every one of a certain set of places this place was sensibly pervaded by some shade of red, and that from every one of the same set of places it is at the same time sensibly pervaded by some shade of green. This, I suppose, would be admitted to be impossible. But it does not cover all that we mean when we say that the same place could not at once be physically pervaded by two different colours. Under this head we should also include, *e.g.*, two different shades of red as well as two different colours, such as red and green. This, however, raises no insuperable difficulty. We have defined the physical *colour* of a place in terms of the *colour* under which all the determinate shades which sensibly inhere in it from a certain set of places fall. It would be quite easy to define its physical *shade* in a similar way. We should say that a certain place was physically pervaded by purple if and only if all the shades which sensibly inhere in it from places which fulfil the required conditions fell within certain limits. If we were prepared to say that this place is physically pervaded by scarlet it is certain that it would have to be sensibly pervaded from the *same* places by *different* shades of red. Since it could not be sensibly pervaded at the same time and from the same place by different shades of the same colour any more than by shades of different colours, it would be impossible for it to be at once physically pervaded by scarlet and by purple on our definitions.

So far we have been discussing a question which may be called "logical", in a wide sense, and certainly not "causal". By this I mean that we have simply been considering the question : "What formal characteristics must the relation of inherence possess if it is to be logically possible to hold that a number of different colours or shades of colour inhere at the same time in the whole of the same region of Physical Space?" The *causal* question is : "Under what conditions will such and such a colour inhere in such and such a place from such and such a place?" To this question I now turn.

In view of what we know of geometrical and physical optics and of the physiology of vision, I think that the following answer is *almost* certain. The *independently* necessary and sufficient *material* conditions for a certain shade of colour to pervade a certain external region from a certain region of projection are all contained in or are close to the region of projection. (I will explain in a moment why I introduce the qualifications which I have italicised.) The direction of the pervaded region is the direction in which a normal human being, whose body is in the projecting region, has to look, in order to get the objective constituent under consideration into the middle of his visual field ; and this is known to depend simply on what is going on in the immediate neighbourhood of his eyes. When a number of people are said to be "seeing the same object directly under normal conditions", *i.e.*, without complications due to mirrors, non-homogeneous transparent media, and so on, their respective lines of sight intersect within a fairly small determinate region. This is where the object is then said to be. But of course there often are mirrors and other complications, and we must be prepared to deal with the general case. When the medium is in fact non-homogeneous, or the vision is indirect, the place which is pervaded by a given shade of colour from a given region of projection is that place in which a suitable object *would* have to be put in order to present the same appearance *if* viewed directly and through a homogeneous medium. In actual fact nothing physically relevant may be going on in this region ; this is the case with mirror images. If I look at the reflection of a luminous point in a plane mirror the region which is pervaded from where I am standing is somewhere behind the mirror ; it is the place where a luminous point would have to be put in order to present the actual appearance, if viewed directly and without a mirror, from where I am standing. And of course nothing physically relevant is happening at this place behind the mirror. The direction of the place is determined by the direction in which the light enters my eye, *i.e.*, by physical events in the immediate neighbourhood of the region of projection. Its distance along this direction is presumably determined by traces left in my brain by past visual situations and correlated bodily movements in cases where the vision really was direct and through a homogeneous medium. Thus I am justified in saying that the position of the pervaded region is immediately determined by events in or close to the region of projection.

Next, the facts which make us ascribe a velocity to light, and particularly the fact of aberration, make it almost certain that the date at which a certain place is pervaded by a certain shade of colour from a certain region of projection is the date at which certain events are happening within the region of projection. When I look at a distant star a certain shade of colour sensibly inheres in a certain distant region of Physical Space from the place which is physically occupied by my body, if the present theory be true. But we know quite well that the star may no longer be physically occupying this distant region; and that, whether it does so or not, the relevant physical events may have happened there hundreds of years ago.

Lastly, and in close connexion with this, we must notice that the particular colour and the particular shade of it which sensibly pervade an external place from a region of projection are almost certainly determined by specific events in the eyes, optic nerves, and brain which now physically occupy this region of projection. Facts about colour-blindness, about the effects of drugs like santonin, and of morbid bodily states like jaundice, make this practically certain.

I have now defended the statement that the *independently* necessary and sufficient *material* conditions which determine that such and such an external place shall be pervaded by such and such a shade of colour from a certain region of projection are physically present within or close to that region. I will now explain what I mean by the italicised qualifications in this statement. (1) The physical events within the region of projection of course have physical causes. Now a necessary condition of a necessary condition of an event may be called a "dependently" necessary condition of that event. There is every reason to believe that the pervasion of a certain region from a certain region by a certain shade of colour has generally *dependently* necessary conditions which are quite remote from the region of projection. When a certain place is pervaded by very similar shades of the same colour from all directions it is generally found that, on walking up to this place, tactual situations arise. And the objective constituents of these tactual situations are generally found to be closely correlated with the objective constituents of the successive visual situations which occur as we walk up to this place. We say then that this place is "tactually occupied". And we have very good reason to believe that such a region is physically occupied by certain microscopic events which are remote and dependently necessary conditions of the pervasion of this region by such and such a shade of colour from places round it. These events determine by physical causation certain events in our eyes, optic nerves, and brains; and the latter events are the immediately necessary and sufficient material conditions of the pervasion of the external region by such and such a shade of colour from the region of projection which contains our bodies. This may be regarded as the normal case; and it is expressed in common language by saying that we are then "looking directly at a certain physical object through a colourless homogeneous medium". But of course this sweet simplicity, though normal, is not universal. Suppose that a number of people "see the same mirror image". Then there is a certain set of microscopic physical events in a certain region of Space; and these do constitute the common dependently necessary condition of the pervasion of a place behind the mirror by similar shades of the same colour from a number of different regions of projection. But the region which contains these physical microscopic events is remote from the region in which these shades of colour sensibly inhere; it is in fact as far in front of the mirror as the pervaded region is behind it.

Let us call the region which contains the common dependently necessary conditions "the emitting region". Then the position may be put as follows: In visual perception we have to consider an emitting region, a region of projection, a pervaded region, and a pervading shade of colour. The pervaded region is immediately determined by events in and near the region of projection. These events also determine immediately the pervading shade and colour. And they are themselves determined by microscopic events in the emitting region. In the cases that arise most often in everyday practical life the pervaded region and the emitting region roughly coincide. But, in the case of mirror-images and the visual situations which arise when we are surrounded by non-homogeneous media, the pervaded region and the emitting region cease to coincide and may be very distant from each other. The pervaded region may then contain no physical events at all ; and, if it does, they will be quite irrelevant. In such cases there will always be a purely optical peculiarity too, viz., that the pervaded region will never be pervaded from *all* directions by similar shades of the same colour. (Cf. the sudden change which happens in the visual situation when we go to the back of a mirror in which we have been viewing the image of a certain object.)

Just as we have contrasted the pervaded region and the emitting region, so we must contrast the "date of pervasion" and the "date of emission". Owing to the very great velocity of light these generally coincide almost exactly in the visual situations of ordinary life. But, when we are concerned with very remote objects, such as stars, the date of emission (which is *always* earlier than the date of pervasion) may precede the latter by thousands of years. In the phenomenon of aberration we have a most interesting case in which the motion of the observer of a very distant object, and the difference between the *date* of emission and the *date* of pervasion, cause a difference between the *place* of emission and the *place* of pervasion.

(2) I have now explained why I used the phrase "*independently* necessary and sufficient conditions". It remains to explain why I introduced the word "*material*" before "conditions" in my original statement. This was simply a precaution. I cannot be completely certain that the sensible inherence of such and such a shade of colour in such and such a place from a given region of projection *may* not have psychical as well as physical conditions. Since we cannot get a brain and

nervous system like ours working properly without a mind like ours, it is obviously impossible to be sure that the latter is irrelevant for the present purpose and that the former is sufficient by itself. And, beside this general consideration, there is a more specific ground for caution. I do not think that the determination of the position of the pervaded region can be completely explained without reference to the persistent effect of past visual and tactual situations and bodily movements, and the associations between them. Now of course these factors *may* now be represented simply by persistent and suitably linked material modifications in the brain and nervous system. But, on the one hand, these material "traces" are purely hypothetical effects of certain causes and causes of certain effects. And, on the other hand, even if they be *now* purely material, it may be that they could not have been formed *originally* without the action of the mind, at least in the form of selective attention. If this be so, we might still say that the *independently* necessary conditions for a certain colour to pervade a certain place from a given region of projection are all material; but we should have to recognise that the past action of the mind is a *dependently* necessary condition, just as much as the past vibrations of distant electrons.

So far the Theory of Multiple Inherence seems to have worked fairly well. But we have left to the end the hardest question with which it is faced. This is the question of "physical" and "sensible" shape and size. We know that different observers, who say that they are all seeing the whole of the top of the same penny, find on careful inspection that the shapes and sizes of the objective constituents of their respective visual situations seem to be different. We know that the same complication arises if a single observer moves about whilst he claims all the time to be seeing the whole of the top of the same penny. And we know that it also arises when the same observer claims to be at once seeing and touching the whole of the top of the same penny. We have dealt with similar difficulties about shades of colour by suggesting that the relation of inherence between a colour and the place which it pervades is irreducibly triadic, and not dyadic, as has commonly been thought. But can we possibly deal with the difficulties about shape and size in the same way? Curiously enough, Dr Whitehead does not, so far as I know, discuss this point. Yet no theory can claim to be satisfactory which does not make some answer to the question.

At first sight it seems evident that we cannot deal with variations in the apparent shape of the same surface in the way in which we have been dealing with variations in its apparent colour. It seems obvious that the proposition " This is round " *could* have been true, even if there had been nothing in the world but this area. In fact the shape of a region seems to be an intrinsic quality of it ; and it seems nonsense to talk of various shapes inhering in a certain region from various places. Plausible as this argument sounds, I believe that it is mistaken. I think that it overlooks a very important distinction, viz., the distinction between a " sensible form " and a " geometrical property ". I shall first try to explain the difference between the two, and to show that they must be distinguished quite apart from the present problem. And I shall then try to show that the distinction enables us to apply the Multiple Inherence Theory to the question of variations of apparent shape and size.

Let us consider circularity, for example. I find it necessary to distinguish a certain geometrical property called " circularity " and a certain sensible form called by the same name, for the following reasons. The geometrical property can be *defined*. To say that a certain area is geometrically circular *means* that all the points on its boundary are equidistant from a fixed point. But, if I wanted to make someone understand what I was referring to by the phrase "sensibly circular", it would be of no use whatever to offer this definition or any other definition. All that I could do would be to proceed by *exemplification*, just as I should have to do if I wanted to make him understand what I am referring to when I use the word "red". I should in fact have to proceed as follows: I might start by getting the man to look straight down on to a penny. I should then cut out geometrically circular bits of paper of various colours and sizes and get him to look straight down on them. I should also cut out bits of paper of the same colours and different geometrical shapes, and get him to look straight down on them. I should then say to him: "You notice that there was a certain resemblance between all the objective constituents of the first series of visual situations in which I placed you, in spite of the differences of colour, etc. And you notice that there was a certain unlikeness between every objective constituent of the first series of visual situations and every objective constituent of the second series. Very well; what I am referring to by the phrase "circular sensible form" is that feature which was present in all members of the first series and absent in all members of the second." In my view it is just as impossible to know *a priori* that a geometrically circular area, when pervaded by a colour and viewed normally, would have the sensible form called "circularity" as it is to know *a priori* that an area containing electrons moving in a certain way would be pervaded by a certain shade of red from a place occupied by a normal human body. Of course some *geometrical* properties are themselves indefinable, *e.g.*, geometrical straightness. But it remains a fact that *all* sensible forms are indefinable, whilst *many* of the geometrical properties which are called by the same name are definable. It is therefore certain that geometrical properties and the sensible forms which are called by the same names must be distinguished.

Let us now apply this conclusion to our present problem. When it is said that the shape of a region is an intrinsic property, and that it is nonsense to talk of it having such and such a shape *from* such and such another region, this is true only of geometrical shape. If an area is geometrically circular it is so intrinsically, and there is an end of the matter. But, since geometrical shape and sensible form must always be distinguished, it does not follow that the sensible form of an area is an intrinsic property of it. It may be that one and the same area is "informed" by one sensible form from one place and by a different sensible form from another place. The relation of "informing" may be irreducibly triadic, as we have suggested that the relation of "pervading" is. If this be so, it may be that it is only from one place or one series of places that an area with a certain geometrical shape is informed by that sensible form which has the same name as the geometrical shape. A like distinction will have to be drawn between geometrical and physical size. The geometrical size of a region will be an intrinsic property of it; but the sensible size may be a property which it only has from another region. It will of course be just as necessary to distinguish tactual form from geometrical shape as to distinguish visual form from geometrical shape. But there may be good reasons for holding that tactual form is a safer indication of geometrical shape than is visual form.

There is every reason to believe that the visual form which informs a certain external region from a certain region of projection is causally determined by events which are physically contained within the region of projection. The determining factors would seem to be the geometrical shape and size of the part of the retina affected by light, and traces in the brain and nervous system left by past visual and tactual situations. Here again it seems to me that we cannot be sure that the mind does not play an essential part, if not as an independently necessary condition, yet perhaps as a remote and dependently necessary condition for the original formation and association of the traces.

I have now sketched and defended to the best of my ability the Multiple Inherence Theory. It is time to ask ourselves: "How much of that primitive belief which is an essential part of every perceptual situation would be left standing if we accepted this theory?" Under favourable circumstances, *i.e.*, when we should commonly be held to be seeing a not too distant object by direct vision through a colourless homogeneous medium, we could go thus far with common-sense. We could hold (1) that the visual situations of a number of observers who say that they are seeing the same object really do contain a common objective constituent, viz., a certain region of Space outside their bodies. (2) That this same region of Space is the common objective constituent of the visual and tactual situations of an observer who would be said to be seeing and touching the same object. (3) That this region really is pervaded now by those sensible qualities and informed by those sensible forms which each observer can detect by careful inspection in the objective constituent of his perceptual situations. (4) That this region really does physically contain a set of microscopic physical events (movements of molecules, vibrations of electrons, etc.) which are the *dependently* necessary conditions for the pervasion of this region by these sensible qualities from the places now occupied by the observers' bodies. This is as far as we could go in agreement with common-sense. We should have to differ from common-sense, even in the cases which are most favourable to its beliefs, in the following points: (1) It believes that the colours which it sees are quite literally spread out over the surfaces of the *physical objects* which it sees and touches. In view of the facts about mirror-images, etc., we can admit only that colours pervade certain *regions of Space*. The latter may or may not contain those microscopic physical things and events which are the dependently necessary conditions of the pervasion of this region by this colour. Even when this is so, *i.e.*, when there is an emitting as well as a pervaded region and the two coincide, we cannot say that the microscopic events and objects have the colour ; we can say only that the region which contains them is pervaded by the colour. (2) Common-sense believes that the pervasion of anything by a colour is a two-term relation between this thing and this colour. In view of the fact that the whole of the top of the same penny may appear brown to me and yellow to you, who have taken santonin, we cannot admit this. If we wish to hold that this one surface really is the common objective constituent of your visual situation and of mine, and that it really has the colours which it seems to you and me on careful inspection to have, we must hold that the sensible pervasion of a region by a colour is at least a three-term relation. It must involve an essential reference to a region of projection as well as to the pervaded region and the pervading colour. (3) Common - sense believes that the independently necessary and sufficient conditions for the pervasion of a certain region by a certain colour are contained in *that* region at the time when it is pervaded by this colour. It therefore holds that this region would be pervaded by this colour at this moment no matter what might be going on elsewhere. This cannot be accepted. The *independently* necessary and sufficient conditions for the pervasion of a certain region by a certain colour are *never* contained in the pervaded region and are *always* contained in or near the region of projection. It is true that, in favourable cases, the *dependently* necessary conditions for this pervasion may *have been* contained in the pervaded region ; viz., when there is an emitting region and it coincides with the pervaded region. But, in the first place, there may be no emitting region at all. (Cf. the visual situations of dreams, or the case of the drunkard and his pink rats.) Secondly, there may be an emitting region, but it may be quite remote from the pervaded region. (Cf. mirror-images and aberration.) And lastly, even when there is an emitting region and it coincides with the pervaded region, common-sense is always wrong about the date of the relevant physical events in this region. It always assumes that they are contemporary with the pervasion, whereas they are always earlier and may be earlier by thousands of years. The net result of all this is that there is the strongest reason to believe that no region would be pervaded by any colour unless some other region contained a living body with a suitable brain and nervous system functioning properly. To the question: "Are things really coloured?" we can make the following answers on the present theory. (i) Colour is not logically an *intrinsic* quality of anything. Its nature is such that it can pervade one place only from another place. We may express this by saying that it is a genuine characteristic, but that it is a "multiply-inherent" one. "To be coloured" is a characteristic which is logically of the same kind as "to be envied." (ii) Things are not coloured, in the sense that their colour is a primitive and causally independent characteristic of them; or in the sense that it is directly determined by their intrinsic characteristics. The colour which pervades a region is directly determined, not by the physical contents of that region, but by the physical contents of a different region. A certain region really is pervaded by a certain colour from a certain other region if and only if the latter contains a suitable brain and nervous system, functioning properly. I express this fact by saying that the colour of a region from a place genuinely pervades it, but is "causally adventitious" to it. (iii) A region may contain such microscopic physical events and objects that a certain shade of a certain colour *would* pervade it from any region which is near enough, *if* the latter were occupied by a normal brain and nervous system in normal working order. I express this by saying that this region has such and such a "potential colour." (iv) If it be asked whether my previous statements imply that colours are "mind-dependent", I answer as follows. The pervasion of a certain place by a certain colour from a certain region of projection is *not* dependent on this colour being perceived by the mind which animates the organism that occupies the region of projection. *Nothing* depends for its existence on being perceived. But it is conceivable that the same events in the brain and nervous system have two effects, viz., that they cause a certain distant place to be pervaded from the region of projection by a certain colour, and that they cause the mind which animates the organism in the region of projection to perceive this colour. If this were so, the colour could not pervade the external place from the region of projection without being perceived by the mind which animates the organism in the region of projection. But it seems to me most unlikely that the bodily conditions which cause the colour to inhere are identical with the bodily conditions which cause the mind to perceive ; and there is certainly no evidence for such a view. If the two sets of conditions be not identical, it is logically possible that a colour should pervade a place from a region of projection without being perceived by the mind which animates the organism in this region of projection. Whether this in fact ever happens is a question to be decided by empirical considerations. We must remember, however, that a colour might be in part mind-dependent without being dependent on the particular mental event of being perceived. As I have said, it seems to me likely that some of the remote conditions of the characteristics of the objective constituents of visual situations are mental ; and it is quite possible that some of their immediate conditions are also mental. It is, *e.g.*, quite arguable that the sensible form and size and distance of objective constituents is in part determined by our predominant interests and beliefs at the moment.

It is evident, then, that the Theory of Multiple Inherence, though it allows us to keep some parts of the primitive belief which is part of every perceptual situation, requires us to modify other parts very profoundly in the case of visual situations. We shall find that the other alternatives are equally upsetting to common-sense. To them I now turn.

(a, β) *Multiple Relation Theory of Appearing*. I shall be able to deal much more briefly with this and the third alternative, because I have brought out in the last section most of the important facts which must be recognised by *any* satisfactory theory. On *any* theory we must recognise that the independently necessary and sufficient conditions of the apparent characteristics of the objective constituents of perceptual situations are contained in or near the place occupied by the percipient's body ; that there may be no external emitting region ; that, if there is one, it may be remote from the region which these characteristics apparently pervade ; and that, even if the two regions coincide, the date of apparent pervasion is later than the date of emission.

There is a close formal analogy between the present theory and the one discussed in the last section. Both of them have to assume a fundamental relation which is at least triadic. The Multiple Inherence Theory supposes that colours inhere triadically in places from places ; and that sensible forms triadically inform regions from regions. The Multiple Relation Theory of Appearing assumes that, if a colour really did inhere in anything, it would inhere dyadically, as common-sense supposes. But it assumes a fundamental relation of "appearing", which must be at least triadic. Thus it assumes, as logically possible, two different kinds of proposition about characteristics like colour, shape, etc. One is of the form "This *is* red " ; the other is of the form "This *looks* red from here ". And, in order to deal with the known facts, it has to assume that the objective constituent of a visual situation can seem from a place to have characteristics which are other than and incompatible with the characteristics which it does have. If the top of a penny literally has a certain colour dyadically, it can have only one shade of one colour. But it certainly seems to have a number of different shades of the same colour, and may even seem to have a number of different colours, from different places occupied by different observers. Hence, if a penny literally and dyadically possesses a colour, the colour which it *has* must differ from all but one of the colours or shades which it *seems* to have; and, it may differ from all of them. Whilst, if it does not literally and dyadically possess any colour, it is still plainer that it seems to have characteristics which it does not in fact have. The same remarks apply to shape, size, and position. On this theory then we may be acquainted in a perceptual situation with a spatio-temporal part of a certain physical object which we are said to be perceiving. But we learn only about the characteristics which it *seems* to have; and the more carefully we inspect the objective constituent the more we learn of its *apparent* properties only. And it is certain that it either does not actually *have* properties of this kind at all; or that, if it does, the apparent and the real properties can be identical only in one specially favoured perceptual situation. And there is of course nothing in any particular perceptual situation, taken by itself, to tell us that in it and it alone the apparent and the real characteristics of the objective constituent are identical.

Let us now consider the points of difference between this theory and the one which we discussed before. Both theories allow that, under suitable conditions, it may be true that there is a common objective constituent to the visual situations of a number of observers who say that they are "seeing the same object". Both allow that there is, under suitable conditions, a common objective constituent to the visual and the tactual situations of an observer who says that he is "seeing and feeling the same object". And both allow, that, under suitable conditions, this common objective constituent may be literally a spatio-temporal part of the object which the various observers say that they are "seeing and feeling". But, at this point, each has to diverge from common - sense in a different direction. The Multiple Inherence Theory allows that the objective constituent really does have those characteristics which it seems on careful inspection by each observer to have. But it can allow this only by supposing that these characteristics inhere in the objective constituent in a way never contemplated by common-sense, viz., triadically. The Multiple Relation Theory of Appearing allows that, *if* the objective constituent did have such characteristics as it seems to have, they *would* inhere in it in the ordinary dyadic way which common-sense recognises. But it can allow this only by supposing that most, if not all, of the determinate characteristics which the objective constituent seems on careful inspection to have do not in fact inhere in it. And both theories, as I have said, have to depart altogether from common-sense when they pass from purely logical to causal considerations. The conditions which immediately determine what colour, sensible form, etc., the objective constituent shall *have* (triadically) on the first theory, or shall *seem to have* on the second, are contained in or near the place where the observer is, and not in or near the place where the objective constituent *is* on the first theory or *seems to be* on the second. And the remote and dependently necessary conditions, in many cases, are neither in nor near the latter place.

(*b*) *The Sensum Theory.* Poor dear Common-sense has not done very well out of the two types of theory which were constructed for its special benefit. Let us now consider the third possible alternative. This theory allows that the objective constituents of perceptual situations really do have all those positive characteristics which they seem on careful inspection to have. And it allows that these characteristics inhere in these objective constituents in the straightforward dyadic way in which common-sense supposes them to do. But, in admitting this much, it is then forced to depart from common-sense. It cannot admit that the visual situations of a number of observers, who say that they are "seeing the same object", contain a common objective constituent. It cannot admit that, when a man says that he is "seeing and feeling the same object", there is in general a common objective constituent to his visual and his tactual situations. And it cannot admit that, when we say that we are "seeing a certain physical object", the objective constituent of our visual situation is in general a spatio-temporal part of the physical object which we say that we are "seeing". On this theory, then, the objective constituents of most, if not all, perceptual situations *cannot* be spatio-temporal parts of physical objects. No doubt they are really extended; they really last for so long; they really have certain shapes, sizes, colours, etc.; and some at least of them stand in spatial and temporal relations to each other. But they are not, in any plain straightforward sense, in the one Physical Space in which physical objects are supposed to be; and between pairs of them which are connected with different observers there are no simple and straightforward spatial or temporal relations. The objective constituents of perceptual situations are, on this view, particular existents of a peculiar kind; they are not physical, as we have seen; and there is no reason to suppose that they are either states of mind or existentially mind-dependent. In having spatial characteristics, colours, etc., they resemble physical objects, as ordinarily conceived; but in their privacy and their dependence on the body, if not the mind, of the observer they are more like mental states. I give the name of "sensa" to the objective constituents of perceptual situations, on the supposition that they are *not* literally parts of the physical object which we are said to be "perceiving", and that they *are* transitory particulars of the peculiar kind which I have just been describing. And I call the theory which assumes the existence of such particulars "The Sensum Theory".

The Sensum Theory is at once faced with the question : "What is the relation between the objective constituent of a perceptual situation and the physical object which we are said to perceive in this situation?" On the two previous theories it was possible to admit that, in favourable cases, the objective constituent of the perceptual situation was quite literally a spatio-temporal part of the perceived object. This cannot be admitted on the Sensum Theory ; the relation must be less direct and more complicated than common-sense believes. On the Sensum Theory the proposition : "The physical object which I am now perceiving appears to have the determinate characteristic c" can be analysed up to a certain point. The analysis would run as follows. This proposition means: "There is a certain sensum s which is the objective constituent of this perceptual situation. This actually has the characteristic c which I can detect in it by inspection, and it has this characteristic in a straightforward dyadic way. And there is a certain physical object o, to which this sensum has a certain relation R which it has to no other physical object. In virtue of this relation the sensum s is said to be "an appearance of" the physical object o. When we say that several people perceive the same physical object o and the same part of it, we must mean, on this theory, that their several perceptual situations contain as objective constituents the sensa s_1, s_2, . . . etc., and that all of them are appearances of the same physical object o. It is plain that these analyses contain an unanalysed factor, viz., the relation R of "being an appearance of". About this relation we can say the following things. (i) It is not the relation of spatio-temporal part to spatio-temporal-whole. (ii) It is a many-one relation, *i.e.*, many different sensa can be appearances of one physical object, and even of precisely the same part of this object; but one sensum cannot, in this sense, be an appearance of several physical objects. There is a certain physical object and a certain part of it which can be called " *the* part of *the* physical object which has this sensum as an appearance ". At this point the Sensum Theory can take one of two courses. It may profoundly modify the common-sense notion of physical objects; *e.g.*, it may hold with Berkeley that what are manifested by sensa are volitions in God's mind; or with Leibniz that what are manifested by sensa are collections of minds; or with Russell that the sensa which are objective constituents of perceptual situations are a small selection out of certain larger groups of interrelated sensa, and that these groups are the only physical objects that there are. Or, on the other hand, it may try to keep as near to the common-sense notion of physical objects as possible. The latter course leads to what I call the " Critical Scientific Theory ", which is the tacit assumption of natural scientists, purged of its inconsistencies, and stated in terms of the Sensum Theory. According to which of these alternative views of the nature of physical objects we choose we shall take a different view of the relation R between a sensum and the physical object of which it is an appearance. *E.g.*, on such a theory as Russell's the relation R is that of class-membership. To say that *s* is an appearance of *o* will mean that *o* is a certain group of suitably inter-related sensa, and that *s* is one of this group. On such a theory as Berkeley's the relation R is that of one part of a total effect to the cause of this total effect. The total effect is all the sensa which would be said to be appearances of a certain thing at a certain time. The cause is a certain volition in God's mind.

Common-sense and the Three Types of Theory. We
have seen in what respects the first two theories agree
with the primitive beliefs of common-sense, and in what
respects they differ from these. Let us now raise the
same question about the Sensum Theory. It agrees
with common-sense in the belief that the objective
constituents of perceptual situations really do have, in
a straightforward dyadic way, all those characteristics
which they seem on careful inspection to have. But
it has to assume that these objective constituents are
particular existents of a peculiar kind, being neither
mental nor physical. And, although it is possible for
it to hold that there may be physical objects in the
ordinary sense of the word, it cannot admit that the
objective constituents of most perceptual situations are
in fact spatio-temporal parts of them. It is thus faced
with a problem which does not arise for the other
theories; viz., to give some account of the relation
between sensa, which are objective constituents of
perceptual situations, and the physical objects which
are supposed to be manifested by these sensa. In order
to give a plausible account of this relation the theory
may be forced to depart very far indeed from the
common-sense notion of a physical object, as has
happened in Russell's theory.

I think that it is now abundantly evident that very
little can be done for common-sense. One theory
requires a kind of inherence which shocks it; the
second theory asks it to believe that the objective
constituents of most, and perhaps of all, perceptual
situations seem on careful inspection to have characteristics other than and incompatible with those which
they actually do have; and the third theory insists that
the objective constituents of perceptual situations are
seldom if ever spatio-temporal parts of the physical
objects which it claims to be perceiving, and presents
it with a peculiar kind of existent which is neither
physical nor mental but seems to have one leg in each

realm. And these results are not due to the wilful perversity of philosophers debauched with learning. They are conclusions to which we are forced most unwillingly by a careful consideration of those facts which common-sense ignores. I think we may say with perfect confidence that, whilst none of the philosophic theories may be true, the primitive belief which accompanies all perceptual situations is certainly to a very large extent false; and that there is not the faintest chance of rehabilitating it. If we reflect on the history and the probable prehistory of human perception, I think we can see that there is nothing in the least surprising in this fact. Perception must have grown up in close connexion with action; and the primitive belief which forms part of the perceptual situation is, on the whole, perfectly satisfactory for practical purposes. It is exactly the belief that a being would naturally reach if he ignored abnormal cases like mirror-images; neglected minor differences, such as we find on careful inspection, between the objective constituents of the perceptual situations of different observers who are said to be perceiving the same object by the same or by different senses; and knew nothing about the velocity of light or the part played in perception by his own brain and nervous system. Now, a being devoted to practical ends naturally would ignore comparatively rare cases, such as mirror-images and other optical illusions. He naturally would neglect the minor differences between the characteristics of various objective constituents, so long as they all guided him to the right place and enabled him to co-operate satisfactorily with his fellows, to avoid danger, and to get what he wanted. From the nature of the case he could not suspect the velocity of light, which needs the most delicate experiments to detect it and a stroke of genius even to think of it. And, as he always carries his brain and nervous system about with him wherever he goes, he would naturally tend to ignore the part which it plays in perception ; just as a person who always wears glasses forgets that he has them on and that he could not see properly without them. These causes, which must certainly have operated in the development of perception, have produced precisely the kind of primitive belief which we might have expected them to produce. And, when we take into account all the factors which were ignored in the development of this belief, but which are none the less real, we naturally find that the belief is far too simple-minded to deal with the extremely complex situation. It is, therefore, in my opinion, simply waste of time to try to rehabilitate naïve realism ; or to regard it as any serious objection to a theory of the external world and our perception of it that it is "shocking to common-sense". *Any* theory that can possibly fit the facts is *certain* to shock common-sense somewhere ; and in face of the facts we can only advise common-sense to follow the example of Judas Iscariot, and "go out and hang itself".

We may now ask ourselves whether there is anything to choose between the three kinds of theory. (1) It seems to me that the Theory of Multiple Inherence, as stated, presupposes a doctrine of Absolute Space-Time, as a kind of fundamental stuff or matrix. It is quite certain that the objective constituents of perceptual situations are particular existents, and not mere universal qualities. And it is quite certain that, if objective constituents of visual situations are really situated where they appear to be, as the theory assumes, they are often situated in places which are not occupied by matter in any ordinary sense of the word. This is often true, *e.g.*, of mirror-images. Now, a mirror-image is as good a particular as the objective constituent of a more normal visual situation. Whence does it get its particularity? On the present theory we must say that it is a particular because it is a certain region of Space, pervaded from a certain other region of Space at a certain date and for a certain time by a certain shade of colour. Now this surely presupposes Space-Time as a kind of omnipresent and eternal substance, every region of which is ready to be pervaded by some sensible quality from some other region. I do not of course suggest that this theory must suppose that Absolute Space-Time is the *only* substance in the material realm. The regions from which colours pervade other regions are occupied in a non-triadic sense by certain physical and physiological events and objects. And the emitting regions are also occupied in a non-triadic sense by electrons, atoms, molecules, etc., and their movements. It is not *necessary* for the theory to hold, *e.g.*, that an electron is just a certain region of Space-Time dyadically pervaded by some physical quality. But, whilst it is not necessary for the theory to hold that Absolute Space-Time is the *only* substance in the material realm, it *is* necessary for it to hold that Absolute Space-Time is *a* substance and that the particularity of the objective constituents of some, if not all, perceptual situations is the particularity of some particular region of Space-Time. This region is marked out by being pervaded by such and such a sensible quality from such and such a region of projection ; and a region thus pervaded and marked out is, on the present theory, that kind of particular which we call "an objective constituent of a perceptual situation".

Now, I do not for a moment suggest that a theory is necessarily wrong because it presupposes the doctrine of Absolute Space-Time as the common matrix of all objective constituents of perceptual situations. But I do think that such a theory starts with rather heavy liabilities, and I do suspect that it has not carried its analysis far enough.

(2) It seems to me that the Theory of a Multiple Relation of Appearing is liable to a similar objection. Suppose I hold up a finger in front of a plain mirror, so that I can see both the finger and the mirror-image of it at the same time. Then it is quite certain that the

characteristic colour of my finger *seems* to pervade the surfaces of two distinct physical objects, one in front of the mirror and the other at the back of it. It is also quite certain that the characteristic sensible form of my finger *seems* to inform two distinct physical objects. Now we have every reason to believe that only one physical object is appearing in this situation. It is therefore not enough for the theory to hold that some part of a physical object which is an objective constituent of a visual situation may seem to have a characteristic which it does not in fact have. It must also assert that what is in fact one physical object in one place may seem to be two physical objects in two places at some distance apart. Now one may admit that a certain particular might seem to have a characteristic which differs from and is incompatible with the characteristics which it does have. But I find it almost incredible that one particular extended patch should seem to be two particular extended patches at a distance apart from each other. There is of course no difficulty in holding that the same shade of colour and the same sensible form may appear to inhere in two places at once, and that one of these places is physically filled whilst the other is physically empty ; provided you hold that colours and sensible forms seem to inhere, not in *physical objects*, but in *regions of Space*. The appearance of two particulars is then accounted for by the fact that there really are two particulars, viz., the two distinct regions of Space in which the same colour and sensible form seem to inhere at the same time. But this presupposes Absolute Space-Time as a substantial matrix whose regions are ready to appear to have such and such characteristics from other regions which are suitably filled. And this was the objection to the Theory of Multiple Inherence.

I think we must say then that, in view of mirror-images, aberration, etc., the Multiple Relation Theory of Appearing must hold *either* that what is in fact a single extended particular can seem to be two distinct extended particulars at a distance apart from each other ; *or* that sensible qualities and forms have the relation of "appearing to inhere in" to regions of Absolute Space - Time, and not to the surfaces of physical objects. The first alternative is difficult to believe ; the second presupposes Absolute Space-Time, which is probably a sign of inadequate analysis.

(3) It is commonly objected to the Sensum Theory that it leaves the existence of physical objects merely hypothetical ; that it introduces entities of a peculiar kind, whose status in the world and relations to physical objects, if such there be, are very difficult to understand ; and that it involves a very odd kind of causation, which is almost creation out of nothing. In this section I shall content myself with showing that the Sensum Theory is in these respects very little worse off than the other two alternatives. It is no doubt true that sensa cannot be parts, in the literal and straightforward sense, of physical objects ; and that, on most forms of the theory, the relation between the two is very indirect. As against this it must be said that the other theories have been found to involve Absolute Space-Time. Now I think that the Sensum Theory can dispense with this. The other theories need this because they require some kind of substance for sensible qualities to inhere in or to seem to inhere in. And, since in the case of mirror-images, etc., this substance can hardly be the surfaces of physical objects, there seems nothing left for it to be except various regions of Absolute Space-Time. Now the Sensum Theory starts with particulars, for each sensum is a particular having those sensible qualities and that sensible form which it seems on careful inspection to have. It therefore does not need to assume Absolute Space-Time, in the sense of a kind of substantial matrix whose various regions stand ready to be pervaded by various sensible qualities and informed by various sensible forms. It can accept a

relational theory of Physical Space-Time; and this certainly seems to me to be a point in its favour. It can start with the sensible spatio-temporal relations of sensa in the same sense-field or the same sense-history, and thus *exemplify* the general notion of a Space or a Space-Time of interrelated particulars. Then, by considering the correlations between sensa in different sense-fields and different sense-histories, and by taking account of the connexion of these with the movements of the observer's body, it can *construct* in thought the concept of a single Physical Space-Time. This Physical Space-Time will be the system of all *physical events* interrelated in the same *kind* of way as are sensa in a single sense-history. The relations in the two kinds of whole differ in detail, but there is enough analogy between them to justify us in regarding the world of physical events as a single spatio-temporal system having a certain kind of " geo-chronometry ". This is the justification of the notion of Absolute Space-Time; but it is no justification for treating it as a substantial matrix, as the other theories have to do. I have dealt with the details of this synthesis to the best of my ability in my *Scientific Thought*, and I must refer the reader to the Second Part of that book for such justification as I can give for the above dogmatic statements.

Let us now consider the objection that the Sensum Theory makes physical objects entirely hypothetical, mere *Dinge-an-Sich*. I shall deal directly with this question in the next section. Here I shall merely consider whether the other theories are much less liable to the same objection. I cannot see that they are. I profess to have proved earlier in this chapter (*a*) that, even if there had been no delusive perceptual situations, it is certain from the nature of the case that no perceptual situation could contain literally as its objective constituent the physical object which we are said to be perceiving in that situation. (*b*) That the existence of totally delusive situations shows that the objective constituent cannot *always* be even a spatio-temporal part of the physical object which we are said to be perceiving. Hence even this modified claim can *never* be accepted at its face-value, since it is made as strongly in the perceptual situations which are certainly delusive as in those which are not known to be so. (c) That, in view of the discrepancies which careful inspection discovers between the objective constituents of perceptual situations when one observer is said to be seeing and touching the same object or when several observers are said to be seeing the same object, even this modified claim *cannot* be true except on the very special assumptions of the Theory of Multiple Inherence or the Theory of a Multiple Relation of Appearing. On *any* view, then, the claims of the individual perceptual situation to reveal a certain physical object and to guarantee its existence must be attenuated to a mere shadow. And, when we come to consider in detail the two theories which are able to admit this attenuated claim at all, we find that the claim must be pared down still more ; as I will now show.

If the Theory of Multiple Inherence be true, all that I can learn from a single perceptual situation is that a certain external region of Space, which may or may not now contain relevant physical events and objects, is at present pervaded by a certain sensible quality and informed by a certain sensible form from the place where my body now is. If I want to get any further than this ; to know whether I am perceiving a "real object" or only an image ; to know what spatial and other qualities I may ascribe to it in itself and apart from its relation to my organism ; I must do this, if at all, by considering the objective constituents of a number of different perceptual situations belonging to myself and to others, and noting the relations between them. And the physical object which I then "know", and to which I ascribe these intrinsic characteristics, is logically (though not psychologically) just a hypothetical entity postulated to explain and systematise these correlations. The position is precisely similar if we adopt the Theory of a Multiple Relation of Appearing. All that I can learn from a single perceptual situation is that a certain surface, which *seems* to be a spatio-temporal part of a physical object, *seems* to have such and such a shape, position and sensible quality. If I want to know whether it *is* part of a physical object; or what kind of physical object this is; or what shape, position and intrinsic qualities it actually *has;* I must do this, if at all, by the same method of comparison and correlation as on the Multiple Inherence Theory. The physical object which I am said to "perceive", and the properties which I ascribe to it, are again logically (though not psychologically) in the position of hypothetically postulated entities.

It is of course open to the supporter of the Multiple Inherence Theory to assert that there may be one specially favourable position (*e.g.*, when one is "looking straight down on a penny from the distance of most distinct vision") in which the geometrical shape and the intrinsic colour of the penny are directly revealed, instead of the colour which it has from a place and the sensible form which inheres in it from a place. And it is open to the supporter of the Theory of a Multiple Relation of Appearing to assert that there may be one specially favourable position in which the qualities which a physical object *has*, and not merely those which it *seems* to have, are revealed directly to the percipient. On such assertions I have the following comments to make. (i) They are in the highest degree unlikely. We are asked to believe that in one special position the physical, physiological, and psychical mechanism produces an utterly different result from that which it produces in all other positions, no matter how close to this specially favoured one. (ii) There is nothing in the nature of any perceptual situation, taken by itself, to reveal to us that it differs in this remarkable way from all the rest.   The unique perceptual situation, if such there be, does not come visibly "trailing clouds of glory behind it".   It would have to be discovered to have this property by comparing it and its objective constituent with other perceptual situations and theirs.   (iii) It is just as possible, logically, for the Sensum Theory to make this preposterous claim as for the other two theories.   It might assert that, from one specially favourable position, the objective constituent is literally a part of the physical object, and that the qualities which we detect in it are literally those of the physical object; whilst, in all other situations, the objective constituent is a mere sensum. I think I may fairly conclude that the objection that on the Sensum Theory the perceived physical object becomes a mere *Ding-an-Sich* applies with almost equal force, if it applies at all, to the other theories.

Let us now consider the objection that the Sensum Theory involves a very odd kind of causation, which is almost creation of particulars out of nothing.   I will first show that the other theories also involve very odd kinds of causation.   The Theory of Multiple Inherence involves instantaneous action at a distance.   When a certain process goes on in my brain and nervous system a certain remote region of Space becomes pervaded by a certain colour from where I am.   So far as we know this is an instantaneous process.   The date of pervasion is identical with the date of the events in my brain and nervous system, though the pervaded place may be millions of miles from the region of projection.   And nothing that may be physically occupying the intervening space is relevant to this process of pervasion; so that we cannot compare this action at a distance with pushing a distant body and making it move instantaneously by means of a rigid rod.   There is in fact, so far as I know, no analogy elsewhere to the kind of causation which the Theory of Multiple Inherence has to postulate. I do not make this an objection to the theory; but I do say that it is in no position to cast stones at the Sensum Theory for having to postulate an odd kind of causation. Exactly the same remarks apply, *mutatis mutandis*, to the Theory of a Multiple Relation of Appearing. Here processes in the brain and nervous system instantaneously cause certain qualities to seem to inhere in places where they do not in fact inhere; or else they make one distant particular seem to be two distant particulars.

I will now consider more directly the special objection to the Sensum Theory on the grounds of the peculiar kind of causation which it involves. The objection is that, if the Sensum Theory be true, physical and physiological processes *create* certain particular existents, viz., sensa, which do not form parts of the history of any physical object. Now it is said that we can understand that a process in one substance may cause a certain quality to characterise the next phase in the history of an already existing substance; but we cannot understand the kind of creation of particulars which the Sensum Theory requires. To this I answer (i) that there are certain forms of the Sensum Theory which do not involve this creative kind of causation but only a selective kind. According to some theories physical objects consist of groups of sensa, and a physical object is perceived when a certain sensum of a certain group becomes the objective constituent of a perceptual situation. On this type of theory the function of the physical, physiological, and psychical mechanism of perception is not to *create* sensa, but merely to *select* from a group of pre-existing sensa a certain one and to make it the objective constituent of a certain perceptual situation. I cannot, however, lay much stress on this answer, because I do not think that a purely selective form of the Sensum Theory is plausible in view of all the facts. I have explained my reasons for this in my *Scientific Thought*, and will not repeat them here.   (ii) The more direct answer to the present objection is the following.   A sensum is not something that exists in isolation ; it is a differentiated part of a bigger and more enduring whole, viz., of a sense-*field* which is itself a mere cross-section of a sense-*history*. Suppose, *e.g.*, that I am aware of a red flash.   This is a differentiation of my total visual field at the moment ; and my total visual field at the moment joins up with and continues my earlier visual fields, forming together with them my visual sense-history.   The sense-history is a continuant ; a kind of substance, though not a *physical* substance.   And the new sensum is not an isolated particular, but an occurrent in this peculiar kind of continuant.   Thus the causation involved in the Sensum Theory, though very different from physical causation, is not the sudden creation of a perfectly isolated and loose particular out of nothing.   It is, to say the least of it, no odder than the causation involved in the other two theories.

The upshot of this discussion seems to me to be that, on the whole, there are no greater objections to the Sensum Theory than to the other theories, and that the other theories have no positive advantages over the Sensum Theory when carefully considered.   And, as the Sensum Theory does not require to assume Absolute Space-Time as a pre-existing matrix, whilst the other theories apparently do, the balance of advantage seems to be slightly on the side of the Sensum Theory.   It remains now to ask: "How much of the common-sense notion of a physical object can we keep ; and with what degree of confidence can we believe that there are things which answer to the various parts of the common-sense notion of a physical object?"

In what Sense can we accept Physical Objects ?   If we consider the common-sense notion of a physical object we can divide it into four logically independent parts. (i) It is supposed to be more permanent than the perceptual situation.   The latter is held to be transitory as compared with the former. (ii) It is supposed to be public to a number of observers, and to be capable of exhibiting different aspects of itself to different senses of the same observer. (iii) It is supposed to be literally extended in Space, having a bounding surface of a certain geometrical size and shape, and standing in straightforward spatial relations to other physical objects. (iv) The objective constituents of the tactual and visual situations in which it is said to be perceived are held to be literally parts of its surface. We have seen reason to reject (iv). The first two are accepted by nearly every one. The average scientist who thinks about the matter accepts the first three and is in an inextricable muddle about the fourth. Berkeley, Leibniz, and Russell accept the first two and reject the rest. It is therefore reasonable to think that there is better evidence for (i) and (ii) than for (iii) and (iv) ; or at any rate that there is less to be said against the first pair than against the last pair.

The evidence for (i) is of the following kind. For long periods of time whenever I look in a certain direction I am aware of very much the same kind of objective constituent, *e.g.*, a visual appearance of my table. Now merely looking in this direction from this place is not a *sufficient* condition for this kind of objective constituent to appear. For sometimes (*e.g.*, when my room is being spring-cleaned) I may look in this direction with quite different results. On the other hand, looking in this direction from this place is a *necessary* condition, over long periods of time, for this objective constituent to appear to me. Now the point to notice is that I can fulfil this condition at quite arbitrary intervals, and that *whenever* I do so during a long stretch of time I am aware of the same kind of objective constituent. The natural interpretation of such facts is that there is another and relatively permanent necessary condition on which all these arbitrarily initiated perceptual situations depend, and that this determines the likeness between their objective constituents. This conclusion is supported by three other sets of facts.

(*a*) When I am not in my room other people may be. And they tell me that they have had visual experiences very much like those which I have when I am in the room and looking in the right direction. This supports the view that there is a relatively permanent necessary condition, which is independent of my presence.

(*b*) I have continually certain kinds of experiences which I ascribe to my own body. Now other people tell me that my body appears to them in exactly the same way as any other physical object. And I have no reason to doubt this, because I know that their bodies appear to me in exactly the same way as other physical objects. I know from internal sensation that my body continues to exist when other people are not seeing or touching it; and I am told by other people that they have the same kind of evidence for the continued existence of *their* bodies when *I* am not seeing or touching them. I have not this kind of direct evidence about chairs and tables; but the analogies in other respects between them and human bodies make it reasonable for me to treat them in the same way. That is, they support the view that something which is *capable* of producing a perceptual situation with a characteristic kind of objective constituent persists, even when no such situation is *actually* being produced, because the other necessary conditions are not being fulfilled.

(*c*) If I look for some time in a certain direction, *e.g.*, "at my fire", as we say, I often find a slow and steady change in the objective constituents of the successive visual situations. If I go out of the room, and, on returning after some time, look again in the same direction from the same place, I shall again be aware of an objective constituent which in the main resembles those of which I was aware before. But there will be certain differences; and in general the differences are such as would have been produced by a steady continuation of that process of change which I observed while I was formerly in the room. Nothing that I can detect in myself during the interval accounts for the difference between the last objective constituent before I went out and the first objective constituent after I again came in. So the natural interpretation is that the original series of objective constituents depended in part on a process outside my body, and that this process has gone on further during my absence.

I do not say that any or all of these arguments amount to a knock-down proof of the view that the objective constituents of perceptual situations are, in many cases, partly dependent on something outside the percipient's body and more permanent than themselves. But I do think that, if it be granted that this hypothesis has any finite initial probability, such facts and arguments do give it a very high final probability. And practically all philosophers have accepted this much of the common-sense view.

(ii) The second part of the common-sense view is that these relatively permanent and necessary, but not sufficient, conditions of perceptual situations are neutral as between different percipients. If this merely means that one and the same set of permanent conditions may co-operate with other conditions which vary from observer to observer, and may produce perceptual situations with correlated objective constituents, this is also highly likely. There are groups of contemporary perceptual situations whose objective constituents are so related to each other that they are all said to refer to the same external object. If we take the case of a number of observers who are said to be seeing the top of the same penny, we find the following correlations. All the observers are looking in such directions that, if they moved along them, they would run into each other at the same place. In the middle of each of their visual fields there is an outstanding patch. All these patches appear to have some shade of brown; they appear to be of different sizes and to have different sensible depths in their respective fields. They appear to have various shapes, but all these shapes are projections of a circle. All the observers will be able to become aware of correlated tactual objective constituents, if they walk up to the place at which their lines of sight intersect. And, as they walk in these directions, each will pass through a series of visual situations; the total objective constituent of each situation will be a coloured field with a brown patch in the middle of it; the shapes of these patches will all be projections of a circle; and the successive patches of each series will be of diminishing sensible depth in their respective visual fields, and of increasing sensible size and clearness.

It is hard to resist the conviction that such groups of correlated perceptual situations depend on two factors. One is a relatively permanent condition, independent of the observers and their bodies. The other is a condition which varies from observer to observer and appears as the position and orientation of the percipient's body. Moreover, the factor in these perceptual situations which seems to be specially closely correlated with this common independent condition is the outstanding patch which is at the middle of each visual field. Suppose that all the observers stand and face as before, and that "the penny is replaced by a tennisball", as we say. Then there will be a simultaneous change in the outstanding central objective constituent of all these visual situations. Thus it seems reasonable to accept the second part of the common-sense view. It is reasonable to hold that the objective constituent in a perceptual situation is in many cases determined by two sets of conditions. One is specially bound up with the percipient and his body; the other is independent of percipients and their bodies. Either can vary without the other. Variations of the latter involve correlated variations in a certain part of the objective constituents of a whole group of perceptual situations belonging to different observers. Variations in the former affect only the objective constituents of the perceptual situations of a single observer. When many people are said to "perceive the same object" we have a group of perceptual situations determined jointly by a *common* independent condition and by other conditions which vary from one observer to another. If this hypothesis starts with a finite initial probability, the facts surely give it a high final probability.

(iii) It remains to consider how far the facts make for or against the third part of the common-sense view; viz., that these relatively permanent and neutral conditions of groups of correlated perceptual situations are literally extended, having geometrical shapes and sizes, and having spatial relations to other things of the same kind. Up to the present all that has been established is equally compatible with the primitive beliefs of common-sense, with the theories of Descartes and the natural scientists, and with the speculations of Berkeley, of Leibniz, or of Mr Russell. For each of these parties admits that such groups of perceptual situations are jointly dependent on a condition, which is relatively permanent and neutral between the percipients, and a variable condition which is specially connected with each percipient. For common-sense this neutral and relatively permanent condition is an extended physical object, of which the objective constituents are literally spatio-temporal parts; the variable conditions simply determine *which* part shall be the objective constituent of a particular perceptual situation. For Mr Russell the neutral and relatively permanent condition is a whole group of correlated sensa; and the variable conditions simply determine *which* member of a certain group shall be the objective constituent of a certain perceptual situation. These two views thus agree in making the variable conditions purely *selective;* everything that could become an objective constituent of a perceptual situation exists already, and the variable conditions simply select a certain part or a certain member from this pre-existing whole and make it the objective constituent of a certain perceptual situation.

The Cartesian, the Leibnitian, and the Berkeleian theories may be called *creative;* for, as usually stated, they assume that the objective constituents do not exist out of the perceptual situations. They assume that, when both sets of conditions are fulfilled, a sensum of a certain kind arises in a certain place in a certain sense-field; but that, when the variable conditions specially connected with the observer are not fulfilled, no sensum of this kind exists. And of course, on every theory except that of Descartes and the scientists, the relatively permanent neutral conditions of groups of interconnected perceptual situations are extremely unlike physical objects, as conceived by common-sense. One cannot say, in any literal sense, that God's habits of volition, or a colony of unintelligent monads, or a group of interrelated sensa, have geometrical shape, size, or position.

Now I have argued that we can never be sure that the objective constituents of perceptual situations *are* literally parts of physical objects, as conceived by common-sense; and that we can be practically certain that they *are not* in most cases. The question then is : " Does there remain any reason for accepting the third proposition of the common-sense view of physical objects when we have rejected the fourth proposition of this view?" Descartes, Locke, and the scientists do reject the fourth and accept the third. The question is whether this is reasonable. Certain general arguments have been brought against the reality of spatial qualities and relations. If these were valid *nothing* could literally have shape, size, or position. It would follow that nothing like the common-sense view of physical objects could possibly be true. But, in the first place, all these arguments seem to me to be plainly fallacious. Secondly, if they be valid at all, they must apply, not only to the supposed persistent and neutral conditions of perceptual situations, but also to the objective constituents of these situations themselves. If there be some internal contradiction in the very notion of spatial qualities and relations it will be as impossible for the objective constituents of perceptual situations to have these qualities or to stand in these relations as for anything else to do so. Now the objective constituents of visual and tactual situations certainly *seem* on careful inspection to have shapes and sizes, and to stand in spatial relations to other contents of the same sense-field. Thus anyone who accepts these general arguments against the reality of spatial qualities and relations must be prepared to hold that we are mistaken, and enormously mistaken, about the *objective constituents of our perceptual situations* as well as about their *neutral and persistent conditions*. It is not merely a mistake about details, as it would be if something which was really round seemed to be elliptical ; it would be a mistake about a fundamental determinable characteristic which seems to belong to the objective constituents of all visual and tactual situations. As I have said, the arguments against the reality of spatial characteristics seem to me plainly fallacious ; but, if I could see nothing wrong with them, I should still venture to think it much more likely that an argument is invalid, though it seems to me sound, than that the objective constituents of visual and tactual situations are unextended, though they seem to have shapes, sizes and positions. For I know from sad experience that I can be taken in by plausible but fallacious arguments, whilst I have no reason to think that the objective constituents of my tactual and visual situations could seem to have shapes, sizes, and positions if they were really unextended. It seems to me then to be practically certain that the objective constituents of certain perceptual situations do have spatial characteristics. It is therefore *possible* that their persistent and neutral conditions may also have these characteristics. The only question is whether there is any positive ground for believing that they do in fact have them.

The only way to answer such a question is to study carefully and in detail the nature of objective constituents and their correlations. In the notion of Physical Space we must distinguish two factors :— (a) the general conception of a Spatial whole having contents of various shapes and sizes at various places in it ; and (b) the special character and contents which are ascribed to Physical Space. I have no doubt that the general conception of a spatial whole springs from our acquaintance with visual fields. Here we do have an extended whole of simultaneous parts ; these parts, viz., variously coloured outstanding patches, do visibly have various shapes and sizes, and do visibly occupy various positions within the whole field. The visual field then is a spatial whole with which we are acquainted in sense-perception, and it is the *only* spatial whole of any importance with which we are acquainted. The physical world, as a spatial whole, is conceived on the analogy of the visual field. Bodies are analogous to outstanding coloured patches. They are conceived to have shapes and sizes, as these patches visibly do have them ; to occupy various positions in Physical Space, as these patches visibly occupy various positions in the visual field ; and to be capable of moving about within Physical Space, as some of these patches visibly do move about within the visual field.

Given the general conception of a spatial whole, many alternative theories about its detailed structure and contents are possible. Our beliefs about the detailed structure and contents of Physical Space are based on experiences of sight, touch, and movement, and on the very complicated correlations which these are found to have with each other. Experiences of movement are interpreted spatially by analogy with the visual field and the visible movements of coloured patches within it, and by means of the correlations between the former and the latter. Conversely, the general conception of Physical Space, which is based on our acquaintance with visual fields, is filled out and specified in detail by our experiences of movement. The hypothesis that what appears to us as external objects and what appears to us as our own bodies are extended and stand in spatial relations, in the sense explained above, accounts for the correlations between objective constituents of perceptual situations and for their variations as we move about. And it is difficult to see that any alternative hypothesis which does not logically reduce to this one will account for such facts. About the minuter details of the physical spatio-temporal order there is room for much diversity of opinion and for much future modification and refinement, as the facts adduced by the Theory of Relativity show. But this much seems to me to be practically certain, viz., that the nature and relations of the persistent and neutral conditions of sensa *must* be interpreted by analogy with visual sensa and their relations in the visual sense-field ; and that they *cannot* be interpreted by analogy with thoughts or volitions and their relations within a mind (as Berkeley held), or with the relations of minds within a society (which, to put it very crudely, was Leibniz's view).

Thus, with suitable interpretations, I accept the first three clauses of the common-sense belief about physical objects. The fourth clause I have to reject, for reasons which I have tried to make plain in the earlier part of this Chapter.

The Status of so-called " Secondary Qualities ". It is of course part of the common-sense view that physical objects literally have colours, temperatures, etc. This is a logical consequence of the view that the objective constituents of perceptual situations literally have the sensible qualities which they seem on inspection to have, and that these objective constituents are literally parts of the surfaces of those physical objects which we are said to be perceiving. If we drop the fourth clause of the common-sense belief it still remains *possible* that the neutral and persistent conditions of perceptual situations literally have *some* colour and *some* temperature. And the colour and temperature *might* be identical with those of the objective constituent of *one* specially favoured perceptual situation. Is there any positive reason to believe that this is in fact true? I do not think that there is. It does not seem to be possible to account for the correlated variations in the *shapes and sizes* of visual sensa without assigning quasi-spatial qualities and relations to the permanent conditions of these variable appearances and to the things which manifest themselves to us by bodily feelings. But, so far as I can see, it is neither necessary nor useful to ascribe to these permanent conditions anything analogous to the *colour* and the *temperature* which we find in sensa. It has been found more expedient to correlate the colours and temperatures of sensa with certain kinds of motion of certain kinds of microscopic parts of their permanent conditions. It is practically certain that the *independently* necessary and sufficient conditions of the colour and temperature of the objective constituent of a given perceptual situation are events within the observer's own body; *i.e.*, within that relatively permanent object which is manifested to himself by a mass of bodily feeling, and to others through certain characteristic visual and tactual sensa. But, in non-delusive perceptual situations, these bodily events are physically determined by certain motions of certain particles in an emitting region; so that these external physical events are the *dependently* necessary and *common* conditions of the colours and temperatures of the correlated sensa of a whole group of observers who are said to be "perceiving the same external object". Provided we are dealing with non-delusive perceptual situations and with normal human observers whose bodies are in a healthy state, we can drop the independently necessary conditions out of account, and confine our attention to these dependently necessary and common external conditions. This of course is what the physical theories of colour and temperature do. Naturally such theories are incomplete, since they presuppose the fulfilment of conditions which are not always fulfilled. But, when we try to complete them we have to do so, not by ascribing a physical colour or temperature in a literal sense to the external conditions, but by considering the structure and processes of the observer's body. Thus, whilst it is not impossible that physical objects may literally have colours and temperatures, there is not the slightest reason to believe that they do. It is of course quite easy to *define* a Pickwickian sense in which a certain physical object may be said to have a certain physical colour. I have already done this in treating the Multiple Inherence Theory, and it is perfectly easy to give a similar definition, *mutatis mutandis*, on the other two theories. But this is quite a different thing from saying that a physical object literally has a certain colour, in the sense in which the objective constituents of visual situations have colours.

I do not know that I have ever seen a satisfactory definition of the terms "Primary" and "Secondary" Quality. It will therefore be of interest to try to give one. I suggest the following definitions. "A Primary Quality is a determinable characteristic which, we have reason to believe, inheres literally and dyadically in some physical object in some determinate form or other." "A Secondary Quality is a determinable characteristic which certainly inheres or seems to inhere literally and dyadically in the objective constituents of some perceptual situations in some determinate form or other, but which there is no reason to believe inheres literally and dyadically in any physical object." A primary quality may, but need not, inhere literally and dyadically in some objective constituent.   On these definitions, colour and temperature are secondary qualities, if I am right about their status.   Shape, size and position are primary qualities which inhere literally and dyadically both in the objective constituents of perceptual situations and in their relatively permanent conditions.   Electric charge, magnetic properties, and so on, are primary qualities which inhere literally and dyadically in physical objects, but do not (so far as we know) inhere in the objective constituent of any perceptual situation.

Before ending this section it will be interesting to see just where Locke and Berkeley were respectively right and wrong, on our view, about primary and secondary qualities.   Berkeley was right against Locke when he said that nothing could possibly be *merely* extended and movable.   (Though Locke, to do him justice, never maintained anything so silly as the proposition which Berkeley refutes.)   This may be expressed by saying that, *if* spatio-temporal characteristics be primary, they cannot be *the only* primary characteristics.   Whatever is extended must have *some* other characteristic, which is capable of covering an area or filling a volume as colour and temperature do in sensa.   But Berkeley was wrong in thinking that this "extensible characteristic", as I will call it, must be colour or temperature or some other quality which literally and dyadically inheres in sensa. It might be mass or electric charge.   Again, Berkeley was right in so far as he held that there is just as good reason to deny that the determinate shapes and sizes of sensa inhere literally in some permanent object, which we are said to be "seeing", as to deny that the determinate colours or temperatures of sensa literally inhere in such objects.   But Locke was right in so far as he held that there is positive reason to hold that the determinable characteristic of extension inheres literally and dyadically in physical objects as well as in sensa, whilst there is no reason to believe that the determinable characteristics of colour and temperature inhere literally and dyadically in anything but sensa. And so Locke was right in thinking that we can and must distinguish between primary and secondary qualities, and he was right in assigning extension and motion to the former class, and colour and temperature to the latter. Both these great men were thus expressing important truths; but they both expressed them imperfectly, because they failed to notice certain important distinctions which we, who have the advantage of standing on their shoulders, are able to see.

The Subjective Factors in Perceptual Situations. I have been considering the belief, which forms an essential factor in every perceptual situation and constitutes its external reference, from a logical and epistemological and not from a psychological point of view. By this I mean that I have been concerned with the propositions believed and not with the act of believing them. I have tried to state clearly what these propositions are; to consider which of them are certainly false and which of them are possibly true; and to adduce and appraise the evidence which can be submitted in favour of the latter. I propose to end this chapter by an attempt at further psychological analysis of the perceptual situation. The remarks which I shall now make are to be regarded as a continuation of the analysis which was begun and carried a certain length in the sub-section on *External Reference*. I there warned the reader of the following points. (i) That the belief which constitutes the external reference of a perceptual situation is not in fact *reached* by inference, even if it can be *defended* by inference on later reflection. (ii) That, psychologically, it can only be called a "belief" by courtesy. We can only say that a man in a perceptual situation acts, adjusts his body, and feels certain emotions; and that these actions, adjustments, and emotions are such as would be reasonable *if* he were explicitly making such and such judgments, which he does not in fact make as a rule at the time. The bodily adjustment itself is of course no part of the subjective factor in the perceptual situation ; but it is impossible to make these adjustments or to start to perform these actions without producing certain characteristic modifications of bodily feeling. These modifications of bodily feeling and these emotions *are* an essential part of the subjective side of every perceptual situation. We have now to see whether we can carry the analysis any further.

A reflective observer, considering one of his own perceptual situations after it has ceased, or considering a contemporary perceptual situation in which he is not personally concerned, would probably propose the following analysis for it. (i) An objective constituent, having certain sensible qualities and forming a differentiated part of a wider sense-field. (ii) A subjective constituent, consisting of a mass of bodily feeling, emotion, etc. (iii) The fact that this objective constituent is intuitively apprehended by the percipient. (iv) The fact that the percipient, who intuitively apprehends the objective constituent and who feels the emotions and bodily feelings, has certain non-inferential beliefs about the objective constituent which go beyond anything that is intuitively apprehended in the situation. I believe this analysis to be substantially correct, though the fourth factor in it is expressed in terms which do not strictly apply to anything so primitive as the perceptual situation but are borrowed from higher cognitive levels. I have already discussed the first factor *ad nauseam*, and I have already given my reasons for wishing to modify the statement of the fourth. What I want to do now is to explain what I suppose to be involved in the intuitive apprehension of the objective constituent and in the quasi-belief about it. I think that the two are probably very closely connected.

The Intuitive Apprehension of Sensa. It is quite certain that there is a difference between the two propositions : "This is a red round patch in a visual field" and "This red round patch in a visual field is intuitively apprehended by so-and-so". Even if as a matter of fact there are no such objects which are not intuitively apprehended by someone, it seems to me to be perfectly certain that it is *logically* possible that there might have been. (I have argued earlier in the chapter that it is also *causally* possible, but it is not necessary for our present purpose that this should be so.) Since it is logically possible that the same sensum should sometimes be intuitively apprehended and sometimes not, or that it should sometimes be intuitively apprehended by A and not by B and at other times by B and not by A, it seems plain that the characteristic of being "intuitively apprehended" is a relational characteristic; *i.e.*, that it consists in the establishment of a certain asymmetrical relation R between the sensum and something else. The question is : "What is this relation, and what is this something else?" A theory has been put forward by the persons who call themselves "New Realists", which would provide a simple answer to this question if it could be accepted. It has also been suggested by Mr Russell, and is therefore worth a degree of attention which it might not otherwise have deserved.

So far as I can understand the theory it comes roughly to this. All the visual sensa of which it would be true to say that A intuitively apprehends them belong to a certain visual field. And of all sensa which belong to this visual field it would be true to say that A intuitively apprehends them. Hence the two properties of "being intuitively apprehended by A" and "belonging to a certain visual field" are logically equivalent. Moreover, the relation of a sensum to a sense-field is asymmetrical. It is then suggested that really we have not two different though logically equivalent properties, but a single property with two different names. To say that " The visual sensum *s* is intuitively apprehended by A " *means* the same as to say that " The visual sensum *s* belongs to a certain visual field f_A." If this were true, the "something else" to which a sensum is related when it is intuitively apprehended would be a certain sense-field ; and the asymmetrical relation of being intuitively apprehended would be that of a part of a sense-field to the sense-field as a whole.

It seems to me perfectly certain that this theory is false. (*a*) No one would admit that a sensum which was part of a sense-field which is not intuitively apprehended would itself be intuitively apprehended. Hence we can hold that " to be intuitively apprehended " and "to belong to a sense-field" *mean* the same *only* if we admit that it is *logically* impossible for there to be a sense-field which is not intuitively apprehended. Now it is quite plain that there is no more logical impossibility in the existence of an unapprehended sense-field than in the existence of a single sensum which is not intuitively apprehended. Hence "to be intuitively apprehended" and "to belong to a sense-field" *cannot* mean the same. (*b*) A visual sensum, a tactual sensum, and an auditory sensum may all be intuitively apprehended by the same person at the same time. They certainly do not all form parts of any one sense-field. Hence, to be intuitively apprehended by a certain person cannot be the same as to form part of a certain sense-field. Still, it is no doubt true that there is *some* relation between those sensa which would be said to be intuitively apprehended by the same person, which does not hold between sensa which would not be said to be intuitively apprehended by the same person. Might it not be suggested then that the theory is right in outline, though incorrect as originally stated? We may admit that "to be intuitively apprehended" is *not* the same as "to be united with certain other sensa so as to form with them a certain sense-field"; but might we not suggest that it *is* the same as "to be united with certain other sensa by a certain relation R"? R might be a quite unique relation, incapable of further analysis or definition ; but it would have to have the following properties. (1) It must be logically possible for a set of sensa which are not all parts of a single sense-field to be related to each other by the relation R. (2) R must be such that two sensa, each of which is related by R to *some* other sensa, need not be related by R to each other. For there are sensa which are intuitively apprehended by A and not by B, and there are sensa which are intuitively apprehended by B and not by A. The modified theory then comes to this. There is a certain relation R which binds certain sensa together into mutually exclusive groups. To be intuitively apprehended means to be a member of some group of sensa bound together by the relation R. Let us consider this theory in its modified form.

So long as the theory is content to regard the relation R as absolutely unique and peculiar I do not think that it can be positively refuted. The moment it attempts to identify R with some familiar relation, such as compresence in a sense-field or a direct relation of simultaneity, it is plainly false. It is obviously logically possible, *e.g.*, that a set of sensa should be directly simultaneous with each other and yet that none of them should be intuitively apprehended. But, although I cannot refute the theory so long as it is willing to take R as absolutely unique and peculiar, I think I can prove that it fails to account for a certain obvious fact so well as alternative theories, and that the motives which led to it are connected with an erroneous belief. This I will now try to show.

(*a*) If the theory be a complete account of the facts, the unity of a set of sensa which are all intuitively apprehended by a certain person is wholly a "unity of system" and not a "unity of centre". I shall have to consider these two types of unity in greater detail when I consider the unity of the Self. At present I will content myself with saying that a family of brothers and sisters is an example of a unity of centre. The relations which they have to each other are due to the fact that they all stand in a common relation to something.(viz., their parents) which is not itself a member of the set. The points on a straight line constitute a pure unity of system ; they are just directly related to each other by the relation of "between", and this relation does not depend in any way on their all being related by some common relation to something which is not a member of the set. Now it is perfectly certain that we all believe, to start with, that the unity of a set of sensa which are all intuitively apprehended by the same person is a unity of *centre* and *not* a pure unity of system. That this is so is proved conclusively by language, and by the extreme air of paradox which the opposite view continues to present even when we admit that it is logically possible. It is certainly a fact then that, *if* the unity of a set of sensa intuitively apprehended by the same person be in fact a pure unity of system, it nevertheless *appears*, and goes on appearing, to be a unity of centre. This fact must be recognised and accounted for on any adequate theory of the subject. Now my objection to the theory under discussion is that it utterly fails to account for this appearance. We must remember that every unity of centre is *also* a unity of system. If x, y, and z all stand in a certain unique relation S to a certain term t there will be an unique, though derivative, relation between x, y, and z. For x will have to y the relation R of "being both of them terms which stand in the relation S to t". And, since S is unique, R will be unique. Thus it is quite possible that what is in fact a unity of centre might appear to be a pure unity of system, especially if the "centre" t were such that it is hard to detect and easy to overlook. But there is no reason whatever why what is in fact a pure unity of system should appear to be a unity of centre. Hence it seems to me that the theory under discussion is quite incompetent to explain a most striking and perfectly indubitable fact. I should therefore consider it absurd to accept such a theory unless there were insuperable objections to the alternatives or great advantages in itself. These claims would be made for the present theory; but I believe that they have no justification, as I will now try to show.

(b) The objection which supporters of this theory make to the opposite view is that the latter involves a "Pure Ego" to be the "centre" which generates the unity. And it is supposed that a "Pure Ego" is so disreputable that no decent philosopher would allow such a thing in his mind if he could possibly help it. I shall have to deal with the alleged indecency of the Pure Ego in a later chapter; here I will merely say that the objection is quite irrelevant because there is no need whatever for the unifying centre to be a Pure Ego. It might be, and I believe is, a mass of bodily feeling. Of course, later on, questions must be raised about the "ownership" of this mass of feeling; and then we might find that the Pure Ego Theory explained the facts better than any other. But, so long as we are merely concerned with the intuitive apprehension of sensa, it is perfectly ridiculous to try to frighten us into the theory under discussion by threatening us with the Pure Ego as a kind of bogey which can be exorcised only by a course of "New Realism".

(c) I think that the advantage which is claimed for the theory is that it is "naturalistic". This, I think, means roughly that it claims to be able to deal with mind without introducing any new and unique entities or relations. I have already shown that the opposite theory has no immediate need of any very mysterious special entity, such as a Pure Ego. There should be nothing very trying, even to the most sensitively naturalistic mind, in a mass of bodily feeling. And I claim also to have shown that the theory cannot dispense with an unique kind of relation. If you identify the relation R with any familiar relation it is perfectly obvious that "to be intuitively apprehended" does *not* mean "to be a member of a group of sensa interrelated by R". On the whole, then, it seems to me that there are grave objections to the theory under discussion and no advantages to outweigh them. I therefore reject it, and accept the common-sense view that when a visual, tactual, or auditory sensum is intuitively apprehended it stands in an unique kind of relation to something which is not an auditory, tactual, or visual sensum. And I believe this "something" to be the mass of general bodily feeling of the percipient at the time.

The quasi-Belief about the Sensum. I am inclined to think that the quasi-belief about the objective constituent, which is the fourth distinguishable feature in a perceptual situation, consists in the fact that certain *specific* bodily feelings (connected with the automatic adjustment of the body), certain emotions, and certain feelings of expectation, are related in an unique way to the apprehended sensum. These are causally dependent on the traces left by past experience. When a sensum of a specific kind is intuitively apprehended certain traces are excited; these arouse certain emotions and induce certain bodily adjustments which are accompanied by specific bodily feelings. They may in addition call up certain images; and, even if they do not do this, they may evoke a more or less vague feeling of "familiarity". These "mnemic consequences" of the apprehension of the sensum do not just coexist with it; they immediately enter into a specific kind of relation to it, which I do not know how to analyse further. And these "mnemic consequences" in this specific relation to this intuitively apprehended sensum constitute the quasi-belief about the sensum, which gives the situation its specific External Reference. Any situation constructed of such materials in such relations, *ipso facto*, has such and such an External Reference. This is the best analysis that I can offer at present of the typical perceptual situation.

It raises one interesting question. Can there be pure sensation without perception? Let us see exactly what this means on our theory. A pure sensation would be a situation in which a certain sensum, *e.g.*, a noise or a coloured patch, was intuitively apprehended, but in which there was no external reference. Now, on our theory, we should expect perception to melt into pure sensation by insensible degrees; we should expect the latter to be an ideal limit rather than an observable fact; and we should expect it to be unstable and transitory, if it happens at all. If the mass of feeling be highly differentiated and certain specific parts of it be specifically related to a certain sensum, we shall have a clear case of a perceptual situation with a definite external reference. If, on the other hand, the mass of feeling be little differentiated, and the apprehension of the sensum fails to excite traces which cause specific modifications in the mass, we shall have a situation which approximates to pure sensation, since its external reference will be very vague. And the same result would happen, even if the mass of feeling were differentiated in the way suggested, provided that for some reason the differentiated parts failed to enter into the proper relation to the apprehended sensum. It seems to me that when we are looking at something with interest our awareness of the sensa towards the edge of the visual field approximates to pure sensation for the first reason. And, perhaps, when we are looking for something and discover afterwards that it was staring us in the face all the time, our awareness of the sensa connected with it approximates to pure sensation from the second cause.

The Categorial Factor in Sense-Perception. One more point remains to be raised. I have said that, when the quasi-belief which is an essential factor in all perceptual situations is formulated in abstract terms, it may be

summed up in certain propositions which I have stated
and criticised.   I rejected the fourth of these, and
defended the first three by an inverse-probability
argument.   But, as a matter of psychology, I asserted
that the belief in them was not in fact reached in this
way.   And, as a matter of logic, I asserted that the
argument gives them a high final probability *only*
if they start with a finite initial probability.   Here then
are certain propositions such that every one acts *as if*
he believed them, and inevitably goes on acting as if
he believed them, no matter what theoretical doubts he
may feel about them while he is reflecting on them.   It
is certain that they do not appear self-evident on reflexion ; that they cannot be deduced by self-evident
steps from premises which are self-evident ; and that
they cannot be defended by probable reasoning except
on the assumption that they have a finite initial probability.   I call such a set of propositions a set of
" Postulates ".   Between them they " define " a certain
general concept, viz. the notion of a Physical Object.
For a physical object just is something that answers to
these postulates.   A general concept which is defined
in this way by a set of postulates such as I have been
describing, I call a " Category ".   From the very
nature of the case the notion of " Physical Object "
cannot have been derived by abstraction from observed
instances of it, as the notion of " red " no doubt has
been.   For the objective constituents of perceptual
situations *are* not instances of this concept ; and it is
only in virtue of these postulates that we can hold that
they are " parts of " or " manifestations of " instances
of this concept.   The concept is not " got out of "
experience until it has been " put into " experience.   It
is best described as an innate principle of interpretation
which we apply to the data of sense-perception.   At
the purely perceptual level " to apply the principle "
simply means to act and to feel as it would be reasonable to act and feel if we explicitly recognised it and

interpreted the data of sense in accordance with it. It is only at the reflective level that we can state in abstract terms the implications of what we have all been doing all our lives.

Summary and Conclusions. In this chapter I have been concerned with two very difficult questions: "What may we believe about our own bodies and about the external world?" and "What is the mind really doing when it is said to be perceiving a material object?" On the first point I have reached the following tentative conclusions. (1) We may believe that there are relatively permanent objects which literally have shape, size, and position; which stand in literal spatial and temporal relations to each other; and which literally move about in Space. (2) We may believe that some of them are animated by minds; and that any one of them which is animated by a mind manifests itself to that mind in a peculiar way, viz., by organic sensations. Nothing manifests itself in this way except to the mind, if there be one, which animates it. (3) We may believe that physical objects, whether animated or not, manifest themselves in a variety of ways to minds which do not animate them. And we may believe that a single physical object may manifest itself at the same time in the same or in different ways to a number of minds animating bodies in various places. (4) We may believe that, by comparison of the objective constituents of various perceptual situations and by reflexion on their correlations, we can determine with high probability the shape, size, and position of the physical object which manifests itself in this situation. And with somewhat less certainty we can determine important facts about its microscopic structure and the movements of its microscopic parts. (5) We must believe that a physical object has other properties beside its purely spatio-temporal ones. It must have at least one quality which is capable of literally covering an area or filling a volume; and it may have many such. (6) We may *not* believe that the objective constituents of perceptual situations are literally spatio - temporal parts of the physical objects which we are said to be perceiving in those situations; or that in general they have the same determi*nate* spatial characteristics as the sensa by which they manifest themselves. (7) We have no reason to believe that physical objects have the same determi*nable* sensible qualities as the sensa by which they manifest themselves. (8) We may *not* believe that the shape, size, spatial position, date, or sensible qualities of a sensum by which a certain physical object manifests itself are *directly* determined by this physical object or by processes in it. On the contrary the *independently* necessary and sufficient conditions of all these characteristics of the sensum are within the region occupied by the percipient's body. At best the external physical object and the processes in it are remote and *dependently* necessary conditions of the sensum and its characteristics. (9) We have, therefore, to recognise a peculiar kind of trans-physical causation, according to which the occurrence of certain events in a certain brain and nervous system determines the occurrence of a sensum with such and such a shape, size, position, and sensible quality, in a certain sense-field of a certain sense-history. (10) We have to admit that certain characteristics of certain sensa are probably not completely determined by physical and physiological events in the body of the percipient; but are in part determined, either directly or indirectly by events in the mind which animates this body.

On the second point I have reached the following tentative conclusions. (1) The perceptual situation contains two constituents, one objective and the other subjective. (2) The objective constituent is a sense-field with a certain outstanding sensum. (3) The subjective constituent is a mass of bodily feeling, together with certain specific emotions, muscular sensations, feelings of familiarity, images, etc. (4) The latter are produced through the excitement of certain traces by the apprehension of the sensum. (5) The sensum is apprehended by entering into a certain specific relation with the general mass of bodily feeling. (6) The situation has a certain specific external reference in virtue of a certain specific relation between the apprehended sensum and its "mnemic consequences" in the way of feeling, etc. (7) It seems likely that pure sensation is an ideal limit, which is approached as the external reference grows vaguer and vaguer, rather than an observable fact. (8) The notion of Physical Object cannot have been abstracted from the data of sense. It is a Category, and is defined by Postulates.

CHAPTER V

Memory

THE word "memory" is highly ambiguous, even when it is not being used in admittedly paradoxical and uncommon senses, as when people talk of "racial" or "ancestral" memory. I call such uses of the word paradoxical because even those persons who hold that in performing an instinctive action we are "remembering" similar actions which were performed deliberately by our remote ancestors would have to admit that, in the ordinary sense of "remembering", we certainly do not remember the actions or thoughts of our ancestors. Even apart from these odd senses of "memory" it is quite certain that the word covers a number of very different acts. We talk of remembering a set of nonsense-syllables; of remembering a poem; of remembering a proposition in Euclid, though we have forgotten the words in which it was expressed when we originally learnt it; of remembering past events; and of remembering people, places, and things. To remember a set of nonsense-syllables is merely to have acquired the power of repeating them at will; and remembering, in this sense, seems to be no more an act of cognition than is the act of riding a bicycle or of swimming. To remember a proposition of Euclid is no doubt to perform a genuine act of cognition; and the same is true of remembering events, persons, and places. But the first kind of act has an abstract and timeless object; whilst the second has a concrete particular object which exists in time. Presumably then the memory of propositions is something quite different from the memory of mere sentences, on the one hand,

and from the memory of events, persons, and places, on the other. This of course is quite compatible with the view that there may be intimate relations of causal dependence between the various kinds of memory, and that there may be something common and peculiar to them all in virtue of which they are all called "memory".

It seems plain that there is one and only one kind of memory which can plausibly be regarded as closely analogous to perception; and this is the memory of particular events, places, persons, or things. Let us call this "Perceptual Memory". My main object in this chapter is to discuss perceptual memory, to compare it with perception, and to consider some of the epistemological problems to which it gives rise. At the end of the chapter I shall say something about the other senses in which the word "memory" is used, and shall consider the mutual relations and the common features (if any) of all kinds of memory.

Memory-Powers and Memory-Acts. I must begin by pointing out an ambiguity which applies equally to all kinds of memory and does not apply to perception. If a man said to me: "Do you see Jones?" and I answered: "Yes", I should be lying unless I were actually at the time subject of a visual situation whose objective constituent I took to be an appearance of Jones. But, if he said to me: "Do you remember Jones?" or "Do you remember Euclid i. 47?" or "Do you remember the first line of the *Æneid*?" I might quite truly answer "Yes" even though I were not at the time performing any memory-act at all. So long as I believe that I *could* remember these things *if* I tried I should be justified in saying that I *do* remember them. If, on the other hand, he had said to me: "Are you remembering Jones?" I should not be justified in saying: "Yes" unless I were at the time actually the subject of a memory-situation with Jones as its epistemological object.

The point may be put shortly as follows. "To remember" is an ambiguous word, which covers both an act and a power. When I say that I remember so-and-so I may be referring either to the power or to a particular present exercise of the power. When I say that I *am* remembering so-and-so I am understood to be referring to a particular present exercise of the power, and not merely to the power itself. We do not use words like "seeing" and "hearing" in this ambiguous way. Whether I say that I see so-and-so or that I am seeing so-and-so I am understood to be referring to a present act of perception, and not to a mere power of perceiving. Thus, in discussing memory and trying to compare it with perception, I must be understood to be talking about particular acts of remembering so-and-so, and not (unless I specially say so) about the general power of remembering so-and-so at will. We must distinguish then between "Memory-acts" and "Memory-powers", and we shall be talking about the former unless we explicitly say that we are talking about the latter.

Perceptual Memory. It will be admitted by everyone that such phrases as "I remember having my hair cut last week", "I remember the tie which my friend wore yesterday", "I remember the feeling which I had when I last went to the dentist", and "I remember hearing Mr Russell lecture", all stand for familiar cognitive situations which do arise from time to time. We will call them "Perceptual Memory-Situations", or in the present section simply "Memory-Situations". It will be noticed that the four examples which I have given differ from each other in the nature of the object which we profess to be remembering. In the first we profess to be remembering an *event* of the *physical* kind. In the second we profess to be remembering a certain physical *thing*. In the third we profess to be remembering a past *feeling*. And in the fourth we profess to be remembering a past *perceptual situation*. Let us first consider the relation between memories of events and memories of things.

Memories of Events and of Things. We have a like distinction in the case of perception. We talk of seeing a flash of lightning and of hearing a clap of thunder ; and we also talk of seeing a cloud and hearing a bell. In the one case we claim to be perceiving a physical event, in the other a physical thing. If we reflect we see that the two kinds of perceptual situation are very closely connected. When we say that we are perceiving a certain physical event, as distinct from merely having an auditory or visual sensation, we mean that we regard the sensum which we are sensing as either a part or an appearance of a part of the history of a certain physical thing. On the other hand, when we say that we are perceiving a certain physical thing, we are really perceiving a physical event or a series of them and regarding them as parts of the history of this physical thing. All perceptual situations refer beyond themselves to physical things ; if we confine ourselves to saying that we perceive a certain physical event we simply leave the further reference rather more vague than when we say that we perceive a certain physical thing. Now the same is true of perceptual memory. I say that I remember the late Master of Trinity, and I say that I remember dining with him. But, on the one hand, I remember *him* only in so far as I remember *events* in which he was concerned. And, on the other hand, when I remember any physical event I, *ipso facto*, remember to some extent the thing in which I believe this event to have happened. Thus I think we may say that to remember a thing or person simply means to remember certain past events and to regard them as incidents in the history of that thing or person. We can, and very often do, remember things which still exist and which we are now perceiving. I both perceive and remember the chairs in my room, in so far as I

perceive certain present events and remember certain
past events and regard them as so many successive
phases in the history of my chairs. So I think that
the fundamental point to be considered in dealing with
perceptual memory is the memory of events. Memory
of things depends on this, and no principles are involved
in passing from the memory of events to the memory of
things which are not equally involved in the passage
from the perception of events to the perception of
things. We may add that the perception of things, in
so far as it involves the belief that the event which I am
now perceiving is the present phase of the history of a
certain enduring thing, is inextricably bound up with
memory of things and therefore with memory of events.

Repetition and Perceptual Memory. It has sometimes
been held that a criterion by which we can distinguish
Perceptual Memory from mere Habit Memory, such as
is involved in repeating a poem by heart, is that
Habit Memory depends on repetition whilst Perceptual
Memory from the nature of the case cannot do so. This
of course would at best be only a distinction between
the conditions under which the two kinds of memory-
power are acquired; it would not be a distinction
between the two kinds of memory-*act*. But it seems to
me to be a rather inaccurate statement; and I think
that those who have made it have failed to distinguish
between perceptual memory of events and perceptual
memory of things. It will be worth while to clear up
this point before going further. In the first place,
repetition is not essential, though it is helpful, for the
establishment of a habit-memory-power. A man, like
Lord Macaulay, with a very quick and retentive verbal
memory, may be able to repeat sentences or sets of
nonsense-syllables which he has met with only once.
Secondly, it is obvious that our power of remembering
a person, place, or thing *is* in some ways improved by
repeatedly perceiving the object in question. It will,
therefore, be well to clear up this question of the relation

between repetition and the acquirement of memory-powers. (1) It is of course perfectly true that the power of remembering a certain definite event cannot be due to repetition, and cannot be improved by repetition. For a definite event with a definite date cannot be repeatedly perceived, although other events very much like it may be perceived at various times. (2) But perceptual memory-power which is concerned with people or things is improved by repetition in two ways. (a) It is improved in content by repetition with variation. I have said that my memory of a thing consists of my memories of various events all of which I regard as so many slices of the history of this thing. Now a thing shows different sides of its nature by being placed in different kinds of situation. I can remember a thing or person better (in the sense that I can know more facts about it by memory) in proportion to the number of events of different *kinds* in which I have perceived it to be concerned. And the same thing can be concerned in a large number of events of very different kinds only on a number of successive occasions. Hence the power of adequately remembering a thing or person does need repetition for its establishment. But the repetition which is needful for this purpose is quite different in kind from that which is helpful in establishing a power of habit-memory. In the former case repetition is important only as a necessary condition for variation. In the latter case what is wanted is pure repetition with as little variation as possible. (b) I think that it is also true that pure repetition without variation plays a part in the establishment and improvement of the power of remembering persons and things ; for I think that an element of habit-memory is involved in perceptual memory   To have an accurate memory of a person or thing it is useful, if not essential, to be able to call up an accurate image. Now the power to call up an image is just a habit, like the acquired power to repeat a sentence which one has learnt by heart. And to establish this power repetition with as little variation as possible is helpful. The perceptual memory-act does not indeed consist in calling up the image ; but the power to do so is an important condition of an accurate perceptual memory. As this power is established and improved by bare repetition, such repetition is so far helpful in establishing a perceptual memory-power.

Nature of Memory-Objects and of Perception Objects. If the reader will refer back to the examples which I gave of perceptual memory-situations he will see that we claim to remember, not only physical things and events, but also feelings and perceptual situations. We claim to remember, not only our friend's tie and Mr Russell's lecture, but also seeing the tie, hearing the lecture, and feeling toothache. Now we do not claim to perceive anything but physical events and objects. I do not think that we ought to exaggerate this difference between the possible objects of memory and the possible objects of perception. If we confine the name "perception" to *sense*-perception, it is true that the objects of memory are less restricted than those of perception. But perhaps this restriction is un-warranted. We certainly seem to have some kind of intuitive knowledge of contemporary feelings and per-ceptual situations, and it is possible that we ought to regard this as a form of perception. I shall deal with this question in the next chapter. In the meanwhile we must recognise that, whilst the objects of memory are certainly less restricted than those of sense-per-ception, they may coincide with those of perception in the wider sense.

It is one of the characteristics of sense-perception that the objects which we claim to perceive are public and neutral. When we remember physical things and events memory claims to reveal public and neutral objects to us. A number of people can remember the same man or the same flash of lightning. When we remember feelings or perceptual situations memory claims only to reveal private and personal objects to us. It might be argued that there is something more private and personal about the object of a memory even of a physical thing or event than there is about the object of a perceptual situation. We can remember only the things and events which *we* have perceived, and only those phases of the past history of things which fell under *our* notice. I think that this does impose a restriction on the *range* of memory as compared with that of perception; but I do not think that it introduces any special privacy into the objects of memory. I can remember only those things and events which I have perceived, and it happens to be true that I perceive many things and events which I cannot remember. But it is also true that I can perceive only those things and events which produce sensations in me, and that many things do in fact produce sensations in me without giving rise to perceptions. This restriction in the range of perception does not make the perceived objects essentially private in character; similarly, the further restriction in the range of memory does not make the remembered objects essentially private in character. In each case the *class* of objects perceived or remembered is determined by factors which are personal to the experient; but each of the individual *members* of the class may still be of such a nature that a number of experients could perceive or remember it.

It is only on one very special theory about memory that it could be maintained that there is something essentially private about the objects even of memories of physical events and things. It might be suggested that, when we say that we remember a certain physical thing or event, what we primarily remember is a past perceptual situation of which we were the subject and the event was the epistemological object. *E.g.*, it might be held that, when I say that I remember a certain lecture being given by Mr Russell, I primarily remember the perceptual situation of myself hearing

Mr Russell speaking; and that my belief that Mr Russell did speak is inferred from my memory of hearing him speak. On this view that what we primarily remember is perceptual situations with ourselves as subjects, and that our memory-beliefs about physical events and objects are secondary and derivative, it would be true to say that the primary epistemological objects of *all* perceptual memories are private and personal in a way in which the epistemological objects of perceptual situations are not. A milder view would be that, although my memory-judgments about physical events and things are not *derived* from a more primitive memory of myself perceiving these objects, yet, in fact, the former kind of memory-situation does not and cannot exist without the latter. On this milder view the *total* epistemological object of any memory situation would be complex; and, since one part of it would always be a past perceptual situation with myself as subject, it would be true that there is *something* private and personal in the epistemological object of every memory-situation even when there is also something public and neutral. I shall have to discuss these two views a little later, when I try to analyse the typical perceptual memory-situation.

In the meanwhile there is one other remark to be made before leaving this part of the subject. We shall find that it is necessary to distinguish between the objective constituent of a memory-situation and its epistemological object, just as we have had to do in the case of perceptual situations. Now it is arguable that the objective constituents of memory-situations are private and existentially dependent on the body, if not on the mind, of the experient. For the objective constituents of memory-situations are generally believed to be images, and images are generally believed to be private in this sense. This, however, would not make any sharp distinction between memory-situations and perceptual situations. For, on the sensum theory, the objective constituents of perceptual situations are sensa ; and there are reasons for thinking that sensa are, in some degree, dependent on the body and perhaps on the mind of the percipient.

We may sum up the discussion as follows : (1) The objective constituents of all memory-situations may very well be private, in the sense that they are existentially or qualitatively dependent on the body or the mind of the subject. But much the same may be said of the objective constituents of perceptual situations. (2) The epistemological objects of *some* memory-situations (viz., of those in which we claim to remember a feeling or a perceptual situation) are undoubtedly private and personal. (3) The epistemological objects of other memory-situations (viz., of those in which we claim to remember a physical thing or event), are, on the face of them, as public and neutral as those of perceptual situations. It is true that the range of physical events and things which anyone can remember is limited by his past perceptions ; but it is equally true that the range of things and events which he can perceive is limited by his sensations. And in neither case does this render the objects themselves private or personal in their essence. (4) There is a certain theory about memory according to which all that is primarily and strictly remembered is past perceptual situations of which the experiment was subject. On this theory it would be true that the *primary* epistemological objects of *all* memory-situations are private and personal to the experient. (5) Even if this extreme view be not taken it remains possible that all memory-situations have a complex epistemological object, one part of which is a past perceptual situation. If this be so there will be *something* personal and private in the complete epistemological object of *every* memory-situation, although there will also be something which is public and neutral in the epistemological objects of memories of physical things and events.

General Analysis of a Memory-Situation. I propose now to analyse a typical perceptual memory-situation, having a physical thing or event for its epistemological object. I shall begin with a rough general analysis, in which I shall try to bring out the apparent analogies between such a situation and a typical perceptual situation. I shall then go into greater detail about certain special points where the two kinds of situation seem to differ fundamentally from each other. Let us compare the two situations which are expressed respectively by the two phrases: "I am remembering the tie which my friend wore yesterday" and "I am seeing a certain penny."

(1) Both are plainly situations with epistemological objects, and in both cases the epistemological object is known as soon as we understand the phrase which expresses the situation. In both cases the fact that the situation has such and such an epistemological object is wholly independent of the question whether there is an ontological object which accurately corresponds with the former. Here I must make much the same warning about the use of words as I did when discussing perception. There are memory-situations which we have good reason to think delusive; *e.g.*, George IV used to say that he remembered leading a charge at the Battle of Waterloo, and there is every reason to believe that he was never within a hundred miles of the battle. Now in common speech we should be inclined to say that he did not "really remember" the event in question, just as we are inclined to say that the drunkard does not "really see" pink rats. But in both cases this is to mix up psychological, epistemological, and ontological considerations in a way which is most detrimental to philosophical discussion. Assuming that the First Gentleman in Europe was correctly describing his state of mind, he was subject of a situation which has just as good a right to be called a memory-situation as a veridical memory of the Duke of Wellington on the

same subject-matter. It was a situation with a certain epistemological object, a certain kind of objective constituent, a certain kind of subjective constituent, and a certain characteristic kind of reference. There is nothing to distinguish it from what we should unhesitatingly call a memory-situation in the case of the Duke of Wellington, except that there probably is an ontological object accurately corresponding to the Duke's situation and that there almost certainly is not an ontological object corresponding to the King's. I therefore propose to call all such situations "memory-situations", regardless of whether there is or is not reason to think them delusive.

(2) In both cases, and for similar reasons, it is impossible to hold that the ontological object, even if there be one which accurately corresponds to the epistemological object, is literally and bodily a constituent of the situation. The most that we could plausibly hold in either case is that each situation contains an objective constituent which is literally a slice of the history of an ontological object that corresponds accurately to the epistemological object of the situation. The objective constituent of the perceptual situation in our example is a certain patch which looks brown and elliptical. To make the analogy as close as possible we will suppose that, when I am remembering my friend's tie, a visual image of it is before my mind. And we will take this visual image to be the objective constituent of the memory situation. Now the strongest claim that the perceptual situation can or does make is that this patch which looks brown and elliptical is literally a contemporary slice of the history of a certain enduring physical object, viz., the penny. And the strongest claim that the memory-situation could make with any plausibility is that the visual image is literally a past slice of the history of a certain enduring physical object, viz., my friend's tie. Whether it is any part of the memory-situation to make even this claim we shall have

to discuss later. But it certainly does not and cannot claim more than this.

(3) An essential feature in both kinds of situation is a belief which refers beyond the situation and its constituents. This belief may not be explicitly formulated ; but we are ready to act in accordance with it if occasion arises, and we are surprised if the results are such as would conflict with this belief. It is an essential factor in the perceptual situation that we believe that the penny now exists and that it is now manifesting certain aspects of itself to us. It is an essential factor in the memory-situation that we believe that the tie has existed and that a certain past phase of its history is now being manifested to us again. I leave the precise content of the memory-belief for more detailed discussion later.

(4) In both cases we may say that the belief is (a) based upon the existence and character of the objective constituent ; (b) refers beyond it to something which is not a constituent ; but (c) is not reached by a process of deductive or inductive inference from the existence and nature of the objective constituent. Memory-beliefs, like perceptual beliefs, not only *are* not reached by inference from the objective constituent of the situation but *cannot* be supported by such inference without logical circularity. When I remember the tie which my friend wore yesterday I do not first notice an image of a certain characteristic shape, colour, etc. ; then recollect the general principle that the power to have an image always originates in a past perceptual experience whose objective constituent resembles the image ; and then infer from these two premises that there must have existed a certain tie and that I must have seen it. And, if I did profess to reach my memory-judgments by an inference of this kind, the validity of my argument would be open to the following attack. How do I come to know the general principle that all images are copies of past sensa, which is an essential premise of the supposed inference? If we say that the general

principle is established inductively, we must suppose that there are *some* cases in which we can remember a past sensum, compare it with a present image, and notice that the latter resembles the former. Now these instances will be useless for establishing the general principle unless, in *these* cases at any rate, we can remember the past sensum *without* using the general principle and making an inference from it. It would therefore be impossible to establish the general principle inductively unless there be *some* non-inferential memory-judgments about past sensa. The only way of avoiding this objection would be to take the desperate step of saying that we know *a priori* that every image must be a copy of a past sensum, and that the power to call up an image must have originated through the sensing of this sensum. It seems to me quite plain that this principle is not *a priori*; and I do not know that anyone has ever asserted that it is so. Even Mr Hume, who had a conviction on the subject which seems to me to be quite unintelligible on his own principles, cannot have regarded the proposition as *a priori*; since he recognises and discusses the possibility of exceptions to it in the case of images of certain shades of colour.

Of course I am not maintaining that particular memory-judgments, like particular perceptual judgments, may not be supported or refuted by argument. They certainly can be. But the arguments always presuppose other memory-judgments which must simply be accepted on their own merits. If I claim to remember that my friend was wearing a tie of such and such a kind yesterday, and I find that he and other people who saw him agree with me, my memory-judgment will be supported. If I find that they disagree with me and agree with each other, my memory-judgment will be rendered improbable. But, in using this test, I presuppose the validity of their memory-judgments. Again, when I claim to remember a certain event, I may test my judgment by inferring what events would be likely to follow

such an event as I claim to be remembering. If I find
that I can remember and perceive these consequences,
my memory-judgment will be supported by inference.
If I find that I remember and perceive events which
are incompatible with these, my memory-judgment will
be made improbable. But, even when I test the
memory-judgment by present perception and not by
memory, I presuppose the general validity of my
memory-judgments. For I start by inferring that I
shall be likely to perceive so-and-so if the event which
I claim to remember really happened. And, if the
chain of inference be of any length, my guarantee for
the conclusion is my *memory* that the earlier stages of
the argument satisfied me. In exactly the same way
we may support or refute particular perceptual judgments by argument; but these arguments always presuppose the general validity of perceptual judgments and
the validity of certain particular perceptual judgments
made by myself or others.

(5) We see then that memory-judgments, like perceptual judgments, are "direct" or "immediate", in
the sense that they are not in fact reached by inference
from the nature and existence of the objective constituent of the situation, and that any such inference
would be logically circular. But there was another
sense in which we said that perceptual situations were
direct and immediate. We contrasted the two statements : "I am hearing the bell" and "I am thinking
about the bell"; and we said that the perceptual situation claimed to bring us into more direct cognitive
contact with objects than the thought-situation. This
we expressed by calling perceptual situations "intuitive"
and thought-situations "discursive". Of course perceptual judgments (like all judgments, whether reached
by inference or not) are "about" their subjects. But,
in the perceptual situation, we claim to be also in
peculiarly direct contact with the subject which the
perceptual judgment is about. Now, very closely

connected with this is the fact that the perceptual judgment is "sensuous". I think that the intuitive character of the perceptual situation lies in the fact that we are directly acquainted with the objective constituent, and that this constituent is regarded as being literally a part of the physical object which we are said to be perceiving. Can we say that the typical perceptual memory-situation is intuitive and sensuous?

(i) Ordinary language suggests that the memory-situation is intuitive and not discursive. We say "I remember my friend's tie", just as we say "I see my friend's tie". In neither case does the verbal expression for the situation contain a preposition like "about" before the phrase which stands for the epistemological object. (ii) The memory-situation often does contain as its objective constituent a visual or auditory image; and an image is obviously very much like a sensum. Nevertheless, it is not clear to me that the memory-situation is so obviously intuitive and sensuous as the perceptual situation. The connexion between the image and the remembered object seems much looser than the connexion between the sensum and the perceived object. In some cases the objective-constituent seems to be merely images of words; and in that case we cannot claim to be in direct contact with a past slice of the history of an object. And, even when the image is visual and is held to resemble a past phase of the remembered object, it is not clear to me that we claim that it is literally a part of the past history of the object. Thus we come here to a point at which the analogy between perceptual situations and perceptual memory-situations begins to fail. In the next section I propose to consider in more detail certain points, such as this, in which there seem to be essential differences between the two.

More detailed Discussion of certain Points. Under this heading I shall consider two closely connected points, viz., (i) the precise content of the memory-belief; and

(ii) the nature of the objective constituent and its connexion with the epistemological object. When I speak of the "content" of a memory-belief or a perceptual belief I mean the propositions which are believed in the typical memory- or perceptual situation. Now, in comparing the content of a memory-belief with that of a perceptual belief, there are two points to be considered. (*a*) Does the total content of one include some proposition to which nothing corresponds in the total content of the other? and (*b*) How far are the parts which may fairly be said to correspond analogous to each other? The latter question forms a transition to the question of the nature of the objective constituent of a memory-situation and its connexion with the epistemological object.

(i, *a*) When I am the subject of a perceptual situation I believe that such and such an event *is happening* and that it *is* part of the history of a certain physical object which still exists. But, so long as I merely perceive and do not begin to reflect on my perception, I do not believe anything about myself and my cognitive situations. When I am the subject of a perceptual memory-situation I believe that such and such an event *has happened*, and that it *was* part of the history of a certain physical object which may or may not still exist. This part of the content of the memory-belief is evidently analogous to the content of the perceptual belief. But is it the whole of the content of the memory-belief? When I remember an event do I not also always believe that I have perceived it as well as that it has happened? If so, there is an essential part of the content of every memory-belief which refers to myself and my past perceptual situations; and there is nothing analogous to this in the content of the perceptual belief.

There is, I think, no doubt that in most memory-situations I judge, not merely that "This happened before", but also that "I have perceived this before"; and that neither of these judgments is inferred from the other or from anything else. And I suppose that I could hardly judge that "I have perceived this before" without, *ipso facto*, judging that "This has happened before." The only question then is this: Are there any memory-situations in which I judge that "This happened before" and do not judge, in the same intuitive and non-inferential way, that "I have perceived this before"? I find this question very difficult to decide, for the following reasons.

In the first place, every one believes that, under normal circumstances, we cannot have direct and non-inferential knowledge of a past event unless we have in fact at some time perceived it. If we ask what can be the evidence for this universal belief, I think we shall find that it has two sources. (1) It is quite certain that, in the vast majority of cases in which I remember an event, I do also remember perceiving it. We might induce from this that, in *all* cases in which I remember an event, I must have perceived it; though, in a small minority, there are special circumstances which prevent me from remembering my perception of it. (2) We have a great difficulty in conceiving the causal mechanism by which we could have direct and non-inferential knowledge of a past event which we had never perceived. When we perceive anything we have a sensation, and this involves a characteristic change in our bodies. We think of this change as leaving a persistent "trace" in our bodies or minds or both, and we think of this trace as carrying with it the permanent possibility of intuitively apprehending the past event. But, if the event did not affect our bodies or our minds when it happened, we find it hard to conceive that it should be causally possible to have subsequent direct knowledge of the event. For my own part I think that there is decent evidence that, in certain abnormal cases, people do have direct knowledge of certain past events which they never perceived in their present bodily life. But the evidence is not known to most people; the phenomenon, if genuine at all, is very rare; and those who are acquainted with the alleged facts would admit that it is dangerous to put too much weight on them. I think then that we may start by accepting the following propositions, one about a matter of fact and the other about the usage of words. (1) It is almost universally held that we cannot have direct knowledge of a past event unless we have *in fact* perceived it, whether we *remember* doing so or not. And (2) if cases could be produced in which there was direct knowledge of unperceived past events, we should refuse to call such knowledge "memory". It is part of the meaning of the word "memory" that a perceptual memory-situation shall in fact be due to a past perceptual situation of the same subject. The question that remains is: Do situations ever arise in which a past event, which has in fact been perceived by us, is remembered whilst our perception of it is not remembered? And would such a situation be called a "memory-situation"?

I think it is certain that situations sometimes arise which it would be natural to describe as follows: "I remember that man's face, though I do not remember seeing it before." No doubt we should immediately add: "I must have seen it before." But this word "must" is the mark of an inferential belief, not of a direct intuitive one; and no doubt the inference is made from the generally accepted premise that I cannot remember anything unless I have at some time perceived it. Now, if this phraseology is to be taken at its face value, such situations *are* called "memory-situations", and the content of the memory-belief does *not* include the proposition: "I have seen this before." But I am not at all sure that this is the right interpretation. Memory-beliefs may be of various degrees of determinateness in at least three respects. In the first place, we may have a more or less determinate memory-belief about the qualities of the remembered object. We may, *e.g.*, remember that it was brick-red, or only that it had some shade or other of red, or only that it was either red or green. Secondly, we may have a more or less determinate memory-belief about the spatial relations and contemporary context of the remembered object. *E.g.*, we may remember that it was to the right of the fireplace in a certain room, or only that it was somewhere in this room, or only that it was somewhere in some room of a certain house, and so on. Lastly, we may have a more or less determinate memory of the temporal relations and the earlier and later context of the remembered object. We may remember that it happened just before dinner on Monday last, or that it happened some time last Monday, or only that it happened some time last week. Now it seems to me quite likely that, when we say that we remember a certain physical event or thing and that we do not remember perceiving it, we really mean only that our memory of our past perceptual situation is extremely indeterminate in these three respects whilst our memory of the event or thing is relatively determinate.

On this view the total belief which accompanies a memory-situation may always include a genuine memory-belief about our own past perception; but in certain cases the latter may be so extremely indeterminate that we say that we remember only the physical event and not the past perception of it. We must, however, recognise the following argument which favours the opposite view. Since we all believe strongly that nothing can be remembered unless it has been perceived by us, we shall almost inevitably infer when we remember an event that we must have perceived it. And we may very well confuse this natural and immediate *inference* with a genuine memory-belief; and thus think that the proposition: "I have perceived this" was part of the content of the original memory-belief, when really it is a reflective and inferential addition. In view of these two considerations which point in opposite directions I do not feel able to make up my mind on the

question ; and I must content myself with saying that
the majority of memory-situations do include a non-
inferential belief that the remembered object has been
perceived by us ; and that this belief may be of any
degree of indeterminateness. I think, however, that
the discussion is enough to refute a view which was
mentioned as possible earlier in the chapter ; viz., that
what we primarily remember is always our own past
perceptual situations, and that our knowledge of the
past physical events which we are said to " remember "
is derived from our memory of the perceptual situations
of which these events were the epistemological objects.
It is difficult to see how highly determinate beliefs
about a past physical event could be derived from a
knowledge of the situation in which it was perceived
which is so indeterminate that many people deny its
existence.

(i, *b* and ii) We have now to consider how far the
memory-belief that " This physical event happened and
formed part of the history of a certain physical object "
is analogous to the perceptual belief that " This physical
event is happening and is a contemporary part of the
history of a certain physical object." It is hardly
possible to discuss this question apart from that of the
nature of the objective constituent and its relation to the
epistemological object. I shall therefore take (i, *b*) and
(ii) together. There are, as usual, two questions, one
purely psychological and the other epistemological.
The purely psychological question is : " What does
the memory-situation *claim* to be the connexion between
its objective constituent and its epistemological object ? "
The epistemological question is : " What view about
the connexion between the two can be *justified* in face
of all the known facts?" I shall defer the second
question to the next section.

I will begin by taking a case where the memory
involves an imitative image. I will suppose that I am
remembering my friend's tie, in his absence ; and that

I have an imitative visual image of a tic. This makes
the analogy to sense-perception as close as possible;
so that any differences that we may discover will be
fundamental. Let us then contrast this situation with
that of seeing a penny, and judging that it is brown
and round. I will suppose that I judge that my friend's
tie was red. Now I think that the most notable difference between the two cases is the following. When I
am simply seeing a penny and making perceptual
judgments about it, and am not philosophising, I draw
no distinction between the objective constituent of the
situation and the surface of the penny. I am acquainted
with a certain particular (the objective constituent); I
regard it as part of the surface of the penny, and I
regard the qualities which seem to be sensuously manifested by it to me as, *ipso facto*, qualities of the penny.
It is true that I find on careful inspection and reflection
that the qualities which I have been ascribing to the
penny are not exactly those that are sensuously manifested to me in this situation, and that there are strong
reasons for refusing to identify the objective constituent
with the surface of the penny. But these views are
reached *only* by careful and critical reflection, and they
exist *only* while we are reflecting. They vanish at once
when we again begin to perceive, and the naïvely
realistic view is reinstated as if it had never been
questioned. Now it seems to me that, when I remember
my friend's tie by means of an imitative image, I do not
regard the image as literally a part of the surface of the
tie which existed yesterday, and I do not regard the
qualities which seem to be sensuously manifested to me
in the image as, *ipso facto*, qualities formerly possessed
by the tie. So far as I can judge, the perceptual
situation *definitely identifies* its objective constituent
with a contemporary part of the perceived object, whilst
the memory-situation *neither* identifies the image with a
past part of the object nor definitely distinguishes the
two. The memory-judgment most certainly is not:

"This, which I am now acquainted with, is a part of the tie as it was." But it also is not: "This, which I am now acquainted with, is numerically different from but qualitatively similar to a part of the tie as it was." It seems to me that both these suggested judgments are reflective theories about the memory-situation, and not judgments which form an essential factor in the memory-situation itself. While we are actually living through the memory-situation, and not philosophising about it, the belief that we have is vaguer than either of these suggested beliefs. If we want to put into words we must use some such formula as follows: "There is *some* peculiarly intimate relation between this, which I am now acquainted with, and a certain part of the tie as it was." And this statement must be taken neither to assert nor to deny that the two may be numerically identical.

The difference which I have been trying to indicate between the memory-situation and the perceptual situation may be expressed as follows. Naïve Realism is not merely a *theory about* perception; it is the explicit formulation of the belief which forms *an essential part* of the perceptual situation as such. But Naïve Realism is merely a *theory about* memory, just as the Sensum Theory is a theory about perception. All that the memory-situation itself claims is that *somehow* the image enables us to have an intuitive non-inferential knowledge of the occurrence of a certain past event and of some of its qualities and relations. That it enables us to do this because it is numerically identical with the past event is neither asserted nor denied in the memory-situation itself. It is perhaps worth while to make the following remark at this stage. The facts which make it difficult or impossible to accept on reflexion the naïvely realistic claims of perception are by no means obvious. In order to recognise them we have to inspect our sensa with special care; to compare notes with others; to know something of the physiology of the nervous system, and of physical optics ; and so on. It is therefore plausible to suppose that, if we start with an innate tendency towards naïvely realistic perceptual beliefs, the tendency will be so strengthened by habit in childhood that no arguments will eradicate it in practice later on. But the difficulties about a naïvely realistic view of memory are glaring, and need no special knowledge or careful inspection to reveal them ; as we shall see in the next section. Hence, even if we started with a tendency to identify the memory-image with the remembered event (which there is no reason to think that we do), it seems doubtful whether it would survive the continual assaults of the objections which would arise almost automatically even in the least reflective mind.

I have so far taken a case in which the objective constituent of the memory-situation is an imitative image, and have argued that even here it is no part of the memory-belief to claim that the image is numerically identical with a certain slice of the past history of the remembered object. I wish now to consider cases in which the memory-situation does not contain an imitative image as a constituent. It seems certain that there are such cases ; and I think that a discussion of them will throw light on the part played by the imitative image in those cases where it is present. Even if it be granted that all perceptual memory-situations contain images of some kind as objective constituents and that these images play an analogous part to that which is played by sensa in perceptual situations, it must be granted that the connexion between the objective constituent and the epistemological object is much looser in the memory-situation than in the perceptual situation. I will now try to illustrate this point.

Suppose that someone says to me : " Was the tie that your friend wore yesterday, red?" I may answer at once : " I remember quite distinctly that it was *not* red, but I cannot remember what its colour was." I

will call this a "negative memory-situation". Now
there is nothing in perception which is strictly analogous
to this. Of course, if my friend is wearing a green tie
and I am looking at it and am not colour-blind, I can
say : "I see plainly that his tie is not red." But I
say that it is not red, and that I see that it is not,
because I *do* see that it is green. I should never say
that I *see* that it is not red unless I also *saw* that it
had such and such another colour. The perceptual
denial of a certain determinate colour depends upon
the perceptual recognition of the presence of another
determinate colour. But the memory-denial of a certain
colour, so far from depending on the memory-recognition
of another determinate colour, may precede the latter
and may exist though the latter never supervenes on it.
Now, in the negative memory-situation at least, the
presence of an imitative image seems quite unnecessary.
It may happen of course that, when the word "red"
is mentioned by the questioner to me, I have a red
image ; but, so long as I understand the meaning of
the word "red" in *any* way, the negative memory-
situation may arise even though there is no red image.
And in many cases I am quite sure that I understand
the meaning of the word and that the memory-situation
does arise in the absence of a red image. Again, it
may of course happen that I have an image which does
in fact resemble my friend's tie in colour ; though it
is evident that I do not recognise the fact at the time.
But it is quite certain that the presence of such an
image is not essential to the negative memory-situation,
and that the latter does in fact quite often arise in the
absence of the former.

When I try to analyse a negative memory-situation
as carefully as I can the essential point about it seems
to be the following. In some way or other a certain
determinate characteristic is presented to me for consideration. It may be presented by an imitative image,
or by actually hearing and understanding the word

which stands for it without using an imitative image, or by calling up for myself an image of the sound or the appearance of this word. The method of presentation seems to be absolutely unimportant so long as it succeeds in making me think of the characteristic in question. The other factor is that I then have a peculiar feeling which can only be described by the phrase : "This doesn't *fit* the object". Of course the feeling is one thing and the judgment is another; but this is the kind of judgment which we consider to express and to be justified by this kind of feeling. Lastly, the belief that the characteristic does not fit the object is not based on a comparison with the object and its remembered characteristics. For, if it were, the negative memory-situation, like the negative perceptual judgment, could not exist apart from the corresponding positive situation; whereas the former certainly can and does exist apart from the latter. The nearest analogy that I can give is that of trying a lock in the dark with a number of keys that do not fit it.

Let us now consider a positive memory-situation. Suppose that I go on trying various suggested colours, red, blue, yellow, etc., and that they all fail to fit. At last, perhaps, I try green and I have a new and unique kind of feeling which I should express by the statement : "This fits the object". I then say that I remember that the tie was green. This feeling, which is naturally expressed by the judgment : "It fits the object", and is regarded as justifying that judgment, is the characteristic mark of a positive memory-situation. And up to this point no imitative image has been needed. There is no more need for the alternative which does fit to be presented for consideration by an imitative image than for the various alternatives which did not fit to be presented in this way. But at this point an imitative image very often does supervene; and then I think we are said, not merely to remember things about the object, but in the strictest sense to remember the object. (Of course, in a looser sense, we are said to remember an object provided we remember anything about it.)

In the examples which I have just been giving we are supposed to be *trying* to remember something, and to succeed after failures. In other cases it seems to me that the imitative image comes first. It floats up; we notice certain characteristics in it which are felt to fit a certain past object, and others which are felt not to fit it. And the two processes may happen alternately. I may begin by merely remembering things about an object; then I may have an imitative image of it; and finally I may read off from the image further characteristics which are felt to fit the object, and so may remember further things about it. The essential point is the felt fitting or non-fitting of suggested characteristics; the way in which these characteristics are presented for our consideration is of minor importance.

I think that I can now state more clearly what seem to me to be the essential points of difference between perceptual situations and even *perceptual* memory-situations. (1) All perceptual denials are based upon perceptual affirmations of determinate characteristics which are incompatible with the characteristic which is denied. But there are *independent* memory-denials, which are not based in this way on corresponding memory-affirmations. This fact should lead us to suspect that there may be important differences between positive memory - situations and positive perceptual situations even where they seem most alike. (2) It is true that we say both that we perceive objects and that we perceive propositions about objects. I see a tie, and I see that the tie is green. But the latter is regarded as dependent on the former. When I say that I perceive a tie I do not seem to mean merely that I know various propositions by perception, such as "This is green", "This is long and thin"; that all these propositions have a common subject; and that the tie is known only as the common subject of all these perceptually known propositions. On the contrary I claim to be directly acquainted with a part of the tie ; and the propositions which I claim to perceive about it seem to be "read off" from the object itself. The object (or, at any rate, a literal part of it) seems to be "given" bodily; and the perceptual judgments profess to "analyse" it. Now, in spite of some appearances to the contrary I believe that the opposite is true of perceptual memory. I believe that what is primarily known by memory is propositions like "This was green", "This was long and thin", etc. ; and that this is true both in positive and in negative memory-situations. Certain groups of such propositions are recognised to have a common subject ; and the object is "remembered" only in so far as it is known as the common subject of such a group of remembered propositions. (3) In many cases an imitative image of the remembered object supervenes at this stage ; and in some cases such an image comes first, and the characteristics which are asserted or denied in the memory-judgments are presented to our attention by it. It is in this last case that perceptual memory is most like perception ; but even here it does not seem to me that we claim to be in direct cognitive contact with an actual fragment of the past history of the object and to be "reading off" the memory - propositions from this fragment. (4) The essential factor in the memory - situation is that peculiar feeling which seems to justify the judgment that a certain characteristic fits or fails to fit a certain past object. The characteristic need not be, and generally is not, presented to our attention by means of imitative images. And the object which the characteristic is felt to fit or fail to fit is not cognised by direct and sensuous acquaintance, as it seems to be in sense-perception, but is presented only to thought as the subject of such and such propositions.

Thus, although perceptual memory agrees with

sense-perception in the fact that the memory-judgment, like the perceptual judgment, is not inferential, I believe that it differs from sense-perception in that it is not strictly intuitive or sensuous. Some perceptual memory-situations certainly seem at first sight to have these latter characteristics; but it seems to me that careful inspection and comparison show that none of them really do so. And I think that the function of imitative images in perceptual memory has been greatly exaggerated. It is perhaps relevant to add that I am myself a strong visualiser, and that memory with me does in fact generally involve imitative imagery; so, if I am wrong on this point, my mistake is certainly not due identifying a personal defect with a law of nature, as the Behaviourists do when they deny the existence of images.

Epistemological Questions about Perceptual Memory. So far I have attempted nothing but a descriptive analysis of perceptual memory-situations, and a careful statement of what they really do claim. I must now consider what claims would be *justified* on the part of the memory-situation. If I am right, the perceptual situation makes a stronger claim than we can admit to be justified. For every perceptual situation claims that its objective constituent is literally a part of the perceived physical object; and this claim is certainly false in some cases and extremely hard to maintain in any. Now it is of course possible that the memory-situation goes to the other extreme and is too modest in its claims. If I am right, it does not claim that its objective constituent is literally a part of the past event which it remembers; nevertheless this claim might be justified, and the New Realists may only be asking on behalf of the memory-situation what it is too modest to ask for itself. There are two reasons for wanting to be as realistic as possible about perception. One is that we are then running with the stream and defending what we all in fact believe except when we are philosophising. The other

is that the rejection of the claim of the objective constituent of a perceptual situation to be literally a part
of the perceived physical object makes it hard to explain
how we can possibly know that there are physical
objects and that perception gives us trustworthy information about them. Now there is not the first motive for
a naïvely realistic view of memory; but there is no
doubt the second motive. Unless the objective constituents of some memory-situations be literally identical
with the events remembered, how, it might be asked,
can we possibly know that there are past events and that
memory gives us trustworthy information about them?
What we have now to consider is whether any such
claim could be admitted even if it were made.

I will first try to show, as I did in the case of perception, that, even if the naïvely realistic view could be
accepted, it would by itself go but a very small way in
meeting the attacks of a sceptic. To be sure that there
are past events or that there are physical objects it is
not enough to be acquainted directly with what is *in
fact* a past event or a literal part of a physical object;
we need in some way to *know* that this is what we
are acquainted with. Now, if there were no delusive
memory-situations, or if it were found on careful inspection that those which are delusive differ internally
from those which are not, it might be suggested that
every memory-situation is accompanied by a kind of
infallible revelation that its objective constituent is
literally identical with some past event. But it is
certain that there are totally delusive memory-situations,
such as that of which George IV was subject. And it
is certain that there is no *inner* difference which distinguishes them from memory-situations which are
commonly believed to be veridical. Hence we must
deny that there is an infallible revelation that we are in
direct contact with the past in any case. And, in the
absence of this, the mere fact (if it be a fact) that the
objective constituents of some memory-situations are

actually past events does not explain how we know that there are past events or how we know that we have trustworthy information through memory about some of them. We shall still have to rely entirely on the *external* tests of agreement or disagreement of one memory-judgment with others, and of agreement or disagreement between inferences from memory-judgments and present perceptions.

The most that we can say then is that the claim which the extreme realists make for the memory-situation *may* sometimes be true, though it is certainly sometimes false. Can we go so far even as this? (1) I will first mention the only point, so far as I am aware, on which the memory-situation is in a stronger position than the perceptual situation in making such a claim. There is nothing in memory corresponding to the *systematic* difference in the apparent shapes and sizes of perceived objects when viewed by observers from different positions. Now it was this which made it so very hard to believe that the objective constituent of a visual situation can be literally a part of the surface of the perceived physical object. Nevertheless there often are positive discrepancies between different people who profess to be remembering the same event, and between successive memories of the same event by the same person. The mere fading of details as the event retreats further into the past presents no particular difficulty for a naïvely realistic view of memory ; but the memory of details which are positively inconsistent with each other on different occasions when we profess to be remembering the same event does present a very serious difficulty.

(2) I will now consider the special objections which might be made against a naïvely realistic theory of memory. (*a*) The first is a general metaphysical objection, which I believe to be baseless. It might be said that, when an event is past, it ceases to exist. Now, when I am remembering a past event, the memory-situation certainly exists and so does its objective con-

stituent. Hence, it is said, the objective constituent of a memory-situation cannot be identical with the past event which is being remembered. This objection seems to me to be mistaken. It depends on a view of time and change which I am forced to reject. It appears to me that, once an event has happened, it exists eternally; all that happens henceforth to it is that, as more and more events occur and take their permanent place in the ever-lengthening temporal order of the universe, it retreats into the more and more distant past. If an event ceased to exist as soon as it ceased to be present it plainly could no longer stand in any relations to anything. But, when we say that it is past, we imply that it does stand in the relation of temporal precedence to the present; moreover, we say that one past event precedes a second past event and follows a third. All such statements would be nonsensical if events ceased to exist when they ceased to be present. It is perfectly true that certain objects which have existed (*e.g.*, the town of Old Sarum) have ceased to *per*sist. But this means only that after a certain time none of the events which happened were such as to continue the history of these particular objects; the earlier series of events which constitute the history of such objects are nevertheless a permanent part of the universe, considered as an existent which is extended in time. There is then no general metaphysical objection to a naïvely realistic view of memory. Past events are always "there" waiting to be remembered, and there is no *a priori* reason why they should not from time to time enter into such a relation with certain present events that they become objects of direct acquaintance. There is no *a priori* reason why a cognitive relation should not bridge a temporal gap, and connect a present mental event with a past event of any kind whatever.

(*b*) The second difficulty is much more serious. Suppose that I remember the same event on several occasions, and that the objective constituent of each of these memory-situations is an imitative image. If the naïvely realistic theory of memory be right, this image is literally and numerically the same in all cases; it *is* the past event or a part of it; and so its date is that of the past event. On the other hand, the image certainly seems to be present on each occasion; and we should certainly judge that we were concerned with as many different and successive images as there are different and successive memory-situations, even though all these images were exactly alike in their qualities. Again, suppose that when I perceived the event I had a twinge of toothache; and that when I first remembered it I had no toothache, but a tickling sensation in my throat. I should certainly judge that the original event was contemporary with this twinge of toothache and preceded the tickling sensation. And I should certainly judge that the image was contemporary with the tickling sensation and not with the twinge of toothache. If the naïvely realistic view of memory be true it would seem that the same event can be both contemporary with a certain other event and can also succeed this event by a long interval.

The present difficulty is evidently analogous to that which arises on the naïvely realistic theory of perception over mirror-images and "seeing double". There we seem to see an object in a place which is remote from its real position, or we seem to see several distinct though qualitatively similar objects in different places, whilst the theory requires that there shall be only one. Here we seem to be aware of a series of distinct images which are separated in time, whilst the theory requires that the objective constituents of all the memory-situations shall be numerically identical and shall have a certain one date in the past. In face of this situation the naïvely realistic theory of memory might take one of three courses. (1) It might suggest that the image only seems to be present, whereas it is really past; and that it only seems contemporary with the tickling sensation, whereas it really precedes it and is contemporary with the twinge of toothache. Or (ii) it might suggest that we are using words in an ambiguous way. Perhaps when we say that the image is present and the original event is past we are using "present" in one sense and "past" in another. The statements may then be compatible with each other. And the same explanation may apply to the statements that the image is contemporary with a tickling sensation, whilst the original event is contemporary with a twinge of toothache and precedes the tickling sensation. *E.g.*, the two statements: "Napoleon was greater than Og, King of Bashan" and: "Napoleon was less than Og, King of Bashan" may both be true if one refers to their relative heights and the other to their respective achievements. Or (iii) it might suggest that we are not using words ambiguously, but that temporal relations are not dyadic, so that the minimum complete statement about the temporal relations of two events is of the form: "x is contemporary with y (or precedes, or follows y) with respect to z." In that case, when we say that the image is contemporary with the tickling sensation whilst the original event precedes the tickling sensation, both statements may be true even though the image is identical with the original event. For we may be using a different third term of reference in the two cases.

I think it is possible that when we say that an image is obviously *present* each time we remember a certain event we may only be justified in saying that it is *presented* each time, *i.e.*, that it is an objective constituent of each situation and an object of acquaintance. Now "being present*ed*" is certainly one of the tests that we use for "being pres*ent*"; but it may not be an infallible test. Now of course, on the usual view of time, the same event cannot be present more than once; but there is no *a priori* reason why it might not be presented to acquaintance dozens of times, and it is of the essence of the naïvely realistic theory of memory to hold that this actually happens. Suppose then that, when we say that the image is present, we are justified only in saying that it is presented. If we think that it is present we shall infer that we must be dealing with a different image on each occurrence of the memory - situation. And yet really we may be dealing with a single entity which is presented many times but is present only once. I think it must be admitted that we have not the same direct and overpowering evidence that we are acquainted with a number of different images in a series of memory-situations with the same epistemological object, as we have for saying that we are acquainted with two distinct sensa when we "see double". In the latter case it is certain that no inference is involved; nothing is needed but inspection. In the former case I am not at all certain that the statement is guaranteed by inspection; I think that it may well rest on inference. And, as I have just pointed out, the premise of the inference might be derived from an uncritical jump from "presentedness" to "presentness." Similarly, when we say that the image is contemporary with the tickling sensation, we may only be justified in saying that both are presented together. And it may be that co-presentedness, though a test for co-presence, is not an infallible test. The original event might be presented (in perception) along with a twinge of toothache and apart from a tickling sensation, and it may be again presented (in memory) along with a tickling sensation and apart from a twinge of toothache. If we think that co-presentation is an infallible sign of co-presence we shall be forced to distinguish between the original event and the memory - image of it, or else to hold that simultaneity is a triadic relation. But, if we admit that the two relations are different, and that the former is not an infallible sign of the latter, we could hold that one and the same event is objective constituent of the original perceptual situation and of the subsequent memory-situation. This event is both co-present and co-presented with the twinge of toothache, whilst it is co-presented but not co-present with the tickling sensation. Thus I think that the naïvely realistic theory of memory could answer the present objection ; provided it is allowed to distinguish between presentness and presentedness and between co-presence and co-presentedness, to hold that the latter can occur without the former, and to hold that one and the same event can be presented at various times to the same mind. This last point leads us to the third possible objection.

(c) It is commonly held that the past cannot change. Would the naïvely realistic theory of memory be consistent with this doctrine? And, if it is not, ought we unhesitatingly to reject it? We must begin by distinguishing between pure qualities and relations. I think that every one would admit that an event cannot change in respect of any pure quality which it had when it happened. If it was, e.g., a red flash, it cannot cease to be red and become green. Again, I think it would be admitted that an event cannot change its relations, in the sense of ceasing to be related in a certain way to contemporary or earlier events and becoming related in different ways to them. But it seems to me that events can and do change, in the sense that they acquire additional relations through the occurrence of later events. This seems to me quite clear about temporal and causal relations. Queen Anne's death now precedes Queen Victoria's by so many years, and will do so for ever ; but there was a time when Queen Anne's death preceded nothing. And, until Queen Victoria had died, Queen Anne's death stood in no relation whatever to the event which we now call "Queen Victoria's death". For there was then no such event ; and an event cannot stand in any relation to a mere nonentity. Again, Queen Anne's death caused a feeling of annoyance in the Duke of Berwick when he heard of it ; but it certainly did not stand in the causal relation to the Duke's feeling of annoyance until the Duke began to feel annoyed, which he did not until he heard of the death. There is then, in my opinion, no objection to holding that past events change, in the sense of acquiring relations to events which follow them. And this is the only kind of change in past events which the naïvely realistic theory of memory absolutely requires. It requires that the same event shall from time to time become a constituent of successive memory-situations. But the memory - situations are simply fresh events which happen after the remembered event is past ; and whenever a past event is remembered it has simply acquired a relation to a certain later event, which it naturally could not do until that later event had happened. It is worth while to remark that even universals and other timeless entities can change in an analogous way to past events. The quality of redness is timeless ; nevertheless it sometimes characterises one thing, sometimes another, and sometimes perhaps nothing at all. Again, it is sometimes thought of by me, sometimes by you, and sometimes perhaps by no one at all. Thus even the timeless may acquire certain additional relational properties through the happening of new events ; and precisely the same is true of the past. It must be admitted then that the naïvely realistic theory of memory necessarily involves the proposition that past events change in certain respects ; but it must also be admitted that there is no objection to the kind of change which it involves in past events. This brings us to the last objection which I propose to consider.

(d) If the objective constituent of a memory-situation were found to differ in some of its pure qualities from the remembered event, it would seem to be impossible to identify the two. For the attempt to do so would involve the proposition that a past event had changed in respect to some of its pure qualities. And this is plainly impossible. I want to make quite clear what kind of qualitative difference between memory-image and remembered event would be fatal to the naïvely realistic theory of memory, and what kind would not, before I consider whether such differences are actually found. (i) A visual sensum must in fact have some perfectly determinate shade of colour ; and so must a visual image. If the memory-image is to be incidental with the remembered sensum it is impossible that the determinate shade of the one should differ from that of the other. But it is one thing for a sensum or image to *have* such and such a determinate shade, and another thing for us to be able to *judge* that it has it. Our judgments about the determinate characteristics of an object may be of various degrees of determinateness, and they are no doubt never completely determinate. Now it might be that, when an event is presented in sensation, we are able to make more determinate judgments about its colour, for instance, than we can do when precisely the same event with precisely the same determinate shade of colour is presented in a memory-situation. If the only difference between the memory-situation and the corresponding perceptual situation is that the former permits of less determinate judgments about the same determinable characteristic than the latter, the memory-image and the remembered sensum may in fact be identical. But, if we can see that the image has a different determinate characteristic from the original sensum, the two cannot be identical ; and the naïvely realistic theory of memory falls to the ground. (ii) Much the same remarks apply to differences of internal detail or external relation between the original sensum and the memory-image. Both must, in fact, be perfectly determinate in these respects. If the difference merely is that we can detect more detail in the perceptual situation than we can in the memory-situation, the image and the sensum may be identical, and the naïvely realistic theory of memory may be true. But, if we can detect details in the images which differ from and are inconsistent with those of the sensum, the two cannot be identical ; and the theory falls to the ground. What are the actual facts?

In the first place, there is a systematic and directly noticeable difference between the corresponding characteristics of sensa and of images. An auditory image never sounds exactly like an auditory sensum, and a visual image never looks exactly like a visual sensum. No doubt there are marginal cases where this systematic difference is hard to detect. A very faint sensum may be hard to distinguish by its intrinsic qualities from an image, and a very vivid image may be hard to distinguish by its intrinsic qualities from a sensum. But in general there is not the slightest difficulty in recognising that an image looks and sounds different from the sensum of which it is said to be a copy. Secondly, when I remember a thing or event by means of an imitative image, I can often say quite definitely that there are certain details in the image which are different from and inconsistent with corresponding details in the original. I may, *e.g.*, call up an imitative image of my friend's head ; and I may be able to say with complete conviction : "His hair is like that, but his nose is not of that shape." And, if I can often detect these positive differences of detail between the memory-image and the original, it is reasonable to suppose that they still more often exist when I cannot be sure that they do. Now it is impossible to believe that a past event actually undergoes a systematic change of intrinsic quality through lapse of time. And it is impossible to hold that a past event can undergo positive changes of internal detail through lapse of time. Hence we must either refuse to identify the memory-image with the remembered event ; or we must hold that the image can seem to have characteristics which differ from and are inconsistent with those which it really does have ; or that the characteristics which we detect when we are subjects of a memory-situation inhere in some different way from those which we detected when we were subjects of a perceptual situation. These three alternatives are analogous to the three which presented themselves when we tried to be naïvely realistic about perception.

I do not think that the theory of two kinds of inherence will help us in defending a naïvely realistic view of memory. It seems quite clear that, if the characteristics which we seem to detect in images really inhere in them at all, they inhere in them in precisely the same way in which the characteristics which we seem to detect in sensa inhere in the latter. There does not seem to be the least reason to believe that the "is" in the two propositions : " This sensum is red " and " This image is green " stands for two different modes of inherence, such that the two statements would be compatible even though " This sensum " and " This image " were identical. A theory of triadic inherence for colours has a certain plausibility in dealing with perception, when we remember that the apparent colour of what we call "the same surface" varies according to the position and internal state of the percipient's body. But what is needed for the present purpose is that the colours, etc., which we detect when we are in a memory-situation shall inhere in some different way from the colours, etc., which we detect when we are in a perceptual situation. And we know of nothing that makes this suggestion plausible. I think then that we may rule out this line of defence for naïve realism about memory. We are, therefore, reduced to saying that naïve realism about memory is possible only on the supposition that memory-images can seem to have characteristics and details which are other than and inconsistent with those which they really do have.

We must note that this last statement needs a little further refinement. The essential point is that, when I remember something which I have perceived, the objective constituent of the memory-situation often seems to have characteristics and details which are, and are recognised at the time to be, other than and inconsistent with certain characteristics and details which the objective constituent of the perceptual situation seemed to have. I make this modification in case anyone accepts the theory that the objective constituent of a perceptual situation does not have the characteristics which it seems to have. Thus we may restate the position as follows. We can identify the memory-image with the original sensum only on the supposition that one and the same event can seem to have one set of details and characteristics when it is the objective constituent of a perceptual situation and can seem to have another set of details and characteristics, partly inconsistent with the former, when it is the objective constituent of a memory-situation. Moreover, I must be able to *know*, with regard to certain determinate characteristics which the object now seems to have, that it did not seem to have these and did seem to have others when I perceived it. *E.g.*, I may remember my friend's face, and I may remember that when I saw him his hair appeared to be bright yellow and his nose straight. Yet the image (which, on the present theory, is identical with the past sensum) may seem to have hair of a washy straw-colour and a crooked nose.

Now it is no doubt theoretically possible to hold that the sensum and the memory-image are numerically identical in spite of the inconsistency between their apparent determinate characteristics in the perceptual situation and in the memory-situation. But I fail to see what advantage accrues to the theory of memory from this supposed numerical identity. On any view I manage somehow to remember the original apparent characteristics by means of the different and incompatible apparent characteristics which are manifested in the memory-situation. If there is any mystery in this, I cannot see that it is in any way lessened by the supposition of a *de facto* numerical identity of image and sensum which is plainly contrary to all the appearances.

I may now sum up what I have to say about the naïvely realistic theory of memory. (i) That the memory-image and the objective constituent of the original perceptual situation are numerically identical is a claim made, not *by* the memory-situation, but *for* it by certain philosophers. Hence this proposition has not the same strong antecedent claim on our belief which Naïve Realism about perception undoubtedly does have. (ii) The motive for a naïvely realistic theory of memory is undoubtedly the belief that, unless we are in direct cognitive contact with past events in memory, it is impossible to explain how we come to have the very notion of "pastness" or how we have trustworthy non-inferential beliefs about particular past events. Now this presupposes that the objective constituent of a memory-situation literally is past; and that we recognise its pastness in the memory-situation just as we recognise the redness of a sensum, which is in fact red, in a perceptual situation. Such a view cannot be maintained in face of totally delusive memory-situations. For in them the objective constituent manifests the very same characteristic which we took to be "pastness" in other situations. And here the objective constituent is not identical with a certain past event which we claim to be remembering, for there is no such event. Thus, even if the objective constituents of some memory-situations be *in fact* past events, it cannot be admitted that there is any infallible revelation of their pastness in the memory-situation. The objective constituent of a memory-situation does no doubt manifest a certain peculiar characteristic which we take as a *sign* of pastness. But the existence of totally delusive memory-situations, and their internal likeness to veridical ones, show that this manifested characteristic *is not* pastness and is not even an infallible sign of pastness. Thus naïve realism about memory, even if it be sometimes true, fails altogether to solve the epistemological problem which gave rise to it.

(iii) The *a priori* objections to a naïvely realistic theory of memory, based on the nature of time and change, are invalid. Past events exist henceforth eternally; there is therefore no *a priori* objection to their being objective constituents of existent memory - situations. And, although the theory requires that past events shall be liable to a certain kind of change, this is not an objection. For it is a kind of change to which past events and even timeless entities may be subject without contradiction. (iv) It is not a conclusive objection to the theory that the memory-image seems to be present each time the same event is remembered and that the memory-image seems to be contemporary with events which the remembered event precedes. There are various ways round this difficulty; and perhaps the simplest and most plausible is to draw a distinction between "presentness" (which cannot be repeated) and "presentedness" (which can), and to hold that the latter is a sign but not an infallible sign of the former. (v) The most serious difficulty is that we can recognise a *general* qualitative difference between any image and any sensum, and *specific* differences in detail and in determinate characteristics between a memory-image and the remembered sensum. This can be reconciled with the naïvely realistic theory of memory only on the assumption that the same event can appear to have different and incompatible details and determinate characteristics according to whether it is the objective constituent of a perceptual situation or of a memory-situation. Such an hypothesis is not impossible; but it entails the conclusion that either in the memory-situation or in the perceptual situation (and possibly in both) an event appears to have determinate characteristics which are other than and incompatible with those which it really does have. The conclusion seems to be that, if the naïvely realistic theory of memory had anything to recommend it, it would be possible to hold it provided we made odd enough supplementary assumptions. But there are, so far as I can see, no reasons direct or indirect for holding the theory.

I must now raise the question which was raised by the naïvely realistic theory of memory, and which the latter failed to answer. If past events be never constituents of memory-situations, or if at any rate they never manifest the characteristic of pastness as sensa manifest colours, etc., how do we come to have the notion of "pastness" at all? It will be remembered that a similar question arose over the origin of the notion of a "physical object". Underlying such questions there is a particular theory about the origin of our knowledge of universal characteristics which is explicitly stated by Mr Hume and tacitly assumed by nearly every one else. The theory may be roughly stated as follows. If a universal characteristic be simple and unanalysable we can form a concept of it only by being acquainted with some particular which has or seems to have this characteristic. If the characteristic be complex and analysable, we may be able to form a concept of it without being acquainted with any particular which has or seems to have *it;* but we must have been acquainted with particulars which between them had or seemed to have all its simple constituents. *E.g.*, red is a simple characteristic; and it seems obvious that we could not have had the notion of redness unless we had been subjects of certain cognitive situations whose objective constituents were or seemed to be red. The really important point is that the particulars in question should *seem to have* the characteristic. For it certainly would not suffice that they should have it without seeming to have it; whilst, so far as we can tell, it would suffice if they seemed to have it even though they really did not have it, if this be possible. Now the trouble is that pastness is certainly a simple characteristic, and that the peculiar characteristic which memory-images seem to have cannot be identified with pastness, for the reasons given above. At most this

characteristic can be taken as a sign of pastness; but
how can I know this unless in some cases I have found
pastness and this other characteristic together? And
how can I have done so if no instance of apparent
pastness is ever presented to my acquaintance?

If we accept Hume's principle the question seems
insoluble. It is even more intractable than the similar
question about the origin of the concept of "physical
object". For it might be argued (though not, I think,
successfully) that the concept of "physical object" is
complex, and is constructed by us from simpler concepts
which are abstracted from sense-experience. But I do
not think that anyone could maintain this view about
pastness. One solution would be to give up Hume's
principle; which is what I have done over the notion
of "physical object". I should then draw a distinction
between "empirical" and "categorial" characteristics.
I should call "red", "hard", etc., "empirical characteristics", and I should be inclined to maintain Hume's
principle about the origin of our concepts of these.
I should count "physical object" "pastness" "causation", etc., as "categorial characteristics", and I should
be inclined to deny Hume's principle about the origin
of our concepts of the latter. I see nothing self-evident
or sacrosanct about Hume's principle; it seems to work
well for empirical characteristics, like colour, and to
cause nothing but trouble over categorial characteristics,
like cause or substance. The two kinds of characteristic
are obviously extremely different, and there would be
nothing in the least surprising in the fact (if it were
a fact) that our concepts of the one arose in a quite
different way from our concepts of the other. I am
not assuming of course that categorial concepts are
"innate", in the sense that we are born thinking of
cause, substance, etc. So far as I can see each such
concept arises only on the occasion of certain specific
kinds of experience, which can be analysed and described with fair accuracy. There are three stages in

the development of these categorial concepts. At the first stage they exist only in the sense that, on the occasion of certain kinds of experience, we act *as if* we were recognising the presence of causation, of substance, etc. This stage is reached by all men and probably by the higher animals. A dog, in the situation described as "seeing a bone", *treats* his visual sensa as appearances of a permanent and present physical object; and, in the situation called "hearing the dinner-bell," he acts *as if* he believed there to be a causal connexion between dinner-bells and food. At the second stage we make explicit judgments involving the categories in question; *e.g.*, "Quinine tastes bitter and gives me a headache." This stage is probably reached by all sane men, and probably not by any animals. Then there is a third stage at which we do not merely act *as if* we recognised the categories, and do not merely make particular judgments which *involve* the categories, but contemplate the categories as such and make reflective judgments about them. This stage is reached only by philosophers while philosophising.

Let us now apply these general remarks to the particular problem under discussion. I suggest that the objective constituents of memory-situations are not in fact past and that they do not even seem to be past. But they do seem to have (and there is no reason to doubt that they actually do have) a certain peculiar characteristic which is not manifested by most images or most sensa. Let us call this "familiarity". Now we are so constituted that, when we are subjects of a cognitive situation whose objective constituent manifests the characteristic of familiarity, we inevitably apply the concept of pastness; and, if we make an explicit judgment, it takes the form: "There *was* an event which *had* such and such empirical characteristics." Familiarity is an empirical characteristic and pastness is a categorial characteristic; but the former "means" the latter to such beings as we are; and this "meaning" is primitive and unacquired, in the sense that it is not, like most meaning, due to the repeated manifestation of the two characteristics together. This is the only account that I can recommend of "how we come to Have the notion of pastness at all". I owe the notion of "unacquired meaning" to Professor Stout; though I do not know in the least whether he would accept my exposition of it or the particular applications which I have made of the notion.

If the reader cannot accept the above suggestion I have only one other to make, and I am not prepared to lay much stress on it. The suggestion is this. The specious present has a certain small temporal extension. Now it might be said that the earlier objective constituents of the specious present are actually past and that they manifest the characteristic of pastness. On this view pastness is an empirical characteristic which is manifested by part of the total objective constituent of a specious present, and we form the concept of "pastness" by abstraction in the same way in which we form the concept of "redness". We then apply this concept beyond the contents of the specious present, just as we apply the concept of redness to things that we have never seen. We might then suppose that the earlier parts of the total content of the specious present manifest both pastness and familiarity, so that familiarity has *acquired* for us the meaning of pastness. The objective constituent of the memory-situation manifests familiarity but not pastness; but we read pastness into it through the association which has been formed between these two characteristics in the case of the contents of the specious present. I do not think myself that this suggestion will work. Apart from any other difficulties the following strikes me as serious. If familiarity has come to represent pastness to us because the two are manifested together in the earlier part of the content of the specious present, I should expect the result of the association to be that, finding the memory-image to seem familiar, we should ascribe pastness to *it*. For in the specious present, on the theory under discussion, what seemed familiar *itself* seemed past. But we do not in fact regard the memory-image itself as past. The familiarity of the image makes us think of some event, *other than* the image, as past; and makes us say that *this* event had or had not such and such characteristics which are suggested to us by the image. I do not see that the present theory will account for this fact.

The question: "How do we come to have the concept of pastness?" is one question, and I have tried to answer it to the best of my ability. The question: "What right have we to believe that we have rightly applied the concept of pastness in any particular case?" is a different one. I have already said that we have no infallible revelation on the subject; that we can indeed test our memory-judgments by comparison and inference, but only on the assumption of the general trustworthiness of memory. I have only one thing to add. There are "secondary signs" of pastness; just as there are "secondary signs" of distance, such as the size, clearness, etc., of the visual sensum. By this I mean simply that there are certain empirical characteristics which are more often found in an image which seems familiar than in one which does not. These become empirically associated with familiarity; whilst familiarity is, in our view, non-empirically associated with the notion of pastness. Hence, by the ordinary process of "telescoping", these other empirical characteristics of images may come to stand for pastness.

Non-Perceptual Memory. I shall end this chapter by considering very briefly some of the other senses in which the word "memory" is used.

(1) It is a fundamental fact about living organisms that, when they have performed a certain set of movements several times, they tend to acquire a more or less permanent power of repeating these movements with

greater or less accuracy from time to time when suitably stimulated. This general capacity of living matter is sometimes called "memory"; and it is in this sense and in it alone that heredity can plausibly be regarded as an extension of memory. It would be better to call this general capacity "retentiveness" or "perseverance".

(2) We may acquire by practice the power of performing at will certain characteristic sets of bodily movements, such as those which are used in swimming. If we find that we can still swim when we get into the water after an interval, we should commonly say that we "remember how to swim" or "remember the movements of swimming". There is nothing cognitive about "memory", in this sense. To say that we remember how to swim is merely to state (a) that we can perform the proper movements after an interval, and (b) that we believe, or that the speaker who observes us believes, this to be due to our having performed them in the past. It would be better to call memory, in this sense, "retention of an acquired motor-capacity".

(3) In precisely the same way we may acquire by practice the power of uttering or writing at will a certain set of noises or marks, as a parrot or a monkey might do. There is no essential difference between this and the last case, if the noises or marks are meaningless to us. What has really been acquired and retained is a certain motor-capacity in the throat and tongue or in the fingers. It is true that, in this case, an external observer would probably say, not only that we remember how to make certain movements in tongue, throat, or fingers, but also that we remember the original words. But this means no more than that the movements in question reproduce noises or marks which in fact resemble those which we had to imitate in acquiring the motor-capacity. I will call "memory", in this sense, "retention of an acquired speech - capacity", using "speech" in a wide sense to include the utterances of a parrot or the imitative scrawlings which a

monkey might make. Here too "memory" is not a form of cognition; it is simply a kind of bodily action such as we perform when we find ourselves still able to swim after an interval.

(4) One peculiar capacity which we may acquire by practice and retain is the power to call up an image which in fact resembles something that we have repeatedly seen or heard in the past. If we can do this, an external observer who knew of the fact would be inclined to say that we are remembering the thing which we have seen or heard in the past which the image in fact resembles. But this would not be an accurate use of the word "memory" unless the image seems familiar to us and leads us to make memory-judgments. Apart from this we have merely acquired and retained a peculiar kind of capacity; and "to remember", in this sense, is no more to perform a special kind of cognitive act than to swim is. The peculiarity of the present case is simply in the nature of the capacity which we have acquired. An image is not a series of movements, and to call up an image is not to move in a certain way. It is of course possible that the calling up of a certain kind of image is causally dependent on the occurrence of certain microscopic movements in the brain and nervous system, and that what we have primarily acquired is the capacity to initiate such microscopic movements at will. But this is purely hypothetical, and therefore it would be paradoxical and rash to count this capacity as a peculiar kind of motor-capacity. I will call "memory" in this sense "retention of an acquired capacity for imitative imagery".

(5) The four kinds of "memory" which I have so far mentioned do not really deserve the name. In themselves they are modes of *behaviour*, and not modes of *cognition*. To call them "memory" is merely to state our belief that the capacity for behaving in these ways arose through our performing similar actions in the

past, or through our having perceived something which resembled the image which we can now call up. Such acquired and retained modes of behaviour may be necessary conditions of genuine memory, but they are nothing more. But it is of course a fact that when I perform such actions as these a genuine memory-situation often does arise. The movements of swimming may seem familiar; so may the sounds which I utter, or the marks which I make, or the images which I call up. I see no reason why this should not happen even with parrots and monkeys. A further stage is that I may then make memory-judgments of various degrees of determinateness. I may judge that this has happened before, or I may definitely remember a certain occasion on which I have formerly swum. I see no reason to suppose that this stage is ever reached by animals. The first stage cannot properly be called "memory", though it approaches nearer to it than the four cases which we considered before. The second stage is definitely memory, *i.e.*, a peculiar kind of cognition in which we seem to be in contact with a part of our own past history and with events which we then experienced. I think that the name "memory" is often applied by external observers to the first four cases because they unwittingly assume that what is in fact a repetition of a past mode of behaviour and is in fact causally dependent on past behaviour or past perception must be accompanied by a feeling of familiarity and a more or less determinate memory-judgment about the past. A very little careful introspection will suffice to show that this is a mistake.

(6) There is one other important sense of "memory" to be considered. In dealing with perceptual memory we had occasion to consider a certain sense in which we "remember propositions". But there is another sense in which we are said to "remember propositions", and it is this which I want now to discuss. We often say that we remember propositions about historical characters, such as Julius Cæsar, which we were taught

at school. Again, I might well say that I remember
Euclid's proposition I, 47, and Euclid's proof of it.
Memory of propositions, in this sense, must be sharply
distinguished from the memory of propositions which
forms a part of perceptual memory. It must also be
sharply distinguished from mere memory of sentences.
We will take these two points in turn.

(i) The propositions which I remember because I
have once upon a time learned them *may* be about past
events, but they need not be. Euclid I, 47 is about the
timeless relations of certain abstract and timeless objects.
Moreover, when the proposition which I remember in
this way happens to be about a past event, I do not say
that I remember the event because I remember the
proposition about it. I certainly do remember that
Cæsar crossed the Rubicon, and I certainly do not
remember the event which is described as "Cæsar
crossing the Rubicon". In perceptual memory the
propositions remembered are always about past events ;
and, when we remember a proposition in this sense, we,
ipso facto, remember perceptually the event which it is
about.

(ii) On the other hand, memory of propositions which
we have been taught or have learnt for ourselves cannot
be identified with a mere power to repeat the sentences
in which these propositions were expressed when we
learnt them, nor with such repetition accompanied by a
feeling of familiarity in the words and by a perceptual
memory-judgment. I remember Euclid I, 47 and his
proof of it through having learnt it. But I certainly
could not reproduce the words in my Euclid book ; and
I should recognise the proposition equally well if I now
saw it stated for the first time in any foreign tongue
that is known to me. Again, I might accurately reproduce a sentence without remembering a proposition.
This might happen if I did not understand the sentence ;
e.g., if it were in Hebrew, a tongue which I do not
understand though I can write the letters. Or it might

happen even though I did understand the sentence when I learnt it, if I have now forgotten its meaning. Lastly, it might happen if I understood the sentence and could again understand it by giving enough attention to it, but I am now repeating it parrot-wise whilst thinking of other things. It is, therefore, impossible to identify memory of propositions with memory of the sentences in which they were originally expressed, for there is not even an invariable and reciprocal connexion between the two kinds of memory.

I am said to remember a proposition which I have learnt provided I have acquired the power of contemplating it at will, and provided that, when I do contemplate it, it seems familiar to me. The first part of this definition might conceivably be fulfilled without the second. If it were, I do not think that the experient would himself say that he remembers the proposition; though an external observer would be very likely to say this of the experient. Now I think it likely that we cannot contemplate a proposition without *some* kind of concrete symbolism, though this may be to the last degree sketchy and vague without apparently interfering with our contemplation of the proposition. But, for the purpose of remembering the proposition, it is a matter of complete indifference what particular form the symbolism takes, and it is quite unnecessary for the present form of symbolism to resemble that which was used for expressing the proposition when we first met with it. No doubt the power to reproduce the original sentence at will is helpful as a means to enabling us to think of the proposition at will; but it is not essential, and it is sometimes positively harmful. Sometimes we have accepted a proposition in the past on authority or because of a process of reasoning which then satisfied us. Perhaps, if we were now to inspect and criticise the proposition, we should no longer accept it; the reasoning might not satisfy us now, and we might have lost our respect for the authority. But,

unfortunately, we have acquired the power of repro-
ducing the original sentence, in which the proposition
was expressed when we first met it, at will.   When we
exercise this power we think that we are thinking of the
proposition, and we remember that we have accepted
it and that we had what seemed adequate grounds for
doing so.   But really we are not contemplating the
proposition at all ; we are just behaving like parrots or
monkeys.   Thus it comes about that intelligent grown
men can honestly believe that they believe the most
preposterous propositions in theology and politics, provided that these continue to be expressed in language
that has been familiar to them since their childhood.

I hope that I have succeeded in this chapter at least
in showing how ridiculous it is to attempt to reduce
memory to "language-habits".   Such an attempt does
not even *seem* to account for perceptual memory ; and
it fails to recognise the elementary distinction between
remembering a sentence and remembering a proposition
which one has learnt in the past.   It is odd enough
that the attempt should have been made ; but it is far
more odd that it should have been hailed as a wonderful
step in psychology and as the last word in "advanced
thinking".

CHAPTER VI

Introspection

UNDER the general heading of "Introspection" I shall discuss the intuitive and non-inferential knowledge which a mind is supposed by many people to have of itself and its states. Here we enter on even more controversial ground than before. No one doubts that there are perceptual situations, and that in them we seem to have intuitive and non-inferential knowledge of physical things and events. But many people deny that we can in any sense "perceive" our own minds or their states. Some hold that we can "perceive" contemporary mental states of all kinds, but not our selves. Others hold that we can "perceive" mental states of one kind, viz., "presentations", but that we have only discursive and inferential knowledge of mental states of another kind, viz., "acts". Yet others hold that we can "remember" certain mental states, but that we cannot "perceive" any kind of mental state while it is happening. I think that the treatment of introspection by philosophers has been much less careful than their treatment of perception, and that many necessary distinctions have been ignored. A great part of the disagreement about introspection seems to me to be due to the ambiguities of the word which arise through the failure to recognise these necessary distinctions. I hope that in this chapter I may at least clear up some of these ambiguities.

General Characteristics of Introspection. I think that it would generally be agreed that, if there is a process which deserves to be called "introspection" at all, the following characteristics must belong to it. (1) It must be intuitive, like perception, and not merely discursive. That is, it must not consist simply of judgments about minds and their states; and minds and their states must not be known simply as the subjects of such and such propositions. No doubt, if there is introspection, there will be introspective judgments; and these, like perceptual judgments will be *about* their subjects. But, if there is introspection, our minds or certain states of them must be or seem to be objective constituents of introspective situations, just as physical events or things are or seem to be objective constituents of perceptual situations. These objective constituents of introspective situations must manifest certain apparent characteristics, as the objective constituents of perceptual situations manifest redness, hardness, etc. And introspective judgments must state explicitly the characteristics which the objective constituents of introspective situations manifest. (2) Introspective judgments must not be reached by inference. Even if they pass beyond the objective constituent of the introspective situation and its manifested characteristics, and are in some sense *based on* the latter, they must not be *inferred from* the latter. (3) If there are introspective situations, their objects are the mind of the subject of the situation or some mental event which is a state of that mind. It is commonly held that no one could have this kind of intuitive and non-inferential knowledge of any mind but himself or of any mental events but his own mental states. Thus the objects of introspection are supposed to be essentially private to the introspecting mind.

The Objects of Introspection. We are alleged by certain people to have introspective knowledge of ourselves and of some of our mental states. And our mental states themselves are divided into two classes,

viz., acts and presentations. Some people hold that
we have introspective knowledge of both; others that
we have such knowledge only of the latter. I will first
consider our alleged introspective knowledge of ourselves, as contrasted with our alleged introspective
knowledge of our states; and I will then consider the
two different kinds of mental states, and our alleged
introspective knowledge or lack of knowledge of them.

Introspective Knowledge of the Self. The distinction
between a self and particular states of it, such as a
certain feeling of toothache or a certain act of thinking,
is obviously analogous to the distinction between a
physical object, such as a chair, and a physical event,
such as a flash of lightning or a certain short phase in
the total history of the chair. Just as a short slice of
the history of a physical object may consist of a number
of different but temporally overlapping physical events,
so a short slice of the history of a mind may consist of a
number of different but temporally overlapping mental
events. The characteristic unity of the successive
slices of the history of a mind is no doubt different from
the characteristic unity of the successive slices of the
history of a physical object. And the characteristic
unity of the temporally overlapping events which
together make up a slice of the history of a mind is no
doubt different from the characteristic unity of the
temporally overlapping events which together make up
a slice of the history of a physical object. But, apart
from these characteristic differences, there is a general
resemblance which enables us to regard each as a persistent substance which passes through successive total
phases, each of which in turn consists of distinguishable
but temporally overlapping events. So far then we may
compare the distinction between a state of mind and the
mind which owns it with the distinction between a
physical object and a certain part of a certain slice of its
history. And we may compare our alleged introspective knowledge of ourselves and certain of our

states with our alleged perceptual knowledge of a physical object and of certain events in its history.

But we must now mention a difference between the two cases, which complicates the present problem. It is very commonly believed that the characteristic unity of the various events in one slice of the history of a self, and the characteristic unity of the successive slices of the total history of a self, depend on the presence of a peculiar *constituent* in every self. This peculiar constituent is called the "Pure Ego". I do not think that anyone seriously holds a similar view about the characteristic unity of a physical object. Now a result of the wide prevalence of the Pure Ego Theory is this. When people talk of the "Self" they sometimes mean the supposed Pure Ego, and not the states which it is supposed to own. Sometimes they mean the complex whole composed, as they believe, of all the states of the self in their interrelations and of the Pure Ego in its relations to these states. And sometimes they simply mean the whole composed of the states in their interrelations, leaving the question of a Pure Ego perfectly open or denying its existence. If, then, people mean three different things by the "Self", it is evident that the question whether we have introspective knowledge of our selves is ambiguous; we might have to answer "Yes" to one form of it, "No" to another, and "It is uncertain" to a third. Let us first consider the self as Pure Ego.

I do not mean to discuss in this chapter whether the Pure Ego theory of the self is true. Here I merely wish to ask the hypothetical question: "If there were a Pure Ego would there be any objection to the supposition that we can have introspective knowledge of it?" Now the Pure Ego might, I take it, be conceived in at least two different ways. (1) We might suppose that the Pure Ego is a single long strand of history of which every slice is exactly like every other slice in all its qualities. On this view the Pure Ego could not possibly be the objective constituent of any introspective situation, since the duration of the Pure Ego stretches from the cradle to the grave, whilst that of any introspective situation is only a few seconds or at most minutes. This, however, would not put the Pure Ego in any less favourable position than the physical object. Various slices of the history of a Pure Ego might be literally objective constituents of introspective situations, just as various slices of the history of a physical object might be literally objective constituents of perceptual situations. We should have to admit that the introspective judgment: "There is a single Pure Ego which lasts without qualitative change throughout my life and owns all my successive states" goes beyond what is manifested in any introspective situation; but we have had to make a similar admission about the perceptual judgment: "There is a penny which is hard and cold as well as brown, and which existed before and will exist after the present perceptual situation." It would not follow that our beliefs about the Pure Ego must be reached by inference. It might be an essential feature of every introspective situation that its objective constituent is believed to be a slice of a longer strand which is qualitatively uniform.

(2) A second possible view is that the Pure Ego is a timeless particular and not a long uniform strand of history. On that hypothesis there is no *a priori* reason why it should not be literally an objective constituent of each one of a whole series of introspective situations.

But, even if we accept a Pure Ego and admit that it might conceivably be an objective constituent of an introspective situation, I think that our actual experience would force us to admit the following two propositions. (1) It is never the *complete* objective constituent of any introspective situation. If it be there at all it is always accompanied by some particular mental event which it owns. (2) It does not manifest empirical qualities in the introspective situation in the way in which the particular mental event does so. Suppose, *e.g.*, that the total objective constituent of a certain introspective situation is a feeling of toothache, together with the Pure Ego (or a slice of the history of the Pure Ego) which owns this feeling. Then it must be admitted that the toothache manifests in the situation (*i.e.*, "seems to have") certain empirical qualities, such as throbbingness, stabbingness, and so on. And it must be admitted that the Pure Ego, or the slice of its history, does not in this sense manifest any empirical qualities. One can think of at least two possible explanations of this. (i) Perhaps the Pure Ego fails to manifest any empirical qualities because it has none to manifest. It may simply have categorial characteristics, such as "being a substance", "being a particular", "being timeless", etc.; and empirical relational properties, such as "owning this toothache", "owning that thought", and so on. (ii) Perhaps the Pure Ego has empirical qualities, but is incapable of manifesting them in introspective situations to the mind of which it is a constituent. There are analogies to this in the case of sense-perception. If we take a naïvely realistic view of sense-perception, a slice of the history of the top of a penny is an objective constituent of my visual situation when I look at the top of this penny. And it *has* the empirical quality of coldness. But it certainly does not *manifest* this quality in the visual situation as it manifests the empirical quality of brownness. Moreover, we should admit that it may have empirical qualities, *e.g.*, magnetic ones, which it fails to manifest in this way in *any* perceptual situation of which we are capable of being subject. We only extend this a little further when we suggest that the Pure Ego may be incapable of manifesting *any* of its empirical qualities in *any* introspective situation. It is no doubt unfortunate that, if it exists at all, it should be so extremely retiring; but its modesty is certainly not a proof that it does not exist or that it cannot be part of the total objective constituent of an introspective situation.

In this connexion I may just mention Mr Hume's famous statement that, whenever he tried to introspect his Self, he always "stumbled upon" some particular mental event instead. I take it that Mr Hume did here mean by his "Self" a supposed Pure Ego which was alleged to own all his mental states. And I think that the conclusion which has generally been drawn from Mr Hume's statement is either that the Pure Ego is a pure myth; or at any rate that, if it exists, our knowledge of it is discursive and inferential. I think that we may accept Mr Hume's statement if we understand it to mean (i) that the Pure Ego is never the *whole* of the objective constituent of any introspective situation, even if the *whole* Pure Ego be part of the objective constituent of *every* introspective situation; and (ii) that, even if the whole Pure Ego be part of the objective constituent of every introspective situation, it *never* manifests any of its empirical qualities, as the other part of the total objective constituent does. Now I think that this does entail the conclusion that, if we know the Pure Ego at all, we know it discursively (*i.e.*, simply as the subject of certain propositions) and not intuitively. But it does not follow that our knowledge of it is inferential; it does not follow that there is no Pure Ego; and it does not follow that the Pure Ego has no empirical qualities.

If we are to hold that we have non-intuitive but non-inferential knowledge of the Pure Ego, I think we shall have to suppose that it arises somewhat as follows. We shall have to suppose that each particular mental event which we become acquainted with in an introspective situation manifests in that situation the relational property of "being owned by something"; that, on comparison and reflexion, we can see that this "something" is the same for all the mental events which we can introspect, whether they be successive or simultaneous, and that it is not itself a mental event or a group of interrelated mental events. The Pure Ego would then be known discursively, but not of necessity inferentially, as the common owner of such and such particular contemporary and successive mental events. Now, since the Pure Ego can be known only in this way even if it be a constituent of all introspective situations, there seems no very good reason for holding that it is in fact part of the objective constituent of any such situation. For, on the one hand, since it manifests no empirical qualities in any introspective situation, there seems to be no direct reason for regarding it as part of the objective constituent. And, on the other hand, if we can have such non-inferential knowledge about it in spite of its manifesting no empirical qualities in introspective situations, there seems no reason why we should not be able to have the same kind of knowledge about it even though it were not part of the objective constituent of any such situation. Thus the conclusion seems to be that, although the Pure Ego *might* be part of the objective constituent of introspective situations, there is no good reason to suppose that it in fact *is*, even if we admit its existence and admit that we have non-inferential knowledge of it.

I have now considered our alleged introspective knowledge of the Self, in the sense of the Pure Ego. Let us next consider our alleged introspective knowledge of the Self, in the sense of the whole complex of contemporary and successive interrelated mental events which together constitute our mental history. If we reject the Pure Ego theory this complex will *be* the Total Self. If we accept the Pure Ego theory the Total Self will be this complex together with the Pure Ego in its relation of ownership to all the events in the complex. Let us call the complex of interrelated mental events the " Empirical Self ". No one seriously doubts the existence of Empirical Selves, whether he accepts or rejects the Pure Ego theory. If a man rejects the Pure Ego theory, the Total Self and the Empirical Self are, on his view, identical. If he accepts the Pure Ego theory, the Empirical Self must still be admitted to exist; but the Total Self will not be identical with it. The Total Self will then be the larger complex which consists of the Empirical Self and of the Pure Ego standing in the relation of ownership to the mental events which are constituents of the Empirical Self. The present question is whether, and in what sense, we can have introspective knowledge of the Empirical or the Total Self.

The Empirical Self is, for the present purpose, precisely analogous to a physical thing; *i.e.*, each is a long strand of history whose successive slices have a certain continuity with each other and are themselves composed of various temporally overlapping events united in a characteristic way. Now I have argued that physical things cannot, as such, be constituents of perceptual situations, quite apart from all questions of delusive perception. For the thing which we are said to perceive is admitted to last longer than the perceptual situation; it is admitted that only a certain part of a certain slice of its history could literally be a constituent of any one perceptual situation; and it is admitted that even this part of this slice does not manifest in the perceptual situation all the empirical qualities which it in fact has. Precisely similar considerations apply to the Empirical Self and to our alleged knowledge of it by introspection. The Empirical Self is something which lasts from birth till death at least; its successive slices differ from each other qualitatively; and each slice is differentiated into a number of distinct but temporally overlapping mental events. A particular introspective situation probably lasts for a minute or so; and it cannot contain as objective constituent more than a certain short slice of the Empirical Self. Moreover, it is doubtful whether it would ever contain the whole of such a slice; it might, *e.g.*, contain a twinge of toothache and a little more besides, but miss out the rest of my contemporary mental states. Lastly, there is no reason to suppose that a mental event which is an objective constituent of an introspective situation must, *ipso facto*, manifest *all* the empirical properties which it in fact possesses. When I introspect my present feeling of toothache it may manifest the quality of throbbingness ; but, even if it be literally an objective constituent of my present introspective situation, there is no reason why it should not have dozens of other characteristics which it does not manifest in this situation.

It is necessary to insist on this last point because of the wide prevalence of a curious superstition. This is the belief that, if there be introspection at all, it must give exhaustive and infallible information. It seems to be thought that, because the objects of *my* introspection are *my* self and *my* states, therefore they can have no qualities which they do not reveal to introspection by me. And it seems to be thought that, for the same reason, my states cannot appear to me to have qualities which are other than and inconsistent with those which they do have. Now the first part of this is simply superstition, and there is nothing more to be said about it. I will not dismiss the second part at present so cavalierly ; it is always difficult to understand how anything can seem to have characteristics which are other than and inconsistent with those which it really does have ; and it may be that there are special difficulties on the assumption that mental events are literally objective constituents of introspective situations. But these difficulties are certainly not due to the fact that the states which *I* introspect are *my* states ; if *anything* can seem to have characteristics which are inconsistent with those which it does have, in spite of its being intuitively known, there is no special reason why *my* states should not seem to *me* to have such characteristics. It is very easy to deny the existence of introspection, if you start out with the principle that introspection must give exhaustive and infallible knowledge of its objects ; and it is therefore important to say firmly that there is no reason to accept the principle.

To return, after this digression, to the Empirical Self. The upshot of the discussion is this. On the most favourable view possible we cannot hold that the Empirical Self as such is the objective constituent of any introspective situation. The most we could say is that the objective constituents of all my introspective situations are mental events which are in fact parts of slices of the history of my Empirical Self, and that the characteristics which they manifest in these introspective situations are *some* of the characteristics which they do in fact possess. It does not of course follow from this that our knowledge of the Empirical Self must be discursive and inferential ; any more than it follows from the similar considerations which we brought forward in the case of perception that our knowledge of physical things must be discursive and inferential. It might be an essential factor in every introspective situation that its objective constituent is believed to be a fragment of a short slice of a long strand of history whose structure is such that we call it an "Empirical Self". I am inclined to think that this is in fact the case. And, for anything that we have seen at present, this belief, which always forms part of the total introspective situation, might always be true. In that case I should say that our introspective knowledge of the Empirical Self was intuitive and non-inferential in precisely the same sense in which our perceptual knowledge of a chair or a penny is so. It will be remembered that, in the analogous case of perception, we had to conclude that our instinctive belief that the objective constituent of the perceptual situation is literally a spatio-temporal part of the physical object which we are said to be perceiving is certainly sometimes false. This was because of totally delusive perceptual situations, such as the drunkard's seeing pink rats. Now, so far as I know, there are no introspective situations which we have reason to believe to be totally delusive in this sense. Let us consider what would be the introspective *analogon* of a totally delusive perceptual situation. Suppose I were subject of an introspective situation whose objective constituent manifested certain characteristics; and suppose that I had a non-inferential belief that this event which manifests these characteristics is a state of my mind, in the sense that it is a fragment of that total strand of history which is my Empirical Self. This introspective situation would be totally delusive, in the sense in which the drunkard's perception of pink rats is so, if and only if there were nothing which corresponds in the least to my notion of my Empirical Self or to my belief that this event is part of the history of my Empirical Self. We call the drunkard's perceptual situation "totally delusive" because we believe that there are no such things in the world as pink rats; or because we believe that, even if there be pink rats somewhere in the universe, the objective constituent of the drunkard's perceptual situation does not stand in any specially intimate relation to a certain pink rat, which the drunkard asserts to be occupying a certain position on his bed at the moment. Now I say that there are no introspective situations which are known to be delusive, in this sense. We have no good reason to doubt that there are such strands of history as we call "Empirical Selves"; we have no good reason to doubt that all the introspective situations of whose existence we know are in fact events in the history of some Empirical Self; and we have no good reason to doubt that the objective constituent of every introspective situation does stand in a certain peculiarly intimate relation to that particular Empirical Self which owns this introspective situation. There is therefore no ground for thinking that the belief which forms an essential factor in all introspective situations is *ever* false in its main outlines.

I must, however, warn the reader at this point against three misunderstandings. (i) I am *not* saying that there is no reason to doubt that *every mental event* stands in this peculiary intimate relation to a certain Empirical Self; I am saying this only of every mental event *which is an object of introspection*. There may be excellent reasons for accepting the reality of mental events which we cannot introspect and which are not connected in this way with any Empirical Self. (ii) I am talking of the *Empirical Self*, and not of the Pure Ego. I do not think that it is any part of the claim made by the introspective situation that its objective constituent is owned by a Pure Ego. And, if it were, I might think that there was good reason for doubting the claim. As I have said, I think that, even if there be a Pure Ego and it be in fact a constituent of every introspective situation, it is not revealed to us in any introspective situation, but is known only by a process of comparison and reflection. (iii) I am not saying that there is no good reason to doubt the claim made by the introspective situation in the precise form in which it is made. I think that the introspective situation does claim that its objective constituent is literally a part of a slice of the history of a certain Empirical Self; and that the characteristics which it manifests in the situation do really belong to it, though they need not be all that belong to it. It may very well be that the claim in this extreme form cannot be upheld in view of all the facts. It may be that we shall find it impossible to hold that the objective constituents of introspective situations are literally *parts* of the Empirical Self; or that we can hold this only on the hypothesis that they can seem to have characteristics which are other than and inconsistent with those which they really do have. Nevertheless, the claim that the objective constituents of introspective situations stand in a certain peculiarly intimate relation to the Empirical Self might be upheld; as we have upheld the corresponding claim of the perceptual situation, in spite of our inability to accept it in the precise form in which it is made. We must therefore consider next our alleged introspective knowledge of particular mental events.

Introspective Knowledge of Mental Events. We must begin by noticing that, under the head of "mental events", a number of existents of very different kinds are included. Various people between them claim to have introspective knowledge of events of all these different kinds. Consequently we have some reason to suppose that, under the head of "introspection" a number of extremely different kinds of cognition may be included.

(1) Many people regard the objective constituents of visual, tactual, and auditory perceptual situations as states of the percipient's mind. Now there are situations in which we specially attend to them and try to describe the characteristics which they seem to have, as distinct from describing the characteristics which the perceived physical object is believed to have. Such people would describe such situations as "introspective".

(2) Some people would hesitate to call the objective constituents of such perceptual situations as these "mental events", and would hesitate to call the act of attending to them and their apparent characteristics "introspection". But they would count bodily feelings, like headache and toothache, as mental states. They would hold that, when we try to describe accurately to a dentist "what our toothache feels like", we are introspecting it. Now, for our purpose, these two cases are so much alike that they may be treated together. (i) It might reasonably be held that, when we have a certain bodily feeling, we are perceiving a certain process in our bodies in precisely the same sense in which we perceive a process in a certain external object when we sense a noise or a coloured patch. No doubt some bodily feelings are accompanied by such vague perceptual judgments about our own bodies that the

situation approximates to one of pure feeling. But it is also true that there are visual and auditory situations which approximate to pure sensation. (ii) The privacy of bodily feelings is no ground for drawing a fundamental distinction between them and the objective constituents of visual or auditory situations. As we have seen, the objective constituents of several visual situations with the same epistemological object always seem on careful inspection to differ in their determinate characteristics, and are probably always numerically different. At most we can say that there is a correlation of their apparent characteristics with each other and with the positions of the observers. The additional privacy of bodily feelings consists only in the fact that there are not groups of correlated bodily feelings, in the sense in which there are groups of correlated visual or auditory sensa. (iii) When we attend to a toothache it manifests, not only such "sensible" qualities as "throbbingness" etc. (which may be compared to redness or "squeakiness"), but also the peculiar characteristic of painfulness. Most noises or coloured patches which we sense do not manifest painfulness or pleasantness when we attend to them. But, after all, some bodily feelings are practically neutral; and some very squeaky noises or very dazzling flashes are distinctly painful. So this introduces no essential distinction. (iv) There is one important feature which is common to the two cases which we have so far considered and is absent in those which we have to consider next. I express this by saying that a toothache, a noise, a flash, and a coloured patch all seem to be *homogeneous* events. No doubt they all have or seem to have temporal parts, and some of them have or seem to have spatial parts. No doubt the different parts may manifest different determinate qualities; *e.g.*, one bit of a coloured patch may seem red and another may seem blue, or the earlier part of a twinge of toothache may seem "dull" and the later part "throbbing", and so on. But all the parts which we can distinguish seem to be of the same *kind* as each other and as the whole which they compose. Moreover, the parts of the whole are united to form the whole by the unique relation of spatial, temporal, or spatio-temporal *adjunction*. This is what I mean by calling toothaches, noises, coloured patches, flashes, etc., "homogeneous events". Now there are other events, which some people say that we can introspect, that are certainly not homogeneous in this sense. *E.g.*, a perceptual situation (*i.e.*, the kind of situation which we denote by such a phrase as "So-and-so seeing such-and-such") is not a homogeneous event in the sense defined. For it is a complex in which we can distinguish an objective constituent, a subjective constituent, and a characteristic relation between them which is not that of adjunction. We may call it a "heterogeneous event". Now some people hold that perceptual situations, and other mental situations which are heterogeneous in the sense defined, can be introspected.

For the reasons which I have just given it seems to me likely that there is *no* essential difference between what is called "introspecting" a bodily feeling and what some people would refuse to call "introspecting" the objective constituent of a visual, tactual, or auditory perceptual situation. And it seems to me likely that there *is* a difference between this and what is called "introspecting" a heterogeneous mental event, such as a perceptual situation or a memory-situation. Now the word "introspection" is generally taken to imply that its object is a state of the introspector's mind. I certainly do not want to use language which would suggest that noises, flashes, toothaches, etc., are states of the mind which senses or feels them; for this is a matter of controversy, and my own view is that they are probably not states of mind. Nevertheless there are situations in which we specially attend to such events and to their apparent characteristics, and *it is* necessary to have some neutral name for such situations. I propose to call such situations "inspective", and not "introspective". Anyone who holds that toothaches, noises, etc., are states of the mind which feels or senses them will simply regard inspection as a species of introspection. Anyone who rejects this view will deny that inspection is a species of introspection. But both parties can agree to use the name "inspection" for the situations which I have been describing, without committing themselves to any special view on this further question.

(3) The third case then that we have to distinguish is our alleged introspective knowledge of heterogeneous mental events such as perceptual and memory-situations. It is necessary to introduce a further distinction under this head, which has often been overlooked. All the situations which we are at present considering have internal complexity; there is an objective constituent, a subjective constituent; and a characteristic relation between the two. But, in addition to this internal complexity, some, if not all, of these situations refer to an epistemological object which is not a constituent of the situation. It is one thing to recognise that a certain perceptual situation, *e.g.*, contains a mass of bodily feeling and a brown elliptical patch related in a certain specific way; and it is another thing to recognise that it refers to a certain epistemological object, *e.g.*, "this penny". Now some people would say that, if we are asked: "What are you seeing; what are you remembering; what are you desiring?" and we answer: "I am seeing a penny; I am remembering the tie which my friend wore yesterday; and I am wanting my tea", we are introspecting in order to answer these questions. Plainly we must distinguish between analysing a situation, describing its various constituents, and noting the relations which subsist between them in the situation, on the one hand; and recognising, on the other hand, that it refers to such and such an epistemological object

which is not a constituent of it. If both these processes are to be called "introspection", they ought to be distinguished by suitable adjectives. We might call the first "psychological introspection" and the second "epistemological introspection". I want now to see whether "epistemological introspection" deserves the name of "introspection" at all.

I think that there are two cases to be considered. (i) The situation may contain as an essential constituent a judgment or some other psychological attitude, such as supposition, whose "objective" (to use Meinong's expression) is a certain proposition or set of propositions. The epistemological object of the situation is determined by these propositions. On this alternative the recognition that the situation has such and such an epistemological object is not an additional cognitive process which may or may not be superinduced on the original situation ; it is an essential part of the original situation itself. In judging or supposing certain propositions I, *ipso facto*, know what are the propositions which I am judging or supposing ; and therefore in being the subject of such a situation I, *ipso facto*, know what is its epistemological object. The most that we can do is to put this judgment or supposition explicitly into words ; and I do not see any reason to call this process "introspection". Now it is important to notice that this process is not infallible, and that in fact it is liable to a certain systematic error which might be called "The Epistemologist's Fallacy". Although we cannot help *knowing* what we are judging, we may find it very difficult to *say* accurately either to ourselves or others what we are judging ; because the subtlety of language is not equal to the subtlety of fact. The systematic error, which I call the Epistemologist's Fallacy, is to substitute a more determinate judgment or supposition for the vaguer and less determinate judgment or supposition which really formed part of the original situation. In addition to the process which

I have been describing we may (*a*) recognise what kind
of attitude we are taking towards the propositions in
question ; *e.g.*, we may recognise that it is judgment
or that it is supposition, or that it is doubt, and so on.
And (*b*) we may recognise the precise relation which
this factor in the situation bears to the other factors in
it, *i.e.*, to the objective constituent, to the subjective
constituent, and so on.   These two processes are of
course particular cases of psychological introspection.
It seems then that, in this case, the so-called process
of "epistemological introspection" splits into two parts.
One is not introspection at all, but is merely the statement in words of certain propositions which are judged
or supposed in the original situation.   The other is a
particular instance of psychological introspection, viz.,
the recognition of the particular attitude which we take
towards these propositions and of the relation of this
attitude to the other factors in the situation.

(ii) The second case is this.   There are certain
situations, notably perceptual ones, which have epistemological objects, but probably do not contain as
constituents judgments or other attitudes towards propositions.   I have described them as best I could by
saying that we adjust our bodies *as if* we had made
certain judgments about what is coming next, and
are surprised and disappointed if something different
happens.   Instead of containing judgments, the situations contain the feelings due to these bodily adjustments related in a characteristic way to the other
constituents of the situation.   In such cases, when we
try to state what is the epistemological object of the
situation, we are really trying to state explicitly those
propositions *in accordance with* which we have acted and
adjusted ourselves.   Here we are quite definitely going
beyond anything that was contained in the original
situation ; otherwise this case is identical with the last
which we considered.

The upshot of the matter is that "epistemological

introspection" is not introspection at all, and need not be further considered. I cannot, however, resist the temptation to remark that the extraordinary confusions which I seem to find in Mr Russell's argument about Desire in the first chapter of his *Analysis of Mind* are due to a failure to distinguish between psychological and epistemological introspection coupled with the superstition that, if there were introspective knowledge at all, it would have to be infallible. Mr Russell is anxious to prove that we do not know our own mental states by introspection. Having discussed this question about other kinds of mental state, he here raises it about Desire. And he thinks it relevant to his purpose to point out (what he need scarcely have gone to the Behaviourists and the Psycho-Analysts to learn) that we are often mistaken in our beliefs about what would in fact satisfy us. This seems to me to be triply irrelevant to his contention that we do not know the mental situation called "Desire" by introspection. (i) It assumes that introspective knowledge, if it existed at all, must be infallible. No reason is given for this assumption. (ii) It would prove only that we do not know "what we desire" (*i.e.*, the epistemological object of the conative situation) by *epistemological* introspection. It would not have the faintest tendency to show that we do not know the mental situation of desi*ring*, and do not recognise its constituents and its characteristic internal structure, by *psychological* introspection. (iii) But the facts adduced by Mr Russell are irrelevant even to epistemological introspection, and even on the assumption that introspection must be infallible if it exists at all. For he has failed to distinguish between the epistemological object and the ontological object of a conative situation. The ontological object of such a situation is that state of affairs which *would in fact* satisfy us; its epistemological object is that state of affairs which *we believe*, while the situation is occurring, would satisfy us. Who in the world ever supposed that *introspection* could give us infallible information about the former, even if he supposed that it could do so about the latter? Mr Russell's argument is thus absolutely irrelevant to his conclusion, even if his conclusion be true ; and he has failed to see this because he has for the moment overlooked the distinctions which I have been drawing. An exact parallel to his argument about desire would be the following imaginary argument about perception : "It is evident that we do not know of the existence and the constituents and the structure of perceptual situations by introspection ; for it is notorious that we may think we are perceiving an Archdeacon when we are really perceiving a scarecrow." The utter irrelevance of this argument is obvious ; but it is irrelevant in precisely the same way and for precisely the same reasons as Mr Russell's argument to prove that we have no introspective knowledge of desire.

The outcome of this sub-section is that we have to recognise two and only two apparently distinct kinds of knowledge which would commonly be counted as introspection of mental events. One is the inspection of sensa, images, bodily feelings, and other homogeneous events. The other is the introspection of heterogeneous mental situations. The so-called "epistemological introspection", which turns up in connexion with situations that have epistemological objects, resolves itself into something which is not introspection, and into something else which is a particular instance of psychological introspection. I propose now to consider inspection and psychological introspection in turn.

Inspection. We must begin by distinguishing a number of different but connected relations in which such an event as a noise, or a patch that appears coloured, may stand to a percipient. Let us suppose that I am looking attentively at a penny. There is a certain objective constituent which, on inspection, will seem to have a certain determinate ellipticity and a certain non-uniform distribution of various shades of brown. This patch will itself be a spatial part of a bigger visual field. Now (i) this visual field as a whole stands in a certain peculiar relation to me which I express by saying that it "is being sensed by me". If another person be looking at the penny at the same time, this visual field will not stand in this relation to him; though there will be another visual field which does stand in this relation to him and does not stand in it to me. Moreover, if I turn my back, this visual field (even if it continues to exist) will cease to stand in this relation to me. These statements will, I hope, indicate what I mean by saying that a visual field is sensed. (ii) It seems to me that when a field is sensed there is always *one*, and there may well be many, "sets of adjoined parts" such that each member of this set is also sensed by me. By a "set of adjoined parts" I mean a set of spatially or temporally or spatio-temporally extended parts which fit together without overlapping to make up an extended whole. It is evident that the same extended whole has an enormous number of different sets of adjoined parts; for this merely means that it can be exhaustively divided up in an enormous number of different ways. (I owe the conception of a set of adjoined parts to Dr M'Taggart.) (iii) On the other hand, it seems to me that when a whole is sensed it may quite well have parts which are not sensed because they are too small or of too short duration. Thus it is possible that a visual field which is sensed may have many sets of adjoined parts such that no member of any of these sets is sensed. And of course there may be sets of adjoined parts of a sensed whole such that some members of any such set are sensed and other members of that set are not sensed. (iv) In our example the visual appearance of the penny and the remainder of the visual field form a set of adjoined parts of the visual field. And both members of this set are sensed. (v) Now, although the visual appearance of the penny and the rest of the visual field agree in the fact that they are both sensed by me, they differ in another respect. I express this difference by saying that the former is and the latter is not "selected by me". Whatever part of a field is selected by me must also be sensed by me ; but there may be parts of the field which are sensed by me without being selected by me. (vi) At this point we come to a parting of the ways. A part of the field which is selected by me may (*a*) be used for perceiving a certain physical object and for learning about *its* physical characteristics, or (*b*) it may become an object of inspection by me with a view to learning accurately *its own* apparent characteristics. We can inspect only what we have selected, and we can perceive only with what we have selected. And we can select only those parts of a sensed field which we sense. But we can *either* inspect or perceive with a part of a field which we sense and select ; and I am inclined to think that we *must* do one or the other. I think that it is vital for the present purpose to distinguish these relations of being sensed, being selected, being inspected, and being used for perceiving ; and to get clear about their mutual connexions.

Inspective situations undoubtedly do arise, though they are of course far less common than perceptual and sensational situations. In ordinary life the most important inspective situations are those in which we select and inspect a certain bodily feeling in order to describe its apparent characteristics as accurately as we can to our doctor or our dentist. Inspective situations which are not concerned with bodily feelings are almost confined to philosophers, psychologists, and those physiologists who study the psycho - physiology of sense-perception. And even these specialists are subjects of such situations only at certain rare intervals when inspection becomes necessary for their investigations. Anyone who has ever put himself in an inspective situation and tried to discover the apparent qualities of his visual or auditory sensa, as distinct from trying to discover the physical qualities of external objects, will recognise how utterly different it is to inspect a sensum and to perceive with it.

There are several questions to be raised about inspection. (1) I have said that, when we select a certain part of a sense-field in addition to merely sensing it, we must *either* inspect *it* or perceive *with* it. Can we do both? Can we perceive with and inspect precisely and numerically the same noise or apparently coloured patch? I think it is very doubtful whether we can. At any rate I find that, when I am tempted to think that I do so, I have really been alternating quickly to and fro between "perceiving with" and "inspecting". Now this raises a problem. My main motive as a philosopher for inspecting a certain noise or·apparently coloured patch is to describe accurately the apparent qualities of the objective constituent of some auditory or visual perceptual situation. But, if what I inspect be probably never numerically the same as what I have perceived with, what right have I to believe that the objective constituent of the past perceptual situation *had* (or *would have* seemed to have) those characteristics which the objective constituent of the present inspective situation *does* now seem to have? To this question I can only make the following answers. No conclusive reason can be given for this belief; it is a memory-judgment, and the correctness of memory in general cannot be proved by argument. It *may* be that the characteristics which the objective constituent of an inspective situation seems to have are always different from those which the objective constituent of the immediately previous perceptual situation had or seemed to have. If it amuses anyone to assert this I cannot possibly refute him. But, on the other hand, there is not the least reason to believe him. If *any* memory-judgment be true, this one would seem to have the strongest possible claims. The numerical diversity of the two objective constituents is of course no bar to complete identity of their actual or their apparent qualities. And the two situations, and their respective objective constituents, are contiguous in time; so that there is the minimum possible opportunity for forgetting.

(2) We can now state our position about the relation between inspection and memory. Inspection itself is not memory. The purely inspective situation does not refer to the past; it merely professes to describe the apparent characteristics of its own objective constituent. But the objective constituent of an inspective situation is very often the objective constituent of a co-existing memory-situation. And the epistemological object of this memory-situation is such that, if anything corresponds to it, this corresponding object is the objective constituent of an immediately previous perceptual situation or of some other immediately previous situation such as a memory-situation. In so far as we profess to be learning by inspection about the apparent characteristics of the objective constituent of a perceptual or memory-situation, we are relying, not on inspection alone, but on inspection and memory. But the conditions are such that, if any memory-situation be veridical, this one may reasonably be expected to be so.

(3) What is the precise difference between trying to learn more accurately about the determinate qualities and the details of a perceived physical object by careful attention, and trying to learn more accurately about the determinate qualities and details of the objective constituent of a perceptual situation by inspection? It seems to me that one very important difference is the following. (*a*) In the former case I do not try to keep the perceptual situation constant. I try to replace it by a certain series of perceptual situations with different objective constituents. And, in particular, I choose certain special situations whose objective constituents are believed to reveal certain details or qualities of the perceived object more fully or determinately than others.

An elementary example of what I mean is looking at the thing from various points of view and approaching it until it is at the distance of most distinct vision. An exaggerated example is looking at the thing through some optical instrument, such as a microscope or a telescope. (*b*) In the latter case I try to keep the perceptual situation as nearly constant as I can, and to inspect the objective constituent of *that* situation or of others as like it as possible. To look through a microscope does not tell me more about the objective constituent of my previous visual situation; it replaces it by another visual situation with the same epistemological object and a different objective constituent. And the new objective constituent is supposed to justify certain more determinate judgments about the details of the perceived object than the old one could do.

(4) There is one other question which I wish to discuss in this subsection. Is inspection infallible; and, if so, in what sense? We must begin by drawing certain distinctions. (i) We must not confuse the pure inspective judgment with the memory-judgment which so often accompanies it and is based on the same objective constituent. Of the latter we can only say that it has as good a chance of being true as any memory-judgment can possibly have, and a much better chance than most memory-judgments have. (ii) We must not confuse the inspective judgment itself with the sentences in which we may try to express it to ourselves or to others. There are many more degrees of determinateness in our judgments than variations in language to express them. Owing to this inevitable limitation of language the most careful formulation of an inspective judgment in words may convey a wrong impression even though the judgment be itself true. (iii) There is no reason to suppose that inspective judgments are infallible in the sense of being exhaustive. Suppose I sense, select and inspect a certain noise or a certain apparently red patch. Such an object is exhaustively

divisible in innumerable different ways into different sets of adjoined parts. Now some of these sets of adjoined parts may consist of members all of which are too small or of too short duration to be sensed or selected or inspected ; yet together the members of any one of these sets make up a whole which is sensed, selected and inspected. We must not suppose then that, because we inspect a certain spatio-temporally extended whole, we therefore, *ipso facto*, have inspective knowledge of all or of most of its parts. (iv) So far as I can see, a certain whole might have a certain characteristic and there might be a certain set of adjoined parts which make up this whole and do not have this characteristic. There might be another set of adjoined parts of the same whole all of which do have the same characteristic as the whole. *E.g.*, a certain patch may appear red as a whole. There is one set of adjoined parts consisting of two halves of this patch ; each member of this set may also appear red. But there may also be a set of adjoined parts of the patch each member of which is too small to appear red or to appear to have any colour at all. Thus the characteristic of "appearing to be red" may belong to a whole and to some of its parts, but this whole may also be composed of a set of adjoined parts *none* of which has this characteristic of "appearing to be red". Nor do I see any reason why the whole and some of its parts should not *be* red, whilst none of the members of a certain set of adjoined parts of this whole *are* red. And, just as a whole may have certain characteristics which *do not* belong to *any* member of a certain set of adjoined parts of it, so *all* the members of a certain set of adjoined parts of a certain whole might *have* some positive characteristic which does not belong to the whole or to some of its parts. A red whole may have a set of adjoined parts none of which is red ; and every one of these parts might, *e.g.*, be a mind, whilst the whole is not a mind. We must not therefore suppose that, because we have inspective knowledge of

certain characteristics of a certain whole, we shall therefore, *ipso facto*, have inspective knowledge of all the
characteristics of all its parts. (v) I have now pointed
out certain common confusions which we must avoid in
discussing our present question, and have shown that
there is no reason to think that inspection will give us
exhaustive information about its objects. The question
that remains is this: "Is there any ground for doubting
that the events which we inspect do have precisely those
qualities which they seem to have and those parts which
we seem to find on inspecting them as carefully as we
can?"

I think that the answer to this last question is that
there is no ground for doubt in any case except when
the apparent characteristics of the inspected event are
ascribed by a memory-judgment to the objective constituent of an immediately past perceptual situation. I
inspect a certain selected patch in my visual field, and I
find that it looks *elliptical*. I make a memory-judgment
ascribing this apparent shape to the objective constituent
of an immediately past perceptual situation in which I
claimed to be seeing the *round* top of a certain penny.
Now, if I insist on identifying the objective constituent
of this recent perceptual situation with the actual top of
the penny, I have two alternatives. (i) I may reject the
memory-judgment. I may say: "The objective constituent of my present inspective situation certainly
appears elliptical; but my memory-judgment that the
objective constituent of my past perceptual situation
appeared elliptical must be mistaken. The latter objective constituent must have appeared round." On this
alternative there is no need for me to suppose that
either objective constituent seems to have a different
characteristic from that which it does have. One was
round and appeared so; the other is elliptical and
appears so; my memory simply deceives me when I
ascribe the characteristic of the second to the first. (ii)
I may accept the memory-judgment. I may say: "The

objective constituent of my present inspective situation certainly appears elliptical ; and my memory-judgment that the objective constituent of my past perceptual situation appeared elliptical is correct. So this latter objective constituent must have been round, although it appeared elliptical." On this alternative it is not indeed positively *necessary* to hold that the objective constituent of the present inspective situation has a different characteristic from that which it appears to have. But it *is* necessary to hold this about the objective constituent of the past perceptual situation. And this would make it very rash *to be sure* that the objective constituent of the present inspective situation *does have* the characteristic which it seems to have. For, if there is certainly this divergence between apparent and actual characteristics in the objective constituent of the perceptual situation, we can hardly feel confident that a like divergence may not exist in the case of the inspective situation.

It will be noticed, however, that both these unpleasant alternatives depend on the assumption that the objective constituent of a perceptual situation must be literally a spatio-temporal part of the perceived physical object. If we reject this assumption, there is no reason why we should not accept both the view that the objective constituent of the inspective situation has the character-istics which it seems to have, and also the memory-judgment that the objective constituent of the previous perceptual situation seemed to have these same char-acteristics. For there is now no reason to suppose that the latter did not have the characteristics which the memory - judgment asserts that it seemed to have. We can therefore accept the memory-judgment without casting doubt on the proposition that the objective constituent of the inspective situation has the characteristics which it seems to have. For, if there be now no reason to doubt that the objective constituent of the recent perceptual situation had the characteristics which we remember that it seemed to have, there is no reason to doubt that the objective constituent of the present inspective situation has the characteristics which it seems to have.

The upshot of the matter is that there is no reason to doubt that inspection gives us information which is accurate, so far as it goes, about certain characteristics which actually belong to the inspected object; and there is no reason to doubt that these characteristics did actually belong to the objective constituent of the immediately past perceptual situation. For the only ground for doubting either of these propositions is the assumption that the objective constituent of a perceptual situation must be literally identical with a certain part of the perceived physical object. And we saw, in discussing Perception, that there are almost conclusive objections to this assumption.

Introspection Proper. It will be remembered that I refused to call the kind of cognition which I have just been discussing "Introspection" because I think it doubtful whether its objects, viz., sensa, images, bodily feelings, etc., can properly be regarded as "states of mind". I am doubtful whether they are even existentially *mind-dependent*, though I think it likely that they are to some extent *qualitatively* mind-dependent. Even if they be existentially mind-dependent it would not follow that they can be counted as states of our minds, *i.e.*, as literally parts of that strand of history which is our Empirical Self. When we reflect I think we find that we do not really regard noises, visual and auditory images, and so on, as literally parts of ourselves or items in our mental history, in the sense in which we do regard "being aware of" a noise or an image as part of our mental history. About bodily feelings I think we are more doubtful. This is because we find more difficulty in distinguishing between a toothache and the awareness of a toothache than in distinguishing between a noise and the awareness of a noise. However this may be I think that every one would admit that what is indubitably mental and indubitably part of our mental history is such events as "being aware of a noise", "contemplating an image", "remembering a past event", "seeing a penny", and so on. If there are situations in which we have intuitive and non-inferential knowledge of such heterogeneous mental events as these there is no doubt that they would be called "introspective situations" *par excellence*.

We must begin by distinguishing these heterogeneous mental events into two classes, viz. (i) those which do, and (ii) those which do not have an external reference to an epistemological object. As we have seen, perceptual and memory-situations belong to the former class. So far as I can see, purely inspective situations would belong to the latter class. So would pure sensation, the mere awareness of an image, etc. Whether situations of the second kind ever exist in isolation is a doubtful point; I am inclined to think that pure sensations, etc., are ideal-limits rather than actual facts. But all situations of the first kind involve situations of the second kind; we cannot perceive without sensing, or remember without being aware of a sensum or an image of some kind. Let us call situations of the first kind "referential" and those of the second kind "non-referential".

As we have said, all referential situations (*e.g.*, perceptual situations) have both an epistemological object (*e.g.* the top of a certain penny) and an objective constituent (*e.g.*, a patch which appears brown and elliptical). They also *involve* a situation which is non-referential but has an objective constituent (*e.g.*, the sensing of this sensum). When I say that they "involve" this, I think I mean something of the following kind. I mean that the perceptual situation could not exist unless I sensed this sensum, whilst it seems *logically* possible that I should sense a precisely similar sensum without perceiving anything. Whether this is *causally* possible is another question; and whether, even if it be causally possible, it ever *in fact* happens is yet another question. I shall say that a perceptual situation is both "objective" and "referential". I shall say that a pure sensation of a noise or a patch would be "objective" and "non-referential"; meaning that it would have an objective constituent, but no epistemological object. Now, in theory there might be mental events which were referential and non-objective; and mental events which were non-referential and non-objective. I do not think that there are or could be instances of the former class. I am inclined to think that a referential situation must also be an objective situation. But I am not at all sure that there are not mental events which are both non-objective and non-referential. Suppose, *e.g.*, that noises, apparently coloured patches, and so on, were literally mental events, as many excellent people have held. Then it seems quite clear that they would be both non-objective and non-referential; for a noise certainly does not contain something else as an objective constituent, as a perceptual situation may contain a noise as an objective constituent. Even if we deny that noises, coloured patches, and so on, are mental events, we might be inclined to hold that toothaches and other more obscure bodily feelings are so. If we do, we must count them as non-objective and non-referential mental events.

We must of course carefully distinguish between being "objective" in the present sense, and being "objectifiable." And we must further distinguish between being "epistemologically objectifiable" and being "psychologically objectifiable". To be "objective" means to be a situation which *has* an objective constituent. To be "epistemologically objectifiable" means to be capable of corresponding to the epistemological object of some referential situation. Now *everything* is in principle epistemologically objectifiable, for everything can at least be thought about, and is thus capable of corresponding to the epistemological object of some thought-situation. To be "psychologically objectifiable" means to be capable of being an objective constituent of some objective mental situation. If a toothache be a non-objective mental event, it nevertheless becomes an objective constituent of a mental situation whenever it is inspected. If a noise be a non-objective mental event, it nevertheless becomes an objective constituent of a mental situation whenever it is sensed, or selected, or inspected, or used for perceiving. Thus, such events as these are certainly psychologically objectifiable even if they be themselves non-objective mental events. On the other hand, there is no reason whatever why *all* mental events should be psychologically objectifiable. It is in fact just those events which are certainly objective, in the present sense, about which we may most plausibly doubt whether they are psychologically objectifiable.

All mental events which we need consider at present are certainly "owned" by some Empirical Self; *i.e.*, they are literally parts of its history. Now owning is not itself a mode of cognition. What is owned may be "felt" or "sensed"; and this is a mode of cognition. But, even if everything that is owned be felt or sensed, and everything that is felt or sensed be owned, the relation of owning differs from that of feeling or sensing. What is felt or sensed may be selected; and what is selected may be inspected or used as the objective constituent of some referential situation, such as perception or memory.

We must then distinguish three kinds of event, of which the following are examples. (i) A noise or a toothache. This is studied by inspection; and, if it be a mental event at all, it will be non-objective and non-referential. Such mental events, if such there be, may be called "purely subjective". (ii) The feeling of a toothache or the sensing of a noise. This is an objective and non-referential mental event. (iii) The perception of a process in one's tooth by means of the felt tooth-ache ; or the perception of a process in a bell by means of the sensed noise. This is an objective and referential mental event. If there be introspection proper, as distinct from inspection, it is concerned with events of the second and third kind. Let us begin by considering our knowledge of objective but non-referential situations, such as sensing a noise or feeling a pang of toothache.

People who deny that we can introspect such situations rest their case on the fact that, when I try to *intro*spect the situation of *sensing* a noise or *feeling* a toothache, I seem to find myself merely *in*specting the *noise* or the *toothache* itself. I imagine that this is what people are referring to when they talk of the "diaphanous" character of "consciousness". Others admit that they seem to find something beside the noise or the toothache, but tell us that this "something more" is merely certain feelings connected with the adjustment of their sense-organs or with the reactions of other parts of their bodies. These men are also inclined to deny that we can introspect the situation of sensing a noise or feeling a toothache. Now it seems to me that the latter set of psychologists are very nearly right in what they assert, and quite wrong in what they deny. If there be such a thing as an objective situation it must presumably consist of at least two constituents, related in a certain specific way by an asymmetrical relation so that one of these constituents occupies a special position (viz., that of *objective* constituent) and the other occupies a characteristically different position (viz., that of *subjective* constituent). Now suppose that there were complexes of this kind, and that I were acquainted with them introspectively, we ought not to expect the relating relation, which makes this a complex of such and such a structure, to be presented to us in the same way as the substantival constituents. The relating relation of a complex never is a constituent of it in the same sense in which the terms are. When I look at a pattern composed of three dots, A, B, and C, arranged in that order on a line, I know intuitively that B is between A and C. But I do not "see" the relation of "between" in the sense in which I "see" the dots; though it would be quite in accordance with usage to say that "I see *that* B is between A and C". Now no one in his senses supposes that the fact that I "see" nothing but the dots proves, *either* that the dots are not in fact related in a certain order by the relation of "between", *or* that I do not know this relation in a perfectly direct and non-inferential way. People who make such facts as we have been mentioning an argument against the possibility of introspective knowledge of objective mental situations are demanding of introspection something which no one thinks of demanding of inspection, and something which is from the nature of the case incapable of fulfilment. If they contented themselves with saying: "When I try to introspect the sensing of a noise or the feeling of a pang of toothache the only *particular existents* which are intuitively presented to me are the noise or the toothache and certain bodily feelings," they might be approximately or exactly right. But it seems to me perfectly clear that these particular existents are presented to me as *terms*, each of which occupies a characteristic position in a *complex* of a certain specific kind. This complex *is* the objective mental situation of sensing the noise or feeling the toothache; and we have direct non-inferential knowledge of its relating relation, as we have of the relating relation of "between" when a pattern of three dots in a line is presented to our inspection. Naturally, further knowledge of the situation will consist largely in learning more about the characteristics of its constituents by *in*-specting them; just as we should learn more about a pattern of dots of various colours by seeing exactly what colour belongs to each dot in each position in the pattern. But, if we were confined to inspecting each constituent, we should never know that they were constituents of a whole of a certain specific structure. And it seems to me that we do know this about the noise or the toothache and the bodily feelings which we find when we try to introspect the situation of sensing a noise or feeling a toothache.

There is one other remark to be made before leaving this subject. Suppose, for the sake of argument, that, when I try to introspect the situation of sensing a noise or feeling a toothache, *no* particular existent except the noise or the toothache itself were presented to my mind as an object. It would still be most rash to conclude that the situation *does not* contain anything but the noise or the toothache, or to conclude that I cannot *know* directly and non-inferentially that it contains more than this. Suppose, *e.g.*, that the situation contained two constituents, one of which is sensed and can be selected, whilst the other is only sensed or felt and cannot be selected or inspected. Then, if we tried to introspect the situation, nothing would be presented to us except the former constituent. But, since the other constituent is sensed or felt by us, though it cannot be selected or inspected by us, we might quite well know with complete certainty that what we are inspecting is not the whole of the situation. We must therefore always be prepared for the possibility that the constituents of a mental situation which we can actually inspect *are not* the whole of its constituents; and we must be prepared to recognise that we may be able to *know* this directly and non-inferentially because the remaining constituents are felt or sensed by us though not selected or inspected.

To sum up. I cannot of course *prove* that we have introspective knowledge of such situations as sensing a noise or feeling a toothache, beside inspective knowledge of the noise or toothache itself. I can only say that it seems to me that I do have it, though it may be very inadequate; and that I do not understand how otherwise I could distinguish between the *existence* of noises and toothaches and the *sensing or feeling* of them. But I do think that I have shown that the reasons which have been brought forward for believing that I do not have such knowledge are utterly inadequate to prove this conclusion or even to make it probable.

I now pass to the case of mental situations which are referential as well as objective ; *e.g.*, perceptual situations, memory-situations, and so on. There is a difficulty here which does not apply to non-referential objective situations, such as we have just been considering. It seems very doubtful whether I can at the same time refer to an epistemological object and also make the mental situation which has this external reference into an objective constituent of an introspective situation. For this would require a division of attention between two very different objects, and it is doubtful whether we can accomplish anything more than a quick alternation of attention backwards and forwards between the two. Here I think we must draw a distinction between two different cases ; viz., (i) attending simultaneously to two objects of the same order, and (ii) attending to a situation which itself involves attending to something else. It is the latter of these which I doubt to be possible ; and this would be involved by the claim to introspect perceptual and memory-situations. The former seems to me to be difficult, but not impossible. Attention has various degrees ; and, although it may be impossible to attend *equally* to two different objects of the same order at the same time, it does seem to be possible to distribute one's attention so that each of them gets some of it, though one gets more than the other. In particular it seems to me to be possible to attend to a situation which does not itself involve attention to something else, and at the same time to use this situation as the objective constituent of a memory-situation which refers to a certain epistemological object. I therefore suggest that what is called "introspecting" a perceptual or memory-situation should be analysed as follows. (*a*) We really do introspect something else, which is now present; and (*b*) we make this "something else" the objective constituent of a memory-situation whose epistemological object is such that, if *anything* corresponds to it, what does so is the immediately past perceptual or memory-situation which we are commonly said to be "introspecting."

The next question is: "What is it that we really do introspect in such cases, and make the objective constituent of a memory-situation?" Let us suppose that we are concerned with a perceptual situation. This contains (*a*) a sensed and selected sensum; (*b*) certain bodily feelings connected with the adjustment and excitement of the relevant sense-organs; (*c*) certain bodily feelings connected with the adjustment of our muscles, etc., in order to respond to the situation; (*d*) *possibly* certain images, and *certainly* vague but characteristic feelings, due to the excitement of traces. The whole of these are bound together into a complex of an unique kind, in consequence of which the whole situation has such and such an external reference. Suppose now that we pass immediately from the perceptive to the introspective attitude. (*a*) There will still be a sensed and selected sensum, continuous with and qualitatively similar to that which was the objective constituent of the immediately past perceptual situation. (*b*) Since the relevant sense-organs will still be adjusted and excited as before, the bodily feelings connected with these will be continuous with and qualitatively like those which were constituents of the perceptual situation. (*c*) On the other hand, we shall no longer be adjusting our muscles, etc., so as to react to the situation practically. Hence the feelings connected with such adjustments in the past perceptual situation will not be continued in the present situation. It is not unlikely, however, that they will be represented by images which resemble them in quality and bear the mark of "familiarity". (d) The traces excited in the perceptual situation will still be excited, so that the present situation will contain images and feelings which are continuous with and similar to those which were due to the excitement of these traces in the perceptual situation. So far then there is probably a great resemblance between the constituents of the present situation, which we introspect, and the immediately past situation, which we remember by means of it. There is probably no constituent of the present introspected situation which does not resemble or continue some constituent of the immediately past perceptual situation. And the constituents of the introspected situation are probably so related that its structure is at least analogous to that of the perceptual situation. But there is this difference. The images, feelings, etc., were purely subjective constituents of the original perceptual situation. The feelings, images, etc., which continue and resemble them in the introspect*ed* situation, are now psychologically objectified ; *i.e.*, they have become objective constituents of the introspect*ive* situation. The latter contains a new subjective constituent, which consists of (or, at any rate, includes) those bodily feelings which are characteristic of the purely theoretic and contemplative situation of introspecting as distinct from the active and practical situation of perceiving. And this new subjective constituent is related in a characteristic way to the introspected situation and its constituents, so that the whole thus formed contains the latter as its objective constituent. In contemplating the constituents and the structure of the present introspected situation we remember the similar constituents and the analogous, but not identical, structure of the immediately past perceptual situation.

This memory-judgment has no more claim to infallibility than any other memory-judgment about equally recent events. Like all such judgments, it cannot be defended by argument against a sceptic who chooses to doubt the trustworthiness of memory *in general*. But there is no *special* reason for doubting the substantial correctness of this particular kind of memory-judgment; and therefore no special reason to doubt that perceptual and other referential situations have substantially the structure and the constituents which we assign to them on the ground of introspection and memory.

Summary of Conclusions. (*A*). (1) If there were a Pure Ego, and it were timeless, it might literally be part of the total objective constituent of every introspective situation. But (2) even if it were so, it certainly does not manifest any of its empirical qualities (if it has any) in any introspective situation. And (3) it is certainly never the whole of the objective constituent of any introspective situation. (4) There is therefore no direct reason to believe that it is a part of the objective constituent of any introspective situation. (5) If it exists, and is known at all, it is known discursively by comparison of contemporary and successive mental events which we introspect. It does not follow from this that its existence and properties are known, if at all, only by inference.

(*B*) (1) The Empirical Self cannot, from its nature, be literally an objective constituent of any introspective situation. But (2) it is possible that every introspective situation might claim that its objective constituent is literally a part of the Empirical Self; and it is possible that this claim might be true. (3) If we distinguish Introspection Proper from Inspection, I think we must admit that this claim is made by all genuinely introspective situations. And (4) there seems to be no positive reason for rejecting it, as there is in the case of the analogous claim which the perceptual situation makes for its objective constituent. (5) This does not imply that there may not be mental events which are not parts of the history of any Empirical Self. It implies only that, if there be such events, they are not possible objects of introspection.

(*C*). (1) The so-called "Epistemological Introspection", by which we know "what we are believing", "what we are desiring", and so on, is not a special kind of introspection. It can be analysed into a process which is not introspection at all, and into another which is ordinary Psychological Introspection. (2) There are situations in which an event, such as an image, a twinge of toothache, a noise, etc., are examined with a view to discovering accurately their own apparent qualities instead of learning about the physical qualities of our own or external bodies. Such situations are called by us "Inspective", because it is doubtful whether the events which are their objective constituents are states of mind at all. (3) If such events be states of mind, they are "non-objective", in the sense that they do not *contain* objective constituents, though they may *be* and often are objective constituents of other mental events. And, on this supposition, inspection will be the kind of introspection which is concerned with non-objective mental events. (4) Introspection proper is concerned with objective situations, such as perceptual and memory-situations, the sensing of sensa, the feeling of toothaches, and so on. These are undoubtedly mental events ; and it is an essential factor of the introspective situation to claim that they are parts of the history of the Empirical Self.

(*D*) (1) There is no reason to doubt that inspection is correct, so far as it goes, in the information which it supplies about the apparent characteristics of its objective constituents. And (2) there is no good reason to doubt that the latter have the characteristics which they seem on careful inspection to have. But (3) there is no ground for supposing that inspective knowledge is exhaustive. An inspected whole may have sets of adjoined parts, such that no member of one of these sets is revealed to inspection. And members of such sets may have characteristics which are not manifested to inspection, which differ from those that are manifested as belonging to the whole, and which differ from those that are manifested as belonging to members of other sets of adjoined parts of the same inspected whole. (4) When we profess to be inspecting the objective constituent of a perceptual situation we are probably inspecting a later event, which is continuous with and qualitatively similar to the former ; and are using it as the basis for a memory-judgment about the former. This memory-judgment is not infallible ; but it has as good a chance of being true as any memory-judgment, and a better chance than most.

(E). (1) The existence of introspection proper has been denied on the ground that, when we try to introspect an objective situation, we find ourselves merely inspecting its objective constituent ; or, at best, this together with certain bodily feelings. (2) This contention has no weight, because it rests on the assumption that, if we have non-inferential knowledge of the structure of a whole, this structure must be presented in the same way as the constituents. And this demand is absurd. Moreover (3) it is perfectly possible that an objective situation may have constituents which cannot be made into objects of inspection. And it is possible that we may know this ; because these constituents, though not capable of being selected or inspected, are nevertheless sensed or felt. (4) It seems likely that we cannot strictly introspect situations which, beside being objective, have also an external reference to an epistemological object. This is not so much because it is difficult to attend to two different objects at once as because it is difficult to attend to a situation which itself involves attention to something else. (5) Here again we have probably to be content with introspecting a present non-referential situation and using this as the basis for memory-judgments about the structure and constituents of the immediately past referential situation. Such memory-judgments are not infallible ; but there is no *special* reason for thinking that they are peculiarly likely to be incorrect.

CHAPTER VII

The Mind's Knowledge of Other Minds

THE proper analysis of our belief in the existence of other minds, and the question of how it can be justified, have been far less thoroughly discussed by philosophers than the corresponding questions about matter and our alleged knowledge of it. Many philosophers have *wanted* to deny the reality of material objects, and have felt that it was a feather in their caps when they succeeded in doing so to the satisfaction of themselves and their followers. But, seemingly, no one *wants* to be a Solipsist; and scarcely anyone has admitted himself to be one. It has been left to rival philosophers to tell him that, on his principles, he ought to be one; and this has generally been regarded as a charge to be repelled and not as a compliment to be thankfully acknowledged. We should be doing too much credit to human consistency if we ascribed this to the fact that all convinced Solipsists have kept silence and refused to waste their words on the empty air. It would seem then that we have a stronger belief in the existence of other minds than in the existence of material things. No one in his senses doubts either proposition in practice; but the philosopher can and does doubt the latter in his study, whilst, even in that chaste seclusion, he seems to be unable or unwilling to doubt the former. I do not think that this difference can be ascribed either to the fact that the evidence for the existence of other minds is more cogent than the evidence for the existence of matter, or to the fact that we have a stronger instinctive belief in the former than in the latter. I think that the real explanation is that certain strong emotions are bound up with the belief in other minds, and that no very strong emotions are bound up with the belief in matter. The position of a philosopher with no one but himself to lecture to, and no hope of an audience, would be so tragic that the human mind naturally shrinks from contemplating such a possibility. It is our business, however, to stifle our emotions for the present, and to follow the argument whithersoever it may lead.

Analysis of the Belief in Other Minds. I wish to begin, as usual, with propositions about which every one will agree. Now, I think it would be admitted by every one that the perception of a foreign body of a certain kind, which moves, alters its expression, makes noises, and so on, in certain characteristic ways, is a necessary part of the basis of our belief in the existence and activity of another mind. The only exception to this statement that I can think of is that some few people have claimed under exceptional circumstances to be in direct communion with God or with other spirits without perceiving a characteristic kind of body moving in characteristic ways or making characteristic sounds. But such claims are rare and hard to test. Setting aside such exceptional cases for the present, I think we may say that the above proposition would generally be admitted.

I want at once to remove two possible misunderstandings. (1) I say only that the perception of such physical objects and events is a necessary *part* of the basis of our belief in other minds. I do not say that it is sufficient. There may be other ingredients which are equally necessary. (2) I say only that the perception of such physical objects and events is a necessary part of the *basis* of the belief in other minds. I express no opinion at present about the nature of the connexion between this perception and this belief. In particular I must not be understood to be asserting that the perceptual judgment forms a *premise* from which the belief in other minds is *inferred*. The sensing and selecting of a certain sensum is a necessary part of the basis of our perceptual belief in the existence of a certain physical object or the happening of a certain physical event. But the two are not connected as premise and conclusion of an argument.

We must next distinguish between our belief that a certain external body is animated by a mind other than our own, and the belief that at a certain moment a certain mental event which does not belong to my mental history is happening in intimate connexion with a certain external body. A mind, in the sense of an Empirical Self, consists of a number of simultaneous and successive mental events united into a whole of a certain characteristic structure. Hence, whenever we believe that a certain external body is animated by a certain mind, we are no doubt equally justified in believing that there is a series of mental events of *some* kind intimately connected with this body. But it might well happen that we believed much more strongly that this body is animated by a mind than that a particular mental event of a certain specific kind was going on in this mind at a certain time and expressing itself by a certain particular perceptible bodily change. I may be practically certain that the body of my friend is animated by a mind ; and yet very doubtful, on a certain occasion when I see him frowning, whether he is angry, or thinking deeply, or in pain. Again, it is very far from certain that all mental events must occur as members of those sets of interrelated mental events which we call "Empirical Selves". We might then strongly believe that a certain movement of an external body is the outward expression of a certain mental event which does not belong to our mind ; and yet we might be very doubtful whether this external body is animated by a mind at all. *E.g.*, I might feel tolerably certain that, when an insect is injured and writhes about, there is a feeling of pain which is no part of my mind and is intimately connected with these writhing movements of the insect's body. And yet I might be very doubtful whether the insect's body is animated by anything that could reasonably be called a "mind". This feeling might be quite isolated. Or, if it be in fact a member of a group of interrelated simultaneous and successive mental events, this group might be so poor in content and so loose in structure as not to deserve the name of "mind". When we contemplate other human bodies and their behaviour (including in this their speech and writing) we do believe both that they are animated by minds and that certain specific mental events are going on in those minds when the bodies behave in certain specific ways. Most men believe that the bodies of cats and dogs are animated by minds, and also that certain specific events are going on in these minds when cats and dogs behave in certain ways. Even if we doubt this on philosophic reflexion, we find it very difficult not to act as if we believed it. But even here I think we are slightly more certain that there are specific experiences connected with certain specific bodily behaviour than that the body of the animal is animated by a mind. If one sees and hears an animal, such as a dog or a rabbit, with its leg caught in a trap, it is practically impossible at the time to doubt that there is a painful feeling which is being expressed by its struggles and cries. But one would feel a little less certain that the body of a dog or a rabbit is animated by anything that could fairly be called a "mind", unless one were already convinced that all mental events must belong to some mind. When we come to living beings which are very different from ourselves, such as insects, we feel rather doubtful about postulating mental events at all; more doubtful about the precise character of the mental event which accompanies a given movement; and extremely doubtful about the supposition that there is a mind which animates the body of the insect.

Let us henceforth confine ourselves to the case of human bodies and their perceptible behaviour. I think it will be agreed that, when we see anything which has the characteristic shape, size, appearance, and movements of a human body, we treat it as if it were animated by a mind like our own. And, if it responds to this treatment in the way in which we expect it to do, we have no doubt whatever on this point. If it does not, we have much the same feeling of shock and surprise as we have when we lift something which looks like a heavy weight but is really made of painted cardboard. Our presumption that this body is animated by a mind is, as I have said, based on its general appearance in the first instance; but it is supported or refuted by the order and connexion (or the lack of these) which we afterwards find in its behaviour. A particular, and vitally important, case of this general principle is that of connected rational speech. If something which looks like a human being talks in a connected way, and makes appropriate answers to questions, it is not practically possible to doubt that it is animated by a mind. Since a mind is a whole of suitably interrelated mental events, it is natural enough that the basis for our belief in other minds should be suitably connected series of physical events rather than any particular isolated physical event.

Besides this general belief that things which look like human bodies and perform certain chains of behaviour are animated by minds, we have more specific beliefs about what is going on in those minds on certain occasions. On observing certain facial expressions, such as frowning, we have a tendency to believe that there is a certain emotion, such as anger, in the mind which animates the body which we are observing. On hearing a human body emit certain sounds we have a tendency to believe that the mind which animates it is suffering a painful sensation, and so on. Here we must draw a sharp distinction between two different ways in which we may come to believe that a certain mind is having a certain experience. (i) The body which we are perceiving may make a series of noises or conventional gestures which form a coherent and intelligible "sentence". This sentence we understand, and we then tend to believe that the mind which animates this body is having the experience which we understand that it is describing to us. In that case we assign to the mind, not only the particular experience which it is describing, but also a certain kind of cognitive experience. When a body emits the series of noises: "I have toothache", we commonly believe that the mind which animates it has this peculiar feeling, unless we have some special reason to think that it is lying. But, in addition to this, we always believe that it is making a judgment of some sort. If it is trying to tell the truth, it is making a judgment about its present experience. And, if it is lying, it is still making a judgment about something. We may call this way of arousing belief in the existence of a certain mental event a "conventional expression". (ii) We ascribe on certain occasions certain experiences to a foreign mind even when it does not and cannot tell us of them. And, conversely, beings who cannot understand spoken or written words probably ascribe certain experiences to other minds on certain occasions. If I see a baby smiling or hear a dog snarling I ascribe a pleasant feeling to the baby and a feeling of anger to the dog, although they cannot describe their experiences to me by any conventional expression. And, on the other hand, it seems most likely that babies and dogs often know when those who surround them are angry or pleased, although such creatures could not understand what we were saying if we tried to describe our mental states to them. I will call this way of arousing belief in the existence of a certain experience in a foreign mind "natural expression". The experiences which most obviously have characteristic natural expressions are certain emotions, such as anger, and pleasant or painful bodily feelings. But I think that there are other experiences which have characteristic natural expressions. If I am doing something and another human body starts to struggle with me and try to hinder me I can hardly help believing that the mind which animates this body has a volition which is opposed to what I am doing. If, on the other hand, the other human body starts to co-operate with me I can hardly help believing that the mind which animates it has a volition which is in accord with what I am doing. Again, if I see another human body performing a chain of actions which seem well adapted to lead up to a certain end; if I see it avoiding obstacles or trying to modify them; I can hardly help believing that this body is animated by a mind which is not only desiring a certain end but is also thinking about the proper means to gain it. Lastly, whenever a body emits coherent and intelligible sentences it is always *naturally* expressing the kind of experience called "judgment" or "supposition" or "questioning", no matter what else it may be *conventionally* expressing. If it says "I have toothache", and I believe what the words mean, this set of sounds conventionally expresses to me the presence of a feeling of toothache; but the mere fact that the words form an intelligible sentence naturally expresses to me the presence of an act of judgment. When I say that I have a certain state of mind I deliberately and conventionally express only that state of mind; but I involuntarily and naturally express in addition the state of mind called "judging". It seems clear that natural expression is more primitive and fundamental than conventional expression, so we will begin with it.

Natural Expression. The question to be considered in this subsection is: "What is the nature of the connexion between perceiving a certain facial expression or natural gesture in a foreign body and believing that there is a certain mental event going on at the time and expressing itself through this bodily event?"

In the first place, I must point out that we are probably intellectualising the situation when we talk of a "belief in" or "judgment about" the mental event. As in the case of perception, it would be truer to say that we act *as if* we believed that such and such an event was happening, and are surprised if the results of our action give us the lie. So we had better talk of a "quasi-belief". A dog acts as it would be reasonable for him to act if he believed his master to be angry when his master shows the external signs of anger; but it is very doubtful whether the dog has the peculiar experience of judging or believing a proposition. And, in most of our intercourse with other human beings, we are in the same position as the dog in the example. The only difference is that we can reflect and afterwards make the judgment "in accordance with which" we have been acting; whilst a dog or a baby presumably cannot.

I can now clear the ground by making certain negative statements. (1) It seems to me to be absolutely certain that the belief in other human minds, and the belief that a certain human mind is having a certain experience on a certain occasion, are not *reached* by inference, even if they can be afterwards *justified* up to the hilt by inference. It is perfectly certain that I do not now make an inference when I see my friend frowning and believe that he is angry. And the notion that, as a baby, I began by looking in a mirror when I felt cross, noting my facial expression at the time, observing a similar expression from time to time on the face of my mother or nurse, and then arguing by analogy that these external bodies are probably animated by minds like my own, which are feeling cross, is too silly to need refutation. If the belief in other minds and other mental events were reached in this way, it might perhaps be entertained as a bold speculative opinion by a few exceptionally ingenious and observant persons at the ripe age of thirty-five. Its actual strength and its universal distribution would be utterly inexplicable on this hypothesis.

(2) Next, I think it is equally clear that our ascription of minds to other human bodies, and our ascription of certain states to these minds on certain occasions, cannot be due to direct associations acquired in the course of our lives. A direct association between a certain facial expression and a certain emotion could arise only in the following way. We should need to have often seen a certain expression (*e.g.*, a frown) on our own faces when we felt a certain emotion (*e.g.*, anger). If this could happen often enough, the visual appearance of this facial change might be associated with this emotion. When we saw a similar expression on another face we might automatically believe in the existence of a similar emotion, and we might locate it in the mind which animates this other body. But (i) the conditions which would be needed for the establishment of such an association are not and cannot in fact be fulfilled. We cannot see our own facial expressions at all except by looking in mirrors; and most of us pass through life with very little direct perceptual knowledge of what we "look like" when we feel angry, or pleased, or in pain. Of course, the same remarks do not apply to the natural expression of states of mind by interjectional noises. A baby who is in pain and howls can hear itself howling. An association might therefore be formed in its mind between the feeling of pain and the sound of howling. If it now heard a similar howl from another baby, it might automatically ascribe a painful feeling to it. Still, it is plain that this will not carry us very far; for many states of mind which have a natural expression are not naturally expressed by characteristic sounds, but by characteristic facial modifications. (ii) Even if

an association were somehow established between the visual appearance of a certain facial expression and the occurrence of a certain state of mind in ourselves, it is not obvious that this would suffice to explain our belief that this state is now happening in another mind when we see this expression on another face. The sight of this expression on another face might simply evoke a mild occurrence of the feeling in my own mind. But, even if it evokes in me the *idea* of that feeling, I might make various uses of this idea. I might just as well think of the *past* occurrence of this feeling in *myself* as believe in the *present* occurrence of this feeling in *another*. We may conclude then that the supposed association could not in fact be formed in the course of our lives; and that, even if it were, it would not suffice by itself to account for our belief that a certain kind of event is happening in another mind when we see a certain kind of expression on another face.

There are two kinds of direct association which *may* be formed in the course of our lives, and must be carefully distinguished from the kind of association which I have just rejected. (i) When I frown, or have any other characteristic bodily modification, there is no doubt a characteristic bodily feeling. It is therefore very likely indeed that an association is quickly formed between certain of my mental states and the bodily feelings which are connected with their natural expression. But this kind of association evidently does not carry me beyond my own mind and its states. (ii) It may be that a certain facial expression in another body which I can perceive has often been followed by overt action on the part of that body, and that this has often ended by producing some characteristic sensation and emotion in my mind. *E.g.*, it might be that, as a rule, when I have seen people frowning, they have followed up their frowns by blows; and these may have caused pain and fear in my mind. An association may thus be formed between the perception of another's frown and the expectation of pain and fear in myself. But exactly the same kind of association may be formed in connexion with objects to which we do not ascribe minds or mental states, as when a "burnt child" learns to "dread the fire." Hence this kind of association cannot suffice to account for our belief in the existence of other minds, or of certain mental states which do not belong to our own minds.

(3) It is now clear that we do not come to believe by a process of inference that other human bodies are animated by minds, and that we do not come to believe this through associations which have been formed in the course of our lives. And it is not in consequence of inference or of acquired associations that we ascribe certain states to other minds on seeing certain facial expressions on other bodies. Hence only two alternatives seem to be left. Either (i) there are certain cognitive situations which actually contain other minds or certain of their states as objective constituents; or (ii) the visual appearance of certain bodily forms, movements, gestures, and modifications, has for us an *unacquired* meaning; so that, from the first, we pass from perceiving such things to believing that the perceived body is animated by a mind, and that this mind is owning such and such an experience. I will now say something about these two alternatives.

For reasons which have been repeated *ad nauseam* in the case of perception and introspection it is not possible that a mind, in the sense of an Empirical Self which may endure for years, can literally be a constituent of a cognitive situation which may last only for a few minutes. So at most we can suppose that the objective constituents of certain of our cognitive situations are mental events which in fact form parts of the history of other Empirical Selves. There is unfortunately no name, corresponding to "perception" and "introspection", for those situations in which we seem to be in direct cognitive contact with other minds and their states. But, as we shall often have to refer to them, we had better invent a name for them. For want of a better word, let us call them "extraspective situations". This name is not to imply any special theory about the right analysis of such situations.

We must next notice that, even if mental events which are not owned by our minds be *parts* of the objective constituent of an extraspective situation, they are never the whole of its objective constituent. The perception of another body and of certain movements or modifications of it is essential to extraspection; and so one part of the objective constituent of any extraspective situation is the visual and other sensa by which the foreign body appears to us in perception. If there be cognitive situations in which a mental event belonging to another mind is the *sole* objective constituent, they must be classed separately. They might be called "telepathic" or "telegnostic", as distinct from "extraspective" situations. It will be remembered that we said that a perceptual situation always involves a sensational situation, and that it is perhaps doubtful whether purely sensational situations actually exist or are causally possible. On the alternative which we are at present considering, some if not all extraspective situations would involve a telegnostic situation; whilst all would involve a perceptual situation. It is of course certain that perceptual situations can and do exist apart from extraspective situations; but a person who accepted the present alternative about extraspective situations might quite legitimately doubt whether purely telegnostic situations exist or are causally possible.

The next point to notice is this. It would not be necessary for an upholder of the present theory to assert that *all* extraspective situations contain a foreign mental event as part of their objective constituent. Suppose that a considerable number of extraspective situations involve telegnostic situations; that they all involve perceptual situations with characteristic objective constituents; and that purely telegnostic situations rarely, if ever, arise. Then an association would be formed between such and such visual and auditory appearances and such and such foreign mental events. Suppose now that a purely perceptual situation were to arise, having for its objective constituents these characteristic visual and auditory sensa. Then this association would probably be excited, and we should automatically believe in the existence of such and such a foreign mental event, though it is not part of the objective constituent of the present cognitive situation. Beliefs reached in this way might often be true; but they might often be false. Thus the present theory is quite compatible with the existence of delusive extraspective situations.

Now the kind of association which would certainly be formed if the present theory be true would presumably work both ways. Suppose then that a purely telegnostic situation were to arise. The association would now tend to call up images of a human being with the facial expression which corresponds to the mental event which is being telegnostically cognised, and it might lead to a perceptual belief that his body is now present to our senses. The result would be to produce an extraspective situation which is delusive on its perceptual side. If the reader will do what most philosophers are too proud and most scientists too prejudiced to do, and will study the evidence for "telepathy" in *Phantasms of the Living*, and the evidence which has accumulated since 1886 as marshalled by Mrs Sidgwick in the *S.P.R. Proceedings* for October 1922, he will see that a large proportion of the cases are of the kind just suggested. There is little evidence for pure telegnosis; but there is a great deal of excellent evidence for the existence of extraspective situations which are delusive on their perceptual side and veridical on their telegnostic side. By this I mean that the mental event which the experient claims to be apprehending really has happened at much the same time in a mind whose body is far away ; but that the apprehension of this event has generally been accompanied by and bound up with an hallucinatory perceptual experience in which this body seems to be present to the experient.

On the other alternative which we have to consider the extraspective situation *never* contains a foreign mental state as part of its objective constituent; *i.e.*, it never involves a telegnostic situation. We must suppose that the innate constitution of human beings (and probably of other gregarious animals) is such that, when one sees any body which *in fact* resembles his own closely enough, he instinctively believes it to be animated by a mind like his own. And we must suppose that, whenever one sees in another a facial expression or hears a noise which *in fact* resembles closely enough the facial expression or noise which in him is the natural expression of a certain kind of experience, he instinctively ascribes a similar experience to the mind which he believes to animate the body of the other. If there be other creatures like ourselves, and if we be largely dependent on them, we could not have survived unless we either had instinctive beliefs of this kind, which are in the main true, or had telegnostic knowledge of some of their mental states.

The next question is whether we can decide between these two alternatives. In the first place, we might accept the positive part of the second alternative, and deny or doubt the negative part. We might admit that there are such instinctive beliefs as the second theory assumes, and that there is also in certain cases genuine telegnosis. And it might be that those particular perceptual situations which call forth the instinctive beliefs are also those which are most favourable to the occurrence of a telegnostic situation. I think we may say at once that an analysis of extraspective situations which accepted telegnosis and denied the existence of these instinctive beliefs would be far less plausible than one which denied telegnosis and accepted the existence of these instinctive beliefs. For it is by no means certain that such instinctive beliefs, eked out by subsequent inference and association interpreted in terms of these beliefs, would not suffice to account for all the known facts about extraspection. After all, such a theory would leave our extraspective beliefs in foreign minds and mental events in no worse position than our perceptual beliefs in external physical events and things, if my analysis of sense-perception be admitted. In fact it would be in a slightly stronger position. For I have argued that we probably do have direct inspective knowledge of *some* mental events, whilst we probably do not have this kind of knowledge of *any* physical events. Thus we do not need any special postulate or category to provide us with the notion of a mental event, or to assure us that there are instances of such things ; whilst, if I am right, we probably do need something of the kind in the case of physical events and things.

If then we had nothing but ordinary extraspective situations to consider, I should be inclined to say that the assumption of a telegnostic factor is unnecessary and ungrounded, though it might still be true. But the actual position is somewhat different. From the study of abnormal phenomena it seems to me to be practically certain that there is such a mental power as telegnosis. It is therefore not a groundless assumption that it may be operative in some normal extraspective situations. And it is evident that, if it were present there mixed up with a perceptual situation and with instinctive beliefs about foreign mental events, it would be almost impossible to detect it. It therefore seems to me quite likely that there may be a telegnostic factor in many normal extraspective situations, *i.e.*, that their objective constituents may include foreign mental events. I do not see that I can prove this, or that anyone else can disprove it ; I merely say that I think there is a faint balance of probability in its favour in view of all the known facts.

Conventional Expression. A complete treatment of this subject would occupy volumes, and would be far beyond the powers of the present writer. I will therefore confine myself to a few remarks which seem specially relevant to our present purpose.

As I have said, all intelligible sentences are *natural* expressions, on the occasion of which we believe that we are in presence of a foreign mind which is owning a process of thinking, judging, and so on. The vast majority of intelligible sentences are not *about* the mental states of the person who utters them, and are therefore not conventional expressions of his state of mind. A sentence is a conventional expression of a state of mind only in so far as it asserts that the person who utters it is having this state. Even those sentences which do conventionally express a state of mind are very likely to be misleading. A man who says that he is having a certain emotion or volition may be intentionally trying to deceive us; or he may have introspected inaccurately, and be honestly mistaken; or he may be unable to find words which adequately express the results of a perfectly correct process of introspection; or we may be stupid and misunderstand the words which he uses. For all these reasons it is rash to believe that a certain man is having a certain experience at a certain time merely because he says that he is doing so. A prudent person checks such statements by noting the natural expressions of the speaker at the time and his subsequent actions and statements.

In fact, for our present purpose, the natural and unintentional expression, which belongs to all intelligible sentences as such, is far more important than the conventional and deliberate expression, which belongs to a small minority of them. The hearing or reading of intelligent and intelligible discourse (whether we accept or reject what it asserts) is *the* occasion *par excellence* on which we feel perfectly certain of the presence of a foreign *mind* as distinct from the presence of mere *mental events*. To avoid an obvious criticism I must here make one important qualification. I say that intelligible discourse is the natural sign of the presence of a mind and of the presence of "thought", in a wide sense. But I am quite well aware that a great deal of intelligible and intelligent speaking and writing is accompanied by very little thought about its ostensible subject-matter. It would not be unfair to say that, while we are speaking and writing most, we are thinking least; and that, while we are thinking most, we are speaking and writing least. Anyone who prepares lectures knows that he was thinking about the subject, and not speaking, during his preparation; whilst he can largely let his mind "go on holiday" (to use an excellent phrase of Descartes) during the actual delivery of the lecture. We must not therefore say that the utterance of an intelligible discourse is a sign that the mind is *now* thinking about what the body is talking about. But we do feel perfectly sure that an intelligible discourse can be uttered only by a body which is animated by a mind that *has* thought and is capable of thinking again. Even here we must make a further qualification. There are many intelligible sentences, uttered in ordinary conversation, which are neither the expression of a present thought about their subject-matter nor the result of past thought about this subject-matter in the mind of the person who utters them. Many "expressions" of political and religious "opinion", which occur in the conversation of quite intelligent men, are of this nature. Nevertheless, these sentences would not have been spoken if someone else at some time in the past had not exercised his mind on these subjects.

This brings us to a point where, as it seems to me, both Behaviourists and Bergsonians have gone wrong through failure to recognise an important distinction. Seeing how much of our alleged "thinking" is just the automatic reeling off of sentences or the mechanical manipulation of symbols, Behaviourists have tended to hold that all "thinking" reduces without residue to this. And Bergsonians have tended to contrast the merely mechanical processes of the "intellect" with a mysterious and superior faculty of "intuition", which is apparently supposed to be manifested in its purest form in the instinctive behaviour of animals. Now it seems to me that we must distinguish between what I call "fluid" and "crystallised" thinking. We must recognise that, whilst the greater part of any so-called process of "thinking" is of the latter kind, it must also contain short spells of the former. And we must recognise that the latter presupposes the previous occurrence of the former in the same mind or in some other mind. Anyone who considers what happens when he solves some problem for himself will recognise the difference. He would commonly be said to be "thinking" about the problem during the whole course of his work. Now, during the greater part of this period, he is certainly only manipulating symbols almost mechanically according to rules. But (i) at the beginning of the work, and at isolated intervals during the course of it, he must cease to do this and must contemplate face to face the actual abstract objects with which he is concerned and their actual relations to each other. When he does this he is performing acts of "fluid" thinking; and no facility in manipulating symbols is any substitute for this. The power to perform acts of fluid thinking constitutes that difference between a man and a well-trained parrot which the Behaviourists (doubtless from excess of modesty) are so loath to admit. (ii) I can now manipulate symbols blindly according to rules, and can feel confident that the result will accord with the real relations of things, only because I or my predecessors directly contemplated the things and their relations and made up a symbolism whose rules of operation were seen to accord with the relations of the things symbolised. Thus the symbolism is just the "crystallisation" of the past fluid thinking of myself or others ; and, if it were not, there would not be the faintest reason to treat these operations with symbols according to rules as anything more than solemn trifling. It is simply unintelligible to me how this fact can escape the notice of any competent person, or why the tacit denial of it should be supposed to mark a wonderful advance in psychology.

The position of the Bergsonians is less silly than that of the Behaviourists ; for the former do at least recognise that mere crystallised thinking will not account for the facts. But why they should *identify* intellectual processes with that mechanical manipulation of words and symbols which I call "crystallised thinking", I cannot imagine. And I am equally at a loss to understand why they should suppose that the missing factor, which I call "fluid thinking", is specially manifested in instinctive actions. For these seem to be extremely like that mechanical reeling off of sentences which is supposed by them to be the special province of intellect, as opposed to intuition.

To sum up. When we hear intelligible and intelligent discourse uttered we cannot help believing, either (*a*) that we are in the presence of a foreign mind which is thinking about the subject-matter of the discourse now, or has done so in the past ; or (*b*) that at any rate there has been a foreign mind which did think about this subject-matter and is an essential condition of the possibility of the present utterance. Which of these alternative beliefs we arrive at depends on the special circumstances in which the words are uttered.

The Logical Status of the Belief in Other Minds. So far I have confined myself to a purely descriptive discussion of extraspective situations. I have tried to show that they certainly do not involve inference ; that our extraspective beliefs cannot be explained by direct associations which have arisen in the course of our lives; that they almost certainly depend on an innate and instinctive meaning which attaches from the first to certain perceived objects and events; and that it is not unlikely that some at least of them actually contain foreign mental events as part of their objective constituents. The purely logical question that remains is: "Granted that such beliefs are not in fact reached by inference, can they be supported by inference?"

The Logical Connexion between Belief in Matter and Belief in Other Minds. I shall begin by considering a question which seems to be of very great interest and to have failed to receive the attention which it deserves. This is: "What logical connexion, if any, is there between the belief in Matter and the belief in other Minds?" This question first forced itself on my attention when reading the philosophy of Berkeley. It will be remembered that Berkeley denies the existence of matter, but is perfectly certain of the existence of himself and of God. He says very little about the existence of other finite spirits; but I think it is certain that he felt no doubt about the existence of other human minds. Now one can see that a Berkeleian has a right to be certain of the existence *either* of God *or* of other finite spirits. For he has certain sensations which are not due to his own volitions, and he holds that the only possible cause of anything is a volition of some mind. Hence he has a right to be sure of the existence of *some* mind other than his own, which has volitions. What seems more doubtful is whether he has a right to believe *both* in the existence of God and in that of other finite spirits. And this raises the general question whether a person who doubted or denied the existence of matter would have as good right to believe in the existence of other finite spirits as a person who accepted the existence of matter and held that we are in cognitive contact with it in perception. Corresponding to this would be the question whether a person who doubted the existence of other finite spirits would have as good a right to believe in the existence of matter as one who believed that there are other finite spirits and that we are in cognitive contact with them in extraspective situations. The second question is the easier of the two, and I will dismiss it before dealing with the first.

If a man doubted or denied the existence of other spirits, it seems plain that he would be deprived of some of the grounds which ordinary men have for believing in matter. One ground which might be alleged for the view that my table is not a mere bundle of sensa, existentially dependent on myself, is that other people tell me that, when they are in my room and I am out of it, they are subject to perceptual situations with a very similar objective constituent to that of my perceptual situation when I am in the room. Another ground which might be alleged for believing in the independent existence of matter is that other people tell me that they know by bodily feeling that their bodies continue to exist when I cease to perceive them. Now suppose that I doubted or denied the existence of other minds. I should of course still hear and understand these utterances which apparently come out of the mouths of other human bodies. But, in so far as they asserted that a mind which animates these bodies has perceived or is perceiving something, I should have to doubt or deny the statement. If my gramophone said to me: "I saw your table all the time you were out of the room," I should not hold that this added any weight to the belief that my table existed in my absence except in so far as I believed that another human being who had been in the room had recorded this observation. Now, on the hypothesis under consideration, all statements uttered apparently by other human bodies will be in the position of statements uttered by gramophones, with the important difference that the "records" will not have been made by bodies which are animated by minds. And there would be no reason to attach any weight to these utterances. Of course the belief in matter is not *reached* by inference. It is, therefore, psychologically possible that a man might cease to believe in the existence of other minds and yet continue to believe just as strongly as before in the existence of matter. But, if he tried to *defend* his belief to himself by arguments, he would certainly be in a weaker position than a man who believed in the existence of other human minds.

We now come to the other and harder question : "Would a man who doubted or disbelieved the existence of matter have as good a right to believe in the existence of other minds as one who accepted the existence of matter and believed that he was in cognitive contact with it in perception?" In order to answer this question let us consider the sensa that we sense and the feelings that we feel, without regard to the question whether they are *really* appearances of our own and of other bodies. We can start by dividing them up into two great groups; viz. (A) those which we naturally regard as appearances of our own body ; and (B) those which we naturally regard as appearances of foreign bodies. The group (B) divides into two sub-groups ; viz. (*a*) those which we naturally regard as appearances of other human bodies, and (*b*) those which we naturally regard as appearances of non-human bodies. We will consider first the resemblances and differences between the contents of these groups.

Group (A) consists mainly of bodily feelings ; but it also contains certain characteristic visual, tactual, and auditory sensa. For I can "see" and "touch" parts of "my own body", and can "hear" "my own voice". Group (B) contains no bodily feelings in either of its sub-groups ; but consists wholly of visual, tactual, and auditory sensa. The contents of sub-group (*a*) resemble that part of the contents of (A) which does not consist of bodily feelings. But it is much richer in content than the corresponding part of group (A) ; for I can "see" and "feel" much more of "other human bodies" than of "my own". The contents of sub-group (*b*) bear no special resemblance in detail to those of sub-group (*a*) or of group (A); for "human bodies" have a characteristic appearance, and "human voices" have a characteristic sound.

Let us next consider the relations of my will to these various groups of sensa which I sense and of feelings which I feel. The great mass of feelings in group (A) is quite independent of my will. But, when I "will to move my body", I initiate certain changes in this mass of bodily feeling (viz., certain muscle- and joint-sensations, etc.). These changes are followed as a rule by certain characteristic changes in the visual, tactual, or auditory sensa of group (A); *e.g.*, I may "hear myself speaking", "see my arm moving", and so on. These may be followed by characteristic changes in the sensa of group (B); *e.g.*, I may "see a chair being moved by my hand" or may "see myself kicking another human body, and hear it cry out". The only way in which I can voluntarily affect the sensa in group (A) or in group (B) is by first initiating certain characteristic changes in the bodily feelings of group (A).

These are the facts which are available for an argument by analogy when we confine ourselves strictly to what we can discover by inspection and introspection. The question which we have now to ask is whether the argument would be weaker or stronger according to whether we do or do not believe that these feelings and sensa are appearances of material things. The only way to test this is to consider in detail how the argument would run on each alternative assumption. I will begin by considering the argument on the common - sense assumption that these sensa and feelings are appearances of material things.

The Argument for other Minds on the Assumption of Matter. On this view the sensa of group (A) will be appearances to me of that material thing which is my own body ; those of sub-group (*a*) of group (B) will be appearances to me of that material object which is another human body. Now, on this supposition, the effect of my volitions is not directly to modify the feelings which I feel or the sensa which I sense. The direct result of my volitions is to produce internal changes in my body ; and the changes which I observe in the feelings of group (A) are collateral results of these internal bodily changes. The physical consequence of these internal bodily changes is certain overt bodily movements of my limbs, tongue, etc. And the changes which I observe in the sensa of group (A) are merely collateral results of these overt bodily movements. Finally, the physical consequence of these overt bodily movements is, or may be, certain changes in external physical things ; and the changes which I observe in the sensa of group (B) are merely collateral results of these external physical changes.

On this view, another mind like mine would be one which animates a body like mine ; which can directly produce changes within this body by willing ; and can thus indirectly produce overt movements in its own body and changes in external bodies. If the other mind is like mine, its body appears to it as a group (A′) of feelings which it feels and of certain characteristic sensa which it senses ; and other bodies appear to it as a group (B) of sensa which it senses. This group (B′) will divide into a sub-group (*a′*) which is the appearance to it of other human bodies, and a sub-group (*b′*) which is the appearance to it of external non-human bodies.

On the present assumption, the argument by analogy for the existence of other human minds would run somewhat as follows. The resemblance of the sensa of sub-group (*a*) to the sensa of group (A), which are appearances to me of the outside of my own body, suggests that the sensa of sub-group (*a*) are appearances of an external body which outwardly resembles mine.

Since it outwardly resembles mine, it is likely that it also resembles mine inwardly. Now the changes which I observe from time to time in the sensa of sub-group (*a*) resemble those which I observe from time to time in the sensa of group (A). The latter are appearances to me of overt movements of my own body, and the former are appearances to me of overt movements of an external body which outwardly resembles mine. So this external body resembles mine, not only in its outward form, but also in its overt movements. It is, therefore, likely that the internal changes which determine the overt movements of this external body resemble the internal changes which determine the overt movements of my own body. Now these internal changes in my own body are determined by my volitions, and appear to me as changes in the bodily feelings which I feel. It is, therefore, likely that the similar internal changes, which I assume on grounds of analogy to be taking place in the foreign body, are due to volitions. Now they are certainly not determined by any volition which I can introspect; and they are often contrary to volitions of mine which I can introspect. Hence it is probable that they are determined by volitions which do not belong to my mind. Now the order and connexion which I find among the changes of sensa in sub-group (*a*) resembles the order and connexion which I find among the sensa in group (A). So probably the overt movements of the external body have a similar order and connexion to that of the overt movements of my own body. But I know that this order and connexion in my own case is due to the fact that the successive volitions which determine the movements are not isolated mental events but are states of a more or less coherent and rational mind. I therefore infer that the postulated volitions are probably not merely isolated mental events, but belong to some mind other than my own, which is connected with the foreign body as mine is connected with my body. Now I know that my body appears to me through a mass of feelings which I feel and of sensa which I sense ; I know that other bodies appear to me through sensa which I sense ; and I know that, when I voluntarily produce internal changes in my body, these appear to me as changes in my bodily feelings. As I have postulated a mind with volitions like mine, connected with a body like mine in the same way in which my mind is connected with my body, I argue by analogy that probably this other body appears to this other mind by feelings which it feels and certain sensa which it senses ; that probably other bodies appear to it through sensa which it senses ; and that probably, when it produces internal changes voluntarily in its own body, these changes appear to it as changes in its bodily feelings.

It is evident that such an argument as I have been describing has *some* weight, if we grant the fundamental assumption that it makes about the connexion of sensa with material objects. And it is evident that this assumption forms an integral part of the basis of the argument. I argue to the existence of another mind like mine by way of the existence of another body which looks like mine and moves like it. And I believe in the existence of this other body because I believe that the sensa of my (*a*)-sub-group are appearances of it, whilst the similar sensa of my (A)-group are appearances of my own body. The next question is whether I could legitimately argue to the existence of another mind like mine from the same facts *without* the assumption that the sensa which I sense and the feelings which I feel are appearances of material objects.

The Argument for Other Minds without the Assumption of the Existence of Matter. It is plain that, on the present alternative, the argument, if it be possible at all, must be very different in detail. We can no longer say that the immediate effect of my volition is to produce internal changes in my body, and that the changes in the feelings of group (A) are merely collateral effects of these internal bodily changes. We shall have to suppose that the *immediate* effect of my volitions is simply to produce changes in the feelings of group (A). Again, we can no longer say that the internal bodily changes produce directly overt bodily movements, and that the changes in the sensa of group (A) are simply collateral effects of these overt bodily movements. Instead we shall have to suppose that the voluntarily initiated changes in the feelings of group (A) directly produce changes in the sensa of group (A). Finally, we can no longer suppose that the overt bodily movements cause changes in external physical objects, and that the changes in the sensa of group (B) are merely collateral results of these external physical changes. We shall have to suppose that the changes in the sensa of group (A) in certain cases directly produce changes in the sensa of group (B).

On this view another mind like mine would not be one which animates another body like mine. And it would not manifest itself to my mind by first directly affecting its own body and then indirectly affecting mine. For neither of us will have bodies. Another mind like mine will simply be one that feels a certain set of feelings and senses certain characteristic sensa, which together constitute an (A')-group. It will moreover sense another group of sensa (B'), and this will divide into sub-sets (a') and (b'). And it will be able directly to affect by its will some of the feelings in its (A')-group, and thence indirectly some of the sensa in its (A')-group, and thence at the second remove some of the sensa in its (B')-group. But none of these feelings and sensa will be the appearances to it of material objects. Can any argument from analogy be founded on such a basis?

So far as I can see it could only take the following form. The sensa of the (*a*)-sub-group of my (B)-group resemble the sensa of my (A)-group. And certain changes which I observe in the former resemble certain changes which I observe in the latter. Now these changes in the sensa of my (A)-group are immediately caused by changes in the feelings of my (A)-group. And these in turn are initiated by my volitions. The (a)-sub-group contains no feelings which I feel, and its changes are not correlated with any volition that I can introspect. Indeed they are often contrary to volitions which I can introspect. Now I might argue from the similarity of the (a)-sensa and their changes to the (A)-sensa and their changes that there is probably a set of feelings which I do not feel, which are related to the (a)-sensa as I know the (A)-feelings to be related to the (A)-sensa. That is, I might argue that probably the (a)-sub-group is really part of a foreign (A')-group as well as being a part of my (B)-group. And I might argue that probably there are volitions that I cannot introspect, and that sometimes conflict with those which I can introspect, which directly produce changes in these hypothetical feelings and thus indirectly produce the changes which I from time to time observe in the sensa of my (a)-sub-group. Having reached this point, I might carry the analogy further. I sense and feel the contents of the (A)-group, and I own the volitions which directly affect the feelings, and thus indirectly affect the sensa, of this group. It is therefore probable that there is another mind which senses and feels the contents of this hypothetical (A)-group of which my (a)-sub-group is a part ; and that this other mind owns the supposed volitions which directly affect the hypothetical feelings of this (A')-group and thus indirectly affect the sensa of this group. The analogy might then be concluded as follows. My mind senses a (B)-group beside sensing and feeling an (A)-group And this (B)-group splits into an (a)- and a (b)-sub-group. It is therefore probable that the supposed foreign mind senses a (B')-group beside sensing and feeling an (A')-group, and that this (B')-group splits into an (a')- and a (b')-sub-group.

I do not know whether this argument from analogy will appear convincing to the reader. At any rate it seems to me to be the only one that could be used on the present supposition. It of course leads to a very different view of the interconnexion of minds from that which is held by common-sense. But this is natural enough, since common-sense believes that sensa and bodily feelings are appearances of material objects, whilst we have been explicitly rejecting this assumption in the present subsection. On the present supposition the group of sensa which I naturally take to be appearances to me of your body and the group of sensa which you naturally take to be appearances to you of your body partially overlap, so that some of them are sensed by both of us. You voluntarily produce certain changes in your feelings, which in turn produce certain characteristic changes in these common sensa. I notice these changes; remark their likeness to certain changes which I voluntarily produce in those sensa which I naturally take to be the appearance to me of my own body; find that they are not connected with changes in my feelings which I have voluntarily initiated, and that they often conflict with my volitions; and so I conclude that they are probably due to a foreign mind, which produces them by first voluntarily affecting certain bodily feelings which it feels and I do not.

It will be noticed that this argument from analogy presupposes that certain sensa which are sensed by me are also capable of being sensed by another mind. Is this essential to the argument on the present supposition? I think that it is. So long as I confine myself to sensa and feelings, and make no assumption about their being appearances of material objects, the only sensa which I khow that *I* can affect voluntarily are sensa that *I* sense. That is, the only voluntary action on sensa with which I am acquainted will be *immanent* voluntary action. If I were to postulate *another* mind, which can voluntarily affect sensa which *I* sense and *it* does not, I should be postulating a mode of action for which I have no positive ground of analogy. For this would be *transeunt* voluntary action. I cannot be sure that the property of "being sensed by M" is not a necessary condition of the property of "being affected by M's volitions". It is of course perfectly possible that this is not so; it is perfectly possible that I do indirectly affect by my volitions sensa which I do not sense. I do not know that I cannot do this. But we cannot take a bare possibility as a ground for an argument from analogy. We must argue from what we know to be true, not from what we do not know to be false. Thus, although it is perfectly possible that there might be a plurality of minds, and that one might communicate with another by voluntarily affecting sensa which are sensed by the latter and not by the former, yet this would remain a bare possibility. I should have no positive ground of analogy for believing anything of the kind, if my only starting point is that *I* can voluntarily affect some of the sensa which *I* sense.

Now it has been held by most philosophers that all sensa are essentially private, *i.e.*, that if a sensum *s* be sensed by a mind M it cannot be sensed by any other mind. I now claim to have proved that, if we hold that sensa are private and also deny that they are appearances of material objects, it is impossible to produce a valid argument from analogy to the existence of other minds. If, however, we keep either of these assumptions and reject the other, it is possible to produce a valid argument for the existence of other minds from analogy. *A fortiori*, if we reject both of these assumptions, it is possible. The advantage for the present purpose of a belief in matter is this. If we believe that sensa are appearances of material objects, then, even if sensa themselves be essentially private, they are signs of the existence of something which is not private. The voluntary action which we observe in our own case is now transeunt from the beginning, for it immediately affects our *bodies* (which are public objects) and not the sensa which we sense (which may be private objects). So the arguments for the existence of other minds really are strengthened by the belief that sensa are appearances of material objects. For the analogy is valid, on this view, whether sensa be private or not; whilst, on the opposite view, it is valid *only* if some sensa at least be public.

A final question remains to be raised. It might be said that it is sufficient for the present purpose that sensa should be assumed to be appearances of *something* public and neutral; it is not necessary that this something should be *matter*. This is of course perfectly true, so far as it goes. But, if we assume that sensa are appearances of something public and neutral, and that this something is not matter, what can it be? The only other plausible alternative is that the sensa which I sense are *directly* appearances of *minds*. Now, if we start with this assumption there is no need to use an argument from analogy to prove the existence of other minds. All sensa will be known from the outset to be appearances of *some* mind, and we shall merely have to seek for reasons for believing that some of the sensa which we sense are not appearances of *our own* minds. How we should set about doing this I do not know; but I do not see that any argument from analogy would be either necessary or useful.

Summary of Conclusions. Our belief in the existence of other minds is not reached by inference; and our belief in the existence of material objects is not reached by inference. Nevertheless, each of these beliefs can be rendered probable by certain inverse or analogical arguments, provided we admit that they have a finite antecedent probability. But the two beliefs are not logically independent of each other. For some, at any rate, of the arguments which support the belief in matter depend on our accepting the statements of other people about their perceptions; and the acceptance of such statements presupposes our belief in other minds. Again, arguments by analogy to support our belief in other minds presuppose either (*a*) that the feelings which we feel and the sensa which we sense are appearances to us of material objects, or (*b*) that some sensa are capable of being sensed by more than one mind. Since the second condition is doubtful, whilst the first is sufficient even if the second be false, it follows that arguments by analogy in support of our belief in other minds are stronger if we believe that sensa are appearances of matter than if we do not.

Do we "perceive" Other Minds? I will end this chapter by trying to clear up a question which seems to me to be largely verbal. Some people are concerned to maintain that we "perceive" other minds; some people are concerned to deny it. And much heat is often engendered by this controversy. What we have to notice is that the question has three possible meanings. There are two senses of it in which the answer is certainly affirmative, and a third sense in which it is a fair matter of controversy. (1) If the question means: "Are there situations in which we believe in the present existence of certain mental states which do not belong to ourselves, and ascribe them to other minds without any process of inference?" the answer is "Yes". (2) If the question means: "Do the objective constituents of such situations have certain peculiar *characteristics* which distinguish them from the objective constituents of other situations?" the answer is again "Yes". For the sensa which are contained in the objective constituent of an extraspective situation always have those peculiar characteristics which lead us to take them as appearances of a human body or a human voice. And they change and succeed each other in perfectly characteristic ways. If (1) and (2) be all that is meant by the question: "Do we perceive other minds?" the answer is that we certainly do perceive them. But

(3) the question may mean : " Do extraspective situations contain a peculiar *kind* of objective constituent, which is not contained in other situations ? " In that case the answer is doubtful. As I have said, I think that it is slightly more probable than not that some extraspective situations involve telegnostic situations, and therefore contain in their objective constituent the foreign mental event which we are said to be extraspecting. If this were certain, it would be certain that we "perceive" other mental events and other minds, even in this third sense. But it is not certain ; and, therefore, if " perception " be taken in this very rigid sense, I can only say that it seems to me slightly more likely than not that we sometimes "perceive" other minds.

SECTION C

Introductory Remarks

" Satyr and Faun their late repose
Now burst like anything ;
Fresh Mænads, turning sprightlier toes,
Enjoy a jauntier fling ;
With lustier lips old Pan shall play
Drainpipes along the sewer's way.

Priapus, long since left for dead,
Is dead no more than Pan ;
Silenus rises from his bed
And hiccoughs like a man.
(There's something rather chaste, between us,
About Priapus and Silenus.)"

(OWEN SEAMAN, The Battle of the Bays)

SECTION C

THE UNCONSCIOUS

Introductory Remarks

IT is admitted by almost every one that the contents of a mind are not all open to introspection, and that the occurrence of those mental events which we can introspect cannot be completely accounted for in terms of other mental events which we can introspect or remember. In admitting this people are admitting facts to which the general name of "The Unconscious" is applied.

But here agreement ceases. People quarrel violently about the general nature of "The Unconscious", and about the reality of particular "unconscious" events which are alleged to happen. It is certain that much of this controversy is due to the scandalous ambiguity with which the term "unconscious" is used. I think it is not unfair to say that "the Unconscious" has been the occasion for a greater flood of more abject nonsense than any other psychological concept, with the possible exception of "Instinct".

In this section I shall first try to distinguish the various senses in which people have used the terms "unconscious mental states" and "The Unconscious". I shall show that, in most of these senses, an "unconscious mental state" is either not unconscious or not mental; and I shall try to define a literal meaning of the phrase "unconscious mental states". I shall then consider the arguments which have been alleged to prove the existence of "unconscious mental states". This will lead up to a discussion of the nature of "traces" and "dispositions", which will bring this Section to an end.

CHAPTER VIII

Various Meanings of the Term "Unconscious"

I WILL first clear out of the way two not very important senses in which we use the words "conscious" and "unconscious". (1) In the first place, we often apply them to distinguish one kind of persistent substance from another kind. We call a stone an unconscious being, and a man or a dog or an oyster a conscious being. By calling a stone an unconscious being I mean that it is incapable of being aware of anything. By calling a man a conscious being I mean that he is capable of being aware of something, even if it should happen that at the present moment he is not aware of anything. So "conscious" and "unconscious", in this sense, mean "capable (or incapable) of being aware of something at some time". I think it would be wise to substitute the words "animate" and "inanimate" for the words "conscious" and "unconscious" when the latter are used in this meaning and with this application.

(2) We must next notice that the words "conscious" and "unconscious" are often used to distinguish two possible conditions in which an animate being may be at different times. A being which is conscious, in the sense of animate, may from time to time be unconscious in the present sense. A man awake and a man in a deep sleep are both "conscious beings", in the sense of animate beings. But we should say that the former is now "in a conscious condition" and that the latter is now "in an unconscious condition".

"Conscious" and "unconscious" in this sense, apply

to the temporary conditions of animate beings and to nothing else. We might be tempted to say that an animate being is in a conscious condition provided that it is actually aware of something, and that it is in an unconscious condition provided that it is not actually aware of anything. A little reflection will show that this definition would not be satisfactory as it stands. Many people hold that there is something which is called "unconscious awareness", and that an animate being can be "unconsciously aware" of certain things. Now they would count a man as being in an unconscious condition, even though he were aware of many things, if his awareness of all these things was "unconscious awareness". To meet the possibility of "unconscious awareness" we must say that an animate being is in a conscious condition when it is "*consciously* aware" of something; and that it is in an unconscious condition when it is either not aware of anything, or, if aware of something, only "*unconsciously* aware" of it. The amended definitions are now *verbally* circular. They are not *really* circular, because a new sense of "conscious" and "unconscious" has turned up. We are in fact defining "conscious" and "unconscious", as applied to the temporary condition of animate beings, in terms of "conscious" and "unconscious", as applied to the process of awareness. But, although the definitions are thus non-circular, they do not tell us much until we know what is meant by "conscious" and "unconscious" as applied to mental events. This is the really important question to which we must now turn.

"Conscious" and "Unconscious" as applied to Mental Events. When a man talks of "unconscious mental events" or "unconscious experiences" he generally assumes that every one understands what is denoted by the phrase "conscious mental events or experiences" I do not of course mean that he assumes that every one would agree about the right definition or analysis of either the adjective "conscious" or the substantive "mental event" or "experience". We all know that people differ violently on these subjects. What I do mean is that we assume at the outset that it is easy to give examples to which every one admits that the name "conscious mental events" or "conscious experiences" can be appropriately and quite literally applied. To feel a toothache which is so acute as to make one seriously contemplate going to the dentist is an event which every one would agree could be literally called "an experience" and could be literally called "conscious". Although there are border-line cases which some people would call "conscious experiences" and other people would refuse to call by that name, there seems little doubt that there are thousands of events which every one would agree to deserve the name of "conscious experiences" in a perfectly literal sense.

Now a literally unconscious experience would be one which differs in a certain respect from these literally conscious experiences and agrees with them in a certain other respect. But, as I have said, the phrase "unconscious experience" is constantly used in a number of senses which are not literal but are highly figurative. By this I mean that a great many events, commonly called "unconscious experiences", are probably *not experiences* at all in the sense in which every one admits that the feeling of an acute pang of toothache is an experience. And I also mean that a great many events, commonly called "unconscious experiences", are certainly *conscious* in precisely the sense in which it is admitted that feeling the acute pang of toothache is conscious. My ultimate object is to try to define, or sufficiently describe, *literally* unconscious mental events. But, before doing this, I want to enumerate and dismiss the various non-literal senses in which the word "unconscious" and the phrase "unconscious experiences" are used. At present the only criterion which we shall be able to employ when we are presented with an alleged case of an unconscious experience is the following : "Is there any reason to think that it resembles admittedly conscious experiences so far as to deserve the name of 'experience'? And is there any reason to suppose that it differs from admittedly conscious experiences so far as not to deserve the name of 'conscious'?"

(1) *Traces and Dispositions.* Far the commonest use of the phrase "unconscious states" in psychology is in reference to traces and dispositions. It is found that, in order to account for many everyday facts about our ordinary conscious experiences, it is necessary to refer to certain conscious experiences which we had in the remote past. Memory is the most obvious example of such a fact. I remember now something which I saw or heard last year and of which I have not consciously thought in the interval. And of course there are numberless other facts about our present experiences which can be explained only by reference to experiences which we had long ago. We may sum up this whole mass of facts under the name of "Mnemic Phenomena", borrowing this phrase primarily from Mr Russell's *Analysis of Mind* and ultimately from Semon. Now, either we must assume a wholly new kind of causation, in which one part of the total cause is separated from the rest and from the effect by a considerable gap which contains no relevant events; or we must fill in this temporal gap with some hypothetical persistent entity which we call "traces". I propose to discuss the alternative of "Mnemic Causation", suggested tentatively by Mr Russell, in a later chapter of this section. For the present we will assume the trace theory, as practically all psychologists have done. It is supposed that experiences leave these traces ; that the latter persist ; and that, when suitable stimuli excite them, they either give rise to new states of mind, such as memories, or else modify states of mind which are in the main due to other causes.

Along with these traces we must include innate "dispositions". These are assumed in order to explain those differences between the experiences and the behaviour of individuals which cannot be accounted for by differences in their past experiences and present external circumstances. They differ from traces in their origin; for they are supposed to be innate, whilst traces are due to experiences which happened to the individual during his present life. They also differ, in one respect at least, from traces in their consequences. Traces may lead, among other consequences, to memories of the experiences which left the traces. Dispositions cannot do this; for, even if they be ultimately due to experiences, these experiences took place in the minds of our remote ancestors. Apart from these differences, traces and dispositions would seem to be very much alike; and, as both are purely hypothetical and are known only by their effects, there seems to be no harm in lumping them together.

Now it is common to call traces and dispositions "unconscious states". Many people go further and call them "unconscious *mental* states" or even "unconscious experiences". They are certainly not conscious, in the sense in which feeling an acute pang of toothache is conscious. And they are no doubt states of something or other. But we have no right whatever to assume that they are "mental states" or "experiences", in the sense in which feeling this pang of toothache is a mental state or an experience. The fact is that we know nothing whatever about the intrinsic nature of traces and dispositions; they are simply the hypothetical causes of certain observable effects, and the hypothetical effects of certain observable causes. True, these observable causes and effects are experiences; but this is no ground for supposing that the traces themselves are of the nature of experiences. This is disguised by the silly metaphor that past experiences are "stored up in the unconscious". I may have had a certain conscious experience which lasted for five minutes and ceased twenty years ago. If we say that this is "stored up in the unconscious", and mean this statement to be taken literally, we must be understood to assert that this same experience has been going on steadily for the last twenty years. Perhaps the original experience was seeing a certain dog for five minutes twenty years ago; if this experience be literally "stored up in the unconscious", I have been literally seeing the same dog in the same situation ever since, though "unconsciously", in spite of the fact that the dog has been dead and buried for the last fifteen years. Of course it will be said that no one does mean to assert anything of this kind when he talks of experiences "persisting in the unconscious". It is quite true that most people hasten to disclaim such preposterous consequences when once they are pointed out. But I think there is no doubt that many people do hold views which, if they could be induced to state them clearly, would be found to lead to these consequences. For instance, Rivers in his *Instinct and the Unconscious* asserts that the *content* of the Unconscious is "suppressed experiences", and he gives as an example of such an experience a fright which one of his patients had had many years before with a dog in a passage. Of course, if anything literally persists, it is not the experience itself but the trace of the experience. And there is no more positive reason to suppose that the trace of an experience resembles it or any other experience than to suppose that persistent deafness resembles the attack of scarlet-fever which left it in the patient.

The plain fact is that we know nothing with certainty about the intrinsic nature of traces, and we ought therefore studiously to avoid all phrases which suggest some particular view of their intrinsic nature. I propose to call traces and dispositions by the innocent name of "mnemic persistents". The reason for calling them "mnemic" is obvious. Our ordinary states of mind may be called "transients"; for they happen from time to time, last for a little while, and then cease. In contrast with these we can call traces and dispositions "persistents"; because they are supposed to last for a long time, and to fill the gaps between our transient states of mind. (I avoid Mr Johnson's terms "occurrents" and "continuants", because they have certain implications which I do not at present wish to assert or deny of traces; and it is a pity to spoil two valuable technical terms by using them loosely in senses which their inventor might not admit.) The phrase "mnemic persistents" has the twin advantage that it does express all that we know about traces and dispositions, and that it does not tacitly imply anything that we do not know about them.

(2) *Inaccessible Experiences*. There is another important non-literal sense in which the phrase "unconscious experiences" has been used. To explain it I will take an example from that excellent book *Instinct and the Unconscious* by the late Dr Rivers.

Rivers quotes the case of a patient who had suffered from claustrophobia for many years. By analysing the patient's dreams Rivers was able to show that the claustrophobia had been started by a terrifying experience which the man had had as a small boy in a narrow passage with a fierce dog. This experience the patient was quite unable to remember by normal means. Now Rivers gives this as a typical example of an unconscious experience; and practically defines "The Unconscious", for his own purposes, as consisting of such experiences. It is clear that this is an entirely new meaning of the phrase "unconscious experience". When the experience originally happened it was in all probability an ordinary conscious experience owned by the patient. There is no reason whatever to suppose that, at the time, the boy was unaware of seeing the dog or of feeling frightened, or at any rate that he could not have been aware of them if he had chosen to introspect at the time. In this the experience contrasts strongly with the case of Livingstone and the lion, which is also quoted by Rivers. Livingstone noticed at the time that he was not aware of any pain or fear while in the jaws of the lion; and the circumstances were such that, if he had been feeling pain or fear, he could hardly have failed to notice the fact. Here we may conclude, either that there was no experience of pain or fear connected with this situation; or that, if there were, it was not a conscious experience of the mind known as "Livingstone".

The case of Rivers' patient is quite different. To say that *his* experience is unconscious means only that he cannot now remember it by normal means; and it does not mean that it was not an ordinary conscious experience which belonged to the boy at the time when it happened. It seems to me to be misleading in the highest degree to use the phrase "unconscious experience" in these two utterly different senses. Rivers would no doubt say that the experience "was conscious" when it happened, and that it "became unconscious" afterwards. This, however, does not alter the fact that the words "conscious" and "unconscious" are being used in two senses which are quite disconnected with each other. In the first sense an experience either is conscious or it is not; and, if it is one, it can never become the other. In the second sense one and the same experience may sometimes be conscious and at other times unconscious. For there might be times when a person could remember it normally, and other times when he could be got to remember it only by technical methods, if at all.

The situation which Rivers is describing is a real and an important one; but the terminology which he uses to describe it is hopeless. I shall substitute for the words "conscious" and "unconscious", when used in this sense, the words "accessible" and "inaccessible" respectively. An experience is accessible when it can be remembered by normal means. It is inaccessible when it can be remembered only, if at all, by special technical methods. One and the same experience may be accessible at some times and inaccessible at others. Also there will probably be degrees of accessibility. Even when an experience can eventually be remembered by normal means it is sometimes harder and sometimes easier to do this. And I suppose that, when technical methods have to be applied, they sometimes succeed easily and sometimes only with difficulty.

Corresponding to this distinction between accessible and inaccessible experiences there will be a distinction between mnemic persistents. Some of these can never by any means be made to give rise to memories of the experiences which originated them. If innate dispositions originated, as some think, in the experiences of our remote ancestors, they fall into this class. And probably some traces fall into it too. Other mnemic persistents will give rise to memories if special technical methods be applied, but not otherwise. And a third class give rise to memories without needing the application of special technical methods. Probably there is no sharp line between the second and third classes.

The work of the psycho-analysts enables us to state one at least of the causes which tend to make certain experiences inaccessible. If the memory of a past experience would be specially painful or shocking to the present self there is a tendency for this experience to become inaccessible. It is sometimes said that the painfulness or shockingness of the original experience is the operative factor; but I think that this is true only in a derivative way. The essential factor is the emotional effect which the *memory* of the experience *would* have if it arose *now*. The memory of many experiences which were quite enjoyable when they happened might be shocking or painful to the present self. Such experiences will tend to become inaccessible in spite of their originally pleasant character. Again, the memories of some experiences which were painful or shocking when they happened might be neutral, or even pleasant and amusing, to my present self. I see no reason to think that such experiences would be specially likely to become inaccessible. All that we can say is that, in a good many cases, the memory of an experience which was painful or shocking when it happened is likely to be itself painful or shocking now. So far, and only so far, as this is true painful or shocking experiences will tend to become inaccessible.

(3) *Ignored, Misdescribed, or Dislocated Desires and Emotions.* There is another non-literal sense of "unconscious experiences", which applies specially to desires and emotions. It is rather closely connected with the sense which we have just been discussing, but it must be distinguished from this. There is no doubt that we have a general undiscriminating awareness of many of our experiences without introspectively analysing and discriminating them. Introspective analysis and discrimination involve a special act of attention which we can make or not as we like. And, if we choose to make it at all, we may take more or less trouble over it and can perform it more or less thoroughly. Even if we choose to make the attempt, and perform the discrimination and analysis to the best of our ability, we can make mistakes about the right analysis of our experiences, just as we can make mistakes in trying to analyse and describe external objects which are presented together in a confused jumble in our field of view. Introspective discrimination is a difficult, tiresome and unwonted process ; and no one who is not used to it is likely to avoid mistakes.

Now there are two classes of experience about which we are specially and systematically liable to make mistakes ; and these mistakes may have several different forms. The two classes in question are desires and emotions. Desires and emotions are the experiences *par excellence* about which we pass judgments of praise or blame on ourselves and others. If we find that we have certain desires and emotions we are obliged to think badly of ourselves ; and, if we confess such desires and emotion to others, they will think badly of us. We thus have a strong tendency not to discriminate these desires and emotions ; or, if we do discriminate them, to misdescribe them to ourselves ; or if we discriminate them and describe them rightly to ourselves, to refuse to acknowledge them to others.

Now, in the case of emotions, we can go wrong either about the mental attitude itself or about its epistemological object. There is perhaps hardly any emotional attitude which is regarded as intrinsically bad ; *i.e.*, as bad, no matter what kind of epistemological object it may be directed to. The rule seems to be that the same emotional attitude is good when directed on to one kind of epistemological object and bad when directed on to an object of another kind. Conversely, of two emotional attitudes which may be directed on to the same epistemological object, one may be good and the other bad. In fact we apply ethical predicates to the whole situation composed of such and such an attitude directed to such and such an epistemological object, and not to the attitude taken in abstraction. It is, *e.g.*, considered virtuous to hate *sin*, but wicked to hate even sinful *people*. And it is considered virtuous to feel *emulation* towards one's rivals, but wicked to feel *envy* towards them. There are thus three methods of saving one's self-respect when one feels a certain emotion towards a certain object and believes that this kind of emotion ought not to be felt towards this kind of object. One method is to ignore the existence of the emotion altogether ; *i.e.*, to refuse to turn our introspective attention in this dangerous direction. A second method is to discriminate the emotional attitude properly, but to substitute for its actual object another pretended object of such a kind that it *would* be respectable to take up this emotional attitude towards *this* object. *E.g.*, I may really hate Germans or capitalists, and may recognise that I am feeling the emotion of hatred. But I may persuade myself, and try to persuade others, that what I hate is not Germans or capitalists as such but is the supposed *special wickedness* of these classes. In order to do this I shall very often have to make up a myth about them, and refuse to contemplate any of the perfectly obvious facts which show that Germans or capitalists are neither much better nor much worse than Englishmen or trades unionists. A third method is to make no mistake about the object of my emotion, and to recognise that I am feeling an emotion towards this object; but to substitute for the emotion which I actually feel, and which I believe that it is not respectable to feel towards that kind of object, another pretended emotional attitude which I believe it would be respectable to feel towards this object. I may recognise, *e.g.*, that I feel a certain emotion towards the success of a fellow philosopher's book; and I may pretend to myself and others that this is the respectable emotion of healthy rivalry when it is really the disreputable emotion of disappointed envy. This third method is easiest when the real and the pretended emotion do resemble each other or contain certain common constituents, as envy and rivalry do. Of course the second and third methods may be, and often are, combined, with the happiest results. The two emotions of malice and of righteous indignation are different; but they certainly contain common factors, for both involve satisfaction at the thought of another's pain. And their appropriate objects are different, but have something in common. If now I actually feel malice towards Smith, I can easily keep my self-respect and the respect of others by persuading myself and them that I am feeling an exalted kind of satisfaction at the thought of Smith's moral purification through suffering. One of the reasons for the extreme popularity of war with childless women and others who are in no immediate personal or family danger is that it renders such substitutions easy, and enables quite ordinary people to go about swelling with pretensions to moral superiority which would be exploded at once in a more normal atmosphere.

The case of desires is, in one way, simpler than that of emotions. There do not seem to be intrinsically different kinds of conative attitude, as there are intrinsically different kinds of emotional attitude, such as fearing and hating. So far as I can see, desires differ from each other only in their intensity and in their epistemological objects ; and the goodness or badness of a desire depends almost wholly on the nature of its object. (It no doubt depends partly also on the intensity of the desire. It would be considered that a very intense desire for knowledge is good, and that a moderate desire for bodily pleasure is good ; but a very intense desire for bodily pleasure would be regarded as bad by many people.) If I entertain a desire for some object which it is considered wrong to desire, there are two courses open to me in order to keep my present high opinion of my moral character and to confirm other people in their high opinion of it. One is to ignore the existence of the desire altogether. Another is to recognise the existence of the desire, but to pretend to myself and to others that it is for some object which it is considered respectable to desire. As our motives are nearly always mixed, this process is childishly simple. It is only necessary to emphasise that part of the desired object which it is considered respectable to want, and to slur over that part of it which it is considered disreputable to want. It is needless to give examples of a process which we are all doing continually.

Such emotions and desires as we have been considering are often given as examples of unconscious experiences. It seems to me that they are quite literally conscious. They are in fact quite ordinary desires and emotions about whose existence, nature, and objects we need make no mistake if we introspect honestly and carefully enough. But, as a matter of fact, we do not do this. We ignore them altogether; or we "dislocate" them, *i.e.*, ascribe to them a different object from that which they really have; or we misdescribe them, *i.e.*, put them into a certain class of mental attitudes when we ought to put them into a certain other class. If there be anything literally unconscious in the whole business, it is not the desire or the emotion itself, but the process of ignoring, dislocating, or misdescribing it. We must therefore consider this process in rather more detail.

If I am going to ignore, misdescribe, or dislocate a certain desire or emotion which I own, I must in some sense know that it is there and that there is a reason for treating it in this way. Now we have simultaneous undiscriminating awareness of many experiences which we do not attentively and deliberately introspect. I suggest that this kind of knowledge suffices to warn us that the ice is thin in certain places, and that we had better not turn our introspective attention in these particular directions. The question might then be raised : "How far is this aversion of discriminating introspection from certain desires and emotions a deliberate and conscious process?" In answer to this I think that the following considerations are important. (*a*) If we have a conscious desire to ignore certain experiences, because we think that they would turn out to be unflattering to our self-respect, this desire is itself an experience which we shall tend to ignore. For it is not flattering to our self-respect to have to acknowledge that we can keep it only by averting our attention from certain of our desires and emotions. It follows that, even if we deliberately and consciously ignore certain desires and emotions, we shall almost certainly refuse to acknowledge this fact to ourselves, and still more so to others. Thus I think that the aversion of our discriminative introspection from certain of our experiences is much oftener a deliberate and literally conscious process than is commonly admitted. I believe that we generally know when we are doing this, and that the extreme "touchiness" which we are liable to display when taxed with it is a sign that we do.

(b) An aversion of introspective attention, which begins by being deliberate, will quickly become habitual. An analogy will make this plain. If I have a tender tooth I shall at first deliberately try to avoid biting on it, and shall sometimes make mistakes and hurt myself. But very soon I shall automatically avoid biting on it. Now emotions and desires tend to recur; and, if I at first deliberately avert my attention from some of them, I shall very soon come to do so habitually. This habit, like any other, may eventually become so strong that it cannot be overcome by deliberate volition.

(c) A method which we very commonly use is to put a ring-fence round a certain region, to label it as dangerous, and to avert our attention from the whole of it. All patriots do this with the whole subject of the virtues of their enemies and the faults of their fellow-countrymen; many scientists put such a fence round all the subjects which are investigated by Psychical Researchers; and the minds of most clergymen appear to be full of regions guarded with barbed wire and a notice that "Trespassers will be Prosecuted". Once this has been done it becomes perfectly easy to assert with complete good faith that we are not deliberately turning our attention away from any assigned desire or emotion which falls within such a region. We can truthfully say that we never thought for a moment of this particular experience, and therefore cannot have *deliberately* ignored it; just as a thief might truly say that he had never touched a certain necklace if he had merely pocketed the case which in fact contains it.

Now I think it is certain that what are called "unconscious" desires and emotions are often simply desires and emotions which we habitually ignore, misdescribe, or dislocate. An experience which is "unconscious" only in this sense is not literally an unconscious experience. And the process of ignoring, misdescribing, or dislocating it is not literally an unconscious mental process. Sometimes it is a conscious and deliberate process which is itself ignored or misdescribed. Sometimes it is habitual. In the first case it is not literally unconscious; and in the second there is no positive reason for thinking that it is literally an experience or series of experiences.

Ignored experiences cannot be identified with inaccessible experiences. Many experiences which have become inaccessible were not ignored when they happened; and many which were ignored when they happened have not become inaccessible. Nevertheless, there probably is a close connexion between ignored and inaccessible experiences. Experiences which it would be painful or shocking to discriminate are generally those which it would be painful or shocking to remember; and these, as we know, tend to become inaccessible. Moreover, the mere fact that an experience is habitually ignored probably tends to make its trace less definite and more isolated, and therefore to increase the difficulty of remembering it by normal means.

I have discussed this subject mainly in connexion with the ignoring of experiences. But exactly the same remarks apply to misdescribed and dislocated experiences. In themselves these experiences, though often called "unconscious", are literally conscious. And the process of misdescribing them or dislocating them is either a deliberate process which we choose to ignore or misdescribe, or it is an habitual process which is not literally an experience at all.

(4) *Unrecognised Needs*. There is another sense in which the phrase "unconscious desires" has been used, in which it does not denote a literally unconscious experience. This has been brought out very clearly by Mr Russell in his *Analysis of Mind;* though I do not agree with his apparent opinion that it covers all that is meant by the phrase "unconscious desire", and I agree still less with the arguments and the conclusions which he bases on it. When we have the experience of desiring something we present to ourselves in imagination some possible future state of affairs to which we take up the conative attitude. And it is an essential part of this attitude that we believe that this state of affairs, if realised, will satisfy us and bring the conative situation to an end. Now, of course, what I now believe would satisfy me may be extremely different both in outline and in detail from what would really satisfy me. I have no infallible revelation about what state of affairs will bring a certain kind of uneasiness to rest. I cannot learn about this by introspection, however careful and thorough ; for this will tell me only about the elements and the structure of my present conative situation. The recorded experiences of others may provide me with the basis for a more or less probable inference on the subject ; but, in the main, the only available policy is to "wait and see."

Now sometimes it is said that what I "really desire" is what would in fact satisfy my present conation. With this terminology it is certain that I am often not conscious of what I really desire. And this fact is expressed by saying that I have an "unconscious desire" for what would in fact satisfy me. I think that this is a most unfortunate and misleading terminology. It is much better to begin by distinguishing between what I "desire" or "want" and what I "need". I may set before myself the idea of a large fortune, and spend most of my life trying to gain it. If so, it is preposterous to say that I only think that I desire money ;

I really do desire it. I have a conative attitude, and the epistemological object to which it is directed is my future wealth. It is true to say that I desire money in precisely the same sense in which it is true to say that the drunkard sees pink rats; and to deny this is to confuse an epistemological object with an ontological object. Now I may find that, when I have made a great deal of money, the same kind of dissatisfaction still persists. And it may be true that this dissatisfaction would in fact have been removed if I had acquired fame instead of money. If so, I *needed* fame. But it is preposterous to say that I *desired* fame, if I never put the idea of fame before myself, or felt any attraction for it, or strove after it. To say that I "unconsciously desired" fame, is like saying that the drunkard "unconsciously saw" the alcohol in his stomach.

What is true then is that needs often give rise to desires, and that the desire which is caused by a certain need may have an epistemological object which fails to agree with the ontological object which would satisfy that need. But needs are not desires, nor are they experiences at all; hence a need of which I am unaware cannot properly be called an unconscious desire, or an unconscious *experience* of any kind. Still, there is no doubt that one of the meanings which is given to the phrase "unconscious desires" is "needs of which a person is unaware". I shall call "unconscious desires", in this sense, by the much less misleading name of "unrecognised needs".

I have now pointed out four non-literal senses in which psychologists use the phrase "unconscious experiences" or at any rate "unconscious mental states". (1) In the sense of traces and dispositions, they seem to have no claim to be called "experiences", and no obvious claim to be called "mental" unless it can be shown that they cannot be simply modifications of the brain and nervous system. (2) In the sense of inaccessible experiences, "unconscious mental states" were literally experiences when they happened. But they were also literally conscious; and no subsequent facts about memory or the lack of it can make them literally unconscious. (3) "Unconscious desires and emotions", in the sense of desires and emotions which we ignore, misdescribe, or dislocate, are certainly experiences. But they are literally conscious. (4) "Unconscious desires", in the sense of unrecognised needs, are, so far as one can see, not experiences at all. And the desires for objects which will not in fact satisfy us, which are often caused by unrecognised needs, are ordinary conscious experiences.

It now remains to try to see what is meant by *literally* conscious and *literally* unconscious experiences or mental states. The existence of " unconscious mental states ", in the four non-literal senses which we have enumerated, is so obvious that people would not have thought of quarrelling about unconscious mental states unless they had had some other and more literal meaning of this phrase at the back of their minds.

Literally Unconscious Mental Events. I will first try to point out what seem to me to be the characteristic marks of a conscious mental state, and I will then describe a literally unconscious mental state as one which lacks some of these marks.

In order that a mental state of mine may be conscious it is certainly not necessary that I should be "conscious of it" when it happens, in the sense of making it the object of an act of introspective attention. I have no doubt that I have been seeing the words of this page as I wrote them down ; and I am sure that my perceptions of the words have been instances of what every one would call "conscious experiences". But I most certainly did not make these perceptual states into objects of introspective attention while they were happening. My attention was taken up with my argument and with the words themselves, and I was not attending at all to the process of seeing the words. No doubt all processes which I introspectively discriminate are conscious, but the converse of this is certainly not true. A conscious experience of mine cannot therefore be defined as an experience of mine of which I was conscious at the time when it happened, if by "being conscious of" you mean "making an object of introspective attention".

Nevertheless, it might be possible to mark off conscious experiences from all other mental events by means of some more hypothetical references to introspective discrimination. Might we not say that every conscious experience of mine is one that I *should* have succeeded in discriminating *if* I had introspected carefully enough while it was happening or immediately afterwards? I think that we are inclined to believe this about all mental events which we should be prepared to count as "conscious experiences" of ours, and that we are not inclined to believe it about anything else. It is therefore plausible to take it as a sufficient description, if not as a definition, of a "conscious experience" of mine.

But, even as à description, it needs some further elaboration. There are certain experiences which probably could have been introspectively discriminated while they were happening, and which would yet be called "unconscious", in a sense which does not fall under any of the four non-literal headings already mentioned. Take dreams, for instance. From one point of view all dreams would be called "unconscious experience". Yet, from another point of view, to see my friend in a dream is as much a "conscious experience" as to see him in waking life. It is certain that many dream-experiences could have been introspected by the dreamer while they were happening; for I have quite often introspected my dream-experiences while dreaming, and I do not suppose that this is at all exceptional in people who are given to introspection. Another example is provided by alleged cases of co-consciousness. Sally Beauchamp, in Dr Morton Prince's *Dissociation of a Personality*, claimed to be aware of most of the things of which B_1 was aware when the latter was in control of the body and the former was not. From Sally's point of view these states of awareness were just as "conscious" as the contemporary states of awareness in B_1; in fact this is precisely what the claim to *co*-consciousness, as distinct from *alternating* consciousness, amounts to. It seems to me that the only way to deal with such cases as these is to introduce a distinction between "relatively" and "absolutely" unconscious mental events. We shall then have to distinguish relatively unconscious experiences from strictly conscious experiences by considering *who* precisely could have introspected them when they were happening. We call the vivid dream of a normal man and the alleged co-conscious experiences of Sally "conscious", because there was *some* mind, viz., my sleeping self in the one case and Sally in the other, which could have introspectively discriminated them if it had tried at the time when they were happening. We call the same experiences "unconscious" simply because the *only* mind which could have introspectively discriminated them at the time when they were happening was a mind which was not then in *control of the body* concerned in the experience. Such experiences as these I shall call "relatively unconscious". An "absolutely unconscious" mental event would be one that could not have been introspectively discriminated at the time of its occurrence by *any* mind, whether in control at the time of a body or not.

I am well aware that even these amended descriptions are open to serious objections. What do we mean by "controlling a body"? And when is a certain mind in control of a certain body, and when is it not? If you press me with these questions, I doubt whether I can give a perfectly satisfactory answer to them. Still, it seems to me that the kind of fact which I refer to under the name of "control" is pretty obvious. There is an important sense in which the mind which is known as "C.D.B." is at present in control of my body, and in which it will not be in control of my body later in the evening when I am in bed and asleep. At that time no mind will, in this sense, be "in control of" it; though it will, no doubt, still be behaving in a somewhat different way from that in which it would behave if it were no longer *animated* by a mind at all. In the case of alternating personality a recognisably different mind is at different times "in control of" the same body, even if there be reason to suppose that all these minds are in a sense parts of a single "mind" which continues to animate this body throughout life.

There is unfortunately one other highly debatable conception which I must introduce before giving a description of literally unconscious mental events which can make any claim to be satisfactory. This is the notion of the "ownership" of a mental event by a mind. To own an experience is evidently not the same as to discriminate it introspectively. It is commonly believed that only mental events which are owned by some mind can be introspectively discriminated, and that the only mind which can introspectively discriminate an experience is the mind which owns it. If this be true, both absolutely conscious and relatively unconscious mental events must be owned by minds. But theoretically there would be two quite different kinds of absolutely unconscious mental events. The first would be owned by a mind which, for some reason, could not have introspectively discriminated them when they happened even if it had tried. The second would have been incapable of being introspectively discriminated by any mind simply because they were not owned by any mind. I have so far drawn no distinction between "experiences" and "mental events". This seems to be a convenient place to do so. All experiences are mental events; but

I think it would be in accordance with usage to say that, if there be unowned mental events, they should not be called "experiences". So I will define an "experience" as a mental event which is owned by some mind. Thus absolutely unconscious mental events will divide in theory into (*a*) absolutely unconscious experiences; *i.e.*, mental events which are owned, but could not have been introspectively discriminated when they happened ; and (*b*) unowned mental events.

Of course many people would deny off-hand the possibility of unowned mental events. They may be right. On the other hand, they may be *defining* "mental event" in some way which includes ownership by a mind as part of the definition. In that case their denial is merely an analytic proposition. Again, anyone who holds that a mind does not require a Pure Ego, but consists simply of a mass of suitably interconnected mental events, can hardly deny the possibility of masses of mental events so poor in content and so loosely interconnected as not to deserve the name of "minds". If so, he can hardly deny the possibility that some mental events are not owned by minds, even if he denies the possibility of completely isolated mental events. For these reasons it is wise to introduce the class of "unowned mental events", even though it may turn out to be a mere blank window.

I must now state more clearly what I mean by "ownership". I do not think that it is definable, in the sense in which I am using it. But it is a highly ambiguous word ; and, by pointing out the senses in which I am *not* using it, I may be able to indicate to the reader what I want him to think about. (1) In the very widest sense we call a mental event "an experience of Smith's" if it is specially connected with the stimulation of Smith's body. And by "Smith's body" we mean the body which is normally controlled by a certain recognisable mind known as "Smith". In this sense a mental event might be called "an experience of Smith's" even if it were not owned by his mind or by any other n.ind. (2) In a slightly narrower sense a mind M might be said to be still owning a mental event if this has left some trace which still affects M's conscious experiences from time to time. In this sense Rivers' claustrophobic patient was still "owning" the experience with the dog in the passage, both before and after Rivers had cured him by enabling him to remember the incident. (3) In a still narrower sense of "ownership" we should say that a mind still owns those and only those experiences which it can remember at will. In this sense Rivers' patient had ceased to "own" the dog-experience for many years, and began to "own" it again only after Rivers had cured him. We have two senses of "ownership" in connexion with personal property, which correspond to the last two senses mentioned above. In the wider sense of "ownership" I am still the owner of a certain umbrella even after it has been lost or stolen. It remains *my* umbrella, though it now rests permanently in *your* hat-stand. In the narrower sense I own it only so long as I can lay hands on it at will. Experiences which are owned in senses (2) or (3) may be said to be "mnemically owned"; because, strictly speaking, their continued ownership by me means only that they continue to affect my conscious experiences. The two senses may be distinguished from each other by calling the former "mnemic ownership *de jure*" and the latter "mnemic ownership *de facto et de jure*".

Now I am *not* using "ownership" in any of these three senses in my attempts to give sufficient descriptions of literally conscious and unconscious mental events. It is in fact evident that there is another sense of "ownership", which is not mnemic. When I look out of the window and see a man passing, or when I feel a twinge of toothache, these experiences are owned by me in a fundamental and probably indefinable sense. This is a sense in which the visual experience ceases to be owned by me as soon as the man passes out of sight, and the other experience ceases as soon as I cease to feel my tooth aching. They may still continue to be owned by me both *de jure* and *de facto*. I may from time to time remember seeing the man or feeling the pain. And, even if I cannot do this, these experiences may continue to modify my later experiences from time to time in some way or other. Let us call this third, non-mnemic, sense of "ownership" by the name of "literal ownership". In my attempts to give sufficient descriptions of literally conscious and unconscious mental events it must be understood that, wherever I use the word "ownership", I mean "literal ownership". It is probable that many mental events which have been literally owned are not mnemically owned *de facto* for more than a negligibly short time; and it is probable that many of them are not mnemically owned *de jure* for long. And it is quite possible that mental events which have never been literally owned by me may be mnemically owned by me *de jure* if not *de facto*.

I will now repeat the descriptions which we have reached. These must be interpreted in the light of the remarks which I have just been making. (1) Mental events are either owned or unowned. All unowned events are incapable of being introspectively discriminated by any mind, and are therefore *absolutely unconscious*. (2) Events which are mental and are owned by some mind are called "experiences". Mental events which are unowned are not to be called "experiences", and therefore not "unconscious *experiences*". (3) Mental events which are owned may be such that the mind which owns them could, or such that it could not, have introspectively discriminated them at the time of their occurrence if it had tried. In the latter case they are *absolutely unconscious experiences* of that mind. (4) Mental events which are owned and could have been introspected may be owned by a mind which is at the time of their occurrence in control of a body, or by a mind which is not in control of a body at that time. In the

former case they are *absolutely conscious experiences*.   In
the latter case they are *relatively unconscious experiences*,
i.e., they are conscious experiences of what would
commonly be called an "unconscious mind". These
results are exhibited synoptically in the table which
follows :

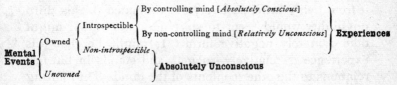

The next point to notice is that I do not pretend to
have given either *definitions* of literally conscious or
unconscious mental events, or *tests* for them.   At most
I claim to have given *descriptions* which suffice to distinguish the two in theory.   I will now say something
more about this first point.   I think that almost everyone would be inclined to say : "It may be that all my
conscious experiences are mental events which I owned
and which I could have introspectively discriminated
at the time ; and it may be that there is nothing else of
which this is true.   But this purely hypothetical proposition about what would have happened if I had
introspected cannot be ultimate.   There must be some
intrinsic difference between those experiences of mine
which I could have introspected and those which I
could not have introspectively discriminated even if I
had tried my hardest.   And this intrinsic difference,
whatever it may be, is what we *mean* by the difference
between a conscious and an unconscious experience."

This may very well be true.   One can think of at
least three circumstances which might tend to make it
impossible to discriminate an experience introspectively.
(1) The difficulty might arise through the experience
being an event all of whose characteristics have an
extremely weak intensive magnitude.   (2) The characteristics of the experience might be reasonably intense,
but it might be part of a larger mass of experiences

which were extremely like it both qualitatively and quantitatively. (3) The experience might have considerable intensity, and might differ from other co-existing experiences both qualitatively and quantitatively to a marked extent; but it might stand in certain special relations to other contents of the mind which prevent it from being introspectively discriminated. This third possibility would seem to split into two. (*a*) It might take a merely negative form. It might be that this experience is relatively isolated, and stands in but few relations to the other contents of the mind. The limiting case of this arises when a mental event is not owned by a mind at all, in the literal sense of "ownership". (*b*) It might take a positive form. There might be some positive relation between this experience and the rest of the mind which positively averts introspective attention from the former. And this peculiar relation might depend on some intrinsic quality in the experience. *E.g.*, the experience may be such that, whenever it begins to be introspected, an intolerably painful feeling begins to arise in the mind which owns it. It seems likely that all these various possibilities are realised in practice in various cases of literally unconscious experiences.

"*Simultaneous Undiscriminating Awareness*" *and* "*Ownership*". I will end this section by raising a rather difficult question which is very closely connected with what we have just been discussing. In our descriptions of literally conscious and unconscious mental events we have used two obviously different relations which may hold between a mind and a mental event, viz., literal ownership and introspective discrimination. The latter seems to imply the former, but the former can evidently hold without the latter. Now there seems to be a third possible relation between a mind and a mental event, which might be called "Simultaneous Undiscriminating Awareness". I want to say something about this, and to consider how it is related to literal ownership.

Let us consider the case of looking for one's spectacles

in a certain drawer, and failing to find them though they were staring one in the face all the time. If I were asked whether I was at the time aware of seeing the drawer and most of its contents, I should answer "Yes", in one sense, and "No", in another. Certainly I *was* aware of seeing the drawer and most of its contents in a sense in which I was *not* aware of seeing the spectacles. On the other hand, I was almost certainly not introspectively discriminating the process of seeing the drawer; for my whole attention was devoted at the time to the drawer itself and its contents, and not to my own mental states. It is evident that, in the vast majority of cases of conscious perception, I am not aware of my perception, in the sense of introspectively discriminating it. Nevertheless, I should certainly refuse to entertain the suggestion that I am not aware, *in any sense*, of my conscious perceptions while they are taking place. I shall say then that the person in our example was aware of his act of seeing the drawer and most of its contents, in the sense that he had "simultaneous undiscriminating awareness" of this mental event. It is also true that he "literally owned" this mental event; it was literally a part of *his* mental history.

It would seem then that literally conscious experiences are always literally owned by a mind, and that the mind which owns them has always simultaneous undiscriminating awareness of them. But, in ninety-nine cases out of a hundred, it does not also introspectively discriminate them. The question now arises: "Do we ever literally own mental events of which we do not have at least simultaneous undiscriminating awareness?"

It will first be necessary to modify the question in order to remove the danger of an infinite regress. If "literal ownership" and "simultaneous undiscriminating awareness" be just two different names for a single relation, it will of course follow that I must have simultaneous undiscriminating awareness of any mental event which I own. And there will be no infinite regress in this assertion. But, suppose that the two names stand for different relations. Suppose I own a certain state *s*, and that I have simultaneous undiscriminating awareness of *s*. This awareness of *s* will also be a state which is owned by me. And, if I must have simultaneous undiscriminating awareness of *every* mental event that I own, I must have it of this state too. We should thus be launched on an infinite regress of awarenesses of awarenesses of awarenesses of . . . . So, unless we take "literal ownership" and "simultaneous undiscriminating awareness" to be simply two names for the same relation, or else modify the proposition which we are investigating, we can be sure that this proposition involves an infinite multiplication of states of mind. I do not maintain that such an infinite series of mental states belonging to a single mind involves any contradiction. But there is not the faintest reason to believe that it is a fact ; and it certainly would be undesirable to accept a proposition which has this implication, unless there were the strongest grounds for doing so.

It is of course quite easy to modify the proposition which we are considering, so that it shall not entail the existence of an infinite series of contemporary mental states belonging to the same mind. We can begin by distinguishing "orders" of mental events. We might call my awareness of the drawer a state of the first order ; my simultaneous undiscriminating awareness of my awareness of the drawer a state of the second order ; and so on. And we might put the proposition into the milder form that I have simultaneous undiscriminating awareness of every mental event which I own, provided that its order does not exceed some finite number *n*. The state of $n + 1th$ order, which is my awareness of a state of *nth* order, would then be owned by me but would not be an object of simultaneous undiscriminating awareness to me. In particular it might be that I necessarily have simultaneous undiscriminating awareness of all mental events of the first order which I own ; but that I do not necessarily have simultaneous undiscriminating awareness of any of my experiences whose order is greater than one. Stated in this form the proposition is intrinsically unobjectionable, whether it be in fact true or not.

We have now to consider whether there is any reason to believe it. For this purpose we had better return to our example about the spectacles. It is plausible to hold that I have simultaneous undiscriminating awareness of all my *conscious* experiences of the first order. The question is whether there may not be *unconscious* experiences of the first order which I own but of which I do not have simultaneous undiscriminating awareness. We must notice that I should not normally use the words "conscious" and "unconscious" at all in describing my experience with the drawer and the spectacles. I should simply say : "I saw the drawer and most of its contents, but I did not see the spectacles." The adjectives "conscious" and "unconscious" are added later, as a result of reflection and inference. I find that the spectacles must have been physically affecting my retina just as much as the drawer and the rest of its contents did. I then perhaps persuade myself that I *must* have seen the spectacles. And I express the obvious difference between the way in which I must have seen the spectacles, if I saw them at all, and the way in which I certainly did see the drawer and the rest of its contents, by saying that I saw the drawer "consciously" and that I must have seen the spectacles "unconsciously", if at all. Now this phraseology does suggest the possibility of first-order experiences which are owned by me, but of which I am not aware even in the sense of simultaneous undiscriminating awareness. When I say : "*I* saw the spectacles unconsciously" or "*My* seeing of them was unconscious", I imply that this experience was owned by me. And, when I say that it was unconscious, I do imply that I was not aware of it even in the sense in which I was aware of seeing the drawer and the rest of its contents. That is, I do imply that I did not have even simultaneous undiscriminating awareness of seeing the spectacles.

But it seems to me very doubtful whether we have any right to accept the verbal implications of this phraseology. The natural thing for me to say is simply: "I did not see the spectacles". And the plain, straightforward meaning of this is that either there was no mental event at all called "seeing the spectacles", or that, *if* there were, it was not literally owned by *me*. Now it does not seem to me that the facts which are taken into consideration on later reflection give us any ground for reversing this view, even if they do give us some ground for accepting the view that a mental event called "seeing the spectacles" did *exist* at the time. The facts which are adduced in favour of the view that a mental event, called "seeing the spectacles", must have existed at the time fall into two main groups. (i) It is argued that the spectacles and my retina were in such relative positions that light from the former must have affected the latter in a way which might reasonably have been expected to produce such a mental event. (ii) It may be that in dreams, or by hypnosis or psycho-analysis or some other technical method, I come to have experiences or to do or say things which are hard to explain except on the assumption that a certain mental event existed in the past and that it is affecting my present experiences or actions. Even if we admit that such arguments make it probable that a mental event of "seeing the spectacles" existed while I was searching in the drawer, there seems no reason to believe that they make it probable that this mental event was literally owned by me. No doubt, if it existed at all, its occurrence depended on the stimulation of *my* body. It is also true that it is a mental event which afterwards affects experiences in *my* mind. But this does not suffice to prove that, when it happened, it was *my* experience, in the plain straightforward sense in which the experience of seeing the drawer and the rest of its contents was an experience of mine.

Now, if this be granted, there would seem to be no very good ground for distinguishing between the first-order mental states which I own and the first-order mental states of which I have simultaneous undiscriminating awareness. The only ground for distinguishing between the two was that certain common phrases do seem to suggest that there are mental events which I literally own but of which I do not have even simultaneous undiscriminating awareness. But we have now seen that, even if there be mental events which arise through the stimulation of my body and subsequently affect my experiences, and of which I have not simultaneous undiscriminating awareness, there is no good reason to think that they are literally owned by *me*. Hence I think that it is quite likely that all first-order experiences which I literally own are also experiences of which I have at least simultaneous undiscriminating awareness; and that all mental events of which I have simultaneous undiscriminating awareness are literally owned by me. This of course leaves it quite possible that literal ownership and simultaneous undiscriminating awareness are different relations; just as size and shape are different qualities, though anything which has either must have both. And I think it is pretty certain that they *are* different relations, for the following reason. If they were just two names for a single relation it would be quite certain that *every* mental event which I own, no matter what its order might be, would be an object of simultaneous undiscriminating awareness to me. This would be an identical proposition. Now it does not seem to be in the least certain that there could not be mental events which I own but of which I do not have even simultaneous undiscriminating awareness. I think that a person who felt quite certain that he had simultaneous undiscriminating awareness of all the first-order events which he owns might feel very doubtful indeed whether he had simultaneous undiscriminating awareness of his simultaneous undiscriminating awareness of his first-order experiences. And, if we press the question on him for experiences of higher orders, I think there will certainly come a stage at which he will feel pretty certain that he could own a mental event without having even this kind of awareness of it. If this be so, "literal ownership" and "simultaneous undiscriminating awareness" can hardly be two names for a single relation. Thus, on the whole, I think the most probable conclusion is that we are concerned with two different relations which, in the case of first-order experiences, always go together. In the case of experiences of a sufficiently high order literal ownership holds without simultaneous undiscriminating awareness.

The Notion of "The Unconscious." We are now in a position to deal with the substantive "*The* Unconscious", after clearing up the meanings of the adjective "unconscious". Here again we find that there are great ambiguities. We must first notice a systematic ambiguity in all such phrases as this. When we talk of "*the* State" or "*the* Internal Combustion Engine" we generally mean a typical idealised state or internal combustion engine. We use such phrases in this way when we are pretty certain that we are dealing with a class, such as states and internal combustion engines, having several quite distinct members which do not combine to form a single complex whole which is itself a state or an internal combustion engine. Each of these members is supposed to be a more or less imperfect approximation to that ideal limit which we call "the State" or "the Internal Combustion Engine", and which Plato would consider to be "laid up in

Heaven". On the other hand, when we talk of "the Sea", we do not as a rule mean a typical ideal sea, but just the whole mass of salt water on earth of which the various seas are so many different *parts*. This ambiguity is inconvenient even when we are talking about "the State" (except to Idealistic Metaphysicians whose more exciting results all depend on juggling with the defects of language instead of trying to correct them). It would be still more so if there were a single international world-state, as there ought to be. For, in that case "the State" might mean an ideal typical state, or it might mean the actual Super-State of which all other states would be constituents.

Now this kind of ambiguity is specially dangerous when we are dealing with something about which we know so little as we do about the Unconscious. It may be that there is only this and that Unconscious, just as there is this and that internal combustion engine; and that the totality of all unconscious mental events has as little unity and individuality as the totality of all internal combustion engines. On the other hand, it is possible that the total Unconscious is not divisible into Smith's Unconscious, Brown's Unconscious, and so on; so that it is only the Unconscious taken as a whole, and without reference to the various origins of various parts of it, which can be treated as an individual unit. Lastly, there is the much more likely alternative that the total contents of the Unconscious do form an important unity, and that they *also* fall into various sub-groups, each of which has a greater internal unity than the Unconscious as a whole. The Unconscious as a whole might be like the United States; and Smith's Unconscious and Brown's Unconscious might be like the State of New York and the State of Nebraska. It is most undesirable that we should use phrases which tacitly prejudge these questions, and tie us down to one or other of the extreme alternatives. It will be wise to introduce at once certain technical terms to avoid these dangers. I will call the whole contents of the Unconscious, taken collectively as a single mass and without regard to the various origins of its various parts, the "Total Unconscious". It is then open to anyone to raise the questions: (*a*) "What are the contents of the Total Unconscious?"; and (*b*) "Does the Total Unconscious possess anything worth calling a 'structure'; and, if so, what kind of structure does it possess?" If the Total Unconscious should contain organised sub-groups, each having an important degree of unity and individuality, these may be called "Unconscious Sub-groups". If, and only if, the Total Unconscious proved to have that kind of structure which characterises minds like our own, we could talk of the "Total Unconscious Mind". If any of the unconscious sub-groups proved to have this kind of structure, it could be called a "Special Unconscious Mind".

The Total Unconscious. One part of the contents of the Total Unconscious will be all mnemic persistents, *i.e.*, all traces and dispositions, no matter whose experiences left the traces or whose experiences these traces and dispositions may subsequently modify. This will be divisible into an accessible and an inaccessible part, in the sense defined earlier in this Chapter. I will call this part of the Total Unconscious the "Total Mnemic Mass". I see no reason to suppose that there is any fundamental intrinsic difference between the accessible and the inaccessible parts of the Total Mnemic Mass. The inaccessible part is mainly dealt with by abnormal psychologists and by psycho-analysts; the accessible part has long been recognised in normal psychology. The importance of the work of the psycho-analysts is not that they have revealed anything absolutely new and unheard of. It is only the extreme ignorance of most of them about all subjects except their own which causes them to make such claims. The real importance of their work is in the following points. (*à*) They have shown that many inaccessible traces or groups of traces do not rest idly. In so far as these fail to produce their normal effects, *e.g.*, memories, they are liable to produce various bodily and mental disorders. (*b*) They have devised several new technical methods for making inaccessible traces accessible. (*c*) They have shown that, when this has been done, the mental and bodily disorders are often (for a time, at least) alleviated. (*d*) They have stated some of the probable causes which tend to make certain experiences become inaccessible. These are great achievements; and it is a pity to create prejudice against them by ignorant pontifications about "the New Psychology". The psychologists of instinct (such as M'Dougall) also deal with the inaccessible part of the Total Mnemic Mass; but I cannot pretend to believe that they have accomplished anything except to revive the faculty-psychology in an extreme form and with an amusingly pretentious parade of "science."

Now, if the whole content of the Total Unconscious be mnemic persistents, there is no reason to suppose that it contains mental events at all. For there is no known reason to believe that traces and dispositions are sufficiently like the only mental events which we know directly (viz., our own conscious experiences) to be called "mental events". And, if the Total Un-conscious does not contain mental events, it cannot possibly *be* a mind or comprise sub-groups which are minds, no matter how complex its structure may be or how definitely it is divided into sub-groups having their own unity and individuality. Thus, on this hypo-thesis, there would be no Total Unconscious Mind, and there would be no Special Unconscious Minds.

If, however, there be literally unconscious mental events, viz. (*a*) unowned mental events, or (*b*) mental events which were literally owned by a mind but which could not have been introspected by it, or (*c*) mental events which were owned and could be introspected only by a mind which was not then in control of a body, these ought to be counted as part of the contents of the Total Unconscious. I propose to call the whole mass of such mental events, supposing that they exist, the "Total Subconscious Mass". In theory then the Total Unconscious will consist of the Total Mnemic Mass and the Total Subconscious Mass. The former consists of traces and dispositions; the latter, if it exists at all, will consist of literally unconscious mental events. If the Total Subconscious Mass exists, and if the mental events which belong to it leave traces, these will presumably belong to the inaccessible part of the Total Mnemic Mass.

Now if, and only if, the Total Subconscious Mass exists, there is a possibility of a Total Unconscious Mind and of Special Unconscious Minds. I do not know how to define a "mind", but I think it is evident that a thing could not be called a "mind" unless it had a peculiar kind of content and a peculiar kind of structure. Its content must be the kind of events which we call "mental" and observe when we choose to introspect. And these mental events must be interconnected in a very peculiar way. It is possible that mental events can exist only as factors in those peculiar complex wholes which we call "minds", but I do not see any very good reason to believe this. It is also possible, and much more likely, that nothing but mental events can be interconnected in the peculiar way which is characteristic of the structure of a mind. Now, among the relations which are characteristic of the structure of minds, a most important place must be given to mnemic relations. It seems essential to the notion of a mind that its contents at one moment shall be largely dependent on its contents at other moments in the *remote* past, and shall not be completely explicable by reference to events within or without it which have happened in the *immediate* past. I do not suggest for an instant that it is a sufficient description of a mind to say that it consists of mental events mnemically interconnected; but there is little doubt that this is an essential part of what we understand by a "mind". Now, unless we assume a quite new kind of causation, the mnemic relations between transient mental events depend on the existence of mnemic persistents. Thus a mind requires a Mnemic Mass. On the other hand, a Mnemic Mass by itself does not suffice to constitute a mind; for a mind must contain experiences, whilst a Mnemic Mass consists solely of traces and dispositions.

In order to prove the existence of anything that could reasonably be called the "Total Unconscious Mind" it would therefore be necessary to establish the following points. (1) That there are literally unconscious experiences, in the sense defined above. If so, there is a Total Subconscious Mass. (2) That these literally unconscious experiences leave traces; *i.e.*, that there is a part of the Total Mnemic Mass which consists of the traces of the Total Subconscious Mass. (3) That, given these two indispensable prerequisites, the mental events which make up the Total Subconscious Mass do in fact have to each other such relations as to form a single individual whole analogous to the minds which we know by introspection. It seems to me most important that people should recognise that the Total Unconscious may contain mental events, and may form a very important unity taken as a whole; and yet that it may be absolutely misleading to call it a "mind". At present anyone who thinks that there is reason to hold that the Total Unconscious has a unity which stretches beyond and between recognised individual human beings, is at once liable to be accused of believing in a Total Unconscious Mind. It is therefore important to point out how much more than this is needed to constitute a belief in the Total Unconscious Mind.

Unconscious Sub-groups. It is commonly assumed that the Total Unconscious falls quite definitely into well marked sub-groups, one specially associated with one human being and another with another. People constantly talk of "My Unconscious" and "Your Unconscious"; and such phraseology would seem to imply the belief just mentioned. So we must now consider the alleged subdivision of the Total Unconscious into one part which is Smith's, another which is Brown's, and a third which is Robinson's.

We will begin by considering the subdivisions of the Total Mnemic Mass. All that we know about traces is that certain experiences leave them, and that they produce or modify certain later experiences. We might therefore classify the contents of the Total Mnemic Mass on either of two principles, viz., by their place of origin or by the place where they produce their effects. Each of these principles can be used in two different ways, thus giving four different methods of subdivision. We might class together (a) all traces left by experiences of Smith's mind; or (b) all traces left by events which happened to Smith's body, or (c) all traces and dispositions which produce or modify experiences in Smith's mind; or (d) all traces and dispositions which cause or modify behaviour of Smith's body. Now it is quite certain that these four equally sensible ways of subdividing the Total Mnemic Mass will lead to different results as soon as we leave completely normal and commonplace phenomena. I will now show this in detail.

(i) If innate dispositions be classified by origin they must be assigned to that part of the Total Mnemic Mass which belonged to our remote ancestors. For, if such dispositions originated in experiences or in bodily processes, it was in those of our remote ancestors and not of ourselves that they must have originated. If, on the other hand, we classify innate dispositions by the minds whose experiences they modify or the bodies whose activities they determine, we must assign them to the Mnemic Masses of contemporary men. Let us then, for the future, confine the discussion to traces.

(ii) If there be literally unconscious mental events, and we classify traces by origin, we shall often reach a different result according as we classify by the mind or the body in which they originated. By "Smith's body" we mean that body which is most usually controlled by a mind with certain marked characteristics, whom we know as "Smith". Now, even if Smith be the most normal person in the world, he is often asleep and sometimes in a swoon. At such times the mind known as "Smith" is not in *control* of the organism known as "Smith's body", even though it be still *animating* the latter. If stimuli act on the body at such times and leave traces, these traces cannot be counted as belonging to Smith's Mnemic Mass, if we mean by this the set of traces left by experiences owned by Smith's mind. For these stimuli, if they produced mental events at all, did not produce experiences which were literally owned by Smith's mind. On the other hand, if by "Smith's Mnemic Mass" we mean traces left by events that happened to Smith's *body*, these traces *will* belong to Smith's Mnemic Mass.

(iii) Generally, when a body is not controlled by the mind which normally controls it, it is not controlled by any mind at all. But in cases of multiple personality the same body may be controlled successively by several recognisably different minds. The phrase "Smith's body" then means the body of which the mind called "Smith" is one of the controlling minds. The fact that it is called "*Smith's* body" is then largely a matter of chance; it will depend on which of these minds is most often in control or was earliest in control. If we classify traces by the bodies in which they originate there will be one group connected with Smith's body. If we classify traces by the minds from whose experiences they originate, this Mnemic Mass will split up into S_1's Mnemic Mass, S_2's Mnemic Mass, and so on. This subdivision may very well not be exhaustive; there may be traces, due to events which happened in

Smith's body, which were not originated by experiences in *any* of the minds which successively control Smith's body.

(iv) I have so far confined myself to the classification of traces by their place of origin ; and have shown that those which originate from experiences belonging to a certain mind will be contained in, but will not exhaust, the group originated by events which happen to the body which is said to be controlled by this mind. I will now point out that classification by place of origin and classification by results will lead to different groupings. Suppose that a certain body B is controlled alternately by minds B_1 and B_2. An experience which is owned by B_1 may leave a trace which afterwards modifies experiences which are owned by B_2. If we classify by origin, this trace will belong to B_1's Mnemic Mass ; if we classify by results, it will belong to B_2's Mnemic Mass. It is of course quite possible that a trace left by one of B_1's experiences may modify the later experiences of both B_1 and B_2. If we classify by origin, this trace will belong to the Mnemic Mass of B_1 and not to that of B_2 ; if we classify by results, it will be common to the Mnemic Masses of B_1 and B_2. There are examples of such facts as these in Dr Prince's account of the Beauchamp case.

(v) So far it has appeared that, even in abnormal cases, all the traces which produce effects in any of the minds which control a certain body were started by events which happened to *that* body. This breaks down in the phenomena of telepathy. So far as I can judge from my own experiences with Mrs Leonard and from what I have read of the experiences of others, telepathy from a sitter to an entranced medium most often concerns past experiences of the sitter which he is not at the moment thinking about. We must therefore suppose that traces of some of the sitter's past experiences now affect the mind of the medium. From the point of view of origin such traces belong to the

Mnemic Mass of the sitter and not to that of the medium. From the point of view of effects these traces are common to the Mnemic Masses of sitter and medium; for the sitter can remember the experience, and the medium can have telepathic knowledge of it.

(vi) Lastly, we have the rare, but reasonably well attested phenomenon of "possession"; where the normal control of an entranced medium ceases to control her body, and the medium begins to speak with a quite different voice, gestures, and mannerisms, which are said to be recognisably characteristic of a certain dead person whom the medium has never met. I have witnessed and taken dictaphone records of one alleged case of this kind. There is no doubt at all of the striking and sudden change which takes place in voice, manner, and subject-matter communicated; but I cannot personally vouch for the resemblance of these characteristics in the so-called "personal control" to those of a certain dead person whom the medium has never met. In the experiments in which I took part the alleged communicator had been known intimately by the other sitter, and not at all by myself; so that I had to take his word for the resemblances between the "personal control" and the alleged communicator. I see, however, no special reason to doubt that the phenomenon in question sometimes does happen. Let us take it as a hypothesis that it does. The most plausible way to explain such phenomena would be to suppose that a set of traces, which originated in the mind or body of a dead person, can persist for a while after the destruction of all that is recognisable of the body; and that this set of traces is capable of affecting in a marked way the speech and bodily behaviour of an entranced medium under specially favourable conditions. Such traces would have to be counted as belonging to the Mnemic Mass of the dead person, if we count by origin; and as belonging to the Mnemic Mass of the medium, if we count by effects.

The upshot of this discussion is that the Total Mnemic Mass almost certainly does contain important sub-groups specially correlated with various recognisably different human minds and bodies. But we must recognise that, since there are several equally reasonable ways of grouping which lead to different results, any such phrase as "Smith's Unconscious" is highly ambiguous until the precise method of selection adopted has been clearly stated. And we must beware of assuming either (a) that all the contents of the Total Mnemic Mass fall into one or other of such groups; or (b) that every pair of such groups are mutually exclusive, so as to have no traces in common; or (c) that there may not be important bigger groups which include several of those smaller masses which are specially correlated with each individual human mind or body. For there are abnormal phenomena, which cannot safely be ignored, which, between them, cast doubt on all these assumptions.

Co-consciousness.—We know that certain personalities claim, not merely to alternate with others in controlling a single human organism, but also to be co-conscious with the rest. It is no part of my present business to discuss the alleged evidence for co-consciousness; but, for the sake of completeness, I must try to define what "co-consciousness" would mean. Let us suppose that a certain body B is controlled in turn by two personalities B_1 and B_2; and that B_1 claims to be co-conscious with B_2. (So far as I know, a claim to *reciprocal* co-consciousness is never made.) This involves making one or more of the three following demands on our belief. (i) That certain stimuli which act on the body B when the mind B_2 is in control of it produce mental events which are not literally owned by B_2 and are literally owned by B_1. Of such events B_2 will not have *even* simultaneous undiscriminating awareness, and B_1 will have *at least* this kind of awareness. (ii) That certain stimuli which act on the common body when B_2

is in control produce either (*a*) two very similar experiences, one of which is owned by B_1 and the other by B_2; or (*b*) produce a single experience which is owned by both of them. If we call these "common experiences", it may be that B_1 introspectively discriminates some of the common experiences which B_2 does not, and conversely. (iii) That B_1 has some kind of *discriminating* awareness of certain mental events which are owned by B_2 and not by B_1 itself. Sally Beauchamp seems to have made all these claims.

I do not think that there is anything wildly paradoxical in the notion of co-consciousness as such. No doubt it is extremely hard to *prove* that it is a fact; but it does not seem to me to be antecedently improbable, as many people think. We commonly identify the mind which sleeps and dreams with the waking mind. In so far as this is legitimate it is certain that what I call "my mind" exists and has experiences at times when it is not controlling my body. Hence there is nothing extravagantly unfamiliar in the notion of a mind, which sometimes controls a body, literally existing and having experiences at times when it is not doing this. Of course one important difference between a co-conscious personality, like Sally, and our minds when asleep and dreaming is that, when Sally is not controlling the body, another mind is doing so; whilst, when we are asleep and dreaming, *no* mind is controlling our body. But, if this were the only difference, it would not be very important. For it is admitted that there are *several* distinct personalities which control the Beauchamp body alternately; and the only question is whether one of these persists and goes on having experiences when the control of the body has been taken over by one of the other personalities. Granted the plurality of personalities, the analogy to the normal dreaming self is enough to make this possibility quite intelligible.

The real difficulties are over the second and third claims. We have very little analogy in ordinary life to the alleged common ownership of certain experiences by two minds. And we have very little analogy in normal life to the alleged direct knowledge by one mind of experiences which belong to another mind and not to itself. Let us first consider the claim to common ownership of certain experiences. I do not think that there is any insuperable *a priori* objection to this, for it can easily be reconciled with either of the three standard theories of the structure of minds. These are the Pure Ego theory; the view that a mind is a peculiar complex of interrelated simultaneous and successive mental events; and the view that the mind is a peculiar complex of interrelated non-mental objects. On the Pure Ego theory an experience would be a complex consisting of a Pure Ego and an object related in some characteristic way. Now, if there be Pure Egos at all, I know of no reason why there should be one and only one of them connected with each human body at a time. Suppose that there were two connected with the Beauchamp body. To say that Sally and Miss Beauchamp had certain experiences in common would simply mean that there are certain objects to which the Sally ego and the Miss Beauchamp ego stood at the same time in the same kind of relation. If the Pure Ego theory be true, it must sometimes happen that two Pure Egos, connected with *different* bodies, stand at once in the same kind of relation to the same object. And, if this be so, there is no antecedent improbability that the same thing should happen when the two Egos are connected with *the same* body.

It is still easier to reconcile the claim to common experiences with the view that a mind is a complex of suitably interrelated mental events. A simple geometrical analogy will make this perfectly clear. Let us represent mental events by points. And let us represent the relations which bind a number of mental events into a single mind by putting a number of points on the same ellipse. A pair of ellipses can cut each other at four points.   If one of these ellipses represents Sally's mind and the other represents Miss Beauchamp's mind, the four points in which the two ellipses cut each other will represent four experiences which are owned in common by Sally and Miss Beauchamp.   It is evident that the claim to common experiences can be reconciled by the same method with the view that the mind is a complex of characteristically interrelated objects.   We have merely to let the points stand for objects, instead of letting them stand for experiences; and the same diagram will represent the alleged facts on this theory about the structure of the mind.   (Of course it is also possible that the "common experiences" are really two different experiences, one belonging to one mind and one to the other, and that their "community" merely consists in the fact that they are very much alike and are produced simultaneously in the two minds by a common external cause.   On that hypothesis there is even less difficulty in admitting the possibility of "common experiences".)

It remains to consider Sally's claim to some kind of direct knowledge of experiences which were owned by other personalities and not by herself.   Really, she professed to have two very different kinds of knowledge of such experiences, both of which fall under the present heading.   (a) She alleged that she could get to know isolated experiences of the personality B_4 by a special method which resembled crystal-gazing.   Of the rest of B_4's experiences she was wholly ignorant.   (b) On the other hand, Sally claimed to be aware, without any special effort except that of attention, of whole masses of experience which belonged to Miss Beauchamp and not to herself.   Thus, when Miss Beauchamp was ill and somewhat light-headed, Sally claims to have been aware of illusory perceptions in Miss Beauchamp's mind and of the fear which these engendered in Miss Beauchamp.   Sally herself did not share the illusions or the fear, though she was aware of the objects in the room, which Miss Beauchamp was misperceiving and consequently fearing.

Now I feel no kind of *a priori* difficulty about the first kind of knowledge. It is closely analogous to ordinary telepathy; and, on her own showing, Sally was throwing herself into a state which is known to be favourable to telepathy when she got this kind of knowledge of isolated events in B_4's mental history. There is no doubt of the reality of telepathy between minds which animate *different* bodies; and it is easier rather than harder to conceive of telepathy taking place between two minds which animate *the same* body. The real difficulty is over the second kind of alleged knowledge. With us introspective discrimination can be applied only to mental events which we own and of which we have simultaneous undiscriminating awareness. Sally's claim practically amounts to asserting that she could introspect experiences which she did not own and which Miss Beauchamp did own, just as we can introspect our own experiences. As we have no analogy to this power anywhere in normal mental life, it must be regarded as antecedently improbable that it exists; though this does not of course prove that it cannot exist.

The upshot of the matter is that, whether there be enough empirical evidence for co-consciousness or not, it ought not to be dismissed *a priori* as antecedently too improbable to be worth consideration. Three out of four of Sally's claims have enough analogy to admitted facts, and are easy enough to reconcile with current theories, to give them a reasonable antecedent probability.

CHAPTER IX

The Alleged Evidence for Unconscious Mental Events and Processes

In the last chapter I pointed out a number of non-literal senses of the phrase " unconscious mental events ", and I tried to give a sufficient description of literally unconscious mental events. Now there are a number of well-known facts, and of familiar arguments based on these facts, which profess to prove the existence of "unconscious mental events". Owing to the ambiguities of this phrase it is uncertain in what sense, if any, these arguments do prove the existence of "unconscious mental events ". In particular it is uncertain whether they have any tendency to prove the existence of *literally* unconscious mental events, as described by us in the last Chapter. In the present Chapter I propose to consider some of the most familiar of these arguments, and to discuss what precisely, if anything, they prove.

Before I begin I want to point out the difference between a sufficient description of an entity and a test for the existence of such an entity. We give a sufficient description of anything when we state a set of properties which together characterise it and do not all characterise anything else. But it may be that some of the properties mentioned in a sufficient description are such that it is difficult or impossible to tell by direct inspection whether they be or be not present in a particular case. Now it may be that there are other properties whose presence or absence can be readily detected by direct inspection. And it may be that their presence or absence involves the presence or absence respectively of those features in the sufficient description which cannot be directly inspected. If so, these properties constitute a test for the entity to which the description applies. Now it is evidently difficult or impossible to know by direct inspection or memory whether we formerly had an experience which we could not at the time have introspectively discriminated. The only test that we can well apply is certain facts about our present experiences, which are supposed to involve the past existence of an experience which we could not at the time have introspectively discriminated. Such tests always assume the truth of some proposition connecting the diagnostic properties with those mentioned in the description; and any doubt about these propositions throws doubt on the test.

Arguments for "Unconscious Sensations." There are certain facts, and certain arguments from them, which have been used since Leibniz's time to prove the existence of "unconscious sensations". Arguments about the roaring of the sea, the stopping of clocks, and so on, are what I have in mind; and they will be familiar to every one. Now, there are certain general remarks which apply to all such arguments, and throw grave doubt on their relevance to prove the existence of unconscious *mental* events.

It will be admitted, I think, that the people who have used these arguments have not as a rule drawn any clear distinction between sensations and sensa. If they have done this, they have, nevertheless, generally assumed that sensa are themselves mental events and experiences of the person who senses them. And, even if they have distinguished between sensations and sensa, and have denied that sensa are mental events owned by the person who senses them, they have generally held that sensa are existentially dependent on being sensed by a mind. I will remind the reader that by a "sensum" I mean such an event as a coloured patch or flash in a visual field, or a noise. And by a "sensation" I mean such a situation as would be expressed by saying: "This noise is being sensed". Now sensa are nearly always outstanding parts or differentiations of spatially larger wholes, which I call "sense-fields". These in turn are generally temporal parts of longer strands of history which I call "special sense-histories". *E.g.*, the sensum which is a certain coloured flash is generally an outstanding feature of a visual sense-field which is a sensibly coloured continuum of coexisting visual sensa. And this visual sense-field is generally a short slice of a longer whole which is a visual sense-history. The reader will find a more elaborate discussion of these conceptions in Part II of my *Scientific Thought*. Now, what the arguments under discussion prove, if they prove anything, is the existence of undiscriminated or undiscriminable sensa in a sense-field. For instance, the argument about the roaring of the sea tries to show that some auditory fields which seem quite homogeneous must yet be highly differentiated into distinct but undiscriminable noises. Now the relevance of such a conclusion to the existence of unconscious mental events depends very much on the view that we take about the nature of sensa.

(1) If we hold that sensa are themselves mental events, an undiscriminable sensum will be, *ipso facto*, an undiscriminable mental event, *i.e.*, an unconscious mental event as described above. But, personally, I see no ground whatever for thinking that a noise or a coloured patch in a visual field is itself a mental event, though of course the total situation which contains such an object as its objective constituent is a mental event.

(2) It might be held that noises and coloured patches, though not themselves mental events, can exist only as objective constituents of mental situations. This is a more plausible view, though I do not think that there are any conclusive arguments for it. Now it might

seem that, if this were true, the existence of undiscriminable sensa would involve the existence of undiscriminable, and therefore unconscious, mental events.
This, however, need be true only in a very trivial
sense. Even if no sensum can exist except as objective
constituent of a situation which also contains a non-
objective constituent suitably related to the sensum, it
does not follow that *each* different sensum needs a
different non-objective factor and a different particular
instance of this relation. Sensa are simply differentiated parts of a larger whole of the same kind as
themselves, viz., a sense-field. If this exists, all its
differentiations exist *ipso facto*. If this whole be sensed,
all its differentiations are thereby sensed ; just as the
fact that Cambridge is north of London involves the
fact that Trinity College is north of London. Thus,
even if all sensa have to be sensed in order to exist,
and even if there be undiscriminable sensa, there is no
need to assume any independent mental event beside
the sensation of the whole field. And this is a literally
conscious experience, since it would be perfectly easy
to discriminate it introspectively if we wanted to.

(3) Lastly, if, as I think most likely, sensa be neither
themselves mental events nor dependent for their existence on being objective constituents of mental events,
it is plain that the existence of undiscriminable sensa
would have no tendency to prove the existence of undiscriminable experiences. We can say at once then that
the arguments under consideration are wholly irrelevant
to the existence of literally unconscious experiences,
unless we accept the extreme view that noises, coloured
patches, etc., are themselves mental events. It may,
however, be of interest to glance at the arguments in
order to see whether they prove the existence even of
undiscriminable sensa.

Arguments for Undiscriminable Sensa. (1) Let us
begin with the familiar argument about the stopping
clock. It is a fact that we may be sitting in a room in

which a clock is ticking; and that, if we be suddenly asked by ourselves or by another whether the clock has been going, we cannot at once answer. But, if the clock should stop, we are liable to look up and say: "Why, the clock has stopped!" This is alleged to prove that we must have been "sub-consciously hearing" the ticking of the clock. What do such facts really suggest?

(i) The negative part, the fact that we could not say off-hand whether the clock has been going or not, suggests that we did not in fact discriminate the ticking noise if it did in fact form part of our earlier auditory fields. If we had been discriminating it, we should almost certainly be able to remember it. (ii) The positive part, the fact that, when the clock does stop, our attention is arrested, does suggest that there is *some* difference or other between our total sense-field just before and just after the stoppage. Now, what the argument would need to prove is the following two propositions. (i) That our earlier fields did contain ticking noises; and (ii) that these ticking noises were not merely undiscriminated but were undiscriminable. Now it seems to me that the argument fails on both counts. If there *were* ticking noises in our earlier fields, there seems to be no reason to suppose that we *could* not have discriminated them if we had tried. All that we can say is that we did not in fact discriminate them, because we were attending to other things such as an interesting book. But it does not seem to me that the argument proves that there were ticking noises at all in our earlier auditory fields. The fact that we notice a difference when the clock stops needs for its explanation no other assumption except that, while the clock is going, it produces *some* modification *somewhere* in our total sense-object, which ceases when the clock stops. This modification might not be auditory at all; it might be simply a vague toning of our general bodily feeling. And, even if it be auditory, it need not take the form of a ticking noise. It might be simply a vague toning of our auditory field as a whole.

It might be objected that, if this be all, why do we at once associate the change with the clock and say that *it* has stopped? To this I answer in the first place that it is doubtful whether we do this as a rule. It seems more accurate to say that we notice a difference, wonder what it is, look about, and finally fix the responsibility on the clock. But, even if we do sometimes immediately attribute the change to the stopping of the clock, this can be explained easily without assuming that there have been undiscriminated ticking noises in our earlier auditory fields. Suppose (to take the least favourable case) that the ticking of the clock simply produced a vague modification of our general bodily feeling. This modification must often in the past have been accompanied by auditory fields in which ticking existed and was discriminated and ascribed to the clock. Hence this kind of modification will have come to suggest by association ticking and clocks. Its cessation would therefore tend to make us look at the clock and ascribe the change to it. Thus, while I have no *a priori* objection to the possibility of undiscriminable sensa in sense-fields which we sense as wholes, I do not think that this argument has any strong tendency to prove that they exist.

(2) I will now consider the argument about the waves of the sea. I will put it in a perfectly general form. When a number of similar physical stimuli are acting together we may be aware of a perfectly noticeable and characteristic sensum. When one of them acts separately, or only a few of them together, we may be unable to notice any sensum of the kind. It is argued that each of them must produce its own special sensum, and that each of these sensa must be undiscriminable.

This is an atrocious argument. It assumes that the effect of a complex cause must be the sum of the effects which each of its parts would produce if acting separately. As a general proposition about causation there is nothing to be said for this. A very simple illustration of its folly is the following. The hearing of a certain note is physically conditioned by a series of compressions and rarefactions in the air which follow each other with a certain frequency. Now each separate compression or rarefaction is physically a part of this total cause. Will it be said that the note heard is the sum of the undiscriminable "notes" due to each separate compression and rarefaction? And, if so, how will you account for the fact that differences of note depend on the characteristic *intervals* between successive compressions or rarefactions?

Even if we accepted this general principle about causation, it would be difficult to apply it to the case of sounds. Sounds have intensive magnitude, and it is not easy to attach a meaning to the statement that loud sounds are the sum of a number of coexisting soft sounds. It might be said, however, that a meaning can be given to this statement by considering the case of an orchestra; and that this example favours the original argument. Let us consider this point. It is true that, in listening to an orchestra, I do not as a rule discriminate the sounds due to the various instruments. But I can do so, if I choose to attend. Here of course each of the instruments would produce a noticeable and characteristic sound if played by itself. Now it might be said: "The sound of the orchestra is the sum of the sounds of the separate instruments; and these separate sounds can be discriminated, although as a rule they are not. When we say that the noise produced by a sufficient number of separately inaudible stimuli is the sum of the undiscriminable noises due to each of them, we mean that the total noise is related to these undiscriminable noises as the sound of an orchestra is related to the discriminable sounds made by the separate instruments. And this is intelligible; because, in the case of the orchestra, you can both hear the whole and discriminate the parts." I think that it would be better to drop the word "sum" and to substitute the word "pattern". The sound of the orchestra might be called a "pattern woven from" the sounds of the separate instruments; and, in this case, we can attend either to the pattern as a whole or to the elements out of which it is woven. The argument would then ask us to believe that a loud discriminable noise, like the roaring of the sea, is a pattern woven out of the many soft and separately indiscriminable noises due to the separate waves. In this case, it would be said, you can attend to the pattern as a whole but not to the elements out of which it is woven. Put in this way the argument is at least intelligible. An intermediate case between that contemplated by the argument and the example of the orchestra would be the following. We might have a number of precisely similar stimuli, *e.g.*, fog-horns, each of which separately would give rise to a noticeable sound. If they were to blow together we should be aware of a louder but qualitatively similar sound. Now, can we regard the noise which we hear when all these fog-horns are blowing together as a pattern woven out of the sounds which each of the fog-horns would make if it were blowing separately, just as we regard a sym-phony as a pattern woven out of the qualitatively dis-similar sounds of the separate instruments? If so, we might fairly argue by analogy that the sound of the sea is a pattern woven from a number of qualitatively similar but separately inaudible sounds due to each wave.

The difficulty in the way of this argument is the following. It seems to me very doubtful whether the noises due to the separate fog-horns do exist within the noise made by all the fog-horns together. I do not think that we could discriminate these supposed separate noises, as we can discriminate the noises of the various instruments in the symphony. And this is certainly not because of their intrinsic faintness, since any one of them could be heard with perfect ease if it happened alone or against a qualitatively different background of sound. Thus it seems uncertain whether we have here an instance of a loud noise being a pattern woven out of a number of softer noises ; for it is doubtful whether the softer noises which would be made by each fog-horn if it were blowing separately exist literally within the louder noise made by all the fog-horns blowing. together. It seems just as reasonable to hold that we have here a homogeneous auditory field, within which no sensa are discriminable because there are none to be discriminated. If this be so, the argument by analogy to prove that the noise of the sea is a pattern woven out of the faint undiscriminable sounds due to each wave, breaks down. Once again I have no *a priori* objection to the conclusion ; I maintain only that the argument fails to prove it.

(3) Before ending the present subsection I wish to point out the complete irrelevance of Stumpf's Argument for the present purpose. Stumpf's argument is perfectly valid ; and it is quite true that it does not, as some of its critics have alleged, depend upon doubtful assumptions about the connexion between sensations and physiological stimuli. Stumpf might (and, for all I know, does) use his argument to the angels in Heaven, who have no bodies. It proves with almost complete certainty that some pairs of sensa, which seem to us to be exactly alike in quality or intensity, must really differ in these respects. But, even if sensa be experiences, no one has ever supposed that the qualities or intensities of sensa or the relations of identity or difference between their qualities or intensities are experiences. The unlikeness of two auditory sensa is not a third auditory sensum or any kind of sensum ; it is a relation. Stumpf's argument merely establishes the fact that we can make mistakes about the relations of qualitative or intensive likeness between sensa which we sense ; just as we may make mistakes about the likeness or unlikeness of anything

else. This has no tendency to prove the existence of unconscious mental events in any sense whatever ; except on two assumptions, one of which is probably false and the other of which is absurd. The first of these is that sensa are experiences owned by the mind which senses them. The second is that, in some sense, we must, *ipso facto*, know all the qualities and relations of our experiences merely because they are *ours*. Stumpf shows that I often judge sensum A to be exactly like sensum B, when in fact they cannot be exactly alike. On the two assumptions just stated I must in some sense know that A and B are not exactly alike if they be not so in fact. Thus, with these two assumptions, Stumpf's argument would prove the existence of *unconscious knowledge* about the relations of sensa, which conflicts with my *conscious beliefs* about the same subject. It would not prove the existence of unconscious *sensations* or of undiscriminated *sensa*, even on these assumptions. And, whatever one may think of the first assumption, the second is too silly to merit a moment's consideration.

Arguments for " Unconscious Perceptions ". We can sometimes be pretty sure, on reflexion that, *if* we perceived a certain object on a certain occasion, this perception must have been unconscious, at least relatively to us. Now the circumstances may have been such that it would be surprising if no preception had existed at the time. Finally, we may afterwards have dreams, or say and do things in ordinary life or under hypnosis or psychoanalysis, which would be most naturally explained by the supposition that a perception did exist at the time. It will be noticed that, in order to establish the existence of an unconscious perception of a certain thing at a certain time, we must prove two propositions, one positive and the other negative : (i) We must prove that a perception of this thing did exist at this time ; and (ii) we must prove that the person who might have been expected to own this perception could not have detected it by introspection at the time, even if he had tried. To prove the first point there are two main lines of argument. The first is that the general situation at the time was such that a perception of this thing might reasonably have been expected to happen then. The second is that some of the later experiences and acts of the person are such as would be likely to follow if he *had* perceived this thing, and not otherwise. To prove the second point we have again two main lines of argument. The first is that the person, not only *does not remember perceiving* the thing, but also *remembers not perceiving* it. (I need scarcely say that these are two very different experiences.) The second is that some of the later experiences and acts of the person are such as would be likely to follow if he had *not* perceived the thing, and would be unlikely to follow if he had perceived it.

A simple example would be one that we have already used, viz., looking for something, failing to find it, and yet discovering afterwards that it had been staring one in the face in the very drawer in which we have been looking. The argument would then run as follows: "If I had recognised at the time that I was perceiving the object, I should certainly have found it. As I did not find it, it seems reasonable to suppose either that I was not perceiving it at all or that, if I was, this perception was not noticed by me. Now, if it existed, it is hardly likely to have escaped my notice by mere inadvertence; for this was the very experience which I was wanting and expecting at the time. Hence it seems probable that, if there was a perception of this object, and if it was owned by me, it was for some reason incapable of being introspectively discriminated by me at the time. Therefore, we must say either that there was no perception of the object at all; or that it was not owned by me; or that it was owned by me but could not have been introspectively discriminated by me at the time. If it was an experience of mine at all it must, therefore, have been a literally unconscious experience." The argument might then continue as follows : "The object was in such a position that light from it must have affected the central part of my retina ; and, therefore, it is very unlikely that it did not produce a perceptual experience at all." Lastly, it might be that in some cases we could add to this presumption something further of the following kind : "Last night I dreamed of the object in a certain place in the drawer ; and when I went this morning and looked again there it was." Or again : "I was hypnotised afterwards and told the hypnotist where this object was, and he found it there." We should then have a pretty strong case, superficially at any rate, for the view that I had had a literally unconscious perception of this object when I was looking for it in the drawer.

Let us now consider whether this case be really so strong as it seems at first sight. I think we may admit that such arguments make it highly probable that, if a perception existed at the time, it was literally unconscious relatively to the mind which was then controlling the body at any rate. So we may confine ourselves to the question : "Is there any reason to believe that a perception of this object existed at all?" The evidence which is given for an affirmative answer to this question is derived, as I have said, from the later experiences or actions of the observer and from the general nature of the situation in which he was placed at the time. That is, we know that most people in the situation in which this man was placed would have had a certain kind of experience, and so we think it likely that he too must have had experience of this kind. And, again, we know that people can generally remember and be affected only by what they have already perceived. So when the man remembers a certain past event under hypnotism, or when he acts in ordinary life as if he had perceived this event, we assume that he must have perceived it. Now these are of course simply arguments from analogy ; and, if the facts can be explained equally well in other ways, they do not carry much weight. Can the facts be explained equally well in other ways?

In the first place, we must notice that the occurrence of an experience in the past is never a sufficient, even if it be a necessary, condition for the occurrence of a memory in the present. No memory will arise unless a trace, whatever that may be, has been left. Now, if a trace exists, it seems reasonable to suppose that it could give rise to mnemic phenomena even if no experience had accompanied its formation. Whether you choose to call any of these mnemic phenomena "memories" or not will be simply a matter of definition. I, therefore, suggest the following hypothesis as a possible explanation of the facts with which we are at present dealing. When stimuli act on our nerves they usually give rise to two results, viz., an experience E and a trace T. But, under certain circumstances, only one of these results may happen; e.g., a trace may be formed, but no mental event may accompany its formation. If this trace be afterwards excited, the resulting experience will be exactly or very much like a memory of the experience E which normally accompanies the formation of the trace T. And, again, the resulting behaviour will be very much like that which normally follows from an experience such as E. Since the stimulus may thus have two alternative effects, it is reasonable to suppose that the total cause is of the form Sxy, where S is the stimulus. Here Sx produces an experience, and Sy produces a trace. We must suppose that the two factors x and y generally co-operate with each other, but that under certain circumstances x is inhibited. We then get a trace formed, but no mental event accompanies it. It is of course theoretically possible that, under other circumstances, y is inhibited. We should then get a mental event, but no trace would be left. Such mental events, if they exist, could never be remembered by any means, and could produce no mnemic effects. It seems to me that this simple and quite plausible hypothesis accounts for the facts perfectly well without the assumption of unconscious perceptions.

I will now go a little more into detail. We must remember that the perception of a certain physical object involves sensation together with at least two other factors. In addition to sensing a certain field and its contents we must select a certain sensum from the rest of its sense-field ; and in addition to this we must recognise this sensum as an appearance of a certain physical object. We might, therefore, fail to find a certain object which we were looking for, and which was staring us in the face, for one of three reasons. (*a*) Because it was producing no sensible appearance in our sense-field ; or (*b*) because the sensible appearance which it was producing was not selected and discriminated from the rest of the field ; or (*c*) because this particular sensum was not recognised by us at the time as an appearance of the physical object for which we were looking. I think it likely that the second and third possibilities are so closely connected as to form in practice only a single alternative. What I mean is this. I think that we select and discriminate certain sensa from the rest of the field largely because they represent certain physical objects to us. If a stimulus does excite certain traces of past experiences we both discriminate the sensum which it produces and take this sensum as an appearance of a certain physical object. If it fails to excite these traces we do not as a rule select and discriminate this sensum from the rest of the field ; and *a fortiori* do not take it as an appearance of any particular physical object.

It seems to me most likely that in the cases under discussion there really was a sensum in the visual field, which was in fact an appearance of the object that we were seeking ; but that for some reason the traces which would usually be excited under such conditions were not excited, or, if they were, failed to produce their normal effect. This sensum was therefore not selected and discriminated from the rest of the field, and was not recognised as an appearance of the object for which we were looking. If this be so, there was no *unconscious* perception, for there was no *perception* at all. But there was an undiscriminated, and at the time probably undiscriminable, sensum in my visual field. This leaves a trace; and afterwards in dreams or under hypnosis the excitement of this trace excites those which failed to operate on the former occasion. We may then get what is, for all practical purposes, a memory of the physical object which we failed to perceive when we were searching for it. Or other mnemic results may follow which usually follow from actual perception. The psycho-analysts have many things of great interest to tell us about the emotional and conative factors which sometimes prevent sensations from developing into perceptions by preventing the usual traces from being excited or by inhibiting the usual results of such excitement.

The conclusion of the matter is that, while I have no *a priori* objection to the existence of literally unconscious perceptions, I do not think that the facts which have been brought forward to prove their existence are adequate for the purpose. These facts can be explained quite as well by another hypothesis which is at least as plausible as the hypothesis of literally unconscious perceptions.

Arguments for "Unconscious Emotions." As an example of the facts which have been brought forward to prove the existence of literally unconscious emotions I will take the case of Livingstone and the lion. Livingstone tells us that he remembers that he felt neither fear nor pain while he was in the jaws of a lion and had given himself up for lost. There are other cases where men have been in extremely dangerous situations, and remember that they felt no fear at the time. Yet afterwards they dream of the incident, and the dream is accompanied by fear amounting to terror. It is reasonable to suppose that in such cases, if the emotion of fear existed at all while the incident was taking place, it must have been literally unconscious relatively to the agent at any rate. If Livingstone's memory be correct he looked at the time for the feeling of fear, which he expected to find, and was surprised to notice that it was absent. It is, therefore, reasonable to suppose that, if this emotion existed at all at the time it was not merely unnoticed by Livingstone but was unnoticeable by him at the time. This argument would not apply so strongly to men who have saved themselves in dangerous situations by their own efforts and resource. They must have been attending intently to external situations with which they had to deal promptly and effectively. They can, therefore, hardly have been attending at the time to their own emotions. When they say afterwards that they "remember not feeling fear" it would probably be much more accurate to say that they "do not remember feeling fear", which is a very different matter. In such cases the emotion, if it existed at all, was no doubt undiscriminated; but there seems no good reason to think that it was undiscriminable. But this explanation will not cover a case like Livingstone's; for he had ceased to struggle and had given himself up for lost.

The evidence for supposing that an emotion of fear existed is twofold. In the first place, the situation was such that a man might be expected to feel fear in it. Secondly, the dreams and other later experiences of the agent are such as might be expected to be consequent on a past feeling of fear. Now this argument can be dealt with in precisely the same way as the argument for unconscious perceptions. I do not think that there is the least need to suppose that there was an emotional experience at all in Livingstone's case, or even that a trace was produced of the kind which an emotional experience generally leaves. All that we need to suppose is that the perception of the situation left an ordinary cognitive trace, and that the emotional experience which would normally accompany such a perception was inhibited. I take it that, although the external situation was such as normally produces pain and fear, the internal state of Livingstone's body at the time was abnormal. The result was that a perception arose as usual, but the emotion which would have accompanied it if the body had been in a normal state did not arise. This perception left a trace, as we know from the fact that Livingstone was able to remember perceiving the situation. When the patient, at some later date, goes to sleep and dreams this trace is excited and produces a dream of the original situation. The abnormal bodily state which inhibited pain and fear on the first occasion has now ceased. Hence the dream is accompanied by the sort of emotion which would normally have accompanied the original perception. There is therefore not the least need to suppose either that there was an emotion when the dangerous situation was being lived through, or that an "emotional trace" was left though no emotion existed. The *cognitive* trace, which was certainly left, is quite adequate to explain all the subsequent phenomena, both cognitive and emotional.

Arguments for "Unconscious Mental Processes." We have so far considered the evidence which has been brought forward to prove *directly* the existence of literally unconscious mental *events*, such as sensations, perceptions, and emotions. We have found this evidence to be quite inconclusive. But we must now introduce a distinction between mental *events* and mental *processes*. I do not pretend that this is an absolutely sharp distinction ; but I think that a few examples will make clear what I have in mind by it. When I deliberately consider a number of possible alternative courses of action, weigh up the *pros* and *cons* of each, and finally decide on one of them to the exclusion of the rest, the whole long event may be called a conscious "mental process". Similarly, when I follow, or make up for myself, a long chain of reasoning the whole long event may be called a conscious "mental process." On the other hand, seeing a dog and feeling frightened of it would hardly be called a mental "process", though it is a mental "event". And feeling a twinge of toothache would hardly be called a "mental process", though it is a mental "event". We might roughly define a "mental process" as a long mental event which has a set of successive parts each of which is a mental event of a different kind from the whole. And the mental process is characterised by the nature of these parts and by the characteristic relations between them within the whole long event. For instance, a process of reasoning is a mental event which is divisible into three successive parts, none of which is itself a process of reasoning; viz. (*a*) contemplating and accepting the premises, (*b*) noticing that they logically entail a certain conclusion, and (*c*) passing from the state of merely contemplating this conclusion to believing it with a feeling of being justified in doing so. (Very likely the analysis could be carried further, but this is enough to illustrate my meaning.) Now it might be that there is good direct evidence for the existence of unconscious mental *processes*, though there is no good *direct* evidence for the existence of un-conscious mental events which are not, in this sense, processes. If this were so, there would be good *indirect* evidence for the existence of certain unconscious mental events which are not processes. For a mental process is a mental event having a set of successive parts which are mental events and not mental processes. We must therefore consider the alleged evidence for the existence of unconscious mental processes. We shall find that this is a somewhat complicated business, which cannot be completed in this Chapter. It will lead us up to the question of the real nature of traces and dispositions, which I reserve for the next Chapter.

The " Unconscious" Factor in Conscious Mental Processes. I think that it is best not to attack the question of the evidence for unconscious mental processes directly, but to make a *détour* by way of the unconscious factors in admittedly conscious mental processes. Suppose we consider an ordinary process of conscious desire which a man follows up to a successful result. When we analyse this we profess to find a process in which the man sets a certain end before himself, feels attracted by the prospect of it, chooses such and such means in order to get it, and so on. But how little of this actually is introspected or is introspectible! While the man is busy carrying out his purpose it is doubtful whether he has any literally conscious idea of the end or any literally conscious feeling of attraction towards it except for short spells separated by long intervals. Most of the time he is thinking of some minute detail in the means which he is using, and is not thinking about the end at all. Yet we say that idea of the end is constantly present, guiding his choice of means; and we say that the attraction which he feels for this end is a factor which is constantly present, making the agent persevere and surmount the obstacles which from time to time arise. Moreover, a conative process is often laid aside for a time, and then taken up again at the point where it was left; and this may go on for years. The writing of this book has been a conscious conative process which has, in a sense been going on for the last two years. But in every day of this period there have been long intervals during which introspection would discover nothing relevant to this conative process. Now here we are dealing with nothing odd or abnormal. I think that such examples show that we cannot *identify* the most normal conscious conation with those scrappy and separated bits of experience of which we have simultaneous undiscriminating awareness, and which we could no doubt introspectively discriminate if we tried. The fullest list of all these fragments with their observable interrelations is no more what we mean by a "conscious conation" than the set of interrelated sensa by which my table from time to time appears to me is what I mean by "my table". We may say that, just as the most ordinary statement about a physical object which I perceive goes beyond the sensa which I sense, so the most ordinary statement about a conscious "mental process" of mine goes beyond the scrappy and jumbled bits of experience which I could introspectively discriminate.

It seems to me then that there is much more analogy between my perceptual knowledge of external physical things and processes and my introspective knowledge of my own mind and my conscious mental processes than is commonly admitted. Poor Locke and Kant have been abused like pickpockets for talking about "internal perception" and comparing it to "external perception". I believe that they were substantially correct; and that their main mistake was that they failed to draw certain very necessary distinctions which really make the analogy stronger than they thought. In ordinary sense-perception we have to distinguish between perception itself and sensation on which it is based. My perception of a chair is based on my sensations of certain interrelated sensa which are appearances of it; and I should not say that I perceived the chair unless I did from time to time sense such sensa. But I mean something more by the "chair" than all these sensa; and I mean something more by "perceiving the chair" than just sensing these sensa. The notion of the chair contains as an essential factor the notion of a persistent something which joins up the various isolated "chair-sensa" which I sense, and which shows itself to me partially and imperfectly through them. Now it seems to me that we must draw a similar distinction in dealing with our introspective knowledge of our own conscious mental processes. In sense-perception we distinguished between (*a*) sensing (*b*) selecting and (*c*) using a sensed and selected sensum for perceiving. I think that we must draw a similar set of distinctions in the case of our knowledge of our own mental processes. We must distinguish (*a*) undiscriminating simultaneous awareness of mental events (*b*) introspective discrimination of certain particular mental events, and (*c*) what I will call "introspective perception" of a conscious mental process by means of certain mental events which I have introspectively discriminated. My introspective perception of an ordinary conscious mental process, such as a conation, is based on certain interconnected experiences of which I do have simultaneous undiscriminating awareness and some of which I may introspectively discriminate. I should not say that I "introspectively perceived" this conation of mine unless I were introspectively aware of these interconnected bits of experience. Nevertheless, I mean something more by my conation than these bits of experience ; and I mean something more by "introspectively perceiving" it than just having simultaneous undiscriminating awareness of these bits of experience or just introspectively discriminating them. The notion of a conation involves as an essential factor the notion of a persistent something which joins up these relatively isolated bits of experience and reveals itself partially and imperfectly to me through them.

I prefer not to call my "perception" of my own mental processes "internal perception", because this name seems to me to apply better to the perceptual knowledge which I have of certain physiological processes in my own body by means of bodily sensations, such as headache or toothache. I prefer to divide Perception into (*a*) Introspective, and (*b*) Sensuous ; and then to divide Sensuous Perception into (i) External and (ii) Internal. I shall say that the introspectible experiences on which I base my introspective perception

of a conscious mental process are "appearances" of the
latter to me. This word is to have no implication of
delusiveness. At present I do not wish to deny the
possibility that the introspectible appearances of a conscious mental process may be literally slices of it ; that
is a question for subsequent discussion.

If the view which I have been suggesting be accepted
it will be seen that there is a close analogy between the
problem of the nature of traces and dispositions and
their relation to introspectible experiences, on the one
hand ; and the problem of the nature of physical objects
and processes and their relation to sensa, on the other.
Now about the latter problem there are, I think, five
possible types of theory ; and corresponding to each of
these will be a possible type of theory about the nature
of traces and dispositions. (1) *Phenomenalism*. This is
the theory that, strictly speaking, there are no physical
objects or processes. There are just the sensa which
we sense and the observable relations between them
which put certain of them into certain groups. Corresponding to this would be Mr Russell's tentative
suggestion of a special kind of Mnemic Causation
which directly connects introspectible experiences and
does away with the need for assuming traces and
dispositions. (2) *Naïve Realism*. This is the theory
that the sensa which are appearances of a physical object
are literally spatio-temporal parts of that object, and
that the spatio-temporal parts of it which are not manifested in sensation are of precisely the same nature as
those which are so manifested. Corresponding to this
would be the theory that the introspectible appearances
of a conscious mental process are literally temporal
slices of the whole process, and that the non-introspectible slices are of precisely the same nature as
those which we can introspect. (3) *Critical Realism*.
This is the theory that sensa are not literally spatio-
temporal parts of the physical objects of which they are
appearances ; that there are certain characteristics which

belong only to sensa and not to physical objects ; and that there are other characteristics which belong to both, though not necessarily in the same determinate form. In the next Chapter I will try to explain the theory about traces and dispositions which would correspond to this. (4) *Agnosticism*. This is the theory that we have no means of telling what are the characteristics of those relatively permanent things and processes which manifest themselves partially to us by the interrelated sensa which we from time to time sense. Corresponding to this would be the view that we cannot tell whether what manifests itself partially to us by interrelated experiences is mental or physical or both or neither. (5) *Mentalism*. This is the theory that the relatively permanent conditions of interrelated sets of sensa are minds or states of mind, *e.g.*, colonies of spirits of a low order of intelligence (Leibniz) or standing volitions in the mind of God (Berkeley). Corresponding to this would be the view that the bits of experience which we can introspect are appearances of purely physical or physiological processes, and that the intervals between these introspectible experiences are filled in with something which is physical or physiological and not in any sense mental. I leave the discussion of these alternatives to the next Chapter.

Wholly " Unconscious Mental Processes ". We are now in a position to consider the arguments for " unconscious mental processes " which are not merely factors in "conscious mental processes." A completely unconscious mental process would be a process of the same kind as those which appear to us or to others as a series of characteristically interrelated experiences, but which does not in fact appear to anyone in that way. It may be compared with a completely unperceived physical object or process, such as an unperceived fire. This is a process of the same kind as those which appear to ourselves or to others as a series of characteristically interrelated sensa, but which does not in fact manifest itself to anyone in this way. Naturally, a belief in a completely unconscious mental process, like a belief in a completely unperceived physical object or process, must rest on inference; and this inference will take the form of an argument from causation and analogy. To illustrate this I will consider the arguments which have led psycho-analysts and others to postulate wholly unconscious conations.

These arguments are logically of the same type as those which led Adams and Leverrier to postulate the existence of the hitherto unperceived planet *Neptune*. In both cases they are arguments by analogy to explain certain observed perturbations and irregularities. We are quite familiar with the conflict between two conscious wishes. Each wish, in the absence of the other, would appear as a certain typical series of conscious experiences, though it would be more than the sum-total of these. When both coexist we can observe that the two series of conscious experiences do not go on side by side, but they are as a rule replaced by a modified series which is in some sense a compromise between the two. This modified series may resemble either of the unmodified series in various degrees, thus showing the relative strength of the two conscious wishes. And the conflict is accompanied by a characteristic conscious experience of strain and uneasiness. All these facts are of course quite familiar and open to introspective observation. Now we may sometimes find one and only one conscious wish; and it may manifest itself to superficial observation as a certain series of conscious experiences which would be the normal manifestation of a single wish. And yet, if we look more closely into our minds or study our actions more carefully, we may find isolated bits of conscious experience or isolated actions which are *not* normal appearances of this conscious wish but are more like the normal appearances of a certain conflicting wish. Or we may find, instead of these isolated and anomalous conscious experiences and actions, another peculiarity. We may find that our actual series of conscious experiences is more like the compromise series which occurs when we have two conflicting conscious wishes than like the pure series which occurs when we have a single conscious wish. Lastly, there will sometimes be a feeling of strain and uneasiness which resembles the feeling that we have when two conscious wishes conflict, although here we can introspectively perceive only one wish. Under these circumstances it is reasonable to suppose that there really are two processes going on, and that they are both such that we should call them "conscious wishes" if they manifested themselves as series of conscious experiences. And it is reasonable to suppose that they have to each other that kind of relation which often manifests itself as a conflict between two conscious wishes. But in this case, for some reason, one of these processes cannot manifest itself in a series of conscious experiences characteristic of a wish. It can manifest itself only by a few isolated and anomalous conscious experiences and actions, or by perturbing and compromising the series of conscious experiences which is the manifestation of one of these wishes. This hypothesis will of course be strengthened if we do have a vague feeling of strain and uneasiness which cannot be explained by any observable conflict between our conscious wishes. So far the argument of the psychoanalysts is exactly like the arguments by which Adams and Leverrier were led to suspect the existence of the planet *Neptune*, and to predict certain facts about it.

The next stage was for astronomers to look for the hypothetical planet ; and, as we know, they were eventually able to perceive it. The psycho-analysts would say that they had followed a similar course with similar results. The astronomers by their special technical methods succeeded in making the planet *Neptune* manifest itself by certain sensa characteristic of a planet such as Adams and Leverrier had suspected to exist. The psycho-analysts profess that, by using certain technical methods, they have in many cases made the previously unconscious wish manifest itself as a series of conscious experiences characteristic of such a wish as they had suspected to exist. If we accept this statement (and I see no reason why we should not) the analogy is complete.

When we are considering the arguments for unconscious mental processes used by psycho-analysts and others, I think we must distinguish three questions. (1) Are the arguments logically of the same form as arguments which we should admit to be valid in other spheres? Here the answer is certainly in the affirmative. As I have just shown, they are of precisely the same form as those used by Adams and Leverrier in astronomy. True, they deal with a subject-matter which is much more complex and about which we know much less. And they cannot be put into mathematical form or tested by making exact measurements. This no doubt reduces the probability of their conclusions, but of their general formal validity there can be no doubt. (2) Do they make it probable that there are certain processes which do not give rise to characteristic sets of inter-related conscious experiences, but which are nevertheless of the same nature and capable of the same mutual relations as processes which do manifest themselves by such sets of conscious experiences? Here again I think there is little doubt that the answer is in the affirmative. (3) Have we a right to call such processes "mental"? This question is ambiguous. If it merely means: "Are they of the same nature as those processes which do manifest themselves as conscious experiences?", the answer is that they most probably are. If it means: "Are they composed of mental events which are of the same nature as the conscious experiences by which other processes of a similar kind manifest themselves?", the answer, if one can be given at all, must be left to the next Chapter. And the answer to it will depend largely on what view we take about the nature of the "unconscious parts" of "conscious mental processes". If we have to regard the "unconscious parts" of a "conscious mental process" as non-introspectible mental events, and the "conscious parts" as differing from them only in being introspectible, we shall have to answer the question affirmatively. Otherwise, we shall have to answer it with a definite negative; or with a confession of ignorance; or by analysing it into several questions, some of which can be answered affirmatively, others negatively, and others perhaps not at all.

I have so far confined my attention to "unconscious wishes" and to the arguments which have been brought forward by psycho-analysts in favour of their existence. There is another set of facts which seem strongly to favour the hypothesis of "unconscious mental processes". These are the cases in which a patient under hypnosis is told to perform a certain act at a certain number of minutes (which may run into hundreds or thousands) after he has been awakened. It is found that certain patients perform the suggested action automatically at or very near to the suggested time. This seems to imply that the time which was given in minutes has been reduced to days and hours by some process of mental arithmetic, and that a watch has been kept for the arrival of the calculated moment. Yet the patient cannot discover this process of calculation and of watching by introspection. Here it certainly seems reasonable to suppose that a process has been going on similar to the processes which manifest themselves as a rule by the series of conscious experiences which we call "making a calculation". This process, for some reason, does not manifest itself in this way to the mind which normally controls this body. Whether the process can strictly be called "mental" depends upon considerations which must be discussed in the next Chapter.

There is, however, one remark which must be made

before ending this Chapter. Suppose that, on again hypnotising the patient, he says that he remembers making the calculation and watching for the calculated moment. If we accept this statement we shall have to suppose that a genuinely mental process has been going on, that it is literally unconscious relatively to the mind which normally controls this patient's body, but that it is literally conscious relatively to the mind which controls this body when it is hypnotised. And of course there may be good grounds for regarding these two "minds" as parts of a single mind which animates the body at both times. Now, supposing that such statements are made under hypnosis, I think that it is certain that *some* weight must be attached to them. We must remember, however, that a person under hypnosis is in an extremely suggestible state, and is very liable to answer questions in the way in which he supposes the questioner to want them answered. Thus I do not think that it would be reasonable to attach as much weight to the statements of a hypnotised person about his own experiences as to the statements of a normal waking person. We should at least need to be very certain that the questions were not put in such a way as to suggest even faintly to the patient that the questioner was wanting a certain kind of answer. I have not enough first-hand knowledge of the facts to feel sure whether these conditions have been fulfilled by the experimenters on this subject.

Somewhat similar remarks apply to the statements made by alternating personalities, who claim to be co-conscious, like Sally Beauchamp. Such a personality, when in control, may tell us that it owned a certain continuous series of conscious experiences while another personality was in control. And this series may be such as to fill the gaps between certain fragmentary and isolated bits of conscious experience belonging to the latter personality. Here we have evidence which, taken at its face-value, would suggest that the "unconscious parts" of a conscious mental process in one personality are literally conscious experiences in another co-conscious personality. And, if we accepted this, we might be inclined to generalise this to normal cases, and to suggest that the difference here is that the co-conscious personality never gets control of the body and therefore never has a chance of telling us about its experiences. Now I think that *some* weight must be given to the statements of personalities like Sally about their own experiences. Moreover, it cannot be said that Sally was particularly suggestible ; she seemed to have a strong will of her own and to be quite capable of resisting unpalatable suggestions. But was the suggestion that she was co-conscious an unpalatable one? One gets the impression that she was very anxious to make herself out to be as important and mysterious as possible. (It will be remembered that at certain stages of the proceedings she claimed to be a " spirit ".) There is obviously a fairly close connection between multiple personality and ordinary hysteria. Now hysterical persons can be extremely obstinate in many respects, as Sally was. But they show an embarrassing readiness to provide evidence for *any* theory about hysteria which they believe to be held by the doctor who is treating them. And probably they would specially welcome any theory which enables them to feel themselves to be mysterious beings who are creating a revolution in current medical and psychological concepts. Thus, although we cannot afford to neglect their statements about themselves and their experiences, we ought to view them with very great suspicion.

CHAPTER X

The Nature of Traces and Dispositions

In the last Chapter we saw that the question whether there are unconscious processes which are *literally* mental involves the question : " What is the nature of those processes which manifest themselves partially through more or less discontinuous series of interrelated conscious experiences, and which presumably fill the temporal gaps between the conscious experiences of such series ? " We have already suggested several alternative possible theories on this point ; and it is now time to consider them in greater detail with a view, to deciding, if possible, between them.

Analogous Facts about Material Substances.—It will be wise to begin by considering the analogies and differences between the mental facts under discussion and certain facts about material substances. Let us take any material substance, *e.g.*, a circular ring of elastic steel wire. We notice that there are certain characteristics which, strictly speaking, belong to its states rather than to it ; and that there are other characteristics, which, strictly speaking, belong to it rather than to any of its states. The wire ring throughout its history always has some shape or other, and it may have the same shape for long periods of its history. If we squeeze it between our fingers it assumes various elliptical shapes ; and, when we let go of it, it goes back to what we call its " natural shape ", which is circular. We should commonly express these facts by saying that " the shape of the ring is sometimes circular, sometimes elliptical and of eccentricity e, sometimes elliptical and of eccentricity e', and so on ". If we divide up the history of this ring into successive adjoined slices there is a certain determinable characteristic which belongs to *all* these slices, viz., the characteristic of "having some shape" or even the more determinate characteristic of "having a shape which is some conic section". This can be said to belong to the thing ; in the sense that it belongs to all the successive states of the thing, and that, if an event did not have this determinable characteristic, it would not be counted as a state of this thing. But the completely determinate forms of this determinable characteristic, *e.g.,* circularity, ellipticity of eccentricity e, etc., belong strictly to the states of the thing and not to the thing. In the first place, one state may have one of these determinate characteristics, and another state of the same thing may have another of them. And, secondly, even if it should happen that all the states of the thing have precisely the same determinate shape, this is regarded as contingent. An event which had a different determinate shape would not *eo ipso* be denied to be a state of this thing.

We have so far distinguished (*a*) certain determinable characteristics which may be said to belong to a thing, in so far as they belong to every state of the thing and in so far as any event to which they did not belong would not be counted as a state of this thing. And (*b*) completely determinate forms of these determinable characteristics. Every state of the thing has one or other of these, and it is possible that all its states may have the same determinate form of a certain determinable characteristic. But this is not necessary ; an event may have a different determinate form of this determinable characteristic without thereby failing to be a state of this thing.

We have now to notice a quite different kind of characteristic, which can be said to belong to the thing

but not to any of its states. The ring in our example
has an inherent tendency to assume an elliptical state of
such and such eccentricity when squeezed in such and
such a way ; and it has an inherent tendency to assume
the circular form when left alone. This might be called
a "causal characteristic" of the ring. The characteristic of having some shape or of having a shape which
is some conic section is not a causal characteristic.
And the determinate forms which this determinable
characteristic assumes in various states of the thing are
not *causal*, though they are *caused* by the causal characteristic and the external circumstances. Now causal characteristics of a thing may change without the thing
being thereby destroyed. If I heated the ring to a
certain temperature and then cooled it in a certain way,
it would lose its elasticity. After this it would stay in
any shape that I squeezed it into, and would have no
tendency to pass into the circular shape when I ceased
to squeeze it. Such facts as these show that we must
distinguish causal properties of various orders in a
material thing. We may say that it is a "first
order" causal characteristic of the ring to pass into
a certain elliptical shape when squeezed and to pass
back into the circular shape when released. And we
may say that, after being heated, it has lost this first-
order causal characteristic and has acquired the first-
order causal characteristic of staying in any shape into
which I may squeeze it. But it is also a causal
characteristic of the ring that, when it is heated and
cooled in a certain way, it loses the former first-order
causal characteristic and gains the latter. This may be
called a "second-order" causal characteristic of the
ring. If we denote the two first-order characteristics
by p_1 and p_2 respectively, we might denote by p_{12} the
second-order causal characteristic that the substance
loses p_1 and gains p_2 under such and such conditions.

Now sometimes such changes as these can be reversed
either by reversing the original process or by some

other means.   *E.g.*, by heating up the ring again, hammering it, and cooling it suitably I could make it lose p_2 and acquire p_1.   If this be so we may say that it has a second-order causal characteristic p_{21} as well as p_{12}.   In other cases a change of first-order causal characteristics is not, so far as we know, reversible.   It is a second-order causal characteristic of an organism that, if you give it a good dose of arsenic, it loses the first-order causal characteristic of "vital response". And we do not know of any way in which this first-order characteristic can be restored.   We must of course recognise the possibility of causal characteristics of the third and higher orders ; but there is no need to go into detail about them.   All that we need say is that the lower the order of a causal characteristic the more is it possible for this characteristic to change without our saying that the original substance has ceased to exist.   Provided that the causal characteristics of higher order remain unaltered, and especially if the changes in first-order causal characteristics be reversible, we tend to hold that the same substance is still existing.

We must next notice the connexion between causal characteristics and internal structure.   So long as a material substance has a certain causal characteristic we are inclined to believe that it must have a certain characteristic internal structure.   The word "structure" must here be taken in a wide sense to include both purely spatial and spatio-temporal structure.   It is a first-order causal characteristic of a pillar-box to look red when illuminated by white light and viewed by a normal eye.   We ascribe this to a certain persistent spatial structure of the minute particles of the pigment, in virtue of which the surface selectively reflects the red constituent of the white light.   If the pillar-box be heated to a high enough temperature it will henceforth appear brown or black under similar conditions of illumination to a normal eye.   Thus this first-order causal characteristic will have changed into a different

one.   We ascribe this change to a change in the
minute spatial structure of the pigment on the surface
of the pillar-box.   Other causal characteristics are
ascribed, not to the mere persistence of a certain spatial
structure, but to the fact that the minute particles of the
body are continuing to move in certain orbits with
certain characteristic velocities.   Magnetic properties
are an example in point.   Here the persistence of the
causal characteristic is correlated with the persistence of
a certain spatio-temporal structure.   It is characteristic
of modern science as contrasted with mediæval science
to correlate causal properties with minute spatial or
spatio-temporal structure, and not to take them as
ultimate facts.   And there is no doubt that, in the case
of material substances, this hypothesis has led to great
advances in knowledge and has been "verified" as
completely as any such hypothesis well could be.

Let us consider the essential meaning of this procedure.   It comes to this.   We correlate a causal
characteristic of a substance with a certain non-causal
characteristic of its successive states.   Let us suppose
that the substance has the first-order causal characteristic p_1 up to and including the moment t, and that it
then loses p_1 and gains p_2 instead.   We assume that
there is a certain determinable non-casual characteristic
π which belongs to all the states of the substance both
before and after t.   And we assume that all the states of
the substance up to and including the moment t have
this determinable characteristic in the determinate form
π_1, whilst all the states of the substance after the moment
t have this determinable characteristic in the different
determinate form π_2.   In the case of material substances
the non-causal determinable π is always supposed to be
some general type of internal spatio-temporal or purely
spatial structure; and the determinates π_1 and π_2 are
supposed to be different specific forms of this determinable spatial or spatio-temporal structure.   Thus there
are really two independent assumptions, viz. (a) that

each causal property of a substance depends upon a certain non-causal characteristic of its successive states, that so long as a causal property of a substance remains unchanged its successive states have the same determinate form of this non-causal characteristic, and that when the causal property changes the later states of the substance have this non-causal characteristic in a different determinate form ; and (*b*) that the non-causal characteristics on which the causal characteristics of substances depend are always certain types of internal spatial or spatio-temporal structure.

There are two important points to notice before leaving this subject. (1) If the non-causal characteristics on which the causal characteristics of a material substance depend be forms of internal spatial or spatio-temporal structure, they are of the same general nature as non-causal characteristics which we can actually observe. For we can observe that material substances have shapes and sizes, that several such substances can be arranged in various spatial patterns, and that they can move about in various ways as wholes. We are thus merely ascribing to the inside of a material substance and to its minute parts characteristics which are analogous to those which we can perceive in its outside and on a large scale. And we assume that the minute structure and the minute movements which we cannot observe are subject to the same laws of geometry and mechanics as the gross structure and the gross movements which we can observe. (If the Quantum Theory be correct we are probably witnessing a partial breakdown of the latter assumption.)

(2) The second point to notice is that we cannot wholly *reduce* causal characteristics to non-causal characteristics by correlating the former with the persistence of a certain type of internal structure. When we say that the movements of the minute internal parts obey the laws of mechanics we are ascribing a certain causal characteristic to them. And when, *e.g.*,. we say that

a certain minute spatial structure of a body causes it to select and reflect the red component of white light we are ascribing a causal characteristic to this structure. The most that we can do by this means is to reduce a number of causal characteristics which seem at first sight to be independent and disconnected to a comparatively few fundamental causal characteristics which are familiar on the large scale and are very general and pervasive.

I think that I have now said enough about the characteristics of material substances, though it would be necessary to go into many more details and to draw many more subtle distinctions if I were professing to give a complete account of this subject. I propose now to consider the analogies and differences between minds and material substances in these respects. In the first place, it is evident that we ascribe causal characteristics to minds as well as to material substances. First of all there are certain general "mental powers", which we regard as characteristic of all minds. For instance there is the power of cognising, the power of being affected by past experiences, the power of association, and so on. These may be compared to the most fundamental causal characteristics of matter, such as inertia, gravitational attraction, etc. Secondly, there are "mental dispositions" which differ from one mind to another and are fairly general in their effects. One man, *e.g.*, is "born good-tempered" and another man is "born irritable". This means that the mind of the former has a causal characteristic such that very few conditions will put it into an angry state, whilst the mind of the latter has a causal characteristic such that very many conditions will put it into an angry state. Now under certain conditions a mind will lose the characteristic of being good-tempered and will acquire the characteristic of being bad-tempered. This may happen suddenly through a wound in the head or gradually through disease or continually irritating surroundings. Here we have an instance of a causal characteristic of higher order belonging to a mind. Some of these changes in the causal characteristics of minds are reversible. A man who has become irritable may be restored to a good-tempered disposition by regulating his liver or by treating him psycho-analytically. "Being irritable" may be compared to "looking red to most people in most lights", and "being good-tempered" may be compared to "looking brown to most people in most lights"; and the characteristic of losing the former and gaining the latter when wounded in the head may be compared to the characteristic of losing one colour and permanently acquiring the other on being heated to a high enough temperature. So far there is obviously a great deal of analogy between the characteristics of mental and of material substances. Let us now consider some of the differences.

(1) Mental substances seem to start mainly with powers to acquire other and more determinate powers. A baby does not at first have the power to talk or to reason, but it has the power to acquire these powers if proper stimuli are applied. And in most cases these stimuli are applied if the baby lives, so that these more determinate powers generally are in fact acquired. I do not think that there is much analogy to this in the case of material substances. And this is not surprising. For a power to acquire some specific power, such as that of talking rationally, could hardly come into action if it were not for the general powers of association and "memory" in its widest sense; and these are common and peculiar to minds. (2) Although some changes in which a mind loses one causal characteristic and gains another are reversible, most of them, so far as we know, are not. On the other hand, most changes in the causal characteristics of material substances are reversible. Of course this difference may simply be due to the fact that we know much more about matter than about mind, and have much greater practical control

of the former than of the latter in consequence. (3) A mind in the course of its history is continually acquiring new and extremely determinate powers. *E.g.*, it is continually acquiring the power to remember a certain definite event, which it did not have before this event happened. Although it also loses many of these determinate memory-powers with efflux of time, yet, on the whole, through many years of its life the number of determinate memory-powers which it possesses is probably steadily increasing. I do not think that there is anything analogous to this in the case of matter. It must of course be pointed out that these contrasts which I have been indicating are at their sharpest when we compare a highly developed mind with a bit of inorganic matter. Organised bodies certainly form a half-way house between mind and matter in these respects.

So far I have been considering differences between the causal characteristics of mental and material substances which are immediately obvious and involve no special theories about these characteristics. I have said that, in the case of material substances, we make two hypotheses which have been amply verified. The first is that, so long as a material substance has a certain causal characteristic, there is a certain correlated non-causal characteristic which belongs to each of its successive states and determines this causal characteristic. The second is that this non-causal characteristic is always a certain type of internal spatial or spatio-temporal structure. Now we do, no doubt, generally assume something analogous to the first proposition in dealing with the causal characteristics of minds. We do assume that, so long as a mind has a certain causal characteristic, there is a certain non-causal characteristic of *something* which determines this causal characteristic of the mind. But it is very difficult to maintain anything like the second proposition. In the first place, a mind, as such, does not seem to be a spatio-temporal whole ; we can, therefore, hardly talk of *its* spatio-temporal structure.   If we want to talk of spatio-temporal structure in this connexion we have to desert the mind and start talking about the brain and nervous system.   Again, the spatio-temporal parts of a material substance are themselves material substances ; *e.g.*, the molecules of a gas are as good material substances as the gas itself.   And the relations of the parts of a material substance within it are analogous to the relations of this material substance to another which is outside it.   *E.g.*, the relations of the molecules of a bit of dust to each other are geometrically and mechanically analogous to the relations of a number of bits of dust dancing about in the air.   Now a theory of mental structure analogous to this would have to be of the following kind.   We should have to suppose that the observable minds of ourselves and our friends are composed of unobservable minds.   And we should have to suppose that the unobservable minds which compose my mind are related to each other within it in the same kind of way as my mind is related to other observable minds to form a society.   Now, of course, this might have been true, but it seems pretty evident that it is not in fact true.   So far as one can judge the unity of an individual mind is not in the least like the unity of a society of minds.

The difficulty then is this.   If we try to correlate the causal characteristics of minds with minute *spatio-temporal* structure we are forced to ascribe this structure to the brain and nervous system and not to the mind itself.   In that case I think we shall have to admit that we can hardly talk of a *purely* mental substance.   The mind, in abstraction from the brain and nervous system, will be a mere set of mental events with many gaps and a very imperfect internal unity.   It might be called an "incomplete substance."   The only complete mental substance will be not merely mental but also material ; it will be the "mind-brain", if I may use that expression. This, of course, is by no means a revolutionary view. St Thomas, though he did not mean exactly what I mean and did not use the arguments which I am using, held that a human soul is in an "unnatural" state when separated from its body, and used this as an argument for the resurrection of the body. If, on the other hand, we try to assign a purely *mental* structure to our minds but otherwise to follow the analogy of material substances as closely as possible, we land in a different kind of trouble. We then have to regard each observable mind as a society of un-observable minds; and this hypothesis seems not to fit the facts. The result of this is that we cannot get away from the much decried "faculty-psychology". We must remember that before Descartes' time there was a "faculty-physics", and that Descartes' greatest achievement was to show that the various causal characteristics of physical things can be connected with each other by correlating them all with characteristic forms of spatio-temporal structure and a few very general and pervasive causal characteristics. No one has succeeded in con-necting the various mental "powers" in any analogous way, and that is why psychology at present hardly deserves the name of a "science". It is, I think, quite certain that psychology will remain in this unsatis-factory state unless and until someone succeeds in doing for it what Galileo, Descartes, and Newton did for physics. And the difficulty of doing anything of the kind is obvious when we remember how difficult it is to conceive of purely mental "structure" or to imagine what can be the few fundamental causal characteristics which, together with differences of "mental structure", will explain and connect the various observable mental powers.

The Theory of Mnemic Causation. This is a theory which abandons all attempts to correlate the causal characteristics of minds with any non-causal characteristic. *A fortiori* it refuses to correlate them with purely mental "structure" or with the spatio-temporal structure of the brain and nervous system. This theory has been tentatively suggested by Mr Russell in Lectures IV and V of his *Analysis of Mind*. He rather unhappily associates it with the name of Semon, who, so far as I can see, never thought of anything of the kind. Semon was anxious to show that mnemic *phenomena* are much commoner and more important than has generally been thought. But his theory of their *causation* seems to be quite commonplace; it is just a theory of traces thinly disguised under the name of "engrams".

I shall have to draw certain distinctions and go into certain details which will not be found in Mr Russell's book. I will begin by trying to give definitions of "mnemic" and "non-mnemic" events, such that there shall be no doubt that there are mnemic events.

Definition of " Mnemic Events". I shall begin with rough definitions, and shall gradually polish them under the friction of criticism. A gas-explosion might be taken as a typical example of a non-mnemic event, and a memory of a past visit to a certain town as a typical example of a mnemic event. What is the relevant difference between them? The gas-explosion could be fully accounted for by reference to the state of affairs which immediately preceded it. In this we should find a certain mixture of gas and oxygen and the striking of a light; and these together are enough to account for the happening of the explosion there and then. No doubt, if we like, we *can* go further back. We could predict the presence of this particular mixture by knowing that a gas-tap had been turned on for so long; and we could predict the striking of the light from the fact that a man had filled his pipe and had just taken out his match-box to light it. But there is no *need* for us to go back to these earlier events. The explosion is directly determined by what immediately precedes it; and it is determined by earlier events only in so far as these determine its immediate antecedents. We will define a "non-mnemic event" as one whose independently necessary conditions are all contained in the state of affairs which immediately precedes it. No one questions that many events are non-mnemic, in this sense.

Now contrast this with the memory which I now have of a visit which I paid to a certain town last year. In order to account for the occurrence of this memory it is not, on the face of it, enough to refer to what immediately preceded it. We should no doubt find there the stimulus which called forth the memory just then. But it is obvious that precisely the same stimulus might have acted and would have called forth no such memory if I had not visited the town at all. Thus, in order to account completely for the occurrence of the memory now, it seems *necessary* to go back to the event of last year, viz., my visit to the town. It might, therefore, seem plausible to define a "mnemic event" as one whose independently necessary conditions are not all contained in the state of affairs which immediately precedes it.

This definition, however, would be unsatisfactory for the following reason. It would leave it uncertain whether there are any mnemic events, and the decision would depend on whether we did or did not accept mnemic causation. This is just what we do not want. On the usual form of the trace-theory all the independently necessary conditions of the memory do immediately precede its occurrence. For this event is supposed to be completely determined by the present stimulus and the present trace which this stimulus excites. On this view the actual visit to the town last year is at most a dependently necessary condition ; *i.e.*, the most that we can say is that the trace would not have existed unless the visit had taken place. So that, if the trace-theory be true, the memory is not really a mnemic event in the sense defined above. In order to avoid this complication I shall have to introduce the words "macroscopic" and "microscopic" into my definitions. Macroscopic events are those which can be directly observed, measured, etc. Microscopic events are those which are supposed to take place in the minute structure of nature, and to be from their nature unobservable by us. These terms were introduced into physics by Lorentz in his *Theory of Electrons*; and I propose to borrow them.

I will now define a "macroscopically mnemic event". This will be an event whose independently necessary *macroscopic* conditions are not all contained in the state of affairs which immediately precedes its occurrence. There is no doubt of the existence of macroscopically mnemic events, in the sense defined. If we make no hypotheses about traces, unconscious mental processes, etc., *i.e.*, about *microscopic* events, and confine ourselves wholly to what we can perceive and introspect, it is quite certain that events in the remote past are independently necessary conditions of memory-experiences. The question at issue between those who accept and those who reject Mnemic Causation can now be stated clearly. "Are those events which are *macroscopically* mnemic *microscopically* non-mnemic, or are they not?" The trace-theory says "Yes", and the theory of Mnemic Causation says "No".

Causal and Epistemological Conditions. We must now notice a distinction which Mr Russell does not explicitly draw. On the ordinary form of the trace-theory, *if* a similar trace could have existed without the visit to the town having taken place, and *if* the same stimulus had acted, I should have had a similar experience though I had never visited the town. And the case of hallucinatory memory-experiences might be quoted in support of this view. But it would be possible to hold a trace-theory, and yet to hold that the existence of the trace and the occurrence of the stimulus are *not* sufficient conditions for the occurrence of the memory-experience. A person who holds the realistic view that, in all memory-situations, there is direct acquaintance with the actual past event remembered would have to regard the existence of the past event as an independently necessary condition of the occurrence of the memory-experience. In order to deal with these possibilities it is necessary to distinguish between the "causal" and the "epistemological" conditions of a macroscopically mnemic event. The causal conditions of a memory-experience are those which *would* make this kind of situation arise at a certain moment *provided* that a suitable object exists to be its objective constituent. The existence of such an object, ready to be the objective constituent of the situation if it arises, is what I mean by the "epistemological condition" of the event. We can now consider the attitude which various possible theories would take up towards a macroscopically mnemic event, such as a memory-experience.

(i) The ordinary form of the trace-theory would hold that both the causal and the epistemological conditions of a memory-situation are non-mnemic when we consider microscopic events and objects. Let us illustrate this, and the alternative theories, by diagrams. Let us represent momentary events by dots, memory-images by circles, persistent traces by crosses, the causal relation by a full arrow, and the cognitive relation by a dotted arrow. Then the ordinary trace-theory of memory is represented by the diagram below.

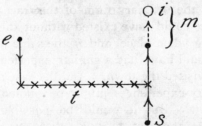

Here e, a past event, produces a trace t which persists. In course of time a stimulus s excites this trace and produces the awareness of a memory-image i which resembles e. The whole situation "being aware of the image i which resembles the past event e" is the memory of this past event. Here the causal and the epistemological conditions are both ultimately non-mnemic.

(ii) Let us next consider the trace-theory combined with a realistic view of memory. The diagram is given below.

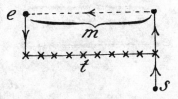

Here, as before, the past event e produces the trace t which persists and is eventually excited by the stimulus s. But here the result is not to make me aware of a present image resembling the past event. The result is to make me cognise directly the past event e which left the trace. The cognitive relation jumps over the time-gap between stimulus and past event, though the causal relation does not. Thus the causal conditions are here ultimately non-mnemic, but the epistemological conditions are mnemic.

(iii) We will next consider Mr Russell's form of the Mnemic Causation Theory. The diagram is as follows:

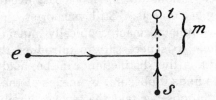

Here the past event e and the present stimulus s together produce by mnemic causation the awareness of a memory-image i which in fact resembles e and is accompanied by a "feeling of familiarity". This constitutes the memory m of the event e. The causal conditions are here irreducibly mnemic, whilst the epistemological conditions are non-mnemic.

(iv) It would obviously be possible to imagine a still more radically mnemic theory, by combining the theory of Mnemic Causation with the realistic view of memory. This is illustrated in the appended diagram.

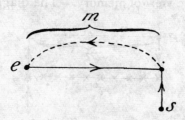

Here the causal conditions are as in (iii); but the result is not to produce the awareness of a present image which feels familiar and in fact resembles the past event. The result is to produce a direct awareness of the past event *e* itself, *i.e.*, a cognitive situation of which *e* itself is the objective constituent. Here then both the causal and the epistemological conditions would be irreducibly mnemic.

Of course there are plenty of macroscopically mnemic events where there is no need to introduce the distinction between causal and epistemological conditions. For many such events are not cognitions at all; and many which are cognitions do not have past events as their epistemological objects. Still, memories are the most striking example of macroscopically mnemic events, and with them it is necessary to introduce the distinction. Perhaps the distinction can be made clear to anyone who finds it obscure, by means of the following analogy. Suppose we take the second possible theory, viz., the trace-theory combined with the realistic view of memory. We might compare the past event, on this view, to a lock; the trace to a key made to fit the lock; and remembering the past event to undoing the lock with the key. The existence of the lock plays two different parts in determining the event of unfastening the lock. (*a*) The lock was originally made; then someone took a wax model of it; and then someone cut a key from this model to fit the lock, and this key is used from time to time to unfasten the lock. (Those of my readers who are either professional burglars or fellows of colleges with a weakness for losing their fellow's-keys will be familiar with the causal sequence which I have been describing.) This corresponds to the original event as an immediate causal condition of the trace and a remote causal condition of the memory. (*b*) The act of undoing the lock with the key cannot occur unless the lock exists in its original form to put the key into. This corresponds to the original event as an independently necessary epistemological condition of the memory.

"*Temporal Separation*" *and* "*Immediate Precedence*". There is one other notion which is involved in our definitions of mnemic and non-mnemic events, which needs to be cleared up. Real events are not momentary, but have a finite duration; *i.e.* they are like lines and not like points. This implies that "momentary events" are not literally constituents of finite events, as short events are of longer ones that overlap them. They are complicated functions of finite events, and have to be defined by Extensive Abstraction in the way which Whitehead has shown us. Again, the time-series is supposed to be continuous; and this implies that, when we "analyse" finite events into "momentary events", no two of these momentary events will be next to each other, as two successive railings of a fence are. When we say that all the independently necessary conditions of an event are contained in the state of affairs which immediately precedes it, we seem to imply (*a*) that all these conditions are "momentary", (*b*) that they all belong to the same moment, and (*c*) that this moment "immediately precedes" the moment at which the event begins. These statements are all Pickwickian, and we must now interpret them.

Let us represent the event e, which is to be the effect, by a short line bc. Let the various conditions which are severally necessary and jointly sufficient to produce e be contained in various earlier slices of the world's history. These may be represented by a number of lines ab, $a'b$, $a''b$, which all end at b the beginning of e. Thus—

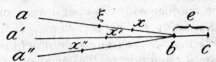

Now take short slices along ba, ba', and ba''; e.g., bx, bx', and bx''. Suppose we find that, no matter how short we make these stretches, they still contain all the independently necessary conditions of e. Then we can sum this up by saying that all the conditions of e are "momentary" and that they all "immediately precede e."

If we did not find this to be true, several alternatives would be possible. (i) We might find that all the independently necessary conditions of e were momentary, but that they did not all immediately precede e. For instance, we might find that the stretch bx fails to contain a certain necessary condition of e, but that the stretch $x\xi$ contains this missing condition, no matter how near ξ be to x. Then we could say that e has a momentary condition which is separated from it by the time-gap bx. (ii) We might find that some of e's conditions are neither momentary nor immediately precedent to e. For instance, it may be that if $x\xi$ be made too short it will fail to contain a certain necessary condition of e. There may in fact be certain characteristics which determine by their occurrence the occurrence of e, and need a certain minimum stretch of duration to inhere in. E.g., if e were partly determined by a certain characteristic rate of vibration, it would seem that this could not inhere in a smaller duration than that taken by one complete period of the vibration. (iii) It might happen that, whilst some of *e's* conditions are not momentary, yet the non-momentary conditions are continuous in time with *e*. This would mean, *e.g.*, that one of the necessary conditions of *e* is the pervasion of a certain finite stretch such as *bx* by a certain non-uniform characteristic, but that this stretch ends at the same moment as *e* begins.

We can now give a more accurate definition of non-mnemic and of mnemic events. A non-mnemic event would be one whose "momentary" conditions (if it has any) all "immediately precede" it, and whose non-momentary conditions (if it has any) are all continuous with it. A mnemic event would be one which has at least one independently necessary condition which is separated from it by a finite gap in time. It does not follow that this gap may not also contain conditions which are necessary for *e's* occurrence ; the point is that they are not *sufficient* without the condition which precedes the gap. We must also recognise the theoretical possibility that a remote condition of an event might be both an independently and a dependently necessary condition of it. Suppose, *e.g.*, that a "momentary" event at *x* determines the filling of the stretch *xb*, and that *e* is a function both of this event and of the filling of *xb*. Then this remote event will be an independently necessary condition of *e* ; but it will *also* be a dependently necessary condition of *e*, in so far as it determines the filling of *xb* which in turn partially determines *e*.

The important point for us to notice is that what is characteristic of mnemic causation is the *time-gap* between an event and some of its independently necessary conditions. The question whether the conditions are or are not "*momentary*" is not the distinguishing mark. And the question whether this time-gap does or does not contain *other* necessary conditions is not relevant, so long as it does not contain *all* the independently necessary conditions. It is important to see this. For it is almost certain that there is causation in which the conditions are not "momentary", in the sense defined above. Therefore, if we confuse mnemic causation with causation in which some of the conditions are non-momentary, we shall be liable to accept the former on grounds which are relevant only to the latter.

Criticism of Mnemic Causation. We may sum up the differences between the trace-theory and the theory of mnemic causation as follows. Whenever we have a macroscopically mnemic event there is a time-gap between the event and some of its independently necessary macroscopic conditions. The trace-theory holds that such a gap cannot be an ultimate fact; all the independently necessary conditions of an event must be continuous with it, if they be non-momentary, and must "immediately precede" it, if they be "momentary". We have explained the Pickwickian phrases in inverted commas. Hence the trace-theory holds that the past experience is not an independently necessary causal condition of the memory of it; and it has to fill the gap by postulating hypothetical microscopic entities, viz., traces, which are produced by the past experience and persist into the present. The mnemic theory, on the other hand, is prepared to accept as an ultimate fact that some of the independently necessary conditions of an event are neither continuous with it nor "immediately precede" it. It is prepared to bridge the temporal gap by postulating a special kind of causal relation.

On a first inspection each theory is seen to have its characteristic merits and defects. One keeps to the familiar kind of causal relation, but has to postulate purely hypothetical persistent entities; the other keeps to events which can actually be observed by introspection, but has to postulate an unfamiliar kind of causal relation. In dealing with matter I do not think that we should hesitate for a moment between the two.

The notion of a hidden minute structure in matter is perfectly familiar to us; we know that our unaided senses cannot distinguish the finer divisions of matter, and that microscopes often reveal a highly differentiated structure in what seems quite homogeneous to the naked eye. Moreover, we know that the details thus discovered very often explain the behaviour of the bodies in which we discover them. Hence the idea of material structure and states too minute for us to perceive even with the microscope is almost forced upon us; and it is reasonable to suppose that the not very numerous macroscopically mnemic phenomena which are observed in the inorganic realm are microscopically non-mnemic. It is much harder to conceive of a microscopic mental structure, and this is the only reason why we are tempted to introduce the theory of mnemic causation into mental phenomena. Since the mind and its states are not in any obvious sense extended, the idea of a structure which cannot be observed because of its spatial minuteness fails us here. The notion of non-introspectible and perhaps unowned series of mental events, which otherwise resemble our conscious experiences, is not easy for us to grasp; and it is hard for us to give a meaning to mental events which do not resemble our conscious experiences. Hence the main motive for considering favourably a mnemic-causation-theory for mental phenomena is simply the difficulty which we have in conceiving the intrinsic nature of traces and dispositions unless we are prepared to regard them as purely material modifications of the brain and nervous system. Against this we might put two considerations. (1) Although the mental events which we can introspect do not seem to be extended they do seem to have different degrees of intensity, and it does seem to be harder to discriminate them introspectively as their intensity decreases. Thus it might be possible to substitute low intensity for small extension, and to conceive of traces and dispositions as being of the nature of ordinary conscious mental events but of very low intensity. (2) Some people would certainly hold that there are *a priori* objections to the whole notion of mnemic causation, and that we *must* therefore adopt a trace-theory, no matter what difficulties we may have in picturing to ourselves the intrinsic nature of traces and dispositions.

I propose now to say something about this last point. In order to discuss it adequately it would be necessary to enter in great detail into the nature of causation in general. This would be out of place in the present connexion. I shall, therefore, confine myself to a few remarks which seem relevant and do not carry us too far afield.

(1) In answering objections against the possibility of mnemic causation Mr Russell assumes that causal laws are merely assertions of regular sequence, and that any true assertion of regular sequence is a causal law. He supposes an objector to say that, in mnemic causation, some of the independently necessary conditions of an event have ceased to exist long before the event begins to happen. And then the objector is supposed to raise the difficulty: "How can anything act after it has ceased to exist for a finite time?" To put the objection in a concrete form:—"According to the theory of mnemic causation my perception of a town which I visited last year literally produces a memory of this event whenever a suitable stimulus acts on me. But the perception is long past and is in no sense continued into the present. It has ceased to exist itself, and nothing now exists which can be regarded as a continuation of it. How then can it *do* anything now?" Mr Russell answers that this objection presupposes the activity theory of causation, which is now rejected by most philosophers. And he goes on to say that causation simply means regular sequence; and that, with this interpretation, there is no *a priori* objection to mnemic causation. By saying that C causes E, on this

view, we simply mean that C is a set of conditions c_1, c_2, . . . c_n, such that (a) whenever they are all fulfilled E happens, and (b) whenever E happens they have all been fulfilled. This says nothing about c_1 . . . c_n being all of the same date and all "immediately preceding" E. Hence, if this be all that we ever mean by saying that C causes E, mnemic causation is antecedently quite as possible as non-mnemic causation; and it becomes a mere question of fact (which could never be conclusively settled) whether there is mnemic causation.

For a complete discussion it would be necessary, first, to consider whether causation does mean nothing but regular sequence. If we found that it did involve something more, the next question would be whether this extra factor would be inconsistent with the possibility of mnemic causal laws. And, lastly, we might ask whether, even if causation is simply regular sequence, it is true to say that past experience and present stimulus are sufficient by themselves to cause a memory of the past event.

(a) It is, of course, impossible for me to give an adequate discussion of the meaning of Causation here. I will simply say that, even if all causation involves regular sequence, I very much doubt whether all regular sequence would be counted as a causal law. I should say that there are many cases where we should admit regular sequence and *unhesitatingly deny* causation; though there are perhaps no cases where we can *unhesitatingly assert* causation in addition to regular sequence. I do not propose to do more here than to show that the line of argument by which the doctrine that causation is simply regular sequence is commonly supported is a very weak one. The argument generally takes the following form. The plain man starts by believing that there is something in causation beside regular sequence. His opponent then asks him to state clearly what this extra factor is. The plain man is then inclined to say that causation involves "activity" or "necessity" or both, in addition to regular sequence. His opponent then tries to show that the notion of "activity" is just an illegitimate extension to all cases of causation of certain characteristics which accompany the very special experience of voluntarily initiating an action.   He also argues, on the lines of Mr Hume, that no causal law is found to be necessary on careful reflection.   Thus the plain man finds that the two marks by which he proposed to distinguish causation from mere *de facto* regularity of sequence vanish under his opponent's criticisms ; and he has to admit that he cannot state any factor which differentiates a causal law from a mere statement of regular sequence.   His opponent then argues that this failure to state the difference is due to there being no difference to state ; and the plain man is reduced to silence, though not altogether to conviction.

If we reflect we shall see that this is a very poor argument for the purpose.   Suppose that causation did involve an unique and not further analysable relation. It might be that regular sequence was not even *part* of what we mean by causation, but was merely a sign (though by no means an infallible one) by which the presence of this other relation is indicated.   If this relation be unique and unanalysable, like the relation of inside and outside in space, for instance, it will be impossible to define it in any but tautologous terms. Thus the failure to define anything in causation except regular sequence may be due, not to the absence of an extra factor, but to its being ultimate and unanalysable. Our extreme unwillingness to admit that causation is nothing but regular sequence, and the extreme paradoxes to which any such views lead (cf. Mr Russell's examples about the hooters at two distant factories which both sound at the same time and therefore are *both* equally causes of *either* set of workmen going to their work) suggest strongly that there is something in causation beside merely regularity of sequence. On the other hand, I think we must admit that, if there be a peculiar relation involved in causation, we are seldom if ever directly acquainted with it as we often are directly acquainted with certain spatial and temporal relations. I cannot perceive the causal relation by any of my senses, as I can perceive that one thing in my field of view is to the right of another thing in my field of view. And I cannot, I think, ever be perfectly certain on reflection that A *causes* B in addition to *regularly preceding* it. (If there be any exception to this, I think it is in my voluntary initiation of certain changes.) But I think that I can be absolutely certain that I do not *mean* the same thing by "A causes B" and "A is regularly followed by B". And I think that I can often be quite certain that A *does not* cause B *in spite of* complete regularity of sequence between the two. *E.g.*, I am quite sure that the hooter of a factory in Manchester does not cause the workmen of a factory in London to go to their work, even though the Manchester hooter does always blow just before the London workmen start to wend their way to the London factory.

(*b*) So far I have suggested that regular sequence may be no part of what we mean by causation, but that it is one of the signs by which we judge with more or less conviction that the causal relation is present. It may be, however, that regular sequence by itself is not an adequate sign of the presence of the causal relation. It may be that only certain kinds of regular sequence are trustworthy as signs of the causal relation. And, again, even if it be held that all causation *is* regular sequence and that there is no specific and unanalysable factor in causation, it might still be held that only certain kinds of regular sequence are cases of causation. I think that this must be admitted in view of our refusal to regard the sequence of the blowing of the Manchester hooter and the movement of the London workmen as an instance of causation. Now the missing factor seems to be a certain spatio-temporal continuity between the sequent events. I am inclined to think that it is the absence of such continuity between the blowing of the Manchester hooter and the movements of the London workmen which makes me so certain that the former is not a cause of the latter. I think that it is the absence of the required temporal continuity between "cause" and "effect" which is the real basis of the objection to mnemic causation which Mr Russell has dismissed as due to the ghost of the activity theory of causation. If such continuity be essential to the notion of causation then "mnemic causation" can be dismissed, even if we admit that there is no specific and unanalysable causal relation. For only certain kinds of regular sequences will count as "causal"; and the sequence of past experience and present memory is not of the required kind. My own view is that I do not *mean* by "causation" *any* kind of regular sequence; but that certain kinds of regular sequence are fairly trustworthy signs of the presence of the causal relation. But the final result is the same. For the sequence of past experience and present memory is not of the kind which I regard as a trustworthy sign of the presence of a direct causal relation between the two.

(*c*) Let us now ask ourselves the question: "Suppose that causation were simply regular sequence, and that any and every kind of regular sequence were causation, should we be justified in holding that a past experience and a present stimulus are the complete cause of a present memory?" Suppose that I visited a certain town two years ago, and that last year someone mentioned its name to me and I thereupon remembered my visit to it. Suppose that some time after this I had a bad illness or an accident; it might well happen that, if the name were now mentioned to me, I should not remember my visit to the town. Such cases are of course very common. It follows at once that the two conditions, past experience and present stimulus, are *not* jointly sufficient, though they may be severally necessary, to cause a memory even on the most extreme form of the regularity-theory of causation. For the memory does not regularly follow on the fulfilment of these conditions and of these alone. In fact, we have made the common mistake of ignoring a condition which is just as necessary as the rest, but is unexciting and is much more often fulfilled than not. We talk carelessly of a gas-escape and a spark as the cause of an explosion. But the presence of Oxygen is equally necessary and much more likely to be forgotten, because this condition is nearly always fulfilled, whilst it is much less common for gas to be escaping or for sparks to be flying about. In the same way something which may vaguely be called "the general integrity of the brain and nervous system" is at least as necessary as the past experience and the present stimulus if the memory is to arise. We forget this condition because it is generally fulfilled while we are alive. Now this condition cannot be given a definite date. If it breaks down *anywhere* between the original experience and the subsequent stimulus, the memory is liable not to arise. It seems to me extremely unlikely that there is any such thing as mnemic causation, even on the extreme regularity-theory which Mr Russell assumes, if by this you mean that a number of conditions separated in time from each other and from the event which they are supposed to cause are jointly *sufficient* to cause this event. And it is perfectly certain that memories are not completely determined by past experience and present stimulus in the sense that they regularly follow on the fulfilment of these two conditions alone. To put the matter generally, I should say that even on the regularity-theory of causation the complete cause of any event involves persistent as well as transient conditions. Even if the transient conditions be separated from each other by temporal gaps these gaps must be filled with persistent conditions which stretch right up to the beginning of the effect. Mr Russell in his account of mnemic causation seems to have made the common mistake of mentioning the transient and forgetting the persistent conditions.

It is, however, quite easy to rectify this oversight, and then we can see precisely where the difference between mnemic causation and ordinary causation would lie. The difference remains considerable. On Mr Russell's theory, as modified to meet the above criticism, there *is* a persistent condition involved in memory, but it is *general* and not *special*. This persistent condition is just the general integrity of the brain and nervous system, which existed before as well as after the past experience and was in no way modified by it. On the trace-theory there is a *special* persistent condition, which·was started by the past experience and would not have existed without it. The two independently necessary conditions of the memory are this special persistent and the stimulus. The difference can be seen most clearly as follows. On the trace-theory, if you were to take a cross-section of the history of the experient's body and mind anywhere between the past experience and the stimulus you would find something, viz., the trace, which corresponds to and may be regarded as the representative of the past experience. On Mr Russell's theory, even when modified to meet the above criticisms, these intermediate slices, though relevant and necessary, would contain nothing which corresponds to and represents the past experience. In mnemic causation we should have the following situation. Although there is continuity between the *total* cause and the effect (since one essential part of the cause is a general persistent condition which fills the gap between its earlier and later transient parts), yet there is not continuity between the effect and *each* independently necessary factor in the cause. The original experience is not joined on to the memory either directly ; or by transmission of a disturbance through a medium, as in the case of light or sound; or by some special persistent which represents it, as on the trace-theory. If the possibility of mnemic causation is to be denied, it must be on the ground that one or other of these special kinds of continuity is needed in addition to the merely general continuity which the integrity of the brain and nervous system provides. I am not prepared to assert that this additional dose of continuity is needed; and, therefore, I am not prepared to deny the possibility of mnemic causation, as modified by us in the course of the discussion.

(2) The second remark which I wish to make about mnemic causation is the following. Suppose that c_1 . . . c_n are independently necessary and jointly sufficient transient conditions for the happening of an event e. We will not now insist that they must all be contemporary with each other, or that they shall "immediately precede" e or be continuous with it. But I do think that we should expect there to be some characteristic time-relation between them. Surely we should expect the law to be at least of somewhat the following form: "Whenever c_1 is followed by c_2 after the interval t_{12}, and by c_3 after the interval t_{13}, . . . and by c_n after the interval t_{1n}, e follows; and e does not happen except when c_1 . . . c_n have all happened with these characteristic intervals between them." No doubt in any causal law the *absolute* dates of the various factors are variable; but one would expect the *relative* dates to be constant **and** characteristic of the law. Now let us apply this to the case of past experience, present stimulus and memory. Assuming the general persistent condition to be fulfilled, we find that the memory arises *whenever* the stimulus is given, so long as it is after the original experience; *i.e.*, there is no characteristic interval between the two transient conditions in the supposed mnemic causal law. Now I should be inclined to suppose that, whenever this is so, we have not got an ultimate causal law but only an empirical generalisation of the very crudest kind.

(3) There is one other point rather closely connected with the above. Suppose we ask ourselves: "What is our usual test for the persistence of anything which is not under continuous observation?" I think that we should have to answer somewhat as follows. Suppose we find that throughout a long period of time *whenever* a certain condition C is fulfilled a certain result E immediately follows. And suppose we know that C by itself is not sufficient to produce E. Then we always assume that there is another *persistent* factor P with which the variable factor C co-operates to give the result E. *E.g.*, one of my main reasons for believing that there is a persistent something, called "my table", in my room is that throughout a long period of time *whenever* I look in a certain direction I become aware of an appearance of the table. I know that the mere fact of looking in this direction is not a sufficient condition of sensing this particular kind of appearance; and I assume that the other necessary condition is the persistent something which I call "my table". But this is almost exactly parallel to remembering my past visit to a certain town *whenever* the proper stimulus is applied. I know that neither the stimulus nor the mere general integrity of brain and nervous system is enough to account for the occurrence of this particular memory at this particular time; and I assume that there must be some other condition which is persistent. The plain fact is then that we have precisely the same kind of reason for believing in persistent traces as we have for believing in the persistence of tables when they are not under direct observation. If this test for persistence be a valid one, we ought to apply it to memory as well as to perception; and in that case we shall have to accept something like the trace-theory. If we refuse to apply the argument to traces we ought not to apply it to tables. We ought presumably to hold that later table-sensations are mnemically caused by the first table-sensation and the subsequent acts of looking in a certain

direction ; and we ought to reject the notion of a persistent physical object as a superstition unworthy of the "Free Man". No one (not even Mr Russell in any of his published works) does in fact take this alternative about the table ; and it seems scarcely consistent to take it about memory and then to refuse to extend it to the precisely parallel case of successive perceptions of what we call "the same thing".

Summary. I will now sum up the results of this discussion about mnemic causation. I have tried to explain clearly the difference between a mnemic and a non-mnemic event, and between mnemic and non-mnemic causation. In so doing I have stated the literal meaning of certain Pickwickian phrases which are used in the definitions. I have distinguished between the causal and the epistemological conditions of memory, and have explained and illustrated the four possible types of theory which arise when we allow the two kinds of condition to be either mnemic or non-mnemic. I then considered the arguments for and against mnemic causation in psychology. The only argument that I could find for it was the difficulty of conceiving the intrinsic nature of traces unless we take them to be purely material and thus pass outside the sphere of pure psychology. On the other side I argued that it is very doubtful whether causation can be reduced to mere regular sequence, and quite certain that not all kinds of regular sequence would be counted as instances of causation. If, then, the objections to mnemic causation can be answered only on an extreme form of the regularity-theory of causation, it is doubtful whether they can be answered at all. I then showed that, even on a pure regularity-theory of causation, it is certain that the past experience and the present stimulus are not jointly sufficient to cause a memory. At the very least a *general* persistent condition, which fills the gap between the two, is needed also. If this be granted, the difference between the trace-theory and the theory of mnemic causation depends on whether a *general* persistent condition is enough or whether a *special* persistent condition, which depends on and " represents " the past experience, is also needed. I did not profess to be able to give a conclusive answer to this last question. But I pointed out that we might fairly expect a genuine mnemic law to involve characteristic time-intervals between the various independently necessary and non-contemporary transient conditions of an event. And we do not find this to be so in the case of memory. On the contrary we have here exactly the kind of situation which anywhere else would make us postulate a special persistent condition.

I do not pretend to have absolutely refuted the possibility of mnemic causation as an ultimate fact in mental life. But I do think that I have shown that we have very little ground for accepting it, and that we have exactly the same kind of evidence for the existence of traces and dispositions as we have for the persistence of physical objects when they are not under continuous observation. Under these circumstances I think we shall do well to accept some form of the trace-theory until some philosopher has successfully applied the theory of mnemic causation, not only to the special case of mental phenomena, but also to all cases where we assume the existence of special persistents in spite of their not being under continuous observation. Henceforth, then, I shall assume that there really are such things as traces and dispositions, *i.e.*, special " mnemic persistents," to revert to a name which we have already introduced. We must now consider the question: " What is the intrinsic nature of mnemic persistents?"

The Nature of Mnemic Persistents.—Let us begin by considering once more the case of material substances. We have agreed that here the causal characteristics are correlated with and dependent upon certain persistent non-causal characteristics. But, if we inquire more closely into the nature of the latter, we find that two different cases arise. (1) We may have both identity of stuff and persistence of structure. Take, *e.g.*, the pillar-box which looks red whenever it is viewed in white light by a normal eye. Here we have *the same* particles persisting, and at each moment they have the *same* spatial structure. (2) Contrast this with the case of an organism. Here we have persistence of structure with continual change of stuff. Matter is continually passing into and out of the organism; and the causal characteristics of the organism depend on the fact that, as new matter comes in, it is continually organised and arranged in the same characteristic way and thus replaces the matter which is continually going out.

A purely Mental Theory of Traces. Now we might have a theory of purely mental traces analogous to the first of these possibilities if we adopted the Pure Ego theory of the self. The Pure Ego itself would be the persistent identical "stuff". And the causal characteristics of the mind might be correlated with various persistent states of the Pure Ego. On this view the existence of a trace would be the fact that the Pure Ego has a certain determinate non-causal characteristic at every moment within a certain period of time. Of course the analogy to the first possibility about material substances is only partial. There we had persistence of stuff and persistence of structure. Here, so far as we know, there would be no question of structure. There is persistence of stuff and an identical determinate quality possessed by this stuff for a certain period of time. But there is no reason to suppose this determinate quality in the possession of a certain internal structure; for the whole notion of internal structure may be nonsense as applied to the Pure Ego.

Could we conceive of a theory of purely mental traces without assuming the Pure Ego theory of the self? I think that we could, and that it would be partially, though not exactly, analogous to the second possibility about material substances. I will begin by pointing out that even a purely physiological theory of traces is incompatible with persistence of stuff. Suppose we compare a scar, due to a burn, with a dent in a leaden ball, due to a blow. The dent is simply a persistent spatial rearrangement of the *same* particles of matter as were present in the leaden ball before the blow dented it. The scar, on the other hand, may persist years after every particle of matter which was in the body when it was burnt has left it and been replaced by other matter. What happens is that the new matter as it comes in is continually arranged so that we still have the scar. Even if traces be purely physiological they must be of the same nature as the scar and not of the same nature as the dent; *i.e.*, they persist through the same *form* being continually imposed on *fresh* matter, and not through the same matter retaining a certain form which has once been imposed on it.

Now I have already said that, in many respects, an organism is a kind of half-way house between an inorganic material substance and a mind. It is, therefore, tempting to see whether we could not conceive of purely mental traces as analogous to scars in organic bodies. I will first point out where it seems to me that the analogy does not hold. Matter enters organisms from outside, is elaborated and arranged within them, remains there for some time, then gradually breaks down and is ejected. If we regard a mind as a complex whole of interrelated mental states, we can hardly suppose that new mental states come into the mind from elsewhere and pass from it after a while. If we take the "parts" of a mind to be its states, we must admit that the "parts" seem to be so dependent on the whole that it is doubtful whether they could have existed before they became parts of this whole or could exist after they have ceased to be parts of this whole. Another difference between a mind and an organism is the following. An organism exists continuously from birth to death, and at any two moments which are reasonably near together a great deal of the matter which composes it is the same. A mind, on the other hand, seems to cease to exist for considerable spells during dreamless sleep or fainting-fits, and then to take up its existence again at the point at which it left it.

If we want to have a purely mental theory of traces we must first fill these gaps with something other than the persistence of a certain structure and the continuance of certain processes in the brain and nervous system. On the Pure Ego theory such gaps are filled by the continued existence of the Pure Ego and by the fact that the Pure Ego has certain determinate qualities throughout the whole period. But we are now trying to do without the Pure Ego theory. The only possible expedient is to suppose that the gaps are filled by literally unconscious and literally mental states and processes, which have to each other relations of the same kind as the conscious mental states and processes of waking life have to each other. These unconscious mental states and processes will not themselves *be* traces ; but, if we are prepared to grant their existence, we can give a theory of purely mental traces without assuming the Pure Ego theory. This can be done as follows. The relations between our ordinary conscious experiences, and the qualities of our ordinary conscious experiences, may justly be called " mental relations and qualities ". But they are not themselves *experiences*, either conscious or unconscious. Now I would suggest the following as a possible theory about traces. Just before a certain moment my total state of mind consists of a set of mental events having certain qualities and standing in a certain characteristic relation to each other. Let us call these events $e_1, e_2, \ldots e_n$, and let us denote the relation which binds them all together into a single state of my mind by R. Then the total state of my mind just before t may be symbolised by R $(e_1, e_2 \ldots e_n)$. Let us suppose that at t a '' new '' mental event happens and forms part of my total state of mind at t. We will call this event E. By calling it "new" I mean that it is not a "continuation" of any of the events $e_1 \ldots e_n$; it might, e.g., be a sensation due to someone suddenly sticking a pin into me. Most of the mental events which compose my total state of mind at t will be continuations of events which composed my total state of mind just before t, but probably some of these will not be continued. Let us suppose that $e_1 \ldots e_m$ are continued as $e'_1 \ldots e'_m$, whilst $e_{m+1} \ldots e_n$ are not continued. My total state of mind at t may then be symbolised by R $(e'_1 \ldots e'_m, E)$. Now I suggest that the presence of E modifies the qualities of $e'_1 \ldots e'_m$, or of some of them, in a characteristic way, so that those of them which are continued into my total state of mind just after t are continued in the specially modified forms $e''_{E1} \ldots e''_{Em}$. It is also possible that there is a characteristic modification in the relation which binds them together, so that it is now R instead of R. On this hypothesis my total state of mind just after t is of the form R_E $(e''_{E1} \ldots e''_{Em})$, assuming for the sake of simplicity that no further "new" experience has taken place. We have now got our "trace" formed. We must next assume that this "E-quality" or this "E-relation" is henceforth imposed on the contents or the structure of each successive total state by the state that precedes it, very much as the scar is imposed on the new matter which comes into an organism from outside. On some such lines as these we can conceive of purely mental traces without needing to assume a Pure Ego; provided we are willing to admit that there are no real gaps in mental life and that the apparent gaps are filled up by non-introspectible mental events, which are of the same general nature and have the same kind of mutual relations as those which we can introspect. The trace is not itself a mental event, but is a characteristic modification in the qualities of mental events or in the relation which binds contemporary

mental events into a single total state of mind.   And
this characteristic modification of quality or structure
is imposed on each total state by the total state which
immediately precedes it.

I do not think that it would be necessary to suppose
that *all* the events in any total state have this characteristic
qualitative modification imposed on them.   So long as
some events in every total state after the occurrence of
the "new" experience are modified in this way, we
have as much as we need.   Again, I do not think that
it would be necessary to assume that the relation which
is modified in a characteristic way is the relation which
binds together *all* the events of a single mental state.
It would suffice if some relation which binds together a
sub-group of contemporary mental events were modified
in this characteristic way and if this modified relation
were handed on from this sub-group in any total state
to the corresponding sub-group in its immediate
successor.

It is then possible to conceive of a purely " mental "
theory of mind without assuming the Pure Ego theory.
A mind will, on this view, be composed entirely of
mental events.   Some of these are introspectible and
others are not.   Again, certain of these mental events
will be related to each other so as to form series of a
characteristic kind.   Such series will be mental processes.
Some mental processes will be wholly imperceptible, *i.e.*,
none of the successive mental events which compose
them will be introspectible.   Others will be perceptible,
i.e., some of the mental events which compose them will
be introspectible and will be objects of simultaneous
undiscriminating awareness.   But there will be imperceptible parts of perceptible mental processes.   On the
present view, the imperceptible parts of perceptible
mental processes, and the wholly imperceptible mental
processes, will be in all other respects of precisely the
same nature as the introspectible parts of perceptible
mental processes.   All mental processes will depend on

traces and dispositions. But these traces and dispositions, though not themselves mental *events* or *processes*, will be purely mental; for they are just certain qualities of the mental events of one total state of mind, which are handed down to the mental events of the next total state of mind, and so on indefinitely. Or they are just certain relations between the mental events composing one total state of mind, which are impressed upon the mental events composing the next total state of mind, and so on indefinitely.

A purely Physiological Theory of Traces. Let us now consider the alternative which lies at the opposite extreme to that which we have been treating above. On this view traces are simply modifications in the minute spatial or spatio-temporal structure of our brains and nervous systems, which are propagated from one state of the brain and nervous system to the next state in the way in which a scar on one's arm due to a burn is propagated for the rest of one's life. I think that the natural complement of such a theory of traces would be to hold that the non-introspectible " parts " of perceptible mental processes are not strictly mental at all, but are purely physiological events. And, in that case, of course they are not, strictly speaking, " parts " at all. The position will be that there are certain physiological processes, some parts of which are accompanied by mental events which depend on them, and other parts of which are not accompanied by mental events at all. And there will be other physiological processes which are exactly like those which are accompanied by mental events except in the fact that they are not accompanied by any mental events. Thus " unconscious mental processes " will not really be mental at all; and the natural accompaniment of a purely physiological theory of traces is an epiphenomenalist theory of the nature of mind. The mind ceases to be a genuine substance theoretically capable of existing in its own right.

I say that this would be the " natural " complement of

a purely physiological theory of traces and dispositions. I do not say that it would be an absolutely necessary consequence of such a theory. It is possible that those parts of a certain physiological process which are not accompanied by introspectible mental events are accompanied by non-introspectible mental events of a similar kind to the introspectible mental events which accompany other parts of the same physiological process. And it is possible that those physiological processes, no part of which is accompanied by introspectible mental events, are nevertheless accompanied by non-introspectible mental events. But, although this hypothesis would be *possible* on a purely physiological theory of traces and dispositions, it would seem to be quite unmotived. At most it could be supported only by arguments from analogy. Since some parts of a certain physiological process are accompanied by introspectible mental events, and since the later of these events seems to be an obvious development of the earlier, it might be argued that the part of the physiological process which fills the gap between two such introspectible mental events must be very much like those parts of the process which are accompanied by introspectible mental events. By analogy it might be argued that probably this part too is accompanied by mental events which fill the gap between those which we can introspect, but which, for some reason, are not introspectible by us. I do not see that this extra hypothesis would help us to explain anything that could not be explained without it ; we must content ourselves with saying that it would be neither necessary nor impossible. The situation is, I think, quite different in the case of a purely mental theory of traces. Here we *must* postulate either a Pure Ego or a continuous series of total mental states ; for, if we do not do this, we have nothing mental to carry the traces. And, since there are certainly gaps in our introspectible experiences, we *must* fill them with non-introspectible mental events if we want to keep to a purely mental theory of traces, and at the same time to avoid the hypothesis of a Pure Ego.

Is there any conclusive objection to a purely physiological theory of traces and dispositions, and to the purely epiphenomenal theory of mind which seems to me to be its natural complement? At first sight there seem to be several objections, and the question is whether they are really conclusive. (1) We have certain experiences in which it seems to us that our minds are acting on our bodies, and we have other experiences in which it seems to us that our bodies are acting on our minds. The voluntary initiation and control of bodily movements is an example of the first kind of experience, and the occurrence of a new sensation is an example of the second kind. Now, it might be said that this distinction between "active" and "passive" experiences could not exist, if epiphenomenalism were true ; for in *all* cases our experiences would be merely idle accompaniments of certain physiological processes, and the latter would be the only real "agents". I do not think that this is the right way of putting the case. It is true that the *interpretation* which we put on this distinction would be mistaken, but it seems to me that the *existence* of the distinction could be explained perfectly well on the epiphenomenalist theory. Let us consider the observable differences between a volition which is followed by the desired bodily movement, and a sensation which arises when someone sticks a pin into me. The volition forms the end-point of a certain conscious mental process, viz., a process of deliberation, which has a characteristic kind of internal unity. It is no doubt succeeded by other mental events, but they do not form a continuation of the process of deliberation. The subsequent events which are specially closely connected with the volition are simply the sensations due to the bodily movement. Now contrast this with the new sensation. This is not a continuation of any conscious mental process which was going on before it happened, though it may form the starting point of a characteristic conscious mental process which succeeds it. The previous events with which it is most closely connected are events in my body which are unaccompanied by conscious mental events. We feel "passive" *par excellence* at those critical points where a physiological process which is not accompanied by consciousness passes into a physiological process which is accompanied by consciousness of a characteristic kind. We feel "active" *par excellence* at those critical points where a physiological process which has been accompanied by a series of mental events so related as to form a single conscious process passes into a physiological process which is either not accompanied by consciousness at all or is accompanied by mental events which are not continuations of the previous conscious mental process. Thus epiphenomenalism would seem to be quite capable of accounting for the existence of the distinction in question.

(2) A rather similar difficulty could be raised over the distinction between mere passive association of ideas and active deliberate thinking, in which we select ideas and control the processes of association. It might be said that the former is compatible with epiphenomenalism and that the latter is not. I think that we can make a very similar answer to that which we made to the previous objection. If epiphenomenalism be true, the process of deliberate thinking is no doubt correlated with a peculiar physiological process, and the association of ideas is correlated with a different physiological process. And, doubtless, the two physiological processes are so connected that (*a*) the latter can go in the absence of the former, (*b*) the former depends for its possibility on the traces and dispositions which are involved in the latter, and (*c*) when the former is going on it greatly and characteristically modifies the latter. A process of the former kind may supervene at a certain stage in the course of a process of the latter kind, and

at that stage we shall pass from mere day-dreaming to active and deliberate thinking. Thus the observable distinction seems to be quite capable of explanation by epiphenomenalism, though the interpretation which we commonly put upon it will not be strictly accurate if epiphenomenalism be true.

(3) A third objection which might be made is the following. "Does not epiphenomenalism amount to saying that conscious mental events and conscious mental processes are 'appearances of' certain physiological events and processes, just as colour and temperature are supposed to be 'appearances of' certain movements of molecules and electrons? And must not an appearance of something be an appearance *to* someone who is not an appearance? Does not the epiphenomenalist theory thus *tacitly* assume the existence of a mind in a sense in which it *explicitly* denies that minds exist? And is it not therefore radically inconsistent?" This objection sounds plausible, but I do not think that there is anything in it. Epiphenomenalism may be taken to assert one of two things. (*a*) That certain events which have physiological characteristics have *also* mental characteristics, and that no events which lack physiological characteristics have mental characteristics. That many events which have physiological characteristics are not known to have mental characteristics. And that an event which has mental characteristics never causes another event in virtue of its mental characteristics, but only in virtue of its physiological characteristics. Or (*b*) that no event has both mental and physiological characteristics ; but that the complete cause of any event which has mental characteristics is an event or set of events which has physiological characteristics. And that no event which has mental characteristics is a cause-factor in the causation of any other event whatever, whether mental or physiological.

It seems plain that neither of these alternative statements of epiphenomenalism involves any tacit reference to the existence of a "mind" in some sense which is inconsistent with epiphenomenalism.   "But," it might be said, "this is not the whole truth about the matter. Some events which have mental characteristics are states of knowing other things. And, again, some events which have mental characteristics do not merely exist but are themselves known by the mind which owns them.   Does not this involve the existence of a 'mind' in some sense which epiphenomenalism cannot accept?" It seems to me that this is not an objection which applies *specially* and *directly* to epiphenomenalism. Epiphenomenalism asserts nothing positive about the qualities and relations of mental events, and it denies only one thing about them.   It simply says that mental events either (*a*) do not function at all as cause-factors ; or (*b*) that, if they do, they do so in virtue of their physiological characteristics and not in virtue of their mental characteristics.   It has no need to deny that certain mental events stand in the cognitive relation to other things ; for the relation of cognising is not, and does not involve, the relation of causation between the terms which it connects.   And it has no need to deny that two mental events may be so related that one is cognised by the other.   Of course epiphenomenalism does tacitly deny the Pure Ego theory, and it does explicitly deny that the unity of a mind is a direct causal unity.   But it denies nothing else.   In particular it has no need to deny that certain contemporary mental events are bound together by unique and very intimate relations, so that they together compose a single total mental state.   And it has no need to deny that certain successive total mental states are bound together by unique and very intimate relations, so that they together form a single mind.   The objection under discussion therefore applies, not directly and specially to epipheno-menalism, but to the view that knowledge (and, in particular, self-knowledge) can be explained without a Pure Ego or without direct causal relations between

mental events. And this is a question which we are
not at present in a position to discuss.

(4) The last objection which I propose to consider is
the following. It might be said that the hypothesis
that there are literally unconscious desires, emotions,
etc., and that they literally interact with each other in
the way in which conscious desires and emotions
appear to interact, is found to be practically useful by
psycho-analysts and others. This kind of hypothesis
does enable them to suggest methods of treatment, and
often to effect cures. The hypothesis of purely physiological traces, dispositions, and processes is not found to
be practically effective. Therefore, probably the former
hypothesis is approximately correct, and the latter is
probably wrong.

I think that there is little or nothing in this argument.
Two conscious desires appear to interact in certain
characteristic ways. If the epiphenomenalist be right,
they do not really interact. But each is correlated
with a characteristic physiological process, and these
physiological processes really do interact with each
other, thus producing characteristic modifications in
the series of observable mental events. Now the
patient observes a certain series of mental events which
is modified in this characteristic way, and he fails to
find any other series of conscious mental events which
seems to account for this modification in the former.
Let us suppose that his psycho-analyst is an epiphenomenalist. Then he would simply postulate the
existence of a physiological process which (*a*) is not
accompanied by any mental events which the patient
can introspect, but (*b*) is otherwise of the same general
nature as the physiological processes which are accompanied by a conscious mental process of conation. If
he chooses to assume that this is accompanied by a
conative mental process which the patient cannot introspect, he is simply using an argument from analogy
which may be good or bad but is quite irrelevant to any

predictions that he may make or to any course of treatment that he may devise. It is no doubt also true that he is not helped in any way by assuming that this process is physiological; but he is also not hindered by this assumption. The point is that, even if the process be physiological, he does not know anything about its physiological details; he knows it only as "the sort of process which would generally be accompanied by a conscious conation or emotion of a certain kind". So long as it *acts* as such a process might be expected to act it makes no difference to his predictions whether its intrinsic nature be physiological or mental or both or neither. Thus the success of psycho-analytic treatment which assumes literally unconscious conations and emotions, and the ill-success of methods of treatment which assume a certain hypothetical structure and processes in the brain and nervous system, seems to me to have no bearing one way or the other on the truth of epiphenomenalism.

The Choice between the Two Theories. I have argued that it is perfectly possible to hold a purely mental theory of traces and dispositions, with or without the Pure Ego theory of the self. And I have argued that it is perfectly possible to hold a purely physiological theory of traces and dispositions. A purely mental theory of mnemic persistents, which does not accept the Pure Ego, *requires* the assumption of literally unconscious mental processes; but there seems to be no conclusive objection to this. A purely physiological theory of mnemic persistents *permits* the assumption of literally unconscious mental processes, but renders this assumption superfluous. There is nothing to choose between the two types of theory so far as concerns our ability to predict and control mental events. Whether traces and dispositions be purely mental, or purely physiological, or both, or neither, we know absolutely nothing about them in detail, and can predict nothing from one hypothesis about their intrinsic nature which we could not predict equally well from any other hypothesis. The fact is that we know what they *are* only from what they *do*, and our knowledge of what they do is equally compatible with either of the four possible theories about what they are. Is there then the slightest possibility of deciding even tentatively in favour of one rather than of another?

If there be no phenomena which give us any reason to believe that minds can exist and operate after the destruction of the bodies which they have animated, I think that there will be some reason to prefer the epiphenomenalist theory on the ground that it involves fewer assumptions than the others. We know that our brains and nervous systems exist throughout our lives, and that they are very closely connected with our minds. We know that our conscious mental life is subject to great interruptions, and we do not know that these gaps are filled by literally mental processes which we cannot introspect or remember. Since the brain and nervous system are capable of carrying the necessary traces and dispositions, and since processes in the brain and nervous system are capable of filling the temporal gaps between our introspectible mental events, it would seem superfluous to postulate *mental* traces and dispositions or literally unconscious *mental* events and processes in addition. Thus, unless there be reason to believe that minds can survive the death of their bodies, I should consider that some form of epiphenomenalism was the most reasonable view to take of the nature of mind and its relation to the body. I have said, and I repeat, that all the arguments against interaction are invalid. I have said, and I repeat, that a purely mental theory of traces and dispositions is perfectly possible with or without the assumption of a Pure Ego. All that I assert here is that epiphenomenalism is also a possible theory ; and that, if there be no reason to believe that the mind ever exists apart from the body, this theory is to be preferred as involving the minimum of assumptions.

It is plain that we can get no further till we have considered the alleged evidence for the doctrine that minds can and do exist apart from bodies. If this evidence produces even a faint probability, it will be rash to accept epiphenomenalism. For epiphenomenalism would seem to be quite inconsistent with the very possibility of the independent existence of a mind. The very essence of this doctrine is that the mind by itself is not a genuine substance capable of independent existence, but either *consists* of events which are also bodily or is absolutely dependent for its existence on such events. Now we have no strong positive ground for accepting epiphenomenalism ; the alternative theories are equally possible, and much more in accordance with common-sense. We have given a tentative preference to epiphenomenalism only on grounds of " economy " ; a theory supported only in this way could be overthrown by a very light blow. In the next section of this book I propose to consider the alleged evidence for the existence of minds apart from bodies.

SECTION D

Introductory Remarks

" By the mere light of reason it seems difficult to prove the Immortality of the Soul. The arguments for it are commonly derived either from *metaphysical* topics, or *moral*, or *physical*. But, in reality, it is the Gospel, and the Gospel alone, that has brought life and immortality to light. . . . Nothing could set in a fuller light the infinite obligations which mankind have to Divine revelation; since we find that no other medium could ascertain this great and important truth."

(HUME, *Essay on the Immortality of the Soul*)

SECTION D

Alleged Evidence for Human Survival of Bodily Death

Introductory Remarks

In this section I am going to consider certain causes which have led people to believe that the human mind can and does sometimes exist apart from the human body. And I am going to consider how far these causes are also adequate reasons. It is worth while to remark that, for our purpose, arguments which led to the view that the human mind existed before it became connected with its present body would be just as important as arguments which led to the view that it exists after the destruction of its body. And arguments which led to the conclusion that a human mind can become temporarily disconnected with its body during life, can function during this interval, and can then again animate the body would be equally important for our purposes. For, if there be reason to believe that a human mind can *ever* exist and function apart from a human body, it will be almost impossible to accept the epiphenomenalist theory of the mind and its relations to the body. I propose, however, to deal only with arguments which claim to prove that human minds survive the destruction of the bodies which they have animated ; the other possibilities will be considered only in so far as they are involved in certain arguments for survival.

I think that men have believed in human survival for five reasons. (1) Some have thought that it was immediately obvious or that they had received a divine revelation which assured them of it. (2) Others have believed it on authority. (3) Some have thought that it could be proved by general metaphysical arguments. (4) Some have thought that it follows from certain ethical premises. And (5) some have thought that there is special empirical evidence in favour of it. I shall say what I have to say about the first three causes of the belief in these *Introductory Remarks*, and I shall devote one chapter to ethical arguments and one to empirical arguments.

(1) Most of us do not find the proposition that our minds will survive the destruction of our present bodies in the least self-evident. And most of us do not claim to have received personally a divine revelation on this or on any other subject. And, if I believe in survival because I believe that it is immediately certain to some-one else or that it has been divinely revealed to someone else, I am believing it on authority. So that it is certain that the vast majority of people who believe in human survival must do so either on authority or because of some kind of argument which seems to them to make it certain or probable.

(2) We all of us believe a great many propositions on the authority of others, and we should be behaving very unreasonably if we did not. We must, therefore, try to distinguish the cases where it is reasonable to believe something on authority from those where it is not reasonable to do so. And we must then consider whether the proposition that human minds survive the death of their bodies is or is not one which it is reason-able to believe on authority. (*a*) My authority may himself believe the proposition as the result of an argument, which is too difficult or unfamiliar for me to follow for myself. I am then justified in attaching con-siderable probability to his conclusion, provided (i) that I accept his premises; (ii) that I can follow and accept simpler arguments of the same kind as he has used to prove this proposition; (iii) that I know that men's

capacities for following arguments of this kind vary, and (iv) that other experts who have looked into the matter for themselves all come to the same conclusion. I am, *e.g.*, justified in attaching considerable weight to any proposition in the Theory of Numbers which Professor Hardy and Mr Littlewood tell me that they have proved.   Now a great many much better philosophers than I (*e.g.*, Plato and St Thomas) have persuaded themselves by argument of the truth of human survival. Ought I then to attach a high probability to this proposition on their authority?   It does not seem to me that I ought.   For (i) I am quite competent to follow their arguments, and they seem to me not to be valid. (ii) They use premises which seem to me very doubtful.   And (iii) there is no consensus among experts either about the validity of these arguments or the truth of the premises.   Kant was a greater philosopher than I, and he thought such arguments involve logical fallacies.   Spinoza was a greater philosopher than I, and he rejected the premises of such arguments.

(*b*) My authority may believe a certain proposition because he has access to facts which I cannot perceive for myself.   These facts may be imperceptible to me simply because I am not placed in a suitable position in space and time for perceiving them ; or because I lack the necessary instruments of precision and the necessary training in using such instruments ; or because my mind or body or both lack certain powers which are possessed by the mind and body of my authority. On the first two alternatives my authority claims only to be perceiving something of the same *kind* as I can perceive ; and there is no reason why I should not be able to perceive it too, if I went to the right place and did the right things.   If I have reason to believe that my authority is a skilled experimenter and observer, and if he is believed to be so by other experts, it is rational to attach considerable weight to what he asserts. This weight will, of course, be increased if other experts perform the same experiments and observations and reach similar results. It is on such grounds as this that it is rational for me to attach considerable probability to statements made by Professor Rutherford or Dr Aston about the experimental splitting of atoms. But, when people are said to believe in survival on the authority of some religious teacher, the situation is not at all closely analogous to this. They suppose that the religious teacher is either himself a divine being or that he has received his information directly from some divine being. The Christian who believes in survival on the authority of Christ is an example of the former case, and the Mohammedan who believes it on the authority of Mohammed is an example of the latter. Let us consider this kind of authority a little more closely.

The ultimate authority in either case is the supposed divine being. Before accepting such statements on authority we must therefore satisfy ourselves (i) that our religious teacher was a divine being or was inspired by one ; (ii) that he has been properly reported ; (iii) that the divine being knows the truth about the question under consideration ; and (iv) that the divine being is not intentionally deceiving us, or accommodating his statements to the current beliefs of the time and place, or speaking metaphorically. Lastly (v) if our authority is not supposed to be himself divine, but only to be divinely inspired, we must be sure that he has not deliberately or unwittingly falsified the message with which he has been entrusted. I can only say that I know of no historical case in which there seems to me to be any strong reason to believe that all these conditions have been fulfilled. The question has been discussed by Mr Hobbes with his usual acuteness in Chapter XXXII of the *Leviathan*, where he writes as follows. "If a man pretend to me that God hath spoken to him immediately and supernaturally, and I make doubt of it, I cannot easily perceive what argument he can

produce to oblige me to believe it. It is true that, if
he be my Sovereign, he may oblige me to obedience so
as not by act or word to *declare* I believe him not; but
not to *think* any otherwise than my reason persuades
me. But, if one that hath not such authority over me
shall pretend the same, there is nothing that exacteth
either belief or obedience." (My italics.) I find nothing
to add to Mr Hobbes's statement or to alter in it.

(3) I pass now to the case of general metaphysical
arguments in favour of human survival. These are
at present somewhat out of fashion; and I think it
would be generally admitted that the older kind of
argument which Kant dealt with in the *Paralogisms of
Pure Reason* really was refuted by Kant. The only
modern philosopher of importance, so far as I know,
who claims to prove the immortality of the soul by
general metaphysical arguments is Dr M'Taggart. He
points out quite rightly that all such arguments have an
a priori and an empirical part. The *a priori* part
consists in proving that anything which had certain
characteristics would necessarily be permanent. The
empirical part consists in showing that the human mind
has such characteristics.   How then do such arguments differ from those which I call "empirical"?
The difference is this. An empirical argument for
survival takes certain special phenomena, viz., those
which are dealt with by Psychical Research. And it
argues that the hypothesis of human survival explains
these phenomena better than any other hypothesis that
we can think of. Such an argument of course uses
a priori principles of logic and probability, as every
argument does. But it has no *a priori* premise. In
this respect it differs fundamentally from such an
argument as M'Taggart's, and is of exactly the same
kind as the arguments for the wave-theory of light or
the constitution of the benzene molecule.

Now I cannot prove that all general metaphysical
arguments for human survival must necessarily be

invalid. I can only say that all that I am acquainted
with seem to be extremely doubtful either in their
a priori part or in their empirical part or in both.
And they are so much bound up with elaborate metaphysical systems, and have persuaded so few men beside
their authors, that I propose to ignore them here. We
are thus left with Ethical Arguments and Special
Empirical Arguments. I shall deal with the former
in the next chapter, and with the latter in the chapter
which follows it. I may say at once that my own view
is that, if human survival can be rendered probable at
all, this can be done only by empirical arguments based
on the phenomena which are treated by Psychical
Research.

CHAPTER XI

Ethical Arguments for Human Survival

IT has been held by many philosophers that all arguments from " value " to "fact" or from "ought" to "is" are necessarily invalid. I have certainly expressed this view myself from time to time. I believe now that this is not true without qualification ; and that, if certain conditions be fulfilled, such arguments are not necessarily fallacious. Whether any of them in fact succeed in proving their conclusions is of course another matter. I will, therefore, begin by discussing in general terms the question whether such arguments can ever be valid, and, if so, what conditions an argument of this kind must fulfil in order not to be logically fallacious.

The Logical Status of Ethical Arguments with Factual Conclusions. An ethical argument is one that uses at least one ethical premise ; we must, therefore, begin by explaining what is meant by an "ethical premise". I assume at the outset that there are certain purely ethical characteristics, *i.e.*, characteristics which cannot be identified with or defined in terms of non-ethical or "natural" characteristics. I should consider that the characteristics of being "intrinsically good" or "right" or "a duty" are examples of purely ethical characteristics. Now presumably some ethical characteristics are simple and indefinable, whilst others can be analysed and defined in terms of other ethical characteristics. *E.g.*, some people have held that a "right action" may be defined as "an action which has as good consequences as any action which is possible to the agent ". Again, even when an ethical characteristic is not definable, there may be synthetic propositions about its properties or about its connexions with other ethical characteristics. *E.g.*, we may say that the goodness of a whole is not necessarily the sum of the goodness which each of its parts would have in isolation. Again, we might hold that both " good" and "right" are indefinable, and yet accept the synthetic proposition that no action is right which does not have at least as good consequences as any action which is possible for the agent. I think that I can now define what I mean by a " purely ethical proposition". It will be a proposition which either (*a*) states that a certain ethical characteristic (*e.g.*, " good ") is indefinable ; or (*b*) analyses it in terms of other ethical characteristics ; or (*c*) states some intrinsic property of an ethical characteristic (*e.g.*, that it is quantitative, that it is not simply additive, etc.); or (*d*) states some synthetic connexion between two or more ethical characteristics.

Now I think that it is certain that no argument *all* of whose premises are *purely* ethical propositions can lead to a factual conclusion. But I am very doubtful whether anyone has ever used such an argument. Now there are other propositions which involve ethical characteristics, which I will call " mixed ethical propositions ". These assert a synthetic connexion between an ethical characteristic and one or more non-ethical characteristics. I will give some examples. " No action can be a duty unless it be physically possible for the agent to perform it." " No state of affairs can be good or bad unless it is or contains as a constituent some conscious mental state." " The goodness of any state of affairs depends on nothing but the balance of pleasure which it contains, and is directly proportional to this balance." All these are mixed ethical propositions ; the first being true, the second highly probable, and the third certainly false. Mixed ethical propositions can always be put into one

of the two forms : " If anything had the ethical characteristic E it would have the non-ethical characteristic
N," or "If anything had the non-ethical characteristic
N it would have the ethical characteristic E." Any
ethical argument with a factual conclusion must contain
a mixed ethical premise of the first kind in order to be
logically valid.

We can now go a step further. The mixed ethical
premise is essentially hypothetical. The conclusion is
categorical. It follows that one premise must be
categorical, if the argument is to be logically valid.
And it is plain that the categorical premise must be of
the form : "Something does have the ethical characteristic E ". We can then conclude that something
does have the non-ethical characteristic N. I have now
stated what Mr Johnson would call the "constitutive
conditions" for the validity of such arguments. We
must now consider what he would call the "epistemic
conditions". If the argument is not to be circular we
must be able to *know* (*a*) that if anything had E it would
have N, and (*b*) that something has E, without having
to *know* beforehand that something has N.

We may divide up ethical arguments on two different
principles, thus getting four different kinds of ethical
argument which might possibly be valid. (i) The
ethical characteristic under consideration might be
"good", or it might be "right" or "duty". (ii) The
factual premise might take the form "Something has
E" or the more determinate form "This has E". *E.g.*,
it might take the form "Some actions are right" or
"This action is right". Of course the latter entails the
former. But it is plain that the argument is stronger if
it only has to use the milder premise. We might be
pretty certain that some actions which have been performed have been right, but doubtful whether any
particular action which was brought to our notice was
right.

This seems to me to be about as much as we can say

about the general question of whether ethical arguments
with factual conclusions can ever be logically valid.
We have seen that they can be if they fulfil certain
conditions, and we have stated exactly what those conditions are.   I propose now to give an example of an
ethical argument which seems to me to fulfil the conditions and to prove its conclusion.   I think that Kant's
argument from duty to freedom is a case in point.   It
may be put as follows.   "If it can ever be truly said
that it is a duty to perform (or to avoid) an act, it must
have been possible for the agent to perform it and
possible for him not to perform it.   Now there are some
acts of which it is true to say that they ought to have
been done (or avoided).   Hence there are some acts
which their agent could have performed and could have
avoided."   It is plain that this argument fulfils the
constitutive conditions.   It seems to me clear that the
ethical premise can be known to be true by merely
reflecting on the conceptions of "duty" and of "possibility", and that it is not necessary to know beforehand
that some acts which have been done could have been
avoided or that some acts which have been avoided
could have been done.   So that the first epistemic condition is fulfilled.   I am also inclined to believe that we
can know that the characteristics "ought" and "ought
not" have application without having to know beforehand that some actions which are done could have
been avoided, and that some actions which have been
avoided could have been done.   It is difficult to be sure
of this because every one does in practice believe the
conclusion of Kant's argument.   Assuming that the
above statement is true, Kant's argument fulfils the
second epistemic condition, and proves its conclusion.
Unfortunately the only conclusion which it certainly
proves is not of much interest.   It no doubt makes it
almost certain that we are *in some sense* "free" in some
of our voluntary actions.   But it is not in the least
certain that the "freedom" required is inconsistent with

determinism. And we could have reached the conclusion that we are "free" in several very important senses without appealing to ethical arguments at all. It seems to me doubtful whether Kant's ethical argument proves that we are "free" in any sense of "freedom" which could not have been established by direct inspection; and all these senses seem to me to be probably consistent with complete determinism.

I will now give an example of an ethical argument which seems to me obviously to fail to fulfil the conditions and to be invalid. We might argue as follows. "Unless God existed it would not be our duty to address private prayers to him. It is our duty to address private prayers to God. Therefore God must exist." (I put in the qualification "private", because it might be my duty to address public prayers to God, even if he does not exist and I do not believe that he exists, if the State of which I am a member orders its citizens to do so by an act which has been properly introduced, discussed, and passed into law.) Now the above argument seems to me to break the second epistemic condition. I do not think that it could possibly be maintained that I can know that it is my duty to address private prayers to God unless I already know that God exists. Hence this ethical argument for the existence of God would be circular.

Professor Taylor's Arguments for Immortality. Now that we understand the logic of ethical arguments for factual conclusions we can consider the special ethical arguments for human survival. These arguments have been stated in many forms. Fortunately the essence of them has been put with admirable persuasiveness, brevity, and clearness by Professor A. E. Taylor in an article called "The Moral Argument for Immortality" in the *Holborn Review*. As I have no expectation of seeing the case put better than Professor Taylor puts it there, I will take this article as the text for my discussion. I think that the article contains two distinct arguments, though Professor Taylor passes from the first to the second without definitely saying that he is making a transition.

The Argument from Duty. Crudely stated, the first argument comes to this. If we and all the human race will eventually die, certain acts which it would be our duty to do on the opposite alternative will not be duties. And certain other acts, which it would be wrong to do if we were immortal, would be harmless and reasonable enough if the lives of ourselves and our fellows are limited to the three-score years and ten which we spend in this mortal body. The duties of a Christian are the right and reasonable behaviour of a man who is going to survive the death of his body ; they are not right or reasonable if we die with our bodies. The reasonable course of life on the latter alternative would be that which is sketched for us in Horace's *Odes*. Now we know that it is right for us to live in accordance with the Christian ethics, and that it is wrong to live in accordance with the Horatian ethics. Since the latter mode of life would not be wrong if we were mortal, we can conclude that we are not mortal. I will deal with this argument first.

It is not in the least necessary for the argument to assume that the Christian ethics are wholly right or the Horatian ethics wholly wrong. I must confess that it seems to me that Professor Taylor allows much too much to the Horatian ethics, even on the assumption of human mortality. He seems to suggest that, if we all die with our bodies, the only reasonable course of action is to enjoy the passing hour. I should have supposed that, even if the belief that I and the race will perish makes it unreasonable for me to trouble about anything but my own pleasure, the reasonable course of life for me might be very different from that which Horace recommends. If champagne gives me a headache I shall be foolish to take too much of it merely because I am mortal. And my mortality will surely not make it my duty to "sport with Amaryllis in the shade" if I find the society of Amaryllis and all her kindred an intolerable bore. If I happen to prefer philosophy, or scientific research, or charity-organisation, to dinner-parties, race-meetings, and night-clubs, there seems to be no reason why I should not indulge these tastes as much as any immortal spirit. Professor Taylor admits that Horace's *Odes* do not make very cheerful reading; surely this may be due, not simply to the fact that Horace believed himself to be mortal, but also to the fact that he acted unreasonably even for a mortal being whose sole aim is to maximise his own happiness. In a good many people the passion for scientific research, for artistic production, or for the construction of engineering works and the organisation of businesses, is extremely strong and largely disinterested. The Horatian scheme forgets these facts. If a man wishes to provide himself with sources of pleasure that will ensure a quiet but strong happiness over the greater part of his life, rather than a few spasms of enjoyment in the earlier part of it followed by years of boredom, he will be most unwise to adopt the "fleeting-hour" plan even if he believes himself to be mortal. His wisest course will be, not indeed to neglect bodily pleasures in the earlier years of his life, but at any rate to indulge in them only to such an extent as will not interfere with the acquirement of sources of quieter but more permanent happiness which can be enjoyed when gout has forbidden port and a failing digestion has vetoed oysters.

Thus, even if we die with our bodies, and if this implies that it is only reasonable to do what will give us pleasure, this will not necessarily make the right and reasonable line of conduct for most of us very different (though it will be somewhat different) from that of a convinced Christian. But of course the mere fact, if it be a fact, that we are mortal has no tendency to make it right to consider only our own pleasure. Suppose that

I and all other men are mortal, this will not alter the fact that, so long as they and I are alive, some states of mind, such as the appreciative hearing of good music, are better than others, such as enjoyment of another's pain. Nor will it alter the fact that it largely depends on our present actions whether I, my contemporaries, and a long series of successors shall experience the one kind of state or the other. Whether we are mortal or not it will still be our duty, I suppose, not to produce a worse state when we can produce a better; not to treat our own pleasure, simply because it is *ours*, as more important than the pleasure of others; and not to show favouritism in the distribution of those materials for a good life which are at our disposal. Thus the duties of Justice, Rational Benevolence, and Prudence remain duties on either hypothesis.

Professor Taylor says that he assumes that "the highest goods are roughly the discovery and knowledge of truth, the attainment and exercise of virtue, and the creation and fruition of beauty". To these he later on adds the relation of love between persons. "All other goods," he says, "are secondary and insignificant as compared with these." I have no quarrel with these statements. The question is whether it would cease to be rational to strive for these goods if we believed that all human beings are mortal and that the race will eventually die out. So far as I can see, the only argument which Professor Taylor uses to support this view is that, on this hypothesis, it will make no *permanent* difference whether we pursue these goods or not. Now I agree that this consequence follows from the assumption that the race will eventually die out. And I agree that it is practically certain that the race will die out unless some individual members of it are immortal. Finally, I agree (subject to certain qualifications which I will mention in a moment) that, if no goods that we can produce are permanent, the world is a poor thing. The qualifications which I have to make are these.

(1) Although every species of intelligent beings may last only for a finite time, yet there might always be some species of intelligent beings existing. And the scientific discoveries and artistic treasures of the human race might be capable of being known and appreciated by the race of intelligent beings whose sun is rising while the sun of the human race is setting. On this hypothesis all values which consist in relations between human beings, or which are stored up in the characters of human beings, would indeed be lost; but a good deal would be saved out of the wreck. The hypothesis which I am suggesting is analogous to what has happened many times in the history of the earth, when one race (*e.g.*, the Greeks) has flowered and decayed, and eventually another race has found inspiration in their artistic, literary, and scientific productions. (2) Professor Taylor holds that, if all the values which the human race has created die with it and are not continued by some other race, the world is *very evil*. This seems to me to be too harsh a judgment; all that is justified is that the world is *not very good*. Suppose that there have not been and never will be any intelligent beings except men, and that the human race lasts for ten million years, reaching a maximum of virtue, happiness, and knowledge, at some intermediate date and then degenerating. On this hypothesis no part of the history of the world before the beginning of this period, and no part of its history after this period, has any intrinsic value. All intrinsic value, positive and negative, is crowded into this ten million years; and this period is no doubt but a moment in the total life of the universe. We must remember, however, that if there is no intrinsic goodness outside these limits of time, there is also no intrinsic evil. Ethically, all but the ten million years may be wiped out; and the moral character of the universe will stand or fall simply by the balance of good or evil within this ten million years. If there be a balance of good in that period, the universe may be

called slightly good; if there be a balance of evil, it may be called slightly bad. But, however great the balance one way or the other within this period, we cannot call the universe as a whole very good or very bad, because the period during which *any* moral predicate can be applied is such a vanishingly small part of the total history of the universe.

After this explanatory digression I return to the main question. Supposing that there will come a time when all our scientific knowledge will be lost, when all our artistic productions will have ceased to exist or will have ceased to be contemplated and admired by any conscious being, and when all the values which are stored up in personal character and in human relationships will have vanished with the human beings who owned them, does it follow that it is irrational for us here and now to pursue those goods and to sacrifice other kinds of pleasure in order to attain them? I cannot see that it does. Let us begin by taking an analogy within a single three-score years and ten. It is certain that no doctor can prevent me from eventually dying. Does this render it irrational for me to go to a doctor if I have an illness in the prime of life, in the hope that he will cure me and enable me to live for many more years in comfort to myself and in useful activities and valuable personal relations to others? Surely it does not. Now, if it is rational to seek to be cured of an illness, though eventually *some* illness is certain to be fatal to me, why is it irrational for me to seek to enlarge scientific knowledge and to produce beautiful objects, though eventually a time will come when this knowledge will be lost and these objects will no longer be contemplated? The human race has probably a very long course before it, and I can certainly affect for better or worse the lives of countless generations of future men. I cannot see the least reason to think that, because the course of human history is not *endless*, it ceases to be my duty to do what I can to assure to these future generations decent social conditions, clear scientific knowledge which they can build upon and extend, and beautiful objects which they can admire and use as an inspiration for the production of yet more beautiful objects. That it will all come to an end eventually is a tragedy ; but this tragedy seems to make no difference to my duty here and now. If you like, it lowers the worth of *every* kind of activity ; but it does not, as far as I can see, alter the *relative* values of various alternative kinds of activity.

No doubt, if one's duties are affected at all by matters of fact, one very important fact which will influence them is the particular place and time within the cosmic process in which one's lot happens to be cast. It would be irrational to start an elaborate scheme of social reform, or a three-volume novel, or a treatise on the theory of functions, if there were reason to expect that the world was coming to an end next week. At least it would be foolish on any other motive than the enjoyment of the activity itself. But it is not obviously foolish, if there be a prospect of a long series of human generations between oneself and the twilight of the earth, so to act that they may have fine works of art, profound scientific speculations, and the opportunity to live in a reasonably ordered community. Even if men were immortal and the human race destined to last for ever, it is certain that my scientific speculations will become obsolete and my artistic productions unintelligible. If they will be appreciated by myself and my contemporaries and will form a basis from which my successors will be able to build something better, it is rational for me to occupy myself in these activities. I am quite prepared to admit that, if the race is going to die out, the duties of a man who is born some millions of years hence may be very different from my duties, and very different from the duties which would be incumbent on him if he believed in immortality. If it were certain that the race had passed its prime, and that nothing now awaited it but a hopeless struggle with an increasingly unfavourable environment, the main duty of a good man might be to preach and to practise contraception and infanticide. But I do deny that the question of mortality or immortality makes any appreciable difference to the duties of a man here and now; and the fact that it *will* make a great difference to the duties of a man born some millions of years hence seems to me to be irrelevant.

It seems to me, then, that the difference between the duties of a Christian and the duties of a man of the present time who believes that he and his fellows are mortal are not nearly so great as has been represented. No doubt there are considerable differences; but these depend on the fact that certain details of the Christian ethics are accepted by Christians on the authority of a supposed divine revelation. Differences of this kind are irrelevant to the present argument, for the following reasons. (*a*) It is needless to prove to Christians that they are immortal from the special features of their ethical system, for they already believe that they are immortal on the same authority on which they accept these special duties. On the other hand, in arguing with non-Christians it is useless to take as the basis for your argument special duties which, since they are believed to be duties only on the authority of the Christian revelation, will not be regarded by non-Christians as duties at all. (*b*) In any case differences of this kind will not be relevant to the argument for immortality. We must find some difference in our duties which depends simply and solely on the question whether we are or are not mortal, if we are to base an argument for immortality on our supposed knowledge of what it is our duty to do. What I have tried to do so far is to show that it is by no means clear that there are any duties which fulfil the two conditions of being regarded as binding by virtuous disbelievers in immortality, and of not *really* being binding unless we are immortal

It would be enough, however, for Professor Taylor's

purpose if a single act can be found which is admitted to be a duty by all competent judges, and would not be a duty if we were mortal. Now, although I do not know of any act which fulfils these conditions here and now, it would be rash to assert that there may not be at least one. Let us assume then, as a hypothesis, that a clear case of such a duty can be produced; and let us then ask whether we should be justified in concluding that we are immortal.

It is plain that the argument fulfils the necessary constitutive conditions. It would run as follows. "I know it is my duty to perform actions of a certain kind. I can show that it would not be my duty to perform such actions unless I were immortal. Therefore I can conclude that I am immortal." The question is whether the argument could fulfil the necessary epistemic conditions. If the argument is to be epistemically valid I must be able to know that so-and-so is my duty without having to know beforehand whether I am mortal or immortal. Now I am extremely doubtful whether the epistemic condition can be fulfilled. Either my duty depends on circumstances or it does not. If it does, how can I know what it is until I know the circumstances in which I am placed? And a very important circumstance will be whether I am mortal or immortal. Thus, if my duty does depend on circumstances, it seems to me almost incredible that I can know what it is while I am ignorant of the relevant circumstances. Now, by hypothesis, the question whether I am or am not mortal, is highly relevant in connexion with the duty on which the argument is based. If, then, my duty does depend upon circumstances, and the question of my mortality or immortality is highly relevant to the question whether so-and-so is my duty or not, I find it hard to believe that I could be certain that so-and-so is my duty at times when I am uncertain whether I am mortal or immortal. I fully admit that there is no logical impossibility here; but I have the gravest doubts whether any actual instance could be produced. If, on the other hand, my duty be independent of circumstances, then there is of course no difficulty in supposing that I can know that so-and-so is my duty at times when I do not know whether I am or am not mortal. But then the other half of the argument will break down. If it be my duty to do so-and-so *regardless* of circumstances, it will be my duty to do it whether I be mortal or not; and, therefore, the fact that it is my duty to do it will not enable me to decide between these two alternatives.

I will now try to state as shortly as possible what I do and what I do not think that I have proved. (1) I have not proved that there is any logical incoherence in Professor Taylor's argument. It is theoretically possible, so far as I can see, that an instance might be produced fulfilling all the conditions which the argument requires. (2) I have tried to make these conditions explicit, and I will now sum them up. In trying to prove to a man M by this argument that he is immortal it is necessary to find some action which fulfils the following conditions. (*a*) M recognises it to be his duty. (*b*) It would not be M's duty unless M were in fact immortal. (*c*) M can *know* that it is his duty without having to know beforehand whether he is immortal or not, in spite of the fact that it can *be* his duty only if he is in fact immortal. (3) I have tried to show that it is uncertain whether any action can be suggested at the present time which fulfils conditions (*a*) and (*b*). And I have tried further to show that, even if an action could be produced that fulfils (*a*) and (*b*), it is most unlikely that it would fulfil (*c*) also.

The Argument that the World would be very evil unless Men are immortal. This is plainly a different argument from that which we have just been considering. The first argument took as its premise that we have certain duties and that these would not be obligatory on us if we were mortal. The present argument is of the following form. "If we and all men die with our bodies the world is very evil. The world is not so evil as this. Therefore some men, at any rate, are immortal." Professor Taylor does not directly discuss this argument. But he has a good deal of importance to say about it. In the first place, he incidentally uses an argument, which seems to me to be invalid in the present connexion, to suggest that the world is not so evil as it seems. Secondly, he argues in considerable detail, not that it is *false* that the world is very evil, but that it is *inconsistent* for a scientist to hold that it is so. I will first consider the argument for myself, and will then consider Professor Taylor's remarks about it.

I think that the argument under discussion could take two forms, one of which applies more directly to the individual than the other. The first form is this. "Men often die quite suddenly at the height of their powers, and other men die when their full powers are not developed. If such men do not survive the death of their bodies they are treated with gross injustice. If there were such injustice the universe would be very evil. Now the universe is not so evil as this. Hence such men do not really die with the death of their bodies." If such an argument were valid at all, it would not directly prove that *all* men survive the death of their bodies or that *any* man is immortal. Some men seem to be provided in this life with ample opportunities to display the best that is in them, and to display nothing that is worth preserving. And it is not obvious that any man needs unending time to display all his powers to the utmost. If you answer that every man *may* have valuable characteristics which need only favourable conditions to develop, and that we cannot be sure that any man could develop his full powers in a finite time, the answer is true but irrelevant. We can argue only from what we know to be true, not from what we do not know to be false.

I have already stated the other form of the argument.

I will begin by making some comments on the first premise and the conclusion. For reasons already given the first premise needs to be stated in a more guarded form. We must not suppose merely that all human beings are mortal and that the race will eventually die out. We must also suppose that there will not be other races of intelligent beings who will be able to take over, appreciate, and develop the science and art of the human race, as one nation of human beings has often done with the science and art of another nation which has died out. If there always will be such intelligent beings, though none of them are immortal, the world need not be very evil; though I think it would be less good than it would be if some individuals, human or non-human, were immortal. Secondly, I am not prepared to say that the world would be *very evil* even on the more detailed hypothesis that there will be no other races of intelligent beings related to the human race in the way suggested. I am prepared to say only that the world would *not be very good* on this hypothesis. It is worth while to remark that the world *might* be very much worse on the hypothesis of immortality than on the hypothesis of mortality. If all human beings be immortal, and most human beings spend eternity in Hell, it seems to me that the world will be very evil; much more evil than it would be on the hypothesis of universal mortality. In fact immortality is a necessary condition (on the present restricted hypothesis) for very great good or very great evil. But it is quite neutral between the two. So much for the first premise of the present argument.

About the conclusion I have to make the same remark as I made about the conclusion of the first form of the argument. So far as I can see, the argument would not prove that every one is immortal; it would prove only that some men must be so. It would be quite consistent with the view that no one who has existed up to the present date is immortal, or that only a small proportion of the men who are alive at any date are immortal.

It now remains to consider the second premise, which is common to the two forms of this argument. Two conditions must be fulfilled if the argument is to be valid. (i) It must be true that the world is better than it would be if all human beings were mortal. And (ii) we must be able to *know* this without having to know beforehand whether all men are mortal or not. It is this second and epistemic condition which renders a perfectly true observation of Professor Taylor's completely irrelevant to the present purpose. He supposes an objector to say that, on the face of it, there is a great deal of evil in the world; and, since the world contains so much evil anyhow, we can feel no confidence that it may not be evil enough to be consistent with universal mortality. To this he answers that a great deal in the world which seems to be very evil would be trivial if we are immortal. This is no doubt true; but it is surely quite irrelevant. If we knew independently that we were immortal this would be a perfectly good argument against the pessimist. But, when we are trying to *prove* that we are immortal, we must surely take the world at its face-value and not import considerations which depend on the hypothesis that we are immortal. Whether we are immortal or not it is certain that pain and cruelty exist, and it is certain that they are *intrinsically* evil. If we are immortal, they may have a great instrumental value which they will not have if we are mortal. But we have no right to assume either that they do or that they do not have this instrumental value when we are trying to prove that we are immortal; the question of their possible instrumental value must here be dismissed as simply irrelevant. It is perhaps worth while to add that, if we are to play fast and loose with our data in this way at all, we may as well do it in one direction as in another. Whether we are immortal or not it is certain that love and pity exist, and it is certain that they are *intrinsically* good. But intrinsically good states sometimes have bad consequences; and, if we are immortal, they may have a great instrumental disvalue which they will not have if we are mortal.

For my own part I believe the objection which Professor Taylor is here trying to answer is a perfectly valid one. There certainly is *some* evil, and I do not know of any general principle by which we could decide, *e.g.*, that toothache is not too bad to be true whilst universal mortality is too bad to be true. Perhaps there may be some general principle which would enable us to draw a line somewhere, if only we knew it. But, so far as I can see, we are not acquainted with any such principle and have not the least idea where this line is to be drawn.

The alleged Inconsistency between holding that the World is "rational" and denying that it is "righteous". Professor Taylor imagines the case of a scientist who should argue as follows. "I see that it is my duty to act in such and such a way. I also know from my study of natural science that the efforts of the human race will all come to naught in the end, whether we do what is right or what is wrong. So much the worse for Nature. It is a fact that it has at a certain stage produced beings who can distinguish between right and wrong and be guided in their actions by this distinction. Such beings can judge the cosmic process and condemn it as indifferent to, and in the end destructive of, all that is valuable. It is a fact that, if men survived the death of their bodies, there would be at least a chance that their efforts and experiences might be of some permanent value. But we have no right to think that this provides any reason for holding that men will survive bodily death; what ought to be and what is fall into two utterly different spheres, and we cannot argue from the former to the latter. Their sole connexion is that the world of what *is* has, under temporary and exceptional circumstances, thrown up for a moment beings who can contemplate the world of what *ought to be*, and can criticise from its standards the material world which has made and will soon break its critics."

Now I understand Professor Taylor's position to be that there is a positive inconsistency in a scientist who combines the view that the world is "rational", in the sense of being coherent enough to be a possible object of scientific knowledge, with the view that it is "irrational", in the sense of being indifferent or hostile to what we know to be ethically valuable. Now we must at the outset distinguish two very different cases. (*a*) That the two propositions : "The world is logically coherent" and : "The world is ethically incoherent" are mutually inconsistent. And (*b*) that *I* should be inconsistent if I believed both of them. The distinction may be illustrated as follows. There is no inconsistency between the two propositions : "Smith is in the dining-room" and : "Jones is not in the dining-room". But, if my sole ground for any determinate belief about the position of either is that the housemaid has told me that both are in the dining-room, *I* shall be inconsistent if I assert that Smith is there and deny that Jones is there. I think it is certain that Professor Taylor claims to prove only the second kind of inconsistency. I will, however, deal with the first before I consider Professor Taylor's arguments for the second.

(*a*) It seems to me quite plain that there is no inconsistency between the two statements that the world obeys the laws of logic and that it breaks the laws of ethics. There appears to be an inconsistency only because of a confusion between two senses of "law" and two senses of "breaking". Murders are committed from time to time ; and this, in a sense, conflicts with the moral law : "Thou shalt do no murder". But it conflicts simply in the sense that something happens which the law asserts to be wrong. It does not conflict with the law in the sense that it is inconsistent with its truth. If every one always and everywhere committed murders, this would not have the least bearing on the fact that murder is wrong, if it be a fact. At most it might make it harder for us to recognise this law. To say then that the world breaks the laws of ethics means only that it contains a great deal of evil ; and, since the laws of ethics make no assertion whatever about the amount of evil which may exist, there is not the slightest intellectual incoherence between this fact and the laws of ethics. There is therefore no difficulty whatever that I can see in believing both that these laws are true and that they are very often or even always broken.

Let us now see what would be meant by saying that the world never breaks the laws of logic. This means that neither the world as a whole nor any part of it can be the subject of two true propositions of the kind which logic asserts to be inconsistent with each other. Is there any incoherence between this statement and the statement that the world or parts of it break the laws of ethics? There would be an incoherence if and only if a breach of the laws of ethics by anything implied that this thing was the subject of two logically inconsistent propositions both of which were true. But we have seen that a breach of the laws of ethics entails no such consequences. If I commit a murder I break a law of ethics, but I do not thereby become the subject of two true propositions which are logically inconsistent with each other. The two true propositions : "I commit a murder" and : " I do wrong to commit a murder" are perfectly consistent in logic with each other.

(b) We may therefore pass to the second question. Granted that there is no inconsistency between the *propositions*: "The world is logically coherent" and "The world is ethically incoherent"; is it inconsistent *of me* to combine the two? I understand Professor Taylor's position to be that I have no positive ground for believing the world to be logically coherent which is not also a positive ground for believing it to be ethically coherent, and that it is therefore inconsistent in *me* to assert the former and doubt the latter. Let us now examine this contention a little more closely. When we say that a man has no ground for asserting *p* which is not equally a ground for asserting *q* we may mean one of two things. (i) We may mean that he has no ground at all for either assertion. Or (ii) we may mean that he has a positive ground for asserting *p*, and that this is just as good a ground for asserting *q*.

The former alternative would mean that the belief that the world is rational is an act of pure faith, and that the belief that the world is righteous is another act of pure faith. Supposing this to be true, all that follows is that A, who believes on no grounds that the world is intelligible, cannot cast stones at B, who believes on no grounds that the world is righteous. Equally, of course, B will not be able to cast stones at A. But, so far as I can see, though A and B could not refute each other, they also could not convince each other. Because I believe one proposition on faith, and another man believes another proposition on faith, it does not follow that I ought to add his belief to mine or that he ought to add my belief to his. Thus, on this alternative, the argument may produce mutual charity but it has no tendency to produce mutual conviction.

The second alternative is that the two beliefs that the world is intelligible and that it is righteous have a common positive ground. If so, it will be inconsistent of me to assert one proposition on this ground and to deny the other. In order to deal with this case it will be necessary to state more clearly what is meant by the proposition that the world is "intelligible" or "intellectually coherent". I think that this involves two points; (i) that the world obeys the laws of logic, and (ii) something more. The first is all that the pure mathematician requires; the second is required in addition to the first by the natural scientist. I will deal with these two points in turn.

(i) It seems to me that my ground for believing that the world obeys the laws of logic can be stated, and that it is obviously quite different from my ground (if any) for believing that it obeys the laws of ethics. Why do I believe that the world obeys the laws of logic? Because I seem to be able to see quite clearly that no term of any kind could be the subject of two true and logically inconsistent propositions. It is true that this belief "has no grounds", in the sense that no reasons can be given for it which do not presuppose it. But it also needs no grounds in this sense; for it is self-evident. It is merely an abuse of language to call it an "act of faith" in the sense in which my belief that my friend loves me in spite of his being sometimes cold and some- times peevish to me may be called an "act of faith". I have this self-evident knowledge of some of the more abstract principles of ethics as well as of the laws of logic. But I have no such knowledge of the proposition that the world conforms to the laws of ethics. So far from its being self-evident that the world conforms to the laws of ethics it is perfectly certain that some parts of it do not. At least it is as certain that the world does not wholly conform to the laws of ethics as it is that there is moral evil in it. It is no answer to this to say that we often meet with apparent contradictions, and that we always feel quite sure that they are *only* apparent and that fuller knowledge would show that the laws of logic have not been broken; so why should not the same thing be true of apparent breaches of the laws of ethics? The two cases are quite different. We *know* beforehand that nothing real can break the laws of logic; we do not know that nothing real can break the laws of ethics. Moreover, additional knowledge will not show that something which I took to be intrinsically evil is not intrinsically evil; at the most it will only show that something which is intrinsically evil is a causal condition of something else which is intrinsically good, or that it is a constituent of a whole which is intrinsically good in spite of the intrinsic badness of this part of it. There is thus no parallel at all between the two cases, so far as I can see.

(ii) There is then not the slightest inconsistency in the position of a pure mathematician, *e.g.*, who believes that all apparent contradictions in mathematics can be resolved and also believes that the world is very bad or not very good. But Professor Taylor was not really considering the case of a pure mathematician. He was considering the ordinary natural scientist; and here his argument has much more plausibility. The intelligibility of the existent world does imply that it and every part of it obeys the laws of logic; but it requires more than this. Nature might obey the laws of logic; but, unless at least two further conditions were fulfilled, it would still be an unintelligible chaos to the scientific investigator. The first condition is that changes shall be subject to general laws, such as the laws of motion, gravitation, etc. This is in no way implied by the fact that nature obeys the laws of logic. But this is not enough. Nature might obey the laws of logic, and every change in the existent might be subject to general laws, and yet nature might be utterly unintelligible. The laws might be too numerous or too complex for us to unravel; they might be such that it was practically impossible for us to isolate any one phenomenon from all the rest even to a first degree of approximation; or again, our situation in nature might be so unfortunate that our sensations came to us in such an order that they failed to reveal the laws which really are present in nature. The scientist who assumes that nature is and will always remain intelligible must therefore assume that nature obeys other laws in addition to those of logic; that these are of such a kind that we shall be able to disentangle them if we try patiently; and that we are not fixed in such an exceptional corner of nature or so badly provided with sense-organs that all our efforts will be vain. These assumptions are not self-evident, like the laws of logic ; and they cannot be proved by any known process of reasoning from any known set of premises which are self-evident. Let us call them "postulates", as contrasted with the laws of logic, which are "axioms".

Of these scientific postulates we may say (*a*) that they cannot be *dis*proved, any more than they can be proved ; and (*b*) that it is practically more advantageous to act as if we believed them than to act as if we disbelieved them. There is no *logical reason* for believing them, but there is a *practical motive* for acting as if we believed them. The practical motive of course is that, if we act on these postulates, we shall go on investigating ; and that if, and only if, we go on investigating, we may discover explanations of what is at present unintelligible. Now I suppose that the corresponding ethical postulate would be that our efforts to do what is right, to discover truth, and to create beautiful objects, have an effect which is *permanently* valuable. I think it is true to say that this (*a*) cannot be disproved, and (*b*) that most men are more likely to exercise themselves in valuable activities if they act as if they believed it than if they act as if they disbelieved it. There is (apart from the special empirical arguments which I reserve for the next chapter) no *logical reason* to believe this ethical postulate, but there is a *practical motive* for acting as if we believed it. It is thus in precisely the same logical position and in precisely the same practical position as the scientific postulate. So much I think we may grant to Professor Taylor.

What is the bearing of this admission on the question of human immortality ? It seems to me to have no direct bearing at all. It is desirable that men should act as if they believed that their efforts will have permanently valuable results. If Professor Taylor be right, the proposition : "Human efforts will have per-

manently valuable results" entails the proposition :
"Some human beings are immortal". All that follows
from this is that it is desirable that men should act as if
they believed a certain proposition which entails the
proposition that some men are immortal. It is plain
that this does not give us any reason to assert that some
men *are* immortal. It does not even justify us in saying
that it is desirable to act as if we believed that some
men are immortal. It may be desirable to act as if we
believed p, and p may in fact entail q ; but it might be
highly desirable that men should ignore this implication.
It is one thing to say that it is desirable to act as if we
believed p ; and it is another thing to say that it is
desirable to act as if we believed both "p" and "p
entails q". And the second does not follow from the
first, even if p does in fact entail q.

All that Professor Taylor's argument justifies us in
asserting is a certain proposition about practical politics.
If people do not *believe* that their efforts will produce
permanently valuable results, or if they do believe something which is inconsistent with this, there is a danger
that they will cease to *act* as if they believed that their
efforts will produce permanently valuable results. And
this will be very unfortunate. Now, if Professor Taylor
be right, those who believe that all men are mortal are
believing something which is inconsistent with the proposition that their efforts will have permanently valuable
results. And of course there is a danger that they may
come to see this ; and may thus cease to *believe* that
their efforts will have permanently valuable results, and
finally cease to *act* as if they believed this. It follows
from this that it would probably be wise for the State to
adopt the immortality of the soul as a fundamental
"myth", and not to allow it to be publicly questioned.
I wholly agree with Plato in thinking that human
society requires to be founded on certain "myths",
which are not self-evident and cannot be proved ; and
that the State is within its rights in forbidding all public

discussion of the truth of these "myths". And I think it is quite possible that the doctrine of human immortality (whether it be in fact true or false) is one of these socially valuable "myths" which the State ought to remove from the arena of public discussion. This of course has no bearing whatever on the question whether the philosopher in his study ought to believe the doctrine of human immortality. He ought only to believe what is either self-evident, or capable of certain or probable proof, or verifiable by sensible or introspective perception.

I have suggested that the view that nature is "intelligible", in the sense in which the natural scientist believes this, is in precisely the same logical and practical position as the view that our efforts can produce results of permanent value. And I have suggested that it is arguable that the State ought to propagate and defend such "myths" as are needed to support the latter belief. Ought I in consistency to suggest that the State should propagate and defend the scientist's "myth" also? I do not think so. In the first place, no one of any influence attacks the scientist's "myth". Secondly, the practical success of the scientific postulate up to the present is much more obvious to the general public than the practical success of the ethical postulate. This of course is not *really* any logical ground for *believing* the scientist's postulate. But it is commonly thought to be so. Hence most people believe that the scientist's postulate is continually strengthened by experience. So long as this logical fallacy is commonly accepted as a truth there is no danger that people will cease to believe the scientist's postulate, and therefore there is no danger that they will cease to act on it. Hence there is no need for the State to take any special precautions in favour of this particular "myth".

Conclusion. The upshot of the matter is that I feel no confidence that Professor Taylor has produced any ground whatever for believing in human immortality. It does not of course follow that there *could* not be a valid ethical argument to prove that some men at least are not mortal. But if, as I think, Professor Taylor has failed to produce one, I should be very much surprised if anyone else were more successful. And, until someone does it to my satisfaction, I shall venture to doubt whether it can be done.

CHAPTER XII

Empirical Arguments for Human Survival

I MUST begin by saying exactly what I do and what I do not propose to discuss in this Chapter. I do not propose to discuss in any detail the special alleged facts (such as the Cross-correspondences in automatic writings) on which empirical arguments for human survival have been based. This is an extremely technical question which must be left to experts and would be out of place in a philosophical book. I do presuppose that the careful work of the Society for Psychical Research has elicited a mass of facts which may fairly be called "supernormal", in the sense that they cannot, if genuine, be explained on the usual assumptions of science and common-sense about the nature and powers of the human mind. And I do assume that a great many of the facts that come up to the extremely high standard of evidence required by the Society are "genuine", in the sense that they have been correctly reported and that they are not simply due to fraud or self-deception. I assume this on the basis of a fairly careful study of the literature; of a knowledge of the kind of persons who have controlled the policy of the Society and taken part in its investigations; and of some investigations of my own. I have, in fact, exactly the same kind of grounds for assuming the existence of genuinely supernormal phenomena as I have for assuming the existence of certain rare physical phenomena which are difficult to reproduce to order, and of certain rare diseases which competent doctors have described. I accept them on a mixed basis of authority and personal experience; and my authority is of the same kind and carries the same weight as the authority on which I accept the rarer and obscurer kinds of physical and medical phenomena as genuine. I do not think it is necessary to argue this point, because I have always found that those who deny it have not carefully read the relevant literature, have conducted very few careful investigations for themselves, and are ignorant of the intellectual calibre and the scrupulous accuracy of such men as Sidgwick, Gurney, and Podmore (to mention only the names of those who are no longer with us). Whenever we are told that "Science *proves* so-and-so to be impossible" we must remember that this is merely a rhetorical form of "Professor X and most of his colleagues *assert* so-and-so to be impossible". Those of us who have the privilege of meeting Professor X and his colleagues daily, and know from experience what kind of assertions they are capable of making when they leave their own subject, will, I am afraid, remain completely unmoved.

I take human survival then to be one hypothesis among others to account for certain reasonably well-established supernormal phenomena. The argument will be of the usual inverse-inductive type. Now, in such arguments we always have to consider the following points. (i) The antecedent probabilities of the various alternative hypotheses. And (ii) the completeness with which the various alternative hypotheses explain the special facts under consideration. If the antecedent probability of h_1 be very much less than that of h_2, then, even though h_1 explains the special facts better than h_2, it may be more prudent to try to make some modification of h_2 rather than to put much faith in h_1. I shall, therefore, begin by considering the antecedent probability of the hypothesis of human survival.

The Antecedent Probability of Human Survival. When we are considering the antecedent probability of a hypothesis put forward to explain certain special facts there are two points to be considered. (i) There is what may be called its "intrinsic probability". This depends on the structure of the proposition itself, and very little can be said about it here. (ii) There is the probability which the proposition has with respect to all known facts *other than* the special set of facts which it is put forward to explain. If p and q be two logically independent propositions, the proposition pq is intrinsically less probable than the proposition p. This is an instance of the first point. If a bishop falls down in the street it is antecedently more probable that this is due to a piece of orange-peel than to direct diabolic agency. For, although both hypotheses explain the observed fact equally well, the former fits in much better with the other facts which we know about the world than the latter does. This is an example of the latter point. I find myself quite unable to say much of importance about the intrinsic probabilities of human survival and its rival hypotheses. But there are a few logical points which are perhaps worth making. (1) Among alternative hypotheses to human survival which have been suggested we may mention (*a*) a very extended telepathy among living men, and (*b*) the action of non-human spirits who personate certain dead men. The second of these would seem to have the least intrinsic probability of the three hypotheses. For we have to postulate minds, for whose existence we have no other evidence, and to ascribe telepathic powers to them. The first hypothesis postulates no minds for whose existence we have not already independent evidence ; but it has to ascribe to them telepathic powers of such great extent that we have little or no independent evidence for their existence. The hypothesis of human survival perhaps makes the minimum assumption of the three ; since it merely postulates the continuance of something which we know independently to have existed, and it ascribes to this only such telepathic powers as we have reason to believe exist in embodied minds. (2) There is one very great logical difficulty which is inherent in the subject. We have not the least reason to believe that the hypotheses that have been put forward are exhaustive or even approximately so. Hence we have no ground for ascribing any very high antecedent probability to any one of them. We believe ourselves to know enough of the general structure of the material world to enable us to rule out all but a few hypotheses about the causation of a physical phenomenon. In such an unfamiliar region as we enter in doing Psychical Research we have not this advantage.

There is just one other remark that I will make before leaving this part of the subject. It is well known that many Roman Catholics and High Anglicans, not content with ascribing the phenomena to non-human spirits, ascribe them to "devils". Now I suppose that a "devil" means a non-human spirit who is morally much worse than the worst man. There appears to me to be absolutely nothing in the phenomena to warrant this hypothesis. (a) There is a certain amount of indecency in some automatic scripts. So there is in the writings of Petronius and in the conversation of many undergraduates; whilst Mr Gibbon informs us that "a learned prelate, now deceased, was fond of quoting . . . in conversation" a passage from Procopius about the Empress Theodora which the historian prudently "veils in the obscurity of a learned language". (b) Most spiritualistic communications which are not merely trivial consist of elevated, but to my mind "twaddling", ethico-religious "uplift". If they be the communications of devils it must be admitted that most devils who communicate are decorous to the verge of dulness; and that the aphorism "Heaven for the climate, but Hell for the company" stands in need of considerable modification. (c) It may be admitted that to personate a dead man and raise false hopes in his friends and relations would not be the mark of a very high morality. It would be a somewhat heartless practical joke.   But it is not necessary to be a devil in order to play heartless practical jokes; such things have been done before now by quite kindly but somewhat thoughtless undergraduates.   (*d*) It may be admitted that a certain number of weak-minded people go mentally and morally to the bad through excessive indulgence in spiritualistic séances.   The same may be said of excessive indulgence in alcohol or religion.   And a devil who chooses this particular method of leading men to damnation when there are so many more profitable alternatives open to him must be extremely incompetent at his own business.   (*e*) There is a certain amount of "roughness" and horse-play at some séances for physical phenomena; there is a great deal more after a bump-supper or at many political meetings. In fact, if we can judge of Hell from those denizens of it whom we meet, on this theory, at spiritualistic séances, we must suppose that it is very much like what I believe is called a "Pleasant Sunday Afternoon" at a Nonconformist chapel, enlivened by occasional bump-suppers.   Its nearest earthly analogy would probably be a Welsh University; and I should suppose that those who pass directly from the one institution to the other must often fail to notice the transition.   To sum up, from a fairly extensive reading of spiritualistic literature, and from a certain amount of personal experience of séances, I should say that the average "spirit" is morally no worse than the average Fellow of Trinity, though there is a very marked difference in the intelligence of the two.

The motives which make the "devil-theory" so popular in ecclesiastical circles are tolerably obvious. In the first place, there is the perfectly legitimate desire to frighten one's congregation away from dabbling in practices which are very unlikely to do good to any of them and very likely to do positive harm to many of them.   The second motive is probably just as strong, but is generally unrecognised or unadmitted.   This is the objection which the members, and especially the officials, of all close corporations have to non-members who claim to perform the same functions. The objection of the orthodox churchman, and particularly the orthodox clergyman, to the spiritualistic medium is the same kind of objection which doctors feel towards "bone-setters" and trade-unionists feel towards blacklegs. It is necessary to disguise this to oneself and to others; and for this purpose the "devil-theory" is very handy, just as doctors find it highly convenient to remind us of the deaths of patients under quacks and to forget that patients sometimes die under doctors.

I propose now to consider whether there are any facts other than the special phenomena dealt with by Psychical Research which make the hypothesis of human survival antecedently probable. Although, as I have said, I do not think that such special propositions as the survival of man fall within the range of proof or disproof by metaphysical arguments, I can see of course that the antecedent probability of human survival will be greatly affected by one's general metaphysical position. If materialism or epiphenomenalism were strict metaphysical truth, survival, though perhaps still abstractly possible, would be in the last degree unlikely. If mentalism, in one of its forms, were strictly true, survival would not indeed necessarily follow. Lotze and Mr Bradley were mentalists; but they held quite consistently that their systems did not necessitate human survival and that it is on the whole improbable. Still, mentalism is decidedly more favourable to human survival than is the view of the world which is taken by common-sense, or by non-philosophical scientists, or by dualistic philosophers. Idealism (which I distinguish from mentalism, though most idealists have in fact been mentalists) is still more favourable to survival. For I take it that the essence of idealism is to hold that what we regard as the "higher" characteristics, such as life and consciousness, are fundamental categories which apply to Reality as such and are not just special and probably transitory features of certain specially complicated and probably unstable parts of Reality. It is possible to be an Idealist and yet to regard human survival as false or highly improbable. This position was taken by Professor Bosanquet. But it must be admitted that idealism would favour the antecedent probability of survival.

It might seem then that, in order to determine the antecedent probability of survival, it would be necessary to make up one's mind between various rival systems of metaphysics. I am certainly not prepared to do this. But I think I have a fairly good excuse. On my view no general metaphysical system can be proved deductively by reasoning from *a priori* premises. Idealism and materialism are just attempts to synthesise all the known facts; and their respective probabilities can be decided only by their respective success in doing this. There is then, in my view, no possibility of *first* deciding between alternative metaphysical systems on general grounds and *then* taking the system which we have accepted as a fixed datum from which to estimate the antecedent probability of survival. The question whether we probably do or probably do not survive the death of our bodies is just the kind of question that has to be answered *before* we can decide (say) between idealism and materialism or epiphenomenalism. What we must do then is to discuss the antecedent probability of survival on data which are common to all men, including the upholders of rival systems of metaphysics. And this means that we must consider the arguments for or against human survival which may be drawn from the constitution of the world as it presents itself to enlightened common-sense; for this is the common basis from which all the rival systems start. If we do this we may consistently use our result as one means of deciding tentatively between the various rival systems.

Now, on the face of it, the most striking feature of the world as we know it in daily life is, for our purpose, that it does not present the faintest trace of evidence for survival. Continued action is a criterion of the continued existence of any substance; and this is conspicuously lacking after death. The body ceases to give the characteristic responses, and very soon it decays and loses even its characteristic shape and appearance. Hence the only evidence that we ever had for the existence of a man's mind has ceased abruptly; and, apart from the alleged facts investigated by Psychical Research, it has ceased for ever so far as our experience goes. We do indeed often believe in the continued existence of substances in spite of long periods during which neither we nor anyone else are aware of them by any of their usual signs. *E.g.*, we believe that silver continues to exist though it be dissolved in nitric acid and kept for years as silver-nitrate. But in such cases we have reason to believe that at any moment we could restore a substance having the properties of the silver which we dissolved, and connected with it by identity of mass and continuity of spatial positions. Every such factor making for belief in the continued existence of dead men is lacking in our ordinary experience; and thus such a belief seems to have nothing whatever in its favour, and to be from a logical point of view a bare unmotived possibility.

Yet of course, as a matter of history, this has seldom seriously militated against the belief in survival. Such a belief has been all but universal. Now, on the one hand, the mere universality of a belief is no proof of its truth. On the other hand, the fact that a belief has been widely held by ignorant and primitive men is no proof of its falsehood. Confronted then by a strong belief which seems to have arisen and persisted in spite of complete lack of evidence in its favour, we must consider what factors may have caused the belief, and whether any of them are *reasons* as well as *causes*.

A primitive man would certainly not accept the statement that there is no evidence in ordinary experience
for survival. He would claim to know of dozens of
cases of men seen and heard after death; and he might
even think that he had met with such cases in his own
experience. Now, without prejudice to the genuineness
of abnormal phenomena in general or to the possibility
that they occasionally happen among savages, we may
be quite certain that in most cases the primitive man is
mistaken in thinking that there is any need to assume
the continued existence of the dead to explain the phenomena which he would regard as evidence for survival.
We may divide such phenomena into two classes. The
first consists of those which are capable of a perfectly
normal explanation; the second of those which would
now be dealt with by Psychical Research. There is no
reason to suppose that the latter will be more numerous
or striking among savages than among civilised men.
The first group provides no evidence at all for survival,
since the facts have simply been misinterpreted. The
second, supposing it to exist, contains no evidence
antecedent to Psychical Research; since, by hypothesis,
it consists of precisely those phenomena which would
now be treated by that science. Hence the primitive
man had simply more *causes*, but no better *reasons*, for a
belief in survival than we have; but a belief irrationally
caused in him may have been handed on to us.

No doubt experiences of fainting and sleeping helped
the belief in survival. In these conditions the mind
gives no external manifestations of its existence, and the
body in many ways resembles a corpse. Yet consciousness returns; and, if we remember our dreams, we
remember that it was not really absent when our bodies
were giving no external signs of its existence. What
more natural then than to suppose that at these times
the mind leaves the body for a while and follows its
own adventures, and that at death it leaves the body
for good? But the differences between sleep and death

make it impossible to accept this undoubted cause of a belief in survival as a valid reason in its favour. If, after dissolving a bit of silver several times in nitric acid and getting it back again, we one day dissolved it in something else and found that no efforts of ours could restore anything with the properties of silver, the inference would be obvious. It was reasonable to think that the silver survived the nitric acid treatment, because it could be restored ; it would not be reasonable to conclude from this that it also survived the treatment after which nothing like it can be again obtained. If we choose to assume that it still exists, our assumption is an unmotived one. So once more we have a cause of belief which is not a reason for belief.

Probably neither of the above-mentioned causes would have sufficed to produce an almost universal belief in survival. Both are to be regarded as interpretations of real or supposed facts in terms of this belief rather than as the original causes of it. The truth is that we have the greatest difficulty in actually envisaging the cessation of our own conscious life. It is easy enough to think of anyone else as having really ceased to exist ; but it is almost impossible to give more than a cold intellectual assent to the same proposition about oneself. In making a will, e.g., containing elaborate provisions for the disposal of one's property after death, it is almost impossible (unless my experience be quite exceptional) not to think of oneself as going to be conscious and able to oversee the working of one's own bequests. I at least can continually catch myself in this attitude, and I should imagine it to be quite common even among people who are intellectually persuaded of their future extinction.

Ought we to attach any weight to this primitive belief which nearly every one has in his own survival? The mere fact that it is held without reasons is no conclusive objection to it ; for, unless some propositions can be known to be true without reasons, no proposition can be known to be true for reasons. We must, therefore, consider the belief on its merits without prejudice. Now it seems perfectly clear that it is not a self-evident proposition like an axiom, which becomes more certain the more carefully we inspect it. Nor can it be regarded as a postulate; *i.e.*, as a proposition which, though not self-evident and incapable of either proof or disproof by experience, has to be assumed in order to organise experience and to furnish a motive for research. Certain propositions which we use in induction seem to me to be postulates in this sense; the proposition that John Jones will survive the death of his body seems to me to be quite plainly nothing of the kind. In fact I think that the belief represents nothing more profound than an easily explicable limit of our powers of imagination. Naturally all my experience of myself has been of myself as conscious and active. There have indeed been gaps during dreamless sleep or fainting fits, but consciousness has revived and the gaps have been bridged by memory. Again, at every moment I have been obliged for practical purposes to think of myself as going to exist at later moments; it is therefore a breach with the mental habits of a lifetime to envisage a moment after which the series of my conscious states shall have finally ended. This practical difficulty, due to habit, seems the sole and sufficient explanation of our primitive belief in our own indefinite continuance; and it obviously provides no evidence for the truth of that belief.

I think then that we must conclude that a mere contemplation of the world as it appears in ordinary experience furnishes no trace of support for the belief in survival. Ought we to hold that the absence of all evidence *for* constitutes evidence *against?* This is a somewhat delicate question. Sometimes the absence of evidence for a proposition makes strongly against it, and sometimes it does not. If I look carefully round a room and, seeing no one, say: "There is no one in the room", my evidence is purely negative; but it is almost conclusive against the proposition: "There is someone in the room ". But the fact that I did not see a tuberculosis bacillus in the room would be quite irrelevant to the question whether there was one there. Finding no evidence for a proposition is evidence against it only if the proposition be such that, if it were true, there ought to be some observable evidence for it.

Now the proposition : "Some men survive the death of their bodies " is not precisely in the position of either of the two quoted above. I know enough about human bodies and about tuberculosis bacilli to be sure that one of the former could hardly be present in a room without my finding it, but that one of the latter could not be seen by the naked eye even if it were present. I know very much less about the conditions under which one human spirit can make its presence known to another ; but I do know something about it. I am a human spirit connected with a body, and all other spirits of whose existence I am certain are in the same position. Setting aside the phenomena treated by Psychical Research, I know that one such spirit can make its presence known to another only by moving its own body, thence agitating the air or the ether, and thence affecting another human body. My friend dies ; I remain alive and connected with my body. Communication with me, therefore, presumably requires the same complex and roundabout series of material changes as before. Its very complexity and indirectness make it not unlikely that, even if my friend has survived, some necessary link in this mechanism will have broken down. Hence the absence of evidence for his survival cannot be regarded logically as very strong evidence against it.

The present position, therefore, is that at the level of ordinary experience there is not the faintest trace of evidence for survival, though there is a pretty general belief in it. The causes of this belief have been enumerated and seen not to be reasons. But the absence of evidence for the belief cannot be taken as strong evidence against it, in view of what we know about the means by which embodied human spirits have to communicate with each other.

Is there at this level any *positive* evidence *against* survival? I think that there are two sets of facts which impress common-sense and are interpreted in this direction. One is the apparently haphazard way in which men are born and die. Human beings are constantly brought into the world thoughtlessly and by mistake; many children live for a few minutes or hours and then die; many are born idiotic. The general impression produced is that the claim to permanence for creatures whose earthly lives begin and end in these trivial ways is somewhat ridiculous. An unwanted child is produced, let us say, in a drunken orgy; and in six weeks dies of neglect or is killed by its mother. Does it seem likely that a being whose earthly career is started and stopped by such causes is a permanent and indestructible part of the universe, or indeed that it survives the death of its body at all?

The second fact which is felt to bear in the same direction is the continuity between men and animals. The bodies of each begin and cease to be animated by minds through precisely similar physical and physiological causes. No doubt the mind of any living man differs, not merely quantitatively, but also qualitatively from that of any living animal; still the most primitive men can hardly have differed appreciably from the highest animals in their mental endowments. Did *Pithecanthropus erectus* and does every Australian aborigine survive the death of his body? If they do, have not the higher animals almost an equal claim? And, if you grant this for cats and monkeys, will you not be forced in the end to grant it for lice and earwigs? If, on the other hand, you deny that any animal survives, on the ground that their minds are not complex or important enough to be permanent factors in the universe, how can you be sure that any man yet born has possessed a mind complex and important enough for survival? The two facts quoted above do, I am sure, exert a considerable influence against the view that men survive the death of their bodies. I am conscious that they affect me personally more than any others. But the question remains: "Have they any logical right to exert this influence?"

I am inclined to think on reflection that the first argument is wholly fallacious. It really involves the illegitimate introduction of a judgment of value into a question of fact. And the judgment of value is itself a rather superficial one. It is thought that, because the occasioning causes of birth and death are often trivial, therefore what seems to begin with birth and to end with death cannot be important enough to survive. But (a) you cannot argue from the triviality of a cause to the impermanence of its effect. (b) The cause is trivial only in the irrelevant ethical sense that it does not involve a considered and deliberate choice by a virtuous human being. There is really no logical transition from: "This is caused by the careless or criminal action or a human being" to: "This is the kind of thing whose existence is transitory". (c) When we say that the cause is trivial we make the common mistake of taking for *the* cause some necessary cause-factor which happens to be specially noticeable or of special practical interest. The complete cause of the birth of a child or the death of a man must be of almost unthinkable complexity, whether the child be begotten or the man be killed carelessly or with deliberate forethought. This is true even if we confine ourselves to the material conditions; and we are not really in a position to say that the *complete* conditions of so singular an event as the manifestation of a new mind through a new body are contained in the material world.

The second argument is of course of a well-known general type. It tries to show by continuity of cases that, if a man asserts one proposition, he ought in consistency not to deny a certain other proposition which he would like to deny. Arguments of this kind can be met in one of two ways. (1) We may point out that an argument from continuity is reversible, and that the direction in which one turns it is arbitrary. We might just as well argue by continuity from the supposed immortality of men to the immor_ tality of earwigs as from the supposed mortality of earwigs to the mortality of men. The actual direction in which the argument is used presupposes that we are *already* pretty certain that earwigs are mortal, and much more doubtful whether men are immortal. This no doubt is true. But it immediately raises the question : "Why are we practically certain that earwigs are mortal?" This question cannot be answered by considerations of continuity, but only by reflecting on the special peculiarities of earwigs. (2) When we raise this question two answers are possible. (*a*) We may find on reflection that we have no good reason for thinking that earwigs are unlikely to be immortal. In that case the argument from continuity to the case of men will prove nothing. Or (*b*) we may find that those characteristics of earwigs which make it very unlikely that they are immortal are obviously not present in men. In that case the argument from continuity will also prove nothing about men. At most it will show that it is difficult for us to say with confidence about certain intermediate forms of living being whether they are likely to be mortal or not. Let us then consider the question why we think it very unlikely that earwigs should be immortal ; and let us also consider whether the reasons, whatever they may be, apply to men also.

In the first place it might be said that an earwig's mind has very little value, and therefore it is unworthy to be a permanent factor in the universe. And it might be argued that it is therefore unlikely to survive. But (*a*) this would be an ethical argument of a kind which we have already dismissed. And (*b*), even if it were valid, it is obvious that most human minds are enormously more valuable than the mind of any earwig; so that it would not be inconsistent to think it likely that human minds are immortal and unlikely that the minds of earwigs are so. All that we should be entitled to say is (a) that it is not certain even that any human mind is valuable enough to be immortal; and (b) that, if it were certain, there would be intermediate cases, e.g., cats, about which the probabilities are about equally balanced.

But the differences between the minds of men and those of the lower animals are never *mere* differences of value. Presumably an earwig's mind has very little unity, complexity, or comprehensiveness. Now it is arguable that such a very simple mind is not very likely to survive bodily death. But (a) I do not think that what we know of nature suggests any straightforward connexion between unity and complexity on the one hand and stability on the other. Both the very simple and the highly comprehensive seem to be fairly stable, though for different reasons. The very simple, like the electron, is stable because of its comparative indifference to changes in external conditions. The highly unified and comprehensive complex, like the solar system, tends to be stable because it contains so much within itself that there is little left over to disturb it. It is therefore quite in accordance with what we know of the order of nature to suppose that the simplicity of the earwig's mind gives it a particularly good chance of survival. (b) Suppose, on the other hand, that we do hold that the simplicity of the earwig's mind makes it very unlikely to survive. Then we must admit that the human mind is enormously less simple and more comprehensive and highly unified. Hence it would be perfectly consistent to hold that the human mind is likely to survive because of its unity and comprehensiveness and that the earwig's mind is unlikely to survive because of its simplicity and poverty of content. Thus on neither alternative does the argument from continuity make it unreasonable to hold that the human mind is likely to survive. As before, all that we can legitimately conclude from the argument from continuity is (*a*) that it is uncertain whether any human mind even is complex and comprehensive enough to survive ; and (*b*) that, if it were certain, there would be cases of intermediate complexity, *e.g.*, cats, about which the probabilities would be nearly equally balanced.

Again, some people no doubt shrink from admitting the possibility of survival to the lower animals out of horror at the immense number of minds which there would be if none, even of the lowest kind, died with the death of their bodies. This shrinking from mere numerical vastness seems to me to be childish. We have no reason to suppose that the universe is conducted in accordance with the Law of Parsimony ; and it may well be that the world exhibits a profusion in the item of minds which would horrify the inhabitants of Aberdeen. Thus I do not think that this consideration makes it specially improbable that earwigs should be immortal.

Lastly, the following argument might be used to suggest that the minds of the lower animals are very unlikely to survive the death of their bodies. The characteristic activities and experiences of animals seem to be specially and exclusively directed to preserving their own lives and those of their offspring. If we judge living things teleologically (and, in practice, it is hard to avoid doing this) it does seem that an animal accomplishes "all that is in it" when it succeeds in keeping itself alive long enough to produce young and to start them in the world. It is hard to see what "purpose" would be served by the individual survival of an earwig which dies at a reasonable age after bringing up a family of little earwigs. I do not know what weight to attach to such an argument as this. The principle of judging living beings and their parts in terms of a supposed "purpose for which they were made" is undoubtedly valuable as an heuristic method ; and it is difficult to suppose that it does not in some way accord with the facts. But fortunately it is not necessary for our purpose to decide on the legitimacy of such considerations. For the position is this. (*a*) If it be not valid, the argument to show that earwigs are very unlikely to survive falls to the ground ; and with it goes the argument from continuity to the probable mortality of human beings. (*b*) If, on the other hand, it be valid, the argument from continuity equally breaks down in another way. For it does seem as if human minds had many powers and faculties which are not merely directed to preserving the life of the individual and the species ; and that the continued existence of certain human minds after the death of their bodies would "answer the purpose for which they seem to be made" in a way in which the continued existence of an individual earwig would not. Hence it would be perfectly consistent to hold, on the basis of this argument, that earwigs are most unlikely to be immortal and that men are quite likely to be immortal. As usual, the argument from continuity would raise a doubt only about certain intermediate cases, such as cats and dogs, where the probabilities might be about equally balanced.

To sum up. The argument from continuity makes against the probability of human survival only on two conditions. (1) There must be some reason (and not a mere prejudice) for thinking that the survival of the lower animals is very improbable. And (2) this reason must not be the presence of some characteristic in the lower animals which differentiates them sharply from human beings. For, if our only reason for thinking it very unlikely that earwigs will survive be some characteristic in which earwigs differ profoundly from men, it will be perfectly consistent to think it likely that men will survive and that earwigs will not. The existence of a continuous series of intermediate forms between earwigs and men will prove nothing except that there are certain intermediate cases in which the probabilities for and against survival are about equally balanced. And there would not be the least trace of inconsistency in the position of a man who should be practically certain that earwigs are mortal and human beings immortal but should be quite unable to make up his mind about cats or kangaroos. Now, so far as I can see, these two conditions are never both fulfilled. The alleged reasons for thinking it very unlikely that earwigs are immortal either are no reasons at all or they obviously depend on characteristics in which human beings and earwigs differ profoundly. Hence I doubt whether the argument against the probability of human survival, drawn from the continuous series of living forms between men and the lowest animals, has any logical validity. The world then, as it presents itself to common-sense and everyday experience, offers no positive reasons for and no positive reasons against human survival. The only reason against it is the utter absence of all reasons for it; and we have seen that this is not a strong argument in the present case. Let us now enquire whether the more detailed investigations of science provide us with any grounds for deciding one way or the other.

Science on the whole does not reverse, but merely amplifies and elaborates, the views of common-sense on the connexion of body and mind. We already knew that body and mind were intimately connected, and that injury to the former may gravely modify or to all appearance destroy the latter. The additional information gained from science may be summed up as follows. (i) More detailed knowledge has been got of the correlation between injuries to particular regions of the brain and defects in certain departments of mental life. Connected with this is the knowledge that many mental processes, which seem to common-sense to be almost independent of the body, have bodily correlates. (ii) We have gained the surprising information that, in spite of the apparent interaction of body and mind, the body and its material surroundings form a closed energetic system from the point of view of the Conservation of Energy. (iii) We know more about the detailed structure and general plan of the brain and nervous system. What bearing has all this on the probability of survival? We find bodies without minds; we never find minds without bodies. When we do find minds we always find a close correlation between their processes and those of their bodies. This, it is argued, strongly suggests that minds depend for their *existence* on bodies; in which case, though survival may still be abstractly possible, it is to the last degree unlikely. At death there takes place completely and permanently a process of bodily destruction which, when it occurs partially and temporarily, carries with it the destruction of part of our mental life. The inference seems only too obvious. I think it is fair to say that our ordinary scientific knowledge of the relation of body to mind most strongly suggests epiphenomenalism, though it does not necessitate it; and that epiphenomenalism is most unfavourable to the hypothesis of human survival.

It is, however, possible to put forward other theories about the mind and its relation to the body, which are consistent with ordinary experience and with scientific knowledge and are less unfavourable to survival than epiphenomenalism. I will call the first of these the "Instrumental Theory."

The Instrumental Theory.—We must begin by drawing a distinction between the existence of a mind and its manifestation to other minds. On the Instrumental Theory the mind is a substance which is existentially independent of the body. It may have existed before the body began, and it may exist after the body is destroyed. For a time it is intimately connected with a certain body; and at such times it can get information about other things only by means of its body and can act on other things only by first moving its body. If the body be injured the mind may be cut off from certain sources of information about other things, and it may be prevented from expressing itself in certain ways; but otherwise it may be uninjured. It is certain that such a theory as this is consistent with a good many of the facts which are commonly held to prove the existential dependence of mind on body. Nevertheless, I think that, in this crude form, it cannot be maintained. Let us take the case of a man who is injured in a certain part of his brain, and for the time loses his power to remember certain events. It can hardly be maintained that, in any literal sense, he still remembers the events; and that all that has been damaged is his power of manifesting this knowledge to others by speech or writing. The latter case does sometimes arise, and it seems introspectively quite different from the former to the patient himself. Again, if the patient recovers these lost memories after a while, it seems to him that a change has taken place in the contents of his mind, and not merely a change in his ability to express to others what was going on in his mind before. We must suppose then that in such cases something more than the power to manifest one's knowledge to others has been injured. The only other alternative is to suppose that all such patients are lying and asserting that they cannot remember certain things which they actually are remembering. If we reject this very violent alternative we must hold that in some cases an injury to the brain does actually deprive the mind of the power to remember certain events which it formerly could remember. Could a supporter of the Instrumental Theory square the facts with his view? He might say that the general power of remembering is unchanged; and assert that all that has happened is that the injury to the body has prevented certain past events from being objects of memory, as blindfolding a man would prevent certain present objects from being perceived. But in that case the mind is reduced to something which has merely certain very general capacities, and any particular exercise of these powers seems to depend on the body.

Let us now take another example. We will suppose that a man is injured in the head; that before the injury he was of a cheerful and benevolent disposition; and that after the injury he is morose and liable to attacks of homicidal mania. Are we to say that the injury has made no difference to his mind; that this remains cheerful and benevolent; but that the change in his brain compels him to express his cheerfulness by scowling and his benevolence by attacking other people with carving-knives? This is scarcely plausible. And, if we accept it, we shall not be able to stop at this point. We shall have to conclude that it is impossible to tell what the character of anyone's mind really is. Lifelong philanthropists may be inwardly boiling with malice which some peculiar kink in their brains and nervous systems compels them to express by pensioning their poor relations and giving pennies to crossing-sweepers. Once more, the mind will be reduced to something with no definite traits of its own, such as benevolence or peevishness, but merely with certain very general powers to express itself in various ways according to the body with which it is provided. It seems to me that what is left of the mind when we try to square the Instrumental Theory with the known facts is so abstract and indefinite that it does not deserve to be called a "mind".

The Compound Theory.—This suggests a modification of the Instrumental Theory, which I will call the "Compound Theory". Might not what we know as a "mind" be a compound of two factors, neither of which separately has the characteristic properties of a mind, just as salt is a compound of two substances, neither of which by itself has the characteristic properties of salt? Let us call one of these constituents the "psychic factor" and the other the "bodily factor".

The psychic factor would be like some chemical element which has never been isolated ; and the characteristics of a mind would depend jointly on those of the psychic factor and on those of the material organism with which it is united.   This would allow of all the correlation between mind and body which could ever be discovered, and at the same time it is not open to the objections which I have pointed out in the ordinary form of the Instrumental Theory.   Moreover, it is in accord with many facts which we know about other departments of nature.   We know that chemical compounds have properties which cannot be deduced from those which their elements display in isolation or in other compounds.   And yet the properties of these compounds are wholly dependent on those of their elements, in the sense that, given such elements in such relations, a compound necessarily arises with such and such properties.   These properties do not belong to either of the elements, but only to the compound as a whole.   Now this does seem to accord fairly well with what we know about minds when we reflect upon them. On the one hand, it seems a mistake to ascribe perception, reasoning, anger, love, etc., to a mere body. On the other hand, as we have seen, it is almost equally difficult to ascribe them to what is left when the bodily factor is ignored.   Thus the mind, as commonly conceived, does look as if it were a compound of two factors neither of which separately is a mind.   And it does look as if specifically mental characteristics belonged only to this compound substance.

It would be unwise to press the analogy to chemical compounds too far.   So far as we know, when two chemical elements are united to form a chemical compound no permanent change is produced in the properties of either.   It would be rash to assume that this is also true when a psychic factor is united with a bodily organism so as to give a mind.   Both factors may be permanently affected by this union ; so that, if they become separated again and continue to exist, their properties are characteristically different from what they were when the two first became connected with each other. Of course many different views would be antecedently possible about the supposed psychic factor. At one extreme would be the view that there is only one psychic factor for all minds. Different minds would then be compounds of this one psychic factor with different brains and nervous systems. Such a view would bear some analogy to Green's theory of the one Eternal Consciousness and the many animal organisms. But the psychic factor on our view would have no claim to be called a "Consciousness"; it would not perform those feats of relating and unifying sense-data which Green ascribed to it ; and there is no reason to suppose that it would deserve honorific titles like "eternal", or be an appropriate object for those religious emotions which Green felt towards it. At the opposite extreme would be the view that there is a different psychic factor for each different mind. Then the question could be raised whether some or all of them can exist out of combination with organisms; whether some one psychic factor can combine successively with a series of different organisms to give a series of different minds; and so on. (It may be remarked that the view that the psychic factor cannot exist out of combination with organisms, and yet that the same psychic factor can be combined with a series of successive organisms, has a pretty close analogy to certain chemical facts. There are groups, such as NH_4, CH_3, etc., which are incapable of more than the most transitory independent existence. Yet one such group may pass successively from one combination to another, and may impart certain characteristic properties to each of these compounds.) Finally, there is an intermediate possibility for which there might be a good deal to be said. It might be suggested that the marked individuality of human minds indicates that there is a different psychic factor as well as a different bodily organism to each co-existing human mind. On the other hand, it might be held that there is only one psychic factor for the whole species of earwigs ; and that the very trivial differences between the mind of one earwig and another are due simply to differences in their bodily organisms. It is obvious that only empirical evidence of a very special kind could help us to decide between these alternatives, even if we accepted the Compound Theory in its main outlines.

Granted that the Compound Theory is consistent with all the facts which are commonly held to prove the existential dependence of mind on body, and granted that it is in better accord with the facts than the Instrumental Theory, is there any positive evidence for it? We have a set of facts which point to the dependence of mind on body. One explanation is that mind depends on nothing but body, *i.e.*, that mental events either *are* also bodily events, or that at any rate they are all *caused* wholly by bodily events and do not in turn affect either each other or the body. The present explanation is that the mind is a compound of the body and something else, and that mental events and mental characteristics belong to this compound substance and not to its separate constituents. Both explanations fit all the normal facts equally well. But the Compound Theory is more complex than the Epiphenomenal Theory, and it would be foolish to accept it unless there were some facts which it explains and which the Epiphenomenalist Theory does not. Now I do not think that there is anything in the normal phenomena which requires us to suppose that a mind depends for its existence and functioning on anything but the body and its processes. We must therefore turn to the abnormal phenomena.

Abnormal and Supernormal Phenomena. I think that it is very important to begin by drawing a distinction which is too commonly neglected, viz., the distinction between *Survival* and mere *Persistence*. It seems to me that a great many of the phenomena which are held to point to the survival of particular human minds point only to the persistence of some factor which was a constituent of a human mind. We are not justified in saying that the mind of John Jones has survived the death of his body unless we have reason to believe that there is still a continuous stream of conscious mental states which may be said to be "further experiences of John Jones". We must suppose that this contains conations as well as cognitions, that it puts ends before itself and tries to realise them, and that it feels elation or disappointment according to its success or failure in doing so. No doubt such a stream of consciousness would be impossible unless past experiences modified later experiences; and no doubt we should not say that John Jones had survived unless he were able to remember some events in his life in the body. But these mnemic phenomena, though necessary to survival, are certainly not by themselves sufficient to constitute survival. If they occur alone, without the continuous stream of conscious cognitions, conations, and feelings, all that we have a right to say is that "some constituent of the mind of John Jones has persisted" and not that "John Jones has survived".

Now it seems to me that the vast majority of mediumistic phenomena which are taken to suggest survival really suggest only persistence. The additional notion of survival is read into them because in our ordinary experience we do not find memories without a pretty continuous stream of consciousness filling the gaps between the memory and the event remembered. The cases that I have in mind are these. A medium goes into a trance. He is then supposed either to be in contact with the spirit of some dead man, or in rarer cases to be directly possessed by such a spirit. In either case he sometimes mentions incidents in the past life of the supposed communicator which are unknown to the sitter and can afterwards be verified. And in the latter case he sometimes exhibits in a very remarkable way some of the mannerisms and even the verbal intonations of the supposed communicator. The evidence for such phenomena is, in my opinion, good enough to make them worth serious consideration by philosophers. Now the ordinary spiritualist interprets such phenomena in terms of the Instrumental Theory; he supposes that a human mind is existentially independent of its body and just uses it as an instrument; that it leaves its body at death, goes on living its own life, and from time to time uses a medium's body for purposes of communication.

But it seems to me that, apart from the intrinsic difficulties of the Instrumental Theory, the Compound Theory fits these supernormal phenomena on the whole much better. One thing which is highly characteristic of the communications of alleged dead men is their singular reticence about their present life, occupations, and surroundings. Such observations as are made by entranced mediums on these subjects seem to me to be extraordinarily silly, and to have every appearance of being merely the crude beliefs about the spiritual world which are current in mediumistic circles. Yet this nonsense is at times mixed up with traits which are highly characteristic of the supposed communicator, and with bits of detailed information about his past life which can afterwards be verified. Now, on the Compound Theory, we can suppose that the psychic factor may persist for a time at least after the destruction of the organism with which it was united to form the compound called "John Jones's mind". This psychic factor is not itself a mind, but it may carry modifications due to experiences which happened to John Jones while he was alive. And it may become temporarily united with the organism of an entranced medium. If so, a little temporary "mind" (a "mind-kin", if I may use that expression) will be formed.

Since this mindkin will contain the same psychic factor as the mind of John Jones it will not be surprising if it displays some traits characteristic of John Jones, and some memories of events in his earthly life. Since the bodily factor of this mindkin is the medium's organism, which is adapted to the medium's psychic factor and not to John Jones's, it will not be surprising if it shows many traits which are characteristic of the medium. And the reason why we can get no information about the present life and experiences of John Jones is that no such mind is existing at all. When the medium is entranced the psychic factor which was a constituent of John Jones's mind forms with the medium's body a mindkin which lasts just as long as the medium remains in trance. At intermediate times, on this view, all that exists is this psychic factor; and this by itself is no more a mind than John Jones's corpse is a mind. To explain the positive part of the phenomena it is plausible to suppose that *something* has persisted, and that this something was an integral part of John Jones's mind. But it is an enormous jump from this to the conclusion that John Jones's mind has survived the death of his body. And the negative part of the phenomena strongly suggests that what has persisted is not a mind, but is at most something which in combination with a suitable organism is capable of producing a mind.

Some of the facts of multiple personality would also be neatly explained by the Compound Theory. Of course mediumistic phenomena are, in the first instance, cases of multiple personality. The peculiarity of them is that one of the personalities professes either to *be* a certain deceased human being, or more usually only to be in communication with one; and that, in some cases, there appear certain characteristic traits of this dead man, or knowledge is shown of some minute details in his past life. But ordinary multiple personality, such as that of the Beauchamp case, might be explained by supposing that the same organism can have two different psychic factors connected with it. We should then expect to find two minds having certain characteristic differences, and yet having a good deal more in common than two minds which differ in their organisms as well as in their psychic factors. Two personalities might be compared to two chemical compounds with one element in common, such as silver chloride and silver bromide ; whilst two ordinary minds might be compared (say) to silver chloride and lead nitrate. I do not think, however, that ordinary multiple personality positively requires the Compound Theory for its explanation. We can never be sure that the organism is in precisely the same state when one personality is in control as it is when the other is in control. Hence it is possible that the facts could be explained on a purely epiphenomenalist theory. It is the apparent persistence of certain traces and dispositions after the destruction of the organism which seems to demand for its explanation something more than epiphenomenalism, and seems to suggest *at least* something like the Compound Theory.

We must now consider (*a*) whether there are any facts which require something *more* than the Compound Theory to explain them ; and (*b*) whether the facts that I have already mentioned could be explained with something *less* than the Compound Theory. It seems to me that we should have grounds for postulating the *survival* of a *mind*, and not the mere persistence of a psychic factor, if and only if the communications showed traces of an intention which persisted between the experiments and deliberately modified and controlled each in the light of those which had preceded it. Now it is alleged that there are signs of this deliberate intention in the Cross-Correspondences which the Society for Psychical Research has been investigating for many years. If all or most of these came up to the ideal type of a Cross-Correspondence, I think we should have to admit that it looks as if a single intelligent being were deliberately trying in an extremely ingenious way to produce evidence of its continuous existence. The ideal Cross-Correspondence would be of the following form. Suppose three automatic writers in different places produce automatic scripts over a series of years. Suppose that they do not communicate with each other, but send their scripts from time to time to an impartial authority for comparison. Suppose that A, B, and C in their scripts get statements which, taken separately, are fragmentary and unintelligible to them ; and suppose further that after such an unintelligible and fragmentary statement in A's script there comes an injunction to refer to what B and C are now writing or will shortly write or have written at some definite time in the past. Suppose that similar injunctions are found in B's and C's scripts after fragmentary and unintelligible passages in them. Suppose finally that when the impartial authority compares the scripts and follows the directions contained in them he finds that these separately unintelligible sentences combine to convey something which is highly characteristic of a certain deceased person who is alleged to be communicating. Then we should have a perfect instance of a Cross-Correspondence ; and it would be difficult to resist the conviction that the phenomena are controlled intentionally by a single mind, which cannot be identified with the conscious part of the mind of any of the automatic writers.

Unfortunately it is not clear to me that most of the alleged Cross-Correspondences accurately exemplify this ideal type. I also cannot help feeling suspicious of the enormous amount of learning and ingenuity which the impartial authority has to exercise in order to find the key to the riddle which the scripts set. Would not the same amount of patience, learning, and ingenuity discover almost as good Cross-Correspondences between almost any set of manuscripts ? I do not say that this is so ; but I should need a good deal of negative evidence, *i.e.*, of failure to discover Cross-Correspondences between other manuscripts which were treated in the same way as these automatic scripts, before I was prepared to stake much on this argument for human survival. So far as I am aware, negative control experiments of this kind have not been tried. It is evident that they would be terribly laborious, and it is hardly to be expected that the same patience and ingenuity would be lavished on them as have been devoted to the interpretation of the automatic scripts in which positive results are hoped for.

There is another remark to be made on the Cross-Correspondences. Suppose that they rendered it practically certain that *some* mind other than the conscious minds of the automatists is controlling the experiments, can we feel any confidence that it is the mind of a certain deceased person who professes to be communicating? Is it not at least equally probable that it might be the unconscious part of the mind of one of the automatists or of one of the officers of the Society for Psychical Research? It would certainly be true to say that some of the automatists (in particular Mrs Verrall) were well aware of the problem of getting evidence for survival which could not be explained away by the hypothesis of telepathy between the living ; that it must have occupied their thoughts a great deal ; and that they must have had a permanent desire to devise some means of solving it. It is also true that the alleged communicators in the Cross-Correspondences had been well known in life to Mrs Verrall and to many prominent and active members of the Society who were not themselves automatists. Now I think that we may take the following propositions as reasonably well established. (*a*) That when a person is greatly interested in a problem this problem is often worked upon and solved by processes which are unconscious relatively to the part of the mind which is normally in control of his body. I need only mention in support of this the quite common experience of solving a problem while asleep, or the post-hypnotic calculations which I spoke of in an earlier chapter. (*b*) That it is extremely probable that telepathy can and does take place between the unconscious parts of living minds. In sittings with Mrs Leonard and other mediums I have met with clear cases of telepathy between myself and the medium when entranced. But I have noticed that these almost invariably involved past events of which I was not consciously thinking at the time. Thus the telepathic influence must have been due to mere "traces", or at most to processes of thought going on in my mind without my being aware of them, *i.e.*, processes which were unconscious relatively to the part of my mind which normally controls my body. (*c*) That the unconscious part of the mind is often extremely willing to "oblige" the conscious part by providing "evidence" for what the conscious part wishes to believe.

Now, if these three propositions be admitted, it is not unplausible to suggest that the unconscious part of the mind of one of the automatists worked out the problem of providing "satisfactory evidence" for survival and telepathically conveyed the fragmentary messages, which were to constitute the "evidence", to the other automatists. Personally I strongly suspect the unconscious part of Mrs Verrall's mind to have accomplished this feat. I am of course quite well aware that such a theory goes far beyond anything for which we have direct evidence ; for it seems to imply that the unconscious part of Mrs Verrall's mind was capable of a kind of *selective* telepathy, conveying so much and no more to one automatist and so much and no more to another automatist. But I must point out that, if we do not ascribe this power to any embodied mind, we have to ascribe it to the disembodied mind of the supposed communicator. So this much must be assumed in any case if we accept the interpretation which the investigators have put on the Cross-Correspondences. And, except on the principle of *Omne ignotum pro magnifico*, I do not see why we should think it more likely that the disembodied mind of a dead man should be able to exercise selective telepathy than that the unconscious part of the embodied mind of a living member of the Society for Psychical Research should be able to do so. In fact the hypothesis that the spirit of the late Dr Verrall is communicating involves the assumption *both* of an otherwise unknown power of selective telepathy *and* of an otherwise unknown substance, viz., a disembodied spirit, to exercise this power. The hypothesis which I tentatively put forward makes only the first of these two assumptions. It therefore has a greater intrinsic probability ; and it seems equally capable of explaining the facts.

I pass now to the second question. Could the facts which we have been considering be explained by something *less* than the hypothesis of a persistent psychic factor? It will be remembered that the facts to be explained are the revelation of certain details in the past life of a certain dead man, which are unknown at the time to the sitter and can afterwards be verified ; or the occurrence of certain characteristic tricks of voice and manner in the entranced medium. Now it must be admitted that it is very rare for a detail about a dead man's past life to be verifiable unless it is known or has been known to someone now living. It must therefore be admitted to be theoretically possible that these phenomena are due to telepathy from the unconscious parts of the minds of living men who are remote from the place at which the sitting is being held. But, although this is conceivable, I cannot regard it as very plausible. It is very difficult to see what can determine the medium to select just those pieces of information from distant minds which are relevant to the supposed communicator. It is true of course that the sitter has generally known the communicator ; and we should have to suppose that the presence of a man who has known X causes the medium to select from other minds bits of information about X and to reject bits of information about other men. On any view some selective action on the part of the sitter must be postulated, since in the main those who are supposed to be communicating when a certain man has a sitting with a medium are people whom the sitter has known. In my own sittings with Mrs Leonard, *e.g.*, the alleged communicator has from the first been one particular man who was described with considerable accuracy and named with approximate (though not complete) accuracy at the first sitting. On the Compound Theory we should have to suppose that the presence of a certain sitter "attracts" the psychic factors of certain dead men who were known to him. On the purely telepathic theory we should have to suppose that the presence of the sitter causes the medium to "select" from various minds scattered about the world certain bits of information which are relevant to someone whom the sitter has known.

Although this hypothesis is possible, there are, I think, two arguments which make slightly against it and slightly in favour of the Compound Theory. (1) On the purely telepathic theory it is difficult to see why mediumistic communications should not be as much or more concerned with one's living friends as with those who have died. This is not found to be so. On the Compound Theory this fact is explicable; for, on this hypothesis, the psychic factor of a living mind is already attached to a certain living organism, and this would presumably make it difficult or impossible for it to enter at the same time into the same relation with the organism of the entranced medium. I think that some weight must be attached to this argument, though it is not conclusive. The main interest and expectation of both sitter and medium is to get messages which purport to come from the dead and not from those who are still alive; and this might account for the fact that the medium "selects" bits of information about dead men, even on the purely telepathic theory.

(2) The second argument is due to Dr Richard Hodgson. He used it against the hypothesis of telepathy from the sitter and in favour of the hypothesis that the messages are due to the disembodied spirits of dead men. I think that the argument can be adapted so that it can be used against the hypothesis of a more extended telepathy and in favour of the Compound Theory. The argument may be put as follows. Suppose that a number of sitters $S_1 \ldots S_n$ sit with a certain medium, and that a number of communicators $C_1 \ldots C_m$ profess to give messages through this medium. On the Compound Theory the adequacy or inadequacy of the communications which purport to come from a certain communicator C_i through a given medium would presumably depend mainly on two things; (a) on the complexity of the psychic factor, and (b) on its adaptation to the organism of the medium. There is no obvious reason why the number and accuracy of the messages which purport to come from a given communicator through the same medium should vary much from one sitter to another; for the main function of the sitter, on this hypothesis, is simply to "attract" a certain psychic factor so that it enters into a temporary combination with the medium's organism. If this happens at all, the subsequent proceedings would seem to depend on the psychic factor and the medium rather than on the sitter. We should thus expect to find certain "communicators" who are good with most sitters, and others who are bad with most sitters; we should not expect to find certain sitters who are good with most "communicators" and others who are bad with most "communicators". On the telepathic hypothesis we should expect the opposite result. For, on this view, the sitter plays a much more active part. His thoughts and interests must determine the particular selection of information which the medium makes from a perfect rag-bag of living minds. And his

power to do this would presumably depend on the peculiar endowments of his own mind and on its adaptation to the mind of the medium with whom he is sitting. On this hypothesis we should therefore expect that there would be some sitters who get good results from most alleged communicators through a given medium ; and that there would be other sitters who get bad results from most alleged communicators through the same medium.

Now Dr Hodgson had an enormous amount of experience of the results of sittings with Mrs Piper extending over many years. And he carefully studied them and classified them from the above points of view. His conclusion was that certain alleged *communicators* gave copious and accurate information to *most sitters;* and that other alleged *communicators* gave fragmentary and incorrect information to *most sitters*. He did not find that certain *sitters* got copious and accurate information from *most communicators;* and that certain other *sitters* got feeble and fragmentary messages from *most communicators*. Thus, on the whole, the actual results are such as might be expected on the Compound Theory and are not such as might be expected on the theory of generalised telepathy from living minds. On the whole then I am inclined to think that there is slightly more to be said for the Compound Theory than for the other alternatives.

Conclusion.—The view that the mind is existentially dependent on the organism and on nothing else is compatible with all the normal facts, and is positively suggested by them, though they do not necessitate it. And it is the simplest possible view to take. The theory that the mind merely uses the body as an instrument is difficult to reconcile with the normal facts ; and it is doubtful whether there are any well-established abnormal phenomena that require it. The theory that the mind is a compound substance, whose constituents are the organism and what I have called a "psychic factor", is compatible with all the normal facts; though it is not suggested by them, and is more complex than the theory that the mind is existentially dependent on the organism and on it alone. This Compound Theory seems to be the minimum assumption that will explain certain fairly well attested abnormal phenomena. Of course, many people will unhesitatingly reject the alleged facts on which I have based the argument of the latter part of this chapter. I am pretty sure that they will be wrong in doing so; but I will confine myself to this remark for their benefit. Anyone who adopts the view that the mind is existentially dependent on the organism alone is taking up a position which is not *necessitated* by the facts which everyone admits, and which can hardly be reconciled with the very *possibility* of many alleged facts for which there is at least respectable *prima facie* evidence. Now this (I should have thought) is not a comfortable position to occupy. It compels one either to ignore all the phenomena in question, or to be continually occupied in explaining them away. The former course is not scientifically respectable; for it is certain that many people, quite as sensible as oneself and far more expert, have personally investigated these matters and have persuaded themselves of the genuineness of these phenomena and of the impossibility of explaining them completely by fraud or mistake. And the latter course may at any moment be barred by some fact which we simply cannot explain away. Now the Compound Theory has at least this merit. It is compatible with all the facts which everyone admits; it has nothing against it except a superstitious objection to dualism; and it leaves open the possibility that these debatable phenomena are genuine. At the same time it does not compel anyone to accept them. It is quite open for anyone to hold that the mind is a compound of the organism and of a psychic factor which is not itself a mind; and yet to doubt or deny that there is any conclusive evidence that a psychic factor ever persists after the destruction of the organism with which it was combined, or that if it does persist it ever combines even for a moment with the organism of some living human being to form a temporary mind. This seems to me to be the great merit of the Compound Theory. It leaves open possibilities, and allows us to investigate alleged facts without an invincible *a priori* prejudice against their possibility. And yet it allows us to be as critical as we like about each of these alleged facts, and about the evidence which is offered for each of them.

I may remark in conclusion that the Compound Theory has certain advantages for those who favour the theory of metempsychosis, as Dr M'Taggart does. Instead of a single *mind* which *animates* a successive series of organisms we should have a single *psychic factor* which *combines with* such a series of organisms to form a successive series of minds. There might be intervals during which a psychic factor has become dissociated from an organism which has died and has not yet entered into combination with an organism that is about to be born. During such intervals this psychic factor might produce those abnormal phenomena which the ordinary Spiritualist takes as evidence for the survival of a certain human mind. I do not know of any facts which strongly suggest metempsychosis; but it is a possible theory, and it has the advantage of dealing with the "origin" of the mind at conception as well as with the "end" of the mind at death. And it seems to me to be much more plausible when stated in terms of a persistent psychic factor, which is not a mind, than it is when stated in terms of a persistent mind which animates successively a series of organisms.

SECTION E

Introductory Remarks

" To conclude, there is nothing in this whole Discourse, nor in that I writ before . . . . as far as I can perceive, contrary to the Word of God or to Good Manners; or to the disturbance of Publique Tranquillity. Therefore I think it may be profitably printed, and more profitably taught in the Universities, in case they also think so to whom judgment of the same belongeth. For . . . . the Universities are the Fountains of Civill and Morall Doctrine, from whence the Preachers and the Gentry, drawing such water as they find, use to sprinkle the same (both from the Pulpit and in their Conversation) upon the People."

(HOBBES, Leviathan, Conclusion)

SECTION E

The Unity of the Mind and the Unity of Nature

Introductory Remarks

In this Section, which will bring this book to an end, I propose first to consider the internal unity of the mind. I shall state and criticise certain theories which have been held on this subject, and shall try to make a tentative decision between them or to show that on the available evidence there is no means of reaching even a probable decision. This will occupy the first chapter of the Section. In the second chapter I shall consider for the last time the status of the mind in Nature; and I shall conclude with a few words about the probable prospects of Mind in the course of future evolution.

CHAPTER XIII

The Unity of the Mind

I SHALL begin by mentioning those facts about the mind which everyone admits and which every theory has to take into account.

(1) It is admitted that the total state of a man's mind at any moment may be, and generally is, differentiated. This differentiation takes two different forms. (*a*) My total state of mind at any moment may consist of mental events of various *kinds*. I may be *feeling* tired, *wanting* tea, *thinking of* my book, and so on. (*b*) There may be in my total mental state at any moment a number of mental events which are of the same kind but have different epistemological *objects*. I may be thinking of my tea, of my book, of the multiplication-table, and so on. We may sum this up by saying that the total state of a mind at any time may be differentiated qualitatively or objectively or in both ways. As we have seen, identity of quality is compatible with diversity of objects. Similarly, identity of object is compatible with diversity of quality. *E.g.*, I might at the same time be thinking of my tea, longing for my tea, and so on. Probably every total state of mind is diversified both qualitatively and objectively; and no doubt there are intimate causal connexions between the two kinds of differentiation. Still, they are distinct forms of differentiation even if they never occur in isolation from each other.

(2) On the face of it there are two fundamentally different kinds of mental events, viz., those which do and those which do not have epistemological objects. Compare, *e.g.*, the two statements "I feel tired" or "I

feel cross" with the two statements "I see a chair" or "I want my tea". The former seem to express *how*, and not *what*, I am feeling. The latter seem to express *what*, and not *how*, I am perceiving or desiring. I will call them respectively "non-referential" and "referential" mental events. (Cf. Chap. VI.) Some people have argued that all mental events are really referential. This may possibly be true; but their arguments do not convince me, and their conclusion seems to me paradoxical. I think it very likely that my total mental state at any moment is never wholly non-referential and never wholly referential; but this is as far as I am willing to go. I therefore assume that there are these two different kinds of mental event, however closely they may always be connected with each other in real life.

(3) At the same time there exist a number of different total mental states, which we say "belong to different minds". It is possible for there to be two contemporary mental events which have exactly the same determinate qualities and the same epistemological object; but these two mental events cannot belong to the same mind. (To this it would generally be added that no mental event can belong to more than one mind, and that every mental event must belong to some mind. But, in view of the facts of abnormal and supernormal psychology, it would perhaps be unwise to insist on this as strongly as on the other points which have been mentioned.)

(4) Certain series of successive total mental states are said to "belong to a single mind". And the events which are differentiations of a pair of total states belonging to the same mind themselves belong to that mind. (It would commonly be held that every total mental state is part of the history of some mind which endures for some time and has other earlier or later total states.)

These are the main facts which every theory has to take into consideration. I now propose to state various theoretically possible analyses of them.

Alternative Theories about the Unity of the Mind.—
We may begin by dividing all theories into two great
groups, viz. (A) Centre-Theories, and (B) Non-centre-
Theories. By a centre-theory I mean a theory which
ascribes the unity of the mind to the fact that there is a
certain particular existent—a Centre—which stands in
a common asymmetrical relation to all the mental events
which would be said to be states of a certain mind, and
does not stand in this relation to any mental events
which would not be said to be states of this mind. By
a non-centre theory I mean one which denies the
existence of any such particular Centre, and ascribes the
unity of the mind to the fact that certain mental events
are directly inter-related in certain characteristic ways,
and that other mental events are not related to these
in the peculiar way in which these are related to each
other.

Now centre-theories may be sub-divided into (*a*) Pure
Ego Theories, and (*b*) Theories that do not assume a
Pure Ego. By a Pure Ego I understand a particular
existent which is of a different kind from any event; it
owns various events, but it is not itself an event. No
doubt the commonest form of the Centre theory has involved a Pure Ego. But it seems conceivable that the
unity of the mind might be due to the existence of a
Centre, and yet that this centre might itself be an event.
It is possible that this is what William James had in
mind when he talked of the "passing thought" as being
the "thinker". So we had better leave room for theories
of this type.

(*A, a*) *Pure Ego Theories.* Theories which assume a
special kind of existent Centre—a Pure Ego—may be
divided according to the view which they take about
mental events. A mental event is certainly a Substantive; *i.e.*, it is the kind of entity which can be a logical
subject of a proposition, but cannot play any other part
in a proposition. But there are two different kinds of
substantives, viz., those which exist and those which

only subsist. A Pure Ego, if there be such a thing, is an existent substantive. A fact or a proposition is a substantive, in the sense defined above. We can say that "The execution of Charles I was a political mistake" or that "It is probable that Edwin will marry Angelina". Here we have facts or propositions functioning as subjects of other propositions. And they cannot play any other part in a proposition. They are therefore substantives. But they do not exist (though they may contain existents as constituents); they merely subsist. Now, granted that mental events are substantives, it might be held (i) that they are merely subsistent, or (ii) that they are existent substantives. Non-centre theories about the mind are obliged to hold that mental events are existent substantives; but Pure Ego theories have already got an existent substantive, viz., the Pure Ego. They can therefore take their choice about mental events. They can regard mental events either as facts about Pure Egos, or as existents of a peculiar kind which stand in specially intimate connexion with existents of another kind, viz., Pure Egos. We will now consider these two forms of Pure Ego theory in turn.

(i) On this view there is a plurality of different Pure Egos. All these Pure Egos have certain causal characteristics or "faculties", *e.g.*, the power of remembering, the power of reasoning and so on. Beside this, each Pure Ego at each moment has some determinate form of some determinable non-causal quality; and each Pure Ego at each moment has some determinate form of some determinable relation to some object or other. A mental event is the fact that a certain Pure Ego has a certain determinate form of a certain determinable non-causal quality at a certain moment; or it is the fact that a certain Pure Ego stands at a certain moment in a certain determinate form of some determinable non-causal relation to a certain object. The first kind of fact is what we have called a "non-referential" mental event; the second kind of fact is what we have called a "referential" mental event. *E.g.*, we might take "tiredness" as one determinable quality, and "crossness" as another. Then the mental event of feeling tired is the fact that a certain Pure Ego has a certain determinate form of the quality of tiredness at a certain moment. Again, perceiving and desiring would be two determinable relations; and the mental event of seeing a chair would be the fact that a certain Pure Ego has this determinate form of the relation of perceiving at a certain moment to a certain chair. Now a Pure Ego can have determinate forms of several different determinable qualities at the same time; *e.g.*, it can at the same time have the quality of tiredness in a certain degree and the quality of crossness in a certain degree. Similarly, it may have the same determinate relation to several different objects at the same time, or it may have at the same time different kinds of relation to the same object. A total mental state would then be the fact that a certain Pure Ego at a certain moment has several different non-causal qualities, stands in non-causal relations of several different kinds, and stands in the same kind of non-causal relation to several different objects. To say that all these contemporary mental events are differentiations of a single total state of a certain mind is just to say that each of them is a fact about the same Pure Ego and the same moment of time and about different qualities or relations or the same relation and different objects.

So much for what we might call the "transverse unity of a cross-section of the history of a mind" on this view. The "longitudinal unity" of a mind, as we might call it, could be explained on this view in two alternative ways. (*a*) The simplest theory would be that the same Pure Ego persists; and that it has different determinate qualities, or stands in different determinate relations, or stands in the same determinate relations to different objects, at different times. To say that two successive total states are states of the same mind is just to say that both of them are facts about the same Pure Ego, about different moments of time, and about the same or different qualities or relations or objects. (β) It would, however, be possible to hold a view which is a kind of compromise between a Central and a non-Central Theory. It might be held that the unity of each total state requires a Pure Ego. But it might be held that the longitudinal unity of a mind does not require that one and the same Pure Ego should be a common constituent of a series of successive total states. It might be held that there is a different Pure Ego for each different total state of the same mind, and that two successive total states are assigned to the same mind because of certain characteristic relations which they have to each other and which they do not have to other total states which would not be assigned to this mind. This second Theory is a Central Theory for the transverse unity, and a non-Central Theory for the longitudinal unity of the mind.

Whichever form of this theory we may take it follows that every mental event must be "owned" by some Pure Ego. For every mental event is a fact about some Pure Ego, and it may be said to be "owned" by the Pure Ego which it is about. I think that it would also follow from either form of the theory that no mental event could be owned by more than one Pure Ego. For a mental event is the fact that a certain Pure Ego has a certain quality or stands in a certain relation to a certain object at a certain moment. Now, although two Pure Egos might have precisely the same quality and stand in precisely the same relation to the same object at the same time, yet it would be one fact that Pure Ego A had this quality or stood in this relation to this object, and it would be another fact that Pure Ego B did so. Hence there would be two mental events and not one. Finally, although on either form of the theory every mental event would be owned by some Pure Ego and no mental event would be owned by more than one, it would be possible on the second form of the theory that there might be mental events which were not states of any mind. For there might be certain mental events which did not stand in such relations to any mental event of earlier or later date that the two could be regarded as successive slices of the history of a mind.

(ii) We will now consider the second great division of Pure Ego theories, viz., those which regard mental events as existent substantives and not merely as subsistent facts about the qualities and relations of Pure Egos. On this type of theory we must suppose that non-causal qualities, such as tiredness or crossness, belong, not to Pure Egos, but to mental events. We must further assume a peculiar asymmetric relation of "ownership" between a Pure Ego and certain mental events. On the first form of Pure Ego theory "ownership" was not a peculiar *material* relation; a Pure Ego owned a state when the state was the fact that this Pure Ego had such and such a quality or stood in such and such a relation at a certain time. Ownership was thus the *formal* relation of a subject to a fact about that subject. On the present form of the theory mental events are not facts about Pure Egos, and the ownership of a mental event by a Pure Ego cannot be dealt with in this simple way.

Let us consider the analysis of a typical mental state on the two forms of the Pure Ego theory. We will begin with the kind of state which is expressed by the phrase "I feel tired". On the first form of the theory this can be analysed into: "A certain Pure Ego has a certain determinate form of the determinable quality of tiredness now." On the second form of the theory it would be analysed into: "There is a mental event characterised by a certain determinate form of the determinable quality of tiredness, and this event is owned by a certain Pure Ego." Next let us consider a referential mental event, such as that which would be expressed by the phrase: "I am thinking of the number

2." On the first form of the theory this could be analysed into: "A certain Pure Ego stands now in a certain determinate form of the determinable relation of 'cognising' to the number 2." On the second form of the theory it could be analysed into: "There is a mental event which stands in a certain determinate form of the determinable relation of 'cognising' to the number 2, and this event is owned by a certain Pure Ego."

There are several points to be noticed about these alternative analyses. In the first place, on both theories there is a relation of the Pure Ego to the mental event, and also a relation of the Pure Ego to the determinate quality, in the case of a non-referential state of mind. On the first theory, the Pure Ego is *characterised* directly by tiredness; on the second theory, the Pure Ego has to the quality of tiredness a compound relation which is the logical product of the two relations of "owning" and "being characterised by". For, on the second theory, the Pure Ego *owns* something which *is characterised by* tiredness. The difference is that, on the first theory, the relation between the Pure Ego and the quality is direct, like that of father to son; whilst, on the second theory, it is indirect, like that of uncle to nephew. Again, on the first theory, the relation of Pure Ego to mental event is the formal relation of a subject to a fact about that subject; whilst, on the second theory, it is the non-formal relation of "ownership" between one existent substantive of a certain kind and another existent substantive of a different kind. Similar remarks apply to referential mental states on the two theories. On the first theory, the Pure Ego stands directly in a cognitive relation to an object. On the second theory, it stands in a compound relation to this object; this relation is the logical product of the two relations of "owning" and "cognising"; for the Pure Ego *owns* something which *cognises* the object. It must, therefore, be admitted that *both* theories are able to deal with all the various relations which any theory has to recognise; they differ here only in the fact that a relation which is direct and simple on one theory is indirect and complex on the other. Secondly, on the present form of the Pure Ego theory it is not logically impossible that there should be mental events which are not owned by any Pure Ego at all; nor is it logically impossible that some mental events should be owned at once by several Pure Egos. On the first form of the theory it followed logically from the nature of mental events that there could not be unowned or common mental events; if this is to be maintained on the present form of the theory it will be necessary to add certain synthetic propositions about the relation of "ownership".

There is one other point which had better be mentioned at this stage. As stated by us, both forms of the Pure Ego theory have presupposed a plurality of different determinable mental qualities and a plurality of different determinable relations to an epistemological object. On the first theory these qualities directly characterise the Pure Ego, and these relations directly connect the Pure Ego with epistemological objects; on the second theory the qualities directly characterise mental events, and the relations directly connect mental events with epistemological objects. Now I do not think that either theory could dispense with a plurality of different determinable mental *qualities*. For there are certainly different kinds of feeling, such as "feeling tired", "feeling cross", etc., and it seems impossible to regard the difference between feeling tired and feeling cross as simply a difference of relation to some object or as a difference in the objects to which something is related. It would seem then as if "tiredness" and "crossness" were so many different non-relational determinables. But, if we once grant a plurality of different determinable mental qualities, it might be suggested that we could do without a plurality of different determinable mental *relations* to objects. We have counted cognising as one kind of determinable relation to an object, and desiring as another kind of determinable relation to an object. But could we not manage with only a single determinable relation to an object, which we might call "objective reference"? Might not the difference between cognising and desiring simply be a difference in the qualities of the term which stands at the moment in the relation of reference to an object? On the first form of the Pure Ego theory this suggestion would work out as follows. Suppose I think of my tea first, and then desire my tea. There would, on both occasions, be simply some determinate form of the general relation of reference between my Pure Ego and my tea. But on the second occasion, *i.e.*, when I desired my tea in addition to thinking of it, my Pure Ego would have a certain characteristic quality which it did not have on the first occasion. A thing would be "desired" when it stood in the relation of being "referred to" by a Pure Ego which had at the time a certain specific quality. On the second form of the Pure Ego theory the suggestion would work out as follows. A desire for my tea would be a mental event which (*a*) has a certain characteristic quality, and (*b*) has the relation of objective reference to my tea. A mere thought of my tea would be a mental event which (*a*) lacks this characteristic quality, and (*b*) has the relation of objective reference to my tea. It may be remarked that all other mental attitudes towards objects presuppose the cognitive attitude; we cannot desire, fear, hate, or love anything, without having an idea of the object towards which we take this attitude. Hence it would be plausible to identify the cognitive relation with the general relation of objective reference; and to suppose that all other mental attitudes consist of the holding of this relation between a Pure Ego or a mental event and an epistemological object, together with the fact that this Pure Ego or mental event has at the time a certain characteristic quality which determines whether the attitude is called "desire", or "love", or "hate" or what not.

Thus we get a cross-division of Pure Ego theories according to whether they do or do not assume a plurality of different kinds of relation of reference to objects. I will now leave the exposition of the various possible forms of Pure Ego theory, and will pass to the theory of a Centre which is an event and not a Pure Ego.

(*A, b*) *Central-Event Theories.* It is evident that these form a kind of half-way house between Pure Ego theories and Non-Centre Theories of the mind. They resemble Pure Ego theories in the fact that the unity of a total mental state at any moment depends on a common relation in which all its differentiations stand to a common Centre. They resemble Non-Centre Theories in the fact that this Centre is itself an event and not a peculiar kind of existent substantive ; it is of the same nature as the events which it unifies. I think that the most plausible form of this theory would be to identify the Central Event at any moment with a mass of bodily feeling. The longitudinal unity of a self through a period of time would then depend on the fact that there is a mass of bodily feeling which goes on continuously throughout this period and varies in quality not at all or very slowly. At any moment there are many such masses of bodily feeling, which are numerically different however much they may be alike in quality. These form the Centres of a number of different contemporary total states of mind. Each of them is a thin slice of a long and highly uniform strand of bodily feeling ; and each of these strands of bodily feeling accounts for the longitudinal unity of one mind.

The transverse unity of a total mental state might be accounted for in two different ways on this theory, which are similar to forms (i) and (ii) of the Pure Ego theory. (i) We might suppose that each cross-section of one of these strands has various other qualities beside that quality in which all adjacent cross-sections of the same strand closely resemble each other. These other qualities may vary sharply between adjacent cross-sections of the same strand. *E.g.*, suppose we take two adjacent sections of a certain strand, each of which lasts for a minute. There may be a predominant resemblance in quality between the two; but the first may have in addition a "toothachy" quality, and the second may have in addition a "headachy" quality. The transverse unity of the total mental state will consist in the fact that the same Central Event has a plurality of different determinate qualities in addition to that quality in which it resembles adjacent Central Events of the same strand. So far we have considered only non-objective mental events. Objective mental events could be dealt with as follows. We might suppose that the same Central Event, which has these various qualities, also stands in various determinate forms of various determinable relations to various objects. The fact that a Central Event stands in such and such a determinate form of such and such a relation to such and such an object will be, on this view, what is meant by saying that such and such a referential mental state is occurring in such and such a mind.

(ii) The other alternative would be to assume a plurality of existent mental events beside those which are bodily feelings and constitute Central Events. These other events would then have characteristic mental qualities and stand in characteristic mental relations to objects of various kinds. And the transverse unity of a total mental state would consist in the fact that a single central bodily feeling stands in a certain common relation to a number of other mental events, each of which has its own characteristic qualities, and some of which stand in characteristic relations to objects.

As in the case of the Pure Ego theory, we might try to do without a plurality of different determinable mental relations to objects, provided we accept a plurality of mental qualities. We might postulate a single determinable mental relation of "objective reference". And we might distinguish the apparently different kinds of objective reference, such as desire, love, fear, etc., by characteristic differences in the quality of the term which stands in the relation of objective reference to an object.

(B) *Non-Central Theories.* These Theories try to dispense with the assumption of an *existent* centre, whether it be a Pure Ego or a Central Event. The unity of a total mental state consists in the fact that a number of contemporary mental events, each with its own characteristic qualities, are directly interrelated in certain characteristic ways. There are other contemporary mental events which are not related in these ways to a given set of interrelated mental events of this kind. These either belong to no mind at all, or to a contemporary total state of some other mind. The longitudinal unity of a mind is due to the fact that certain non-contemporary total mental states, of the kind just described, are related to each other in characteristic ways. It is obviously logically possible on such a theory that there should be mental events which do not belong to any total mental state, and total mental states which do not belong to any mind.

There are several remarks of a general logical character to be made on the relation between Central and Non-Central Theories. (i) If a number of terms stand in a common relation to a certain other term it necessarily follows that they will stand in a symmetrical relation to each other. *E.g.*, if A and B be both children of X, they necessarily stand in the relation of "brother-or-sister" to each other. This consequence may be called merely "analytic", since the relation of "brother-or-sister" between A and B just *means* that A is a child of someone who is a parent of B. But (ii) the fact that a number of terms stand in a common relation to a certain other term *may* entail a consequence about the relation of these terms to each other which is not merely analytic. Suppose, *e.g.*, that four points A, B, C, and D are all

at the same distance from a point X.   Then it necessarily
follows that the angle ABD is equal to the angle ACD.
This consequence about the relations of the points cannot
be called merely analytic ; for it is certainly not a mere
restatement or weakening of the statement that A, B, C,
and D are all at the same distance from X.   It might
have been recognised by a person who had never suspected that there was a point X from which these four
points were equidistant.   We must, therefore, admit
that the direct relations which we discover between
a number of terms may in fact be entailed by their
standing in a common relation to some other term.
(iii) If a number of terms be interrelated directly in a
characteristic way it follows analytically that there is
something to which they all stand in a common asymmetrical relation, even though there be no Existent
Centre in the system.   For each of them is a constituent
in the *fact* that they are all related to each other in this
particular way ; and so this fact stands in a common
asymmetrical relation to all these terms.   Thus, even if
a number of interrelated terms have no Existent Centre,
there is always a certain substantive, which subsists
though it does not exist, which stands in a common
asymmetrical relation to all of them and might be called
their " Subsistent Centre ".   (iv) What has just been
asserted is merely an analytic consequence of the fact
that the terms in question are interrelated.   But the fact
that a number of terms are directly interrelated *may*
entail the synthetic consequence that there is an Existent
Centre which stands in a common asymmetrical relation
to them all.   If the four points A, B, C, and D be so
related to each other that the angle ABD is equal to
the angle ACD it follows that these points are concyclic,
i.e., that there is a certain point X from which they are
all equidistant.   And this is not a mere restatement or
weakening of the original statement about the equality
of the two angles.   It must, therefore, be admitted that
the direct relations which we discover among a set of

terms *may* in fact entail that there is a certain Existent Centre which stands in a common asymmetric relation to all of them. Lastly (v) we must notice that theories of the Non-Central Type are not obliged to hold that the relations which bind certain contemporary mental events into a total mental state, or the relations which bind certain successive total mental states into a mind, are dyadic relations. Both kinds of relation might be irreducibly polyadic, like jealousy or trusteeship.

I have mentioned these purely logical points for two opposite reasons. On the one hand it is often objected *in limine* against Non-Central Theories that our use of personal pronouns, like "I" and "You", presupposes that we recognise the existence of Centres ; and that Non-Central Theories are necessarily incapable of accounting for this fact. We see that this preliminary objection is baseless. Even on Non-Central Theories there is necessarily something which can be called "I" or "You". This something is a substantive, and it stands in a common asymmetrical relation to "my" state or to "your" states respectively. The only difference between Central and Non-Central Theories is about the logical nature of this substantive. On Central Theories it is a particular existent, either a Pure Ego or a Central Event. On Non-Central Theories this substantive is a Fact about certain mental events and their interrelations, and so its mode of being is subsistence and not existence. What the opponents of Non-Central Theories have to prove is, therefore, not simply that the unity of the mind involves an entity other than its states, which stands in a common asymmetrical relation to all these states ; but that this entity is an *existent* and not merely a *subsistent* substantive.

On the other hand, it is often objected *in limine* to Central Theories (and, in particular, to Pure Ego Theories) that all that we can observe is mental events and their direct relations to each other. We cannot observe Pure Egos and their relations to mental events or to objects. As against this preliminary objection it was worth while to remark that, if there were an Existent Centre, this fact might entail synthetically the subsistence of certain direct relations between the mental events which it unifies. And conversely that the subsistence of certain observable relations between a set of mental events might entail that there was an Existent Centre to which they all stood in a certain common relation. In this connexion the following remark may be of interest by way of analogy. The existence of conic sections was recognised, and many of their properties were worked out, long before it was known that to each conic section there is a peculiar point (the Focus) and a peculiar straight line (the Directrix) and that all the other properties of any conic entail and are entailed by the fact that every point on it is such that its distance from the focus bears a fixed ratio to its distance from the directrix.

It remains to be noticed that Non-Central Theories, like Central Theories, may take two different forms according to whether we assume a plurality of different determinable relations of objective reference, such as cognising, desiring, loving, etc., or content ourselves with a single determinable relation of objective reference and a plurality of different determinable qualities in the terms which stand in this relation to objects. We must remark here, however, that a still further degree of simplification has been attempted by certain philosophers, such as William James and Bertrand Russell. All forms of all theories which we have so far mentioned have distinguished sharply between the *constituents* of a mind and its *objects*. The objects of the mind were never supposed to be also constituents of it, except possibly in the very special case where the mind is introspecting and making one of its own states into an object. On the first form of the Pure Ego theory the mind can hardly be said to have constituents at all. The Pure Ego *is* a constituent of a number of facts, and the objects of the mind are constituents of some of these facts. But this does not make the objects constituents of the mind. On the second form of the Pure Ego theory the constituents of the mind are the Pure Ego and the mental events which it owns. Some of these mental events are constituents of certain facts of which the objects of the mind are also constituents. But this again does not make the objects constituents of the mind. On the theories which reject the Pure Ego, which we have so far considered, the constituents of the mind are mental events. Some of these mental events are constituents of facts of which the objects of the mind are also constituents ; but this does not make the objects of the mind constituents of it. The form of Non-Central theory which we have now to mention holds that the mind is *composed of* its objects interrelated in certain characteristic ways. A total state of mind just is the fact that a certain set of objects are related to each other at a certain moment in a certain way ; and a particular mental event just is the fact that at a certain moment a certain object stands in certain relations to certain other interrelated objects.

Discussion of the Alternative Theories. I have now stated and tried to explain all the alternative theories about the unity of the mind with which I am acquainted. It will be seen that they are very numerous ; and that none of them, with the possible exception of the third form of Non-Central Theory, is so obviously silly that it can safely be dismissed without discussion. And even this third form of Non-Central Theory has been held by such eminent men that it would be impertinent to ignore it.

Plurality of Relations of Reference. I will begin by considering a question which arises on all the alternatives, viz., whether it is necessary to assume a plurality of different determinable relations of reference to an object as well as a plurality of different determinable mental qualities. It seems to me that it would not be possible to dispense with a plurality of different determinable relations of reference on the first form of the Pure Ego theory. Let us consider, *e.g.*, the two attitudes of loving and hating. It is impossible for the same mind to love and to hate the same object at the same time. If then we suppose that the statement " X loves A " means " X has the quality *l*, and stands in the relation of reference to A ", and that the statement " X hates A " means " X has the quality *h*, and stands in the same relation of reference to A ", we shall have to suppose that the qualities *l* and *h* are incompatible with each other. But it is quite certain that X can love A and hate B at the same time. And, on the present analysis, this would seem to require X to have at the same time the two inconsistent qualities *l* and *h*. Now, if X be a Pure Ego, we cannot avoid this by supposing that one *part* of X has the quality *h* and another part has the quality *l*; for X will not have parts. Hence it seems impossible to accept this analysis on the first form of the Pure Ego theory. The same result may be brought out in a different way. It is certain that I may cognise both A and B, and desire A and not desire B at the same time. Now, if " X desires A " means " X cognises A and has the quality *d* ", it would seem to follow that, when X cognises both A and B and desires only A, X must both have and not have the quality *d*. And this seems to be impossible if X be a Pure Ego. Thus I think we may conclude that the first form of the Pure Ego theory requires a plurality of different determinable relations of reference as well as a plurality of different mental qualities.

This kind of difficulty does not arise on any theory that admits of a plurality of existent mental events in the same total mental state. Take, *e.g.*, the second form of the Pure Ego theory. Here the statement that " X cognises A and B, desires A, and does not desire B " may be reduced to " X owns the events e_A and e_B; e_A and e_B both stand in the same relation of reference to the objects A and B respectively; and e_A has, whilst *e* lacks, the quality *d*." There is no inconsistency in this. Omitting for the present the third form of the Non-Central Theory, I think we may say that it is logically possible for all the other theories to account for the facts without assuming a plurality of different determinable relations of reference. Can we go any further than this?

When I try to analyse introspectively such referential situations as seeing a chair, wanting my tea, loving my friend, and hating nationalism, and when I compare them with each other and with other situations which I can introspect, I seem to be pretty certain of the following propositions. (1) That in all these situations an object is being cognised by me. (2) That in each of them something is present beside this object, and that there is an asymmetrical relation between this something and the object. (3) That there is a qualitative difference between the four situations which does not consist in the fact that the objects differ in quality. For I find that desiring my tea and merely thinking of my tea differ in this way, although their objects are the same. And I find that thinking of my tea and thinking of my chair do not differ in this way, although their objects differ very greatly in quality. But I do not find that introspection tells me with any certainty whether this qualitative difference is (*a*) simply a difference in the quality of the non-objective constituents of the situations, or (*b*) simply a difference in the asymmetrical relations between the two constituents, or (*c*) a difference in both. Still (4) there are some facts which make the alternative (*a*) somewhat plausible. There are states which I can introspect, which are called "emotional moods", such as crossness, restlessness, etc. These seem to be non-referential mental states. And it seems that certain emotional moods bear a strong qualitative resemblance to certain emotions, which are referential mental situations. *E.g.*, there is an obvious connexion between the emotional mood of crossness and the emotion of anger at some definite object. And it would be plausible to express this relation by saying that anger is a state of crossness "directed at" a certain cognised object, that desire is a state of restlessness "directed at" a certain cognised object, and so on. It seems plain to me that the relation of "cognising" is not the same as the relation of "being directed at"; but it does seem plausible to suggest that no relations are involved in the various kinds of referential situation except the two relations of "cognising" and "being directed at" an object; and that the characteristic differences between various kinds of referential situation are wholly due to differences of quality in that which cognises and is directed at the object.

I do not suppose for a moment that this argument is conclusive. In the first place, emotional moods may really be emotions with highly indeterminate objects. *E.g.*, being cross may consist of being angry with "things-in-general". In that case the suggestion that the various kinds of emotion are just so many different kinds of emotional mood "directed at" objects breaks down. Secondly, it is perfectly possible that the relation which the emotional mood of crossness bears to an object in the emotion of anger is a different relation from that which the emotional mood of restlessness bears to an object in the state known as "desire". I do not think that introspection is capable of refuting either of these possibilities. So the upshot of the matter is this. Except on the first form of the Pure Ego theory there is no logical impossibility in the attempt to do without a plurality of different determinable relations of reference to objects. Introspection, so far as I can see, has also nothing conclusive to say against the suggestion. And there are certain facts open to introspection which slightly favour it. The only other point in its support is the methodological principle that entities are not to be needlessly multiplied. But this is *only* a guide for *our* procedure; it is not a law which is binding upon Nature.

Referential and Non-Referential Situations and the Third Form of Non-Central Theory. I must now remind the reader of a distinction which we drew in Chapter VI, which I have so far kept in the background in this chapter in order to avoid excessive complication. It will be remembered that we distinguished situations into (*a*) those which do and those which do not refer to epistemological objects, and (*b*) those which do and those which do not contain objective constituents. These two distinctions we expressed respectively by the phrases "referential" and "non-referential" and by the phrases "objective" and "non-objective". It will be remembered that we said that there are probably mental events which are non-objective and non-referential, *e.g.*, vague feelings; that probably all mental situations which are referential are also objective; and that possibly there are mental situations, such as pure sensations of sounds, coloured patches, etc., which are objective but non-referential. Finally, we must remember that, in perception, memory, etc., the objective constituent of the situation cannot be identified with the epistemological object of the situation or with the ontological object (if there happens to be one) which corresponds to this epistemological object. The position is that to "refer to such and such an epistemological object" is a *property* of any situation which has such and such a structure and such and such an objective constituent. There may be no ontological object corresponding to this: and, even if there should be one, it cannot as a rule be identified with the objective constituent of the situation. And we have seen grave reason to doubt whether, even in the case of veridical perceptual and memory-situations, the objective constituent is ever literally a part of the ontological object which corresponds to the situation.

Bearing these facts in mind, we can see that the various alternative theories have been stated too simply as regards referential situations. Such an event as "I am seeing a chair" cannot really consist in the fact that a certain Pure Ego is now standing in a certain relation to a certain chair ; at best it can only consist in the fact that a certain Pure Ego is standing in a certain relation to a certain sensum. If the perceptual situation be veridical this sensum also stands in a certain peculiar relation to a certain chair ; but at that stage we have left the *psychological* analysis of minds and mental events, and are entering the region of epistemology and ontology. Similar remarks apply, *mutatis mutandis*, to referential situations on all the alternative theories. Suppose we hold that a referential situation consists in the fact that a certain *event*, and not a certain Pure Ego, stands in a certain relation to a certain object. We must still recognise that the object to which the event stands in this relation is *not* the chair, or table, or what not, which corresponds to the epistemological object of the situation ; even if there be such a thing, as there often is not. The object to which the event stands in this relation is a certain sensum or image ; and the further question whether there is an ontological object corresponding to the epistemological object of the situation, and, if so, how the sensum or image is related to this ontological object, does not arise in the psychological analysis of the situation.

Since these remarks apply equally to all theories about the structure of the mind they do not directly help us to decide between the various alternatives. But they enable us to say something further about the third form of the Non-Central theory, *i.e.*, the view that a mind is composed of its objects, suitably interrelated, and that it has no other constituents. The natural interpretation of this theory would be that the mind consists of the chairs, tables, people, pink rats, unicorns, etc., which it is said to be "aware of"; *i.e.*, that its constituents are the objects which it refers to, and that it has no other constituents. Now this is certainly false.

When a drunkard perceives a pink rat it is impossible that one of the constituents of his mind can be the pink rat that he is perceiving; for there are no pink rats to be constituents of anything.   And in general we may say that, even when there is an ontological object corresponding to a referential state of mind, *this* object is not a constituent of the state and, *a fortiori*, is not a constituent of the mind.   Thus the theory that the constituents of the mind are what would commonly be called its "objects" has no plausibility whatever if by "its objects" you mean the things to which it refers in its referential states of mind.   The theory is worth discussing only on the assumption that by "its objects" we mean the *objective constituents* of its objective states of mind.   The difference between the two alternatives is roughly this.   On the first interpretation the theory asserts that the constituents of the mind are the *things* that it perceives, the *events* that it remembers, and so on. This, as I have said, may be rejected at once as absurd. On the second interpretation the theory asserts that the constituents of the mind are the *appearances to it* of the things that it perceives, of the events that it remembers, and so on.   This, so far as I can understand, is the form of the theory which Mr Russell defends in his *Analysis of Mind;* and it is certainly the only form of it which is capable of defence.   Now, such a theory makes certain assertions and certain denials.   (1) It asserts that sensa and images are constituents of minds.   (2) It denies that they have any other constituents.   (3) Mr Russell further asserts that sensa are constituents of physical objects, though he is not bold enough to assert that images are constituents of past events.   We may leave this third assertion, which is not strictly relevant to our present discussion, and confine ourselves to (1) and (2).

The assertion (1) would not commonly be regarded as particularly startling.   Probably most philosophers in the past have regarded sensa and images as constituents of minds. The difference between them and Mr Russell here is simply that he regards sensa as being constituents of physical objects as well as being constituents of minds, whilst they would almost certainly have held that what is a constituent of a mind cannot also be a constituent of a physical object. It is in the denial (2) that Mr Russell's theory would commonly be held to be paradoxical. It would commonly be held that any mind contains other constituents beside sensa and images. In so far as Mr Russell denies that a mind contains a perfectly unique constituent—a Pure Ego—in addition to sensa and images a great many psychologists and philosophers would agree with him. But most people would say that, if the mind had no constituents except sensa and images, it would be impossible to account for the distinction between non-objective mental events, such as feeling cross or tired, and objective mental events, such as sensing a flash or seeing a gun. I am not at all clear what answer Mr Russell would make to this objection. At certain points in his *Analysis of Mind* he makes great play with "feelings" of various specific kinds, *e.g.*, "belief-feelings", "feelings of familiarity", "feeling of reality", and so on. But he does not seem to make it very clear what he supposes these "feelings" to be. Are they supposed to be sensa or images of a peculiar kind? If so, the words "sensum" and "image" are being used with so wide a meaning that the statement that the *only* constituents of the mind are sensa and images is hardly worth making. For it amounts to little more than a denial of the Pure Ego theory; and Mr Russell presumably intended to do more than flog what most of his contemporaries rightly or wrongly regard as a dead horse. I notice that whenever Mr Russell is dealing with a plainly objective mental state, such as a memory or a belief, he introduces a "feeling" in addition to a group of ordinary sensa and images. Moreover, it is of no use to say simply that a belief, *e.g.*, is such and such a group of sensa or images "accompanied by" such and such a feeling. This phrase "accompanied by" must stand for some more specific relation than mere coexistence within the same total mental state. For, at a given moment I may believe one proposition and merely suppose another proposition. If a belief-feeling "accompanies" the first set of images and sensa, it must equally "accompany" the second set, unless "to accompany" means something more specific than to "coexist with in the same total mental state". And it is evident that Mr Russell *must* mean something more specific by "accompaniment"; for the belief is to be distinguished from the contemporary supposition by the fact that a certain feeling "accompanies" the one set of images and does not "accompany" the other and coexistent set of images.

Now, I understand Mr Russell's programme in the *Analysis of Mind* to be roughly the following. I think he wants to show (*a*) that the ultimate constituents of a mind have no qualities which are not also possessed by constituents of things which are not minds. In support of this he asserts that the only constituents of a mind are sensa (which he believes to be also constituents of physical objects) and images (which, though not constituents of physical objects, are supposed to differ from sensa only in their causal characteristics and their spatio-temporal relations and not in their qualities). (*b*) That the characteristically "mental" property of reference to such and such an epistemological object is completely analysable into causal and other relations, which occur separately or in other combinations among physical things. (*c*) That the characteristic qualities of certain groups of sensa and images within a mind, and the characteristic relations of such groups to each other, are completely analysable into qualities and relations which occur separately or in other combinations among groups of sensa which are not contained in minds. And (*d*) that, consequently, even if introspection be possible, it has nothing special to teach us. I hope that this is a fair account of what Mr Russell is trying to do.

Now it seems to me that, so long as such a cloud of darkness hangs over the nature of "feelings" and the nature of the relation of "accompaniment", it is doubtful whether Mr Russell has even begun to fulfil this programme. If a "belief-feeling", *e.g.*, be neither a sensum nor an image, then presumably some of the ultimate constituents of the mind do possess qualities which are not possessed by the constituents of physical objects, and section (*a*) of the programme is abandoned. Nor is the case very much better if we suppose that a feeling is either (*a*) a single sensum or image, or (*β*) a certain group of sensa or images, which possesses a peculiar "feeling-quality" in addition to the ordinary qualities of sensa and images. It is extremely hard to believe that a sensum could possess the quality of "familiarity", *e.g.*, when it was only a constituent of a physical object and not a constituent of a mind. And, if "familiarity" or "conviction" be qualities of certain groups of sensa or images, it is extremely hard to believe that they can be anything but *emergent* qualities of such groups ; *i.e.*, qualities which *are possessed by* groups having such and such a structure and such and such constituents but are not *deducible from* a knowledge of the structure of the group and the qualities of its constituents. On either alternative there will be specific and unanalysable *mental* qualities. And this directly wrecks section (*c*) of Mr Russell's programme, and indirectly wrecks section (*d*). For, if "familiarity", *e.g.*, be a quality which attaches to a sensum *only* when it becomes a constituent of a mind, or if it be an *emergent* quality of groups of sensa or images which occur *only* within minds, introspection will have something to teach us which we can learn from no other source. Introspection will not indeed disclose any ultimate existent constituent which we might not have met with in ordinary perception; but it will disclose certain qualities which we could never have met with otherwise, and it will disclose the fact that these qualities belong to groups which have such and such a structure and such and such constituents.

Finally, I think it is extremely likely that there are characteristically "mental" forms of structure, which cannot be analysed in terms of relations which hold between sensa that are not constituents of minds. At any rate I cannot see that Mr Russell has produced any ground for doubting this proposition. Let us take an example. We are told that the difference between a mere "sensation" and a "perception" consists in the fact that in one case a sensum occurs without, and in the other case with, certain "accompaniments" in the way of other sensa, bodily feelings, images, etc. And we are told that these "accompaniments" are explicable by mnemic causation, which is not peculiar to minds but occurs in purely physiological and biological phenomena also. To this I answer that the blessed word "accompaniment" tells us nothing. The essential point is, that in the perceptual situation these various factors do not merely coexist, but are related in a perfectly unique way to form that perfectly unique kind of whole which we call a "perception of so-and-so". The uniqueness of this kind of whole is in no way impugned by the statement that it is due to mnemic causation and that mnemic causation occurs also outside the mind. It is no doubt true that the other factors in a perceptual situation would not be added to the sensum which is its objective constituent unless the mind had the powers of retentiveness, reproduction, and so on. And it is no doubt true that we find powers of retentiveness, reproduction, and so on, in living bodies as well as in minds. This does not alter the fact that, in the perceptual situation, these various factors which are due to mnemic causation are fused with each other and with the objective constituent in a perfectly unique and characteristic way, to which (so far as we know) there is no analogy outside the mind. Thus it seems to me that Mr Russell has failed to show that there are not specific and unanalysable "mental" relations between different constituents of the same mind.

I may now sum up my remarks on the third form of the Non-Central theory as follows. (1) It is, of course, open to any general objections which there may be to Non-Central theories as such. (2) If it be taken to assert that the constituents of the mind are the objects that it perceives, the events that it remembers, and so on, it is certainly false. For in many cases there is no ontological object which corresponds to a perceptual situation, and no event which corresponds to a memory-situation. And, even when such situations are veridical and have ontological objects which correspond to their epistemological objects, these ontological objects are not constituents of the situations, and, *a fortiori*, are not constituents of the mind which owns the situations. (3) The theory must, therefore, be accepted, if at all, in something like Mr Russell's form of it, which makes the constituents of the mind to be the sensa and images which are appearances to it of the objects that it perceives and the events which it remembers. But, even in this form, it requires "feelings" in addition to ordinary sensa and images; and specific relations between certain feelings and certain groups of sensa and images. And at that stage it differs very little from the other forms of Non-Central theory. The difference consists mainly in the fact that Mr Russell regards sensa as constituents of physical objects, whilst most philosophers who would admit that sensa are constituents of the mind would deny that they are also constituents of physical objects. But this is a difference about the nature of physical objects, and not a difference about the contents and structure of the mind. (4) I have also tried, incidentally, to show that Mr Russell has accomplished little, if anything, of his attempt to get rid of the uniqueness of mind. The fact is, that the more one insists on the community of *stuff* between mind and its objects, the more one will have to insist on the radical differences of *structure* between the two, and on the emergence of new *qualities* in those structures which are peculiar to mind as contrasted with matter.

Central and Non-Central Theories. We can now consider the great division of theories about the unity of the mind into Central and Non-Central theories. I will begin with two preliminary remarks : neither of them is conclusive, and they bear in opposite directions. (1) The *prima facie* presumption in favour of Central theories and against Non-Central theories is the common usage of language, which strongly suggests the existence of a Centre. We say : "*I* am thinking of this book, and wanting my tea, and feeling tired, and remembering the tie that my friend wore yesterday." This certainly suggests that " I " is the proper name of a certain existent which stands in a common asymmetric relation to all those contemporary mental events. We say further : "*I*, who am now doing and feeling these things, was yesterday doing, thinking, wanting, and feeling such and such other things." And this certainly suggests that " I " is the proper name of something which existed and was a centre yesterday as well as to-day. Now, as I have said before, it is unwise either to follow blindly the guidance of language or to ignore it altogether. Supporters of Non-Central theories can reply that they too admit that there is something which can be called " I ". It is not indeed a constituent of my empirical self ; it is the whole complex of interrelated mental events which are said to be "mine". To this I think that the following answer must be made. No doubt the ordinary man would find it difficult or impossible to tell us what he is referring to when he uses the word "I" ; but it is extremely doubtful whether he means to refer simply to the fact that the mental events which he calls "his" are interrelated in certain characteristic ways. I doubt whether anyone except a philosopher engaged in philosophising believes for a moment that the relation of "himself" to "his tooth-ache" is the same relation as that of the British Army to Private John Smith. Now, I am not suggesting that we should accept a theory because it seems to be implied by the statements of plain men. God forbid! But I do suggest that any satisfactory theory must account for the fact that plain men and philosophers in ordinary life express themselves in language which strongly favours one alternative. Now, as I have said in Chapter IV, I can quite understand that a unity of centre might appear to be a pure unity of system if the Centre were such that it could not be directly inspected. But I cannot imagine any reason why what is in fact a pure unity of system should appear to be a unity of centre. That the mind does *appear* to be of the latter kind seems pretty certain. And I think that this fact must be regarded, *pro tanto*, as favouring Central Theories.

(2) The main preliminary argument against Central theories and in favour of Non-Central theories is the alleged fact that no Existent Centre can be directly observed; that the Centre is in fact postulated *ad hoc* to explain the observed unity, and, if the unity can be explained without it, so much the better. This kind of argument has been used at two different stages in the history of the subject. (*a*) It has been used in favour of Non-Central theories as against Central theories. (*b*) In these latter days it has been carried further, and used in favour of the third form of Non-Central theory. For, it has been said that we cannot directly observe relations between the mind and its objects. When we try to *intro*spect, it is alleged, we find ourselves merely *in*-specting what I have called the "objective constituents" of mental situations, *i.e.*, sensa and images. Hence it is more prudent to take the view that the mind consists of nothing but such objective constituents interrelated in certain characteristic ways. I have dealt incidentally

with both these arguments in the chapter on Introspection. The fact that the Centre never becomes an
object of introspection is no objection to the existence
of a Centre unless a Centre be the sort of thing which
we might reasonably hope to be able to introspect
if it existed. Now, if there were a Centre which is a
non-objective constituent of *all* our mental states, it
seems unreasonable to expect that it could *also* be an
objective constituent of some of our states. To put the
matter generally : — The relation of acquaintance is
essentially asymmetrical, and this implies that the term
which has acquaintance cannot be identical with the
term with which it is acquainted. Thus, if there were a
Centre, it could not be acquainted with itself as a whole.
Now, if the Centre were a Pure Ego, it would have no
parts ; hence, if it could not be acquainted with itself as
a whole, it could not be acquainted with itself at all.
On the other hand, it might be acquainted with facts of
which it is a constituent ; and, by comparing and reflecting on these facts, it might come to a discursive
knowledge of its own existence and nature. If the
Centre were not a Pure Ego, but were a Central Event
of long duration and very uniform quality, there is no
reason why situations should not arise, in which the
non-objective constituent is a later slice of this long
event and the objective constituent is an earlier slice of
this same long event. But then it is by no means
certain that such situations do not arise. If the centre
be a continuous strand of very uniform bodily feeling it
is by no means certain that I cannot now remember the
particular slice of this strand which formed the Centre of
my total mental state some time ago. It seems to me
therefore that there is very little in this preliminary
objection to Central theories.

As regards the further extension of this argument in
favour of the third form of the Non-Central theory I can
only repeat what I said at the end of Chapter VI. The
argument seems to assume that, if objective mental

situations consisted of an objective and a non-objective constituent related in a certain way, the relation (which is an universal) must be known in the same way as the objective constituent (which is a particular). And this demand is absurd. It also seems to forget that some of the constituents of a total situation may be sensed or felt though they cannot be selected or inspected. In that case they may *be* there in addition to the objective constituent, and we may *know* that they are there (as it seems to me that we do), although we do not at the time *inspect* anything but the objective constituent.

So much for the two preliminary arguments. Neither is very strong and they cut in opposite directions ; so that at worst we may regard them as neutralising each other. But, on the whole, the argument *for* Central theories from the facts of language seems to me to be slightly stronger than the argument *against* Central theories from alleged negative facts about introspection. For the first argument does remind us of a certain very persistent "appearance" which any satisfactory theory about the unity of the mind will have to "save"; and it is certainly easier to "save" it on the Central than on the Non-Central type of theory. And the second argument does seem to consist in doubting the reality of something merely because it is not known in a particular way in which, from the nature of the case, it *could not* be known *even if it were real*.

I pass now to what seems to me to be the really crucial question between Central and Non-Central theories of the unity of the mind. This question concerns the nature of mental events, and may be put as follows : "Can we take the notion of 'mental event' as fundamental, and define the notion of 'mental substance' in terms of mental events and certain relations between them ? Or must we conceive a 'mental event' as consisting in the fact that a certain Centre has at a certain time such and such a determinate quality, or such and such a determinate relation to other things ? "

In order to deal with this question it will be wise to consider the partly (but only partly) analogous question of material events and material substances. It seems easier to take the notion of "material event" as fundamental and the notion of "material substance" as derivative than to do likewise with the notions of "mental event" and "mental substance". But I believe that this is due to the fact that most of us tacitly assume something like the Newtonian theory of Absolute Space. I shall (i) show why this is so; (ii) show that, on this view, we have not really got rid of a plurality of existent substances as a fundamental notion; and (iii) show that, on this view of material events, there is no very close analogy between them and mental events; so that, even if we could take the notion of "material event" as fundamental and the notion of "material substance" as derivative by this means, we should have no reason to suppose that we could do likewise with the notions of "mental event" and "mental substance."

(i) If we think of Space as a kind of pre-existing substance, we can of course think of a material event as the fact that a certain region of Space is characterised throughout at a certain moment by a certain determinate form of a certain determinable quality (*e.g.*, by a certain shade of a certain colour). Now the same region of Space can be characterised throughout at the same moment by determinate forms of a number of different determinable qualities (*e.g.*, by a certain shade of a certain colour, by a certain degree of temperature, and so on). Thus we can suggest with some plausibility that the unity of a total state of a certain material substance at a certain moment consists in the fact that at this moment a certain region of Space is characterised throughout by determinate forms of certain determinable qualities. Again, at a given moment, a number of separated regions of Space may each be characterised throughout by the same (or different) determinate forms of the same determinable qualities; and the intervening regions, which surround and separate these, may not be characterised by these determinable qualities at all. We can thus suggest with some plausibility that a plurality of contemporary total states of different co-existing material substances consists in the facts just mentioned. Finally, a certain region of Space may continue for some time to be characterised throughout by the same (or by continuously varying) determinate forms of the same determinables; and may continue to be surrounded by regions which are not characterised by these determinables. It is plausible to suggest that this is what we mean by saying that a certain material substance has persisted and has rested for so long in a certain place. Or, alternatively, the same (or continuously varying) forms of the same determinable qualities may successively characterise a set of regions which together make up a continuous region of Space, which is surrounded by regions that are not characterised throughout this period by these determinables. It is plausible to suggest that this is what we mean by saying that a certain material substance has persisted and has moved about during this period.

No doubt every one would admit that something more than this is needed to complete the notion of persistent material substances. But it might be suggested that the "something more" is merely a causal unity between those successive events which are counted as successive total states of the same material substance. This causal unity would consist in the fact that the variations in the determinate forms of these determinable qualities which characterise successive total states of a single material substance follow certain laws.

(ii) There are considerable difficulties in this view, as I pointed out in Chapter I, when we remember that some material substances are homogeneous fluids and not solid particles with definite boundaries separated by regions of empty Space. But the point on which I want to insist here is a different one. Even if it be granted that by this means we make the notion of particular material substances (like "this penny" or "that electron") derivative as compared with the notion of material events, we must admit in turn that the notion of a material event is not simple and that it involves the notion of something which can only be called a "substance." For what is a material event, on this theory, but the *fact* that such and such a region of Space is characterised throughout by such and such determinate forms of such and such determinable qualities? And what is a region of Space, on this theory, but a timeless particular in which sometimes one quality, sometimes several qualities, and sometimes perhaps no qualities, inhere? And what is the plurality of different regions of Space, in terms of which the plurality of coexisting material substances is defined on this theory, but a plurality of timeless particulars which differ *solo numero*?

(iii) It is plain that no form of Non-Central theory about mental events and mental substances could be at all closely analogous to the above theory about material events and substances. For the theory just described is essentially a peculiar form of Central Theory. At any given moment each total state of each material substance has its own Centre, viz., a certain region of Space which the substance is said to "occupy" at that moment. But (*a*) successive total states of the same material substance may have different Centres. For, when a material substance is said to "move about", the Centre of each of its successive total states is the region which it is said to "occupy" at each successive moment. And (*b*) the same Centre may at different times unify total states of different material substances. This happens if one material substance "moves out of a certain place" and another material substance "moves into this place". For the region in question would be first the Centre of an earlier total state of the first material substance, and then the Centre of a later total state of the second material substance.

An analogous theory about mental events and minds would be a peculiar case of the first form of Pure Ego theory. Every total mental state would be the fact that a certain Pure Ego has such and such determinate forms of such and such determinable qualities at a certain moment. If there be a plurality of coexisting total mental states, each of them will belong to a different Pure Ego. But (a) successive total states of the same mind might belong to different Pure Egos; and (b) the same Pure Ego might be the Centre of successive total states of different minds. (These cases could arise only if there were changes in the mental realm analogous to motion in the material realm; and there might of course be no reason to believe this, or positive reason to disbelieve it.)

I will now sum up the argument as far as it has gone. (a) The view that material events are logically prior to material substances is rendered plausible by the tacit assumption of something like Absolute Space, in Newton's sense. (b) But the analogous view about mental events and substances would be a form of Pure Ego theory, and not a form of Non-Central theory. Hence (c) however successful this type of theory may be for material events and substances, its success cannot be used to support by analogy a Non-Central theory of the unity of the mind. On the contrary, the analogy would support the first form of Pure Ego theory, though it would suggest certain possibilities which have not generally been contemplated by upholders of the Pure Ego theory.

The next stage in my argument is this. I shall consider (i) whether the theory that material events are logically prior to material substances can be stated and rendered plausible without the assumption of something like Absolute Space in Newton's sense. And then (ii) I shall consider whether, even if this be so, mental events and their qualities and relations bear enough analogy to material events and *their* qualities and relations to make a similar theory about mental events and substances plausible.

(i) We must of course begin by admitting the *facts* which have already been described on the assumption of Absolute Space in Newton's sense; and we must then try to reinterpret them without this assumption. Probably there are several alternative ways of doing this; but the following seems to me to be the easiest to state briefly, and to be theoretically possible.

(*a*) I begin by distinguishing two fundamentally different, though intimately connected, kinds of determinable quality, viz., Positional and Non-Positional Qualities. There are two generally recognised determinable Positional Qualities, viz., Temporal and Spatial Position. A Non-Positional determinable quality can only be defined negatively as any determinable quality, such as colour or temperature, which is not positional like "being in such and such a place" or "being at such and such a date". (*b*) A completely determinate form of any Non-Positional Quality can characterise a number of numerically diverse particular existents. Any particular existent which is characterised by some determinate form of some Non-Positional Quality will be called "an instance of that quality". It will also be called an instance of that determinate form of this quality which characterises it. (*c*) Every particular existent is characterised by some determinate form of the determinable quality of Temporal Position. (*d*) All the instances of certain Non-Positional Qualities must *also* be characterised by some determinate form of the determinable quality of Spatial Position. Such Non-Positional Qualities will be called "Material Qualities". There are other Non-Positional Qualities whose instances are not necessarily characterised by any determinate form of the quality of Spatial Position. These will be called "Immaterial Qualities". (*e*) The same particular existent cannot be characterised by different determinate forms of the quality of Temporal Position;

i.e., every particular existent is instantaneous. (*f*) If a particular existent is characterised by the quality of Spatial Position it cannot be characterised by two different determinate forms of this quality; *i.e.*, all particular existents which are instances of Material Qualities are punctiform as well as instantaneous. We may therefore call them "Point-Instants". (*g*) There can be a plurality of particular existents having the same determinate quality of Temporal Position and the same determinate form of the same Non-Positional Quality. If they be instances of a Material Quality they will of course have to have different determinate forms of the quality of Spatial Position. (*h*) There can be a plurality of particular existents having the same determinate form of the quality of Spatial Position and the same determinate form of some Non-Positional Quality. They will of course have to have different determinate forms of the quality of Temporal Position. (*i*) The same particular existent may be characterised by determinate forms of a number of different Non-Positional Qualities. It is to be noted that nothing that we have said precludes the possibility that the same particular existent may be an instance both of Material and of Immaterial Qualities. It is true that, if it be characterised by a Material Quality it *must* be also characterised by the quality of Spatial Position; and that, if it be characterised by an Immaterial Quality, it *need not* be characterised by the quality of Spatial Position. But we have not said that what is characterised by an Immaterial Quality *cannot* be characterised by the quality of Spatial Position. (*j*) Every particular existent is an instance of some Non-Positional Quality in addition to being characterised by some determinate form of the determinable quality of Temporal Position.

So far we have considered only the instantaneous and the punctiform. We take the fundamental constituents of the material world to be instantaneous punctiform particulars, each of which has a determinate quality of

Temporal Position, a determinate quality of Spatial Position, and determinate forms of one or more Non-Positional Qualities. *Paulo majora canamus*. (*a*) The various determinate qualities under the determinable of Temporal Position form a continuous one-dimensional order, as, *e.g.*, do the determinate qualities under the determinable of Temperature. (It used to be assumed that all point-instants fall into a single temporal series. The facts on which the Special Theory of Relativity is based suggest that this is probably not true. They suggest that, while every point-event falls into *some* series of this kind, they do not all fall into *the same* series. But we need not bother about these complications for the present purpose.) (*b*) The various determinate qualities under the determinable of Spatial Position form a continuous three-dimensional order, as, *e.g.*, do the determinate qualities under the determinable of Colour. Point-instants are thus ordered in various ways, and stand in various temporal, spatial and spatio-temporal relations to each other in virtue of the determinate qualities of Temporal and Spatial Position which characterise each point-event. (*c*) Now there are certain determinable qualities which cannot characterise an individual point-instant, but which can and do characterise certain complex wholes composed of point-instants related to each other in certain ways in virtue of their various Positional Qualities. I will call these "Extensional Qualities". (*d*) The only Extensional Quality connected with Temporal Position and the relations which it generates is Duration. If a set of point-instants vary continuously in their qualities of Temporal Position, the whole composed of them has a certain determinate duration, which depends upon the determinate relation between the determinate qualities of Temporal Position which characterise the first and the last point-instant of the set. (*e*) The Extensional Qualities connected with the quality of Spatial Position are more complicated, because the determinates under the determinable of

Spatial Position form a three-dimensional order. We have here the two interconnected determinable Extensional Qualities of Shape and Size. There is no need to go into elaborate details. If a whole composed of point-instants is to have shape and size the first condition is that all the point-instants shall have the same determinate Temporal Position. The other condition is that the determinate qualities of Spatial Position possessed by the various point-instants of the set shall vary continuously. The determinate shape and size possessed by this complex whole will then depend on the determinate relations between the determinate qualities of Spatial Position which characterise the various point-instants which form the boundary of the set. We might sum the matter up by saying that Extensional Qualities are emergent from the relations between different determinate forms of a determinable Positional Quality. Positional and Extensional Qualities might be classed together under the general name of "Structural Qualities"; and they might then be distinguished from each other by the names of "Primitive" and "Emergent" Structural Qualities respectively.

(f) We must now draw some rather similar distinctions among Non-structural Qualities. We may divide them first into those which can characterise individual point-instants and those which cannot. The former may be called "Primitive" and the latter "Non-primitive". The Primitive Non-structural Qualities can be subdivided into (1) those which can characterise only point-instants; and (2) those which can characterise both point-instants and extensional wholes composed of suitably interrelated point-instants. These might be distinguished as "Non-extensible" and "Extensible" Non-structural Qualities respectively. The Non-primitive Non-structural Qualities might be subdivided into (1) those which can characterise any extensional whole, no matter what may be its determinate duration, shape, or size; and (2) those which can characterise only extensional wholes which have a certain minimum size, or duration, or a certain determinate shape, etc. The former might be called "Homogeneous" and the latter "Non-Homogeneous" Non-structural Qualities.

Granted all this, we can see how the notion of a material substance can be defined. We will begin with the simplest possible case, and gradually complicate it. (*a*) Imagine a set of point-instants which fulfil the following conditions: (1) They all have the same determinate quality of Spatial Position. (2) Their determinate qualities of Temporal Position form a continuous series, so that the whole composed of these point-instants has a certain determinate duration. (3) Each of them is an instance of several determinable Material Qualities, the same in each case. And each of them is an instance of the same determinate form of any given one of these Material Qualities. A whole of this kind is a material particle which endures for a period, stays in one place for that period, remains unaltered in quality throughout the period, and at each moment has a plurality of different states. (*b*) We can now keep all the conditions as before, except that the various point-instants are to have different determinate values of some of the determinable Material Qualities which characterise them all. We now have a material particle which endures, stays in one place, and has a plurality of states at each instant, but changes in some respects during the period. (*c*) Now alter condition (1). Let the various point-instants of the series no longer all have the same determinate quality of Spatial Position. Instead let the determinate qualities of Spatial Position of the successive point-instants vary continuously from one to another. The whole composed of these point-instants is now a material particle which endures, has at each instant a plurality of different states, changes qualitatively as time goes on, and also moves about. (*d*) We can now further complicate matters by considering successive sets of contemporary point-instants. Suppose that each set consists of point-events which are exactly alike in all respects except that they have different determinate qualities of Spatial Position. And suppose that these determinate qualities of Spatial Position vary continuously from one point-instant of the set to another. Then the set as a whole will have some determinate size and some determinate shape ; it will form a line, or an area, or a volume. Suppose now that every point-instant in this set is a member of a series of successive point-instants of the kind which we have called a "material particle" and have described in (a) to (c). Suppose further that every set of contemporary point-instants, such that one point-instant of the set belongs to each of these material particles, is a whole of the kind which has Shape and Size. Then we have got a persistent *body* of finite spatial dimensions. And we could quite easily define the conditions under which we should say (1) that this body rests and keeps its shape and size constant, or (2) that it rests and alters in shape and size, or (3) that it moves and keeps its shape and size constant, or (4) that it moves and alters its shape and size. Lastly (e), having got our finite persistent bodies, we can introduce Non-primitive Non-structural Qualities ; some of them might be Homogeneous, as perhaps mass is ; others might be spatially Heterogeneous, *i.e.* requiring a whole of a certain minimum size to inhere in, as is probably the case with electric charge ; and others might be temporally Heterogeneous, *i.e.*, requiring a whole of a certain mimimum duration to inhere in, as is probably the case with magnetic properties.

I have now tried to show in detail how it would be possible to take the notion of a material event as fundamental, and to construct the notion of material substances out of it, *without* assuming Absolute Space in Newton's sense. It is to be noted that, in another sense, we have assumed both Absolute Space and Absolute Time. We have assumed that there are spatial and temporal positional *qualities*, and that spatial and temporal relations depend on them. Thus our theory of Space and Time is absolute, in the sense that it is not purely relational. But it is not absolute, in the sense that it makes the points of Space and the moments of Time to be existent substantives of a peculiar kind, as Newton's theory does. The only existent substantives which we assume are instantaneous punctiform particulars, which have determinate qualities of Spatial and Temporal Position and determinate forms of determinable Non-positional Qualities. Certain sets of these form wholes which have the qualities of shape, size, and duration, in virtue of the relations between their Positional Qualities. Adopting a distinction of Mr Johnson's, we may say that we have assumed an "adjectival" and not a "substantival" form of the Absolute Theory.

(ii) I can now pass to the second part of my argument. Granted that it is possible to take the notion of a material event as fundamental and to derive the notion of a material substance, without smuggling back the notion of substance under the guise of Absolute Space in Newton's sense, is it possible to do likewise with mental events and mental substances?

First of all, what are the relevant differences between the facts in the two cases? The fundamental difference seems to be this. Mental qualities are what I have called "Immaterial"; *i.e.*, although any existent particular which is an instance of a mental quality must have some determinate quality of Temporal Position, it need not (and, so far as we know, does not) have any form of the quality of Spatial Position. It follows that, although a series of instantaneous mental events may form a whole which has the Extensional Quality of duration, a set of contemporary mental events will not form a whole which has the Extensional Qualities of size and shape. Now, if two contemporary *material* events have the same determinate form of the same Non-positional Quality, we know that they must have different determinate forms of the quality of Spatial Position. It is logically possible for there to be two contemporary *mental* events which have the same determinate form of the same Mental Quality (*e.g.*, it is *logically* possible that there might be two precisely similar contemporary thoughts of the same object, even if there is reason to think that this is *causally* improbable or impossible). Now there seem to be only two alternative ways of explaining this fact. The two precisely similar thoughts must either belong to different Pure Egos, or there must be some non-spatio-temporal Positional Quality of which they possess different determinate forms.

I said that there are only two *commonly recognised* determinable Positional Qualities, viz., Temporal and Spatial Position. We now see that, if we want to make up a theory of mental events and substances analogous to that which we have suggested for material events and substances, we must assume a third determinable Positional Quality which we might call the quality of "Mental Position". We must suppose that every mental event is an instantaneous particular which has a certain determinate Temporal Position and a certain determinate Mental Position. Two mental events may agree in every other respect, provided that they differ in Temporal Position; and two mental events may agree in every other respect, provided they differ in Mental Position; but they must have different determinate forms of one or other of these Positional Qualities. With this assumption it would, I think, be possible to take the notion of "a mind" as definable. A total state of mind would be an instantaneous particular existent, which (*a*) has a determinate quality of Temporal Position, (*b*) has a determinate quality of Mental Position, and (*c*) is an instance of several different Mental Qualities. Suppose now that there were a set of instantaneous events, having the following characteristics. (*a*) They all have the same determinate quality of Mental Position. (*b*) They all differ in their Temporal Position, and their determinate qualities of Temporal Position form a continuous series, so that they form a whole which has a certain determinate duration. −(*c*) They all have the same determinable Mental Qualities. (*d*) They all have the same determinate form of some of these Mental Qualities. (*e*) Some of them have different forms of some of these Mental Qualities, but these different determinate forms of the same determinable Mental Quality vary continuously from one instantaneous event of the set to another. Then the whole thus formed might fairly be called a "mind", which endures, has a number of different mental "states" at each moment, changes its states as time goes on, and so on.

It will be noticed that the kind of enduring whole which I have just been describing as a "mind" is analogous, not to a body, but to a material particle. And, for reasons which will appear in a moment, it will be better not to call this very simple kind of mental whole a "mind". We will call it a "mental particle" instead. I will now explain why I make this suggestion. We know that the determinate qualities under the determinable of Spatial Position form a continuous manifold of three dimensions, like the determinate qualities under the determinable of Colour. Now I suggest that the determinate qualities under the determinable of Mental Position may form a manifold of more than one dimension ; and that, if this be so, we can form a conception of the phenomena of the Unconscious, of Multiple Personality, of Telepathy, and so on, in terms of the present theory. A body consists of a number of material particles, such that any set of contemporary point-instants chosen from each of these material particles forms a whole which has a certain size and shape. And the condition for this is that the determinate qualities of Spatial Position of these point-instants vary continuously from one point-instant of the set to another. Now substitute mental particles, as defined above, for material particles; and substitute Mental Position for Spatial Position. Then, if the determinate qualities under the determinable of Mental Position form a manifold of more than one dimension, a mind may be analogous to a body and may have something analogous to size and shape. Two entirely different minds might then be analogous to two entirely separate bodies. Now two bodies may come into contact at certain times, and they may touch each other at a point, or along a line, or over an area. Similarly, if the determinates under the determinable of Mental Position form a manifold of more than one dimension it will be possible for there to be "mental contact" of various kinds between minds, if a mind be what I am now suggesting that it is. This might be what happens when telepathic communication takes place between two minds.

I will now consider how the facts of Multiple Personality might be explained in terms of such a theory of mind as I am now suggesting. It is not unreasonable to suppose that all the mental events connected with a certain living brain and nervous system have determinate qualities of Mental Position which fall within certain limits or are interrelated in some special way. Let us suppose, e.g., that the relative mental positions of all the mental events connected with a brain and nervous system at a given moment are such that these mental events may be represented by points on the surface of a certain sphere. It would be reasonable to suppose that the determinate mental positions of all the mental events that belong to a single personality are interrelated in some still more special way. Let us suppose, e.g., that the relative mental positions of all the mental events that belong to a single personality at a given moment are such that these mental events may be represented by a *continuous series* of points forming a *great circle* on the surface of the sphere. Now it might happen that the mental events connected with a single brain and nervous system at a certain moment can be divided into three sub-groups, as follows. (A) Those whose representative points form a continuous great circle A on the sphere. (B) Those whose representative points form another continuous great circle B on the sphere. (C) Those whose representative points are isolated dots on the sphere. The diagram below will make this plain.

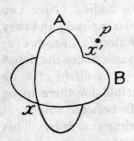

Then the great circles A and B will represent two contemporary total states of two personalities A and B connected with the same body. The points x and x' in which these two great circles intersect will represent mental events which are common to the two personalities at this moment. And the isolated dots, such as p, will represent mental events which are connected at the moment with this brain and nervous system but do not belong to any personality. It would of course be possible to represent any number of different personalities connected with the same body by introducing other great circles continuously filled with mental events. On this representation the relations between the personalities are symmetrical; but it would be easy to devise a representation of the case in which A shares all B's mental events and has other mental events which are not shared by B. *E.g.*, B might be represented by the same great circle as before; A might now be represented by the upper hemisphere which stands upon this, supposed to be continuously occupied by mental events; whilst events that belong to neither might be represented by isolated dots on the lower hemisphere.

It is needless to go into further detail. The essential point to notice is that it would be difficult to deal with the facts of abnormal and supernormal psychology if we identified a mind with a single mental particle, whilst it is easy to deal with them on the following two assumptions. (*a*) That the determinates under the determinable of Mental Position form a manifold of several dimensions; and (*b*) that a mind consists of a number of mental particles, such that the mental positions of contemporary mental events from each particle vary continuously from one mental event to another, so that a mind has something analogous to size and shape.

There is one other point to notice. It is almost certain that the Immaterial Non-Positional Qualities which we are familiar with in the case of minds are non-homogeneous in respect to time. By this I mean that they cannot characterise single instantaneous mental events, but only wholes which are composed of certain continuous series of mental events and have a certain minimum duration. I think it very likely too that the Mental Qualities with which we are familiar can characterise only wholes which have a certain minimum of "Mental Extension"

Conclusion. So far as I can see then, there is no *a priori* objection to the view that the notion of "mental event" can be taken as fundamental and that the notion of "mind" or "mental substance" can be derived from it. It remains to be seen whether there are any special empirical facts which make for or against this view. (1) I think that it would have no particular advantage over the Pure Ego theory if we were confined to the psychology of normal human minds. But it does seem to have great advantages over the Pure Ego theory when we are concerned with the facts of abnormal and supernormal psychology; just as the corresponding theory about material substances has very great advantages when we are concerned with abnormal physical facts, such as mirror-images. If then it be equally capable of explaining the facts of normal mental life, it is on the whole to be slightly preferred to the Pure Ego theory. (2) If one of these facts be the appearance of a Centre to each total mental state, the present theory is quite capable of dealing with it. For it can allow of a Central Event in every total state of mind, though it cannot allow that the Centre is a Pure Ego. (3) I think that one empirical fact on which supporters of the Pure Ego theory have relied is the fact of Personal Memory. Now this fact has two sides to it, viz., a causal and an epistemological side. (*a*) Causally considered, it is just a particular case of the fact that an event which has happened to a substance in the remote past may partially determine a present event in the same substance, although there has been nothing to show for it in the interval. This kind of causation is not peculiar to minds. And, granted that it involves the persistence of something which we call a "trace", I have tried to show in Chapter X that it is quite easy to conceive the persistence of a trace as the handing on of a certain structural or qualitative modification from one total event to the next total event in a successive series of specially interconnected total events. It does not involve of necessity tne persistence of a certain substantial constituent. Hence the Pure Ego is not required to account for memory on its causal side. (*b*) Epistemologically the peculiarity of memory is that the memory-situation claims to give us non-inferential and intuitive knowledge of an event in our own past history. Naturally, memory differs from all non-mental mnemic effects in the fact that it consists of a *cognitive* event; for the power to cognise is characteristic of minds. But this peculiarity by itself does not necessitate the assumption of a Pure Ego, unless cognition as such is impossible without a Pure Ego; and I do not think that this has been maintained. Thus, if Personal Memory requires a Pure Ego, it must do so, not because it is causally dependent on persistent traces, and not because it is a form of cognition, but because it claims to be a non-inferential and intuitive cognition of an event *in one's own past history*. Now there are two distinct points to be considered here, viz. (i) that I claim to have *present* acquaintance with a *past* event; and (ii) that I claim to know that this past event was a state of *my* mind.

(i) I do not see that the hypothesis of a Pure Ego is relevant to the first claim. This claim is that there are cognitive situations which, as wholes, are present, and which contain as their objective constituents events which are past. Supposing this to be possible at all, I do not see that the hypothesis of a Pure Ego helps us to understand the possibility of such situations. If a situation can be present in spite of the fact that one of its constituents is past, it does not seem to matter whether the other constituent be a timeless Pure Ego or a present event. In fact it is slightly easier to understand the position on the latter hypothesis than on the former. For, on the latter hypothesis, the situation which is present contains a constituent which is present; whilst, on the former, it contains no constituent which is present.

(ii) If Personal Memory requires a Pure Ego this cannot then be because in Personal Memory I claim to have present acquaintance with a past event; it must be because I claim to recognise this past event as having been a state of *myself*. Now, on the Pure Ego theory to recognise that a past event was a state of myself is to recognise that its subjective constituent is numerically the same Pure Ego as that which is the subjective constituent of my present act of remembering. On other theories it consists in recognising that the past event stands in certain relations of qualitative resemblance, causal connexion, and identity or continuity of mental position, with my present act of remembering and with other intermediate states which I can remember. I cannot see that there is any more difficulty in supposing that we could recognise the one kind of fact than the other; and I cannot see that the power of recognising the second kind of fact requires the presence of a numerically identical substantial constituent common to all our successive total states.   Hence I do not think that the facts of memory require the hypothesis of a Pure Ego.

The upshot of the matter is that I can see no conclusive reasoning for rejecting or accepting the Pure Ego theory; and that I think that it is perfectly possible to state a theory of the unity of the mind which does not involve a Pure Ego.   And, as the latter theory seems better adapted to deal with the facts of abnormal and supernormal psychology than the former, I am inclined slightly to prefer it.

CHAPTER XIV

Status and Prospects of Mind in Nature

It is now time to gather together the various threads of the earlier chapters, and to see whether we can come to any conclusions about the probable position and probable prospects of Mind in the Universe. It appears to me that *seventeen* different types of metaphysical theory are possible theoretically on the relation between Mind and Matter. I will first proceed to justify this very startling statement, and to enumerate, classify, and name the theories. Afterwards I shall consider the strong and weak points of each, and see whether we can come to any tentative decision between them.

The Seventeen Types of Theory. In order to understand the discussion that follows the reader should refer back to the section on Pluralism and Monism in Chapter I, where I defined the notion of " Differentiating Attributes " and distinguished them from other kinds of attribute. He should also refer to Chapter II, where I distinguished between those non-differentiating attributes which are " Emergent " and those which are not. I propose here to call non-differentiating attributes which actually apply to certain things in the world, but are not emergent, "Reducible Attributes". It will be necessary to introduce one further distinction which we have not so far made use of. Some attributes have application, *i.e.*, there are things in the Universe which have these attributes in some determinate form. Other attributes have no application. The characteristic of being a fire-breathing serpent, or of being mistress of the Duke of Bletchley, applies to nothing in the world. Now it is held by many people that there are characteristics which do not in fact apply to anything but which seem to some or all men to apply to something. *E.g.*, if Dr M'Taggart be right, it can be proved that the characteristic of being extended cannot apply to anything. But it certainly seems to all men as if there were extended things. I propose to call a characteristic which seems to apply to certain things, but does not in fact apply to anything, a "Delusive Characteristic". I am going to use words in such a way that Differentiating Attributes, Emergent Qualities, and Reducible Qualities, are to be understood to have application and therefore not to be delusive. With these preliminary explanations we can pass to our classification of theoretically possible types of metaphysical theory about Mind and matter.

We have to consider the two attributes of "mentality" and "materiality". We at once find three great divisions of possible theories. (1) Both mentality and materiality might be differentiating attributes. (2) One might be a differentiating attribute and the other not. Or (3) it might be that neither is a differentiating attribute. We now proceed to divide up these three types of theory in turn.

(1, 1) Both mentality and materiality may be capable of belonging to the same substance; or (1, 2) it may be that no substance can have both these differentiating attributes.

(2, 1) Mentality might be a differentiating attribute and materiality not; or (2, 2) materiality might be a differentiating attribute and mentality not. We now further subdivide these alternatives as follows. (2, 11) Materiality, though not a differentiating attribute, might still have application; or (2, 12) materiality might be a delusive characteristic. Similarly (2, 21) mentality, though not a differentiating attribute, might still have application ; or (2, 22) mentality might be a delusive characteristic. The alternatives (2, 12) and (2, 22) need no further subdivision ; but the alternatives (2, 11) and (2, 21) both need further subdivision. Let us begin with (2, 11). It might be that materiality is (2, 111) an emergent characteristic ; or (2, 112) that it is a reducible characteristic. Similarly, it might be (2, 211) that mentality is emergent ; or (2, 212) that it is reducible. This completes the subdivisions of alternative (2).

We pass now to the subdivisions of alternative (3). Granted that neither mentality nor materiality is a differentiating attribute, there are three alternatives open. (3, 1) Both attributes might have application ; or (3, 2) one might have application and the other be delusive ; or (3, 3) both might be delusive. The last alternative needs no further subdivision ; the first two require to be further subdivided. We will begin with (3, 1). If mentality and materiality both have application, they may (3, 11) both be emergent ; or (3, 12) one may be emergent and the other reducible ; or (3, 13) they may both be reducible. The first and third of these alternatives need no further subdivision, but the second divides into two. It may be (3, 121) that mentality is emergent and materiality reducible ; or (3, 122) that materiality is emergent and mentality reducible. It remains to subdivide (3, 2). If one of the attributes has application and the other is delusive, it may be (3, 21) that mentality has application and materiality is delusive ; or (3, 22) that materiality has application and mentality is delusive. Each of these latter alternatives subdivides into two viz., (3, 211) that mentality is emergent ; or (3, 212) that mentality is reducible ; or (3, 221) that materiality is emergent ; or (3, 222) that materiality is reducible.

We have now got our seventeen alternative theories, which I will recapitulate and name.

(1, 1) Mentality and materiality are both differentiating attributes which can belong to the same substance. This I will call "Dualism of Compatibles".

(1, 2) Mentality and materiality are both differentiating attributes, but they cannot both belong to the same substance. This I will call "Dualism of Incompatibles".

(2, 12) Mentality is a differentiating attribute, but materiality is delusive. This I will call "Pure Mentalism".

(2, 22) Materiality is a differentiating attribute, but mentality is delusive. This I will call "Pure Materialism".

(2, 111) Mentality is a differentiating attribute, and materiality is an emergent characteristic. This I will call "Emergent Mentalism".

(2, 112) Mentality is a differentiating attribute, and materiality is a reducible characteristic. This I will call "Reductive Mentalism".

(2, 211) Materiality is a differentiating attribute, and mentality is an emergent characteristic. This I will call "Emergent Materialism".

(2, 212) Materiality is a differentiating attribute, and mentality is a reducible characteristic. This I will call "Reductive Materialism".

(3, 11) Neither mentality nor materiality is a differentiating attribute, but both are emergent characteristics. This I will call "Emergent Neutralism".

(3, 13) Neither mentality nor materiality is a differentiating attribute, but both are reducible characteristics. This I will call "Reductive Neutralism".

(3, 121) Neither mentality nor materiality is a differentiating attribute, but mentality is an emergent characteristic and materiality is a reducible characteristic.

(3, 122) Neither mentality nor materiality is a differentiating attribute, but mentality is a reducible characteristic and materiality is an emergent characteristic. I class these two alternatives together under the name of "Mixed Neutralism".

(3, 211) Neither mentality nor materiality is a differentiating attribute, but mentality is emergent and materiality is delusive.

(3, 212) Neither mentality nor materiality is a differentiating attribute, but mentality is a reducible characteristic and materiality is delusive. I class these two alternatives together under the name of "Mentalistic Neutralism".

(3, 221) Neither mentality nor materiality is a differentiating attribute, but mentality is delusive and materiality is an emergent characteristic.

(3, 222) Neither mentality nor materiality is a differentiating attribute, but mentality is delusive and materiality is a reducible characteristic. I class these two alternatives together under the name of "Materialistic Neutralism".

(3, 3) Neither mentality nor materiality is a differentiating attribute, and both of them are delusive. This I call "Pure Neutralism".

We have now got our seventeen alternative possible theories about Mind and Matter definitely stated. I propose now to take them in order, to explain more fully what each of them means, and to consider the strong and weak points (if any) in each of them. It may then be possible to make a tentative decision between them.

Discussion of the Seventeen Types of Theory. It will save time and simplify the discussion if we begin by eliminating those alternatives which are quite plainly impossible. It is easy to see that any theory which makes mentality a delusive characteristic is self-contradictory. For to say that mentality is a delusive characteristic is to say that it in fact belongs to nothing, but that it is misperceived or misjudged to belong to something. But, if there be misperceptions or misjudgments, there are perceptions or judgments; and, if there be perceptions or judgments, there *are* events to which the characteristic of mentality applies. This enables us at once to eliminate (2, 22) Pure Materialism ; (3, 221) and (3, 222) the two forms of Materialistic Neutralism ; and

(3, 3) Pure Neutralism.   We have thus reduced our alternatives to thirteen.

There are two other types of theory which, I believe, can be positively refuted.   These are (2, 112) Reductive Mentalism, and (2, 212) Reductive Materialism.   So far as I am aware, Reductive Mentalism has never been held ; but Reductive Materialism flourishes to-day under the name of "Behaviourism".   I will therefore take the latter theory first, and try to prove that it is absurd.

Reductive Materialism or "Behaviourism".   This theory holds that there really are material objects, and that materiality is a differentiating attribute.   And it also holds that the characteristic of being a mind or being a mental process *reduces to* the fact that a certain kind of body is making certain overt movements or is undergoing certain internal physical changes.   Of course many writers who call themselves "Behaviourists" are really Epiphenomenalists, and Epiphenomenalism is an entirely different doctrine ; but there is a residue of quite genuine Behaviourists, and it is with their views which we are now concerned.

Behaviourism in psychology may be compared to mechanism in biology.   But there is a very important difference between the problem of life and that of mind, which makes Behaviourism in psychology much less plausible than mechanism in biology.   The one and only kind of evidence that we ever have for believing that a thing is alive is that it behaves in certain characteristic ways.   *E.g.*, it moves spontaneously, eats, drinks, digests, grows, reproduces, and so on.   Now all these are just actions of one body on other bodies.   There seems to be no reason whatever to suppose that "being alive" means any more than exhibiting these various forms of bodily behaviour.   That is why Substantial Vitalism, which is the biological analogue of Cartesian Dualism in psychology, is a dead issue ; and why the whole controversy about life is really between Emergence and

Mechanism.   But the position about consciousness, certainly seems to be very different.   It is perfectly true that an essential part of our evidence for believing that anything but ourselves has a mind and is having such and such experiences is that it performs certain characteristic bodily movements in certain situations.   *E.g.*, we observe it avoiding obstacles, repeating some series of movements again and again with suitable variations until a certain end is gained, giving appropriate answers to questions, and so on.   When external bodies behave in these ways, we are inclined to associate minds and mental processes with them ; and, when they do not, we are inclined to deny these to them.   Now, if this were the only evidence that we ever had in any case for the existence of minds and mental processes, it may be admitted that the latter could, at most, be regarded as purely hypothetical causes of certain kinds of bodily behaviour.   And it might then be plausible, though it would certainly not be logically necessary, to suggest that "having a mind" simply *means* "behaving in such and such ways".   But it is plain that our observation of the behaviour of external bodies is not our only or our primary ground for asserting the existence of minds and mental processes.   And it seems to me equally plain that by "having a mind" we do not mean simply "behaving in such and such ways".   These points can be made clear as follows.

(*a*) We certainly ascribe mental processes to ourselves as well as to others, and it is perfectly certain that here our ground for saying that we are having such and such an experience is *not* the fact that we have observed our bodies to be behaving in such and such ways.   When I say that I am seeing a chair or hearing a bell I am asserting the occurrence of an experience.   Now it is possible that, whenever I have the first kind of experience, my body is behaving in one characteristic way ; and that, whenever I have the second kind of experience, my body is behaving in a characteristically different way.

But, even if this be in fact true, it is perfectly certain that this is not my ground for saying that I see a chair or hear a bell. I often know without the least doubt that I am having the experience called "seeing a chair" when I am altogether uncertain whether my body is acting in any characteristic way. And again I distinguish with perfect ease between the experience called "seeing a chair" and the experience called "hearing a bell" when I am quite doubtful whether my bodily behaviour, if any, on the two occasions has been alike or different. If then the Behaviourist argues that mental processes, in so far as they differ from bodily behaviour, are purely hypothetical causes of such behaviour; and that we shall keep nearer to the observable facts by dropping these hypothetical entities altogether; the answer is to deny his premise. If we confine ourselves to bodily behaviour it is perfectly certain that we are leaving out something of whose existence we are immediately aware in favourable cases.

(b) However completely the behaviour of an external body answers to the behaviouristic tests for intelligence, it always remains a perfectly sensible question to ask: "Has it really got a mind, or is it merely an automaton?" It is quite true that we have no available means of answering such questions conclusively. It is also true that, the more nearly a body answers to the behaviouristic tests for intelligence, the harder it is for us in practice to contemplate the possibility of its having no mind. Still, the question: "Has it a mind?" is never silly in the sense that it is meaningless. At worst it is silly only in the sense that it does not generally express a real doubt, and that we have no means of answering it. It may be like asking whether the moon may not be made of green cheese; but it is not like asking whether a rich man may have no wealth. Now, on the behaviouristic theory, to have a mind just means to behave in certain ways; and to ask whether a thing which admittedly does behave in these ways has a mind would be like asking whether Jones, who is admittedly a rich man, has much wealth. Since the question can be raised, and is evidently not tautologous or self-contradictory, it is clear that when we ascribe a mind or a mental process to an external body we do not mean simply that it behaves in certain characteristic ways. If the Behaviourist answers that, whatever we *do* mean, this is all that we *ought* to mean, I have two comments to make. (i) We have a right to mean more, because we know that in our own case there is more. (ii) I would invite the Behaviourist to explain how, on his own theory, we can ever have come to make the mistake which he says that we do make. If in fact we can observe nothing but bodily behaviour in ourselves and others, how did we ever come to entertain the hypothesis that there is something more than these ; and how did we come to suppose that there are better grounds for assuming the presence of this extra factor in some cases than in others? On the ordinary view this fact is easily explicable. We know that there is something more than bodily behaviour in our own case, because we can directly observe it. We find that certain kinds of experience in ourselves are accompanied by certain types of bodily behaviour. If we find external bodies which resemble our own behaving in the way in which ours behave when we have a certain kind of experience, we assume that there is a similar kind of experience associated with these bodies. And we feel more confidence in this conclusion the more closely the external body and its behaviour resemble our own. Of course such an inference may be wrong in any particular case ; it is even possible theoretically that it is wrong in all cases. But it is at least intelligible, on the ordinary view, how we come to make this hypothesis, and why we feel more certain of it in some cases than in others. All this would be completely inexplicable, it seems to me, if Behaviourism were the whole truth. If Behaviourism be true we all make a mistake which it would be impossible for us even to think of unless Behaviourism were false.

I propose now to go rather more into detail about the behaviouristic analysis of certain special kinds of mental process. But, before I do this, I must clear up a certain ambiguity about the meaning of "bodily behaviour". When the Behaviourist says that all mental processes reduce without residue to the fact that the body is behaving in a certain specific way he does not mean to confine himself to gross overt actions, like shrieking or kicking. His attempts to reduce all mental processes to bodily behaviour would have no plausibility at all if he were restricted to this narrow sense of "behaviour". He always includes also at least such bodily movements as changes of blood-pressure, incipient movements in the tongue and throat, convergence and accommodation of the eyes, and so on. This, I think, is quite legitimate; for there is no essential difference between movements which are difficult to observe simply because they go on inside the body and those which are overt and easily observable without special instruments of precision. I will lump together all such changes under the name of "molar behaviour", as contrasted with "molecular behaviour"; and I will call a Behaviourist who thinks that all mental processes can be reduced without residue to molar behaviour a "molar Behaviourist".

But it is very difficult to get the Behaviourist to stop at this point. When overt behaviour, supplemented by changes of blood-pressure, incipient movements in the throat, etc., seems inadequate to make the behaviouristic analysis of some mental process seem plausible, the Behaviourist is very liable to appeal to hypothetical molecular movements in the brain and nervous system. If you say to him that two obviously different mental processes, A and B are accompanied by indistinguishable molar behaviour, or that qualitatively indistinguishable mental processes are accompanied on different occasions by obviously different kinds of molar behaviour, he is liable to say: "Well, at any rate, the correlated molecular changes in the brain and nervous system must have been different in the one case and exactly alike in the other." As no one knows anything about these, no one can deny that this may be true. The Behaviourist then proceeds to *identify* the mental process with the supposed molecular changes. This I will call "molecular Behaviourism". In this form of course there is nothing new about Behaviourism; it is just old-fashioned materialism which has crossed the Atlantic under an *alias*. It is true that all Behaviourism is a form of Reductive Materialism; but it does at least claim to be a new form. And this claim can be upheld only if it be interpreted to mean molar Behaviourism· Of course, what happens is that a man starts as a Molar Behaviourist and is then pushed back by criticism into Molecular Behaviourism, at which stage his theory has lost most of its interest.

I am now going to consider the behaviouristic account of perception, because perception is the mental process to which Behaviourism can most plausibly be applied. If it fails to give an adequate account of perception, it is incredible that it should give an adequate account of memory, imagination, or abstract thinking. I will first explain why I hold this. If a certain kind of mental process is to be *reduced to* a certain kind of bodily behaviour it is evidently a necessary, though by no means a sufficient, condition that there shall be a one to one correlation between the two. That is, it must be quite certain that this mental process never happens without this bodily behaviour, and that this bodily behaviour never happens without this mental process. If either ever happens without the other it is certain that the two cannot be identical; though of course they might not be identical even if one never did happen without the other. There is a one to one correlation between the events in the life of Augustus and the events in the life of the second Roman emperor, because the name "Augustus" and the phrase "the second Roman emperor" denote the same person. There is also a one to one correlation between the movements of the needles of two connected telegraphic instruments. But these are nevertheless two different sets of movements, and not a single set with two different names. The Behaviourist has to show that mental and bodily events are connected as incidents in the life of Augustus and incidents in the life of the second Roman emperor are connected. He will have done nothing relevant if he shows only that they are connected as the movements of the two telegraph-needles are connected.

Now I do not see the least reason to believe that there is any kind of molar behaviour which always goes on when I am thinking and never goes on at any other time; and the same remarks apply to remembering and imagining. I see still less reason to believe that there is one kind of molar behaviour which always happens and only happens when I am thinking of Cleopatra's Needle, and another kind which always happens and only happens when I am thinking of the Binomial Theorem. If you say that there may be molecular differences in these cases I cheerfully admit it, since neither you nor I can possibly know anything about the matter. It seems to me then that the irreducible minimum of conditions necessary for applying Behaviourism to thinking, remembering, and imagining, are plainly lacking in the present state of our knowledge. On the other hand, it is more or less plausible to hold that there is a certain type of bodily behaviour which always happens and only happens when I am perceiving something. And it is more or less plausible to hold that this behaviour differs in a characteristic way according to whether I am perceiving A or B. What I propose to do is to show (a) that there are cases where we should be said to be perceiving a certain thing, and where it is by no means certain that there is any characteristic molar behaviour which might not have taken place when we were not perceiving this thing; and (*b*) that, even where there is a one to one correlation between my perception of a certain object and certain molar behaviour, there is something more involved in the perception than the mere occurrence of this molar behaviour.

(*a*) Whenever we perceive we perceive some definite object, *e.g.*, a chair on one occasion and a cat on another occasion.   A complete account of the act of perceiving in behaviouristic terms must therefore do two things· (i) It must mention some special kind of bodily behaviour which is always present when we are perceiving and is never present when we are merely imagining or thinking or remembering.   And (ii) this kind of behaviour must be such that a meaning can be given to the statement that one bit of behaviour of the perceptual kind refers specially to a certain chair and that another bit of behaviour of the perceptual kind refers specially to a certain cat.

If I am already moving about I shall no doubt as a rule avoid those obstacles which I perceive, and I shall stumble into objects which lie in my way and which I do not perceive.   In such cases there is no doubt certain bodily behaviour which has a specific relation to those objects which I am said to perceive.   And there is no bodily behaviour having this specific relation to objects which I am said not to perceive.   It is in such cases as these that the behaviouristic analysis of perception has most plausibility.   For here we may admit that at any rate the irreducible minimum of conditions for the possibility of such an analysis seems to be fulfilled. But even these examples are subject to the following criticism.   We are not dealing here merely with the perception of an object, but with the perception of an object which is an obstacle to some already intended and initiated course of movement.   Surely, as I walk about a room (and, still more so, as I stand still), there are

many objects which I perceive and in reference to which
there is no specific molar bodily behaviour of the kind
mentioned.   There are plenty of objects which I neither
avoid nor stumble over, because they are not in my
way or because I am not moving about.   And yet I
may be perceiving them.

Perhaps the most plausible kind of bodily behaviour
to take as present in all cases of perception, and as
specially correlated with the object which is said to be
perceived, would be the convergence and accommodation of the eyes on to the place where the object is.
But, in the first place, this applies only to visual perception.   Secondly, since it is admitted that I can see
two things in different places at the same time, though
not perhaps with equal clearness, it is evident that my
perception of one at least of them cannot be accompanied
by the convergence of my eyes on to the place which it
occupies.   Lastly, even when we find a man blundering
into an obstacle, it is not safe to assume that he did not
perceive it unless we know what his intentions and
wishes are at the time and that his body is under the
control of his will.   No doubt it is *generally* safe to
assume that a person does not want to be dashed to
pieces.   And no doubt it is *generally* safe to assume
that, if a person did not want to fall over a precipice, he
could stop himself from doing so when it stares him
in the face.   Subject to these conditions it would no
doubt be reasonable to conclude that a man who walked
over a precipice had not perceived it.   But it is perfectly
notorious that people sometimes do walk over precipices
which they perceive, because they want to be dashed to
pieces.   And it is probable that some people walk over
precipices which they perceive, although they do not
wish to be dashed to pieces, because the height exercises
a fascination over them which paralyses their wills.
Such happenings are relatively uncommon because the
wish to be dashed to pieces is much rarer than the wish
not to be, and because contra - voluntary ideo - motor

actions on this scale are very rare indeed. But they do happen. It is thus very doubtful whether we can find any kind of molar bodily behaviour which always takes place when a person would be said to perceive a certain object and which never takes place when a person would be said not to perceive this object. And, unless this can be found, the attempt to *reduce* perception to some kind of molar bodily behaviour which has some special reference to the perceived object fails *in limine*.

(*b*) I propose now to waive this objection, and to assume for the sake of argument that careful enough investigation of a man's body would disclose some specific kind of molar behaviour which always takes place when he perceives A and never takes place when he does not perceive A. I shall now show that, even if this be so, there is always something involved in the statement that this man perceives A over and above the fact that his body is behaving in this specific way. It is quite certain that, whenever it is true to say that I see something, it is true that I have a sensation of colour; that, whenever it is true that I hear a bell, it is true that I have a sensation of a noise; and so on. In fact every perception involves a sensation as an essential factor, although it involves something else as well. Perception, therefore, cannot be reduced to the fact that my body is behaving in a certain way towards a certain external object unless the sensational element in it can be reduced to bodily behaviour. This quite obvious fact may be illustrated as follows. There is a perfectly specific relation between the movements of a compass-needle and those of a magnet held near it. On a purely behaviouristic analysis of perception there can be no possible reason to doubt that the compass-needle perceives the magnet. Yet, as a matter of fact, nearly every one would deny that the needle perceives the magnet; and the few people who would suggest that it does would admit that this is a paradoxical proposition which needs to be recommended by an elaborate set of arguments such as those used by Spinoza or by Schopenhauer in establishing their peculiar metaphysical systems of hylozoism. This is because we know that a sensational element is an essential factor in what we understand by a "perception", and because we are very doubtful whether there is anything of the kind in the case of the needle and the magnet.

Now can statements of the form: "I am aware of a red patch" or "I am aware of a tinkling noise" be reduced to statements of the form: "This body, or some part of it, is behaving in such and such a way"? If not, behaviourism has manifestly failed even in the cases which are antecedently most favourable to it.

Let us suppose, for the sake of argument, that whenever it is true to say that I have a sensation of a red patch it is also true to say that a molecular movement of a certain specific kind is going on in a certain part of my brain. There is one sense in which it is plainly nonsensical to attempt to reduce the one to the other. There is a something which has the characteristic of being my awareness of a red patch. There is a something which has the characteristic of being a molecular movement. It should surely be obvious even to the most "advanced thinker" who ever worked in a psychological laboratory that, whether these "somethings" be the same or different, there are two different *characteristics*. The alternative is that the two phrases are just two names for a single characteristic, as are the two words "rich" and "wealthy"; and it is surely obvious that they are not. If this be not evident at first sight, it is very easy to make it so by the following considerations. There are some questions which can be raised about the characteristic of being a molecular movement, which it is nonsensical to raise about the characteristic of being an awareness of a red patch; and conversely. About a molecular movement it is perfectly reasonable to raise the question: "Is it swift or slow, straight or circular, and so on?" About the awareness of a red patch it is nonsensical to ask whether it is a swift or a slow awareness, a straight or a circular awareness, and so on. Conversely, it is reasonable to ask about an awareness of a red patch whether it is a clear or a confused awareness ; but it is nonsense to ask of a molecular movement whether it is a clear or a confused movement. Thus the attempt to argue that "being a sensation of so and so" and "being a bit of bodily behaviour of such and such a kind" are just two names for the same characteristic is evidently hopeless. And this is what the Behaviourist has really got to do.

Of course, when a man says that all mental states are reducible to bodily behaviour, he may not mean anything so radical as this. He may admit, *e.g.*, that to be a sensation of red is one characteristic and to be a molecular movement of a certain kind is another characteristic. He may merely wish to deny that the two characteristics belong to different events or substances. He may wish to maintain only that there is one event which has the two characteristics of being an awareness of a red patch and of being a molecular movement of a certain kind ; that there are events which have only material characteristics, and none which have only mental characteristics ; and that the mental properties of those events which do have mental properties are completely determined by the material properties which these events also have. Such a doctrine, whether true or false, cannot be dismissed at once as plainly absurd. But it is certainly not Behaviourism, and is not a form of *Reductive* Materialism ; it is a form of the theory (2, 211), *i.e.*, of *Emergent* Materialism.

It seems to me then that Reductive Materialism in general, and strict Behaviourism in particular, may be rejected. They are instances of the numerous class of theories which are so preposterously silly that only very learned men could have thought of them. I may be accused of breaking a butterfly on a wheel in this discussion of Behaviourism. But it is important to remember that a theory which is in fact absurd may be accepted by the simple-minded because it is put forward in highly technical terms by learned persons who are themselves too confused to know exactly what they mean. When this happens, as it has happened with Behaviourism, the philosopher is not altogether wasting time by analysing the theory and pointing out its implications.

Reductive Mentalism (2, 112). Reductive mentalism would be the counterpart of Behaviourism. It would consist in holding that the material characteristics of being extended and public, of having position, motion, etc., are *reducible to* combinations of purely mental characteristics. And there is precisely the same reason to deny this as to deny the opposite doctrine of Reductive Materialism. So far as I know, the present theory has never been held. All mentalists with whose works I am acquainted have held that material characteristics are delusive *appearances* of certain mental characteristics. This is obvious in the case of Leibniz, Hegel, Ward, Bradley, and M'Taggart. Berkeley's theory, on the face of it, is somewhat different. He holds that *sensa* really do have some material characteristics. They really are extended, coloured, hot, etc., and they really do move about in sense-fields. But (*a*) they are also mental events. And (*b*) they do not have all the characteristics of matter. For they are private, fleeting, and incapable of interacting with each other. (*c*) The remaining characteristics of matter are ascribed to God's habits of volition by Berkeley. These are permanent, neutral, and capable of causal action. But they are not extended or movable; and they are mental. Thus, in the end, materiality is a delusive characteristic for Berkeley as for other mentalists. There is *nothing* which has all the characteristics of materiality; though there are some things which have some of these characteristics, and other things which have the rest of them. For

Berkeley materiality is a delusive characteristic, in the sense in which the characteristic of being a mermaid is delusive ; *i.e.*, it is a compound characteristic which applies as a whole to nothing, though it can be analysed into factors each of which does apply to something. For M'Taggart or Hegel materiality is delusive in a still more radical sense. It is a compound characteristic some of whose factors apply to nothing. *E.g.*, nothing, on their view, is really extended.

Are Mentality and Materiality compatible Characteristics? We have now reduced our original seventeen candidates to the more wieldly number of eleven. Can we make a further reduction? The most promising question to raise at this point is the following. Granted that mentality and materiality are distinct and mutually irreducible characteristics, could any substance or event possess both of them? If we could answer this in the negative, if we could show that it is as absurd to suppose that the same event or substance could be both mental and material as to suppose that the same material substance could be at once red and blue all over, we could make a considerable clearance. We should certainly get rid of (1, 1) Dualism of Compatibles ; (2, 111) Emergent Mentalism, and (2, 211) Emergent Materialism. The effect on the various Neutralistic Theories would be less marked ; it would, I think, still be possible to keep them by a suitable statement. We should simply have to suppose that mental and material characteristics both emerge from certain arrangements of the same Neutral Stuff ; but that they never both emerge from the same arrangements of this Neutral Stuff.

Opposite answers have been given to the question at issue by different philosophers of eminence. Mr Locke saw no reason why God should not have endowed a material substance with the power to think. Descartes and Dr M'Taggart held that it is impossible that the same event or substance should be both mental and material. The argument against the compatibility of the two characteristics is this. Suppose a certain event were both mental and material. Since it is material it must have a certain shape and size. But is it not plainly nonsense to talk of a circular thought of an inch in diameter? Again, suppose that at a certain moment I am wanting my tea and thinking of the square root of minus-one. If this volition and this thought be also material events they must have spatial positions and stand in spatial relations. But is it not plainly nonsense to talk of a volition being two inches to the north-west of a thought?

I should like to believe that these arguments were conclusive, because it would greatly simplify our problem if they were. But I cannot honestly say that they seem to me to be conclusive. I admit, of course, that such statements as have been made above sound very odd, and that no one ever thinks of making them. But these facts seem capable of explanation. Suppose for the moment that it were true to say of a certain event both that it occupies a circular region in a brain and that it is someone's desire for his tea. It would have to be admitted that the two characteristics of this one event are known in quite different ways. There is one and only one person to whom its mental characteristics are directly manifested, viz., the person whose desire it is. Its material characteristics *never* manifest themselves to this person; and, strictly speaking, they do not manifest themselves to anyone. For no one *perceives* the position, shape, and other physical characteristics of this event. If the latter characteristics be known at all, they are known only to physiologists by an elaborate and precarious process of hypothetical and analogical reasoning. Now, since no one is acquainted with the material characteristics of any mental event, even if such events do have material characteristics, and since every one is acquainted with the mental characteristics of some mental events, it is not surprising that it should sound odd to ascribe determinate spatial qualities and relations to those events which are thoughts, volitions, etc. We may admit (*a*) that the presence of mentality does not *entail* the presence of materiality in the same object, as, *e.g.*, the presence of colour entails that of extension. So far as one can see, an event *could* have been mental without being extended or material. (*b*) That nothing which manifests mentality also manifests materiality. There is thus no direct empirical evidence that what has mentality ever has also materiality, as there is direct empirical evidence that what is red may also be hot. But the real question is: "Does the presence of mentality in an object entail the absence of materiality from it?" We may admit (*a*) and (*b*) without admitting that this question must be answered in the affirmative.

Now I cannot see by direct inspection that what is material cannot also be mental. Is there any indirect way of proving this proposition? It might be said that there is a fundamental difference between mentality and all those qualities which admittedly can belong to extended objects. Every non-spatial quality which admittedly can belong to an extended object is an extensible quality; *i.e.*, it is such that any object which possesses it *must* be extended. It is obvious that colour, temperature, etc., are extensible qualities in this sense. Now it is certain that mentality is not an extensible quality, in this sense. For, as we have seen, it is plainly logically possible that an event might have mentality without being extended. Now it might be suggested that it is a self-evident proposition that every non-spatial quality of an extended object must be an extensible quality. If this be accepted, it follows that mentality cannot be a quality of any extended object, and therefore that mentality and materiality are incompatible characteristics. But I do not find the suggested proposition self-evident on careful inspection. I do indeed find it self-evident that every extended object must have *some* non-spatial extensible quality ; but this is quite a different proposition from the suggested principle that every non-spatial quality of any extended object must be an extensible quality. Hence I see no impossibility in the supposition that one and the same thing or event may have both mental and material characteristics. And I can see what causes may have made men think that the two characteristics are incompatible even if they be really compatible.

It might perhaps be admitted that, so long as we confine ourselves to isolated mental events, we cannot see why they might not also be material. But it might be said that, when we consider that mental events are states of mind whilst material events are states of body, and that the characteristic interrelations of mental events within a mind are utterly unlike the characteristic interrelations of material events within a body, we see that it is necessary to assume two sets of events and not just a single set of events with two different characteristics. This again is not obvious to me. If two events have each two different determinable characteristics A and B in the determinate forms $a_1 b_1$ and $a_2 b_2$ respectively, they can obviously stand at the same time in two very different determinable relations to each other, one in virtue of the determinable A and the other in virtue of the determinable B. *E.g.*, two musical notes may be identical in temporal position, whilst one is an octave lower than the other in pitch. It therefore seems perfectly possible that a set of events, each of which had both material and mental characteristics, might form a whole of the material kind in virtue of the relations which depend on the material characteristics of the events, and might also form a whole of the mental kind in virtue of the relations which depend on the mental characteristics of the events. Thus a series of notes is at once a tune, in virtue of the relations of pitch which depend on the auditory characteristics of the notes ; and a series of events each of which lasts so long and is separated by such and such a time-gap from its neighbours, in virtue of the temporal characteristics of the notes.

I should like to point out that the doctrine that every event which is mental is also material would in no way entail the view that all causation is physical causation. To say that the event e_2 is determined by purely physical causation would mean that the necessary and sufficient condition of the occurrence of e_2 is the occurrence of an event e_1 having a certain determinate material characteristic θ_1. This event *might* also have a determinate mental characteristic ψ_1; but, if the causation be purely physical, the possession of ψ_1 by e_1 will be causally irrelevant to e_2. Now it is obvious that this is only one of three possible alternatives. In the first place, the possession of θ_1 by e_1 might be necessary but not sufficient to determine e_2. It might be that the possession of ψ_1 by e_1 was also necessary, and that the complete cause of e_2 is the occurrence of an event e_1 with the material characteristic θ_1 and the mental characteristic ψ_1. Secondly, it might even be the case that the possession by e_1 of θ_1 was causally irrelevant to e_2 and that the occurrence of an event e_1 having the mental characteristic ψ_1 was necessary and sufficient to determine e_2. This might be true even if in fact there are no events which have mental characteristics without having material characteristics. We can call these two alternatives which we have just been mentioning " mixed causation " and "purely mental causation " respectively. I have thus shown that the types of theory at present under discussion do not preclude mixed causation and purely mental causation, as might perhaps be thought by some.

On the whole, then, I can see no conclusive objection to the possibility that one and the same event should have both mental and material characteristics or that one and the same substance should be both a mind and a body. Hence I cannot reject off-hand the three types of theory which imply that this possibility is realised.

So we are still left with the eleven alternatives with which we started this subsection.

Theories which make Materiality delusive. We have seen that no theory which makes mentality delusive can be accepted. We cannot reject on the same grounds theories which make materiality delusive. Nevertheless we might be able to reject such theories on other grounds. Let us consider this question next. We are left with three types of theory which make materiality delusive, viz. (2, 12) Pure Mentalism, and (3, 211) and (3, 212) the two forms of Mentalistic Neutralism.

Of these theories I believe that Pure Mentalism, both in its less radical Berkeleian form and in the more radical form in which it is held by Leibniz, Hegel and M'Taggart, may be rejected. The theory has a negative and a positive side. The negative side is that materiality is a delusive characteristic. The positive side is that things which have nothing but mental qualities and relations are misperceived to have material qualities and relations. Now I see no reason to believe the negative proposition, and strong reasons to doubt the positive proposition. Materiality is a complex characteristic, which I have analysed in Chapter IV. (*a*) All the arguments to prove that some of the constituent characteristics of materiality (*e.g.*, extension) are delusive seem to me to be plainly fallacious (like Bradley's) or to depend on premises which I see no ground for accepting (like M'Taggart's). (*b*) The arguments to prove that, whilst none of the constituent characteristics of materiality are delusive, materiality as a whole is delusive seem to me to prove *something* important, but not *this* proposition. I therefore see no ground to believe that materiality is delusive either in the more radical sense of M'Taggart and Leibniz or in the less radical sense of Berkeley. (*c*) It seems to me most unlikely that things which had nothing analogous to spatial qualities and relations and did not form a quasi-spatial order of at least three dimensions could present that particular system of interconnected appearances which external objects do present. And I do not see that minds or mental events, connected by the only mental relations with which we are acquainted, would fulfil these conditions. If you say that there may be many mental relations with which we are unacquainted I of course agree. But why call these particular relations "mental" if they do not resemble any *mental* relation that we are acquainted with, and do resemble *spatial* relations?

My detailed reasons for making these assertions will be found in Chapter IV, and especially in the subsection headed: *In what Sense can we accept Physical Objects?* On the whole then I think we may reject Pure Mentalism, and thus reduce the number of theories which are worth serious consideration to ten.

Would the arguments which I have used against Pure Mentalism apply to Mentalistic Neutralism? They would apply to any form of Neutralism which refuses to allow quasi-spatial qualities and relations to the neutral stuff itself or to certain combinations of this neutral stuff. But they would not be fatal to such a form of Mentalistic Neutralism as Mr Russell puts forward in his *Analysis of Mind*. For Mr Russell mentality is not delusive, since it does belong to certain groups of suitably interrelated sensa. And materiality is delusive, in the less radical sense in which it is so for Berkeley, though not in the more radical sense in which it is so for M'Taggart. For Mr Russell's neutral stuff is sensa; and these really are extended and spatially related to each other, though they lack the remaining characteristics which are essential to materiality. These other characteristics really do belong to certain groups of interrelated sensa; but these groups are not literally extended. Hence every characteristic involved in materiality has application, though materiality itself has no application. Mr Russell's theory is therefore a form of Mentalistic Neutralism. And it is a form to which my arguments do not apply, since his neutral stuff really does have spatial qualities and relations. It is therefore possible for Mr Russell to "save the appearances", whilst, so far as I can see, it is not possible for a Pure Mentalist to do so. So we cannot rule out the two forms of Mentalistic Neutralism at this stage, provided that they are suitably stated.

General Remarks on Neutralistic Theories. It will be noticed that six of the ten theories which we still have on our hands are forms of Neutralism. It will therefore be wise to consider now the general conditions which any neutralistic theory must fulfil, in the hope that these may exclude some of the suggested forms of Neutralism. I understand by Neutralism the doctrine that neither mentality nor materiality is a differentiating attribute, so that the fundamental stuff of which the existent world is made consists of one or more substances which are neither mental nor material. This fundamental stuff must have some differentiating attributes, and by hypothesis these are neither mentality nor materiality. Now of course it might be suggested that the differentiating attributes are utterly unknown to us. In that case we could hardly deny the possibility of any of the six remaining forms of Neutralism. But this purely agnostic Neutralism is not worth serious consideration; for it is useless to trouble about a theory which, from the nature of the case, could explain nothing. I shall assume then that the differentiating attributes of the fundamental substance or substances are attributes which we are acquainted with.

In that case the possible suppositions about the nature of the fundamental stuff are very restricted. We are directly acquainted at most with two kinds of existent, viz., sensa or images and sense-fields, on the one hand, and mental states and minds, on the other. The only empirical attributes with which we can claim to be acquainted are the qualities of each of these two kinds of existent, the relations of sensa or images to each other in sense-fields, the relations of mental states to each other in minds, and the relations of mental states to sensa or images. In addition to these empirical characteristics, which we become acquainted with by abstraction from instances which manifest them to us, there are, I think, certain categorial characteristics, such as the relation of substance and state, cause and effect, etc. We become acquainted with these on reflection when suitable material is presented to us by our senses or by introspection; but we do not reach our knowledge of them simply by abstraction from instances which manifest them to us. Now these empirical and categorial characteristics are the only materials that any human being has or can have for constructing a theory of the Universe. It follows that the Neutralist who is not content to be merely agnostic about his neutral stuff can ascribe to it nothing but a selection from these characteristics. The neutral stuff must be supposed either (a) to have some of the factors included in materiality and none of those included in mentality; or (b) to have some of the factors included in mentality and none of those included in materiality; or (c) to combine some of the factors of mentality with some of the factors of materiality. Let us now consider the effects of these three hypotheses on the six forms of Neutralism which still remain.

Before we can do this a little preliminary explanation is needed. I have admitted that materiality is a complex characteristic. The fundamental factor involved in it is extension. This, if I am right, carries with it *some* extensible quality, but not any particular extensible quality. The other characteristics are publicity, persistence, and existential independence of any observing mind. It is therefore easy to understand what is meant by the supposition that the fundamental stuff has some but not all the characteristics involved in materiality. It presumably means that extension, at any rate, is ascribed to it, and existential independence of any observing mind. But the corresponding supposition about mentality needs some further explanation.

So far I have neither asserted nor denied that mentality is a complex characteristic. Some people would no doubt hold that it is simple. If this be so, the hypotheses (*b*) and (*c*) are ruled out, and the Neutralist is left with hypothesis (*a*). But I think that it is arguable that mentality is a complex characteristic, and that it may be analysed somewhat as follows. (i) The irreducible minimum involved in mentality would seem to be the fact which we express by the phrase "feeling somehow", *e.g.*, feeling cross or tired or hungry. It seems to me to be logically possible that this characteristic, which we might call "sentience", could belong to a thing or event which had no other mental characteristic. But this possibility depends partly on the view that we take about the proper analysis of "feeling somehow"; and I can discuss the question better when I have mentioned the other factors involved in mentality.

(ii) There is plainly a difference between the fact that something *exists* and *has* such and such qualities and relations and the fact that something *manifests* its existence and *manifests* certain qualities and relations. Now the converse of manifestation is acquaintance, such as we have in sensing and in imaging. I think that some people would claim to reduce sentience to acquaintance with certain peculiar existents and their qualities. It might be held, *e.g.*, that there are certain peculiar qualities, called "tiredness", "hungriness", "crossness", etc., and that these qualities characterise certain things from time to time. When this happens something *is* tired or hungry or cross. Now a thing which is tired or hungry or cross may manifest itself to itself, or to something else which is uniquely connected with itself, as having these qualities. We then say that "tiredness is felt" or that "there is a feeling of tiredness". I introduce the two alternatives of "manifesting itself to itself" and "manifesting itself to something which is uniquely connected with itself ", because there seem to be two alternative forms of the theory under discussion.   (*a*) It might be held that tiredness, crossness, etc., are qualities which belong to *minds*, and that to feel tired is to be acquainted with one's own *mind* as having the quality of tiredness at the moment.   Or (*β*) it might be held (and it apparently is held by Professor Laird and Professor Alexander) that tiredness, crossness, etc., are qualities which belong, not to minds, but to *living organisms*.   In that case to feel tired is to be acquainted with one's own *organism* or with some part of it as having the quality of tiredness at the moment.   Of course a complete account of all feelings might need to combine both these alternatives.

If we accepted either of these alternatives we could take acquaintance as the fundamental characteristic involved in mentality.   My tentative statement that there might be things which had sentience and no other mental characteristic would then have to be modified as follows.   We should have to say that there might be things which had no mental characteristic except acquaintance with themselves or their organisms as having certain peculiar qualities, such as tiredness, crossness, etc.

(iii) Whether sentience be a mental characteristic distinct from acquaintance, or whether it just be acquaintance with certain special objects as having certain special qualities, it is plain that mentality as we know it in ourselves involves a further characteristic.   This may be called " referential cognition ".   We believe in the existence of things and events which we are not at the moment acquainted with, and we believe them to have certain qualities and relations which they are not manifesting to us at the moment.   I have tried to show that even perception is referential cognition. It seems clear that there could be no referential cognition without acquaintance ; and it seems to me logically possible that there might be things which have sentience and acquaintance without referential cognition.

We must next notice that we find in ourselves two different kinds of referential cognition, which I will call "intuitive" and "discursive". When I perceive a chair or a pink rat, my perception is an instance of intuitive referential cognition ; when I merely think of a chair or a pink rat, my thought is an instance of discursive referential cognition. I can have both intuitive and discursive referential cognition of certain objects ; but there are many objects, such as Julius Cæsar or a Hydrogen atom, of which I can have only discursive cognition. Now I think it is impossible for there to be referential cognition of the discursive kind in a being which has not referential cognition of the intuitive kind ; but it seems logically possible that there should be things which have intuitive referential cognition without discursive referential cognition.

(iv) Finally, we find in ourselves what may be called "affective attitudes". Conations and the various kinds of emotions are examples of these. An affective attitude consists in "feeling some*how towards* some*thing*". Now, if I am to be able to take up an affective attitude towards something, this something must fulfil one of the following conditions. (a) It may be a feeling which is felt by me. *E.g.*, I may dislike my present feeling of hunger. (β) It may be something which I am acquainted with, and which is not a feeling of mine. *E.g.*, I may be pleased with the brightly coloured visual sensa which I am acquainted with when I see a firework display. (γ) It may be the epistemological object of an intuitive referential situation of which I am subject. *E.g.*, a drunkard may be frightened at the pink rats which he sees. And (δ) it may be the epistemological object of a discursive referential situation of which I am subject. *E.g.*, I may desire the dinner which I am now thinking of. It is therefore logically impossible that any affective attitude should exist in a thing that did not possess any other mental characteristic ; but it does seem possible that any or all the three mental characteristics previously enumerated should exist in a thing which did not have any affective attitudes whatever. Again, there are certain affective attitudes, such as volition, which could occur only in a being which has discursive cognition ; there are others, such as anger, which presuppose at least intuitive, but not necessarily discursive referential cognition ; and there are others, such as mere liking and disliking, which presuppose no more than acquaintance or mere sentience.

The upshot of this discussion is as follows. If "mentality" means the peculiar characteristic of human minds, we must admit that it is complex. Its factors may be divided first into Affective Attitudes and Other Factors. The relation between them is that it is logically possible for the Other Factors to occur without any of the Affective Attitudes, whilst it is not logically possible for any of the Affective Attitudes to occur without at least one of the Other Factors. Secondly, we can arrange the Other Factors in a hierarchical order, such that the earlier could occur without the later but the later could not occur without all the earlier ones. This order is Sentience, Acquaintance, Intuitive Referential Cognition, and Discursive Referential Cognition. We can now see exactly what would be meant by ascribing some but not all of the factors of mentality to the supposed neutral stuff. In the first place, it would mean that the neutral stuff was supposed to have the earlier but not the later factors (of this hierarchy). And, secondly, the Neutral Monist might ascribe or refuse to ascribe affective attitudes to his neutral stuff. (There are some affective attitudes, such as volition, which he *must* refuse to ascribe to it if he refuses to ascribe the higher members of the hierarchy of Other Factors to it.)

We are now in a position to consider the three hypotheses, and to note the effects of each on the six remaining forms of Neutralism. I will first try to show that no form of Neutralism which makes mentality a *reducible* characteristic is compatible with any of the three hypotheses. It is immediately obvious that no such form of Neutralism is compatible with hypothesis (*a*), which ascribes to the neutral stuff no characteristics except some of the factors of materiality. For we have already argued that mentality cannot be reduced to materiality as a whole ; and, if this be so, *a fortiori*, it cannot be reduced to a part of materiality.

It is easy to show that such forms of Neutralism are also incompatible with hypothesis (*b*), which ascribes to the neutral stuff no characteristics except some of the factors of mentality. If mentality is to be a reducible characteristic on this hypothesis we must suppose that the higher terms in the hierarchy of mental factors can be reduced to the lower terms of this hierarchy. Now it seems to me that this is plainly impossible when we clearly understand what is required. Let us take an example. There is a certain event which has the characteristic of being a perception of a pink rat. Let us make the most favourable assumption possible for the reductive type of theory. Let us suppose that this perception has no existent constituents except events which are feelings and events which are acquaintances with sensa and images. We are to suppose then that this perception consists of such events interrelated in certain characteristic ways, and of nothing else. It seems to me that it would still be impossible to *deduce* from the fact that it has this structure and is composed of these constituents, and from laws which are entirely about *feelings* and *sensations*, that this event will be the *perception* of an epistemological object and that this epistemological object will be a pink rat. Unless we had actually met with events which were perceptions and had epistemological objects I do not see that we could possibly have suspected that a whole composed of feelings and sensations interrelated in certain ways would have the property of being the perception of a certain epistemological object. Thus the characteristic of being a perception is not a reducible characteristic, like the behaviour of a clock, but is at best an emergent characteristic, like the behaviour of silver-chloride. Similarly, I do not see the least reason to believe that the characteristic of being a discursive cognition could be reduced to characteristics which come lower in the hierarchy of mental factors. If such reductions can be effected it is quite certain that no one has made even a plausible beginning of performing the reduction. I conclude then that all forms of Neutralism which make mentality a reducible characteristic are incompatible with hypothesis (*b*) as well as with hypothesis (*a*).

What about hypothesis (*c*), which ascribes to the neutral stuff some of the factors of mentality and some of the factors of materiality? The forms of Neutralism at present under discussion could be consistent with (*c*) only on the supposition that the higher factors of mentality, though not reducible to the lower factors alone, are reducible to these eked out with some of the factors of materiality. And I cannot see the least reason to believe that the addition of these factors of materiality would help the proposed reduction. I am therefore inclined to reject all forms of Neutralism which make mentality a reducible characteristic, on the ground that they are inconsistent with all the intelligible hypotheses that we can make about the neutral stuff. We thus get rid of (3, 13) Reductive Neutralism, (3, 122) the second form of Mixed Neutralism, and (3, 212) the second form of Mentalistic Neutralism.

We are thus left with three forms of Neutralism, viz., (3, 11) Emergent Neutralism, (3, 121) the first form of Mixed Neutralism, and (3, 211) the first form of Mentalistic Neutralism. We must now see how the three hypotheses affect these three alternatives. We find that hypothesis (*a*) is consistent with all of them. The same is true of hypothesis (*c*). But hypothesis (*b*) would exclude all but the first of them, as I will now show. In the first place, if no characteristic be ascribed to the neutral stuff except some of the factors of mentality, it is plain that no form of Neutralism which makes materiality a *reducible* characteristic can be accepted. For we have already argued that materiality cannot be reduced to mentality as a whole; and, if this be so, *a fortiori*, it cannot be reduced to a part of mentality. This removes (3, 121) the first form of mixed Neutralism. Moreover, this hypothesis is incompatible with any form of Neutralism which makes materiality a delusive characteristic. For we have argued that it is almost incredible that what has nothing but mental qualities and relations should appear to have spatial qualities, motion, and spatial relations. If this be true, it is, *a fortiori*, incredible that what has only some of the factors of mentality should appear to have spatial qualities, to move, and to stand in spatial relations. This removes (3, 211) the first form of Mentalistic Neutralism. Thus we may finally classify the three surviving forms of Neutralism as follows. (I) Theories compatible with all the alternative hypotheses :—(3, 11) Emergent Neutralism. (II) Theories compatible with (*a*) and (*c*) but not with (*b*) :—(3, 121) the first form of Mixed Neutralism, and (3, 211) the first form of Mentalistic Neutralism.

The Seven remaining Types of Theory. We have now reduced our original seventeen types of theory to a modest seven. I shall now take these seven survivors in order, and mention what seem to me to be the strong and weak points to each.

(1) We will begin with the two forms of Dualism. If I am right in holding that materiality and mentality are both complex characteristics analysable into several factors, it cannot strictly be said that either is a differentiating attribute. For it is part of the definition of a differentiating attribute that it shall be simple and unanalysable. What then must we understand the two types of Dualism to mean when they say that mentality and materiality are "differentiating attributes"? I think

it is fairly easy to see what they mean. Dualism means to assert of materiality the following propositions. (*a*) There is something which possesses *all* the factors of materiality, so that materiality is not in any sense a delusive characteristic. (*b*) None of the factors of materiality are reducible to or emergent from the other factors of materiality, or mentality, or a combination of both. This is of course quite consistent with the belief that there may also be some things which have some of the factors of materiality and not others. It merely insists that, if there be such things, the remaining factors of materiality are neither reducible nor emergent qualities of certain complex wholes composed of these things. *E.g.*, sensa would have some but not all the factors of materiality, and Dualism is not compelled to deny the existence of sensa. But it is compelled to assert that there are *also* material things, and that the characteristics which these have and sensa lack are not emergent or reducible characteristics of certain groups of interrelated sensa.

I take it that Dualism asserts a similar pair of propositions about mentality. It asserts (*a*) that there is something which possesses *all* the factors of mentality. And (*b*) that the higher factors of mentality are neither reducible to nor emergent from the lower factors of mentality, or materiality, or a combination of both. This is quite consistent with admitting that there may be things that have only some of the lower factors of mentality. *E.g.*, the minds of oysters might have nothing but sentience. But Dualism is compelled to assert that there are some things which have all the factors of mentality. And it is compelled to assert that the characteristics which human minds have and the minds of oysters lack are not emergent or reducible characteristics of certain groups of interrelated things which have nothing but sentience.

We now understand what is asserted in common by theories which make mentality and materiality both "differentiating attributes". It is evident that, if we accept Dualism, five alternative views are possible about the relations between mentality and materiality. (*a*) They may be incompatible with each other. (*b*) The possession of materiality may entail that of mentality, but not conversely. (*c*) The possession of mentality may entail that of materiality, but not conversely. (*d*) The possession of either may entail that of the other. And (*e*) the possession of one may entail neither the possession nor the absence of the other. Now I have argued that the theory that the two are incompatible, though plausible at first sight, is really quite groundless. I therefore reject (1, 2) the Dualism of Incompatibles, which was Descartes' theory. We can therefore confine ourselves to (1, 1) the Dualism of Compatibles, which includes the remaining four alternatives. I see no reason for, and strong empirical reasons against, both (*b*) and (*d*). On the face of it there are plenty of things which are material and have none of the factors of mentality. I do not know that (*b*) has ever been maintained. But I understand Spinoza to have asserted (*d*); if so, he appears to me to have produced no reasons good or bad for his belief. We are thus left with (*c*) and (*e*). Let us begin with (*c*).

It is certain that we have no empirical evidence in normal experience for the existence of anything which possesses any factor of mentality without being also material. Thus the empirical facts are all *in accordance with* the view that the possession of mentality entails that of materiality. But, in the first place, they do not *require* this view. It might be that mentality and materiality are logically indifferent to each other, and yet that, in the actual world or in the only part of it that comes under our observation in this life, it is a fact that mentality is always accompanied by materiality whilst materiality is sometimes unaccompanied by mentality. In the second place, the empirical facts would suggest *causal* rather than *logical* dependence of mentality on materiality. For the only things which exhibit signs of mentality are organisms, *i.e.*, certain very special and complex material structures. Now this would make mentality, not a "differentiating attribute", even in the wider sense in which we are at present using the phrase, but an *emergent* characteristic. Finally, when I reflect on mentality and materiality as carefully as I can, I cannot see that the presence of the former logically entails that of the latter. I do not find the least difficulty in conceiving of a being which had all the factors of mentality and none of the factors of materiality. Some philosophers (perhaps St Thomas) seem to have taken an intermediate view. They seem to have held that some of the lower factors of mentality (*e.g.*, sentience) entail materiality, whilst some of the higher factors (*e.g.*, discursive cognition) do not entail it. And some philosophers seem to have gone further, and to have maintained that the higher factors of mentality exclude materiality. I see no ground for holding either alternative. I cannot see any *a priori* reason why an immaterial being should not have sentience and sensation; or why a material being should not have discursive cognition.

We are thus left with alternative (*e*), viz., that mentality and materiality are logically indifferent to each other. This supposition divides into five *factual* alternatives analogous to the five *logical* alternatives which we have already discussed. (*a*) Nothing in fact has both mentality and materiality. (*β*) Everything which has materiality has in fact mentality, but there are some things which have mentality without materiality. (*γ*) Everything which has mentality has in fact also materiality, but there are some things which have materiality without mentality. (*δ*) Everything that has mentality has in fact materiality, and everything that has materiality has in fact mentality. And (*ε*) some things have mentality without materiality, some things have both characteristics, and some things have materiality without mentality. Now we must admit that all direct empirical evidence of the normal kind favours (γ). We are not acquainted with anything that is certainly mental and certainly immaterial. And we are acquainted with many things which seem to be material and do not show the least sign of being mental. Of course it remains possible that there may be things which are mental and immaterial (*e.g.*, angels), but that they cannot or do not manifest themselves to us. But, in that case, there can be no direct empirical evidence for their existence. Again, it remains possible that those minds which do manifest themselves to us are immaterial, but that they stand in specially intimate relations with organisms and have to manifest themselves by means of these organisms. But, unless we hold that it is logically impossible for what is mental to be also material, there seems to be nothing in the normal phenomena to suggest this. And I have argued in Chapter XII (i) that there are serious difficulties in squaring this Instrumental Theory of the relation of body and mind with the known facts, and (ii) that the abnormal facts dealt with by Psychical Research do not on the whole support it and do in certain respects conflict with it. The existence of immaterial mental substances therefore remains a mere possibility for which there appears to be no evidence whatever, normal or abnormal, *a priori* or empirical.

Again, there is plainly no direct empirical evidence for the view that everything which is material is in fact also mental. If we accept it at all we must accept it as a hypothesis which goes beyond and appears to conflict with the observable facts. We must therefore ask (i) whether this hypothesis has any appreciable antecedent probability, and (ii) whether it explains anything that could not have been explained equally well without it. (i) I do not think that anyone has had the hardihood to ascribe *all* the factors of mentality to *every* material substance. At most they have regarded some of the lower mental factors, such as sentience, as differentiating attributes which belong to all bits of matter.   But even this seems rash to the last degree.   It is no doubt true that the evidence for sentience fades gradually away as we go lower in the scale of organisms.   It is therefore quite possible that sentience extends below the point at which direct evidence for it ceases.   But everything which we have the least ground for believing to be sentient is a living organism ;   *i.e.*, a highly complicated material structure consisting of millions of molecules. Moreover, every organism is composed of a comparatively few chemical elements, viz., Carbon, Oxygen, Hydrogen, Nitrogen, Sulphur and Phosphorus.   It is an enormous extrapolation to ascribe any kind of sentience to inorganic matter which does not consist of these elements.   Thus the antecedent probability of the hypothesis of universal sentience seems to me to be vanishingly small.

(ii) I think that the only empirical ground that anyone has ever had for ascribing some of the factors of mentality to all material objects is indirect.   It looks as if things which obviously have mentality had developed in the course of time from things which obviously had materiality and seem not to have had any factor of mentality.   And it is thought that this alleged fact could be more easily explained if we assumed that non-living matter really has some of the factors of mentality in spite of all appearances to the contrary.   We can deal with this contention very shortly.   Any theory which regards mentality as a "differentiating attribute", even in the looser sense defined in this subsection, *ipso facto*, renounces all hope of "explaining" its occurrence.   For, by definition, it holds that none of the higher factors of mentality are reducible to or emergent from the lower factors of mentality alone or in combination with materiality.   Hence it is not of the least advantage to a Dualistic Theory to ascribe some of the factors of mentality to all matter in the hope that it will thereby explain the occurrence of the complete characteristic of mentality in certain material objects.

I therefore conclude that the only form of Dualism for which there is the least evidence, either direct or indirect, is (γ) which asserts that everything which has mentality has also materiality, whilst some things which have materiality have no factor of mentality. Is there any good reason to accept Dualism in this form? I do not think that there is. All the empirical facts which make it unreasonable for the Dualist to accept any but this particular form of Dualism make it unreasonable for him to accept Dualism at all. We find that nothing exhibits mentality except living organisms, and that all living organisms of a certain kind and degree of complexity do exhibit a certain number of the factors of mentality. As we pass to more and more complex organisms we find that higher factors of mentality are exhibited by them. This suggests most forcibly that *all* factors of mentality are emergent or reducible; or, if not, that only the lowest factor of mentality is a differentiating attribute, whilst the higher factors are reducible **to** or emergent from it alone or in combination with materiality. The normal facts seem to me to be altogether against Dualism, and the abnormal facts seem to me not to require a Dualism of mentality and materiality. We may therefore pass on to the five types of theory which still remain.

(2) We can at once dismiss (2, 111) Emergent Mentalism. For this makes mentality a differentiating attribute; and I have just argued that this is most improbable, even when it is interpreted in the looser sense in which we had to interpret it in order to make it possible at all. Hence the only type of theory which remains for discussion under (2) is (2, 211) Emergent Materialism. This asserts (*a*) that materiality is a differentiating attribute, and (*b*) that mentality is an emergent characteristic.

I have already explained what a person must be understood to mean by calling materiality a "differentiating attribute" in spite of its being a complex characteristic. He must mean that all the factors of materiality are differentiating attributes, and that there are in fact some things which have them all. Now I have argued in Chapter IV that this is possible and even highly probable. I have therefore no objection to the first part of the Theory of Emergent Materialism. The second part needs a little further explanation. It might be held in a more or a less radical form. The more radical form would assert that even the lowest factor of mentality, viz., sentience, is an emergent characteristic of certain kinds of material complex. The higher factors of mentality would of course be emergent characteristics of complexes composed of complexes which have the lower factors. The less radical form would make sentience a differentiating attribute, which in fact belongs only to material things and perhaps only to some of them. The higher factors of mentality would, as before, be emergent characteristics of complexes composed of complexes which have the lower factors.

I see no reason to prefer the less radical form of Emergent Materialism to the more radical form. If the higher factors of mentality could be *reduced to* the lowest factor there might be something to be said for making sentience a differentiating attribute which belongs to some or all material things and to nothing else. But actually no factor in the mental hierarchy can be reduced to any or all of the lower factors, whether taken by themselves or combined with material characteristics. And, since we therefore *must* postulate emergence at every stage but the first, there seems to be no advantage in refusing to postulate it at the first stage too.

If there were no facts to be considered except the normal ones, and we rejected all the alleged abnormal facts dealt with by Psychical Research, I should regard Emergent Materialism as on the whole the most reasonable view to take of the status and relations of matter and mind in Nature. The only question would be whether one of the forms of Neutralism might not be preferable. I shall ignore the alleged abnormal facts for the present, and shall discuss the three forms of Neutralism which still remain.

(3) Of the three remaining forms of Neutralism the only one against which I have a positive objection to offer is (3, 121) the first form of Mixed Neutralism. This type of theory makes materiality a reducible characteristic. We have agreed that it could not be reduced to any or all the factors of mentality. Hence the only question that remains is whether there are some factors of materiality to which the remaining factors of materiality could be reduced. If this were so it would be possible to ascribe only the fundamental factors of materiality to the neutral stuff; and to hold that materiality as a whole is reducible, in the sense that its remaining factors could be proved to belong to certain complex wholes composed of elements which have only these fundamental factors. So far as I know, this cannot be done. At any rate no one has done it, or, to the best of my knowledge attempted to do it. I shall therefore reject (3, 121) the first form of Mixed Neutralism.

The two remaining forms are (3, 11) Emergent Neutralism, and (3, 211) the first form of Mentalistic Neutralism. Both these types of theory have actually been held by distinguished philosophers. Professor Alexander's theory in *Space, Time and Deity* is a form of Emergent Neutralism. Mr Russell's theory in the *Analysis of Mind* is a form of the first kind of Mentalistic Neutralism. Now Emergent Neutralism takes materiality to be an emergent characteristic, and the first form of Mentalistic Neutralism takes materiality to be a delusive characteristic. Either view appears to me to be possible, but I do not see any good reason to believe either. I have argued that it is possible and even probable that materiality is a " differentiating attribute ", in the sense that there are some things which have all the factors of materiality and that none of these factors are either reducible or emergent.   There are not the same strong empirical reasons for refusing to take materiality as a differentiating attribute, in this sense, as there are for refusing to take mentality as a differentiating attribute in a similar sense.   So far as I can see, the only merit of these two remaining forms of Neutralism is that they introduce rather more unity into the world as a whole than we could admit on other theories.   But this seems to me to be a very minor virtue, and quite insufficient to justify any strong preference for these theories.

It will be noticed that Professor Alexander's theory may be regarded as a more radical form of Emergent Materialism.   Emergent Materialism regards materiality as a "differentiating attribute" in the looser sense, and it regards mentality as an emergent characteristic of certain material aggregates.   Professor Alexander, so far as I can understand him, ascribes to his neutral stuff only some of the factors of materiality, viz., spatio-temporal characteristics, and none of the factors of mentality.   Now, if this be the right interpretation, I have a positive objection to Professor Alexander's form of Emergent Neutralism.   For it seems to me to be impossible for anything to have *only* spatio-temporal characteristics; it seems to me that anything that has spatio-temporal characteristics must also have some extensible quality.   This, however, is a minor point for the present purpose.   If Professor Alexander admitted this objection it would be quite easy for him to ascribe some non-spatio-temporal extensible quality to his neutral stuff and then carry on as before.

In calling Mr Russell's theory a form of the first kind of Mentalistic Neutralism I am aware that I am being perhaps too charitable.   It is indeed quite certain that he regards materiality as a delusive characteristic, in the milder sense in which Berkeley did so.   That is, he holds that nothing has all the characteristics of matter, though he admits that each characteristic of matter belongs to something. What I am not certain about is whether he regards mentality as an emergent characteristic or as a reducible characteristic. I am sure that he would *like* to hold the latter view, because it would shock more intensely more of the people whom he likes to shock. If he really does hold this view his theory is a form of the second kind of Mentalistic Neutralism, and I have rejected this long ago.

The upshot of the discussion is that, if we confine ourselves to normal phenomena, Emergent Materialism, Emergent Neutralism, and the first form of Mentalistic Neutralism are all possible; and that there is nothing to suggest any theory which would give to Mind a more important and self-subsistent status in Nature. As between these three theories I prefer Emergent Materialism to any form of Emergent Neutralism or Mentalistic Neutralism with which I am acquainted. This is partly because I think it possible and probable that materiality is a differentiating attribute, in the sense there are some things which have all the factors of materiality and that none of these factors are emergent or reducible. And it is partly because I think that there are difficulties in the only two forms of Neutralism with which I am well acquainted, viz., Professor Alexander's and Mr Russell's. But it is quite possible that these difficulties will some day be removed by these learned men themselves, or by successors who will enjoy the advantage of their pioneer work. In the meanwhile, if I were forced to choose between the two, I think I should give a slight preference to Mr Russell's form of Neutralism. If I am not to regard materiality as a "differentiating attribute", in the looser sense, I think it is more profitable to regard it as a delusive characteristic, in the milder sense of Berkeley and Russell, than as an emergent characteristic. The former view seems to me to fit better into the facts of perception than the latter.

Final Considerations. It only remains to consider what

effect the abnormal and supernormal facts, which I have so far ignored in this Chapter, will have on the above tentative conclusions. For this purpose I must refer the reader back to the latter part of Chapter XII. I suggested there that, in the present state of Psychical Research, there is some evidence for *persistence* after bodily death, but hardly any that justifies a belief in *survival*. And I suggested that the facts which are at present reasonably well established are best explained by a peculiar form of the view that mentality is an emergent characteristic. This theory I called the "Compound Theory". The essential point of it is that mentality is an emergent characteristic of a *compound* composed of a living brain and nervous system and of something else which is capable of persisting for some time after the death of the body and of entering into temporary combination with the brain and nervous system of certain peculiarly constituted human beings called "mediums". This something else I called a "Psychic Factor".

About the nature of this Psychic Factor there is very little that can at present be said with certainty. We can say positively of it that it must be capable of carrying traces of experiences which happened to the mind of which it was formerly a constituent. And negatively we can say that there is at present no reason to believe and strong reason to doubt that it has the higher factors of mentality. It remains possible that it may have some of the lower factors of mentality, such as sentience; but I do not see anything in the facts to require or to suggest this hypothesis. Could it have materiality as a whole, or any of the factors of materiality? It certainly has the factor of persistence; but this is common to all substances and is not peculiar to matter. If we say that it is material we must admit that it is an unusual kind of matter. It is not destroyed by the breaking up of the body with which it was connected; it does not manifest itself to sense-perception; and it does not produce ordinary physical and chemical effects.   On the other hand, there is no reason why it should not be material in spite of these peculiarities.   If the Psychic Factor be material, and if it have none of the factors of mentality, the Compound Theory is a form of Emergent Materialism.   Thus a slightly modified form of Emergent Materialism is compatible with all the well-established supernormal facts, so far as I can see. *A fortiori*, these facts will be compatible with slightly modified forms of the two kinds of Neutralism which I have admitted to be possible.

It is perhaps just worth while to mention that, if the alleged phenomena of materialisation and telekinesis were well established, we might be able to see our way to a more definitely materialistic view of the Psychic Factor.   For the so-called "ectoplasm", which is alleged to be involved in these phenomena, would be a peculiar kind of matter associated with the ordinary matter of the living human body.   It would then be plausible to suggest that the ectoplasm, which is involved in the physical phenomena of Psychical Research, is identical with the Psychic Factor, which is required to explain some of the mental phenomena of Psychical Research.   At present, however, the physical phenomena do not stand on the same evidential level as the mental phenomena.   It is much harder to rule out all possibility of fraud in the former than in the latter. And it is harder to make fraud impossible in the case of alleged materialisation than in the case of alleged telekinesis.   I therefore do not wish this suggestion to be regarded as any more than a pure speculation.

The upshot of the discussion is that such abnormal phenomena as are at present reasonably well established do not require us to accept anything more than a slightly modified form of one of the three types of theory which we accepted as possible in the last subsection.   They do not give us any reason to ascribe to Mind a more important and self-subsistent status in Nature than we were prepared to give it when we confined ourselves to the normal phenomena.   It is of course possible that in future we might get empirical evidence for *survival* as distinct from mere *persistence*.   Some people, who have much more extensive practical experience of Psychical Research than I have, would say that we have such evidence already ; but, as I have tried to show in Chapter XII, this is doubtful.   In that case we might be forced to look with more favour on Dualistic theories which make mentality a differentiating attribute.   But we must estimate probabilities on the evidence that we have, and not on the evidence which our successors may have.   And, on all the evidence which is available to me, which I have tried to state as fairly as I can to the reader in the course of this book, I judge the most likely view to be some form of the Compound Theory which is compatible with Emergent Materialism.

Prospects of Mind in Nature.   I shall end this book by saying something about the probable prospects of Mind in Nature.   This is a question which could not be profitably asked until we had formed some opinion of the status of Mind in Nature.   But it does not follow that we can make any very definite answer to it even now.

The first point that I want to make is that there is nothing in Mentalism as such to justify an optimistic view of the prospects of Mind, and nothing in Materialism as such to justify a pessimistic view of the prospects of Mind.   Let us consider, *e.g.*, the Leibnitian form of Mentalism.   If this be true there are certainly many minds which are so stupid and confused that aggregates of them appear to us as material objects.   And, although we are not so confused as this, we are confused enough to misperceive such aggregates as material objects though they are really mental.   Now it is quite consistent with Mentalism as such that all the minds in the Universe should be getting steadily more and more stupid and confused. It is quite possible that the minds which are now so confused that aggregates of them appear to us as material objects were once minds like our own. And it is quite possible that our minds were once clear enough not to misperceive aggregates of very confused minds as material objects. Mentalism seems to be an optimistic theory only because it is confused with Idealism.

By "Idealism" I understand the doctrine that the nature of the Universe is such that those characteristics which are "highest" and most valuable *must* either be manifested eternally or *must* be manifested in greater and greater intensity and in wider and wider extent as time goes on. It so happens that most Idealists have been Mentalists; but, as I have just shown, Mentalism is no guarantee of Idealism. Leibniz and Berkeley were both Mentalists; but their optimism was based on the fact that they were Theists, and not on the fact that they were Mentalists. And it is perfectly possible to be a Theist without being a Mentalist, or a Mentalist without being a Theist.

I will now show that, just as Mentalism as such does not entail Idealism, so Idealism is not incompatible with Materialism as such. Suppose that mentality is an emergent characteristic of certain complicated material aggregates. It remains quite possible that the actual configuration of matter in the Universe and the actual laws of matter are such that aggregates of this kind *must* grow more and more complex, and that a larger and larger proportion of matter *must* be aggregated in this way as time goes on. In that case we should have an Idealistic view of the Universe combined with a Materialistic view of the status and nature of Mind. Materialism is supposed to be incompatible with Idealism only because it happens to be associated with a particular view about the actual laws of matter and the actual configuration of matter in the Universe. And, as we have seen, the former theory about the status of

Mind does not entail any particular view about the laws and configurations of Matter.

It is perhaps worth while to remark before going further that Mentalism would make it probable that pain and frustration are much more widely distributed in the Universe than there is any reason to suppose on a materialistic or dualistic theory. We all treat what we regard as bits of inorganic matter wholly as means. Now, if the Leibnitian form of Mentalism be true, what we take to be lumps of coal and pokers are really colonies of spirits of low intelligence. These spirits must presumably have at least sentience; for this is the lowest factor of mentality. Yet, when I burn a bit of coal in my fire and poke it with my poker, I certainly treat all these confused but sentient spirits merely as means. And it seems quite possible that, under these circumstances, their sentience will be tinged with pain. This pain would be absent if Materialism or Dualism were true.

I claim now to have shown that there is no special connexion between Mentalism as such and a cheerful view of the prospects of Mind, and no special connexion between Materialism as such and a depressing view of the prospects of Mind. The question that remains is whether we know anything about the laws and configuration of Matter which would throw any light on the probable prospects of Mind, supposing that some form of Emergent Materialism is true. But, before we discuss this final question, there is a more fundamental issue to be faced. Some philosophers, *e.g.*, Mr Bradley and the Dean of St Paul's, have held that the whole notion of perpetual progress is *logically* impossible. If this be so, it is obviously needless to discuss the question whether it is *causally* possible. And it would be still more futile to discuss the question whether it is likely or unlikely to be a fact.

Is Perpetual Progress logically possible? We must begin by drawing some distinctions which are commonly overlooked. (i) I distinguish between *perpetual* and *uniform* progress. The latter implies the former, but the former does not imply the latter. To say that *s* uniformly progresses means that every later state of *s* is better than every earlier state of *s*. To say that *s* perpetually progresses is to assert the following two propositions. (*a*) If *x* be any state of *s* there is a state of *s* which succeeds *x* and is better than *x* itself and all *x*'s predecessors. And (*b*) if *x* be any state of *s* there is no state of *s* which succeeds *x* and is worse than *x* itself and all *x*'s predecessors. This of course leaves it quite open that some of the successors of any state of *s* are worse than this state or than some of its predecessors. The definition is meant to allow of fluctuations of value, provided that their maxima increase and their minima do not as time goes on. I need hardly say that perpetual progress, thus defined, is perfectly compatible with the view that the value of no state of *s* will surpass a certain finite magnitude. For, although the successive maxima always increase, they may increase at a diminishing rate as time goes on. It is also consistent with the definition that the successive minima should continually decrease, and that they should approach the same limit as the successive maxima. In that case *s*, though perpetually progressing, would perpetually approach (though it would never exactly reach) a permanent condition of constant finite value. Now I think that most philosophers who have objected to the notion of perpetual progress have done so because they supposed that this would entail (*a*) a *uniform*, and (*b*) an *unlimited*, increase in the value of the thing which is said to be "perpetually progressing." We now see that this is just a gross mistake, which these persons might have avoided by half an hour's study of any decent introduction to mathematics even if they were not acute enough to avoid it for themselves. I may add that personally I see no logical objection even to the notion of uniform and unlimited progress ; but it is not necessary to defend this view, since it is not entailed by the notion of perpetual progress.

(ii) There is another important point about progress which we have so far ignored. We have spoken as if the whole value of a thing resided in its successive states. And we are even liable to talk as if the whole value of a thing were concentrated in its final state, if it has one. This is of course a mistake. The value of a thing does not reside in any one of its states ; nor is the value of a thing the sum of the values of its successive states. It would obviously be absurd to identify the value of the Byzantine Empire with the value of that slice of its history which occupied the last second before Constantinople was taken by the Turks. And it would be equally absurd to identify the value of the Byzantine Empire with the sum of the values of all the successive slices of its history from the foundation of Constantinople by Constantine till its capture by Mahomet II. For it is plain that one important factor in the value of the Empire is the fact that after a time it went from better to worse and not from worse to better. The value of a persistent thing is a quality which inheres in its whole history from its beginning, if it had one, to its end, if it has one. If it be still existing its value is a quality which inheres in its history up to and including its present state. No doubt the value of a thing does depend in some complicated way on the values of its successive states ; but it does not depend on this alone. It is plain that the temporal order in which the states happen, and other relations between them, make a great difference to the value of the persistent thing of which they are successive states. It is necessary to modify our definition of "perpetual progress" in the following way to meet these facts. The more accurate definition will run as follows. To say that s perpetually progresses is to assert two propositions ; viz., (a) If x be any state of s then there is a state y of s which succeeds x and is such that the value of the whole history of s up to and including y is greater than the value of the whole history of s up to and including x. And (*b*) if x be any state of s then there is no state y of s which succeeds x and is such that the value of the whole history of s up to and including y is less than the value of the whole history of s up to and including x.

This would of course leave it possible that some later patches of the history of s are worse than *some* earlier patches of its history. I think it would even leave it possible that some later patches of the history of s are worse than *all* the earlier patches of its history. Suppose that Ax is the history of s up to and including x. And suppose that xB is a patch of the history of s which immediately succeeds Ax. Suppose further that xB is worse than Ax and than every slice of Ax. It is nevertheless theoretically possible that the whole AB, composed of Ax and xB, should be no worse than Ax. For the value of a whole is not in general the algebraic sum of the values of its parts. *E.g.*, Ax might be an early life of continual sin, and xB might be the appropriate amount of regret in the mind of the sinner for this particular kind and amount of sin. Then I should say that AB is better than Ax. And yet xB might be worse than Ax. The pain without the sin might have a greater disvalue than the sin without the pain. It is certainly arguable that sin without sorrow may be less bad than that state of sorrow for purely imaginary sins which occurs in religious melancholia.

Now it is sometimes objected by philosophers to the notion of perpetual progress that it places the whole value of a thing in a last state which, by hypothesis, can never be reached. If the notion involved this it would no doubt be self-stultifying. But we have just seen that it involves nothing of the kind. Hence this objection is quite irrelevant. And I think we may safely conclude that there is no purely logical objection to the notion of perpetual progress,

Is Perpetual Progress causally possible? Granted that perpetual progress is *logically* possible, it only remains to ask whether it is *causally* possible on that view of the status of Mind which has seemed most probable in the light of all the facts which are at present available.

I will first remind the reader that the view about the status of Mind which I have asserted to be most probable on the available evidence is that mentality is an emergent quality of a compound composed of a living brain and nervous system and another constituent which is not always at once destroyed when the brain and nervous system are broken up. As we obviously know extremely little about this other constituent, I will say what I have to say about it at once, and clear it out of the way. It *may* have some of the lower factors of mentality, though there is no need to suppose that it has. And, whether it has any of the factors of mentality or not, it may be matter of a peculiar kind. All that we positively know about this constituent is that it is capable of carrying traces of past experiences and of certain personal peculiarities. We do not know how persistent it may be, and we do not know what conditions, if any, are capable of destroying it. But we do know that it is not immediately destroyed by those processes which destroy brains and nervous systems.

It is therefore possible that, even if a cosmic disaster were to destroy all living organisms (and therefore, on our view, all minds) in the Universe, the other constituents of these minds might persist indefinitely. We might imagine them blowing about the Universe for millions of years, like seeds or spores or uncombined chemical elements, waiting for suitable material conditions. Eventually the necessary and sufficient conditions for the existence of living organisms might once more be fulfilled in some part of the Universe, and some of these constituents might unite with them to form those compounds which have mentality as an emergent characteristic. And the new minds, thus formed, might derive certain advantages from the traces left by the experiences of the old minds. The new minds might then develop for millions of years, thus adding fresh traces to the persistent constituents of the wholes of which they are emergent characteristics. Another cosmic disaster might eventually happen, and the process described above might be repeated. Such a series of events as I have been imagining would be quite consistent with *perpetual*, though not with *uniform*, progress.

I have spoken as if these persistent constituents merely *waited* passively for the development of living organisms, and then combined with them. This may be true. But it is also possible that they play a more active part. It is possible that the development of living organisms out of inorganic matter depends on the agency of such persistent constituents as well as on the fulfilment of certain conditions in ordinary matter. We never find highly developed organisms without minds, any more than we find minds without organisms. It therefore seems not unlikely that the persistent constituents of minds act as cause factors in the original production of living organisms from inorganic matter.

It remains to consider brains and nervous systems, the other and more familiar constituents of those compounds which have the emergent characteristic of mentality. On our view they are just as necessary for the existence of minds as are the persistent constituents which we have been discussing. Even if the persistent constituents persist indefinitely, a time will come after which there will be no more minds, if the laws and configurations of ordinary matter be such that after a time there can be no more living organisms. And, unless the laws and configurations of ordinary matter allow of perpetual progress in the complexity of living organisms, there is no likelihood of perpetual progress in the mental realm. (I say "no likelihood" and not "no possibility" here, because it must be admitted that a great deal of mental progress can be secured merely by improved social organisation and recording of experiences, without any fundamental change in the individual human organism or its mind.)

Now, so far as I can see, the situation, according to our present knowledge about matter, is roughly as follows. (1) There is one and only one alleged law of physics which would seem to make it very probable that, after a certain time, there will be no more living organisms, or only organisms of uniformly decreasing complexity. This is of course the law which asserts a perpetual decrease in the amount of *available* energy in the Universe. Now there are two remarks to be made about this alleged law. In the first place, it is a statistical law. All alleged laws of nature are only probable; but this law is peculiar in that it is a statement about probability, which most laws are not. It says that a process by which the available energy of the Universe should be increased is not causally impossible but is extremely unlikely to happen at any given moment. It does not follow that it is extremely unlikely to happen at some moment or other within a sufficiently long period of time. It is extremely unlikely that a person will be involved in a railway accident on any assigned day, but it is by no means unlikely that he will be involved in one some day or other if he travels by train every day for a hundred years. It seems not improbable that the Universe as a whole may pass through successive phases of "running down" and "winding up"; or that, while one part of it is "running down", another part of it may be "winding up". And perhaps the fact that there still is available energy supports the view that such processes of "winding up" do happen from time to time or from place to place. A full discussion of this last point would take us into difficult questions about finite and infinite duration, and about (what is quite a different thing) having a beginning or having no beginning in time. I do not propose to enter into this subject at the end of a long book which is mainly concerned with quite different problems.

Secondly, even if the amount of available energy in the Universe continually diminishes, it does not seem to me to be impossible that there should always be organisms and that they should perpetually grow more complex. It is very easy to commit a fallacy here. We can see that, if any *existing* organism were put into conditions very different from those in which it has lived and in which its immediate ancestors have lived, it would die or degenerate. And we are liable to conclude from this that *no* organism could live or be highly developed in these supposed conditions. This argument forgets that, if the conditions change slowly enough, the organisms may have time to adapt themselves to the new conditions, and that this adaptation need not take the form of degeneration. It is certain that no existing organism, or only very simple kinds of existing organism, could live if suddenly placed in conditions in which there is much less available energy than there is at present. But it does not follow from this that, if the available energy slowly diminished, the descendants of complex organisms might not be able to live and flourish under the new conditions. It is quite certain that there is no very close correlation between the mere *size* of the brain and nervous system, or the mere *strength* of the organism, and high intellectual development. If anyone denied this he might be advised to " go to the ant, to consider her ways, and be wise ". For here we have very high intellectual development accompanied by a very small brain and very feeble bodily strength. On the whole then I do not think it is by any means certain that the law of the degradation of energy precludes the possibility of perpetual mental progress, in the sense defined by us.

(2) Granted that the *laws* of physics oppose no insuperable bar to the perpetual progress of Mind, it might still be true that the special *configurations* of matter

in the actual Universe do so.   About this possibility I
have the following remarks to make.   We have to take
the ultimate laws of matter as unalterable data ; but the
configurations of matter are certainly to some extent
under our control.   And they certainly come more and
more under our control the better we understand the
laws of matter.   In particular we are able to make
material complexes which have new emergent qualities ;
this happens whenever we synthesise a new chemical
compound.   I have already pointed out that we cannot
set limits to the automatic power of adaptation possessed
by organisms, provided their environment changes
slowly enough.   I wish now to point out that the
existence of minds which understand the laws of matter
makes a great difference to the environment itself.
There are, *e.g.*, thousands of chemical compounds now
existing which probably never existed before in the
history of the Universe, and which almost certainly
would not have existed if there had not been minds which
came to understand the laws of chemical combination
and the properties of the chemical elements.   Now the
greater part of the mind's knowledge and control over
inorganic matter is quite new.   It dates from the time
of Galileo and Newton.   Such as it is, it has been
gained under the most unfavourable circumstances by
the work of a comparatively small group of men, surrounded, influenced, and often opposed by a majority
whose minds are warped by the superstitions and heated
by the emotions of patriotism and religion.   If so much
control over inorganic nature has been gained in so short
a time and under such unfavourable conditions, it would
be rash to set limits to the possible developments of this
control in the future.

The next point to notice is that the human mind has
not as yet gained any comparable degree of knowledge
of and control over living organisms.   When we remember how long it was before it understood the
fundamental structure of the inorganic world, and how

much this understanding depended on the insight of a few men of genius, like Galileo, Newton, Dalton, and Maxwell, we shall not be surprised at this. And, when we remember how quick and cumulative has been the growth of our control over inorganic matter since Newton's time, we need not despair of a similar growth of control over living organisms. We must remember, however, that, even if we had enough knowledge of biology, physiology, and genetics, to produce healthier and healthier bodies and better and better brains, there might be insuperable *psychological* difficulties in applying it. For here we come against a solid mass of primitive emotions and superstitions, many of which are crystallised in theological dogmas and supported by the authority of vast ecclesiastical organisations like the Church of Rome. This leads me to the last remark which I wish to make.

The beginnings of a genuine science of organisms exist, and progress in this science might at any moment become rapid. Supposing that Europe does not relapse into barbarism before America has emerged from it, it is quite possible that the next two hundred years may witness as great an advance in our knowledge of living matter as the last two hundred years witnessed in our knowledge of inorganic matter. But, so far as I can see, there are not even the beginnings of a scientific psychology of the individual or of communities. And, unless this defect can be remedied, there seems to be no hope either of devising a stable yet progressive social system or of making the vast alterations in men's minds which would be necessary before they could work such a system and live happily in it.

Now undoubtedly the greatest immediate threat to the further progress of the human mind is the *unequal development* of these three branches of knowledge; *i.e.*, the relatively high degree of our control over inorganic nature, combined with our still very rudimentary knowledge of biology and genetics, and with the complete absence of a scientific psychology and sociology. The first and least obvious danger of this state of affairs is that our environment and mode of life are changed deliberately, profoundly, and very quickly by the application of physical and chemical knowledge. The human organism has had no time to adapt itself spontaneously to these changes; for the spontaneous evolutionary adaptation of organisms is an extremely slow process. It therefore seems not unlikely that there is a great and growing disharmony between human organisms and their environment; and that, unless this can be corrected, the physical and mental qualities of the human race may degenerate. Now it cannot be corrected except by a *deliberate* modification of human organisms, which shall proceed as fast as the deliberate modification of their environment now proceeds. And this is possible only if we have a scientific knowledge of biology, physiology, and genetics comparable in extent and accuracy to our knowledge of physics and chemistry.

The more obvious danger of this unequal development of our knowledge lies in the fact that human control over inorganic nature provides men with means of destroying life and property on a vast scale; whilst the present emotional make-up of men, and their extraordinarily crude and inept forms of social organisation, make it only too likely that these means will be used. This danger, so far as I can see, could be averted only by deliberately altering the emotional constitution of mankind, and deliberately constructing more sensible forms of social organisation. And it is quite useless to attempt the latter without the former. In order to do this a vast development of scientific psychology would be needed for two different reasons. In the first place, it would obviously be needed in order to know how to alter the emotional make-up of the individual. But this would not be enough. We might know how to do these things, and yet it might be quite impossible to get people to submit to having these things done to them. For this purpose we should need an enormous development of what Kant calls "the wholesome art of persuasion"; and this could arise only on the basis of a profound theoretical knowledge of the factors which produce, modify, and remove non-rational beliefs.

Conclusion. The conclusion of the whole matter seems to be that perpetual mental progress is certainly not logically impossible, and certainly not causally inevitable, in the sense of being bound to happen whatever we may do. On the other hand, there seems to be no positive reason to believe that it is causally impossible, in the sense that it is bound not to happen whatever we may do. So far as we are concerned, the possibility depends on our getting an adequate knowledge and control of life and mind before the combination of ignorance on these subjects with knowledge of physics and chemistry wrecks the whole social system. Which of the runners in this very interesting race will win, it is impossible to foretell. But physics and death have a long start over psychology and life.

INDEX